Sport Facility
Management

The Jones and Bartlett Series in Health and Physical Education

Sport Facility Management

Marcia L. Walker, PhD
University of Northern Colorado

David K. Stotlar, EdD
University of Northern Colorado

Jones and Bartlett Publishers
Sudbury, Massachusetts

Boston   London   Singapore

Editorial, Sales, and Customer Service Offices
Jones and Bartlett Publishers
40 Tall Pine Drive
Sudbury, MA 01776
(508) 443-5000
info@jbpub.com
http://www.jbpub.com

Jones and Bartlett Publishers International
Barb House, Barb Mews
London W6 7PA
UK

Library of Congress Cataloging-in-Publication Data
Sport facility management / [edited by] Marcia L. Walker, David K.
   Stotlar.
       p.   cm.
     Includes bibliographical references and index.
     ISBN 0-7637-0283-8 (pbk.)
     1. Sports facilities—Management.   I. Walker, Marcia L.
   II. Stotlar, David Kent.
   GV401.S626   1997
   725'.8043—DC21   96-39659
                                                                    CIP

Vice President and Acquisitions Editor: Joseph E. Burns
Production Editor: Martha Stearns
Manufacturing Manager: Dana L. Cerrito
Typesetting: University Graphics, Inc.
Cover Design: Hannus Design Associates
Printing and Binding: Hamilton Printing Company
Cover Printing: Henry N. Sawyer Company, Inc.

Printed in the United States of America
01 00 99 98 97   10 9 8 7 6 5 4 3 2 1

CONTENTS

Chapter 6   Risk Management and Litigation   71

Marc Rabinoff

Chapter 7   Events   84

Bernie Goldfine, John Schleppi

Chapter 8   Control and Security   103

Rob Ammon, Jr.

PREFACE

The rationale for writing this text was twofold. First, there is a limited amount of published work in the area of sport facility management. Second, a proliferation of both graduate and undergraduate sports management programs have been introduced in recent years that require courses in facility management and design.

The focus of this book is on managing facilities where sport occurs, therefore entertainment facilities such as theaters, convention centers, and public assembly halls are not directly addressed.

This comprehensive sport facility management text includes examples in physical education, athletics, recreation, health/ fitness, and aquatics. Illustrations and examples have been included to enhance the reader's understanding. Some overriding issues such as affirmative action, gender equity, and ADA are addressed from various standpoints in different chapters.

Although this book was originally intended for graduate-level students, instructors will also find it useful for upper-level undergraduate courses. In addition, it is a practical guide and a valuable reference for the manager of a general facility. Part I presents the basic concepts of planning and managing a sport facility and includes specific case studies. Part II follows with an in-depth look at the management of specific areas in a facility and special groups.

ABOUT THE AUTHORS

MARCIA L. WALKER

Marcia L. Walker is an associate professor of sport administration at the University of Northern Colorado in Greeley, Colorado. She received her PhD in sports administration from the University of New Mexico in Albuquerque in 1989. She is the past chairperson of the Council on Facilities and Equipment in the American Alliance for Health, Physical Education, Recreation, and Dance (AAHPERD), and is active as a facility consultant. A frequent presenter at both the national and regional levels, she has published in the areas of facility management and design and is the co-author of *Sports Equipment Management*.

DAVID K. STOTLAR

David K. Stotlar serves as the director of the School of Kinesiology and Physical Education at the University of Northern Colorado. He teaches on the faculty in the areas of sport management and sport law. He has published more than forty articles in professional journals and has written several textbooks and book chapters on sport, fitness, and physical education. He has made numerous presentations at international and national professional conferences. On several occasions, he has served as a consultant to fitness and sport professionals; and in the area of sport law, to attorneys and international sport administrators. He was selected by the USOC as a delegate to the International Olympic Academy in Greece and the World University Games Forum in Italy.

He has conducted international seminars in sport management for the Hong Kong Olympic Committee, the National Sports Council of Malaysia, Mauritius National Sports Council, the National Sports Council of Zimbabwe, the Singapore Sports Council, the Chinese Taipei University Sport Federation, the Bahrain Sport Institute, the government of Saudi Arabia, the South African National Sports Congress, and the Association of Sport Sciences in South Africa. Dr. Stotlar's contribution to the profession includes having served as the chair of the Council on Facilities and Equipment of the AAHPERD, and as a board member and later president of the North American Society for Sport Management (NASSM).

CONTRIBUTORS

Rob Ammon, Jr.

Rob Ammon is an assistant professor at Slippery Rock University, Slippery Rock, Pennsylvania, where he teaches in the Sport Management Department. He teaches graduate and undergraduate courses in sport facility and event management, sport law, sport promotion and fund-raising, and management of sport. Dr. Ammon's areas of research include risk management at sports events and facilities, spectator violence, alcohol and sport, crowd management, and legal liabilities involved in sport. For eight years, before entering the academic arena, Rob was involved in intercollegiate athletics as a coach and administrator. In addition, he has been associated with events as a practitioner since 1976, serving as a consultant and supervisor for a national crowd management company. He has worked various Super Bowls, collegiate athletic events, and hundreds of concerts across the United States. He has also directed crowd management services in Kansas City, Denver, and Seattle.

Frank B. Ashley, III

Frank Ashley is currently an associate professor and chair of the Kinesiology Division in the Department of Health and Kinesiology at Texas A&M University, College Station, Texas. Dr. Ashley teaches courses in sport management, sport business and personnel management, administration of health, physical education, and athletics, and sport facility planning and management, and co-ordinates the Sport Management Program. He is a member of NASSM and served on its executive council from 1991 to 1995 and on its program committee from 1990 to 1995. In addition, for the Texas AAHPERD, Frank serves as chair of the Sport Management Division and has organized and hosted 1994 and 1995 "Southwest School of Sport Management" Conference for Graduate and Undergraduate Sport Management Studies at Texas A&M University. Frank has made numerous state, national, and international presentations including seminars in the United States, South Africa, Hong Kong, Malaysia, and Singapore. He is also well published in sport management and physical education journals.

Wendy Busch

Ms. Busch has an extensive background in exercise science as well as the travel and tourism industry. She is currently pursuing a degree in physical therapy at the University of Puget Sound, Washington, and intends to remain active in the fields of exercise and physical therapy.

Shannon Courtney

Ms. Courtney currently serves as an athletic trainer at the University of Northern Colorado and holds the rank of assistant professor. She has been involved in NATA certification testing and program design. Shannon earned both her BA and MA at the University of Northern Colorado.

Bernie Goldfine

Bernie Goldfine is an associate professor of sport management at Kennesaw State University in Georgia. Serving as a high school athletic director for thirteen years, Dr. Goldfine oversaw the design, planning, and management of a wide array of athletic facilities. He has taught undergraduate courses in the area of facility design and management and has made presentations on these topics at the NASSM and the AAHPERD conventions. In addition, Dr. Goldfine serves as a consultant on athletic facility projects.

Scott Hall

Scott Hall is the head coach of men's and women's track and field at the University of Northern Colorado, was North Central Conference Coach of the Year in 1989 and 1991, has coached thirty-six NCC individual champions, seventy-two NCAA Division II national qualifiers, thirty-one All-America, and six NCAA II champions in nine years. He also coaches on the USA VISA Decathlon team staff, at the USA Emerging Elite decathlon camp, and was an assistant coach at the US Olympic Festival in 1994. Dr. Hall also coached at St. Lawrence University (New York), Idaho State University, and Northfield-Mt. Hernon (Massachusetts) High School. He received a BS in physical education from St. Lawrence University, an MA from Idaho State University, and his EdD from the University of Northern Colorado.

Virginia L. Hicks

Virginia Hicks is currently an assistant professor of human performance, leisure and sport on the School of Education Graduate and Undergraduate Faculty, and Basic Instructional Program Coordinator at New Mexico Highlands University. Dr. Hicks received her BS and MA at the University of Iowa and her PhD at the University of New Mexico. She is active in AAHPERD, NMAHPERD, NWA, ACSM, UIAA, and NMPHA. Dr. Hicks has been consultant to Community Wellness Programs, Springer Boy's School, Las Vegas Schools, and the Public Health Division–District II at the New Mexico State Department of Health. She is also co-investigator (Research Manager) for American Indian Men Body Composition studies at the University of New Mexico. Dr. Hicks has had numerous publications and has presented many papers at national conventions such as AAHPERD and ACSM.

Diane B. Krogh

Diane Krogh is the coordinator of all physical education and athletic facilities and game manager of home athletic events at the University of Northern Colorado. Her experience includes athletic administration in the Fargo, North Dakota, public schools and at Moorhead State University in Minnesota. Diane also taught undergraduate and graduate courses in physical education administration at the University of Nevada-Las Vegas and coached cross country and field hockey at Moorhead State. She earned a BS in physical and health education at Moorhead State in 1975 and an MA in physical education and athletics at the University of Northern Colorado in 1986.

Richard J. LaRue

Richard LaRue received his undergraduate degree from the University of Northern Iowa and both his master's and doctorate from Springfield College in Massachusetts. Dr. LaRue is an associate professor and past chair of the Sports Science Department at Colby-Sawyer College in New Hampshire, and a visiting scholar in the School of Public Health at Harvard University. Dr. LaRue is a past chair of the Council on Facilities and Equipment and a regular presenter on facilities topics ranging from ADA to OSHA. As a facilities consultant, Rich has served several institutions with their facility design and management, including the YMCA Walter Schroeder Aquatic Center in Milwaukee, Wisconsin, and the Hogan Sports Center in New London, New Hampshire.

Kathryn Malpass

A former fitness director and assistant manager of Bethesda Racquet and Health Club, Kathryn has taught aerobics for more than sixteen years, including four in the public schools. While at the University of Northern Colorado, she taught courses in fitness management, sport law, and methods of teaching dance. She has made several presentations on sport liability and risk management including a session at the 1992 Colorado Parks and Recreation Association and programs at the 1990, 1991, and 1993 AAHPERD conventions. Her publications include three chapters for a national training manual and a section in a book about marketing sports. She is a member of the International Dance Exercise Association, NASSM, National Golf Educators of America, and the AAPHERD. Kathy has her BS from Wake Forest University, North Carolina, and an MA from Indiana.

Alison Osinski

Alison Osinski's educational background includes a PhD from the University of Maryland, an MS from Florida International University and a BS in physical education with a specialty in aquatics from Hillsdale College (Michigan). She is active in several national and regional aquatic organizations and currently serves as an officer or advisory board member of the National Swimming Pool Foundation, Council for National Cooperation in Aquatics, Professional Pool Operators of America, Aquatic Associates, and International Association of Aquatic Consultants. Dr. Osinski is an author of more than seventy publications, a workshop coordinator, and a frequent speaker at national aquatic conferences. Alison Osinski is currently the principal-owner of Aquatic Consulting Services, located in San Diego, California, specializing in aquatic risk management and aquatic facility design, management, and operation.

Marc Rabinoff

Marc Rabinoff is a professor of human performance, sport and leisure studies at Metropolitan State College of Denver and President of Rabinoff Consulting Services, Inc., of Littleton, Colorado. Dr. Rabinoff has more than twenty-six years of experience in teaching, coaching, administration, and supervision of sport, fitness, physical education, and recreation activities. Dr. Rabinoff has authored, co-authored or been interviewed for more than ninety publications and media segments including The Oprah Winfrey Show, The Today Show, Good Morning America, Hour Magazine, and Special Reports TV with Joan Lunden. He has testified or consulted in more than 100 litigations involving issues of instructor qualifications, standards of care in facility operations, equipment design, warnings, and the use of Safety Inspections and Risk Management. Based on this work and resource data, Dr. Rabinoff has written text chapters on risk management, professional liability, and the insurance industry. Additionally, Marc lectures at colleges, recreational facilities, civic organizations, and public schools on these issues, as well as serving on the advisory board of the National Academy of Sports. He is also certified as a forensic examiner in human performance by the American Board of Forensic Examiners and serves on their technical and scientific advisory board and editorial review board.

Tom H. Regan

Tom Regan is an assistant professor of sports business at the University of South Carolina. He brings with him a wealth of experience in regional economic impact analysis and event development in sports and entertainment. His research emphasis is regional economics and sports and development of entertainment events. His recent accomplishments include a leading research study on the Economic Impact of the Denver Broncos on the Denver Colorado Metropolitan Area, and a business/marketing plan proposed for luxury box seating at Notre Dame Stadium. Other economic impact studies include golf courses across the state of South Carolina, the University of South Carolina athletics on the Columbia metropolitan area, and numerous studies for local and regional events. Dr. Regan's experience includes working as a staff accountant for Fox and Co., CPAs, and eight years as a comptroller for a fully integrated oil and gas company. He is currently under contract to complete a textbook on managing sport and special events. Dr. Regan's education includes bachelor's and master's degrees in accounting from the University of Wyoming and a doctorate in sports administration from the University of Northern Colorado.

John Schleppi

John Schleppi coordinates and teaches in the sport management program at the University of Dayton. His background includes working with the organization of activities in the following areas: wrestling and soccer tournaments, the archery competition at the 1987 Pan American Games, the National Rifle matches, and many years with long-distance running events.

Todd Seidler

Todd Seidler received his PhD in sports administration from the University of New Mexico and is currently the coordinator of the graduate Sports Administration Program at Guilford College, North Carolina. He is a past chairman of the Council on Facilities and Equipment of the AAHPERD and is active as a consultant on facilities and risk management for sport and recreation. Dr. Seidler presents, publishes, and frequently teaches classes in facility planning and design, facility management, and risk management.

Jeff Steffen

Jeff Steffen has been involved in adventure activities in teacher preparation programs for ten years. He has assisted in the design, development, and implementation of numerous ropes courses and climbing walls in K–12 schools. Jeff has also served as chair of the Council of Outdoor Education. He has published in a variety of professional journals in the area of adventure facilities and safety. Jeff has his BA from Dakota State College and his MA and PhD from the University of Iowa and is currently an associate professor of physical education at the University of Wisconsin-LaCrosse.

Ed Turner

Ed Turner is a professor of health, leisure, and exercise science at Appalachian State University in North Carolina. Ed received his undergraduate degree from Pennsylvania State University and both his master's and PhD from the University of Maryland. He has taught a graduate facilities design class for twenty-seven years and has served as a facilities consultant on numerous projects. He has written extensively in journals and texts on the topic of facility design and planning and made many professional presentations about facilities. He is currently involved in planning the Appalachian State's $30 million convocation-academic center.

Greg Waggoner

Greg Waggoner serves as athletic director at Western State College in Colorado and is in the process of a sport facility design and renovation of the athletic, kinesiology and recreation fieldhouse. Greg received his EdD in sport management from the University of Northern Colorado in 1994. Greg spent eleven years as the head wrestling coach at WSC where his teams consistently ranked nationally in the NCAA II. Greg has taught in the Kinesiology and Recreation Department at Western State College for ten years, including sport management classes. As athletic director, Greg is very involved with facility design, facility management, fund-raising, and corporate partnerships.

Newton Wilkes

Newton Wilkes has twenty-eight years of experience in various educational settings. He was a coach/teacher, assistant principal, and principal for eight years in the Jefferson Parish School System of New Orleans, Louisiana. He served in the Bureau of Personnel Evaluation in the Louisiana State Department of Education for one year. He was responsible for developing the Teacher/Systems Personnel Evaluation instrument and guidelines for teacher/system personnel accountability. After his tenure in Jefferson Parish, Newton served eighteen years in institutions of higher education.

Fourteen years were as assistant/associate professor in the School of Health and Physical Education at the University of Southern Mississippi in Hattiesburg, Mississippi. Four years have been spent as head of the Department of Health and Human Performance at Northwestern State University of Natchitoches, Louisiana. Dr. Wilkes has had responsibility managing educational physical plants and their upkeep; additionally, he has served on facility planning committees and has taught facility management, planning, and design classes at the collegiate level.

PART I

Concepts of Facility Management

1

The Planning, Design, Construction, and Management Process

Marcia L. Walker

Managing sport programs successfully requires a basic knowledge of managing a sport facility. This is critical because facilities are where sport occurs. Because the type of facility dictates the management of it, the focus of this chapter is on the planning and design of it. This process consists of the preliminary planning or predesign phase, the design development phase, the construction phase, and the management preparation or training phase (see Figure 1–1).

PHASE 1: PRELIMINARY PLANNING

Program Analysis

The preliminary planning phase begins with establishing a need for the facility and requires a thorough analysis of the programs to be offered. If there is a preexisting building and programs are already in place, an examination of these areas is needed. Information can be acquired from usage or attendance records, previous program and event schedules, maintenance reports, and equipment ledgers. Deficiencies and inadequacies should be noted. The organization's mission, program objectives, and short- and long-range goals must be considered. Finally, one needs to examine current trends and probable future developments.

This data, along with feasibility studies, should be closely analyzed to determine whether it would be best to build a new facility or to renovate an existing one. In this regard, "experience has shown that if it will cost 50 percent or more to rebuild than to build new, it is better to construct new" (Horine, 1987).

This information can also be used later to justify the financial expenditure for the project. A thorough appraisal with written documentation is necessary to gain approval of a project. The data must be well organized and presented in a professional manner.

The Planning Committee

Next in this phase is the appointment of persons for the planning committee. In some cases the committee is formed prior to the needs analysis. The important point is to proceed through the process in a logical order that is appropriate to the specific organization.

It is highly recommended to include in the planning process everyone who is interested and all who play critical roles. This is often referred to as participatory planning. Involving many in the planning process need not be a cumbersome task. Some organizations conduct public forums to obtain the views of concerned citizens. Other agencies solicit information through client or student surveys. Figure 1–2 depicts the results from a student survey. The input from surveys such as this provide essential data for the planning committee to consider.

The institutional planning committee should be limited in size to hasten the process. Initially, the members of the committee must include the owner or manager of the facility and key individuals such

Figure 1–1
This flowchart shows the process of planning, designing, building, and opening a sports or recreation facility.

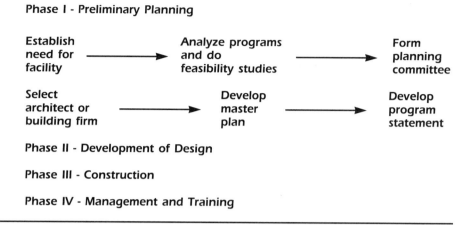

Phase I - Preliminary Planning

Establish need for facility → Analyze programs and do feasibility studies → Form planning committee

Select architect or building firm → Develop master plan → Develop program statement

Phase II - Development of Design

Phase III - Construction

Phase IV - Management and Training

as the program coordinator and the equipment manager. Once the architect has been hired, he or she will also be a member of the committee.

Designing and building a sport facility is quite different from designing and building other types of structures. Therefore, if possible, hire an architect who has experience in building sport, physical education, or fitness facilities. If it is not possible to acquire an architect with such experience, it is essential to hire a consultant who has had experience in designing such a facility. The consultant provides insight into the unique aspects of sports programs and needs that are specific to them. The Council on Facilities and Equipment of the American Alliance for Health, Physical Education, Recreation, and Dance provides a list of consultants on sport and physical education facilities.

Others who should be considered as potential planning committee members include program specialists, administrators, and users. Two persons who could add substantially to the committee are the equipment manager and the head of maintenance. They can provide "common sense" information that might easily be overlooked. To approve budget decisions, persons in positions of authority (other than the owner or manager, who are already involved) should also be included.

The Architect

It is important to note that the hiring of the architect does not have to take place immediately. In some cases the architect is not hired until late in the predesign phase. Meagher (1990) suggests that "to turn too early to an architect can be a serious mistake, for you may then end up with a building that suits the architect rather than one that meets the needs and aspirations of the building's owner and clientele." He identifies "four phases in the development of a new construction or renovation proposal: The identification, prioritization, conceptualization, and realization phases" and recommends the architect not be hired before completion of the first three phases.

An organization may decide to hire either an architect or a building and design firm. Before making this decision, acquire background information on all prospects. In regard to this issue, Oommen and Maynard (1989) suggest "if the quality is determined by a program, and if quality can be monitored, design/build can be a good choice if money and schedule are the key factors. If you have a clear program document and an architect who will follow that program, an architect may be the right choice."

In the search for the right architect or design firm, it is also helpful to visit facilities they have built. Spend the time investigating, asking questions, and looking at both the positive and the negative features.

Conduct interviews with the top candidates and check their references. Get a feeling as to whether they are professional and easy to work with. Examine their credentials, philosophy and approach, experience, cost, potential contracts, and proposed timetable for building. Architectural firms will provide a detailed plan for their "project

Figure 1–2 A student survey at The University of Northern Colorado indicated the popularity of particular activities, as this graph shows.

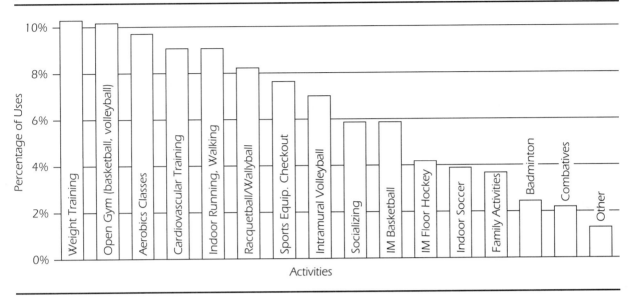

approach." Figure 1–3 presents a diagram of a proposed plan for a university student recreation center solicited by an architectural firm.

After weighing all the data carefully, select the person or firm who best meets the needs of the organization. At this point a written agreement should be set between the two parties. This agreement lists the responsibilities of both sides. Further information and standard agreement forms are available from the American Institute of Architects.

The Master Plan

After the committee is formed, the next step is the development of a comprehensive or "master plan" for the facility. The master plan is the accumulation of all information needed to assist in developing the project. Flynn (1993) describes the plan as "a formal, comprehensive building scheme that identifies the organization's facility needs and establishes the priority in which construction of new or the renovation of existing facilities will occur." This scheme includes collecting data from the various feasibility studies, assessing the needs and demands for a new facility, examining budgetary plans, observing trends, and analyzing the organi-

zation's purpose and objectives including short- and long-term projections.

The generation of the master plan is a complex process and should not be rushed. Spending the time creating a sound master plan saves time and money later on in the development process. The master plan provides the structure from which to work and keeps the planning team focused on the main direction of the project. Throughout the composition of the master plan, a number of points must be considered:

1. The primary focus throughout the development of the master plan is on the purpose for which the facility is being built. Develop the facility to accommodate programs rather than adapt programs to fit a facility.

2. Plan for the best building your organization can afford, which should be determined through a thorough investigation of its financial resources.

3. Avoid biased and restrictive points of view. Be open to new and different ideas and approaches. Research innovations and new technology in design.

4. Do not compromise with the architect or give up essential aspects of the design that are important to the program.

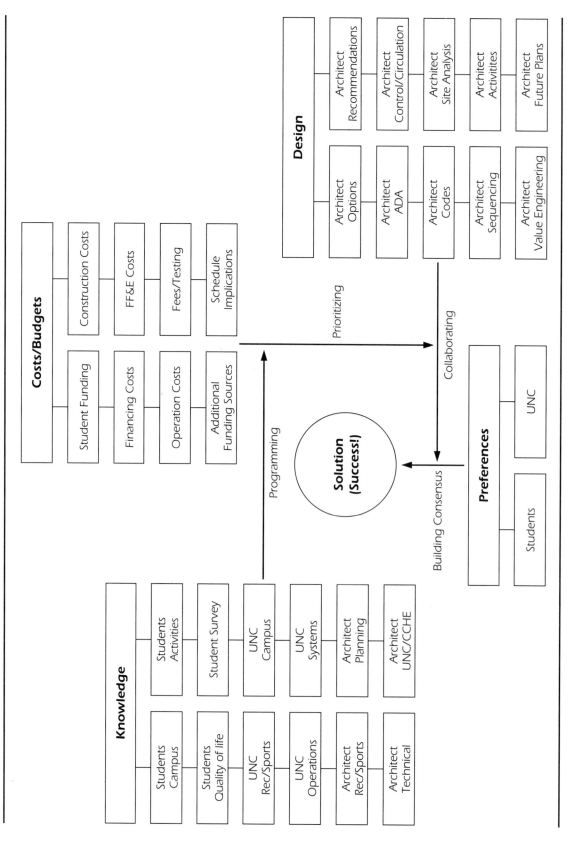

Figure 1-3 This chart of the project approach to building a university recreation center illustrates the many roles played and their interrelationships. (Courtesy of The University of Northern Colorado, Greeley, Colorado)

Figure 1–4 An example of a bubble design.

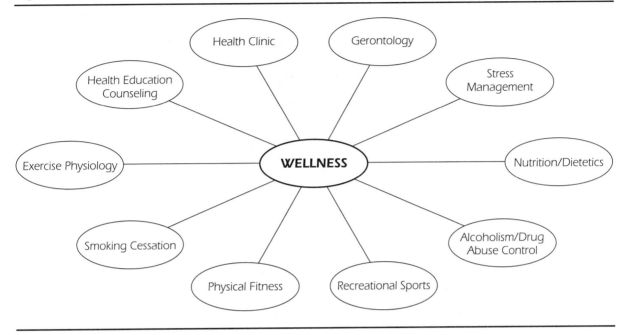

5. Include complete accessibility of the building within the plan. Research requirements of current legislation and the Americans with Disabilities Act (ADA).

6. Avoid costly errors and omissions by being thorough in planning. Include feasibility studies in all related areas: legal, site, user-usage, design, financial, and administrative.

7. Identify the spaces that are needed and map out how those spaces interface. Bubble designs may be useful in ascertaining the types of programs desired. Figure 1–4 is a sample bubble design for a wellness facility. The connecting bubbles represent the major areas that will be in the facility.

8. Consider how the facility will be controlled and managed. Build these management and control features into the design itself.

9. Visit similar facilities and inquire about the best and worst features of the design and use.

10. Examine current trends and plan for the future. It is recommended to project twenty years ahead in the plan for building.

11. Pay close attention to the environmental impact that the building project will have on the community and surrounding area.

The Program Statement

The next step in the preliminary phase is the creation of a written report that may be called a "program plan," a "case statement," or a "program statement." This report is prepared primarily for the architect and represents a summary of the major components of the master plan. In some cases a program statement is prepared for other purposes, such as presenting to groups to influence them to support the project (see Figure 1–5).

Obviously, the program statement that is prepared for the architect is comprehensive and detailed and begins with a needs statement. Both Flynn (1993) and Patton, Grantham, Gerson, and Gettman (1989) present sample program plans that account for the following categories: (1) program objectives; (2) basic assumptions; (3) trends affecting planning; (4) current and proposed programs; (5) preliminary data-design specifications

Figure 1–5 A widely distributed brochure makes the case for a new student recreation center. (Courtesy of the University of Northern Colorado, Greeley, Colorado)

On April 13–14, all UNC students will have the opportunity to vote on whether to financially support the construction and operation of a new Student Recreation Center.

A new Student Recreation Center is being proposed due to the inadequacy of the current recreational facilities on campus and the possible expansion of programming by the College of Health and Human Sciences into Gunter Hall. A new campus center will offer multiple recreational opportunities throughout the day, and provide activities and programs, which are not available as part of the current offerings.

The proposed Recreation Center has been a student-driven process from its inception with the Student Representative Council (SRC) serving as the guiding force behind this effort. In 1992, a total of 85 percent of students who completed an SRC survey (647) responded positively to the proposal to construct and operate a Student Recreation Center funded from student fees. The survey also addressed the types of activity spaces and amenities the students believed would meet their needs; these are reflected in the facility features listed in this flyer.

Sixty percent of the Recreation Center steering committee are students. At various times before students vote on construction, they will have the opportunity to react to the plans and to the process during open public forums.

If the proposal is approved, a facility advisory board comprised of students and administrators will be established to set operating policies.

Shortcomings of our current facilities

- Gymnasiums in Gunter Hall and Butler-Hancock are not available for recreational use before 6:30 P.M. Monday through Thursday.
- Overcrowding and competition for space at Gunter Hall are major problems. The current levels of use far exceed the capacity for which the building was designed.
- After 6:30 P.M. a variety of groups—athletics, intramurals and open recreation, physical education classes, club sports and special units—compete for the available space in both Gunter and Butler-Hancock. Oftentimes there is no space left for free play, once the formal programs have been scheduled.
- There is inadequate space to expand existing programs or create new ones.
- The weight and fitness rooms in Gunter Hall are small and poorly ventilated. Space for additional pieces of equipment is limited. Much of the existing weight training equipment needs to be replaced and/or upgraded to meet current use.
- The racquetball courts, located in Butler-Hancock, are currently in disrepair, and no state funds are available to refurbish them.

Benefits of a new center

- A recreational facility where students are given the top priority in scheduling
- A facility where the students control the decision-making process
- A major expansion of the recreational facilities available on campus
- A state-of-the-art upgrade of the facilities available on campus
- A safe and healthful recreational and social environment
- A substantial expansion of options for evening and weekend activities

Indirect benefits

- Improved recruitment and retention of students, potential rental income during downtimes, and supplemental income for the student recreation budget with the sale of passes to faculty/staff

Facility features

The areas listed below are included in the preliminary floor plans. However, this plan will be discussed at all forums and suggestions from students will be incorporated before the referendum. Your input will be greatly appreciated.

- 2 Multipurpose Gymnasiums: The space available could accommodate 5 basketball courts or 7–8 volleyball courts.
- 1 Conditioning/Fitness Room: approximately the size of Gunter 107
- 1 Aerobics/Multipurpose Room: approximately the size of Gunter 107
- 1 Multipurpose Meeting Area: with dividers to create 3 separate rooms
- 4 Racquetball/Handball Courts: with viewing area above
- 1 Jogging Track: above the large gymnasium
- 1 Suite of Offices: with a conference room
- 1 Game Room
- Lounge and Study Areas
- Hot Tub and Sauna Area
- Storage Spaces: for all check-out and program equipment
- Small Concession Area
- Campuswide Bike Path System

Project cost

The total estimated cost of the Student Recreation Center is $6.5–8 million. Revenue bonds would be sold to

Figure 1–5 *(continued)*

cover this cost and would be repaid from student fees over a period of 30 years.

Student fees

The fee assessed to students would be approximately $42 per semester. This translates to a per-day user fee of only $37 per student based on current enrollment. For comparison, student membership fees at local clubs and recreation centers range from $85 to $110 per semester.

The exact amount will depend on: (1) the final floor plan, based on student input and (2) construction costs, which will vary with the type of facility selected and fluctuations in the cost of building materials.

If approved, all students will be assessed the fee as part of the student fee package; however, students will not pay the fee until the facility actually opens for use.

Timetable

If approved in April 1993, the projected opening date is Spring 1995.

For more information

Students Forums will be announced in the "Mirror", and will be publicized at the UC and at the Intramural Office, Gunter 109.

If you have questions, contact the following individuals:

- Student Representative Council members
- L.J., director, Student Recreation
- C.K., assistant director, Student Recreation

---

and space allocations; (6) space needs and relationships; (7) activity, auxiliary, and service facilities; (8) facility usage; (9) equipment and furniture list; (10) environmental necessities; and (11) other considerations.

PHASE II: DEVELOPMENT OF DESIGN

The second phase in the planning process is design development. The program statement is presented to the architect as the representation of the program needs. Communication between the architect and the planning committee is crucial at this point. A thorough understanding must exist between the two parties prior to continuing the building process.

Preliminary schematic designs will be prepared by the architect for consideration and approval by the planning committee. These include a plot plan, floor plans, and elevation drawings. Models of the proposed facility may also be constructed to provide an example of the finished product.

The planning committee must thoroughly review the preliminary designs and clearly communicate with the architect concerning additions or adjustments needed. It is wise to ask questions and not make assumptions at this juncture. Be sure the designs reflect the purpose of the facility and support the programs it is intended to house.

In examining the preliminary designs, look specifically for:

1. *The placement of rooms* in relation to other rooms. For example, locker rooms should be located with entrances adjacent to aquatic areas, so users do not have to track through dry areas after leaving the pool.

2. *Noise level.* Consider the separation of racquetball courts, aerobics rooms, and weight training areas from offices, classrooms, or conference rooms.

3. *Security and management control.* Assess the designs with regard to control and management concerns. Determine if the number of staff working at any time will be able to manage the entire facility. Ask questions: Are there potentially unsupervised areas? How does one gain access to the building? Are there emergency and escape routes?

4. *Storage rooms.* Analyze the plans for adequate storage space. Storage areas are needed for offices, audiovisual materials, equipment issue areas, maintenance closets, and large equipment on-site storage in activity rooms.

5. *Specification sheets.* Specification sheets give detailed information regarding the types of materials to be used in the facility. There should be specification sheets for construction materials, interior and exterior finishes, mechanical and electrical

Figure 1–6 This program schedule is the design team's timetable for the first phase of planning the student recreation center. (Courtesy of the University of Northern Colorado, Greeley, Colorado)

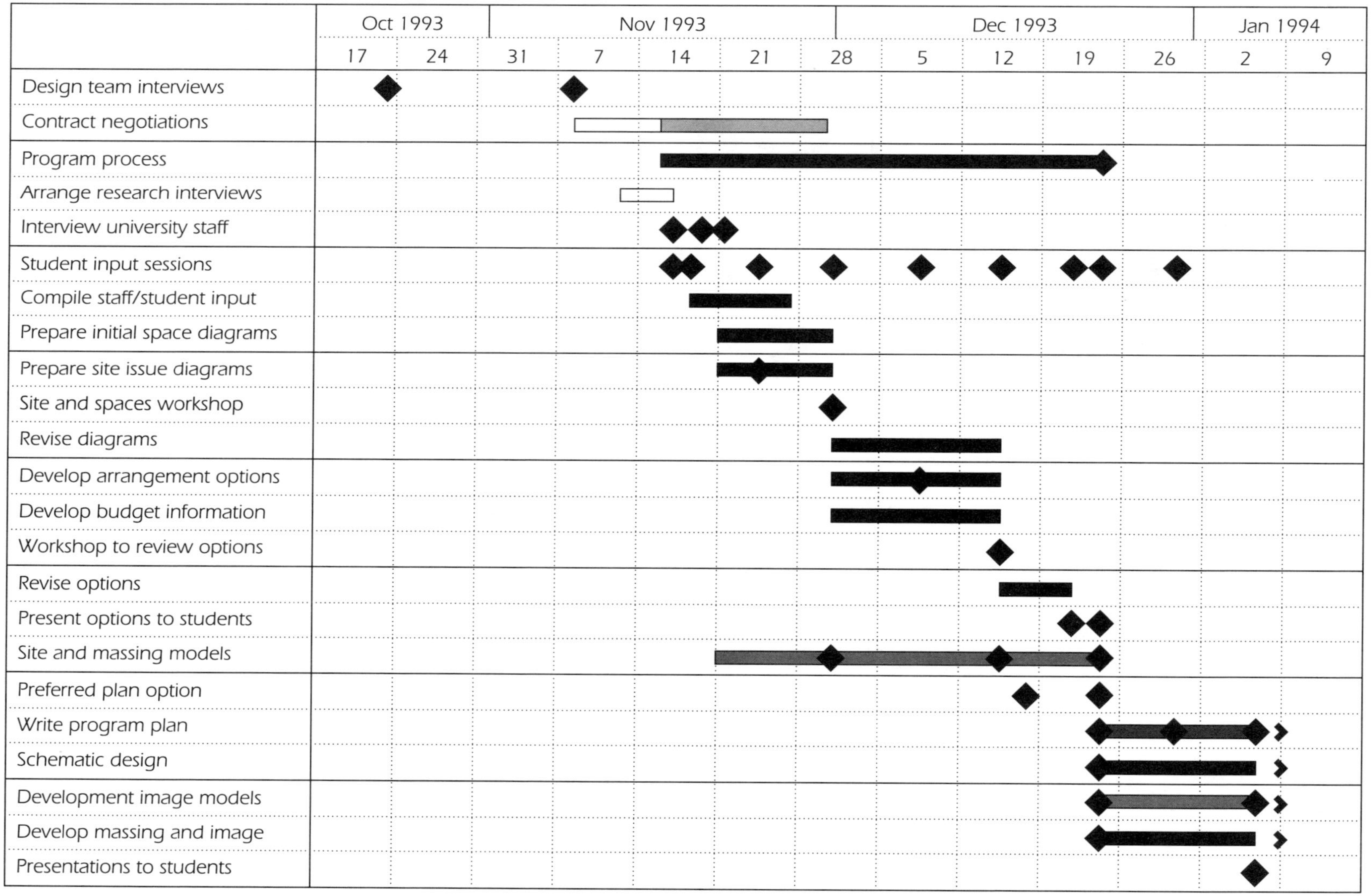

Figure 1–7 The triad represents the primary participants in the construction process and their relationships.

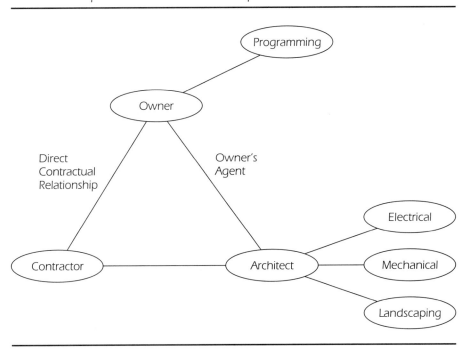

---

systems, doors and windows, appliances and fixtures, and furniture and equipment.

6. *Environment and surroundings.* Examine the impact of the placement of the facility on the surrounding area. It should fit in with the architectural design of nearby buildings. Parking and traffic areas must be considered, as well as ramps for wheelchair-bound persons.

Another important part of the design development phase is to create a realistic timetable that includes planning, construction, and staff training schedules. Plan for problems that may arise by allowing more time for the project than should be necessary. Creating a preliminary countdown schedule may help simplify the task, by working chronologically backwards from the proposed opening date. The amount of time required will vary, however Balling (1992) recommends a period of "30 months or $2\frac{1}{2}$ years from the idea stage until opening."

The timetable is a working document and should be consulted frequently. The architect is responsible for developing a detailed program sched-

ule for the planning and construction phases. In some instances, the architect and owner or planning committee may decide to use a "fast track" in completing the building. It is more costly, but may be worth the expense to speed up the completion time.

A sample timetable in Figure 1–6 represents the design team's program schedule that encompasses only one part of the overall timetable (approximately four months).

Another important component that must not be overlooked during this phase is site selection. The location for a facility is crucial and should be near the persons it will serve. The basic requirements in selection of the proper location for a facility are (1) financial factors (assets and tax considerations); (2) physical resources (adequate water and utilities supply); (3) environmental factors (impact on area, climate, extreme temperatures, humidity, solar possibilities); (4) physical factors (contour of site, soil conditions); (5) zoning requirements (available or restricted site, type of building including height and lot size, parking, traffic flow, environmentally controlled areas, and use/purpose of building); (6) accessibility (easy access for construction crews getting equipment and materials to the site); and (7) other considerations (egress/ingress, visibility, and demographics).

Pomeroy (1992) expresses the importance of designing a sports facility to the site. He states: "The key consideration in designing The Solana Club (a sports/fitness club in Dallas, Texas) was ensuring it worked architecturally within the entire development, yet maintained its own unique character."

The final, and most important, element to consider during the design development phase is producing a cost estimate. This information is critical in determining whether it is financially possible to construct the building.

The cost estimate is based on the space needs for the building. Space needs are determined by evaluating the kinds of programs to be offered and the number of persons expected to use the facility. This information should already be available in the data acquired during the preliminary planning phase.

Estimates of square footage should be obtained for all areas including both activity and ancillary space. Ancillary space represents all types of space that support activity areas such as locker rooms, equipment storage, offices, rest rooms, and so on. Using multipurpose designs and functional layouts may provide more usage within a smaller area. More information is provided on space management in Chapter 5.

For specific recommendations on the size of rooms, there are a number of standards and guidelines available. Keep in mind that competition areas must be specific sizes according to the governing body for that sport. It is not within the scope of this text to provide a list of all the space standards; there are several texts devoted exclusively to this. Refer to the References and Suggested Readings for further resources.

Once the total square footage has been estimated, this number is then multiplied by the average cost for construction materials in the vicinity. This figure is a rough cost estimate from which to work. For example, the estimated square footage (75,000) is multiplied by the average construction cost ($100/ft.) to equal $7,500,000. If the estimate is more than the available finances, then the planning team may need to eliminate parts of the orig-

inal design. Choose wisely at this point, being careful not to eliminate essential elements.

Later on, the architect and contractor will supply a document obtaining exact construction costs. There should be a construction contingency built in to the figure to account for additional charges that may occur. Patton, Grantham, Gerson, and Gettman (1989) recommend: "Even the most accurate cost estimate can be wrong by as much as 4% to 6%. For this reason the recommended contingency for the construction of a new facility is 8% to 10%; the contingency for a renovation is 12% to 15%."

Other costs that should be added into the facility construction cost estimate are site costs, equipment costs, financial costs, and management and maintenance costs. Often these expenditures are overlooked. There have been instances where new sports facilities have been built and the management teams were unable to open them due to a lack of funding provided for these areas.

PHASE III: CONSTRUCTION

The responsibility for the construction phase is primarily that of the architect and contractor. The architect prepares the necessary construction documents that include the drawings and specifications mentioned previously. During this phase the construction schedule should be reviewed and updated if necessary.

In addition, the architect works with the planning committee in hiring the contractor, which can be accomplished (1) through a competitive bidding process; (2) by hiring a construction manager and subcontractors (many architectural firms provide a joint service by providing their own construction manager); and (3) by negotiating a contract among the architect, owner, and construction company.

Figure 1–7 provides an example of the relationships among the owner (planning committee), contractor, and architect. A simple triad exists with each primary participant relating to the other two. The architect serves as the owner's agent and the contractor serves in a direct contractual relationship.

The contractor will create detailed shop drawings from the architect's plans and specifications. "Shop drawings are the life blood of the construction phase, and must be reviewed closely" (Meyer, 1981). It is essential that members of the planning committee are able to read and understand blueprints and that they stay attuned to changes that are made. Remember that the later changes are made in the construction process, the more it costs.

PHASE IV: MANAGEMENT AND TRAINING

While construction of the facility is under way, consideration for the management of the facility must be taken and training should begin. Many times this phase is overlooked or minimized, which is a critical mistake. As mentioned, the management

aspects should be considered from the beginning of the planning project. Given the appropriate attention, proper planning can save time, effort, and money after the building is completed and open for use. For example, building in a barcode-operated turnstile relieves staff members from the responsibility of checking identification cards.

Training personnel prior to opening the new or renovated facility saves time and confusion. The ideal situation is to hire the staff and allow enough time to have thoroughly trained them by the final stage of the construction phase. When the construction is completed, the staff is trained and ready.

The remainder of this text provides details on the specific components of facility management.

Managing a sports facility such as the Gostomski Arena at St. Mary's College in Winona, Minnesota, is as complex as the sports that are played in it. (Photo courtesy of the architects Toltz, King, Duvall, Anderson and Associates; Don F. Wong, photographer.)

SUMMARY

The process of planning, designing, and developing a facility is quite complex. The four major phases are preliminary planning, design development, construction, and management preparation and training. It is of primary importance to remain focused on the main purpose for the facility throughout all the phases of the planning and development process.

QUESTIONS

1. Describe the phases of the planning and development process.
2. List the primary participants who should be included in the development of a facility. Describe their roles.
3. What is the main focus that must be followed throughout the planning, design, and development process?
4. What precautions should be taken to avoid costly mistakes during the building process?
5. Compile a list of areas for potential feasibility studies.

ACTIVITIES

1. Develop a multipurpose sports/fitness facility for a small college. Facts that apply to this assignment: enrollment (5,000 undergraduate students); programs using the facility (physical education—priority 1; NCAA Division III athletic program—priority 2; leisure services—priority 3; community groups—priority 4). You provide information about location, funding, and so on.
2. Upon completion of the first exercise, develop a list of management policies that would be appropriate for the designed facility.
3. Visit a few sports facilities and compare designs.

SUGGESTED READINGS

American Hospital Association. (1986). *Fitness facility planning: Resources and recommendations*. Chicago: American Hospital Association.

Anderson, D. L. (1984, September). Sports facility checklist: A pre-design guide. *Athletic Business*, pp. 84, 86.

Bucher, C. A., and Krotee, M. L. (1993). Facility management. In *Management of physical education and sport*, (10th ed.) (pp. 246–279). St. Louis: Mosby-Year Book.

Castaldi, B. (1994). Foundations and principles of educational facility planning. In *Educational facilities: Planning, modernization, and management*, (4th ed.) (pp. 130–159). Needham Heights, Mass: Allyn and Bacon.

Clayton, R. D., and Thomas, D. G. (1989). *Professional aquatic management* (2nd ed.). Champaign, Ill.: Human Kinetics.

Crane, R., and Dixon, M. (1991). *The shape of space: Indoor sports spaces*. New York: Van Nostrand Reinhold.

Sol, N., and Foster, C. (1992). *American College of Sports Medicine's health/fitness facility standards and guidelines*. Champaign, Ill.: Human Kinetics.

Warren, R., and Rea, P. (1989). *Management of aquatic recreation resources*. Worthington, Ohio: Publishing Horizons.

REFERENCES

Balling, C. (1992, August). Public preparedness. *Athletic Business*, p. 46.

Flynn, R. B. (Ed.) (1993). *Facility planning for physical education, recreation, and athletics* (pp. 2, 9–10). Reston, Va.: American Alliance for Health, Physical Education, Recreation and Dance.

Horine, L. (1987, January). Planning sport facilities. *Journal of Physical Education, Recreation, and Dance*, p. 22.

Meagher, J. W. (1990, August). 43 steps to a successful facility. *Athletic Business*, p. 42.

Meyer, J. (1981, June). Owner's role in construction process? Working with people. *Athletic Purchasing & Facilities*, p. 32.

Oommen, G., and Maynard, L. (1989, August). How to select the right architect. *Athletic Business*, p. 42.

Patton, R. W., Grantham, W. C., Gerson, R. F., and Gettman, L. R. (1989). *Developing and managing health/fitness facilities* (pp. 92–94, 129). Champaign, Ill.: Human Kinetics.

Pomeroy III, L. F. (1992, October). Design to the site. *Fitness Management*, p. 35.

Stotlar, D. K. (1990). Facility management. In J. B. Parks and B. R. K. Zanger (Eds.), *Sports & fitness management: Career strategies & professional content* (pp. 35–42). Champaign, Ill.: Human Kinetics.

2

Organizational Structure and Staffing

David K. Stotlar

The profession of sports facility management is in a state of rapid change. Owners and operators are faced with rising building and maintenance costs and management is experiencing increased pressure to produce revenue in excess of operating expenses. Furthermore, facilities once reserved solely for sport use have disappeared in favor of facilities that can accommodate a multitude of different events. In this environment, the organizational structure selected for the operation is critical. This chapter concentrates on the theories and concepts pertinent to organizing the personnel and management functions for sports facilities, arenas, and stadiums. Sport facility management, as a business, is typically categorized into three distinct sectors: private facilities, municipal facilities, and college and university facilities.

The uniqueness of the facility management business has been characterized by Finfrock (1990). He said the primary responsibility of the facility manager is to "operate [the facility] with quality service, responsiveness and benefit to the general public, the taxpayer, or owner in the case of a privately owned facility and for the tenant whose fees for leasing space will produce revenues of a magnitude to provide management with a favorable 'bottom line' " (p. 2). Within this paradigm, the manager is responsible for governing and managing the facility and interpreting the stated mission and purpose of the facility.

The implementation of philosophy is evident in the organizational structure and administrative design. Sports facilities have been constructed for a variety of purposes, which must be articulated through the director. Some sport facilities are funded by specific user groups (i.e., college campus recreation buildings, private sport clubs), therefore, special attention is needed regarding the requirements of that group. In other situations, one specific sport team may be a primary tenant (e.g., Denver Nuggets in the publicly owned McNichols Arena) and would, therefore, have priority in use and scheduling. Initially, all of these elements impact organizational structure.

Although many characteristics are shared by public, municipal, and college sectors, substantial philosophical differences are also apparent. The role and function of a facility in the private sector emphasizes return on investment and profit. It is expected to generate reasonable revenues in excess of expenses. Managers in this environment need polished business practices and excellent marketing and financial management skills. Your job as the manager may be tied to the profit-and-loss statements. "Putting people in the seats, shows on the floor, and dollars in the stock holders' pockets is the name of the game" (Stotlar, 1990, p. 37).

In the municipal sector, the operating philosophy emphasizes serving a public function. Managers in this environment need to be politically astute to negotiate and work effectively with elected politicians. More recently, however, the trend in municipal facility management is for managers to run the facility more like a business and less like a public service enterprise (Stotlar, 1990). Traditionally, college and university sport facility managers acted as liaisons between the athletic director and the facility's staff. Although many of their facilities were designed to be used predominantly for the conduct of collegiate contests in football and basketball, with a few nonrevenue sports thrown in for good measure, many college and university operations are moving toward revenue production through events that result in increased profits. Added services such as parking, concessions, and souvenirs (merchandising) have also been introduced to increase revenue (Stotlar, 1990).

THE ROLE OF MANAGEMENT

Bridges and Roquemore (1992, p. 21) define management as "the optimal utilization of human resources to achieve predetermined goals and objectives." This concept is just as important in the management of sport facilities as in the management of any other business or organization.

The role of management and the administrative structure of an organization depend on the size, purpose, philosophy, mission, objectives, and goals of the organization. For example, the management of a small private college gymnasium used for academic and athletic programs might have a different management structure than would a large muncipally owned stadium used exclusively for professional sports events. Likewise, a privately owned and operated health and fitness center would probably have a management structure quite different from a city recreation center.

To become a successful facility manager, you must acquire competencies in various management skills. In a study by Lambrecht (1987), sport and athletic club managers ranked the competencies required for successful management in a commercial sport setting. This investigation found that the highest ranked competencies were communication with clientele, employee motivation, handling complaints of customers, staff communication, decision making, supervision, evaluation, time management, strategic planning, and budget preparation.

LEGAL STATUS

Determining the legal status of the sport facility's business structure is an important management consideration. The vast majority of sports facilities in the United States have been publicly funded and are operated under the auspices of local government authorities. Municipally owned sport facilities are often operated by the branches of city government designated as "stadium districts" or "sports authorities." The entire structural scope of these quasi-public operations vary widely and therefore, cannot be addressed in this limited section. However, a typical model of organizational structure in the industry is Denver Metropolitan Major League Baseball Stadium District. In general, the provisions of the legislation (Colorado Revised Statutes 32-14-101 1990) indicate that:

1. The district shall be governed by a seven-member Board of Directors, none of which shall be an elected official.
2. Board members shall be appointed by the governor and serve four-year terms.
3. In addition to other powers granted by the legislation, the Board has the power and authority to:
   (a) contract for the construction, equipment, preservation, operation and maintenance of a stadium and all of the necessary incidental works.
   (b) enter into and execute all contracts, leases, intergovernmental agreements, and other instruments necessary for the accomplishment of the purposes of this article.
   (c) establish criteria for a stadium site and a stadium and to acquire, on behalf of the district, the selected stadium site and other such lands as may be necessary.
   (d) exercise all powers necessary and requisite for the accomplishment of the purposes for which the district was organized.
4. The district shall make every reasonable effort to obtain funding for a target amount of at least 50% of the total cost incurred by the district in the acquisition of a stadium from monies acquired from sources other than the levy and collection of the sales tax authorized. Such moneys may include, but are not limited to, private donations or the revenues acquired by the issuance of special bonds.
5. The Board shall pursue opportunities for privatizing the costs of acquiring a stadium site, the costs of constructing a stadium, or the costs of operating a stadium in order to minimize the use of sales tax revenues to the greatest ex-

tent possible. Such methods to be pursued include, but are not limited to:

(a) the sale or lease of stadium seat rights.

(b) the sale or lease of stadium luxury suites.

(c) the sale of long-term advertising, parking, and concession rights.

(d) the sale or lease of the name of the stadium, any symbol or image of the general design, including trademarks, service marks, or logos.

6. The Board shall negotiate and enter into one or more management agreements for the management and operation of the stadium with independent contractors having experience, expertise, and specialization in the management of sports, entertainment, or convention facilities.

In recent years, some sports facilities have been built totally with private funds. Joe Robbie Stadium in Miami, Florida, is a large-scale sports facility that was constructed recently using private funding sources. These business operations are typically run as a corporation. The formation of a corporation is a complex and time-consuming proposition because of the complicated tax structure, cost of legal services, and governmental regulations. You should be familiar with some of the overriding concepts and principles. Three basic types of business structure exist under the law and many sport facility managers will be interested in the following material describing the formation of a corporation.

Corporations, as governed by state laws, constitute the primary type of business structure for sports facilities that are not municipally owned. Corporations become a legal entity in the eyes of the law. They also exist independent from the owners, which allows the assets or the entire corporation to be easily sold or transferred. The corporation authorizes the issuance of shares, the distribution of which determines the percentage of ownership. There is generally a board of directors whose members are elected by a majority of the shareholders.

To form a corporation, you must choose a name for the company (a name that has not already been registered) and file a notice of incorporation with the state. As always, there are fees to be paid, forms to be completed, and the state will ask for a "registered agent" so that it will have someone to contact for business affairs.

The major advantage gained in forming a corporation is that creditors (both business and legal) can only access the assets of the corporation if bills are owed or judgments granted. The personal assets of the corporate officers, board members and shareholders are generally off limits. For this reason alone, most businesses establish corporations.

For some small sport operations such as health clubs and commercial recreation companies, other options may be attractive. A sole proprietorship is, as the name implies, a business owned and operated by a single person. Any income or losses from the business activity of a sole proprietorship are legally attributable to the owner/operator. Forming a sole proprietorship establishes a legal right to conduct business and supplies the owner with a legal title to the business. Because many sport facilities are often large and expensive businesses, this structure is not common in the industry.

A partnership is another form of business structure. A partnership is created when two or more people agree to operate a business and share profits and losses. It could include a group of people who wish to work together or possibly a fitness instructor who becomes a partner in the ownership of a club. Business relationships in a partnership are best accompanied by a "Partnership Agreement," which includes stipulations of the structure for authority, the rights of the partners, the performance of each partner, the contributions of each partner, buyout clauses, the distribution of income, and responsibility for debts. Especially important is whether the partnership is a general partnership or a limited partnership.

The general partnership functions such that all partners are fully liable for the actions of the business. In a limited partnership partners are classified as either "general" partners or "limited" partners. A general partner can be any individual in the business and often runs the day-to-day operations of the business. A limited partner is normally someone who has invested in the business, but has a desire to limit his or her liability to the amount of money invested. Limited partners are usually prevented by law from taking an active role in the management of the business. Under the law, there must be at least one general partner in a limited partnership.

Partnerships (both general and limited) have the same tax advantages as does the sole proprietorship, that is, the profits are taxed at personal rates. This is popular with investors because tax losses, credits, and deductions can be passed on to investors, while giving limited partners many of the legal protections of a corporation.

MODELS OF ORGANIZATIONAL STRUCTURE

However diverse sport facilities may be, as public assembly facilities, the critical factors that influence the organizational structure are quite similar. Within this context, an organizational structure must be designed for the accomplishment of varied tasks. According to Chelladurai (1985, p. 75) organizational structure exists to provide the means by which an organization can coordinate efforts for the completion of the stated mission. Specifically, organizational structure affects performance in two distinct areas, individual accomplishments and organizational functions (Nadler, Hackman, and Lawler, 1989). Many people think that sound structure translates into organizational effectiveness. However, Chelladurai (1987) suggests that organizational effectiveness is difficult to measure and that the theories tying structure to effectiveness are both complex and controversial. He forwards several theoretical perspectives from which organizational effectiveness can be viewed and, in turn, organizational structure can be designed.

Sport facility managers could chose a "goals model" wherein the specific goals and objectives of the organization determine effectiveness (Megginson, Mosely, and Pietri, 1992; Chelladurai, 1987). These objectives are typically output based and defined in clearly measurable terms. A limitation of this model lies in the fact that not all measures of organizational effectiveness are output based.

Another model, the "system resources model," views effectiveness in terms of an organization's ability to attract and secure valuable resources. In the case of a sport facility, this could be operating capital, physical resources, and highly competent personnel. Chelladurai also offered a "process model." This model expresses effectiveness as a function of the internal processes and decisions made in an organization.

Yet another model looks outside the organization for measures of effectiveness, the "multiple constituency model." Here, the organization is judged, not by internally generated goals for process, but by the constituencies which the organization serves (Chelladurai, 1987). Within the sport facility industry, this could include spectators, resident teams, sport promoters, vendors, and stockholders.

The reality of the industry is that no one model best conforms to the organizational complexity of a sport facility management. Each has inherent weaknesses. The goals model is limited by the clarity and consistency of goal statements and the degree to which employees embrace them as meaningful objectives. The resource model is often a difficult fit for sport organizations because some organizations, such as a municipal recreation department, exist within an environment where the resources are externally controlled. The major issue with the process model is the degree to which the processes are linked to the outcomes. In many organizations, this link is not clearly delineated. The criticism of the multiple constituency model is that constituents often have contradictory and disparate values, which they seek to impose on the organization (Chelladurai, 1987).

Chelladurai (1987) recognized the complexity of sport organizations and recommended that sport managers adopt a multidimensional model wherein managers must consider the applicable components of each model and ascertain the ability of each constituency to thoroughly assess organizational effectiveness. Therefore, the experts (Nadler, Hackman, and Lawler, 1989; Chelladurai, 1987) recommend that sport managers use a combination of the above theories adjusted to fit the complexity of the organization and parameters of the operational environment.

Nadler, Hackman, and Lawler (1989) indicate certain issues to address when making decisions regarding organizational structure. They recommend that managers consider the effect of structure on reporting relationships, information management, task performance, and communication patterns. Organizational structure (see Figure 2-1) also exists to facilitate decision making in the accomplishment of organizational tasks. In particular, formal management structures establish the communication channels for effective decision making.

Organizing an effective unit is a function common to most facility management positions (Bridges and Roquemore, 1992). Nadler, Hackman, and Lawler (1989, p. 187) stipulate, however, that "there

Figure 2-1 A typical organizational chart for a sports arena.

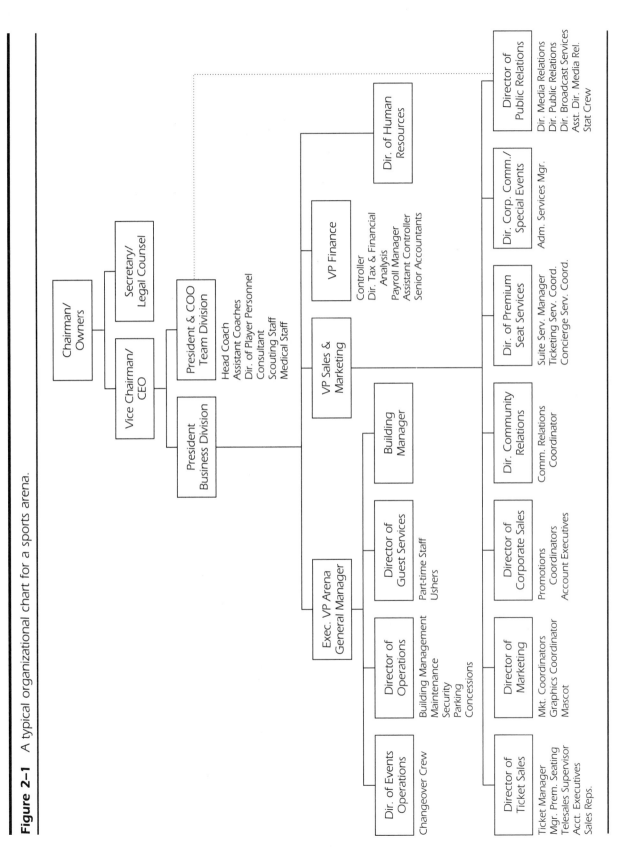

Chairman/Owners

Secretary/Legal Counsel

Vice Chairman/CEO

President & COO Team Division
Head Coach
Assistant Coaches
Dir. of Player Personnel
Consultant
Scouting Staff
Medical Staff

President Business Division

VP Finance
Controller
Dir. Tax & Financial Analysis
Payroll Manager
Assistant Controller
Senior Accountants

VP Sales & Marketing

Dir. of Human Resources

Building Manager

Exec. VP Arena General Manager

Dir. of Events Operations
Changeover Crew

Director of Operations
Building Management
Maintenance
Security
Parking
Concessions

Director of Guest Services
Part-time Staff
Ushers

Director of Ticket Sales
Ticket Manager
Mgr. Prem. Seating
Telesales Supervisor
Acct. Executives
Sales Reps.

Director of Marketing
Mkt. Coordinators
Graphics Coordinator
Mascot

Director of Corporate Sales
Promotions
Coordinators
Account Executives

Dir. Community Relations
Comm. Relations Coordinator

Dir. of Premium Seat Services
Suite Serv. Manager
Ticketing Serv. Coord.
Concierge Serv. Coord.

Dir. Corp. Comm./Special Events
Adm. Services Mgr.

Director of Public Relations
Dir. Media Relations
Dir. Public Relations
Dir. Broadcast Services
Asst. Dir. Media Rel.
Stat Crew

19

is no one best way to structure an organization." The classical determinants for organizational management include specialization, span of management, departmentalization, unity of management, and responsibility and authority (Bridges and Roquemore, 1992; Megginson, Mosely, and Pietri, 1992; Chelladurai, 1985). Specialization means that there are individuals who perform very specific and diverse tasks within the sport facility, much as there are specialists in the electrical, carpentry, and plumbing trades. On the management side, it could be applied to personnel management, sales, marketing, and finance. As Chelladurai (1985) points out, limiting the number and diversity of tasks a person must perform increases the quality of the output.

Span of management relates to the number of people under the direction and control of a manager. In upper management, the ratio is about 1 to 4, while at the lower levels it can be as high as 8 to 1. Some research indicates that seven is the optimum number of subordinates for one manager to supervise (Chelladurai, 1985). The actual number of subordinates assigned to a manager often has more to do with the type of work that must be done rather than simply the number of people supervised. Generally, supervisors responsible for employees performing complicated tasks (e.g., building engineers) often have a smaller span of management because of the high level of supervision required, whereas supervisors of employees with less complex tasks (e.g., ticket sales people) may have more people to supervise. Other factors affecting the span of management include similarity of work and geographical proximity of the work group. When the work tasks are similar and the geographical area is small, one supervisor can oversee more employees (Megginson, Mosely, and Pietri, 1992). This assignment of supervisors by type of work leads to the concept of departmentalization.

Departmentalization is the grouping of work into homogeneous units under the control of one manager (Megginson, Mosely, and Pietri, 1992; Chelldurai, 1985). Within the management area you may have departments of Human Resources, Sales and Marketing, Events Management, and Box Office. In the operations area you may find departments of Carpentry, Painting, HVAC (heating, ventilation, air conditioning), Engineering, and Maintenance. The primary organizational divisions for sport facilities are frequently classified as either administrative or operational.

Unity of Management (or Command) is a principle that dates back to the early 1900s and the scientific approach to management. Nevertheless, it is still important for today's managers. Simply stated, this principle means that workers should report to only one superior (Megginson, Mosely, and Pietri, 1992). Complications can result that include ambiguity of role and competition between superiors for the employees' time.

STAFFING

The practice of assigning authority commensurate with responsibility becomes crucial when the entire organization, supervisors and subordinates, is considered (Chelladurai, 1985). According to Chelladurai (1985, p. 80) "individuals cannot carry out their duties if they do not have the authority to make decisions relating to their tasks." Therefore, all positions should be structured with authority commensurate with required tasks.

Designing Jobs

"In any organization, the total work must be broken down into simple, well-defined tasks, and these tasks must be distributed to members as official duties" (Chelladurai, 1985, p. 81). To accomplish this task, the facility manager must become competent in analyzing and designing jobs. A job analysis is "the process of gathering information and determining the elements of each job through observation and study" (Megginson, Mosely, and Pietri, 1992, p. 345). This process enables facility managers to thoroughly understand the work environment and the position to be filled.

The term *job* should be used to refer to a unit of work that must be performed. A position is the individual(s) assigned to perform the necessary jobs within an organization. Therefore, a job may require several position assignments and a position may be assigned several jobs. Although the clarity of this statement is not essential for the employees, it is a concept that managers need to fully understand.

When referring to a position in the organization many people talk about a job description. Many times this is an all-encompassing term for what an employee does and brings to the job. As a management term, however, it needs to be more narrowly defined. "A [position] description is a written statement of all the duties and responsibilities to be performed in a particular [position]" (Bridges and Roquemore, 1992, p. 237). Position descriptions, therefore focus on duties and tasks and use action words to describe them. On the management side, personnel could be asked to engage in *planning, analyzing* data, and *reporting* to superiors within the organization. Personnel in facility operations could have action words in their position descriptions referring to *assessing* event operations, *calculating* materials for repairs, and *developing* maintenance budgets.

The effective facility manager must also be sure that the employee has the requisite skills to perform the tasks and responsibilities assigned. This requires the development of job specifications. Here the focus is on the qualifications required of a person to complete an assigned job. Job specifications are developed using possessive words for defined skills. In this case the job specification may mandate that your accountant be a Certified Public Accountant or have five years experience as a carpenter. Management personnel are often required to possess excellent oral and written communication skills. Operations personnel could be required to have HVAC computer-programming skills. Typical managerial duties included in job descriptions include (Bridges and Roquemore, 1992):

Planning	Creating	Prioritizing
Evaluating	Leading	Interpreting
Controlling	Deciding	Staffing
Budgeting	Organizing	Problem solving
Motivating	Implementing	Coordinating
Hiring	Reviewing	Scheduling
Firing	Instructing	

While the above list is not exhaustive, it does provide a sample of duties you may consider for creating job descriptions. Below are some examples of the phrases you could use in writing the job specification of a vacancy notice:

Ability to . . .	Certification in . . .
Degree in . . .	Competence in . . .
Capacity to . . .	Skills in . . .
Proficiency in . . .	Background as . . .
Knowledge of . . .	Master of . . .
Experience in . . .	Aptitude with . . .

By using these terms and phrases, you can build a vacancy notice that provides a clear picture of the expectation for the employee and establishes

meaningful criteria upon which to base the employee's evaluation.

The organizational structure and available positions in the sport facility business do not vary significantly among the sectors. Most sports facilities have a director, operations manager, box office manager, personnel manager, stage manager, concessions manager, building engineer, and general clerical support staff. Some examples of position descriptions and specifications are outlined below:

Facility Director

Position Description. The Facility Director

- is responsible for the complete operation of the facility
- reports directly to the Executive Board
- establishes appropriate goals and objectives
- conducts long-range planning
- supervises sales, marketing, finance, and personnel operations staff
- conducts annual employee evaluations
- prepares and manages budget and financial operations

Position Specifications. To qualify for the position of Facility Director, the applicant must have

- a minimum of a college degree in sport management
- exceptional political and interpersonal skills
- effective oral and written communication skills
- experience in labor and contract negotiation
- three years experience in managing a profitable sports facility
- successful experience in media management
- a philosophy consistent with the organization

Operations Manager

Position Description. The Operations Manager

- reports to the Facility Director
- is responsible for event operations and financial management
- conducts human resource planning
- manages day-to-day operation of the facility
- supervises concessions, ticketing, and engineering personnel
- supervises trade, security, and medical personnel during events
- oversees the conduct of sports and entertainment events

Position Specifications.   Requirements for the position of Operations Manager include

- experience in labor relations
- the ability to calculate work-hour requirements
- exceptional political and interpersonal skills
- effective computer and communication skills
- three years experience in facility operations
- successful experience in event management
- a philosophy consistent with the director

Box Office Manager
Position Description.   The Box Office Manager

- reports to the Operations Director
- is responsible for box office management, operations and maintenance
- controls all ticketing functions including receipt, distribution, and sales
- is responsible for the selection, training, supervision, and evaluation of box office personnel
- prepares box office statement following each event and assists other management personnel with interpretation
- works closely with promoters and lessees by providing data regarding ticket counts and financial reports
- coordinates and oversees off-site ticket sales for all events
- handles problems and complaints associated with box office operations

Position Specifications.   To qualify for the position of Facility Director, the candidates must have

- experience in box office management
- proficient skills in public relations
- the ability to supervise hourly employees
- effective communication skills
- demonstrated knowledge of and skill in computerized ticketing systems
- experience with creating financial reports
- a philosophy consistent with the facility management team

Job Analysis

If the organization is new or if a vacancy in personnel occurs, it is the responsibility of the facility manager to recruit a capable person for the organization. In this process, it is imperative to carefully analyze the organization for job and position needs.

Too often, managers simply replace a departing worker without examining the needs. If Chris left the organization, we simply hired another Chris. This results in a wasted opportunity. The opportunity presented by the departure of an employee is to examine the functions performed by that person and determine if they are still required. Maybe another person in the organization has developed new skills and would enjoy taking over those responsibilities, or perhaps the functions can be computerized. Another possibility is that the functions could be contracted to part-time or temporary employees. Regardless, this occasion presents management with an opportunity to evaluate the organization for the effectiveness of its personnel.

If the decision is made to hire a replacement worker, the manager must find the most competent person for the new vacancy. Employment practices for government agencies and federal contractors require that Affirmative Action/Equal Employment Opportunity (AA/EEO) procedures be followed. (Although substantial discussion occurred within federal and state governments in 1995, the requirements were still mandatory at the time of publication.) Private employers are not legally bound to follow AA/EEO procedures, yet many choose to do so in an effort to avoid discrimination and civil rights claims.

The equal opportunity laws are based on the Civil Rights Act of 1964 and its subsequent amendments and are designed to deter discrimination in hiring and employment practices. When combined with the Equal Pay Act of 1964 and the Americans with Disabilities Act of 1994, many of the staffing functions in an organization are closely regulated. Federal enforcement of these laws is typically entrusted to the Department of Labor's Equal Employment Opportunity Commission or the Justice Department's Office of Civil Rights (Megginson, Mosely, and Pietri, 1992).

The legal requirements typically require that the vacancy be made known to all qualified candidates regardless of race, religion, national origin, age, or gender. The best way to accomplish this is to advertise nationally. You can have the vacancy announcement put in newspapers and specialty trade magazines to ensure a wide readership. Remember, your task is to find the best available candidates.

Once the advertisement has been circulated, you must begin processing the applications. Your first responsibility is to notify all applicants that their materials have been received. Next, you must develop a screening mechanism to sort the most qualified person from the other candidates. In all cases, this process should bring you back to the position description and specifications. Special care should be taken in reviewing the credentials. Many applicants want their applications and materials to be confidential. It is recommended that applicants complete an application for employment that includes information related specifically to the position. You may question the need to ask candidates to transfer information from their résumé to an application for employment. The reason is based in the legal system. A person's résumé is not a legal document, it is only that person's representation of his or her qualifications and credentials. As hard as it may be to imagine, some people fabricate information for their résumés. Having all applicants record the information on an application for employment, complete with a signature attesting to the accuracy of the information, creates a legal document. It is also easier to review candidates when a standard format exists.

Background investigations are also important in the employee selection process. Official educational transcripts and letters of recommendation are customary requirements in the application process. You should read these carefully while looking as much for what is not there as for what is presented. For instance, you read a line that said "No one would be better for the job." Does this mean that there are no better candidates or that the job would be better left unfilled when compared to hiring this person?

Although it may be legal, contacting a person's immediate supervisor without permission is unprofessional. When you would like to do so, the candidate should be asked for permission. Many managers also believe that essential information can be gained from talking to a candidate's references over the telephone. This procedure usually puts the candidate in a more comfortable position and sometimes a better overall impression can be obtained. All of your questions should show a reasonable relationship to the work assignment and no questions should be developed regarding race, religion, age, gender, or national origin. To comply with legislative guidelines, an accurate record of these conversations should be kept for at least one year.

The importance of pre-employment interviews has been the subject of substantial research. In general, the research shows that interviews are valued by most employers, but are not particularly effective in differentiating candidates' qualifications (Boucher, 1984). Therefore, you should structure your interview to provide the desired results. The best interviews are called "patterned interviews." Here the interviewer asks exactly the same questions of all candidates. Additional depth can be achieved though systematic investigation of content areas. This process allows the answers from different candidates to be objectively compared. The questions constructed for the interview should emerge from and reflect the position description. For example, you could ask the candidate, "How do you normally handle . . . ?" or "What would you develop for . . . ?" or "How would you describe your planning of a . . . ?"

Interviews for trade positions should include work sampling. It is not effective to ask potential employees if they have computer ticketing skills. They should be asked to demonstrate their skills in the work environment. For example, a lighting specialist could be asked to operate a spotlight for a simulated pregame show.

Performance Evaluation

The purpose of performance evaluations is generally to encourage individual excellence and achievement. One of the manager's top priorities is to get the best out of the people whom he or she supervises and the evaluation process is a tool to assist in this process. Many managers are uncomfortable evaluating employees because they are typically not well trained for this task. A basic, yet overlooked rule for performance evaluations is to start with the employee's job description. It states precisely the tasks that should form the basis for evaluation. In this light, one of the best methods to conduct the evaluation is to construct a rating form based on the specific duties and tasks in the job description.

Some managers choose to construct a rating form with scaled (i.e., 1 to 10) responses to each item. Another popular approach is to list each task and then provide statements about the quality of performance on each task. This is often called a behaviorally anchored rating system. Qualitative statements that describe excellent, good, average, below average, and unacceptable performance must be created for each aspect of the employee's job. The manager then observes the employee and selects the proper statement to describe the observed performance. This system, while very time consuming to construct and implement, provides excellent feedback to the employee (Lewis and Appenzeller, 1985).

For example, in regard to a job responsibility for material and resource utilization, the behaviorally anchored ratings could include:

1. Unacceptable performance—the employee does not use available material and resources to assist with work assignments.
2. Below average performance—the employee makes marginal use of available material and resources to assist with work assignments.
3. Average performance—the employee appropriately uses available material and resources to impact work assignments.
4. Good performance—the employee plans and coordinates material and resources to enhance job performance.
5. Excellent performance—the employee seeks and develops material and resources to optimize job performance and organizational success.

Performance evaluations should be used to reward employees who meet certain levels of performance and to assist those not achieving at a satisfactory level through professional development. However, the most frequent application of performance review is to decisions about salary, promotion, and retention. Use for retention decisions is the most feared by employees while achievement appraisal is the most beneficial to the organization.

Other methods of evaluating employees include those conducted by subordinates or self-evaluations. A discussion of these methods will not be attempted in this book. Each method of personnel evaluation has specific benefits and drawbacks; the best systems use the advantages of different methods and mold a system to fit the unique situation in the organization.

Compensation

Compensation should be directly tied to the position descriptions. The objectives of a compensation management system should be to attract high quality people to staff the facility. The question which always arises is "How much are you worth?" Because pay, in our culture, is a measure of relative worth, your compensation system can cause conflict if not properly designed. A well-defined system also reduces the need to defend actions related to pay.

There are several systems for managing compensation. According to Megginson, Mosely, and Pietri (1992), the three most common methods are hourly wage, commission, and salary. Most sport facilities employ all three systems and, at times, combinations of the three. Factors that influence compensation include the worth of a particular job, the value of each employee, the general labor market, and an examination of comparable positions in similar facilities.

For example, most sports facilities pay concession vendors according to the number of units they sell (Megginson, Mosely, and Pietri, 1992). This is also the standard pay scheme for people selling group tickets and advertising. Managers customarily receive a designated salary and trades workers are paid hourly wages negotiated through their union. However, there are exceptions and variances among and across sport facilities.

For instance, salespeople are also needed to work at ticket windows and they are normally paid an hourly wage. Some managers receive a salary and then a profit-sharing bonus if the organization meets or exceeds projected revenues. Some marketing and salespeople are compensated with both a base salary and commissions (when targeted sales figures have been reached). In general, administrative employees are paid on a salary basis, salespeople receive a commission, and laborers are compensated at an hourly rate.

Within the salary system, a job factors approach can be implemented for facility employees. This method of salary determination depends on the calculation of an employee's contribution to the facility. Areas examined in the process include the extent of responsibility, complexity of the job, span of supervision, education or training required, extent of contacts with the public, physical effort demanded, working conditions, and level of confidentiality required. Points are awarded in each area and are totaled for each position. Positions with the lowest scores for responsibility and complexity should have the lowest salaries, while those with higher point totals should receive higher compensation. All positions within the facility could be placed on a wage curve graph (see Figure 2-2). If an appropriate calculation has been made, the graph shows a linear progression from low to high.

OPERATIONAL POLICIES

Within the scope of this chapter, operational policies are presented to assist in forming the managerial foundations for sports facilities. This global view of policy can be contrasted with the policy information in Chapter 3 on operations management where day-to-day operational policies are detailed. According to Finfrock (1990), facility managers must be fully versed in policy formation and implementation. He indicated that a policy defines the philosophy under which the facility operates.

Williams (1990) indicates that the development of an operational policy starts with an examination of the facility's purpose. In his estimation, that re-

lates to serving customers through the provision of the highest quality service possible. All aspects surrounding every event should be performed to high levels of professional standards.

Quality Management

Quality management has been defined as the process of ensuring that an organization's services meet the expectations of their clients/customers (Megginson, Mosely, and Pietri, 1992). According to Finfrock (1990), the main point to remember in sport facility management is that audiences pay to see and hear the event with ease and without frustration. Therefore, managers must focus on attaining customer satisfaction through the provision of high quality services.

In the past decade, the concept of Total Quality Management (TQM) has been incorporated by a variety of companies across the United States, including sport organizations. Law (1993, p. 24) de-

Figure 2–2   In this graph of wages, point values calculated for each position are plotted against their respective salaries.

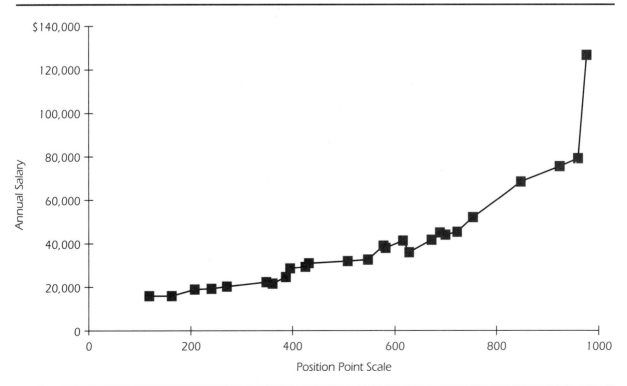

fines TQM as "a process of continuous improvement that is focused on responding to customer needs, basing decisions on data, and allowing everyone to participate in the process." The concept is based on the work of American W. Edwards Deming in post–World War II in Japan. Deming's quality control theories advanced the quality of manufacturing systems and were based on fourteen management principles:

1. Establish a constant organizational purpose or role in satisfying customers.
2. Commit to the new quality control philosophy.
3. Cease inspection of the final poduct or service, but seek improvement in the process instead.
4. Disregard the cost in securing the best quality in organizational resources.
5. Continually improve the process of providing goods and services through statistical analysis of performance data.
6. Institute training and development programs for employees.
7. Select leaders who enable people to excel rather than directing or punishing workers' behavior.
8. Drive out employees' fears about asking questions, seeking assistance, or making mistakes, or they will continue to do things wrong or not at all.
9. Eliminate barriers between organizational work units to eliminate conflicting competition, or one unit may cause performance problems for another.
10. Eliminate organizational slogans and targets for workers; let them create their own.
11. Eliminate numerical quotas; they do not account for quality or methods.
12. Encourage pride of work by acknowledgment of intrinsic excellence and elimination of management's standards of performance.
13. Encourage retraining and self-improvement through education in new methods, teamwork, and statistical techniques.
14. Take action so the organization's managers and all employees can create the new quality system (U.S. Office of Personnel Management, 1991).

The implementation of TQM in the sport facility industry can be accomplished through quality circles. These "circles" are teams of employees in specific areas who work to solve problems in the pro-

vision of the organization's services. Megginson, Mosely, and Pietri (1992, p. 669) recommend that the following steps be used by quality circles to propose and implement quality control measures.

1. Identify problem areas.
2. Select problem to solve.
3. Study the problem.
4. Plan its improvement.
5. Present improvement to management.
6. Implement improvement.
7. Study the results.
8. Decide if successful.
9. Make change permanent.

For sport managers, TQM principles should be of special interest because, according to Mawson (1993), sport consumers in the spectator, commercial, and club business have come to expect quality in service and products. Mawson (1993) recommends that sport managers who adopt TQM techniques need to include all employees in the development process. "Adherence to TQM principles could make the difference in the viability of a sport organization" (Mawson, 1993, p. 105).

Within the industry, operation and management of a sport facility must be centered on the quality of services offered. Recent research has indicated that "service quality is one of the most important problems facing management" (McDonald, Sutton, and Milne, 1995, p. 9). Their research examined various factors involved in customer satisfaction at professional basketball games. Spectators were surveyed in the sport facility and asked about their satisfaction with the services provided. The specific factors included (1) tangibles—the physical facilities, equipment, and appearance of personnel, (2) reliability—their ability to perform promised service dependably and accurately, (3) responsiveness—their willingness to help customers and provide prompt service, (4) assurance—the knowledge and courtesy of employees and their ability to inspire trust and confidence, and (5) empathy—the individualized attention provided to customers (McDonald, Sutton, and Milne, 1995). Their research found that the overall quality of service provided to the NBA fans was good as indicated by a rating of 4.86 points on a scale of zero to 7 points.

The concept of TQM has been around for decades, yet it has not been fully implemented in the sports facility management industry. In sport and public assembly facilities, you must be able to define TQM in operational terms. You must answer the question, "What are the standards by which we will be judged?" Most marketing executives will tell you that the best way to assess quality is through the consumer. What does the consumer want? How does the consumer develop opinions about your facility's operations? What can be done to assure that the consumer is pleased with the services provided? Excellence must exist at all levels of service. From the parking lot to the ticket window, from the concession stand to the ushers, and culminating in the traffic control officers encountered when exiting the facility, people expect and deserve the best.

Bernie Mullin, when serving as Vice President of Operations for the Colorado Rockies baseball club, constantly referred to the fans as "guests." This philosophy, originated by the Walt Disney Company, was applied by Mullin such that each person who attended a Colorado Rockies game deserved to be treated like a guest in your home. Maybe due in part to this philosophy, the Colorado Rockies broke all major league attendance records in their first season of operation.

Taking a similar approach to customer satisfaction, one collegiate athletic director actually drove to the outskirts of the city on the day of a football game and entered the traffic flow into the stadium. The unpleasant experiences encountered during this trip lead to major changes in the traffic operations on game days. Remember, you do not want the customers angry even before they come through the doors of your facility.

As the manager, you will want to create a system for gathering and managing customer and employee information regarding the quality of service. This can then be incorporated into the overall management of the facility. If you don't exist to serve customers through excellence in service, then why do you exist? In summary, you should operate a first-class sport facility with your customer as the focal point by using an effective structure, well-trained and courteous employees, and a competent staff.

PRIVATIZATION AND CONTRACTING

There has recently been an emerging trend that deserves the attention of a prospective facility manager. There is a move toward the professional management of sports facilities. The primary advantage of professional management is that a company that specializes in sports facility management is hired to independently manage and run the center, as opposed to having it managed by individuals employed by the city or college. This outside firm typically brings a level of management expertise with advanced training and skill and can therefore manage the facility very effectively (Howard and Crompton, 1995). This trend is also occasionally referred to as privatization.

Another specific advantage of privatization is reduction in labor costs. Howard and Crompton (1995) indicate that private firms typically have overhead (benefit) costs of 12% of salaries, whereas the average overhead costs for government agencies is 30% to 35% of employee pay. The difference of 18 to 23% is a substantial management savings. Public entities often must operate within agreements reached between labor union and governments. In one example, privatization reduced labor expenses by 50% for a golf course in California (Howard and Crompton, 1995). One final advantage of contracting facility management to outside companies is that liability risks are reduced. Government agencies can reduce their risk of litigation by requiring that the outside corporation indemnify (hold harmless) the municipality through insurance.

Difficulties have arisen with outside contractors when quality of service has been an issue. At times, contracted companies have not delivered service at the level of quality that in-house employees have provided. In some organizations employees consider the facility "their building" and, as a result, take substantial pride in its maintenance and operation. Another shortcoming of contracting for facility operations is that, on occasion, personnel turnover has been high. When an organization hires full-time employees, the same person is working at the facility from one day to the next. With contracted services, you often have a high variation in personnel assigned to the facility. It has been estimated that 10 to 15% of the nation's municipally owned sports facilities are currently operated by private companies. By the end of the 1990s this is expected to be near 40% (Stotlar, 1990).

Many sport facilities also contract portions of their operations to private firms. Those areas most typically available for private contracting are security, concessions, ticketing, novelty sales (merchandising), housekeeping (custodial), and advertising (Williams, 1990). Several situations may give rise to contracting facility services to outside firms. A shortage of cash or a financial emergency may be one reason to pursue an outside contractor. In these situations, you need only to pay for the services actually used. If you need only five hours of janitorial work, you simply contract for only that amount. In this situation, you don't have to pay for employee benefits or recruiting and training costs. In addition, your contract with the employment agency can specify the hours and dates for which the service is needed. This differs from hiring employees who prefer a standardized work schedule and demand overtime pay for atypical assignments and hours.

However, when you obtain contract workers, you may not get the same workers for all assignments. Therefore, the worker's familiarity with your facility and events is lower than that of employees. In some instances the loyalty of the contract worker has also been questioned. Some facilities have sought outside contractors when they have not been capable of providing a high standard of service. For example, in the area of ticketing, expensive equipment may be needed and the facility may not be able to afford the up-front expenses, yet a ticketing company could offset the capital outlay over the life of the contract.

Because the operational situations are unique for each facility, it may be wise to evaluate the potential advantages and disadvantages of contracting and private management. If you choose private management, you must establish a close working relationship with the firm providing the service.

CURRENT DEVELOPMENTS

In addition to the competencies that facility managers must have, there are always current developments that impact managers' decisions. Due to their impact, a few of the more important developments are briefly discussed here and are more thoroughly explained in other parts of the text.

Technology is exploding. Never has there been a time when things changed so rapidly. Therefore it is imperative that facility managers know about technological developments and the impact they

will have on the management of sport facilities. As an example, managers must ascertain ways in which computers can assist employees in performing their duties. There may also be new systems and software to expedite energy conservation or facility security.

The general trends regarding the influence of current technological developments are related by Naisbitt and Aburdene (1990) in *Megatrends 2000*. They state that "computers are turning buildings into 'smart' buildings that monitor and run themselves and connect occupants with the rest of the world" (Naisbitt and Aburdene, 1990, p. 307).

Ethics and principle-centered leadership are still impacting managers. Employees are demanding that managers operate within the very highest standards of morality and principle. Bridges and Roquemore (1992, p. 60) define ethical behavior as "taking the action that is right and just and that conforms to accepted standards for behavior." Managers must develop a social responsibility and a professional demeanor that include ethical behavior.

In setting policies and enforcing rules and regulations, managers are faced with an array of controversial decisions. Many of the decisions are difficult because they are based on ethical judgments and individual rights. Smoking policies are a prime example. Managers in a number of professional stadiums and arenas administer rules that prohibit smoking on the property. The rules stem from either legislative statute or locally generated policy. In fact, several states have voted to ban smoking in all places of public accommodation. If there is no governmental law regulating your facility, these decisions will be left to the manager. The decision-making process must, therefore, be undertaken with the utmost sensitivity to individual rights and the rights of the general public.

Another controversial area is the advertisement of alcohol and tobacco. In order to enhance revenues, many sports facilities sell facility signage. Yet, many of these same sports facilities provide a number of programs for youth. Also, many people feel that it is unethical to promote products that are considered unhealthy. Furthermore, some sport organizations and leagues prohibit alcohol and tobacco signage in venues where their events are conducted.

Another highly debated issue that you may encounter as a sport facility manager is the rental of the facility by groups who espouse racial or sexual discrimination. Others share this responsibility, as well, including owners, directors, government officials, and attorneys. Based on the U.S. Constitution, publicly owned facilities may not be able to deny access to individuals or groups based on their beliefs or restrict their freedom of speech. Regardless of the ethical issue, managers constantly deal with people and owe their constituents an elevated standard of ethical behavior.

SUMMARY

The ultimate goal in facility management is to provide the highest standard of service to all clients of the facility. This includes employees, contractors, promoters, entertainers, owners, and patrons. This goal can be accomplished with consideration of clients' needs through attention to quality and the operation of a comprehensive, well-planned facility. Both Lambrecht (1987) and Bridges and Roquemore (1992) conclude that the competency to manage personnel is one of the most important management tasks because "managers manage people."

The information in this chapter was designed to assist you with the effective organization and staffing of a sport facility. Your success will depend on your ability to design an efficient operational structure; hire, train, and motivate capable employees; and implement appropriate operational policies.

QUESTIONS

1. How do the operating procedures and philosophies of a sports facility in the public sector differ from those of a facility in the private sector?
2. What critical factors influence the development of an organizational structure for operating a sport facility?
3. What is the difference between a job specification and a job description?
4. What are some of the advantages and disadvantages of privatizing the management of sports facilities?

ACTIVITIES

1. Interview the manager of a facility in one of the three sectors—private, municipal, and college/university. Request information on the organizational structure

and inquire as to how and why this structure has evolved.
2. Write a job description and specifications for two positions in facility management—one for a person in management, one for a person in operations.

SUGGESTED READINGS

Facility management (1985). In Appenzeller and Lewis *Successful Sport Management*, Part 5. Charlottesville, Va: Michie Company.

REFERENCES

Appenzeller, H., and Lewis, G. (1985). *Successful sport management*. Charlotte, NC: Michie Company.

Boucher, R. (1984). The utility of the pre-employment interview. *Journal of Organizational Behavior*, pp. 195–98.

Bridges, F. J., and Roquemore, L. L. (1992). *Management for sport/athletic administration*. Decatur, Ga: ELS Books.

Chelladurai, P. (1985). *Sport management: Macro perspectives*. Victoria, B.C.: Sport Dynamics.

Chelladurai, P. (1987). Multidimensionality and multiple perspectives of organizational effectiveness. *Journal of Sport Management*, 1:37–47.

Finfrock, D. (1990). *Establishing operation procedures*. Irving, Tex: International Association of Auditorium Managers.

Flynn, R. B. (1993). Facility planning for physical education, recreation, and athletics. Reston, Va: American Alliance for Health, Physical Education, Recreation and Dance.

Howard, D. R., and Crompton, J. L. (1995). *Financing sport*. Morgantown, WVa: Fitness Information Technologies.

Lambrecht, K. W. (1987). An analysis of the competencies of sports and athletic club managers. *Journal of Sport Management*, 1(2):116–128.

Law, J. E. (1993, April). TQM and me: Why is it important? *School Business Affairs*, pp. 24–27.

Lewis, G., and Appenzeller, H. (1995). *Successful sport management*. Charlottesville, Va: Michie Company.

Mawson, L. M. (1993). Total quality management: Perspectives for sport managers. *Journal of Sport Management*, 7, pp. 101–106.

McDonald, M. A., Sutton, W. A., and Milne, G. R. (1995). TEAMQUAL: Measuring quality in professional team sports. *Sport Marketing Quarterly*, 4(2):9–15.

Megginson, L. C., Mosely, D. C., and Pietri, P. H. (1992). *Management: Concepts and applications*. New York: HarperCollins.

Nadler, D. A., Hackman, J. R., and Lawler, E. E. (1989). *Managing organizational behavior*. Boston: Little, Brown.

Naisbitt, J., and Aburdene, P. (1990). *Megatrends 2000*. New York, NY: William Morrow.

Stotlar, D. K. (1990). Facility Management. In B. K. Zanger and J. Parks, (Ed.), *Sport and fitness management*. Champaign, Ill: Human Kinetics.

Williams, S. (1990). *Patron services and event staffing*. Irving, Tex: International Association of Auditorium Managers.

U.S. Office of Personnel Management. (1991). *Federal total quality management handbook: Introduction to total quality management in the federal government*. Washington, DC: U.S. Government Printing Office.

3

Operations and Maintenance

David K. Stotlar

Operations management of sports facilities is a complex process that involves numerous administrative tasks and management procedures. Given the recent changes involving sport facilities presented in Chapter 2, the manager is responsible for governing and managing the facility and implementing the stated mission and purpose. Sports facilities have been constructed for a variety of purposes, which must be articulated through operations management. Some sport facilities are funded by specific user groups (i.e., college campus recreation buildings, private sport clubs), therefore, special attention is needed regarding the requirements of those groups. Municipally owned facilities are generally charged with serving the needs of the community's citizens. In some situations, one specific sport team may be a primary tenant (e.g., the NBA's Denver Nuggets in the publicly owned McNichols Arena) and would therefore have priority in use and scheduling. Implementation of the mission follows through policy formation and issues of operations management and control.

POLICIES AND PROCEDURES

According to Appenzeller and Lewis (1985), managerial control of a facility is typically determined at the time of construction. Whoever pays for construction has the control. Facility control is operationalized through statements of policies and procedures (Appenzeller and Lewis, 1985; Flynn, 1993; Finfrock, 1990). These parameters guide the manager in day-to-day operations. Finfrock (1990, p. 1) has defined policy as "the philosophy under which a facility is operated. It should generally take the form of a 'mission statement' which can be the basis for establishing all aspects of the operational procedures." Managers must therefore rely on the mission statement to generate procedures. Procedures are defined as the "series of steps to be followed by the staff members in order to carry out their assigned duties" (Finfrock, 1990, p. 1).

The importance of policies and procedures has been stressed by many authors (Appenzeller and Lewis, 1985; Flynn, 1993; Finfrock, 1990). They must be created prior to the first event scheduled in a facility. It is too hard to gain control after the facility begins operation. Another benefit of creating the policies and procedures early is that they can be used in the training of the facility's staff. Most policies and procedures are contained in an operations manual, which can clarify operating guidelines and position descriptions for the staff. It can also assure consistency among staff members when services are provided to patrons. Finfrock (1990) adds that "after the policies and procedures are written, but prior to their enactment and prior to the printing of the manual, it is important that each item be evaluated and examined from many and varied perspectives. Have them thoroughly examined by your legal counsel and especially by your staff members who are going to have to enforce them" (p. 8).

ORGANIZING OPERATIONS AND MAINTENANCE

Organizing, as a management function, involves transforming the established organizational structure into the daily operations of the facility. Proper management of functions can lead to substantial financial savings. These savings can be achieved in labor, material, maintenance, shop equipment, and capital investment. Unfortunately, operations and maintenance requirements are invariably not given adequate consideration when facilities are being designed. Architects are typically concerned with the artistic and structural facets of construction. The operations and maintenance managers in an organization are usually so far down in the management hierarchy that few planners consider the importance of their participation in design review. In addition, maintenance is often considered so mundane, that it should not present a challenge to the facility designer.

Therefore, it is the responsibility of operations and maintenance managers to convince upper management to include them in all planning, design, and organizing decisions. Some of the items that should be considered during the design phase are lockers for maintenance and janitorial personnel, janitorial closets, building hardware and fixtures, power and water sources, logistics operations, storage areas for maintenance, and the location of building equipment, tools, and supplies.

Basic Functions

Several basic operations and maintenance functions affect cost and performance. Managers must determine the nature of the work to be performed by specifically defining each department's role and function. This includes making decisions regarding the grouping of the functions to be performed and determining when the operations and maintenance tasks are best accomplished. It is also important to remember that operations and maintenance managers must interact with other departments like finance, personnel, accounting, and purchasing. Organizing operations and maintenance tasks should be ongoing and managers should be prepared to reevaluate them periodically because the conditions under which the facility must operate do not remain constant (Stotlar, 1990).

In most maintenance operations two methods are available for organizing required functions. One method entails assigning functions by geography (location), and the other method separates the functions by task (specificity). Either method can be efficient. Grouping functions according to where they take place results in a decentralized de-

A mechanical equipment area

partment, usually with a supervisor assigned to each location. One example is a city sports facility department organized into northern and southern sections, each having a full complement of personnel and having the capacity to carry out all maintenance tasks necessary for facility operation. The advantages of geographical organization usually include reduced travel time to and from jobs, more intimate knowledge of the equipment through repetitive experience, and more familiarity with the specific needs in the area serviced. For all of these reasons, improved relations are generated between the users of the facilities and the maintenance department. Improved job performance can also result from the close alliance formed through working in the smaller groups.

The main disadvantage with geographically zoned maintenance is the potential for inefficiency. Duplication of shop equipment and tools with a low rate of use can also result as each location endeavors to be self-sufficient. Inefficiency can also result if significant differences exist in the ages of sport facilities. Maintenance personnel assigned to older facilities could be overworked, whereas those in newer and more modern buildings may be less burdened.

The alternative organizational scheme whereby workers are organized around specific tasks and trade skills typically results in a structure that is more centralized. A centralized shop organization can benefit from more qualified technical supervision within trade specializations. A supervisor with training and experience in electrical engineering can better supervise the group of electricians than could a structural engineer who was the only supervisor at an off-site location. Improved training and higher quality equipment can also help justify larger central maintenance facilities. Other advantages of this organizational method generally include greater ease in dispatching specialized tradespeople and craft workers to match the demands of specific tasks. Central control often creates a better network among the varied trades or craft areas. Finally, the determination and administration of plantwide priorities is facilitated with a centralized system of control.

The layout and operating conditions of the facilities and maintenance department should be carefully analyzed to determine the required degree of centralization or decentralization. Managers must be able to identify the factors that impact this decision. A centralized organization is appropriate when travel time to and from the job site is short or when it can be minimized by proper scheduling and planning. Other factors are the convenience offered by a centralized location for single-site delivery of materials and increased availability of required tools. Geographically segmented maintenance should be used when distances between the buildings are large and when specific and intimate knowledge of each facility is essential for proper maintenance. Also, a geographically segmented system relies on radio/computer dispatch or prearranged telephone contacts, but a central maintenance shop allows constant communication between supervisors and operatives.

Inventory and Purchasing

Regardless of the system selected, it is essential for the operations and maintenance manager to establish support sections with specialized activities. One such section is the stockroom operation to control and manage maintenance inventory. Generally, inventory can be classified into two groups. "Standard stock" consists of items that are used regularly and have a relatively low unit value. Items that are used continuously (e.g., standard nuts, bolts, screws, nails, and other hardware) and materials that are used regularly (e.g., lubricants, paint, wood, wire) are generally referred to as standard stock items. For these items a minimum on-hand quantity is established and stock replenishment is initiated when the quantity on hand reaches the specified limit. These items can usually be handled on an "open-stock" basis. Open stock refers to a system whereby workers can obtain goods directly from supply bins without the use of a stock requisition form. This is a matter of the cost of paperwork. Does it cost more in work-hours, storage, and aggravation to process requisitions for nuts and bolts than the cost of occasional theft? Management must make that decision.

"Special-buy" items tend to have a higher unit value than standard stock items and are usually held on a closed-stock basis (under lock and key with limited access). As special-buy items, they are obtained on the basis of individual procurement requests, because there is no provision for a minimum quantity or automatic stock replenishment.

Typical stockroom operations include the following:

1. Issuing stock
2. Processing returned stock
3. Receiving standard and special stock, materials and supplies from vendors
4. Stocking shelves and bins
5. Certifying, receiving, and invoicing documents (interface with finance)
6. Conducting physical inventories
7. Reporting stock outages
8. Initiating stock orders
9. Declassifying items as standard stock (low turnover)
10. Identifying and disposing of surplus inventory
11. Identifying items that should be added to the standard stock inventory (usually highly repetitive special buys).

A typical tool crib in a university facility

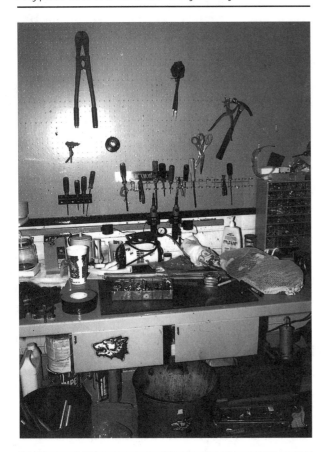

Occasionally, the maintenance department may find itself doing purchasing for the whole organization. In this case, you may need to establish a procurement department. A procurement department normally performs the following services:

1. Preparing purchase requisitions or purchase orders for special-buy and standard-stock materials, tool crib items, and capital equipment
2. Coordinating deliveries with vendors
3. Coordinating vendor services such as pest control, drapery cleaning, and carpet cleaning
4. Locating sources of supply
5. Coordinating the evaluation of new products

Because of the close relationship with the stockroom operation regarding standard-stock materials and supplies that constitute the largest portion of the procurement workload, the procurement section is frequently combined with stockroom operations. If they are not combined, both supervisors should report to the same person to facilitate coordination between the two operations in fulfilling the overall supply function.

Most operations and maintenance departments have a "tool crib." The purpose of a tool crib is to provide a storage area and inventory control for portable tools and equipment that are not assigned to individual workers on a permanent basis. The specific responsibilities that should be assigned to a tool crib operation are as follows:

1. Issuing items
2. Maintaining sign-out records
3. Receiving and inspecting returned tool crib items
4. Initiating action to service or repair tool crib items
5. Initiating action to retire or replace tool crib items
6. Monitoring usage and obtaining additional tool crib items as needed

In a maintenance department organized by area, a tool crib operation may be established in each area in addition to a central crib to support facility-wide needs. When tool crib operations are decentralized, there should be a consolidated as well as an onsite inventory control system. Without such a system, each tool crib will have a tendency to promote its own needs and refuse to cooperate in sharing its items even to meet emergencies. This can result in substantial duplication of items with an attendant low usage rate and a reluctance to lend items if one crib's item is being repaired. Tool crib operations can be combined with stockroom operations, which permits cross-training and use of personnel in both operations, and provides economies of scale in handling the combined workload.

If operations and maintenance personnel are assigned to keep track of costs, you have the beginning of finance functions. Coordinating the planning of expenditures, finalizing departmental budgets, and keeping costs within the budget are of vital importance. The responsibilities of an operations finance staff in this scenario include:

1. Coordinating the preparation of department budgets and justifications
2. Analyzing cost performance against budgets
3. Investigating deviations from budgets to determine causes
4. Coordinating the preparation of budget revisions
5. Working with the accounting department

Because accounting departments often have little concern about how well their chart of accounts and reports match the information needs of the maintenance department, they typically place costs of all supplies (whether T-shirts or nails) into one account. Therefore, operations and maintenance managers must keep their own specific and well-documented records.

Transportation Services

Transportation services are often assigned to the operation and maintenance division because of the logistics and nature of the service. In a large organization that has a substantial inventory of various types of vehicles (cars, trucks, scrubbers, forklifts, mowers), the transport function is frequently specialized within the maintenance department. The transportation-related duties typically include:

1. Ordering additional or replacement vehicles (leasing, buying or renting)
2. Servicing and repairing vehicles
3. Coordinating the retirement of vehicles
4. Managing fleet inventory (what types of vehicles are needed in the inventory)

Standardization of vehicle type can provide for interchangeable use of vehicles according to a repair cycle or on a pool basis. Because of the requirements for team travel, sports programs, and facil-

ities operations, some sports maintenance operations warrant an in-house garage to perform service and repairs. To facilitate coordination, the garage operation should be part of the transport services section in the maintenance department.

As mentioned previously, many operations and maintenance factors should be addressed in the planning stages. People involved in design of the facility must take into account maintenance operations early in the design phase. For instance, two methods are usually available for window cleaning, "over the roof" and "ground up." In both cases, special equipment is going to be required for any structure higher than one story. The ground-up system requires a hose and squeegee, whereas the over-the-roof method calls for an expensive scaffolding. Plans for installing water and electrical power sources for the window-washing equipment would have to be instituted during the construction of the facility. The frequency of cleaning required depends on many variables such as weather (rainfall, snow), the surrounding environment (amount of smoke and dust), and how dirty you are willing to let the glass get (quality of maintenance effort).

Janitorial Services

Another major factor to be considered in building design is a determination of the number of janitorial closets required in a facility. Some general rules in planning are that there should be at least one janitorial closet per floor in addition to one per restroom complex. Locating janitorial closets next to, or in restrooms is ideal because the restroom can provide the water source and sewage system for the mop sink. Also, restroom supplies can be stored in the immediate area, which facilitates replenishment of dispensers.

Depending on the use of the area being serviced, other cleaning supplies require storage space. For example, office areas require dust cloths, upholstery and fabric cleaners, furniture polish, and glass cleaner, while locker rooms require space for mop buckets, sponges, clothes, cleaners, and soaps. In addition, washer and dryer hook-ups should be situated nearby because the maintenance department is often the one to whom laundry functions are delegated. Because a weekly or monthly contingent of supplies needs to be stored, security is a factor. Therefore, automatically locking doors should be planned from the onset. In many instances, the U.S. Office of Safety and Health Administration (OSHA) also requires chemical storage areas to be locked. Storage space should also be planned to accommodate floor-finishing equipment. If your building has tile floors, scrubbing equipment will be required. Facilities with carpeted areas must plan storage space for vacuum cleaners. In large facilities, locker space with controlled access should be provided for janitorial and maintenance personnel. Without lockers there could be pilferage of personal property such as coats, jackets, wallets, and lunch buckets. Substantial long-term savings in operating and maintenance costs can accrue through adequate consideration of the needs for proper organization and accessibility to equipment for use, service, repair, and replacement.

Costs

Estimating operations and maintenance cost depends on three factors: the cost of maintenance labor costs, the cost of equipment to perform the maintenance, and the cost of expendable materials and supplies. The initial step in estimating these costs is planning the maintenance effort. Effort depends on the required level of sanitation, the acceptability of "downtime" in the facility, and the overall appearance of the facility.

A rudimentary approach to maintenance is to wait until something breaks down. Here you simply try to repair buildings and equipment as they wear out. This system creates substantial downtime and typically generates higher costs. Abiding by a system of preventive maintenance will help you provide a continuous basic level of maintenance.

To create a periodic preventive maintenance schedule for all building systems and equipment, you must start by establishing a list of all tasks to be performed. Manufacturers' maintenance standards are often included in the operating manuals that accompany most equipment. Attention to these standards is required so that the warranties remain intact. Experience is also important and experienced workers and engineers frequently add their servicing recommendations to the manufacturer's minimum standards. Next, the frequency of each type of service is recorded along with the trade skills necessary to accomplish the tasks. An estimate of the amount of time to perform each servicing task is then computed. The total hours by craft are then compiled for an annual figure.

The data can then be used for estimating total maintenance costs. This process also provides base-level personnel data needed for staffing decisions.

The first step in calculating maintenance costs is reviewing each of the operations identified above. The tasks prescribed, the number of trade workers, and the time required to perform each function are then used to compute the labor hours needed for the job. Table 3.1 shows the average percentage of available maintenance time (hours) allocated to various maintenance functions.

As an example of how to determine labor costs, assume that your calculations show that you need 2,200 hours of scheduled electrical repair, service, and construction projects per year. You need to increase the total by 15% to account for emergency repairs, which yields 2,530 hours of required electrical services. Next, you have to compute the number of hours per year that one electrician could work. Start with the average 40-hour week. With 52 weeks per year, one electrician provides a total of 2,080 work hours. However, if you are going to allow for 2 weeks vacation, you are now down to 2,000 hours (2,080 − 80). Most organizations allow workers to accumulate sick leave. A typical figure is two 8-hour days per month. Your available pool is now reduced to 1,808 hours (2,000 − 192). Workers do not really like to work on government holidays either so you need to subtract another 10 days from your available hours, which leaves 1,728 hours (1,808 − 80) per electrician per year.

To arrive at your personnel expenses for this area, you now need to determine the wages for this work. Continuing with our example, you know that you will pay the electrician for 2,080 work hours (although the worker will only be working for 1,728 hours but will be paid for sick days, holidays, vacations). Your investigation indicated that electricians typically receive a wage of $20.00 per hour.

Table 3–1   Maintenance department allocation

Type of work	Average effort
Emergency repairs	10%
Scheduled service/inspection	39%
Scheduled repairs/documentation	24%
Construction/projects	10%
Paid nonwork days	17%

To this you must add approximately 20% for fringe benefits including sick, holiday, and vacation time, health insurance, worker's compensation, and pension plans. As a result, your cost for the electrician is $24.00 per hour ($20.00 + $4.00 = $24.00). In summary, the cost for one electrician for one year is $49,920 ($24.00 × 2080). The next task is to deduce the number of electricians needed for the facility.

Since we had determined the total number of electrical hours to be 2,530, we need to divide that number by the number of hours that one worker would provide in a year (1,728). Our figures tell us that we need to hire 1.5 electricians. We now have a classic management dilemma. You can hire one electrician and pay him or her overtime wages for the extra work required, you can hire two electricians and have some hours assignable to other functions, or you can hire part-time employees to fill in the extra hourly demands. The best of these alternatives depends on the unique nature of your facility. (Because this book is not intended to be a personnel management text, a complete discussion of this decision is not pursued here.)

The same process needs to be followed for each of the operations and maintenance areas. To complete the budget picture, you add in the costs of tools, equipment depreciation, and expendable supplies. You should also remember that a span of control (workers per supervisor) of around 5 to 1 is common for this function of sports facility management. Also note that these data are not static. As equipment ages, it requires increased levels of maintenance. Similarly, if you replace a faulty pump, for example, maintenance hours decrease because new equipment does not require a high degree of servicing. Hence, the use of historical records as models or guidelines must be done with care and in consideration of the present set of circumstances. Likewise, your records must be complete and current to contribute both to ongoing monitoring and to future budget planning.

SCHEDULES

One of the most popular staffing methods for sports facilities is a system of shift assignment, whereby maintenance tasks are assigned in blocks of time or by shifts. The first shift is usually the normal business hours of the facility. As much work as possible should be handled on the day shift; lowest total maintenance costs and minimum downtime result from using the least amount of coverage that can be tolerated on the other shifts. This situation is attributable to the fact that suppliers, support services, and full supervision are available during the day shift. During the second, or after-hours, shift janitorial and painting tasks are usually performed because they are nonpeak times and the building may be empty. Although this is the general rule, the nature of sports facilities gives rise to other considerations. In the majority of sport facilities, a substantial amount of the activities takes place after "normal" working hours and on weekends. Maintenance coverage has to be adjusted to accommodate these needs.

Efficient staffing patterns are best accomplished through a planning staff. The basic rationale for a planning staff is that the skilled laborers who are engaged in maintenance tasks should not have to interrupt their activities to plan job sequences. This same concept carries through to the separation of job performance from other functions, such as ordering and stocking supplies, maintaining administrative records, and preparing departmental budgets.

The functions of a planning staff vary, but some of the tasks normally assigned are:

1. Processing work orders
2. Scheduling work
3. Reviewing plans and specifications
4. Planning jobs
5. Applying job standards
6. Estimating costs (budgetary and planning)
7. Coordinating construction by in-house crews
8. Supervising construction contractors
9. Planning human resources

The work of an efficient planning staff can actually lower your department's expenses. In some operations, productivity of in-house maintenance crews have improved in excess of 25 percent.

The size of a crew on a given shift depends primarily on the type and amount of work to be performed. To avoid paying overtime wages to provide coverage for facilities used seven days per week, the techniques of designated relief workers and crews with an odd number of workers can be applied. Again, the nature of sport facilities (used during off-hours) creates an impact.

Table 3–2 Three-person maintenance crew

Day	Person 1	Person 2	Person 3	Daily crew size
Monday	X		X	2
Tuesday	X		X	2
Wednesday	X	X	X	3
Thursday	X	X		2
Friday	X	X		2
Saturday		X	X	2
Sunday		X	X	2

With a three-person crew, you always have an overage in crew size for one day. The schedule in Table 3.2 calls for an extra person on Wednesday. Careful planning can make this "extra" person very helpful. For example, if you have special events that run every Friday, you can adjust the schedule to have additional coverage on that day. On the other hand, you may want three people to work on Monday to recover from high use on the weekend and to prepare for the week ahead. As you can see from Table 3.3, a seven-person crew rotation produces a consistent level of support.

Properly planned, a periodic maintenance program can effectively schedule routine and emergency inspection and maintenance of building equipment, distribution systems, janitorial services, painting, and groundskeeping for sport facilities.

DOCUMENTATION

Documentation time allocated in Table 3.1 is likewise critical. For all repairs, maintenance and inspection workers need to provide written feedback to assist supervisors in completing their reports to management. Often graphs depicting the data will dramatically show the maintenance needs to senior management, and are valuable when combined with periodic written reports. Facility operations can also be enhanced by "Work in Progress Files." These files track ongoing work authorizations and allow supervisors to keep track of current work in the facility. These reports form the basis for planning and human resource allocation.

It is crucial that maintenance schedules be coordinated with schedules of other departments. Think how tragic it would be if your schedule called for refinishing the indoor tennis courts on the same dates a program director had a tournament planned. What if your staff drained the swimming pool when a major swimming competition or revenue-generating program had been booked? This coordination with other departments takes a great deal of preplanning and cooperation. There should be a written maintenance calendar to serve as a ready reference after a schedule has been determined in conference. Follow-up notices such as newsletters or postings on bulletin boards are also helpful reminders to the facility staff.

Work Orders

All operations and maintenance procedures must be managed and controlled. The primary mechanism for accomplishing this control is the work order. A work order, as the main operational document, serves as a notice that a specific operation is to be performed. It provides authorization for the expenditure of labor and materials necessary for proper performance of the work. A completed

Table 3–3 Seven-person maintenance crew

Day	Person 1	Person 2	Person 3	Person 4	Person 5	Person 6	Person 7	Daily crew size
Monday	X		X		X	X	X	5
Tuesday	X		X	X	X	X		5
Wednesday	X	X		X	X	X		5
Thursday	X	X		X	X		X	5
Friday	X	X	X	X			X	5
Saturday		X	X	X		X	X	5
Sunday		X	X		X	X	X	5

work order also provides a record that the operation was successfully performed. Cost and labor forecasts are also facilitated with feedback regarding materials used and actual work hours expended.

COMPUTERIZED OPERATIONS

The process for establishing a computer-based maintenance system (CMS) involves a team approach. Trade workers, supervisors, and facility engineers all need to have input into the system. Common elements in computerized facility operations include maintenance tasks for each facility, personnel required for each task, time required to complete the task, time interval for required maintenance, and generation of work orders. Climate and lighting control are functions that have traditionally been reserved for mainframe computers, however, with the recent upgrades in memory these functions can now be accommodated on stand-alone personal computers (PCs).

Generally, two options are available for the introduction of computers to operations management. You can have a program written for the task at hand through a programming consultant or purchase a prepackaged commercial program that can be adapted for your specific tasks. The current market has several high-quality facility and maintenance management programs, so this option is recommended. If you have very special needs, you may have to seek competent programming assistance, which may be available in another department of your organization. The major problem with dedicated programs is that the user is not generally able to make program alterations and the programmer must be rehired for even minor changes.

The power of the computer can be seen in the manner in which it can be used to manage complex information in facility management. The computer can search, find, and print specific information. For example, it might find bookings made by a specific user or find and print all reservations made for a certain playing field in the month of May. Some of the programs have a feature that also prints a reservation card for the person making the request.

One of the major tasks in the operation of any sport facility is scheduling. The variety of things that are scheduled is amazing. We schedule staff, buildings, fields, meeting rooms, weight rooms, swimming pools, and all maintenance functions. This information can be processed quickly and accurately by the computer and can be easily modi-

Computerized systems control is often tied in to building design.

fied as bookings and demands change. The scheduling of hourly employees is a task that can be expedited by the computer. Through these programs the names of the workers can be entered beside the times that they are scheduled to work. Lists of tasks for each person can be generated along with daily or weekly blocks of time. Any changes that become necessary can be made quickly, and new schedules can be printed with relative ease. Information (e.g., forms, schedules, lists) that is used repetitively can be duplicated and the minor changes can be made as needed (e.g., daily, weekly, monthly, annually).

Scheduling is not the only task the computer can complete regarding facilities. Equipment inventory and equipment ordering can also be accomplished with microcomputers. The primary capabilities of the program should include the ability to monitor current inventory, locate inventory items, control reordering and lead time, produce inventory lists and reports, and provide assistance for forecasting and planning. Separate files can be created for each area or unit and a data base program could be used to organize the information. Each piece of equipment and its location can be documented and recorded. While individual computers may perform functions at stand-alone sites, communications software can provide a network for the entire facility's operation. Computers can be used to keep accurate records of maintenance and repair through the development of a computerized maintenance system. This system provides information on "(1) equipment status, (2) maintenance due, (3) maintenance history, (4) maintenance budget, and (5) performance and services history" (Horine, 1985, p. 329).

A variety of operations and maintenance functions related to financial management can be accomplished through the use of computerized systems. They include accounts receivable, accounts payable, general ledger, payroll, and cost forecasting. Financial management packages are usually designed for general business operations but have formats that are relatively flexible and can be adapted for facility management. The accounts receivable segment usually performs the following functions: preparation of invoices, maintenance of customer accounts, and production of sales and other reports. The features that often appear in this function are purchase order control, invoice processing, check writing and control, purchase forecasting, and vendor information analysis. In the operations and maintenance setting, these features should satisfy the needs and desires of the manager.

On a larger scale, some operations and management functions involve enormous projects that span several years. Project planning has been done for many years and various computer programs are available to assist managers in this area. These programs feature a time-line representation of start and stop dates, slack time, holidays, and deadlines

Computers are especially useful in controlling facility operations.

for up to 300 tasks. A multitude of different computer-generated reports can be produced covering project tasks, cost estimates, staffing levels, downtime, earliest start dates, latest finish dates, and deadlines for project tasks. The interactive time chart and the reports assist facility managers with investigating tradeoffs among staffing, dollars, and time. A critical path capability indicates which group of tasks directly affect the overall length of a project schedule. If any task along the critical path is not accomplished on time, completion of the overall project will be delayed. Projects can be displayed in graphic form or via text and can be arranged in a variety of ways: by date, critical path, or task classification. The value of this type of computerized program in planning, maintenance, and construction of sport facilities should be readily apparent.

The duties of sport facility managers have changed so dynamically in the past few years that the use of a microcomputer is a necessity. The staggering growth and expansion of information generated with regard to programs, staff, maintenance, equipment, and scheduling makes it obvious that a computer can assist with information-based decision making. Managers need a computerized systematic method for processing the overload of information they receive. The purpose of computerized information systems is to provide the facility manager with the necessary data for making intelligent decisions. The system cannot make decisions, but it can make information available quickly, accurately, and in a form that managers can interpret. Through computer-based systems, information can be retrieved much faster than through traditional methods. Among the areas that lend themselves to computerization are event scheduling, work order management, equipment inventory management, user/client data, and fiscal management. It is imperative that when administrators are required to make decisions, they make informed decisions based on current information. All managers must make decisions, but the success of the decision often depends on the quality of the information on which they base their decisions.

SUMMARY

Sport facilities are constructed and designed to serve various community and commercial func-

tions. The variety often presents difficult decisions for facility managers. Outcomes from these configurations determine the operational guidelines for managers. Given the parameters implicit in this situation, managers must organize facility functions to optimize program delivery and cost savings. These savings can be achieved in labor, material, and capital investment. Facility managers should expedite efficient operations by defining the role and function of the maintenance units. This includes making decisions regarding the grouping of the functions to be performed and determining when tasks are best accomplished in coordination with other departments.

Practices that are essential for proper management of operations and maintenance functions include the following. ·

1. *Planning:* Planning involves determining what maintenance work should be performed on a periodic basis and establishing staffing levels and schedules for all work required. As mentioned previously, your planning staff determines the tasks and schedules to be employed through the reference to the building's history, personal experience, and manufacturer's warranties.

2. *Preparing work orders:* Work orders can be prepared on an automated or manual basis. Regardless of the method, work orders should be prepared in advance of the scheduled dates for performance of the operations. If the paper work authorizing the work is not available for distribution, the schedules become meaningless. Forms should be devised and printed to meet your particular requirements.

3. *Distributing work orders:* Work authorization orders should be dispensed from a central location at a designated time each day. All workers would be required to pick up their orders for the day. If the operation is decentralized, a supervisor may be assigned to retrieve the orders for each remote location. With due consideration given to the amount of work being assigned, work orders for a skilled craftsperson should be grouped by geographical area or building to reduce travel time whenever possible. Completion notices should be forwarded at the conclusion of each job assignment. They should be filed with the same office/location that distributed the work order.

4. *Tracking:* Proper tracking is necessary to ensure that the assigned work was indeed completed. There should be a method for identifying work orders for which no completion notice has been received so that corrective action can be initiated. Another aspect of tracking work orders is that the information recorded can provide comparison of the actual performance time with an assigned standard. The key questions are whether the worker is able to complete the tasks within the assigned time and whether the quality of the work is within acceptable standards.

5. *Collecting and integrating data:* An integrated maintenance system requires more than completion of a given item of work and posting of cost and service data. Completed work orders should be processed for the purpose of closing out the "open order" files, maintaining historical maintenance records on selected items, and compiling actual costs of material and labor expended. Integration of these data into a centralized system allows managers to make future decisions based on reliable information.

QUESTIONS

1. What are the applications of computer technology in managing sport facilities?
2. What are the advantages and disadvantages of assigning maintenance functions by geographical location rather than by task?

ACTIVITIES

1. Schedule an appointment with the building engineer of a major sports facility and ascertain his or her most critical challenges.
2. Investigate the existence of an operations and policy handbook at a collegiate sports facility in your area. If you can acquire a handbook, discuss with a small group the various policy statements for the facility.

SUGGESTED READING

Farmer, P. J., Mulrooney, A. L., Ammon R. (1996). *Sport facility planning and management*, Morgantown WV: Fitness Information Technologies.

REFERENCES

Appenzeller, H., and Lewis, G. (1985). *Successful sport management*. Charlotte, NC: Michie Company.

Finfrock, D. (1990). *Establishing operation procedures*. Irving, Tex: International Association of Auditorium Managers.

Flynn, R. B. (1993). *Facility planning for physical education, recreation and athletics*. Reston, Va: American Alliance for Health, Physical Education, Recreation and Dance.

Horine, L. (1985). *Administration of physical education and sport programs*. New York: Saunders College.

Stotlar, D. K. (1990). Facility management. In J. B. Parks, and B. K. Zanger, *Sport and fitness management*. Champaign, Ill: Human Kinetics.

4

Financing Facilities

Tom H. Regan

Sport and recreation facilities throughout the country are integral parts of communities. Schools, community organizations, teams, leagues, and special interest groups use the facilities for sports, entertainment, and business. Professional teams (major and minor), colleges and universities, high schools, and all educational entities use facilities for a variety of sport and non–sport-related activities. The media has made famous major stadiums such as Camden Yards in Baltimore, The Ballpark in Arlington, Comiskey Park in Chicago, and Jacobs Field in Cleveland. However, many more small sport and recreational facilities are being built by local and regional communities throughout the United States.

This chapter focuses on the financial methods used to build sport and recreational facilities. The financial arrangements of the project are often the foundation for a successful facility. Budgets, cash flow, and financial statements depend on the facilities' debt service arrangements. The objective of sport financial management in the public sector is to minimize public subsidy, which translates into maximization of municipal cash flow. The objective of private sport management is to maximize shareholder wealth, which translates into maximization of stock price. It is important to understand how the facility is financed either publicly or privately. The objectives differ and therefore the financial arrangements also differ.

FINANCING OPTIONS

Financing sport- and recreation-related facilities often requires public, private, and joint public/private financing (see Figure 4–1). Each facility manager needs to determine the best financial arrangement for the facility. State, regional, and local government officials are involved in both public and private facilities. The community must determine if the need exists for a facility. Community leaders exert influences on the government officials to determine how a stadium, arena, recreation center, convention center, or related facility could be built. Government officials then contact experts to determine the most favorable financial arrangement for the community.

The Public Interest

It is important for government leaders to attract professional, collegiate, and interscholastic events and teams to their region or city. In the United States, cities compete to attract and retain professional sports franchises, major sports events, and facilities to their tax district. Federal, state, and local governments subsidize the financing of sports facilities. Financing arrangements are a key element attracting teams and investors. A key element of the funding plans is the exemption from federal, and most state and local, income tax on the interest earned on qualified municipal securities (munis) that could be issued to finance these stadiums. The borrower can then sell bonds at a lower interest rate than if the interest were taxed.

Government authorities are usually proponents of stadiums, arenas, and multipurpose recreational facilities. They claim without the necessary local support, teams and special sport and entertainment events might choose to relocate and the

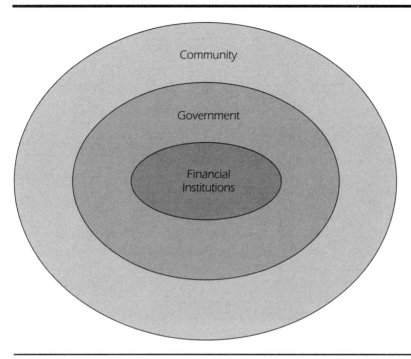

Figure 4-1 Successful financing for a sports facility draws funds from several sources.

cities would lose employment, tax revenues, and other indirect benefits. Opponents claim that benefits are probably overstated and likely future costs understated, making probable the need for even more public support in the future.

Sport arenas, stadiums, and multipurpose facilities are large capital projects for municipalities. Several mechanisms are used in structuring public sector participation in sports facility development, expansion, and renovation. Among the most common public financing instruments are bond issues backed by general obligations and/or dedicated revenues, lease appropriations bonds (certificates of participation), and tax increment bonds (see Figure 4-2).

State and local governments issue bonds in the capital market to finance their capital spending programs such as construction of arenas, stadiums, and parking lots, and upgrades of infrastructure. Infrastructure improvements include roads, water/sewer, and other utility needs. Investors call these bond issues *municipals* because they are issued by municipalities, subdivisions of states; they are also called *tax-exempts* because the interest investors receive is exempt from federal taxation. Most states exempt state income tax as well on the interest

earned from their bonds. Each state differs on how interest earned on bonds is taxed on a state basis. For example, in South Carolina citizens do not pay state income tax on bonds issued by a state municipality, however, bond interest earned from out-of-state bonds is subject to South Carolina state income tax.

General Obligation Bonds

General obligations bonds, backed by the full faith and credit of the issuing body (state, local, or regional government) generally require the use of ad valorem taxes. *Ad valorem* taxes are property taxes. This means taxes are levied according to the value of one's property; the more valuable the property, the higher the tax, and vice versa. The underlying theory of ad valorem taxation is that those owning the more valuable properties are wealthier and hence able to pay more taxes. General obligation (GO) bonds typically result in lower costs of issuance and higher credit ratings and the bond size is often reduced because a debt reserve fund is not always required. However, in some cases the bonding capacity of the municipal unit for other capital needs can be reduced.

Revenue Bonds

Revenue bonds are special obligations in public financing that are payable solely from a particular source of funds, which may include tax/surcharge revenues from hotel/motel, restaurant, sales, liquor/beer, cigarettes, and rental cars. (See Table 4-1). No pledge of state, regional or local ad valorem tax revenues is required; however, the typical revenue bond does carry a higher interest rate and requires a higher debt services coverage ratio as well as debt service reserve.

Certificates of Participation

Certificates of participation (COPs)—This public financing mechanism involves the governmental entity creating a corporation to buy (build) a public facility such as an arena or convention and visitors' center. The corporation then issues certificates of participation to raise money to buy (build) the public facility. The government leases back the building, and the lease payments are supposed to pay back the bonds. All this happens without a public vote.

Table 4–1 Sources of funding for a public facility

Hotel tax	Business license tax
Meals tax	Utility tax
Liquor tax	Road tax
Sales tax	Public and private grants
Auto rental tax	State appropriation
Property tax	Taxi tax
TIF districts	Team tax

Though certificates of participation (COPs) seem like traditional bonds, they are *not* backed by the full faith and credit of the government entity that issues the bonds. In a recession-hammered environment, certificates of participation and lease appropriation financing become popular with local governments looking to fund projects as real estate values decline, and with them property tax collections. Because these securities are not backed by the full faith and credit of a municipality, they are

Figure 4–2 Public financing of a facility includes several options.

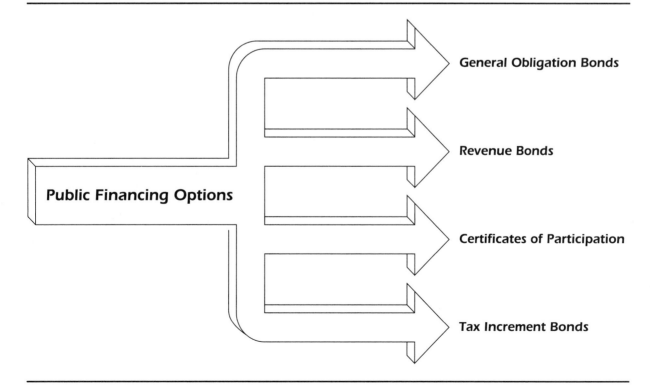

a greater risk than a general obligation bond and rated a full step lower.

Tax Increment Financing

Tax increment financing (TIF) transactions are based on the incremental property tax value of the ancillary economic development projects that are triggered by a major new facility. The tax base of a defined area identified as the tax increment financial (TIF) district surrounding the capital project is frozen and any increases in the tax base are used to repay tax increment financing bonds. The area surrounding the facility may be one county/parish or several counties/parishes.

The economics of any tax increment financing district are highly dependent on the development potential of a chosen site and its surrounding land. It is essential to anticipate future revenues on increases in ad valorem taxes or funding sources listed in Table 4–1.

Other Contributions from the Public Sector

The general public indirectly subsidizes sport organizations in other ways. There are a number of ways facilities have obtained additional public funding or government has directly reduced interest costs or borrowing requirements. A few of these mechanisms include the purchase or donation of land; funding of site improvements, parking garages, or surrounding infrastructure; direct equity investments or construction of related facilities, either directly or through an independent authority; and lending the government's credit by guaranteeing payment on new debt. Public sector

---

Table 4–2 Private sector revenue streams

Premium seating
Building rent
Corporate sponsorship
Lease payments
Vendor/Contractor Equity
Parking fees
Merchandise revenues
Advertising rights
Concessions revenue
Naming rights
Food and beverage serving rights

---

financing is extensive in professional sport franchises. Cities, states, and regional communities have financed the construction of major arenas, stadiums, and related convention centers for the benefit of the economic community. A recent trend is a joint financial arrangement described in the next section.

Private and Joint Public-Private Financing

The trend is leaning towards joint public-private partnerships. Public-private partnerships have been set up to finance major public assembly projects, particularly sports facilities. Typically, the public sector lends its authority to implement project funding mechanisms, while the private sector contributes project-related or other revenue sources. The expanded revenues generated by the facilities and their tenants have resulted in increases in the level of private participation in facility financing. Several of the private sector revenue streams (sources of revenue recorded in the income statement) that have been used in structuring facility financing include the items in Table 4-2.

Recent examples of joint public/private participation are illustrated in Table 4-3. It is clear that there has been extensive state and local government interest in the development of sports and other public assembly facilities in recent years, and there are a variety of means with which to structure the financing for those facilities. Expanding building operating and tenant revenue streams have encouraged a public/private partnership whereby public

---

Concessions—are they considered a part of the sport facility market?

General merchandise sales—are they a part of the sport facility market?

sector financing vehicles (various bonding techniques) are supplemented with private sector revenue streams. Creative financial arrangements allow communities to benefit economically and create a lifestyle conducive to positive public opinion. Table 4-3 provides examples of how communities created a financial vehicle to build sport and entertainment facilities.

For example, the Alamodome in San Antonio, Texas, is a 77,000 seat domed arena. The Alamodome was completely funded by an additional 1/2% sales tax on all retail sales. The $170 million project was completed in 1993 and is now debt free. Therefore, the facility now only has to cover operational expenses, not bond premium and interest expense.

Another example concerns the Colorado Rockies, the newest major league baseball team in the National League. The Rockies attracted more than four million six hundred thousand fans during the 1993 season. Coors Stadium, completed for the 1995 season opener in Denver, cost approximately $180 million. Financing the stadium required a vote by the public to collect one-tenth of one percent sales tax on all taxable retail sales within the jurisdiction of a special tax district. The special tax district included six Colorado counties—Adams, Arapahoe, Denver, Jefferson, Boulder, and Douglas. Colorado state legislators allowed the special tax district to be created in H.B. No. 90-1172, thereby creating a financial mechanism to provide a sales tax revenue stream to finance the revenue bonds necessary to build Coors Stadium.

The "Big Stadium," as the French refer to the proposed sight of the 1998 World Cup is in Saint Denis, France, outside of Paris. The stadium will be the largest outdoor facility in France with a seating capacity of 80,000. The World Cup Committee required France to build a stadium of this size to host the 1998 World Cup. Stadium cost will be approximately 2.4 BFF (Billion French Francs) or US $480 million dollars (at current rate of exchange).

Table 4–3 Examples of facilities financed by public/private partnerships

Facility	Public financing	Private financing
Alamodome, San Antonio, Texas	City revenue bond backed by 1/2% sales tax	Arena revenues
America West Arena Phoenix, Arizona	City revenue bonds backed by excise taxes	Naming rights Arena revenues
Bradley Center Arena Milwaukee, Wisconsin	Land donation purchased with general bond issue	Donations by local families
Charlotte Stadium (proposed) Charlotte, North Carolina	Land donation	Naming rights Arena revenue Premium seating deposits Luxury suite revenue
Coors Stadium, Denver, Colorado	Special tax district revenue bond secured by sales tax increase (1/10) of 1%	Naming rights Arena revenues
Delta Center Arena Salt Lake City, Utah	City tax increment financing bonds	Private loan secured by building revenue Naming rights
Cleveland Cavaliers Arena Cleveland, Ohio	County general obligation bonds Luxury tax allocation	Private donations and foundation contributions Premium seat deposits and revenue
The "Big Stadium" Saint Denis, Paris	City of Paris, land State, tax increase Region, tax increase City, tax increase	Private donations and contributions Club seating
Ballpark in Arlington Arlington, Texas	City revenue bond secured by sales tax increase Infrastructure improvements	Luxury suite revenues Ticket surcharge Seat options Concessionaire payments

The Big Stadium is an outdoor facility. The plan for financing the stadium is shown in Table 4-4. Although France has a sports lottery to fund and develop sports in the country, the lottery cannot be used to finance construction of sports facilities such as the Big Stadium.

The French method of financing the stadium is unique: they directly tax the citizens of the city, county, region, and nation to finance the stadium, infrastructure, equipment, and transportation. The liability is not long term (20 to 30 years) but should be quickly paid off during the construction period of the facility. This differs from the American way of financing most stadiums and arenas. The United States prefers to bond the taxing district over a longer period of time corresponding to the estimated life of the facility.

A key element in financing sport-related facilities is the relationship between government and entrepreneurial sport owners. A public/private partnership exists between the parties to create an

Table 4–4 Sources of financing the Big Stadium in France

Amount	Source of funds
200 MFF land (no estimated value)	City and County of Saint Denis City of Paris
300 MFF	Regional government
590 MFF	State (federal) government
1.3 BFF	Private or public/private funds

entertainment and economic opportunity for the regional economy. Without this relationship, few professional or collegiate programs could financially exist. Financing facilities and the revenue streams shared between the tenant and the municipality are essential for retaining and attracting sport franchises, special events, and fans.

The proper financial team needs to be assembled in order to design, organize, and finance a public, private, or public/private facility. Components of a successful team should include the following members:

- Issuer or owner
- Facility management
- Feasibility consultant
- Examination accountant
- Business plan consultant
- Financial advisor
- Architect
- Cost estimator
- Designer/Contractor
- Construction manager
- Senior underwriter
- Co-underwriter
- Bond council
- Issuer's legal counsel

The financing team must work together to obtain the goal and objective of the community or owner. The scenario for each facility is different and requires study and analysis. Successful facility financing is a partnership between the regional community, the owner/tenant, government, and the financial institutions.

A recent trend is for major facilities to be privately funded. Private ownership can only occur if all revenue streams from the facility go to the owner. The owner will not share income from parking, concessions, club seats, luxury box seating, advertising, and memorabilia sales with a second party. Private ownership does not mean a public subsidy did not assist the development of the stadium or arena.

Financing public/private sport and recreational facilities is a fascinating area of sport business. Each facility is financed differently depending on the government involvement and the needs of the region. Sport facilities continue to be built as professional sports expand and new minor leagues become established. It is a great time to be creative in developing financial plans for sport facilities.

Financing Daily Operations

Public/private sport facilities require operational financing. Daily operations require a commitment of funds to provide salaries, repairs and maintenance, equipment purchases, and various miscellaneous expenses. A consistent cash flow is required to provide money to the facility for these purposes.

Budgeting is the foundation for determining the financial commitment of a facility. It is not the scope of this chapter to develop the budgeting concepts necessary to properly administer the operational expenditures for a facility. Examples of revenue sources used for facilities include:

- Sales tax revenue
- Lottery revenue (from state)
- Hotel/motel tax
- Transportation tax
- General fund (government funded)

Budgets are an essential key to assist management in developing a sound financial plan for a facility. Facilities should not be built or remodeled if operational expenditures are not calculated into the tax structure necessary to build the facility.

SUMMARY

Public assembly facilities are necessary to attract fans to sport and entertainment events. Private, public, and combination financial arrangements provide various tools and options for governmental entities to pursue. The usual form of financing has been public subsidy from the city, county, or state governmental units. The federal government does subsidize sports stadiums and arenas by the implications of the federal tax exemptions provided to municipal debt issues.

QUESTIONS

1. Why do cities, counties, and state governmental entities build or assist in funding stadiums for sport organizations?

2. What types of public financing are available for constructing a stadium or arena?

3. What are the advantages and disadvantages of each public-financing option?

4. The trend is toward public/private facilities for major sport organizations. Why?

5. What is the advantage of a totally private facility compared to a public facility? (Consider finance, management, and community image.)

6. Bond indebtedness is either tax free or taxable to the investor. What advantage is a tax-free bond? Who can issue these bonds? Why is it important to maintain this advantage?

7. Cash flow is essential to repaying debt on municipal facilities. How important is it for a facility manager to be able to program the facility for various events, not only for team sports?

ACTIVITY

The Best Football Conference school needs to expand their stadium in order to compete for college recruits and due to competition from professional football in the region. They need to add 10,000 seats, new football offices, luxury and club seating, and a new press box/media center. The cost of the 10,000 seat addition is $12 million, the few football offices cost $3.8 million, and the luxury/club seat addition and press box area will cost $8.9 million. The total capital expenditure is $24.7 million. The school can only borrow $20 million from the municipal bonds available for capital projects. The athletic department must find the shortfall of $4.7 million. It looks toward revenue from ticket sales. Football has seven games this year and six games in alternating years.

The ticket prices are $22.00 per game and all are presold. The prime rate is 7.5% and is invested by the athletic department in secure accounts.

Can the cash flow from the additional ticket sales accommodate the additional borrowing to complete the capital expenditures necessary for the stadium? Discuss the types of borrowing that are available and present a proposal.

SUGGESTED READINGS

Goff, B., and Tollison, R. (1990). *Sportometrics* (1st ed.). College Station, Tex: Texas A&M University Press.

Gorman, J., and Calhoun, K. (1994). *The name of the game*. New York: John Wiley.

Staudohar, P. D., and Mangan, J. A. (1991). *The business of professional sports*. Urbana and Chicago: University of Illinois Press.

Zimbalist, A. (1992). *Baseball and billions*. New York: Basic Books.

REFERENCES

Cooley, P., and Roden, P. (1991). *Business financial management*, (2nd ed.) Hinsdale, Ill: Dryden.

Hurt, Richardson, Garner, Todd and Cadenhead. (1993). *Stadium leases arrangement*. San Antonio, Tex: International City Managers Association, Sports and Special Events Conference.

Regan, T. H. (1993). *Financing stadiums and arenas in the United States and Europe*. Paris, France. Proceedings from the 4th Annual International Conference on Sports Business. Columbia, SC: University of South Carolina.

5

Programming and Scheduling

Richard J. LaRue, Marcia L. Walker, Diane B. Krogh

This chapter presents another important function of the facility management process—programming. Programming refers to the procedure of planning and/or preparing programs, establishing schedules, and managing space.

STRATEGIC PROGRAM PLANNING

One of the methods used in the development of program plans is strategic program planning. Bridges and Roquemore (1992) define strategic planning as "the process of determining an organization's long-run goals and objectives in compliance with its mission and formulating the proper plan of action (strategy) that will guide efforts to achieve the desired end results over the long run."

Using the strategic program planning process, programs are developed that specifically relate to the philosophy of the organization. This philosophy is usually evident through the association's mission, strategies, and goals.

For instance, if the mission, strategies, and goals of a youth sports program stress that all baseball players who participate in the summer program have equal opportunities to practice and play, then it is critical that there are enough baseball fields, equipment, and coaches to conduct such a program. Likewise, if a private sport club's mission is to provide "state-of-the-art" programs that make a considerable profit, then the programs should incorporate cutting-edge ideas and innovative technology in a sound plan designed to make money.

According to Patton, Grantham, Gerson, and Gettman (1989), "A strategic management plan is a four-step, iterative process that involves

1. assessing needs and interests,
2. planning the programs,
3. implementing the programs, and
4. evaluating the programs to ensure that the organization's health/fitness mission is well organized and purposeful."

Needs Analysis

To acquire information for the planning process, management should conduct a "needs analysis" to ascertain the needs and interests of the clients or participants who use the facility. Primarily, this data is acquired through an internal managerial investigation and through external surveys of clients or participants. Examples of information collected for a needs analysis include programs and activities desired, facilities available, competitors, discretionary moneys, records of current facility usage, client/participant information, hours available for use, available staff, and current trends.

Obviously, the data sought must be based on the type of program for which it will be used. For instance, the needs of a private fitness facility are quite different from the needs of a municipal recreation and sport center; therefore, the programs should be different. Figure 5–1 is an example of a survey used to collect data from students for a leisure and fitness facility.

Figure 5–1 A survey of interests helps to program and schedule a college's facilities. (Courtesy of Richard J. LaRue)

STUDENT SURVEY OF LEISURE AND FITNESS INTERESTS

General Information:

Class: Freshman _____ Sophomore _____ Junior _____ Senior _____ Continuing Ed _____
Gener: Female _____ Male _____
Student Status: Full-time _____ Part-time _____
Housing: On campus _____ Off campus _____ [location] _____

Preferred Hours of Use: Please designate interest using **WD** for week day and **WE** for week end

	Pool Rec/Lap Swim	Fitness Center	Racquet Courts	Jogging Track	Fieldhouse	Tennis Indoor/ Outdoor
6:00–8:00 A.M.	_____	_____	_____	_____	_____	_____
8:00–11:30 A.M.	_____	_____	_____	_____	_____	_____
11:30–1:30 P.M.	_____	_____	_____	_____	_____	_____
1:30–3:30 P.M.	_____	_____	_____	_____	_____	_____
3:30–6:00 P.M.	_____	_____	_____	_____	_____	_____
6:00–8:00 P.M.	_____	_____	_____	_____	_____	_____
8:00–10:00 P.M.	_____	_____	_____	_____	_____	_____

NOTE: The Athletic and Recreational Center has the following fitness and support spaces: fieldhouse (basketball, volleyball tennis, etc.), indoor jogging track, Universal wgt. equipment, two racquetball courts, one squash court, six-lane 25-yard swimming pol, locker-room facilities, sports medicine/training room, and the Van Cise Fitness Center.

Programs/Classes: Please designate interest with a check mark.

Aquatic Programming
_____ Instructional swimming
_____ Lifeguard certification
_____ Swimming instructor certification
_____ Lifeguard instructor certification
_____ Synchronized swimming
_____ Springboard diving
_____ Other: _____

_____ Skin diving
_____ SCUBA diving
_____ Competitive swimming
_____ Therapeutic swimming
_____ Water exercise/aerobics
_____ Water polo

Fitness Programming
_____ Dance aerobics
_____ Starter fitness
_____ Fitness testing
_____ Weight training
_____ Other: _____

_____ Stress reduction
_____ Healthy back exercises
_____ Injury rehabilitation
_____ Aerobic training

Figure 5–1 (continued)

Sports Skills Programming

____ Gymnastics	____ Recreational games	____ Wallyball
____ Racquetball	____ Nordic skiing	____ Bicycling
____ Handball	____ Softball	____ Golf
____ Squash	____ Soccer	____ Alpine skiing
____ Basketball	____ Field hockey	____ Lacrosse
____ Martial arts	____ Volleyball	____ Badminton
____ Self-defense	____ Tennis	
____ Archery	____ Wrestling	
____ Other _____		

Intramural Sports Programs

____ Flag football	____ Soccer	____ Swimming
____ 2-on-2 volleyball	____ Golf	____ Water polo
____ Volleyball	____ Table tennis	____ Wallyball
____ Floor hockey	____ Innertube water polo	____ Badminton
____ Softball	____ Wiffleball	____ Bowling
____ Road races	____ Tennis	____ Handball
____ 3-on-3 basketball	____ Ultimate frisbee	____ Racquetball
____ Squash	____ Weight lifting	____ Wrestling
____ Other _____		

Sport Camps

____ Resident	____ Volleyball	____ Soccer
____ Basketball	____ Tennis	____ "All sports"
____ Day	____ Swimming	
____ Other _____		

PROGRAM DEVELOPMENT

In addition to the types of sports program and its philosophy, a number of other components impact program development. These components are listed as either internal factors or external factors. The internal factors include personnel policies and attitudes, physical resources (facilities and equipment), and the users and participants. The external factors involve professional governing organizations and agencies, laws and legislation, environment and geography, social influences, and trends.

Policies and Attitudes

The personnel, including both the management and the staff, have a lot of influence on program development. In fact, they should be involved in the development of the programs and the policies that govern those programs. The sports facility manager must be careful to avoid biases when selecting programs to offer. He or she should be open-minded and willing to try innovative activities and new trends in the profession.

Program development is also affected by the qualifications of the manager and the staff. Some programs cannot be offered without certified or licensed personnel. Other programs may present high-risk activities, in which case staff members responsible for such activities must have specific training and experience. In providing new sports or other types of physical activities, the manager may find it difficult to find qualified instructors.

Physical Resources

The physical resources available have a severe impact on the development of programs. Physical resources, in this case, refers to facilities and equipment. Many managers find that the organization's physical resources, the facility itself, dictate the programs. Unfortunately, this is not good management. Ideally, the programs should determine the type of facility needed, as described in Chapter 1. However, in most situations, managers and other personnel who develop programs are more transient than the buildings that house those programs. So, most program planners end up adapting or changing their desired programs to fit less-than-perfect surroundings.

Users and Participants

The type of persons using the facility impacts the program development. Demographics of the facility users should be available from the surveys collected during the needs analysis. Look closely at who the users are, including their ages and ability levels; what types of activities or specific programs they desire; and what time periods they prefer.

As an example, if the user information acquired through the needs analysis shows a dramatic increase in the number of older citizens in the local community, the impact on a public health and fitness club may be significant.

Governing Organizations and Agencies

Among the external factors that affect program development are the various organizations and agencies that govern specific sports and programs. These organizations and agencies exist at all levels and include government agencies, national and state associations, private voluntary organizations, and corporate groups.

Governmental departments regulate educational institutions through certification programs, such as North Central Association of Teacher Education (NCATE) and the Colorado Commission on Higher Education (CCHE). Within their jurisdiction, they control the curriculum that must be offered to obtain licenses and/or certification for

teaching or coaching. Therefore, their requirements must be met by offering certain courses that, of course, impact programming at a college or university offering these types of degrees.

Other organizations that influence programming by establishing regulations and standards include Aerobics & Fitness Association of America; American College of Sports Medicine (ACSM); American Alliance for Health, Physical Education, Recreation, and Dance (AAHPERD); Council for National Cooperation in Aquatics; National Collegiate Athletic Association (NCAA); National Federation of State High School Athletic Associations (NFSHSAA); and the National Operating Committee on Standards for Athletic Equipment (NOCSAE).

Laws and Legislation

A number of federal laws affect program development. For instance, Title IX of the Education Amendments of 1972 was enacted to prohibit sex discrimination. It states: "No person in the United States shall, on the basis of sex, be excluded from participation in, be denied the benefits of, or be subjected to discrimination under any education program or activity receiving federal financial assistance" (Bridges and Roquemore, 1992).

In addition, several laws exist that must be understood in regard to staffing, such as Title VII of the Civil Rights Act of 1964 and the Occupational Safety and Health Act (OSHA) of 1970.

Another major legislative act, the Americans with Disabilities Act (ADA), was passed in 1990. This law assures that persons with disabilities have the right to all employment and educational opportunities. In the first year following the enforcement of ADA, more than 11,000 discrimination charges were filed with the federal Equal Employment Opportunities Commission (EEOC) (Recreation Resources). The ADA, and other related legislation such as the Architectural Barriers Act of 1968, are discussed in detail in Chapter 16, "Facilities for Impaired Persons."

Environment and Geography

There is a great impact on program development from both environmental and geographical factors. Programs located in warm climates can schedule outside activities year-round, whereas programs located in cold climates must find indoor facilities in which to conduct those activities. It is wise also to use the geographical area to benefit the program, if possible. For instance, programmers for a fitness/sports club located near a wilderness area or rocky terrain might offer adventure and wilderness activities. Keep in mind, however, that many activities once considered only outdoor activities are now popular in indoor settings. An increasing number of rock-climbing clubs have been established throughout North America that offer artificial rock walls and other climbing apparatus. The successful sports manager uses the surrounding environment to the advantage of the program and offers activities that are popular and conducive to the area.

Social Influences and Trends

In a rapidly changing world, social influences and trends help shape the program. What is "in" or popular may influence your program choices. The fitness boom made it popular to "work out." Country and western dance classes have seen a huge boost in enrollment due to the popularity of line dancing. There is tremendous growth throughout the nation for youth soccer. New types of sports and recreational activities are constantly being invented with varying success. Many technological advances have impacted certain sports and recreational activities. In order to program effectively, it is critical for the program manager to be aware of the trends and to use the best forecasting possible in making program decisions.

IMPLEMENTATION OF THE PROGRAM

When new programs are initiated, several points must be taken into consideration. First and foremost, someone must assume the leadership role in introducing and guiding the new program. This may be either the manager or someone with a thorough understanding of the program itself. It is critical that this person have the power to make decisions during the development and implementation of the program and to make adjustments whenever necessary.

A second point in regard to program implementation is there must be adequate resources to conduct the program. As previously noted, facilities, equipment, and staffing must be considered. In addition, one must determine if the necessary financial support exists. The programmer should establish if the proposed program will require extra capital to run and, if so, if it will take valuable resources from other programs already in place. In other words, are you merely shuffling the resources instead of expanding them? If this is the case, then a decision should be made as to whether it is better to spread the finances thin to be able to offer more activities or to provide fewer activities that are financially stable and have enough support to be highly successful.

Finally, in regard to program implementation, enough time must be allowed in which to fully prepare, institute, and conduct the program. Many times programs are dropped too quickly, before they have had sufficient time to succeed. If the program is worth offering, then it is worth giving it time to flourish. An ongoing evaluation should be conducted with adjustments made throughout the process. Remember also, how well the program is promoted and marketed has a direct link to successful implementation.

EVALUATION OF THE PROGRAM

"Evaluating is defined as the process of assessing the degree to which the organization as a whole and various units and individuals have accomplished what they set out to do" (Chelladurai, 1985). The facility manager may be responsible for measuring the effectiveness of the overall organization, parts or units of the organization, or individual performances within the organization. In reality, it is wise to conduct several types of evaluations. It is also important that program supervisors (middle management) and other front-line employees and clients be questioned regarding issues surrounding a particular program.

The results of the evaluations may then be used as rationale for changes in the program or activities. Many evaluation systems are available for the manager's perusal depending on the area to be evaluated. The critical point here is that the evaluation must be appropriate for the area to be evaluated. It is also important to remember that an evaluation will not fully serve its purpose unless the results are communicated to the parties involved. In most instances, the feedback from evaluations is most useful when it is immediate. If corrections are needed, action can be taken without further delay or loss of productiveness.

SCHEDULING

Scheduling is a major component of programming. Whether to use one person or a team to schedule the use of a sports facility may depend on a variety of factors including the size of the institution or business as well as the number of groups who have primary use of the facility. There are advantages and disadvantages for both scheduling methods. The ultimate goal of any system is to make it work whether there is one primary user group (e.g., all of the clients of a fitness facility) or several user groups sharing facilities (e.g., university athletics, academic programs, and campus recreation groups). Figure 5–2 is a sample schedule for a college setting.

The manager in charge of a small sports club might be responsible for coordinating the scheduling of various facilities among all user groups. Obviously, the task of scheduling becomes more complex as the size of the facility, the number of programs, and the number of clients or participants increases. For example, the person in charge of scheduling a private volleyball club facility would need only to schedule for one sport in one facility with no changeovers between sports. (More information about changeovers is provided later in this chapter.) Of course, even the scheduling here becomes more complex if the number of teams using the facility suddenly jumps from 10 to 100 for a major tournament.

In comparison, one might find a more team-oriented scheduling approach similar to that found at Michigan State University. Michigan State University employed three members of three departments to coordinate the scheduling of athletic facilities for 25 varsity teams, 90 sections of physical education classes per term, and 29 intramural sports (Grinczel, 1989). This team worked to establish time zones in which the facilities were to

be used by each of the three departments. The physical education department used the facilities from 8 A.M. until 2 P.M. Intercollegiate athletics took over from 3 P.M. to 6 P.M., and intramural competition was scheduled from 6:30 P.M. until 1 A.M. (Grinczel, 1989). Fortunately, Michigan State University has enough playing fields and gyms for every in-season team to have its own field/facility to practice on from 3 P.M. to 6 P.M. daily.

Management should determine who is in charge of scheduling and be sure that everyone is aware of that person's responsibility. The person who does the scheduling should be capable of making quick decisions that may impact a large number of people. The scheduler should not show favoritism toward certain groups or programs. It is extremely important for this person to have the power to enforce scheduling decisions or, at critical moments, chaos may ensue.

It is necessary to create a policy regarding priority usage of the facility (see the section Establishing Priorities). If the chief executive officers—whether college presidents, athletic directors, or business owners—have assisted in creating a priority schedule, then one person should be able to enforce their policy. Other times, a committee might need to be convened to decide what activities should be acceptable in a facility and what the priority for use will be.

Facility schedulers should remember that changes in philosophy and personnel affect scheduling. What has worked in the past may not work in the present or the future.

Grinczel (1989) suggested several other ideas for those responsible for scheduling facilities:

1. Once the P. E. facility schedule is set, it is cast in stone. Changes are seldom made to accommodate class instructors. The schedule may change if a conflict arises and there are both time and space available to make a switch.
2. In-season athletic teams get first priority for their usual playing field or their usual time slots for practice. Teams in the preseason portion of their schedules are next on the priority list.
3. Varsity sport coaches are held to their practice time if there are not other times or places available to switch.

Figure 5–2　A schedule for activities at a college's gymnasium (Courtesy of Richard J. LaRue)

GYMNASIUM "A" SCHEDULE

DAY/TIME	SUNDAY	MONDAY	TUESDAY	WEDNESDAY	THURSDAY	FRIDAY	SATURDAY
6:00–7:00	CLOSED	Adult Open 6:15 A.M.–8:00 A.M.					CLOSED
7:00–8:00							
8:00–9:00		Activities Time Please See Activity Board for Schedule. 8:00 A.M.–11:00 A.M.					
9:00–10:00	All Member Rec. 9:15–11:00						Sports Classes 9:15–11:00
10:00–11:00							
11:00–12:00		Adult Open 11:00 A.M.–1:00 P.M.					
12:00–1:00							
1:00–2:00	All Member Rec. 1:00–3:30	Activities Time Please See Activity Board for Schedule. 1:00 P.M.–3:30 P.M.					
2:00–3:00							All Member Rec. 1:00–6:00
3:00–4:00		Athletic Team Practice 3:30 P.M.–6:00 P.M. (unless posted otherwise)					
4:00–5:00							
5:00–6:00							
6:00–7:00	Adult Open 6:00–7:30	Adult Open 6:00 P.M.–7:00 P.M.					Adult Open 6:00–8:30
7:00–8:00		Athletic Team Practice 7:00 P.M.–9:00 P.M. (unless posted otherwise)					
8:00–9:00	CLOSED						
9:00–10:00	Indoor Soccer 9:00–11:00	Intramural Sports 9:00 P.M.–11:00 P.M.		Indoor Soccer 9:00–11:00	I. M. Sports 9:00–11:00	CLOSED	CLOSED
10:00–11:00							

This schedule is subject to change due to contests and/or special events.

For questions regarding the gymnasium schedule, please contact Dr. Rick Larue, Director of Facilities.

A facility coordinator must be prepared to schedule and monitor activities that take place in the facility on a regular basis (over the course of a quarter, semester, or season) or that are a one-time event such as a concert or tournament. This person needs to be well-versed in the many different activities that might be scheduled either inside or outside of the facility. He or she must understand the specific requirements of different activities. For instance, what type of room or space is needed for a karate class? What kind of safety equipment and what type of space would be appropriate for an indoor archery class? Knowledge of how to efficiently conduct different types of programs in a safe environment is essential for good scheduling.

Depending on the type of sports or fitness facility, programs offered may vary from traditional team and individual sports such as volleyball and racquetball to aquacize, aerobics, kayaking, body building, rock climbing, and exercise prescription and weight control.

Scheduling is needed not only for areas such as the gymnasiums and natatoriums, but also for classrooms, conference rooms, and laboratories. It also requires expertise in related areas such as the type of surfaces and lighting required, equipment and fixtures needed, audiovisual demands, and perhaps even making arrangements for spectator seating and concessions for special events.

Scheduling and Planning the Facility

As noted in Chapter 1, when planning the construction of a sport facility, the person responsible for scheduling should have input along with the other on-site experts. It is important to furnish the architect with information on the kinds of activities that constitute the programs, the teaching stations needed, lighting and temperature requirements, minimum square footage for various activities, and storage and equipment areas needed for all of the activities that will be scheduled in that facility. The success of a facility depends heavily on a careful layout to maximize usage while maintaining adequate clearances for safety and movement (Whitney, 1992).

The facility coordinator may be asked to provide input on gymnasium floor surfaces as well (e.g., comparing maple, prefabricated PVC flooring, and poured urethane surfaces). Berg (1994) asserts that cost should not be the only factor in choosing a sports surface. A gymnasium with a maple floor is an excellent surface for basketball, volleyball, and aerobic activities, but is less versatile than synthetic flooring to accommodate indoor track and baseball practices during inclement weather. Operators of multipurpose facilities may be inclined to choose a synthetic surface, regardless of life-cycle cost (Berg, 1994).

If an indoor track is part of the facility, then with the addition of a netting/gym divider curtain, it is conceivable to schedule the basketball team practice on the main court at the same time that the track team is "running" around it. The curtain itself should have about eight feet of solid fabric at the base with open mesh above, which helps discourage climbing on the nets (Viklund, 1993). On the other hand, in order to save space, some facilities are designed to have the track overlap the basketball court thereby eliminating the need for a divider curtain. Viklund (1993) points out that net dividers have no acoustic value. Consequently, if sound is a concern, a full-height movable wall system is the only appropriate alternative.

Establishing Priorities

Prior to opening any facility, a committee should be organized to write a manual of guidelines for building hours of operation and the use of the space (who, when, how much, why). The "who" addresses user groups (in-house or outside, free versus those who might be charged rent), the "when" addresses the process of deciding when certain groups will be given first priority, the "how much" refers to the amount of time allotted, and "why" refers to justification of the guidelines.

The guidelines that are developed should be signed by major facility users including representatives from central administration. This document then becomes the best reference available in regard to the needs of the users as well as those who manage the facility.

Prioritizing the Scheduling Process

The committee charged with developing a policy on scheduling must determine the priority times that different groups will be scheduled to use the facility.

For example, if the main gymnasium facility is considered multipurpose and exists to support the entire fitness club, then all major user groups should be considered when developing the priority schedule. If possible, the schedule should accommodate all their needs.

In an example of an educational setting, first priority is probably given to academic needs such as physical education classes, second priority to athletic practices and games, and third to recreational users.

The list may continue with club sports next in priority, then on-campus groups, then off-campus groups. One should not assume that needs of on-campus groups are for a recreational or sport nature. A multipurpose sport facility is often the site of graduations, speeches, banquets, and concerts.

There are several reality checks involved with the scheduling process. Regular physical education classes rarely displace athletic or recreational events; however, occasional athletic competition may affect the physical education and recreation programs. A national college athletic tournament scheduled for a Friday and Saturday might preempt all physical education classes on Thursday (for set-up needs) and Friday for contests. As an illustration, a midwestern university hosting a two-day teacher fair every year in a multipurpose facility preempts all physical education, athletic, and recreation needs.

Once the schedule has been prioritized, it is up to the facility coordinator to follow the policy. This person must honor those times that have been previously determined and also decide at what point to return to the primary users and renegotiate the schedule or seek a compromise.

To assist in the scheduling of activities, many high schools and colleges have chosen to schedule basketball doubleheaders as a means of boosting attendance and giving media better access to both men's and women's teams. Another benefit, according to Mendel (1993), is financial—cutting costs by staffing two games for the cost of one; the whole crew of ticket takers, concession stand workers, security staff, and ambulance personnel only have to work one night instead of two.

A fourth benefit for scheduling doubleheaders is the savings on facility space, which can be crucial at schools where active intramural programs or heavily used multipurpose facilities make space and time a precious commodity (Mendel, 1993).

The facility scheduler should protect the programs of the primary users from too many distractions from outside user groups wanting to rent or use the facility. Do not overlook the fact that your clients have paid to use the facility. Facilities that exist to make money are jeopardizing their business when they overlook the individual customer.

The facility coordinator should develop a management strategy that includes (1) striving to do what is best for the greatest number of users, (2) being consistent with all user groups, (3) trying constantly to improve, (4) continually evaluating the scheduling processes, and (5) taking into account activities that are consistent with the organization's mission.

Requests to Use the Facility

Scheduling problems may occur at times when groups with permission to be in a facility are confronted by an unauthorized group, especially if there is no paper trail. One method of solving this scheduling nightmare has been the adoption of a facility request; in simple terms, a permission slip is distributed by the scheduler to groups who have permission to use the facility.

Facility requests are issued to all user groups when they are scheduled into their facility time slots. Any time additional groups are scheduled into the facility, a facility request is typed up and sent to them. For example, when two groups show up at the skating rink at the same time, the group with the pre-approved facility request has the official authorization to use the facility.

Rental Rates for Special Groups

How are rental rates for special groups determined? A facility committee may look at developing rental rates for activities. Groups scheduled solely to make money (e.g., Harlem Globetrotters basketball games, Royal Lippizan Stallion shows, musical concerts, etc.) would pay a higher rate than charitable events to which no tickets are sold, and the event is strictly organized as a fund-raiser for the community. Also, the facility coordinator may negotiate a higher rental rate for a business that expects to make money.

Some flexibility in rental rates may be suggested for summer (hot weather requires air conditioning, which costs more than heating, to maintain) versus winter scheduling, as well as the difference in the types of set-ups, cleanups, and additional situations needed to organize the event. Events that require complicated set-ups and very difficult breakdowns will cost more than much simpler events.

Evaluation of an Event

The job is not complete when a user group walks away from the facility. The facility scheduler or manager must do a follow-up evaluation for events scheduled in the facility. The evaluation should determine both the positive and the negative aspects and what could be done to improve the event in the future. Both formative and summative evaluations should be prepared.

Bigger events require detailed records (notes of meetings, tour of facility, and telephone calls), contracts, and other items of importance kept on file from year to year to establish a history.

Changeovers

The transition to change the room or area between events or classes to accommodate a different activity is called *changeover*. When a facility schedule exists and is followed, the changeover becomes a manageable task. However, the facility manager must have also planned for a reasonable amount of time for each transition, equipment changes (take-down, removal, replacement, or set-up, safety inspections), changes in space supervision or program leadership, and so on. The transition time increases or decreases (much like a pit stop in an auto racing event) depending upon the availability of equipment, the distance to adequate storage, and the staff's training. (Storage and equipment are discussed later in this chapter.)

Staff training is a critical component of the successful changeover. Your staff should fully understand the proper installation of equipment (and flooring), be aware of where the equipment is stored, and appreciate the need to be prompt and work as a team. Even relatively simple equipment installations require directions. Facility staff should be required to read and practice the directions for setting up equipment. Further, a set of directions, along with any special notations about installation or storage, should be kept with the equipment or posted in the adjacent storage closet. Finally, facility staff need to be trained to regularly

check that floors are clean and equipment is in proper and safe working order.

In large facilities requiring major changeovers, the amount of time required for the transition ultimately affects the profitability of the facility. Major stadiums, such as the Super Dome, employ numerous persons whose entire job responsibilities are to set up for an event and take down after the event is over. The changeover in most instances requires even a change of the surface. Artificial turf may be installed for a football game one day and removed the next day to set up for a home and garden show.

Changeovers must be accomplished on time because most major sporting facilities, such as stadiums, are booked solid and will lose hundreds of thousands of dollars if the next event is not ready when it is supposed to be. This is critical not only for financial reasons, but also for the reputation of the facility.

In another setting, college or high school academic schedules give students and teachers a 10- to 15-minute break between class periods. This extra time allows the facility coordinator or instructor to set up equipment or to break it down for storage without affecting the next scheduled activity.

The facility schedule should reflect the needs of all user groups and the demands their activities have on the scheduling process. Setting up seven badminton courts for the first activity, breaking them down for a one-hour basketball class, and having to set up the seven badminton courts again for the next hour is not only poor time management, but also promotes unnecessary wear and tear on the equipment.

If possible, some specialized activities should have a space dedicated to them. Gymnastics is a prime example. The equipment is heavy and takes a lot of time to set up or to take down. The equipment is also quite expensive and wears out much faster when it has to be moved.

Other specialized equipment such as mats for wrestling are heavy, bulky, difficult to move, and require a large storage space. They must be disinfected prior to and after each use, which makes it extremely difficult to remove them quickly for another class or event.

It is important to set aside a reasonable amount of time between these activities. Ten to fifteen minutes to set up wrestling mats is probably not considered a reasonable amount of time. The amount

Setting up for an event requires considerable lead time.

of time should be determined from actual experience and kept on record for future use.

BARRIERS TO INSTRUCTION

There are a number of barriers to instruction that should be avoided. Noise affects the quality of instruction or communication in an area. Some of it can be avoided through proper design such as not building classrooms next to racquetball courts and not placing offices on the floor beneath a free weight area. Other noises are not so easy to avoid, such as aerobic music playing in a room next to a room where tennis balls are being hit against the adjoining wall. Other noise distractions include heating and ventilation fans and activity or instruction areas that are not designed with acoustics in mind.

Another type of barrier that affects the facility's atmosphere, as well as quality of instruction, is an offensive smell. Areas with poor ventilation or with no air exchange to remove perspiration odors become extremely stale and offensive. This

can also present a changeover problem, because more time is required to eliminate and remove such odors from the room. As an example, a wrestling coach found that if he sanitized the wrestling mats immediately following the team's daily practice, lingering odors dissipated quicker than if the team just left the room at the end of practice without trying to remove the stale air.

SCHEDULING MAINTENANCE

Scheduling proper maintenance is necessary to extend the life of a facility, indoors or outdoors. Proper maintenance also plays a vital role in reducing liability.

Michigan State University wedges maintenance and custodial care around physical education, intramural, and athletic needs; priority is given to the programs (Grinczel, 1989).

Other facilities schedule routine cleaning during the day when the facility is open. One hour of the day is set aside for the custodial crew to clean the pool, then move to the racquetball courts which are closed down the next hour for cleaning, and so on throughout the building. This permits custodians to be on hand throughout the day to assist with emergency cleanups as they are needed.

The facility scheduler needs to regulate the amount of use on the natural turf fields. Regardless of the level of maintenance, athletic fields are only able to withstand a certain amount of wear and tear. No turf can withstand the daily pounding of hundreds of soccer, football, and softball players. The risk of injury to all users increases as the underground portion of the field is pounded to a concretelike consistency. Field use should be scheduled and regulated in such a manner that the field is not used to the point where the turf is no longer able to recover (Hodnick, 1991).

In addition, fields should be scheduled for "downtime," periods when the fields are not available for any use whatsoever. During these times, major repairs (like resodding or reseeding) or renovations (aeration or top dressing) can be performed or the grass simply given time to "heal" itself to prevent deterioration (Hodnick, 1991).

The demand for safe, well-maintained athletic fields continues at an ever-increasing rate. People responsible for green space are finding themselves caught between the demands of the public for more fields and trying to maintain the fields in good condition (Hodnick, 1991).

Turman and Allen (1990) asked the question: "Am I getting all I can out of my facility?" The key to answering that question is continuous evalua-

A multipurpose court in the Gangelhoff Center at Concordia College, St. Paul, Minnesota (Courtesy of the architects Toltz, King, Duvall, Anderson and Associates; Don F. Wong, photographer)

tion. The first step is to keep organized records in the following categories: use/space facility allocations; numbers of participants using the facility; and frequency of use related to time, periods of inactivity, and seasonal demand. In addition, Turman and Allen (1990) suggest that the facility manager perform site inspections, meet regularly with maintenance/custodial personnel and seek opinions, ideas, suggestions, and complaints of the users as well as colleagues.

Facility maintenance is a primary concern of all employers and employees. Everyone should contribute to providing a clean and safe environment. Oversight and inattention by upper management sets a negative precedent and sends a message diluting the importance associated with maintenance.

SPACE PLANNING AND MANAGEMENT

A realistic approach to the task of planning space is to evaluate the space you have and get to work planning all that you can do. The space that you are managing, adequate or not, is what you have to work with.

Planning is the essential operation component of successful space management. The facility manager must manage the space available, efficiently, and ensure that both the staff and users are kept well-informed.

Space is usually designated for either multiple or single use, however most sport facilities today are multiple use or commonly called multipurpose. Some single-use areas are still designed primarily for one major activity. Indoor tennis courts (especially clay courts) are designed for tennis. It is possible that other activities, within reason, can be accomplished in this kind of single-use space. Court activities like badminton or volleyball could be played in these areas with little damage to the floor surface or risk of injury to users.

A multiple-use area, large enough for volleyball, basketball, badminton, indoor soccer, and so on, may also serve as space for tennis. Functional components, such as the type of floor installed, determines the nature of play. Most multiple-use areas have composition floors over concrete. Composition floors afford great flexibility in programming, but limited quality for some specific activities. Wood is generally the preferred surface for basketball, however wood is generally considered too "fast" a surface for tennis.

When there is adequate storage and a sound budget, some multiple-use facilities have a portable wooden floor that is temporarily installed over the existing floor whenever required by the change in activity. However, this arrangement demands additional staff and extra time for installation.

Another significant functional component related to space is the overhead clearance. Properly designed multiple-use spaces must consider a variety of spatial issues. For lack of a few feet over head, or in width/depth, a multiple-use space can be disqualified from service as a competition-quality space. Sports-specific standards of space are available from most sports organizations.

Diagrams of space utilization (Figures 5–3 and 5–4) show how multiple-use facilities can be used for a wide variety of activities. A multipurpose facility that is about 100′ × 124′ (including an intercollegiate-sized volleyball and basketball courts located in the center of a gymnasium) can accommodate three side-by-side recreation basketball courts or 5 to 7 volleyball courts or 6 to 8 badminton courts (Figure 5–5).

Seidler (1992) has developed a "Think Table" for facility planning (Figure 5–6) that affords the user the opportunity to consider the significant function(s) and relationship(s) to each area in a facility. From this table, the user can then construct a "bubble diagram," similar to that described in Chapter 1, that visually describes the flow of the facility. When designing a new facility, the Think Table can be used to consider the initial placement of areas in your space. The Program Diagram (Figure 5–7) is representative of a bubble diagram designed to meet the program needs for a proposed facility at Bradford College. Program diagrams are essential to successful space planning. In an existing facility, an understanding of the multiple spatial relationships assists the facility manager with the challenges described previously. And, when designing a new facility, the program and bubble diagrams ensure that the spatial integration of all areas in the space meet the needs of the program, from the start.

As mentioned, the one type of space that is frequently overlooked and consistently inadequate is the storage space in facilities. If you have too

Figure 5–3   A plan for use of space in a multipurpose facility, a fieldhouse of 27,000 square feet
(Courtesy of Richard J. LaRue)

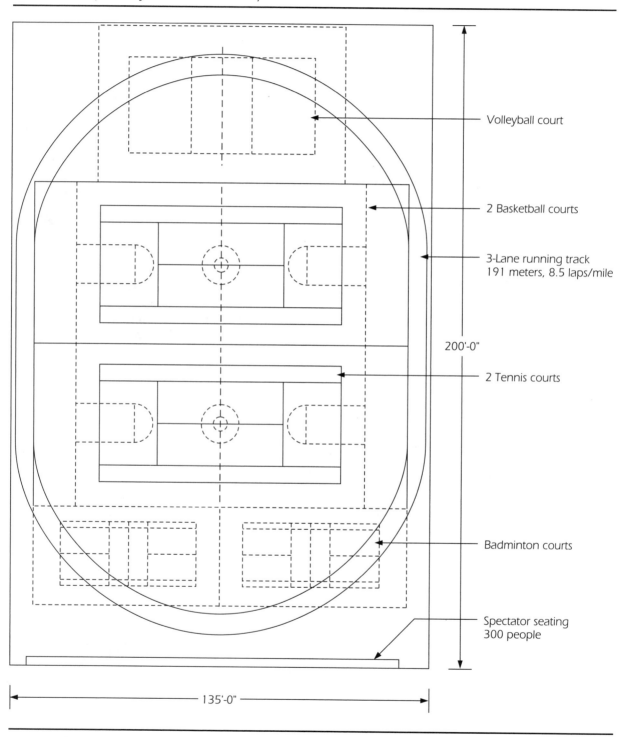

Volleyball court

2 Basketball courts

3-Lane running track
191 meters, 8.5 laps/mile

200'-0"

2 Tennis courts

Badminton courts

Spectator seating
300 people

135'-0"

Figure 5–4 Alternative plans for use of a swimming pool (Courtesy of Richard J. LaRue)

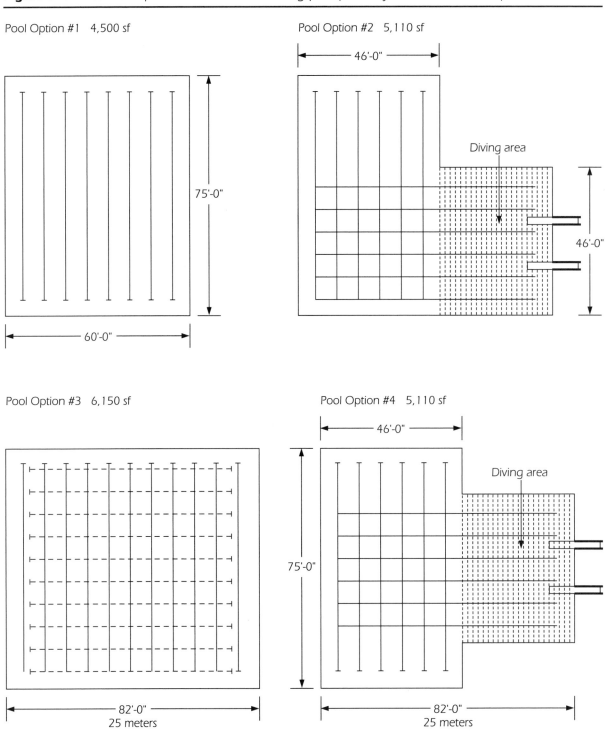

Pool Option #1   4,500 sf

Pool Option #2   5,110 sf

Pool Option #3   6,150 sf

Pool Option #4   5,110 sf

Figure 5–5 A general-use model shows how an area of 124' × 100' can accommodate several court layouts. (Courtesy of Todd Seidler)

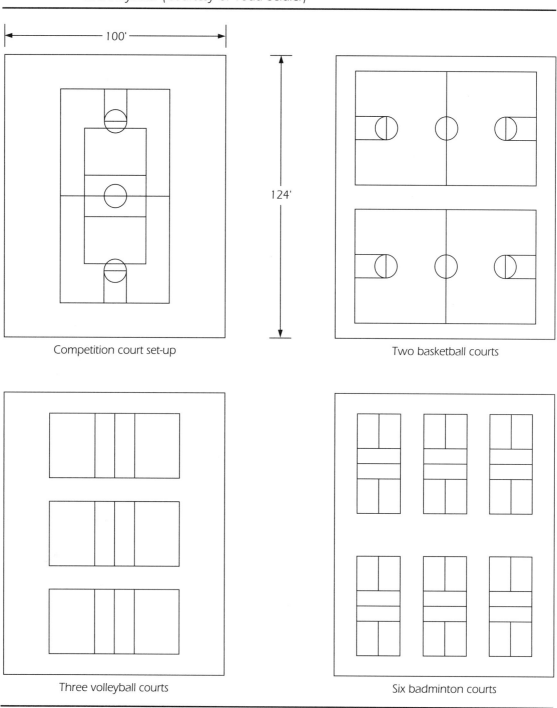

Competition court set-up

Two basketball courts

Three volleyball courts

Six badminton courts

Figure 5–6   Facility planning think table (Courtesy of Todd Seidler)

THINK TABLE		
Area	Function	Relationships
Gymnasium	**Dimensions**	Gymnasium
Auxiliary Gym	Floor Area	Auxiliary Gym
Other Gym	Ceiling Height	Other Gym
Wrestling		Wrestling
Dance	**Air Handling System**	Dance
Racquetball Courts	Temperature	Racquetball Courts
Natatorium	Circulation	Natatorium
Weight Area	Humidity	Weight Area
Fitness Area		Fitness Area
Classroom	**Lighting**	Classroom
Storage	Amount of Light	Storage
Offices	Color of Light	Offices
Locker Room	Lighting Controls	Locker Room
Shower Area	Natural Lighting	Shower Area
Drying Area		Drying Area
Varsity Team Room	**Surfaces**—Material/Color	Varsity Team Room
Visiting Team Room	Floor	Visiting Team Room
Staff Locker Room	Wall	Staff Locker Room
Training Room	Ceiling	Training Room
First Aid	Acoustics	First Aid
Laundry		Laundry
Equipment Issue	**Spectator Seating**	Equipment Issue
Lobby	Permanent	Lobby
Ticket Booth	Portable	Ticket Booth
Concessions		Concessions
Maintenance Areas	**Security**	Maintenance Areas
Public Rest Rooms	Access	Public Restrooms
	Traffic Control	
	Supervision	
		Parking Lots
	Miscellaneous	Student Parking
	Water	Faculty/Staff Parking
	Drains	Outdoor Fields
	Electrical Outlets	Outdoor Storage
	Provisions for Disabled	
	Clocks	
	Telephone Line	
	Data Line	
	Sound System	
	Intercom	
	Doors–Types & Dimensions	

Instructions: Select an area from the first column. Then go down through the second column and consider each of the functions for that area. Next look at the third column and consider each of the space relationships.

Figure 5–7 A typical program diagram (Courtesy of Richard J. LaRue)

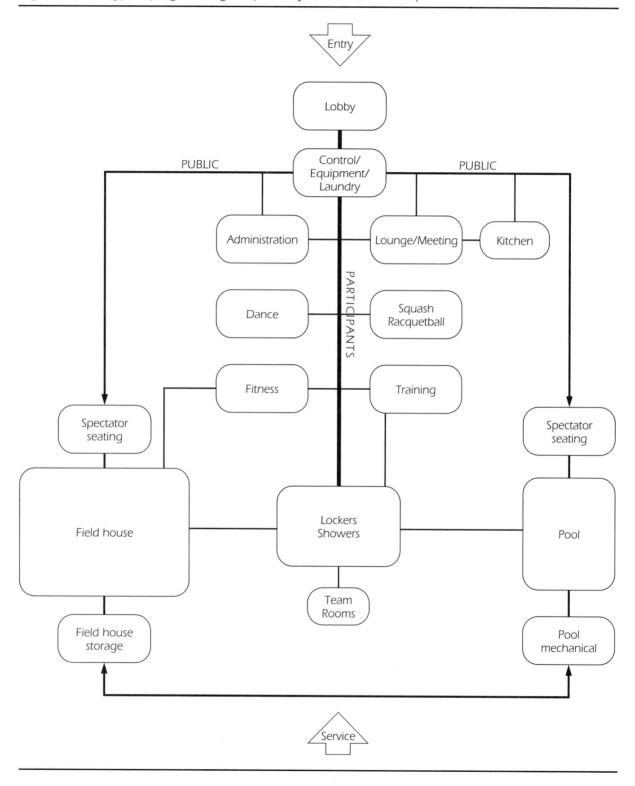

little storage space, consider the space management options below:

1. Organize stored items. A highly organized storage room allows a quick inventory to assess if equipment is missing, allows better management of equipment, and provides needed space.

2. Be creative in storing items. Use shelves, hooks, pulleys, and so on. Is there available space above the usual storage areas?

3. Purchase equipment designed to take less space when stored, or purchase equipment that is multipurpose, such as sets of posts that can be used for volleyball, tennis, and badminton.

4. Find spaces in your facility that can be remade into storage space. Some storage spaces require limited access. When a storage space must be made secure, you want a separate room with doors. However, some kinds of equipment can be stored safely and efficiently right in your program areas without any concern for security. Volleyball nets can be hung neatly from hooks installed at a safe height along one wall of a gymnasium. Hanging the net stretched out maintains the net (and cable) better than rolling it up each time after use and allows for quick changeovers. In multiple-use spaces, equipment that can be raised and lowered safely with winches and cables (e.g., basketball hoops, batting cages) can also eliminate the need for storage. Remember that any equipment intended for overhead suspension must be regularly inspected by a certified specialist to ensure against suspension failure.

5. Build new storage space. Many larger spaces have exterior walls that allow for some expansion. Adequate storage is so important that you might consider "expanding" your storage space with a building addition. However, because of the significant costs, this is likely a last resort.

SUMMARY

Programming is a complex and necessary function of facility management. Successful programmers develop thorough program schedules that are based on sound priorities. They establish strategic program planning policies and follow them.

In addition, they find ways to use the space they have in the most productive and effective ways possible. Managing your space is like managing your time. If you become good at managing your time, you begin to enjoy the time you have. If you become good at managing your space, you begin to enjoy the space you have. It evolves into a matter of quality. The initial investment of time in planning will not be wasted if it is committed to the careful analysis of your space and its functionality, and if it considers your current and future program needs. With successful planning, the demand on your time for space management should diminish so that you can direct your energy toward other meaningful and necessary challenges of facility management.

QUESTIONS

1. What is the strategic program planning process?
2. What major components impact program development?
3. How important is scheduling, including prioritizing, from the manager's standpoint?
4. In what ways do changeovers affect scheduling?
5. What measures can create more space in a facility?

ACTIVITIES

1. Create a planning schedule for a multipurpose sports facility. The programs are aerobics, basketball, body building, floor hockey, gymnastics, modern dance, racquetball, swimming, volleyball, walleyball, and weight training.
2. Upon completion of the schedule, examine the schedule for potential problems and find ways to eliminate those problems.
3. Compare schedules for different types of sport and fitness facilities.

SUGGESTED READINGS

Dethlefs, D. (1991). Multiple cheers. *College Athletic Management*, 3(3):30–31.

Gimple, J. (1992). Indoor facilities: Laying the foundation. *Athletic Management*, 4(5):32.

Haney, M. W. (1991, October). Creative operations. *Fitness Management*, pp. 48–49.

Johnson, R. J. (1991). All in one. *College Athletic Management*, 3(3):28–33.

Nyvall, P. (1991, Fall). Is your facility fit? *YMCA Property Management News*, 8:1.

Peterson, J. A., and Tharrett, S. J. (1991, October). Making your facility environmentally sound. *Fitness Management*, pp. 44–46.

Strand, B. N. (1988). A space analysis of physical education activity areas and ancillary areas in big ten universities. Unpublished doctoral dissertation, Albuquerque, NM: University of New Mexico.

REFERENCES

Berg, R. (1994, April). Floored. *Athletic Business*, p. 9.

Bridges, F. J., and Roquemore, L. L. (1992). *Management for athletic/sport administration*, pp. 88, 262.

Chelladurai, P. (1985). *Sport management: Macro perspectives*, p. 171.

Grinczel, S. (1989, January). Share and share alike. *Collegiate Athletic Magazine*, pp. 51–53.

Helm, S. (1989, January). Planning time away. *Collegiate Athletic Magazine*, pp. 28–29.

Hieber, J., and Van Der Kamp, S. (1994, February/March). A mutual structure. *Athletic Management*, pp. 58–64.

Hodnick, M. (1991, May). Playing it safe. *Athletic Business*, pp. 57–60.

Mead, W. (1988). *Program diagram: Bradford college athletic facility*. Boston: Shepley, Bulfinch, Richardson, Richardson, and Abbot.

Mead, W. (1988). *Field house: Space no. 1.00*. Boston: Shepley, Bulfinch, Richardson, and Abbot.

Mendel, B. (1993, May). Back to back billing. *Athletic Management*, pp. S12–S19.

Patton, R. W., Grantham, W. C., Gerson, R. F., and Gettman, L. R. (1989). *Developing and managing health/fitness facilities* (p. 202). Champaign, Ill: Human Kinetics.

Seidler, T. (1992). *Example of how a general use module 124' × 100' can accommodate several different court layouts.* A handout from a panel presentation on Facility Problems and Solutions at the 1992 AAHPERD National Convention. Indianapolis, Ind.

Seidler, T. (1992). *Facility planning think table.* A handout from a panel presentation on Facility Problems and Solutions at the 1992 AAHPERD National Convention. Indianapolis, Ind.

Turman, J., and Allen, D. (1990, July). Evaluating for efficiency. *Collegiate Athletic Magazine*, pp. 53–56.

Viklund, R. (1993, July). This old gym. *Athletic Business*, pp. 29–34.

Whitney, T. (1992, March). A house divided. *Athletic Business*, pp. 44–51.

6

Risk Management and Litigation

Marc Rabinoff

Litigation, contract negotiations, risk management, and the insurance industry, for many sport/fitness managers are the "dark sides" of the management of sport facilities.

MAJOR COMPONENTS

To fully understand and appreciate the complexities of these areas of management, there are four major components to be studied.

1. The litigation process
2. The use, development, and implementation of a risk management program
3. The art of contract negotiation for all personnel and activities, as well as the proper documentation of files
4. The insurance industry—how to select a carrier, deal with the carrier, and evaluate coverage

While sport managers depend on coaches, fitness instructors, and equipment managers, to provide much of the data for administrative decisions, ultimately the manager is responsible for the actions of subordinates. This is commonly known as *respondeat superior* (Wong, 1994), that is, the negligence of the employee is imputed to the corporate entity. It should be noted here that at times this doctrine of respondeat superior becomes negated as a result of the specific actions of an employee. This situation as well as any state immunity statutes can place the employee in a "stand alone" status for the purpose of the litigation process.

We know that the manager is certainly responsible for dealing with all the activities in a fa-

cility, including equipment usage, maintenance, supervision, and purchasing, so it is wise of him or her to learn how the litigation process works. This would include a sound working knowledge of the process from time of injury to the courtroom and beyond. Data indicate that we are living in a time of increasing litigation. Our litigious society often seeks to address issues in court rather than through other means such as arbitration (Appenzeller, 1993; Rabinoff, 1994). Litigation in sport has followed this trend and has increased substantially both in the number of litigations filed and the amount of the awards (Appenzeller, 1993; Rabinoff, 1994; Wong, 1994). In 1990, there were 703 verdicts for $1 million dollars or more, resulting in a total of 5,032 verdicts of $1 million or more since 1962 (Jury Verdict Research, 1990).

THE PARTIES OF THE LAWSUIT

In the litigation process, each state has civil rules of procedure that must be followed by attorneys for all parties. All managers should be aware of this, so they can keep abreast of the process as time moves along. Once a summons is served on the facility by the plaintiff's attorney the litigation process begins. Remember, the *plaintiff* or *plaintiffs* are the people bringing forward the lawsuit. They are the people claiming that they were injured or victim of a civil wrong and need the courts to address their issues (Wong, 1994).

The summons illustrates the issues of liability, and states damages being sought through the courts by the plaintiff for the suffering caused by some situation that allegedly caused an injury. An example of such a summons is in Appendix A-1.

Once the summons is served the defense of the entity begins. However, the insurance carrier is notified in writing by the plaintiff's attorney, early in these proceedings, prior to filing the lawsuit, so that a settlement can be reached before the actual litigation begins. Remember, the *defense* is the entity or persons named in the claim as being, in part or wholly responsible for the injury or other damages to the plaintiff or plaintiffs (Wong, 1994).

The insurance carrier then begins its investigation of the facts. During this investigation, the carrier may obtain the services of an expert in the particular field, so a report can be filed as to whether there is liability on the part of the entity or whether the liability is questionable. Should the carrier decide not to settle, it will obtain the services of a law firm to provide legal defense against the claim. The trend of insurance carriers today is to try the litigation and not to settle as easily as they have in the past (Jury Verdict Research, 1990).

THE DISCOVERY PHASE

During the "discovery" phase of the litigation process, both plaintiff and defense attorneys are attempting to discover information favorable to their respective clients. They seek documents covering any and all operations policies—procedures, manuals, meeting minutes, research, communications, photos, reports and personnel records—because they may yield evidence that could be admissible in court or that could be used to convince all parties named that a settlement is a viable option (Wong, 1994).

THE EXPERT WITNESS

Since attorneys are not experts in the field of sports, fitness, physical education, recreation, or equipment standards of care, they obtain the opinion of an expert. The *expert witness* is a person who by education and or experience (and this definition can vary greatly from jurisdiction to jurisdiction) can review the data, evidence, and statements, as well as depositions (sworn testimony) and offer their opinions as to how the injury oc-

curred and who might have been at fault. The term *forensic examiner* refers to a professional who performs a systematic analysis, investigation, test, inspection, or other reasonable inquiry in an attempt to reach conclusions that will be the foundation for the expert's opinion (Rabinoff, 1996).

Once a report is filed by an expert, that report is delivered to the opposing attorney. The opposing attorney then has an opportunity to "depose" that expert. The same is true for the other side, and so there are now two professional opinions for the court to consider in the litigation. Again, the use of written reports varies from jurisdiction to jurisdiction, and in some states is not needed at all (Rabinoff, 1996).

In recent years, the use of the expert witness has been challenged and re-evaluated by our federal courts and as of 1 December 1993 the Federal Rules of Civil Procedure that govern how an expert can testify have been changed significantly. These changes reflect a growing concern as to the determination of an expert and how the evidence and foundation of experts' opinions are reached and presented to juries (Rabinoff, 1996).

LEGAL CONSIDERATIONS

Plaintiff's Arguments

As the litigation proceeds, which may take years, the main issues examined fall under four basic legal considerations: (1) duty to perform, (2) breach of the duty, (3) proximate cause of the injury, and (4) damages.

Further examination of these four concepts can result in the plaintiff's attorney deciding that there is enough evidence that liability exists and that the lawsuit should be filed and pursued (Wong, 1994; Champion 1993).

Defense Arguments

The facility or entity named as a defendant has basically four avenues of defense: (1) deny the allegations, (2) comparative negligence, (3) exculpatory clause, and (4) lack of reasonable foreseeability.

These four avenues, as well as the "assumption of risk" doctrine will, in most cases, constitute the legal issues for this type of litigation. The common law defense of assumption of risk is put forth by the defense when they claim that the plaintiffs themselves knowingly put themselves in the road toward the potential of injury. According to tort law statues in most states, a person assumes the risk of injury if he or she voluntarily or unreasonably exposes himself or herself to injury or damage with knowledge or appreciation of the danger and risk involved (Wong, 1994).

According to Struthers (1993) there are "mountains to climb and bridges to cross," as a plaintiff's attorney devises the legal strategy for the client. The concepts mentioned above must be viewed clearly and then the evidence must be presented in a manner that is convincing to the judge and jury at trial, or in settlement hearings. In other words, it is not an easy task for the plaintiff's attorney to argue liability.

The defense attorney has a similar predicament in that he or she must refute all allegations that can result in a verdict in favor of the plaintiff. The position is illustrated in the four areas above as defenses.

In denying the allegations, the facility or entity admits no wrongdoing by fact or by standards. Simply put, it did what it was supposed to do and that all blame for the injury and damages be placed on the plaintiff or other named parties. Recently, defendants have chosen to bring into these litigations third-party defendants, such as the equipment manufacturers. The sport/fitness manager needs to recognize that for the manufacturer to be brought into a product liability suit, three legal theories can apply: (1) negligence, (2) breach of warranty, and (3) strict liability (Wong, 1994).

PRODUCT AND FACILITY LIABILITY

Although the plaintiff's attorneys can name manufacturers as defendants, they have been somewhat reluctant to do so. The reason for this reluctance is that litigation for product failure and/or defect is very costly, moreso than a simple issue of liability as discussed previously. To further illustrate the difficulty in filing and winning a product liability litigation, it was reported that during the period between 1987 and 1992, the chance of winning such a litigation dropped from 54% to 41% (Jury Verdict Research, 1990).

The position of many manufacturers today has been to vigorously defend their equipment and at times countersue the parties in such litigations.

In some litigations the issue of equipment defect or failure is combined with the legal doctrine of "dangerous condition." This condition deals with the facility being used when a physical condition constitutes an unreasonable risk of harm to the safety or health of the user. In some respects this doctrine is similar to that of "foreseeability" in that the environment was not in a proper operating condition as could have been determined by the professional staff at the time of use (Appenzeller, 1993; Wong, 1994). The design of the facility alone cannot constitute a dangerous condition.

COMPARATIVE NEGLIGENCE AND TORT REFORM

Comparative negligence requires that each party be examined as to their specific roles and responsibilities, if any, that might have contributed to the cause and damage results of the injury. In many states, the plaintiff must prove that his or her negligence was less than 50% or the defense wins the case. If the plaintiff does prove to a jury that he or she was less than 50% at fault, they will receive that percentage of the damages less their own negligence. The courts have become more humane with the emergence of comparative negligence, especially with some states implementing tort reforms, which have sought to balance the scales for plaintiff and defense. Some argue that tort reform has been anticonsumer and probusiness, but at least the changes through tort reform have opened the eyes of the public to question how much we are to accept responsibility for our actions in society (Wong, 1994; Champion, 1993).

Since the 1980s most states have initiated some form of tort reform. *Tort Reform* is the movement to revisit the issues that surround the tort laws in each state and at the federal government level. This new look at these laws will possibly provide a more balanced view of the roles of plaintiffs and defendants as to their comparative responsibility as determined by the injury. In recent years, some tort reforms have resulted in laws preventing a person from filing a lawsuit against certain entities, such as ski resorts or horseback riding centers, and places limits on the liability of other professions such as physicians (Rabinoff, 1994).

THE EXCULPATORY CLAUSE, AND RELEASES AND WAIVERS

The sport/fitness manager needs to understand what a tort is in order to appreciate the complex issues of tort reform. *Tort* is a legal term meaning a wrongful act by which a person can bring a civil lawsuit against another to recover damages. This is a civil wrong, other than a breach of contract. Negligence is a tort, as are theft, assault, trespass, and defamation, as well as others (Wong, 1994; Champion, 1993).

The *exculpatory clause* has been used for decades as a means of protection for the facility or entity. This clause is written into all contracts for members who join health clubs, fitness centers, and in many recreational activity settings. This clause informs the potential user of the facility or participant in the program activity of inherent risks he or she may encounter while engaging in the activity. It also states that the entity or facility will not be responsible for any and all injuries to the participant, even injuries caused by the negligence of the entity or any of its employees, and that the participant waives his or her right to file a litigation against the facility or entity (Wong 1994; Schubert, Smith, and Trentadue, 1986).

Some states, notably New York, have ruled that the exculpatory clause is not valid and therefore not a defense against a claim of negligence. In contrast, Colorado and many other states use a four-prong test to determine the validity of the exculpatory clause (Wong, 1994). This test involves:

1. The existence of a duty to the public
2. The nature of the service provided
3. The fairness between the parties when the contract was signed
4. The clarity and lack of ambiguity of the wording

These provisions in the contracts that members sign when they join health clubs, fitness, or recreation facilities are often upheld as unconscionable or contrary to public policy. The facility's manager needs to seek legal advice as to how this clause is viewed in his or her state or jurisdiction. (A sample "Acknowledgement, Assump-

tion of Risk, Consent, Waiver and Release" form can be found in Appendix A-3.) Furthermore, releases and waivers are most often held to be valid only with regard to simple negligence, regardless of any attempts to obtain additional protection against more aggravated kinds of negligence. However, if the conduct of the entity's personnel is charged with punitive, willful, or wanton conduct, the waiver may be nullified (Reinig, 1993).

This type of release is viewed by the courts in a narrow and strict sense. They may or may not cover all the people that the facility manager may think they do. To overcome this problem, the facility's manager must write releases or waivers that specifically speak to all people to be covered, and have them clearly enumerated on the form itself (Reinig, 1993). Remember, this strict position by most courts also pertains to the plaintiff as well (Wong, 1994; Champion, 1993; Schubert et al., 1989).

Furthermore, the issue of whether these clauses are valid or are being upheld in the courts should not be the deciding factor as to whether you as a manager will use them. The use of an exculpatory clause is still a strong defense document, because it shows a jury or a judge that you as a professional cared enough about the participant to explain the risks at least as you saw them.

Waivers for Minors

Waivers or releases for minors are not effective, even if the minor lies about his or her age. However, the defense of assumption of risk can be used if the risk that caused the injury was "ordinary" as associated with the specific activity being done at the time of the injury (Wong, 1994; Appenzeller, 1993; Rabinoff, 1994).

Remember, minors can receive all the benefits of the contract without any of the responsibilities. The exception to this concept is that the minor is bound by all contracts for necessities. Necessities usually refer to food, housing, or clothing.

WILLFUL AND WANTON CONDUCT AND FORESEEABILITY

Willful or wanton conduct is acting in a manner that was intentional and with no regard for the welfare of the injured party. This could include actions involving a fight in the stands where one patron deliberately injures another. *Foreseeability*, related to our ability as professionals to be concerned about the environment we provide our participants, is an assessment of how much probable injury or damage can reasonably be expected in given circumstances. The concept of foreseeability is discussed later in this chapter.

THE TRIAL OR SETTLEMENT

Once all discovery is completed, the time line has been set by the courts as the rules of civil procedure dictate, and no settlement has been reached, the litigation is set for trial. During the trial witnesses are called, experts appear, and a variety of exhibits presented; then the jury or judge, depending on the court's earlier motions, render a verdict. The losing side has the option to appeal. This continues the issues on to a higher court, which can also take years. Once the appeal is reviewed and a court ruling announced, the losing side at this stage can appeal to the state's supreme court. In most cases the ruling at the state supreme court level will end the litigation, although it is possible in certain circumstances to file a further appeal to the federal court (Wong, 1994).

It is important to note that if the litigation is settled at any time prior to the original trial, there will be no admission of guilt or liability by any party, and the issue is finished (Wong, 1994; Rabinoff, 1994).

CLAIMS OF INJURY

There seen to be some consistent trends in results of litigations claiming personal injury. Most such litigations deal with the concepts mentioned above. Specifically, they surround the sport/fitness management issues of (Appenzeller, 1994; Schubert et al. 1989; Wong, 1994; Rabinoff, 1994):

1. Lack of supervision
2. Poor instruction
3. Failure to warn
4. Foreseeability

The standards for supervision can be found in numerous publications, professional organizations' position papers, textbooks, and in proceedings from professional conferences, conventions, and symposia. Because these standards at times are controversial, it mandates that sport/fitness managers attend professional meetings, read journals, and belong to organizations that are recognized as authoritative on these matters. The methods of class organization, sport team practices, or recreational activities need to be well thought out to assure that the placement of the participants in relationship to the teacher, coach, or supervisor meets these standards (Wong, 1994; Schubert et al., 1989).

The issue of *poor instruction* could take volumes of pages to discuss, but for purposes of this chapter, the concern falls in three major areas:

1. Progressions of skill development
2. Currency (up-to-date?) of theories or practices for skill development
3. Qualifications of professional staff

In the commercial fitness industry, health clubs, fitness centers, and spas, the issue of unqualified instructional staff is a serious violation of professional standards, and a major factor in juries reaching verdicts for the plaintiff (Reinig, 1993).

In claims against the physical educator or recreation professional, the use of outdated theories or practices, especially in sport settings, seem to be the most vulnerable aspect of the defense arguments, and the major factor resulting in a verdict for the plaintiff. In claims against coaches, the progression of skills development seems to be the most vulnerable area by the plaintiff attorney, and thus the most dangerous for the defense.

The *failure to warn* issue has been used by plaintiffs for decades, but has only recently been applied to the sport/fitness industry. It has been determined by many court rulings, verdicts, and settlements that the profession and the professional has the duty to warn the participant of any and all inherent risks associated with a specific activity, facility, or equipment prior to allowing the participant into the setting (see Figure 6–1). The trends in the courts seem to illustrate that these warnings must meet certain criteria. These criteria include, but may not be limited to issues of size, color, placement, wording, and in some circumstances the use of pictures, or foreign languages. With this in mind, it would be prudent for the sport/fitness manager to know how warnings are implemented in his or her facilities (Farmer, Mulrooney, and Ammon, 1996).

Figure 6–1 Warning signs like this sample from a weight room are part of a comprehensive risk management program.

WARNING

Serious injuries can occur if struck by falling weights or moving parts of machines and by improper technique or use of equipment.

You assume a risk of injury every time you use free weights and machines. This risk can be reduced by always following these guidelines and rules:

1. Do not use any equipment without **QUALIFIED SUPERVISION**. When in doubt about proper use or technique, **ASK!**
2. Always warm up properly before lifting heavy weights. This consists of exercising large muscle groups as well as practicing the lift or activity with minimum poundage.
3. When using free weights, **ALWAYS HAVE A SPOTTER**. Use 2 spotters when lifting maximum poundages in overhead lifts.
4. The use of weight belts is highly recommended to prevent lower back strain or injury.
5. Rely on leg power rather than back strength in lifting weights from the floor by keeping the hips low and the back as vertical as possible.
6. Use and tighten clamps/collars on bars at all times.
7. Keep the floor area clear to avoid falling over other weights. **NEVER LEAVE WEIGHTS ON A BAR!** **ALWAYS** return weights to the weight tree of the same color when finished.
8. Before using, **INSPECT EQUIPMENT** for loose, frayed, or worn parts. If in doubt, do not use until parts are repaired or replaced. Using damaged equipment can cause injury.
9. If weights, pulleys, or other parts become jammed, **DO NOT** attempt to **FREE BY YOURSELF** because weights might fall unexpectedly. Obtain spotter's, supervisor's, or instructor's assistance immediately.
10. When machines are in use, selector keys must be **FULLY INSERTED AND LOCKED**. Do not allow the plates to drop; set them down gently.
11. To reduce chance of injury, **KEEP HEAD AND LIMBS CLEAR** of weights and moving parts at all times. Don't be careless. **STAY ALERT.**
12. Remember: The weight room is not a play room. Concentrate on completing your workout and avoid "playing around."

Violation of these guidelines and rules may result in suspension from the weight room.

Thank you for your cooperation!

As mentioned earlier, the sport/fitness manager needs to develop the skill to evaluate the risk of a setting for injury to people engaged there in an activity. The concept is known as *foreseeability*. The issue of "should you have known or could you have known" has played a major role in the arguments of plaintiffs in claims for relief as a result of not having been provided the appropriate, safe environment to conduct the activity or program. Providing such an environment is, at least in part, the responsibility of the manager and staff members.

Remember, you can be sued by anyone, anytime, anyplace, for anything. This comment along with the fact that as a sport/fitness manager you cannot waive your liability, will keep your focus on the constant vigilance of your facility and professional staff.

RISK MANAGEMENT

Now that the litigation process and the legal system have been examined, the question a sport/

fitness management professional must ask is, How can we work toward a safer environment for our participants? The answer is Risk Management. Through the establishment of a sound program of risk management, the facility's manager can provide an environment that will conserve assets and resources in a systematic manner to minimize losses that would likely result if situations were out of his or her control (Appenzeller, 1993; Farmer, et al., 1996).

Developing a Risk Management Program

A systematic approach to risk management includes any and all reasonable actions that can be taken to prevent, reduce, or eliminate the potential for injury to participants/users. According to Van der Smissen (1990), a sound program of risk management involves the following steps:

1. A complete safety or risk analysis of the facility (This step must include a checklist; see Appendix A-4 for an example.)
2. A complete analysis of the programming usage of the facility, including a section devoted to future planning needs.
3. A complete review of all policies and procedures for the operation of the facility, including a review of contracts and other business-related matters
4. A complete review of the staffing patterns, and appropriate professional qualifications and or experience
5. A complete review of the history of accidents, injuries, and litigations
6. Establishment of a safety committee or assignment of a professional staff member as risk-management specialist
7. A complete review of relevant laws such as ADA, OSHA, Affirmative Action, Equal Pay Act, and Public Law 94-142
8. Familiarity with usual practices and recommendations of experts in your field.

Note that on a checklist, there must be space for comments and suggestions for situations that need change, repair, or modification. This is the most critical portion of the document because it clearly shows what the analysis revealed, and also shows a plaintiff's attorney what condition needed to be corrected.

Once these steps are taken, a sound reasonable program of risk management can be implemented from year to year, thus providing the facility or entity with a written record of the attempts to provide the best environment possible for all users and participants. Remember that risk management is ever changing, never stagnant. What was the standard last year, may not be the standard this year. Therefore, there must be a serious commitment by all professionals and the entity to continuously identify areas of risk and work toward making them safer (Appenzeller, 1993).

When a manager begins to evaluate the facility, programs, and equipment, he or she must be aware, for example, of the American Society of Testing and Materials (ASTM), which meets each year to establish, review, or suggest voluntary compliance to standards in many industries. This organization provides a forum for producers, manufacturers, and consumers of these products to meet and write standards for materials, products, systems, and services. Included are standards that address the exercise and fitness equipment industry and sport equipment usage and design, such as applies to trampolines, weight training, conditioning, and other sport/fitness-related equipment (Van der Smissen, 1990).

The sport/fitness facility's manager must assure that if there are standards for equipment, the facility's equipment meets or exceeds such standards. This requested information can be written into the purchasing agreements as part of the specifications for the equipment or products being bought (Wong, 1994).

With Affirmative Action Programs under federal review, the question of the value of continuing such programs has yet to be resolved. This is an issue that will be with the sport/fitness manager for quite some time to come. Furthermore, meeting the needs of Americans with disabilities and the standards that a facility manager must meet to comply with the ADA laws is, again, ever changing (Farmer et al., 1996).

NEGOTIATING CONTRACTS

Negotiation is the chance to convince or persuade someone to think your way. The sport/fitness facility's manager must do his or her homework and prepare for all problems and information that may

---

Figure 6–2 Sample warning sign designed for a facility where a trampoline is in use

---

WARNING! CRIPPLING INJURIES CAN OCCUR DURING SOMERSAULTS.
Somersaulting should never be attempted without an overhead safety harness operated by a trained instructor. Refer to instruction manual. Almost all benefits and enjoyment of the trampoline can be obtained by learning the non-somersaulting, twisting skills and routines provided in the manual furnished with this trampoline.

Any activity involving motion or height creates the possibility of accidental injury. This equipment is intended for use ONLY by properly trained and qualified participants under supervised conditions. Use without proper supervision could be DANGEROUS and should NOT be undertaken or permitted. Before using, KNOW YOUR LIMITATIONS and the limitations of this equipment. If in doubt, always consult your instructor.

Always inspect for loose fittings or damage and test stability before each use.

---

come up at such negotiations. If negotiations are conducted in an ethical, honest, and professional manner, with respect and appreciation for all parties, the result will be beneficial for all involved and may lead to future contracts.

As sport/fitness managers, a major role is that of negotiating contracts for facilities, staff, and equipment.

A *contract* is an agreement between two or more parties that sets out conditions and obligations to perform or not to perform certain actions. In most cases, the contract begins with an offer from one party with an acceptance by the other party or parties. Although, contracts can be verbal, sometimes known as an implied-in-fact contract, they are most often in writing because they will be easier to enforce should disagreements arise at a later date between the parties. Note that courts do not distinguish between a written (expressed) contract and an implied-in-fact contract (Wong, 1994; Schubert et al., 1989; Champion, 1994). According to Schubert and colleagues (1986):

> All the formalities of a contract need not be present to establish an action in quasi-contract; the critical element is unjust enrichment. When one party has been unjustly enriched at the expense of the other, quasi-contract provides a legal basis for the recovery of the value of that benefit. (p. 43)

In most employment situations, contracts to perform are informal, with job descriptions providing the scope of professional duties. In return for the successful performance of these duties, the employee receives compensation, usually in salary or benefits, until termination. There are employees who use a written contract, which can include incentive benefits for work completed and provide a sense of continued employment for the professional. At times an employer may want to set conditions such as a non-compete clause in the contract. This clause would prohibit the employee from entering into a competing business upon termination. This clause seems to be used more by private fitness trainers than in educational settings.

A TYPICAL FACILITY CONTRACT

A sport/fitness facility's manager must be well versed in negotiating a facility's lease agreement. Therefore, he or she must consider various issues before signing such an agreement with an outside organization or agency. Some of these issues include the following:

1. Know your client.
   A. Can your facility meet all league rules for competition?
   B. Can your facility meet all the mechanical needs of the event (e.g., electric, sound, stage, playing surfaces) as well as repairs, fixed operations costs, and administrative expenses as agreed upon?
   C. Can your facility meet the revenue requirements of the user for the event?

1. Advertising
2. Scoreboards
3. Seats
4. Ticket sales
5. Concessions
6. Parking
7. Sponsorships
2. Know your politics.
   A. Can your facility support the specific event given your established purpose and intended usage?
   B. Can your facility withstand the potential damage to its areas while still supporting other events, activities, and programs?
3. Know the media and your community.
   A. Can your facility and management work with the media in presenting the events that are to take place?
   B. Can your community assist with the event or support it?
4. Know your legal issues.
   A. Can you provide complete access to the facility for minority or disabled persons?
   B. Can your facility conduct business with other organizations without affecting the agreement with existing organizations?
   C. Will the entity wanting to use your facility sign an indemnity clause?

A TYPICAL EMPLOYMENT CONTRACT

A typical employment contract should contain the following (Wong, 1994; Schubert et al., 1989) elements:

1. Clause describing the job responsibilities and duties
2. Provisions for salary and other compensations
3. Duration of the contract and causes for termination
4. Method of reimbursement for expenses
5. Any non-compete clauses
6. Any rights the company will retain, should the employee develop new products or research while in the employ of the company

The most critical aspect of an employment contract from the sport/fitness manager's perspective is that of responsibilities and duties the professional is to perform according to standards

in the industry. Therefore, it requires that the sport/fitness manager be available to supervise and assist professional staff, especially when the staff are in direct contact with participants.

There seems to be on the horizon a new breed of sport facility manager who will be responsible for not only the day-to-day operations of the facility, but also for the long-term agreements that are entered into by the entity and individuals, including coaches, and athletes. In today's work of big business in sport, the stadia, arenas, and other sport facilities must be able to meet the contractual agreements of the teams, sports, or individuals who will be competing in these venues or lose that portion of the business revenues that would have been generated.

CONTRACTS FOR PROFESSIONAL COACHES

The United Educators Insurance Risk Retention Group, Inc., developed the "Athletes Liability: Self-Assessment Audit" (cited in Appenzeller, 1993, p. 38). In this audit, five questions concerning contracts for professional coaches are raised:

1. Are the contracts for all coaches reviewed by the institution's counsel?
2. Are the contracts for coaches subject to the institution's procedures concerning termination and appeal?
3. Are the assistant coaches apprised of any clauses or agreements in the head coach's contract that allow for their termination at will?
4. Do contracts clearly specify perks, such as the use of owned or loaned vehicles, permission to operate summer camps as independent contractors, and so on?
5. Are athletics department personnel routinely advised of the institution's personnel policies and procedures?

THE COURTS AND SPORT/FITNESS CONTRACTS

In commercial settings, the courts have been active since the late 1980s. As a result, many states have enacted legislation governing and regulating the commercial fitness center or health club or spa industry.

Van der Smissen (1990) states that

> the focus of the laws is upon the rights of the buyers, specifically upon provisions of the contract for services, which must be written and have very specific rights related to cancellation of the contract. (p. 148)

Indemnity is defined as "an obligation or duty resting on one person to make good any loss or damage another has incurred while acting at his request or for his benefit. By a contract of indemnity one may agree to save another from a legal consequence of the conduct of one of the parties or of some other person" (Metzger et al., 1986).

REMEDIES FOR CONTRACT DISPUTES

The contract is an employer-employee relationship or an entity-paying participant relationship. In all cases, there are remedies should a contract matter be disputed and not reconciled. Usual remedies include (Wong, 1994; Schubert et al., 1989):

1. Money damages
2. Restitution for specific performance or lack thereof
3. Punitive damages (intentional tort)

The courts have been reluctant to award punitive damages, however the latest trend for the award of punitive damages is in the area of insurance law. The courts have viewed the status of the insured as unequal in bargaining power to the insurance company and therefore, the insured can file a bad-faith breach-of-contract litigation against the carrier. There is some evidence in recent years that the courts are beginning to look at the relationship between the student-athlete and the institution in the same light as the insured and the insurance company. This trend should move all sport/fitness managers to reevaluate how they conduct business, when dealing with participants.

In the final analysis, the sport/fitness manager must be aware of how to finalize a contract. The basic steps include (Wong, 1994; Schubert et al., 1989; Appenzeller, 1993):

1. Always put the contract in writing.
2. Always get the contract signed prior to actual performance of the responsibilities or duties of the professional.
3. Have all contracts reviewed by legal counsel.
4. Never agree to anything not spelled out in the contract; add to the contract, when applicable.
5. Always attach additional items such as informed consents, liability waivers, assumption-of-inherent-risks statements, and any other forms deemed appropriate (see Appendix A).

Remember, a contract is only as good as the parties who entered into it want it to be.

THE INSURANCE INDUSTRY

The sport/fitness manager is confronted with a dilemma if litigation is filed due to an injury that occurred in the facility or in relationship to a program offered by the entity. We have examined the litigation process, the use, need, and purpose of risk management and the matter of the contract; let us now assume that a lawsuit has been filed and you and your facility are named as defendants.

At this point, the insurance carrier is notified, or has been notified, and will begin its role in the legal system. (For more information about the evolution and present thinking of the insurance industry, see Rabinoff (1994). This chapter explores the insurance industry's role in our discipline from 1977 to 1992, and includes an extensive list of selected readings.) Schmid's (1993) article provides additional information on this topic.

Once you realize you must deal with insurance agents, be aware of the type of coverage you or your facility have purchased, and how the carrier will attempt to defend you (manager, professional staff, or the facility). According to Cole (1993), there are ten common pitfalls athletic departments fall into when attempting to use insurance coverage. They are:

1. Failure to commence treatment at or near the time of the injury
2. Failure to properly establish the date of the injury
3. Failure to provide complete primary insurance information
4. Failure to apply primary insurance
5. Failure to exhaust primary insurance coverage

6. Failure to provide coverage for "overuse" injuries
7. Failure to educate parents, athletes, and coaches of proper insurance procedures
8. Failure to properly complete the claim form
9. Failure to define limitations of the athletic department's secondary insurance coverage and its obligation for medical bills
10. Failure to establish conclusion of care

PITFALLS IN CHOOSING AN INSURANCE POLICY

When considering an insurance policy, some critical points to keep in mind as you select coverage, to avoid the ten pitfalls discussed by Cole, are:

1. Who is covered?
2. When are you covered?
3. What is covered?
4. Limits of insurance
5. Premiums to be paid, and the amount of the deductible
6. Type of premises and operations of programs to be offered
7. What is not covered, if expressly mentioned by the carrier?
8. Additional insured such as managers or lessors of premises
9. Endorsements that change the policy
10. Clear effective and expiration dates of the policy

In addition the sport/fitness facility's manager should conduct an event audit in relation to insurance, study the carrier's status, examine the policy closely, and be aware of any and all independent contractors who will be working at the event or programs.

When executing a contract for an independent contractor, the sport/fitness facility's manager should include the following subsections (Wong, 1994; Van der Smissen, 1990):

1. Parties to the contract between
2. Mutual promises or covenants
3. The nature of the work
4. Compensation
5. Status of the independent contractor
6. Soliciting clients after termination

7. Competing with the entity
8. Return of entity's property
9. Status of records and documents produced by the entity
10. Status of referrals
11. Status time frame for the independent contractor to recruit employees after termination
12. Status of liability and indemnification clauses
13. Tax responsibilities for independent contractor payments
14. Length of the contract
15. Remedies for breach of contract
16. Severability and additional conditions for the agreement to be valid, if any
17. A place for all appropriate signatures

Jerry Tegan, executive vice-president of marketing for an insurance group, stated "Ten years ago, I'm not sure anyone specialized in this business. Everyone did a small piece of it—one company would do some pro sport teams, but nothing else. It was piecemeal." (Schmid, 1993, p. 39).

LIABILITY OF PARTICIPANT AND PREMISE

The most important part of the coverage should be to include "participant legal liability," as well as premises and casualty coverage. Catastrophic injury coverage must also be included; the damages from such a lawsuit can be devastating to the future of the facility. In addition to all this coverage the sport/fitness manager and the entity should consider any "excess" policy, which requires a deductible but covers other health and accident insurance such as covering the athlete during practices as well as in games.

The funding for potential liability is known as *risk transfer*. Risk transfer is the transferring of the loss to another party or entity. Therefore, it is extremely important that the manager review all contracts to determine the exposure of risk when renting a facility or equipment to another party. Through contractual means, the manager should, whenever applicable, attempt to transfer the risk. This can be accomplished in two ways (Van der Smissen, 1990).

The first is using the *Hold Harmless Agreement*. This Hold Harmless Agreement basically means that one party agrees not to involve the other party in the event of a lawsuit, as a contributing entity to the damages or injury to the plaintiff. Tenant/landlord contracts are the most common of this type of transfer of risk.

The second method of risk transfer is the purchasing of insurance. This method tends to be cost-effective in terms of premiums. From the insurance carrier's viewpoint, there are some positive aspects that can reduce your premiums. One area is that of your loss experience. This refers to the number of claims against your facility, staff, or operations. Another aspect is the use of a safety checklist from a site inspection and a risk management program. There are professional consulting firms that provide site inspections, and review or develop risk management plans and programs for facilities.

The insurance industry has become very active in the sport, fitness physical education, and recreation industry. Numerous insurance companies offer this type of coverage. The question arises, Which company offers the best product to protect the entity and the professional?

When selecting an insurance carrier, choose a carrier that has a long and stable track record in this industry. Your homework in this area can avoid problems in what was covered, not due to any wrongdoing on the part of the carrier, but perhaps to the inexperience of the carrier to understand the unique nature of the sport/fitness industry.

RATING INSURANCE COMPANIES

To assist the sport/fitness manager in selecting the best insurance company for his or her needs, there are five rating services of insurance carriers:

1. AM Best
2. Standard and Poor's
3. Moody's
4. Duff and Phelps
5. Fitch Investors Services

Most insurance experts recommend that you work with a carrier that has been rated by at least two of these rating services. These rating services, however, do not offer guarantees, but they certainly have a close eye on the insurance industry.

That could be useful when comparing the performance of one carrier to another.

Ken Reinig (1993), a health club insurance specialist, listed a few of the common-sense questions the health club owner should ask about potential exposure to an injury and lawsuit. They include:

1. Is your staff trained to handle accidents?
2. Do you use an accident report?
3. Does your staff show genuine concern when someone is injured?
4. Does the club have regular maintenance schedules for all equipment?
5. Does the staff acquaint all new members with the proper use of the exercise equipment?
6. Does the staff make sure that the equipment is used only as to manufacturers' intended use?
7. Does the membership agreement have information outlining risks and inherent dangers involved with working out?
8. Does the club staff act immediately to repair or place out of service equipment that is damaged or broken?
9. Does the club have someone on duty at all times who is certified to perform CPR and First Aid?
10. Does the club have warning and safety signs posted?
11. Does the club keep the entire facility clean?

Although these questions cover a broad area of potential lawsuit arguments, the list is endless because each facility has unique needs. For this reason the manager must be aware of the industry, trade, and professional standards of care in operating these facilities and programs.

SUMMARY

We are in a most litigious society. When all is said and done, the most effective and efficient, as well as safe, facilities and programs are those conducted by professional sport/fitness managers who have studied the litigation process, appreciate and follow the trends in the courts, understand the use and importance of risk management and contracts, and have a reasonable working knowledge of the insurance industry.

QUESTIONS

1. What are the legal complexities of operating a sport facility that its manager must understand to be successful?

2. What purpose does a contract serve? Who benefits from it?

3. What are the four legal arguments presented in the majority of injury claims against a sport facility?

4. What are the critical aspects of the contract from the perspective of the sport fitness facility manager?

5. What are the risks a facility manager must take into consideration?

6. Describe the critical elements of a contract.

ACTIVITIES

1. Using the Risk Management Facility Survey, visit a sport/fitness facility and conduct the survey. Do this with a member of the facility's staff or management who will be able to provide all the information to complete the survey.

2. Visit an actual trial. Reflect on the atmosphere of the courtroom, the judge, jury, parties in the lawsuit, and the proceedings. Submit a short conceptual report of your observation, and how you would react if you were the defendant.

3. You are a sport facility manager who wants to develop a major source of revenue for supporting your present programs and to expand your offerings. You decide to invite the general public into your facility to use your equipment, and participate in your programs. Establish the policies and procedures for such a change in operations. What issues should you discuss with your insurance agent? What changes to warnings or user information will you need? What organizations could you contact to obtain additional information as to standards of care, conducting such programs, and hiring qualified staff to supervise these new consumers in your facility?

4. You are being asked by your insurance carrier to survey your facility's risk level. Your facility is less than three years old and does not have a long or significant history of injury to users. The insurance carrier needs to know where the most exposure to injury and potential lawsuits exists. What do you do first? Who do you rely on to provide this information to you and then the insurance carrier? How will you use the risk management facility survey?

SUGGESTED READINGS

Bledsoe, R., Johnson-Freese, J., and Slaughter, D. (1985). *Legal research handbook*. Dubuque, Iowa: Kendall/Hunt.

Flynn, R. (Ed.). (1993). *Facility planning for physical education, recreation and athletics*. Reston, Va: AAHPERD Publications.

Management of risks and emergencies—A workbook for program administrators. (1983). Kansas City, Mo: Camp Fire.

Weiler, P., and Roberts, G. (1993). *Cases, materials and problems on sports and the law*. St. Paul, Minn: West.

REFERENCES

Appenzeller, H. (1993). *Managing sports and risk management strategies*. Durham, NC: Carolina Academic Press.

Cole, P. (1993, November). Falling grades. *Athletic Business Magazine*, pp. 41–43, 46.

Champion, W. (1993). *Sports law*. St. Paul, Minn: West.

Farmer, P., Mulrooney, A., Ammon R. (1996). *Sport facility planning and management*. Morgantown, WVa: Fitness Information Technologies.

Graham, P. (1994). *Sport business*. Madison, Wis: Brown and Benchmark.

Metzger, M., Mallor, J, Barnes, A., Bowers, T., and Phillips, M. (1986). *Business law and the regulatory environment*. 6th ed., Homewood, Ill: Irwin. Appendix, p. 215.

Plaintiff Recovery Rates for Sport Liability. (1990). Salon, Ohio: Jury Verdict Research, Inc.

Rabinoff, M. A. (1996). *The forensic expert's guide to litigation*. Horshem, Pa: LRP Publications.

Rabinoff, M. A. (1994, January). Our Legal system and the insurance industry: The two most effective facets of society affecting sports in America. In P. Graham (Ed.), *Sport Business*. (pp. 121–131). Madison, Wis: Brown and Benchmark.

Reinig, K. (1993, spring). Protecting your club from lawsuits. *National Fitness Trade Journal*, p. 26.

Schmid, S. (1993, April). Premium coverage. *Athletic Business Review*, pp. 39–44.

Schubert, G., Smith, R., and Trentadue, J. (1986). *Sports law*. St. Paul, Minn: West.

Struthers, D. (12 November 1993). Trends in sport and recreation litigation. The Furman Griffiths Symposium on Legal Liability of the Human Performance and Leisure/Recreation Professional held at the Metropolitan State College of Denver, Colorado.

Van der Smissen, B. (1990). *Legal liability and risk management for public and private entities*. Cincinnati: Anderson.

Wong, G. M. (1994). *Essentials of amateur sports law*. Westport, Conn: Praeger.

7

Events

Bernie Goldfine, John Schleppi

This chapter provides general guidelines and principles for managing events including sport competitions (with special emphasis on tournaments), concerts, speakers, and special presentations. The "how tos" of event management discussed here are written especially for athletic directors, community recreation directors, and others whose experience in this realm may be limited or who are seeking ideas to improve their event management skills.

BASIC PRINCIPLES

Prior to addressing specific areas of event management, it is imperative to delineate some general principles that are paramount to the detailed information presented in this chapter. Keeping these guiding tenets in mind when planning an event is the essence of event management. The specific information presented in this chapter is simply a logical extension of the ten general principles that follow.

1. Event management, like all other types of management, is directing, working with, and overseeing human resources and motivating professional spirit and cooperative efforts towards fulfillment of goals (Horine, 1991). Therefore, how you, as the event manager, manage others and inspire their best efforts is the key to running a successful event. Interpersonal and leadership skills are at the core of managing an event. How does one inspire others to perform at a high level? One leadership principle, often overlooked yet funda-

mental, is to treat others the way you would like to be treated.

2. A proactive rather than reactive approach to planning an event is critical to the success of that event. In other words, you must try to anticipate problems and have contingency plans ready when obstacles present themselves. Being proactive requires a great deal of event preplanning. Furthermore, the ability to be a proactive event administrator demands that you foresee possible unsafe conditions that might contribute to the injury of spectators or participants. Thus, being proactive should be foremost in the minds of event managers.

3. Event management may follow several corollaries to "Murphy's Law":

- Everything takes longer than you plan.
- If several things could go wrong, the one that will do the most damage will—and often at the last possible moment.
- Left to themselves, things tend to go from bad to worse.
- Human beings tend to regress toward being mean.
- Every solution creates new problems.
- And, finally, the scientific consensus on Murphy's Law: Murphy was an optimist (Kelly, 1985).

What is to be ascertained from these Murphy corollaries? Simply that the individuals charged with event management must remain calm when faced with crises and must convey a sense of confidence to those under their direction.

4. Organization is important to running an event. First, in a managerial sense, the seemingly endless list of tasks that must be accomplished need to be delegated to those who can be trusted with such responsibilities. Organization is simply deciding who accomplishes which tasks, and when. Second, the event coordinator must personally address multiple tasks. The tasks must be written, not kept on a "mental" list, and prioritized.

5. Ongoing and terminal critical evaluations of the management of an event by all parties involved (i.e., spectators, participants, security officers, managers, etc.) is essential to improve management for the next event. Event managers should learn from both their successes and their failures. An event, no matter how successful, can always be managed better the next time.

6. To manage an event is to provide a service to customers. All customers voice concerns, com-plaints, and kudos at one time or another. Their input provides keys to improving the event-management process. Listen to your customer.

7. Always invoke the concept of equifinality. Equifinality is the notion that there is no "best" way to manage an event and, in fact, employing different processes may achieve identical results. Event managers who are locked into only "their" way of accomplishing objectives (a) run the risk of inadvertently alienating others involved in the management of an event, and (b) fail to be open to better, more efficient ways of managing events.

8. Communications must be maintained among all members of the event management team during preplanning, event execution, and postevent evaluation.

9. The safety of spectators and participants supersedes all other aspects of event management. Event managers have an ethical and legal obligation

Conducting a successful event requires good planning and organization. (Courtesy of architects Sink Combs Dethlefs; Greg Hursley Photography)

to be diligent and obsessive in this regard. Also, accidents due to negligence may jeopardize future events or result in lawsuits.

10. Regularly convey expressions of appreciation and goodwill. You can never bestow enough "thank yous" or expressions of appreciation upon those involved with an event, including participants, customers, sponsors, and those who helped manage the event—especially the volunteers.

PLANNING AN EVENT

The primary issue in planning an event is determining its purpose or purposes. Establishing and clarifying goals provides a framework for managing the event. Examples of event goals are:

1. To make a profit or raise funds
2. To achieve a specific attendance figure or fan support for a particular sport team or event
3. To expose the institution or community to a specific type of entertainment
4. To raise awareness, sensitivity, and/or money for a particular cause (e.g., Special Olympics)
5. To improve organizational image and visibility in terms of creating a positive image or overcoming a negative one

After the goal(s) of an event have been discussed and defined, a marketing plan must be created that clearly states the event's purpose, timelines, budget, target audience, means of promotion, advertising, public relations, media relations, and possible sponsorship.

Following the establishment of the event's goals, it is important to develop a timetable for the event. How this timetable is structured depends on the time available leading up to the event. For annual events, preliminary planning should take place during the twelve to seven months prior to the event date. The timetable should be viewed as a countdown or "check off" of when various tasks should be completed. Table 7–1 is an example of a preliminary timetable for an annual dance marathon.

For a first-time event or an event for which little preparation time is available, there is less opportunity to contemplate and design a detailed plan. In such pressured situations, simply executing the event, rather than ensuring its quality, can become the manager's focus. If possible, it is still sound practice to devise a less formal plan with timelines.

In addition to a timetable, written guidelines, responsibilities, and codes of operation should be created. These documents clarify roles, responsibilities, expectations, and conduct for leaders, paid personnel, and volunteers. One-time or last-minute

Table 7–1 Timetable for an annual dance marathon

12 months prior January 1, 1999	Evaluate the management of the just-completed dance marathon.
11–10 months prior March 1, 1999	Establish organizational and committee structure for the next dance marathon. Begin to garner sponsorships and inform various media of the date and details of next dance marathon.
9–7 months prior June 1, 1999	Begin to execute public/community relations campaign. Start to re-enlist former and recruit new volunteers.
6 months prior July 1, 1999	Send notification sheets to last year's participants.
3 months prior 12/15 October 1, 1999	Send entry forms to last year's participants. Advertise event and distribute entry forms for recruiting first-time participants.
3 weeks prior December 8, 1999	Send out reminders to all possible participants.
Countdown Days	Put management plan into action.
January 1, 2000	Dance Marathon!

Figure 7–1 A precise descriptive job advertisement

PARKING ATTENDANTS NEEDED TO WORK ROX DIAMOND CONCERT ON AUGUST 14, 4:00 P.M., AT MEADOWS COMMUNITY COLLEGE PAY IS $5.50 PER HOUR

Hours: 4:00 P.M.–11:00 P.M.
Job Requirements: Must be 18 years old and possess a valid driver's license.
Responsibilities: Assist in setting up parking areas, directing traffic, and parking automobiles.

---

events run more smoothly if even a very brief, noncomprehensive document of guidelines is developed and implemented. Regardless of whether an event is annual, one-time, planned in detail over time, or put together at the last minute, such documents help to (1) avoid duplication of effort, which may lead to internal conflict; (2) increase cooperation among groups; and (3) standardize workers' training.

When all those involved in the planning and execution of an event are cognizant of their roles, the event's goals, a general idea of how the event is being marketed, and the deadlines for the various tasks, there is a greater probability that the event will be successful.

PERSONNEL

The quality of an event is only as good as the people working it. Therefore, one of the most essential aspects of event management is personnel management. As an event manager, you must be concerned with recruitment, selection, training, supervision, motivation, and evaluation of both paid personnel and volunteers. Other vital aspects of personnel management are understanding how to delegate work and recognizing the qualities necessary for the specialization of workers.

The quality of the recruitment and selection of paid personnel is a function of the time available prior to an event. Ideally, job descriptions should be advertised through the local media, including newspapers, radio, and community cable-access chan-

nels. Furthermore, these descriptions can be posted at job placement agencies, service organizations, and other highly visible community locations.

Job descriptions should be clearly worded and informative. The more precise the description regarding event information, job responsibilities, requisite experience, and wages, the more likely those who apply will be qualified and able to work the necessary hours. Figure 7–1 is an example of a precise, descriptive job advertisement.

If a job requires managerial or complex technical skills, the selection process must be rigorous. Résumés should be elicited, then interviews and reference checks should be conducted for the top candidates selected from the pool of applicants. Jobs that do not require such expertise, such as ushers and parking attendants, should also have a selection process. If possible, applicants for these positions should be screened based on previous job experience, brief interviews, and employment or character references.

In addition to hiring paid employees, the event manager must secure volunteer assistance. Volunteer workers are essential to the success of any event. The media and community outlets used to advertise paid positions can also be used to attract volunteers. In addition, volunteers can be recruited from local community service organizations such as the Rotary Clubs, Boy Scouts, or University Clubs. The first time a special event is conducted in a venue, it may be difficult to recruit volunteers. However, once a volunteer base has been established, and if those individuals have been treated well and shown appreciation, the odds are that they will offer their services again and persuade others to volunteer as well. Creative gifts of recognition such as T-shirts, mugs, gift certificates, or free vacations can be extremely motivating. Thus, recruiting volunteers can be less demanding if previous volunteers believe that their services were valued and recognized.

The event manager must look for certain qualities when recruiting and selecting individuals for both paid and volunteer positions. For example, ushers should have excellent interpersonal skills. The most frequent problems ushers face are customers who are in the wrong seats or who are disrupting other customers' ability to enjoy the event. Ushers must be diplomatic and quick-thinking to facilitate solutions to such problems.

Cashiers for parking, concessions, programs, or merchandise sales must possess good basic mathematical skills. If these individuals can quickly calculate and dispense change, lines will move quickly. Roving vendors (hawkers) are part of the personnel at some events. These individuals must have outgoing and pleasant dispositions if concessions and merchandise sales in the stands are to be lucrative.

The qualifications of the more specialized roles are specific: public address announcers should have excellent public-speaking skills and should be knowledgeable of the event or contest; scoreboard operators should have a thorough understanding of basic computer operations; electricians must be familiar with the venue's power supply and wiring; and those who serve the media should have good public-relations and communications skills.

Committees and Leadership

The magnitude and variety of work entailed in managing an event requires assigning tasks to various committees. Each committee should have a well-defined mission such as registration of participants, media relations, facility setup and takedown, hospitality, concessions, security, budgeting, or programming/scheduling.

Selecting committee chairpersons who are able to effectively guide volunteers can be challenging. These chairs should have a keen interest in the event. Ideally they are good at managing human resources. These leaders may be recruited from sponsoring organizations, city governments, the corporate community, and local universities.

Although there is no definitive code of operations for committees, some general guidelines for such groups include the following:

1. Keep the number of committees to a minimum. A good small group is always preferable to a large unwieldy one.

2. Allow committee chairs to select the persons with whom they will work. Given autonomy in the selection of volunteers, committee chairs are likely to recruit volunteers with whom they can work well. This ability of the committee to interact well facilitates the accomplishment of its given tasks. Furthermore, committee chairs should develop their own chain of command.

3. Prepare written outlines of committee responsibilities and dates and times of tasks to be accomplished. Chairs should maintain close contact with committee persons and their tasks to ensure all assigned tasks are accomplished.

4. Regular meetings of the event manager and committee chairs (the executive committee) should be scheduled for the purposes of planning, assessing progress toward event preparation, and coordinating efforts among committees. David Wilkinson (1988) offers the following excellent suggestions to enhance the planning process:

   - Planning should be done in a comfortable environment, without distractions.
   - Everyone in a committee should be drawn into the planning process, including the quiet individuals, so that all possibilities and alternatives are discussed.
   - Key points should be written, displayed (on a flip chart or board), and recorded (p. 2).

5. Develop a calendar of tasks to be completed. The calendar should begin with the first day the event is confirmed and continue through execution of the event and final wrap-up after the event.

Figure 7–2 is an organizational chart for the management of an event.

Figure 7–2 Organizational chart for event management

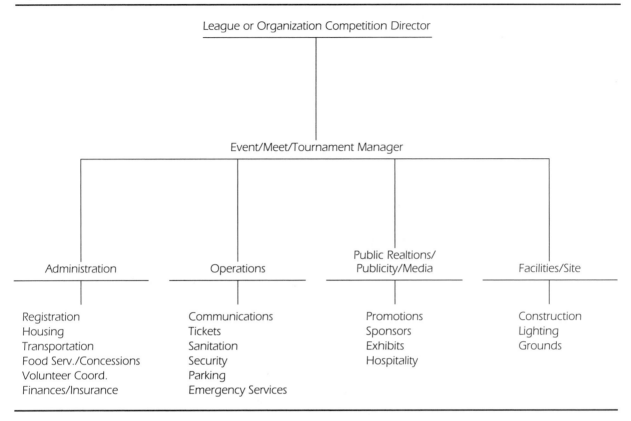

FACILITIES AND EQUIPMENT

A number of concerns are common in the site preparation for all events. The foremost is an assessment of whether major alterations or repairs are necessary for the event to take place.

After addressing major adaptations of the site, one of the best ways to assure a site is adequately prepared for an event is to use facility and equipment checklists. These checklists should be comprehensive and include site-preparation tasks such as cleaning the facility, providing adequate parking and special areas for emergency vehicles, testing the public address equipment and lighting, assuring proper signage for pedestrian and vehicular traffic, providing sufficient ticket-sales areas which operate in an efficient manner, examining the availability and readiness of first aid/medical facilities, making proper provisions for concessions and merchandise stands or vendors, inspecting the permanent seating and addressing any supplemental seating, stocking the restrooms adequately, providing areas for on-site storage and repair of equipment, setting aside special rooms for sponsors and official meetings, addressing the needs of the media including providing communications equipment (e.g., phones, fax machines, photocopiers, etc.), and developing a system for on-site communications among personnel.

When the event involves athletic competition, some other concerns to address in a checklist are providing high-quality practice venues near the competitive site(s), furnishing changing rooms for participants and officials, providing game balls and equipment for practices and contests, making provisions for water, assuring scoreboards are in working order, and designating reserve parking areas for competitors and game officials.

Attending to the needs of visiting teams is often neglected. Providing clean towels and shower facilities, adequate changing rooms, and some post-competition refreshments/snacks are small gestures that do much to bolster a host's good reputation.

The needs of individuals with disabilities should be addressed in the most diligent of manners. Entrances and exits should be easily accessible, as should seating, restrooms, drinking fountains, phones, and concession stands. The Americans with Disabilities Act (ADA) access standards of 1992 clearly delineate facility guidelines for accommodation. A common misconception is that disabled individuals are confined to wheelchairs. Event coordinators need to consider disabilities in a broader sense—to include individuals who are hearing, visually, or mentally impaired—and address accordingly their needs.

Finally, one economical way to ensure that all equipment needs are met is to rent or borrow equipment. It is less expensive to rent items such as tents and additional seating than to purchase them. Often, wrestling and gymnastics equipment,

volleyball standards, and public address systems can be borrowed from community recreation departments or schools.

MARKETING THE EVENT

Marketing is the process of promoting the event through a coordinated set of activities. Specifically, event marketing includes (1) determining if the potential event matches customers' interest (will it draw people?), (2) planning events aimed at satisfying customers' interests, (3) budgeting, and (4) planning advertisements and promotions to inform the public about the event. These and other elements of marketing an event are illustrated in Figure 7–3.

Attracting customers (participants, fans, or both) requires research to determine if a proposed event has appeal. Ideally, customer interest should be determined through marketing research conducted by marketing research specialists; however, this is not always possible. Therefore, you may have to resort to collecting

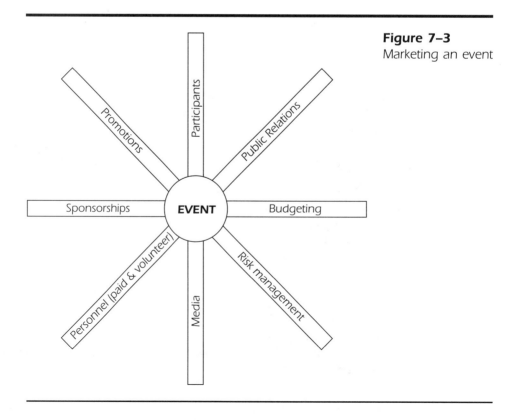

Figure 7–3
Marketing an event

this data on your own. Regardless of the means to accomplish this research, it is essential to have information that accurately portrays customers' sociodemographics (age, income, gender, marital status, address, etc.) and psychographics (interests, attitudes, etc.) in order to attract customers and sponsors to an event.

According to event marketing specialist Viginia Davis (1991), when an event is held annually, the 80/20 rule of recruitment for special events should be kept in mind (i.e., 80 percent of marketing should be geared toward recruiting new participants or fans, and 20 percent should be aimed at maintaining the previous year's participants or fans). Good strategies of promotion to attract new recruits include (1) placing posters and event brochures or information sheets in high-traffic locations; (2) ensuring all local publications (e.g., newspapers, sports publications, and newsletters) have your event dates listed in their general calendars of events; and (3) placing paid advertisements in the media at least three months prior to the event.

Budgeting

Budgeting for an event should be based on the goals established at the outset of planning. Some events are held specifically to make significant amounts of money (e.g., a bike-a-thon to garner funding for athletic equipment). Other events, however, operate at a financial loss but achieve goals such as increased visibility for an institution or cause.

To determine expenses and identify sources of revenue, the event manager should seek the advice of others who have held similar events. For a first-time event, the event manager and committee chairpersons should prioritize the various event-related expenses (e.g., publicity, programs, facilities, equipment, etc.). Once a budget has been established, several particulars of the event finances must be clarified and conveyed to appropriate personnel.

1. Who is responsible for paying bills? Who authorizes purchases? Is there a petty cash fund?
2. Will you require insurance for your event? What type? How much?
3. Are there contingency funds for an emergency?

4. How are purchases and receipts processed? Who is authorized to make purchases?

Expenses may be incurred for promotions, facility or field rental, equipment purchase or rental, transportation, accommodations, supplies, security, publicity, postage, advertising, performers' fees, telephone, stationery, typesetting, printing, officials, and personnel. According to special event marketing authority Davis (1991), overall, promotions should account for at least 20 or 25 percent of an event's budget. Advertising is the most expensive means of promoting an event. Advertising space in newspapers, magazines, or the electronic media can be expensive and, therefore, should be used discriminately. Print, visual, or audio promotions can be selected based on the budget and target audience.

When operating on a limited budget, funds can be maximized through bartering. For example, a local newspaper may sponsor your event in exchange for being named the title sponsor, receiving free tickets, and being given special recognition at the event. Also, to save on advertising and publicity costs, the various media can sponsor one another. For example, a newspaper may sponsor a local television station and vice versa, thus providing each other exposure through print and electronic media at no cost to the event's organizers.

On the opposite side of the ledger, revenues can be obtained at various times in various ways. Prior to the actual event, pre-event series packages for special prices bring in operating moneys. A first-time event needs a "bank" to pay early bills (e.g., printing, advertising) and early intake of funds allows essential jobs to be completed. Other areas of potential revenue, depending upon the event, are entry fees, ticket sales (on-site), sponsorships, grants, lotteries or raffles, trades of "in-kind" services (i.e., bartering) such as printing services for complimentary tickets, parking, concessions, and souvenirs.

Finally, an important consideration is that the "further out" the planning of an event from its actual date (such as one to two years), the greater the chances that costs will exceed the initial budget. Thus, contracts for purchases or services (such as hotels), to be received later at current prices should be well understood at the outset. Contingency funds can help meet the rising cost of goods and services.

Promotions

Promotions, when properly timed, draw attention to an event and enhance anticipation. Luncheons, displays, concerts, theater events, and exhibition-related events (such as 3-on-3 contests or foul-shooting contests for a basketball tournament, or a short run by youngsters to promote a marathon) are just a few promotional ideas that can spark interest in an event.

Advertising is also an important aspect of promoting an event. The visual advertisements should vary in size and color and be eye-catching. Direct-mailing information sheets and brochures that have a catchy event title and logo are other effective promotions. T-shirts that highlight the upcoming event can be worn by people involved in the event as a less formal means of advertising.

Sponsorship, another type of promotion, can be a tremendous source of revenue. Whenever possible, sponsorships should be matched to the needs of participants or spectators. For example, transportation could be sponsored by automobile dealers, accommodations through local hotels, and food and drink concessions matched with appropriate food vendors.

To garner sponsorships, you must create personalized sponsorship packages that delineate (1) a mission statement, (2) event specifics, (3) advertising plans, (4) a demographic profile of the participants and spectators, and (5) what the sponsor will receive in exchange for sponsorship (e.g., tickets, free parking, advertising, etc.). Finally, you should formally recognize sponsors immediately after an event (e.g., a luncheon) and through periodic correspondence (e.g., Christmas cards). Such gestures of goodwill foster positive, friendly relations and may lead to future sponsorships.

Although sponsorships are important, it is the media that can make or break an event. Therefore, all event staff who will interact with the media should be instructed to emphasize the same promotional aspects of the event. Furthermore, they must present confident and positive images to members of the media.

One commonly overlooked medium is the promotional video. Either a professional production company or someone with good videotaping and editing skills can produce a promotional tape. Such tapes can either be sold or given to a local television network or access cable channel.

Community relations must be considered when executing an event. Event organizers must think of the potential impact of the event on the local community. Questions should be asked such as: Will traffic patterns be disrupted? Will neighbors be subjected to unusual noise or lights? Will any person's lifestyle be impinged on in any way? If the answer to any of these questions is yes, the event managers must devise creative solutions to minimize or avoid negative consequences such as bad publicity. For example, neighbors who might be inconvenienced could be given free tickets to the event or be recognized publicly for their cooperation in allowing the event to take place.

Thus, marketing is an essential part of successful event management. Although it may not be possible to conduct formal marketing research, develop comprehensive promotional plans, draw a great deal of media attention, solicit numerous sponsorships, or have an extensive community relations plan, even modest attempts in these areas will enhance the chances of executing a successful event.

RISK MANAGEMENT

Risk management is discussed thoroughly in Chapter 6 of this text. The intent here is simply to accentuate some critical aspects of risk management pertaining to the management of an event. Event risk management should be viewed as an evolutionary process; that is, each event should be examined to determine how risks could be addressed better during succeeding events. The risk management plan for an event should be documented carefully and updated continually based upon data regarding problems, hazards, and injuries. The solutions to these problems should also be recorded.

The four aspects of event risk management of special concern to event managers are (1) insurance, (2) facility inspection and monitoring, (3) crowd management, and (4) first aid and emergency. When investigating insurance, the event manager must address the needs of participants and fans, personnel, and the sponsoring facility and institution. A wide variety of insurance options are available, from comprehensive policies for all parties to self-insurance. The event manager must carefully weigh these options against the particular needs of the event in order to develop the optimum insurance package.

The second significant risk management concern is facility inspection and monitoring, which includes ingress and egress. Ingress (entrance) and egress (exit) should facilitate the most efficient flow of pedestrian traffic in and out of a facility. Sufficient entrances, exits, and personnel to assist and direct people are essential to avoid overcrowding. Furthermore, all entrances and exits must be clearly marked.

Facility inspection includes physically examining all facilities—both for spectators and participants—before an event. Bleachers and seating should be checked to ensure they are secure; this is a particular concern if temporary bleachers have been erected. All walkways and stairs should be inspected for adequate traction. Event managers must be especially vigilant in cold-weather climates where icy conditions can create extremely dangerous footing for spectators. Facilities for participants are equally important. For a basketball tournament, for instance, the floor should be cleaned so that it provides adequate traction and the integrity of the basketball standard supports, backboard padding, and rims should be inspected.

The third key risk management concern is crowd control. The event manager should develop a complete crowd management plan that is appropriate to the magnitude of the event. Crowd management plans are especially critical to the safety and success of an event. The highly publicized 1993 debacle at the University of Wisconsin following their football victory over the University of Michigan, where fans were crushed while rushing the field after the contest, illuminates the need for prudent planning.

To assist with crowd management, law enforcement and trained security personnel should be assigned specific areas, be immediately available by walkie-talkie, and have access to backup officers when necessary. One or more police officers, in uniform, with "arresting authority" should be present and visible at all events (California Interscholastic Federation, 1990). Also, for large events, a central command should be established.

Security personnel and ushers play an important part in crowd management; therefore, they must understand their roles in interacting with law enforcement officials. The primary objective of the security staff and ushers is to maintain a safe environment for spectators, licensees (e.g., concessionaires), and participants. They must keep aisles and walkways clear and intervene when there is a conflict between spectators.

Events that require a public-address announcer introduce another facet of crowd management. The announcer can help set the tone for sportsmanship (at athletic contests) and crowd behavior. Furthermore, announcers can inform the spectators of emergency exits and first aid stations, and direct them in the most efficient means of dispersing at the conclusion of the event.

Unfortunately, some events are marred by fights between fans, participants, or both groups. When a fight breaks out and appears to be out of control in an enclosed venue, all exits must be opened immediately, and the public-address announcer must instruct all individuals to exit in a calm and orderly manner. Most spectators do not wish to be involved with these incidents, and the event's management staff must take immediate actions to protect them and clear the premises.

The fourth and final key risk management concern of an event manager is first aid and emergencies. Establishing first aid and medical emergency procedures is a critical part of pre-event planning. Every event should have a designated, well-stocked triage area to accommodate both spectators and participants (in the event there are no training room facilities). The first aid station should be manned by a qualified nurse or, at the very least, someone with first aid and current CPR certification. Ideally, all event staff personnel are trained in first aid and CPR.

All event staff members should know their roles in a well-established emergency plan. They must know the location of phones to call for emergency medical personnel. When required, an ambulance should be on-site at the event (e.g., football games). In the event of a major disaster (e.g., an earthquake), there should be an emergency disaster plan that delineates the roles of all event personnel relative to transportation, egress of noninjured individuals, tending to the injured, traffic, and so forth. More details are presented on this in Chapter 8.

THE DAY OF THE EVENT

Setting up or "staging" an event requires considerable lead time to accomplish the numerous pre-event tasks. To ensure all necessary tasks are being addressed, you should develop a master checklist of tasks that includes the times and by whom the tasks are to be performed. This master checklist can then be coordinated with checklists for each of the key areas of event planning (e.g., parking, registration, area of competition, ticket and program sales, security, souvenirs and concessions, and so forth.)

Athletic contests have unique requirements the event manager must address. That is, arrangements must be made for (1) visiting teams, (2) game officials, (3) auxiliary game management personnel (e.g., scorekeepers, clock operators, and statisticians), and (4) members of the media.

Accommodating visiting teams is one of the most overlooked aspects of event management. Extending hospitality to visiting teams often takes a low priority in relation to the other aspects of contest management that are essential to the competition. However, treating visiting teams and spectators well fosters appreciation, sportsmanship, and cooperation.

Hospitality begins with communication prior to the contest. Visiting coaches and/or administrators should be given good directions to the playing facility, be provided adequate parking, and be apprised of other essential information. The event manager should designate personnel to greet arriving teams at a convenient area and immediately escort them to their locker room. At this time, the host(s) should orient visiting coaches to other facilities they may need, such as the training room, designated meeting room for half-time or between periods, storage areas, and telephones. During contests, visiting teams should be provided towels, water, plenty of disposable cups, and access to ice. At the conclusion of a contest, a classy but uncommon gesture is to provide refreshments for opposing team members while engaging in a brief, friendly, social encounter. Such encounters enable the participants to develop friendships and an appreciation for the ability of others (Pestolesi, 1978).

Game officials should be treated courteously. They should be directed to their dressing areas and given an orientation to the facilities. It is considerate to pay officials *prior* to the contest rather than forcing them to seek out payment in the mayhem that follows many games. Officials should be offered towels and refreshments. If necessary, security should be designated to escort officials from the playing area during intermission and at the conclusion of the contest.

Auxiliary game management personnel (i.e., contest operations personnel) need to be highly skilled at their responsibilities. Alternative personnel should be designated to fill in if an emergency prevents someone showing up to perform his or her duties. Those in charge of the scoreboard and game clock should be familiar with the operation of this equipment. Scorekeepers and statisticians must have a thorough knowledge of the game. Other auxiliary personnel (e.g., timers for cross-country races and line judges for volleyball matches) should receive thorough training before serving in these capacities. Accurate timekeeping and line calls can avoid controversy and chaos.

Members of the media should be shown the utmost hospitality. Such treatment helps to ensure that future contests will receive coverage. The local media should be provided seating at the scorer's table or in the press box and be given game statistics at half-time and after the game. Furthermore, the media should receive ample access to electrical hookups, telephones, and fax machines. Finally, food and drink should be provided to all members of the media.

Thus, to ensure a well-orchestrated event, the athletic event manager must ask the following questions:

1. Are all personnel (security, ushers, parking, program and ticket sales, etc.) in place prior to the contest? Do these individuals know their responsibilities, from pregame through postgame?
2. Are security and police adequate? Do they know their roles and how they will interact?
3. Should certain areas be cordoned off? How will this be done?
4. Are team benches, equipment, towels, and drinks in place?
5. Are scoreboards, game clocks, official's equipment, and so forth functioning properly?
6. Is someone assigned to meet teams or competitors?
7. Are ceremonies, promotions, and intermission plans ready?
8. Are game personnel (such as scorekeepers, public-address announcers, and ball retrievers) assigned?

9. Have areas been set aside for photographers and the media?

10. Have provisions been made for security to cordon off areas to get teams and officials safely on and off the playing area at the start, during extended breaks, and at the end of the contest?

11. Are maintenance personnel in place to maintain playing surfaces, such as mopping gym floors or dragging a baseball infield?

12. Have arrangements been made for postgame clean-up, exit of competitors, box office check, storage of sales items, concessions, and other necessities?

13. Is there a system for postcontest evaluation by representatives of all aspects of contest management?

CONCERTS AND SPEAKERS

Concerts and speakers may require particular arrangements, especially if there is controversy or emotionalism attached to a speaker. Security, sound, seating, and press interview areas must be arranged. Transportation may also be needed for featured speakers and their aides. Because of the intensity and volubility of concerts, all chairs or benches should be fastened down so that they cannot be moved into aisleways or hurled by concertgoers.

Always be aware of provisions in contracts pertaining to opening acts, merchandise sales, loading and unloading procedures, and technical riders that require specific power, risers, stage arrangements, and lighting. Technical riders are additions to an agreement, similar to an addendum, and usually refer to the technical and dressing room needs of a performer (International Association of Arena Managers, 1993, pp. 4–5). Arrangements for dressing rooms and catering should be in the contract. A "backstage rider" for complimentary passes, sponsorship, billing, or production rights is also part of the contract.

For outdoor summer concerts or shows in particular, weather can be an interrupting factor— from rain to excessive heat. If possible, a back-up indoor facility should be arranged. Procedures should be developed regarding a decision to switch venues, how tickets will be honored, how staff will be notified, whether concessions and souvenirs will be moved, how the switch will be publicized, and what the provisions will be if the

event is canceled (e.g., whether "rain checks" will be issued).

TOURNAMENTS

Tournament management can vary considerably depending on their purpose and organization. Two broad classifications of tournaments are (1) extramural, when teams outside an institution or organization are invited to compete and (2) intramural, when teams within an institution compete. Because managing extramural tournaments involves many of the same considerations discussed in the previous section, the focus of this section is intramural tournaments.

The first consideration for an intramural tournament is its goals. Some participants may simply want to enjoy the camaraderie and get a little exercise. Others may be seeking a high level of competition and are most concerned with winning. Having teams or individuals with such disparate objectives within the same tournament can detract from the satisfaction each is seeking. One solution to this dilemma is simply to hold two tournaments that have different, well-defined objectives (e.g., recreational or competitive divisions or brackets), assuming the number of entrants allows for such organization.

When an organization decides to hold a tournament, the event manager and tournament committee must choose the model best suited for the competition. For example, if you have an intramural, club, youth tournament, or similar event, small-sided games (as 5 versus 5 soccer, 3 versus 3 basketball or volleyball) are an excellent alternative to traditional full-sided contests. Small-sided games allow more action per player; thus, it is not surprising that they have gained popularity in recent years.

The following are examples of the most common forms of tournaments and the advantages and disadvantages of each.

Round Robin. Table 7–2 is an example of an eight-team round robin tournament. Team 1 remains fixed as the others rotate clockwise for each game. In this type of tournament, all teams have an equal opportunity to play one another; therefore, a true champion is determined. However, keep in mind that the more teams entered, the longer it takes to determine a champion. Also, the longer competitive period can increase expenses for personnel and facilities.

Table 7–2   Order of team play in a round robin tournament

A.		B.		C.	
1 vs. 5		1 vs. 2		1 vs. 3	
2 vs. 6		3 vs. 5		4 vs. 2	
3 vs. 7		4 vs. 6		8 vs. 5	
4 vs. 8		8 vs. 7		7 vs. 6	

D.		E.		F.	
1 vs. 4		1 vs. 8		1 vs. 7	
8 vs. 3		7 vs. 4		6 vs. 8	
7 vs. 2		6 vs. 3		5 vs. 4	
6 vs. 5		5 vs. 2		2 vs. 3	

G.	
1 vs. 6	
5 vs. 7	
2 vs. 8	
3 vs. 4	

Figure 7–4   Order of team play in a single-elimination tournament

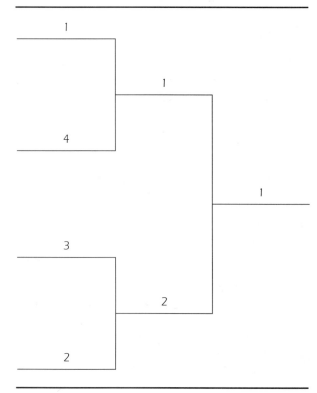

Single Elimination.   The single elimination format (Figure 7–4) is probably the most easily managed type of tournament. The only difficulty arises when an uneven number of teams or teams of demonstrated superior ability (determined by their season records) are given advantageous positions in the brackets. This type of tournament is an efficient use of time, space, and facilities. Unfortunately, it limits playing time for all teams and good teams may be eliminated early through upset losses.

Single Elimination with an Uneven Number of Teams.   Examples of single elimination tournaments with an uneven number of teams are given in Figures 7–5 and 7–6, respectively, for a five-team tournament and a six-team competition. In these tournaments, the stronger teams should be given byes. The proper number of byes is gained by subtracting the number of contestants from the next highest power of two (e.g., for an 11-team tournament, $16 - 11 = 5$ byes).

Single Elimination with Seeds.   In a single elimination tournament with seeds (Figure 7–7), the objective is to have the two strongest teams in the final game. Coaches or a committee determine an order of strength among the teams (based on records and schedules) and place the stronger teams at the far ends of the brackets in the first round.

Single Elimination with a Consolation Round.   A single elimination tournament with a consolation round requires more time and possibly more facilities but allows increased playing time for teams. Furthermore, defeated teams can contest for third place. The example presented in Figure 7–8 shows Team 6 as the third place winner.

Double Elimination.   In a double elimination tournament, all teams play until defeated twice. Thus, a strong team defeated early in the competition or upset later in the tournament has another chance for victory. This type of tournament, illustrated in Figure 7–9, requires more time and facilities and may require teams to play consecutive games.

Pools.   The pool tournament (Figure 7–10) is used for a number of sports such as soccer, volleyball, and fencing. Small (usually groups of four) round robin tournaments are played as preliminaries to quarter- or semi-final rounds. The seeded teams may be divided among the pools to ensure they do not meet until later in the competition. One or two teams from each pool may advance to the next round. This type of tournament allows more competition in limited time. The opportunity for more

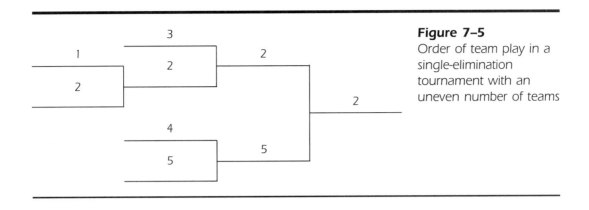

Figure 7–5
Order of team play in a single-elimination tournament with an uneven number of teams

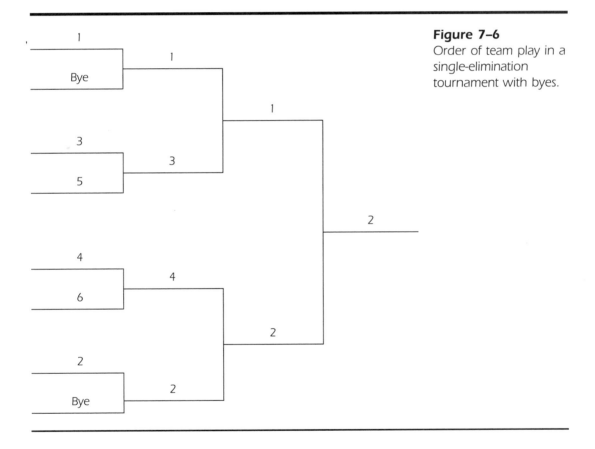

Figure 7–6
Order of team play in a single-elimination tournament with byes.

play time is especially appealing if teams must travel a long distance to participate.

Ladder. The ladder tournament (Figure 7–11) is used in individual competition for an ongoing tournament, usually with limited numbers (e.g., in class or in intramurals). Participants may challenge others directly above them on the ladder. If a challenger is successful, the two participants merely exchange positions on the ladder. Thus, the tournament is continuous; however, a time limit must be set. If the tournament continues indefinitely, interest will decrease significantly.

Pyramid. The pyramid (Figure 7–12) is similar to the ladder tournament; however, it can accommodate more players. Participants can challenge anyone in their row; the winner can challenge any

Figure 7–7 Order of team play in a single-elimination tournament with seeds

Figure 7–8 Order of team play in a single-elimination tournament with a consolation round

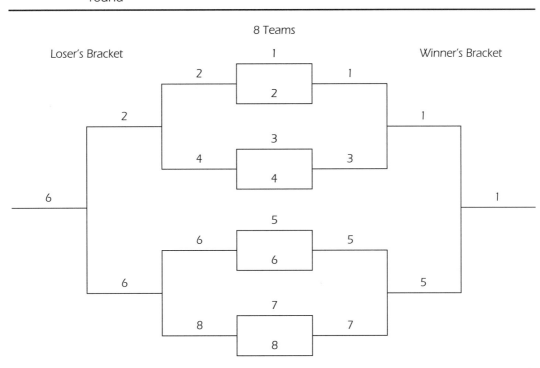

competitor in the row above. The pyramid provides much movement among players and thus more interest; however, like the ladder, a limited time period must be specified to maintain interest.

Various types of awards or recognition can be given to participants of intramural contests. Trophies, T-shirts, dinners at local restaurants, movie tickets, and writeups in the campus newspaper are the most common ways to recognize them. Local businesses may even donate awards. For example, if a business is permitted to add its logo to the event's T-shirts, it may be willing to donate the T-shirts. Also, restaurants may be willing to offer gift certificates.

EVENT WRAP-UP AND EVALUATION

A final evaluation should be made to obtain a complete picture of an event's success. Provisions for this evaluation must be in place well before the event is finished, and a timetable for completing the evaluation must be developed. The following are several items to consider when developing an evaluation:

I. Purpose
   A. Evaluate "worth" of event
   B. Check against initial written goals for event
   C. Learn from mistakes and successes
   D. Gain support for future events
   E. Improve
II. Considerations
   A. Who is involved in evaluation
   B. What instrument is used for evaluation
      (1) Written
      (2) Check sheet
      (3) Brainstorming
      (4) Interviews

Figure 7-9 Order of team play in a double-elimination tournament

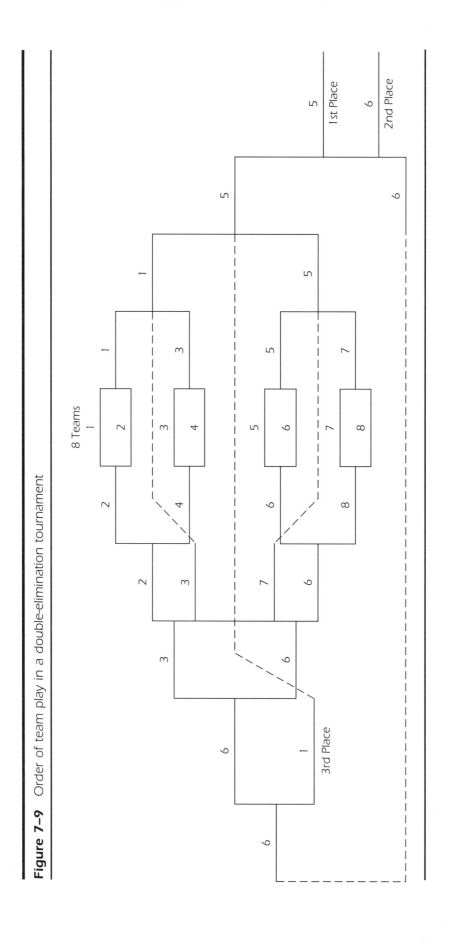

Figure 7–10 Pools tournament—order of play for 16 teams

POOL W	POOL X	POOL Y	POOL Z
1 vs. 2	5 vs. 6	9 vs. 10	13 vs. 14
3 vs. 4	7 vs. 8	11 vs. 12	15 vs. 16
1 vs. 3	5 vs. 7	9 vs. 11	13 vs. 15
2 vs. 4	6 vs. 8	10 vs. 12	14 vs. 16
1 vs. 4	5 vs. 8	9 vs. 12	13 vs. 16
2 vs. 3	6 vs. 7	11 vs. 10	12 vs. 14

Figure 7–11 Ladder tournament in racquetball

Figure 7–12 Diagram of a pyramid tournament. The numbers represent participants' levels. Lower level players challenge higher level players and replace them if they beat them.

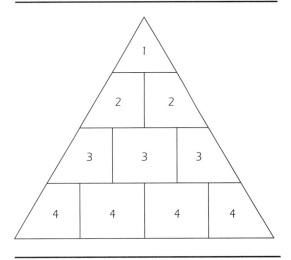

III. Procedure
  A. Report includes
    (1) Introduction and background of goals and purpose
    (2) Recommendations
    (3) Statements
      (a) Financial
      (b) Equipment and facilities
      (c) Personnel
      (d) Organizational structure
      (e) Reports from various committees
      (f) Materials (final disposition or storage of and access for future events)
      (h) Recommendations
      (i) When preparations for next event should begin and how

SUMMARY

With proper planning and organization, managing an event can be an enjoyable experience. Good personnel management, comprehensive marketing, sound budgeting, and prudent risk management are essential aspects of conducting a successful event.

QUESTIONS

1. What are the five basic principles of event management?

2. What are several major concerns of an event manager?

3. How can volunteers be recruited for a special event?

4. What is the 80/20 rule of event marketing?

5. What are some risk-management issues in conducting an event?

ACTIVITIES

1. If you had to initiate, organize, and oversee a 3-on-3 youth (ages 10–15) basketball tournament, what steps would you take to ensure its success?

2. How would you promote a one-day, collegiate intramural, co-ed indoor soccer tournament?

3. Your community is bidding for an international bicycling championship. In cooperation with the chamber of commerce, your organization conducts a series of races for men and women, ranging from 5 miles to 100 miles. The city wishes to showcase its new waterfront and work with surrounding suburbs in a cooperative effort. Delineate as many considerations as possible that will need to be addressed in order for the event to be successful.

4. Your athletic department is hosting a regional volleyball tournament for sixteen elite teams. However, at the last minute two of the teams cancel, leaving you with fourteen teams. You have four courts available and were originally planning to use pool play. Address the following concerns:

   A. How will you determine play among teams? How will you determine the tournament champion?

   B. How will you finance this event?

   C. How will you market this event?

   D. What arrangements will you make regarding spectators, players, officials, coaches, and the media?

   E. What could have been done to discourage teams from dropping out?

5. A regional track meet is being held at your college during the summer break. The athletes will be housed in the school's dormitories. Men's and women's competitions will be held over four days throughout the day and evening hours. Crowds are expected to average between 1500 to 2000. There will be a fitness and conditioning conference held at the same time on the campus in conjunction with and sponsored by the track association. Approximately 300 people will attend this convention. What arrangements need to be made for food for athletes, officials, media, spectators, and any others connected with these events? What will you have to consider in terms of risk management? How will you market this event?

SUGGESTED READING

Champion, W. T. (1993). *Sports law in a nutshell*. St. Paul: West.

REFERENCES

Brown, S. C., Sutton, W. A., and Duff, G. D. (1993). The event pyramid: An effective management strategy. *Sport Marketing Quarterly*, II(4).

Bucher, C. A. (1988). *Management of physical education and athletic programs*. St Louis: Times Mirror/Mobsy.

California Interscholastic Federation (CIF). (1990). *Effective game management: A handbook for school site administrators*. La Mirada, Cal: CIF.

Davis, V. (1991). *How to market special events*. A presentation at the American Alliance for Health, Physical Education, Recreation and Dance (AAHPERD) Convention in San Francisco, California, April 4, 1991.

Horine, L. (1991). *Administration of physical education and sport programs* (2nd ed.). Dubuque, Iowa: Wm. C. Brown, p. 2.

International Association of Arena Managers (IAAM) Glossary. (1993, May). Irving, Tex: IAAM.

Jensen, C. R. (1988). *Administrative management of physical education and athletic programs* (2nd ed.). Philadelphia: Lea & Febiger.

Kelly, J. R. (1985). *Recreation business*. New York: Wiley, p. 407.

Pestolesi, R. A. (1978). *Creative administration in physical education and athletics*. Englewood Cliffs, NJ: Prentice-Hall.

Road Runners Club of America. (1993). *The road runners club of America handbook*. (5th ed. rev.). Alexandria, Va: Author.

University of Dayton. (1992). *NCAA division I basketball tournament manual*. Dayton, Ohio: Author.

Wilkinson, D. G. (Ed.). (1988). *Manual*. Toronto: The Event Management and Marketing Institute.

8

Control and Security

Rob Ammon, Jr.

Management of athletic facilities has changed dramatically with the influx of television revenue and national exposure. Due to the popularity and importance of sport in American society, today's competitions are highly publicized, revenue producing, and sometimes dangerous extravaganzas.

While many fans' attention remains focused on the activity, other individuals are working behind the scenes to ensure the protection and safety of all who attend. These individuals, who range from facility managers to ushers, although typically not individually responsible, assist with implementing policies and practices paramount to the success of the athletic event.

You as a facility manager guide the organization and supervision of stadium administration. Because of the litigious nature of American society, however, your institution, once immune from litigation, now must protect itself. The lack of consistent and validated game management practices could result in unnecessary injuries, countless law suits, decreased revenue, and a negative impact on your facility's public relations.

EXPLANATIONS FOR VIOLENT BEHAVIOR

Violence occurs at athletic events throughout the world and the United States is not without its share of violent outbursts. After the Florida versus Florida State football game in 1982, victorious Florida fans swarmed onto the FSU field to tear down the goal posts. Florida State fans rushed onto the field to prevent this from happening. The en-suing altercation involved an estimated 800 people and sent 25 police to the hospital (Neff, 1985). After the Detroit Tigers won the 1984 World Series, more than 10,000 people took to the streets in a wild destructive celebration. This riot left 1 dead, 80 injured, 41 arrested, and over $100,000 in damages. In another incident the same year, 8,000 fans rioted after the Kansas versus Kansas State football game (Leo, 1984). Anyone who follows sports realizes that the phenomenon of spectator violence is increasing, especially when witnessing recent destructive celebrations after the Super Bowl in Dallas, the Stanley Cup in Montreal, and the NBA Championship in Chicago.

Sociological Theories

What causes these violent actions by seemingly normal spectators? There are several theories, but most sociologists maintain that the social background and psychological make-up of the fans are critical factors regarding their deviant behavior (DeBenedette, 1988). Fredrick Koenig, professor of social psychology at Tulane University, theorized that the European crowds are made up of young macho males, most of whom are out of work and believe society has given them a raw deal. Supporting a soccer team gives them a sense of identity or belonging. Koenig believes that this close identification with the team gives the "hooligan" a vicarious sense of victory or defeat (DeBenedette, 1988).

Gordon Russell, social psychologist at Alberta's University of Lethbridge, has a different belief: combative sports, which involve "interpersonal aggression," actually stimulate hostilities during and after the sporting event. Athletes are rewarded for aggressive play and their fans learn that violence is condoned. Russell's interviews found that hockey fans registered approval when witnessing verbal abuse and fist fights (Birchall, 1982). Dr. Stanley Cheren, of the Boston University School of Medicine, has similar beliefs. He believes that as people become more experienced with violence, they need more excessive violence to stimulate their hunger for violence (Appleson, 1982).

Delia S. Saenz, a social psychologist at the University of Notre Dame, describes the irrational behavior of spectators as arousal that leads to loss of self control. She terms this manifestation *deindividuation*. Everyone becomes part of the crowd, no one is an individual, and no one person is responsible for the abnormal behavior (Leerhsen, 1988).

Location and Design

The United States does not have the same problems with crowd violence that plague Europe because of two factors: geography and architecture. In Europe, the big soccer games are an inexpensive train ride away. Athletic teams participating in the United States, however, are often separated by long plane trips. The exception occurs when intrastate schools play each other and the possibility of violent outbreaks increases.

The second reason relates to facility design. The stadiums in Europe have large open areas or "terraces" where there are no seats and spectators mill about in large groups. Gammon (1989) explains that many in Europe believe that this ancient stadium design is a leading cause of poor crowd control.

The United States does not have stadiums with this type of design and, in most instances, the stadium seating is individually reserved and fairly expensive. In this setup, spectators rarely condone violent behavior. Geoffry Alpert, director of the Center for Law and Society at the University of Miami, asserts that most fights in ancient Rome occurred at the chariot races. Few violent outbreaks occurred at the gladiator matches because they were frequented by the wealthy upper class (DeBenedette, 1988).

Other Factors

Crowd management disasters have occurred in the United States. Though they involve concert crowds and are not sports related, some of the inherent dangers for facility managers are the same. *Festival seating*, (a misnomer since no seats exist, just open floor space), which allows spectators to crush up against the stage in a general admission setting, has proven tragic in several instances.

In 1979, 11 patrons were killed as a result of festival seating and the facility doors not opening on time (*Bowes v. Cincinnati Riverfront Coliseum*, 1983). In 1991, three teen-agers died as a result of a crowd surge at an AC/DC concert, in Salt Lake City (Lewis, 1992). Festival seating existed at the concert even though legislation prohibited its use. Later the same year 5,000 patrons tried to cram into a 2,700-seat facility for a charity basketball game on the campus of City University of New York, resulting in 9 deaths and 29 injuries (Newman and Dao, 1992).

CROWD MANAGEMENT

To protect the organization's assets, a facility manager must recognize the importance of a crowd management plan. Such a policy is created to assist in *managing* crowds, not in trying to *control* them. Trying to control a crowd is a very tenuous and nearly impossible venture, while managing a crowd is more feasible.

The main reason for implementing a successful crowd management policy, however, is the safety and comfort of your spectators. An effective crowd management plan assists you, as the facility manager, by providing the best environment for your fans while diminishing the possibilities of litigation. Representatives from all agencies involved with game management need to have input in order to insure your fans' safety and comfort. In addition, your plan should include individual circumstances, history, information from other facilities, and sometimes a little bit of luck (Oshust, 1985).

Foreseeable Duties

One of the most important aspects of crowd management is the concept of "foreseeability"; this aspect is also a key element in the determination of negligence (Miller, 1993; Sharp, 1990; van der Smissen, 1990). As an administrator or manager you are expected to take reasonable care to avoid acts you can reasonably foresee as possibly leading to injuries (Hudgins and Vacca, 1979). If an injurious situation has occurred in the past, then "foreseeability" dictates the circumstances may occur again and "due care" needs to be implemented.

Sharp (1990) believes that one of the more pressing concerns for your occupation is the protection of spectators from foreseeable negligence by third parties. She describes an incident which took place at an Oregon girls' basketball game. A plaintiff attending the game was attacked by three individuals; the school district was not found negligent by the court. Though the only supervision was provided by the two head coaches, the court believed that the lack of prior violence or rivalry precluded additional personnel.

An additional concept that permeates liability relates to the fact that as the facility manager you do not guarantee a patron's safety; you only have a duty to provide safe premises (Berry and Wong, 1986; Champion, 1990; Wong, 1988).

An additional example involving the courts and foreseeability occurred when a male plaintiff attended a high school football game during which he was beaten and robbed. He sued the school district for not providing safe premises. The court found there had been no prior attacks; therefore, there was no duty to protect the patron against the unforeseeable violence (*Gill v. Chicago Park District*, 1980). Generally, while you have a duty of care to provide safe premises to your patrons, that duty of care to protect does not extend to unforeseeable acts committed by third parties (van der Smissen, 1990).

Bearman v. University of Notre Dame (1983), a case described further in the alcohol policy section, is the landmark case pertaining to foreseeability (Berry and Wong, 1986; Miller, 1993; Sharp, 1990; van der Smissen, 1990; Wong and Ensor, 1985; Wong, 1988). During ensuing litigation the facts of the case demonstrated that intoxicated individuals posed a general danger to university patrons. The court found that the university had a duty to protect their "invitees" from negligent acts of third parties.

The duty of care owed to your spectators depends on their status. Most fans and athletes are classified as "invitees." An invitee enters the property of another, with the owners' encouragement and usually gives the owner a monetary benefit. These individuals are owed the greatest degree of care from any known defects. You do not guarantee these spectators from all injuries, however, only from those risks that should have been discovered by exercising reasonable care (Wong, 1994).

What Is Crowd Management?

Modern crowd management involves a great many facets and is one of the most vital components of game management. Every element of the event from the design of the facility to the game itself is part of crowd management (Antee and Swinburn, 1990). Van der Smissen (1990) classifies crowd control as part of the duty facility managers owe their patrons to protect them from unreasonable risk of harm from other individuals.

The frequency and the intensity of crowd and spectator violence is increasing (Nygaard and Boone, 1989). In Philadelphia a professional football game between the Eagles and the Dallas Cowboys was delayed because of snowballs thrown by fans. Early in the game a referee was knocked down by the icy missiles; the doctors trying to assist him were pummeled; and the cheerleaders were driven from the field (American Survey, 1989). In another case a spectator was seriously injured after a Harvard–Yale football game when she was struck by the goalposts as they were pulled down. The university and city police had agreed not to try to stop the crowd and allowed them to tear the goalposts down. A reported settlement of $900,000 was reached in the case (*Cimino v. Yale University*, 1986).

The components of an effective crowd management plan are similar, regardless of whether a concert or a football game is being conducted. Miller (1993) listed seven criteria that juries have evaluated to determine if the crowd control measure were adequate and appropriate: (1) type of event, (2) surrounding facilities and environment, (3) known rivalries among schools, (4) threats of violence, (5) existence and adequacy of emergency plan, (6) anticipation of crowd size and seating configuration, and (7) use of security personnel and ushers.

Components of a Crowd Management Plan

A basic crowd management policy should parallel your facility's philosophy of providing a safe, enjoyable, and secure environment for all invitees. This may be accomplished through the implementation of five components. First, a *trained and competent staff* must be employed to carry out the crowd management policy. Using trained personnel who have progressed through a licensing program provides you as the facility director with better qualified employees. Employing licensed personnel also serves as a partial protection against frivolous lawsuits because most courts recognize the training process for securing the license.

A second vital component of the crowd management plan should address *the procedures to eject* disruptive, unruly, or intoxicated patrons. Ushers should never be delegated this duty. Ushers are an integral part of a game management policy, however, their responsibilities should be to enhance communication and customer satisfaction (Miller, 1993). Since ushers are not trained to handle these disruptive behaviors, they may injure themselves or cause the problem to escalate (van der Smissen, 1990). The author recommends that ushers never be delegated crowd management duties, especially those involving ejections. The ejection duties

This sign at Tiger Stadium in Detroit informs the media of time limits so they will be able to get interviews before games. (Courtesy of Rob Ammon)

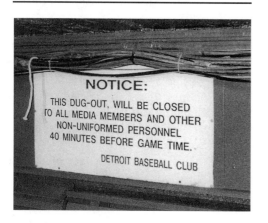

should remain the responsibility of the crowd management staff.

As previously mentioned, the prime focus of an effective crowd management plan should be to provide for the safety and security of the fans, which includes protection from violent third parties. While a facility operator is not responsible for all injuries that occur at his or her stadium, the operator must take reasonable precautions (Wong, 1988). Therefore, the removal of any disruptive or intoxicated fans will provide a safer environment for the remaining spectators and help to protect the stadium director from potential litigation.

As a facility director you must be prepared to document your ejections with some type of paperwork. This is an extremely crucial step in the ejection process because it serves to protect the crowd management employee and your facility's administration from subsequent litigation. An additional step is to photograph the person being ejected. This measure gives an accurate portrayal of the condition of the ejected and further protects the employees from unnecessary legal harassment.

The third component for an effective crowd management policy should be adequate *signage*. These types of informational and directional signs build a support network between fans and your staff. Spectators appreciate being treated fairly and will normally abide by facility directives if previously informed.

A fourth element in your crowd management plan is the *services provided for the disabled*. The Americans with Disabilities Act (ADA) must be strictly adhered to in order to provide disabled fans a safe and secure environment. The existence of a written emergency evacuation plan for the disabled is a vital concern that every stadium director must address. These evacuation policies should be designed, implemented, and practiced along with the normal evacuation plan.

A second area of concern with the ADA pertains to the seating of the disabled and specifically people in wheelchairs. As Fenley (1992) indicates, the ADA requires wheelchair locations to be scattered throughout the facility providing wheelchair-bound fans the opportunity to purchase "prime" seat locations. Facility managers without such procedures need to comply and provide the required services to prevent federal litigation. In addition, wheelchair-bound fans must be able to be accompanied by those who use fixed seats.

The fifth and final component for an effective crowd management plan pertains to your *implementation of an effective communication system*. The foundation of this system will consist of multichanneled radios that allow simultaneous communication among various employees. In addition, the creation of a centralized area for representatives from each group (facility, medical, security, and law enforcement) will facilitate communication and improve decision making. This area, often known as the *command post*, is normally in, or on top of, the press box.

Communication, as mentioned earlier, has been found to be a critical aspect in guaranteeing the safety, enjoyment, and security of the spectators. Establishing a command post in the press box is paramount for effective communications to occur. Disruptive or intoxicated patrons are identified by the command post operators, through the use of binoculars, and the patron's location is then communicated to the responsible crowd management team. In addition, medical emergencies, and traffic congestion can be observed from the command post. By dealing with these situations swiftly and firmly, your patrons recognize the serious tone the crowd management plan conveys.

Every facility requires a crowd management plan (Antee and Swinburn, 1990; Appenzeller, 1993; Baley and Matthews, 1984; Miller, 1993; Sharp, 1990; van der Smissen, 1990). This plan provides the blueprint for a safe and enjoyable environment for all your spectators.

POLICY ON ALCOHOL

Many individuals attend football games as social outings and are sometimes involved in drinking. While millions of sport fans drink alcohol responsibly, a minority are irresponsible and their "good times" may become a major headache for you as a facility manager. If you manage the sale and consumption of alcohol properly, few problems may occur; improperly managed, a litigious nightmare may await.

A comprehensive policy on alcohol must be an integral part of your overall game management plan. Intoxicated patrons cause many problems because of the safety concerns brought onto themselves and others. You and other facility managers must be aware of the potential problems that exist with large events and alcohol abuse.

Implementation of two methods used by many other sports facilities may assist in limiting operational risks. First, station trained crowd management personnel at the entrances to prevent intoxicated individuals from entering the grounds. Second, instruct these personnel to prohibit patrons from entering the stadium with alcoholic beverages. These two procedures assist your controlling the alcohol consumption of the spectators.

The Pros and Cons of Alcohol Sales

Many individuals in the sports industry argue that substantial revenue generates from beer sales at football games and therefore is worth the risks. In addition, some programs, especially universities with small attendance figures, find it difficult to generate a profit if not for the sale of beer at home games. Other facilities determined alcohol sales not worth the liabilities associated with the increased revenue. Wong and Ensor (1985) pointed out that (1) the NCAA banned the sale of alcohol at all championship and tournament events back in the 1970s; (2) the New Jersey Sports and Exposition Authority adopted several new policies aimed at limiting the abuse of alcohol; and (3) in 1984, Foxboro Stadium in Foxboro, Massachusetts, began offering low alcohol beer; the Metrodome in Minneapolis, Minnesota, started selling only 3.2% beer; Three Rivers Stadium in Pittsburgh, Pennsylvania, allowed families to sit in alcohol-free sections and; Shea Stadium in Flushing, New York, and Tiger Stadium in Detroit, Michigan introduced low alcohol beer in 1985.

Legal Liabilities

As a facility manager you must implement alcohol management strategies to prevent your patrons from drinking too much. Many states have legislation that allows injured plaintiffs to bring suit against the defendants, in addition to the owners of the establishments that allowed the defendants to become drunk. Some states allow plaintiffs to sue liquor establishments under these statutes, often called "dram shop laws," others allow recovery by common negligence theory, and some states allow both (Chafetz, 1990; Miller, 1993).

"Social host liability" is a second ordinance that you as a sport facility manager should monitor. This type of statute provides injured plaintiffs with the opportunity to prefer charges against both the host of the party where the defendant became intoxicated and the inebriated individual (Chafetz, 1990). However, although these situations exist, not all courts follow this line of thinking. In one case a superior court in New Jersey ruled that an intoxicated fraternity student, at a Rutgers football game, was responsible for his own injuries since Rutgers did not serve or sell alcohol at their football games (*Allen v. Rutgers The State University of New Jersey*, 1987).

As mentioned, deploying trained crowd management personnel at facility entrances prohibits intoxicated individuals from entering the facility and also prevents spectators from entering the facility with alcoholic beverages. These two procedures will assist you in controlling alcohol consumption, thus protecting your facility from social host liability suits.

Foreseeable Risks

As a facility manager you need to be aware that foreseeability is, again, a key determinant in court decisions, especially in cases involving alcohol-related incidents. The ability to foresee risks associated with alcohol is a reasonable way to reduce liability (Miller, 1993).

Measuring foreseeability requires you as a facility manager to document incidents and then review the records to determine which problems occur more often than would be expected by random chance. Your implementation of preventive measures to guarantee these incidents do not recur must then be undertaken. When liability results from foreseeable risks, it usually indicates that the facility manager inadequately used all procedures at his or her disposal (Maloy, 1988).

For example, a court case relating to the concept of foreseeability and alcohol involved a man and his companion who, while bowling, argued with a group of intoxicated individuals in the next lane. The plaintiff complained to the bowling alley's manager about the unruly individuals. Later, one of the drunks assaulted the plaintiff by savagely attacking him in the parking lot. The United States Court of Appeals stated the bowling alley failed to protect the plaintiff from an obvious and foreseeable danger. The court's opinion stated the bowling alley's manager should have stopped selling beer to the intoxicated group and should have provided safe passage for the plaintiff to his vehicle (*Bishop v. Fair Lanes Georgia Bowling Inc.*, 1986). This decision creates serious implications for managers of many various facilities.

A second demonstration of foreseeability occurred in *Bearman v. University of Notre Dame* (1983). In October 1979, Christenna Bearman and her husband were walking across a parking lot after leaving a Notre Dame football game. An intoxicated fan fell on Bearman from behind, breaking her leg. No security or facility personnel were present at the time of the accident. Bearman sued Notre Dame stating she was an invitee, therefore the University had a duty to protect her from the negligent acts of a third party. Notre Dame maintained that the incident was an unforeseeable accident. The University, however, was aware of alcohol being consumed during "tailgate" parties, and that some individuals would become intoxicated and pose a general danger to others. Therefore, the Indiana Court of Appeals found Notre Dame had a duty to protect those spectators from the negligent acts of third parties (Wong and Ensor, 1985).

In a third case involving foreseeability, the plaintiff was a sixteen-year-old girl knocked down by a drunk at a sports pavilion. She sustained a catastrophic injury from the incident. The court found that since the facility did not serve alcohol, neither the injury nor the intoxicated patron were foreseeable (Miller, 1993).

Alcohol Training Programs

The implementation of two national programs may assist you as the facility manager, by training individuals who serve alcohol and/or handle intoxicated patrons. *Training for Intervention Procedures by Servers of Alcohol (TIPS)*, a program funded by General Motors, received the National Commission Against Drunk Driving Award for Education and Prevention (Chafetz, 1990). Techniques for Effective Alcohol Management (TEAM), formed in conjunction with the International Association of Auditorium Managers (IAAM) and several other organizations, provide successful training to individuals in effective alcohol management (Antee and Swinburn, 1990).

A designated driver program is encouraged at Jacobs Field in Cleveland. (Courtesy of Rob Ammon)

In order for you to administer an effective game management plan, the plan must treat spectators in a humane fashion and assist in providing a safe environment for all. Designated Driver programs provide a popular service by building rapport with football fans. Your incorporation of a similar program increases individual awareness of the need to drink responsibly. Designated Driver programs help patrons recognize the problems with alcohol abuse, remind fans of their limits with alcohol, and assist in reducing alcohol-related accidents (Miller Brewing Company, 1992).

Criteria to Control Alcohol-Related Problems

The potential for litigation involving alcohol is obvious. Many administrators in the sports facility industry are alarmed at the liability possibilities and, therefore, eliminate sales of alcohol. Chafetz (1990) believes this reaction is analogous to eliminating cars because of their potential to be involved in accidents. Individuals learn to drive responsibly and they can learn to drink responsibly as well.

Your implementation of certain measures assists in curtailing irresponsible actions. Controlling sales of alcohol in the facility, limiting and supervising tailgate activities in the parking lots, and providing security inside and outside the facility help ensure that concerns about alcohol are addressed (Wong and Ensor, 1985). Miller Brewing Company (1992) lists several elements that, if implemented, may assist you in curtailing alcohol-related problems:

1. Determine the type of crowd.
2. Make spectators aware that the only drinking allowed in the facility is responsible drinking.
3. Keep the emphasis on the sport, not on the drinking.
4. Require servers and security to be TIPS or TEAM trained.
5. Check identification (for age) thoroughly and put a wristband on everyone legal to drink.
6. Limit the number of beers sold to one person at one time.
7. Reduce the size of servings to 12 ounces.
8. Cut off beer sales at a specific point during the game.
9. Offer lots of food and nonalcoholic beverages.
10. Encourage families to attend and everyone to be on good behavior.

Alcohol signage at Edmonton Stadium in Edmonton, Alberta, Canada, gives proper notice to all spectators about policies enforced in the stadium. (Courtesy of Rob Ammon)

MEDICAL PLANS

Medical services are an additional element for facility management personnel. Trying to cut corners by minimizing the medical budget is unwise, as well as potentially litigious (Berlonghi, 1990). A slow response by the facility's emergency personnel can mean the difference between life and death. Van der Smissen (1990) mentioned that, from a legal perspective, improper or inadequate medical services and assistance by the facility, may be determined by the courts to represent negligence. She states that the courts scrutinize the availability of medical care and its immediacy, and determine if either availability or immediacy were the proximate cause in the seriousness of injuries.

Designing the Medical Plan

Devising a comprehensive plan is a preliminary condition to providing adequate medical services. Your detailed analysis must identify several important components. Ricardo Martinez, a leading expert in spectator care, identified two vital segments to be included in a viable plan: injury control and medical response (Carlson, 1992).

Control of injuries may be enhanced in several ways. First, the design of your facility should be evaluated to determine if any structural changes need to be made to eliminate potential injuries. Signage is a second way you may minimize injuries. These signs direct individuals to first aid stations, ambulances, and life support units. It is imperative that these signs by simple, easy to read, and placed in highly visible locations (Berlonghi, 1990; Carlson, 1992). Identification of potential medical problems is a third method for controlling injuries. Alcohol abuse and related injuries, breathing problems, heat exhaustion, cardiac arrests, insect stings, twisted ankles, and broken bones are a few of the common medical problems that may arise at your events (Berlonghi, 1990). Recognizing these common occurrences allows you as the facility manager to prepare for all eventualities.

The second component of a medical plan identified by Martinez (Carlson, 1992) is medical response. Staff members and personnel must be aware of their individual responsibilities for providing adequate medical care to thousands of spectators attending an event such as a football game. The plan cannot be carried out by one or two individuals; everyone must work as a coordinated unit (Richter and Murphy, 1989).

As van der Smissen (1990) explains, once a patron has been injured, prompt care is important to reduce potential for liability. Your medical team's goal should be to provide basic life support within four minutes, advanced life support within eight minutes, and transportation to the hospital within twenty minutes (Carlson, 1992). To achieve these goals, you must have an efficient communications system in place. Nonmedical personnel must have the ability to contact the command post to initiate the process for immediate emergency medical assistance.

As Antee and Swinburn (1990) state, communication is at the heart of effective crowd management. A well-developed communications system includes emergency telephone numbers, an adequate telephone system installed in the command post, an efficient network of walkie-talkies, hand signals for medical assistance, and a pre-event meeting to discuss communication (Richter and Murphy, 1989).

The quality of care provided during a medical situation is an important concern for you as a facility manager. The standard of care in similar situations is normally established by experts in the field. The standard of care required by the courts for individuals providing medical assistance, however, depends on the person's training and qualifications. A higher standard of care is expected from individuals who provide skills beyond those of an untrained person (Wong, 1988).

Physicians are extremely helpful in case of a medical emergency and other individuals, including ambulance personnel and paramedics, legally fall under the physician's directions. However, potential difficulties arise when the physician has less experience related to emergency medical care than do the emergency medical technicians or paramedics (Richter and Murphy, 1989).

Status of Personnel

Medical personnel attending events are most often classified as independent contractors and not as employees. Normally, this relieves you as facility management of liability from negligent acts perpetrated by medical personnel (Wong, 1988). An exception to this theory occurred when a team physician made an erroneous statement regarding a Philadelphia Eagles football player. The player brought suit against the Eagles and the NFL for defamation and intentional emotional distress. The courts awarded the player $10,000 in compensatory damages and $60,000 in punitive damages because of the inaccurate remarks made by the doctor (*Chuy v. Philadelphia Eagles*, 1977).

CRISIS MANAGEMENT AND EVACUATION PLANS

For any sporting event, the medical plan should anticipate a disaster (Carlson, 1992). The plan should be written, available to all personnel, and reviewed on a regular basis (Miller, 1993). Planning for a major disaster such as an earthquake or a big fire is an integral step in the medical plan. In addition, a plan is not complete unless it is practiced. Practice is important because it lessens evacuation time and allows you, as the facility manager, a chance to determine the fastest flow of patrons out of the facility, thereby reducing the risk caused by uncertainty and panic in a real situation (Berlonghi, 1990).

Considerations for the Disaster Plan

The hazards you should consider in a disaster plan consist of bomb threats, severe weather, earthquakes, fires, terrorist actions, and individual disturbances. Planning for these types of incidents is paramount.

The most critical aspect in an emergency situation that you as a facility manager must control is panic (Berlonghi, 1990). Your game management personnel are instrumental in setting the tone to prevent this from occurring. If they react in a calm, professional manner, the crowd will respond. Communication and tone setting are vital aspects during an emergency evacuation (Antee and Swinburn, 1990). Appenzeller (1993) recommends that your personnel avoid using words such as "fire," "explosion," or "bomb" during an emergency situation.

The priorities during a disaster, however, differ from those in a medical emergency. The first priority is to determine if the area is safe. The second priority is to distinguish between the "salvageable patients" and the "unsalvageable pa-

tients." Third, a comprehensive plan with a formal chain of command must be implemented (Martinez, 1991).

Designing an Evacuation Plan

Detailed emergency evacuation outlines need to be prepared by your facility management team with specific directions for every potential disaster. Each of the outlines should state the reasons for the evacuation and provide directions for the public (Berlonghi, 1990). A chain of command should already exist to authorize the person who makes the decision to evacuate the facility (Appenzeller, 1993). Once a decision has been reached to evacuate the stadium, your game management personnel and all other employees must know exactly what their responsibilities entail.

Berlonghi (1990) discusses several responsibilities that must be delegated during an evacuation to ensure the safety of everyone. First, some of your personnel must be positioned at each exit, making sure all doors are open and obstructions removed. Once evacuated, your spectators should not be allowed back into the stadium until you as the facility manager have given the "all-clear" sign. Also, personnel should be assigned to assist the disabled, especially wheelchair-bound patrons.

Game personnel should be positioned at all ramps, escalators, and aisles to instruct patrons to exit in a calm, orderly fashion. Positioning your ushers in seating areas to direct patrons to the nearest exit is important as well. Another important strategy is to station your security personnel at each elevator to prevent access. Elevators should never be used except by emergency personnel. In addition, several of your most tactful game management personnel should be deployed to VIP areas to assist in their protection during the crisis.

Once outside the facility, your parking attendants should assist in instructing patrons to remain calm as they reach their vehicles. As spectators begin leaving the parking lots, additional law enforcement officials should be present to control the traffic. Finally, you should deploy barricades around the facility to allow access for emergency vehicles and their crews.

Evacuating sport and public assembly facilities can be an extremely volatile and risky undertaking. By employing these few strategies you as a facility manager can help protect your fans and provide them with a secure egress from the facility.

PARKING AND TRAFFIC CONTROL

An additional area of concern for facility managers relates to the ingress and egress of vehicular traffic and parking for fans at athletic and entertainment events. Several requirements mentioned in previous sections pertain here as well. First, a comprehensive traffic control plan should be developed and then implemented. This plan should be a cooperative effort between you as the facility manager and state and local law enforcement officials.

Berlonghi (1990) identifies several major concerns when reviewing traffic control plans. As with every type of plan, the various traffic control groups (campus, city, county, and state patrol) must provide input to the traffic plan. The intersections that have higher-than-normal accident rates must be identified and extra personnel should assist out-of-town fans through these problem areas. Posting adequate signs on major thoroughfares to direct and inform spectators also decreases problems. Altering the duration of signal lights during ingress and egress assists vehicular traffic through most congested areas. Also, by providing bus lanes, alternative methods of transportation decrease the number of vehicles parking at your event. In addition, notifying local residents and businesses of game-day traffic plans helps community relations. Finally, by establishing emergency routes for police, fire, and medical personnel, dangerous situations may be quickly and safely overcome.

The Traffic Control Plan

Your well-planned traffic policy, with input from all agencies should ensure a smooth and safe progression of vehicles from city streets to parking lots. Congestion leads to irritability and anger, which may jeopardize the safety of drivers and pedestrians. The elimination of accidents and timely arrival of all spectators are objectives to be attained by your traffic control officials.

The author believes several components must be included in all traffic plans. First, the safety and well-being of all spectators should be considered before you implement any plans. Second, main roadways should be used in as expeditious a fash-

ion as possible when monitoring the flow of vehicles to and from the stadium.

Third, the ingress and egress of traffic must occur in a timely fashion, with the least impact on the local community. Sometimes this point is carried to an extreme. In order to reduce congestion during the 1984 Olympics in Los Angeles, an attempt was made to move California's Founders Day to create a three-day holiday. An uproar ensued because many people were irate that the holiday was to be moved from September 10 to August 6 (Kirshenbaum, 1984).

Parking

You as a facility administrator have a duty to maintain the parking lots in a reasonably safe condition and to provide warnings of dangers that may exist. Your failure to post warnings of known or foreseeable risks may be construed by the courts as willful and wanton misconduct (Maloy, 1988).

Parking inside your facility must be closely monitored. Deliveries to the facility for vendors, concessionaires, and other suppliers should not occur less than one hour before the gates open (Miller Brewing Company, 1992). All vehicular traffic must be parked in designated spots before the gates open and only emergency vehicles should be allowed to move during the game.

Legal Precedents

Three court cases illustrate the issues pertaining to parking. Not all cases pertain, however, to the conditions of the premises. As previously mentioned in *Bearman v. Notre Dame*, 1983, the courts found for the female plaintiff, because Notre Dame had been aware of the actions of its "tailgaters." Though this case normally pertains to alcohol-related incidents, it also demonstrates that a facility has a duty to protect patrons from the negligent acts of third parties in their parking lots.

In the second case, an individual walking in a lot adjacent to Dolphin Stadium in Miami, Florida, fell over some concealed railroad ties. He sued the Dolphin football organization for the dangerous condition of the premises and the failure to warn an invitee of danger. The court found for the football club, stating that the city and not the Dolphins had control of the lot (*Rodgers v. Miami Dolphins, Ltd.*, 1985).

Foreseeability must be constantly evaluated by your facility's parking management. It is paramount for you as the facility manager to identify all foreseeable problems. The potential for crimes in the lots must be minimized through security and adequate lighting (Berlonghi, 1990).

A third case identified the importance of foreseeability when a spectator was stabbed in the parking lot after a Jai-Alai match. The court found the facility's management negligent, due to foreseeability, because similar acts had previously occurred, because the facility was in a high-crime neighborhood, and because no steps to remedy the situation had been undertaken (*Fernandez v. Miami Jai-Alai*, 1980). Spectators must have the opportunity to travel from their vehicles to the facility in a reasonably safe condition. You do not have a duty, however, to warn of an obvious danger if the patron is aware of the dangerous condition (van der Smissen, 1990).

The Parking Plan

To create a smooth transition, parking must be a coordinated effort between law enforcement officials and employees in your facility's parking lots. Since your parking employees are the first individuals with whom spectators come in contact, first impressions are extremely important. These individuals must establish the "tone" as to the proper behavior condoned by facility management (Antee and Swinburn, 1990). Polite but firm parking employees assist in these endeavors. Proper signage is helpful in directing and informing spectators and is therefore a necessity for the success of your game management plan.

Several other important concepts should be emphasized in your facility's parking plan. First, parking areas for the disabled, VIPs, media and press, recreational vehicles and busses must be identified and publicized (Berlonghi, 1990). Second, every vehicle's owner should pay for parking or possess a parking pass. Third, you want your facility parking to be a break-even operation, so trustworthy individuals must be employed. Finally, the facility's insurance for fire, theft, vandalism, and negligence should also apply to parking operations (Berlonghi, 1990).

In conclusion, Berlonghi (1990) identifies several major objectives to be considered when devising parking plans. First, an accurate estimate of required parking spaces is important to determine if the present parking lots will accommodate the kind and number of expected vehicles. A fairly accurate number of parking spaces can be ascertained by dividing the estimated attendance by 2.0 or 2.5 people per car. Second, diagrams of all lots should be sent to season ticketholders, be available at ticket outlets, and be published in the newspaper the day of the game. In addition, access for fire, police, and medical vehicles must be open at all times. Fourth, tailgate parties and loitering after the game are potential sources of litigation. They should be monitored closely and curtailed if necessary. Finally, security personnel need to be present in the lots to deter speeding, thefts, vandalism, and any other major problems that might arise.

SUMMARY

The social mores and values of the surrounding community influence the decisions of administrators in all industries, including facility management. As a facility manager, you will usually attempt to answer the needs of your community in order to maintain good public relations, thus increasing attendance.

Because the success of a multi-event facility depends heavily on community support, the philosophy you adopt as the facility administrator is vital. While communities have activities and events ranging from tractor pulls to rap concerts, a basic aim for all facility administrators must be to provide a safe and secure environment where spectators, employees, and participants can enjoy themselves. These individuals must be confident that their health and well-being are paramount concerns to you as the facility operator. Once these groups become aware of your interest, they will reward the facility with loyalty and return for many more events.

Finally, as a facility manager you need to be aware of the continuing research in this field. Only through your support and assistance will the industry's problems be identified and their solutions found.

The main points presented here regarding facility control and security are the following:

- Depending on the facility's philosophy, the facility manager should decide if alcoholic beverages will be sold during events.

- If the facility's manager authorizes the sale of alcohol, a written policy regarding the consumption and sale of alcoholic beverages should be devised including limitations on the size and number of beverages permitted per sale. It is also recommended that sales be stopped at the beginning of the third quarter, last inning, or some such suitable time before the final segment of the event.
- Alcohol management training such as TIPS or TEAM should be provided, paid for by the facility's management, to employees involved in sales of alcohol.
- The facility's manager should implement procedures prohibiting alcoholic beverages from being brought into the facility, and denying entry to the facility to anyone judged to be under the influence of alcohol.
- "Tailgating" should be permitted only in the parking lots under supervision from law enforcement officials. The participants engaged in these activities should be advised that quantity of alcohol, length of stay, and intensity of celebration will be limited at the discretion of the facility's management.
- A crowd management policy should be written that provides for the facility's manager to employ the people providing services. These employees should be required to participate in training and orientation on a quarterly basis.
- The facility's manager should establish written policies regarding the ejection of unruly, disruptive, or intoxicated fans. An "incident" form should accompany each ejection, describing in detail what actions preceded the ejection; a picture of the ejected person(s) should accompany each incident form.
- Various signs should be used around the facility to (1) direct fans to various locations and services, (2) identify items that are prohibited from being brought into the facility, and (3) direct fans on major roadways to the facility and the appropriate parking lots.
- The facility's administrators should implement fully the policies of the Americans with Disabilities Act.
- The facility's manager should design and implement a communications system to link the various agencies involved in game management. This communications net should use multichanneled radios. The facility should provide a command post, during events, where representatives from the agencies are in communication with each other.
- A written medical services plan should be established by the facility's manager. This plan should include the procedures for emergency medical transportation and be coordinated with local law enforcement officials.
- The facility's manager should have an emergency evacuation plan. The plan should identify the specific conditions necessary to cause an evacuation, the person responsible for making the evacuation decision, the information to be announced, and the means of disseminating information to the spectators. The plan should be practiced at least once a year by all personnel who would be involved in any way in an evacuation.

QUESTIONS

1. Why hasn't the United States been plagued with crowd violence similar to that in Europe? Why doesn't Europe adopt measures similar to those employed in the United States?
2. What is foreseeability? How does it influence crowd management plans? How can you foresee problems?
3. Explain the difference between "dram shop laws" and "social host liability." As a facility manager, which will affect your policies regarding alcohol?
4. What factors must be taken into consideration when designing a comprehensive medical plan? How would these factors be different if you were a facility manager at an indoor sports arena rather than at an outdoor stadium?
5. What is the biggest danger during a facility evacuation? How can your crisis management plan be designed to control this situation?
6. Why is maintenance of the facility's parking lots an important responsibility of the facility manager? Provide legal precedents to back up your answer.

ACTIVITIES

1. You are the manager of an 18,000-seat arena in a mid-sized city in the central United States. Present an argument either for or against the sale of alcohol in your new building. The city council's decision as to

whether alcohol will be served will depend on the thoroughness of your argument. Be certain to include *all* information required to make this decision. You need to *convince* the council of your position.

2. Upon graduation you secure employment as an event coordinator at a 65,000-seat indoor stadium in the south central United States. Part of your job description is to train newly hired ushers, door personnel, and unarmed security. Organize an oral presentation for these individuals explaining the facility's crowd management plan. Be certain to include such variables as specific duties for each hired position, the ejection policy, types of patron searches, refund policy, signage, and ADA policy.

3. You have been hired as the facility manager for a field house at a mid-sized Division II university located in the eastern United States. You are in charge of the 8,000-seat indoor facility, which is used for several intercollegiate sports as well as university physical education classes. Design an emergency evacuation plan for the field house. Be thorough and include answers to such questions as, Who will make the decision to evacuate? How will patrons evacuate the facility? Where will the patrons go? Who will make the announcement to evacuate? What wording will be used to evacuate?

SUGGESTED READINGS

Adams, S. H., Adrian, M. J., and Bayless, M. A. (Eds.). (1987). *Catastrophic injuries in sports: Avoidance strategies* (2nd ed.). Indianapolis, Ind: Benchmark Press.

Ammon, Jr., R. (1993). Risk and game management practices in selected municipal football facilities. Doctoral dissertation, University of Northern Colorado, 1993. *Dissertation Abstracts International*, 54, 3366A–3367A.

Appenzeller, H. (1970). *From the gym to the jury.* Charlottesville, Va: The Michie Company.

Appenzeller, H. (1978). *Physical education and the law.* Charlottesville, Va: The Michie Company.

Champion, W. T. (1993). *Sports law in a nutshell.* St. Paul, Minn: West.

Christiansen, M. L. (1986). How to avoid negligence suits: Reducing hazards to prevent injuries. *Journal of Physical Education, Recreation & Dance*, 57(2):46–52.

Clement, A. (1988). *Law in sport and physical activity.* Indianapolis, Ind: Benchmark Press.

Cotten, D. J. (1993). Risk management—A tool for reducing exposure to legal liability. *Journal of Physical Education, Recreation and Dance*, 64(2):58–61.

Football identity card: Nasty rough boys. (1989, January). *The Economist*, p. 59.

Gilbert, B., and Twyman, L. (1983, January). Violence: Out of hand in the stands. *Sports Illustrated*, pp. 62–72.

Girvan, G. A. (1990). The development of an instrument to assess how risk management practices are addressed in intercollegiate athletic programs. Eugene, Ore: Microform Publications, College of Human Development and Performance, University of Oregon. UO91316–UO91317.

Guard, S. (1992, May 18). Collapsed: A temporary grandstand at a soccer stadium in Bastia, Corsica, killing 13 persons and injuring more than 700 others. *Sports Illustrated*, p. 85.

Hobbs, D., and Robins, D. (1991). The boy done good: Football violence, changes and continuities. *The Sociological Review*, 39(8):551.

Kaiser, R. A. (1986). *Liability and law in recreation and sports.* Englewood Cliffs, NJ: Prentice-Hall.

Kozlowski, J. C. (1988, September). A common sense view of liability. *Parks & Recreation*, pp. 56–59.

Maloy, B. P. (1993). Legal obligations related to facilities. *Journal of Physical Education, Recreation and Dance*, 64(2):28–30, 64.

Patterson, A. (1988). Sports and the courts: How athletic directors and coaches can survive the "lawyer's game." *Interscholastic Athletic Administration*, 15(2): 6–7.

Williams, J., Dunning, E., and Murphy, P. (1984). *Hooligans abroad.* Boston, Mass: Routledge & Kegan Paul.

Williams, J., Dunning, E., and Murphy, P. (1988, March). Football's fighting traditions. *History Today*, pp. 5–7.

Yasser, R. L. (1985). *Torts and sports: Legal liability in professional and amateur athletics.* Westport, Conn: Quorum Books.

REFERENCES

American Survey. (1989, December 23). Brotherly love on ice. *The Economist*, p. 30.

Antee, A., and Swinburn, J. (1990, January/February). Crowd management: An issue of safety, security, and liability. *Public Management*, pp. 16–19.

Appenzeller, H. (1993). *Managing sports and risk management strategies.* Durham, NC: Carolina Academic Press.

Appleson, G. A. (1982). Spectator violence: What they see is what they do? *American Bar Association Journal*, 68(4):404.

Baley, J. A., and Matthews, D. L. (1984). *Law and liability in athletics, physical education, and recreation.* Boston: Allyn & Bacon.

Berlonghi, A. (1990). *The special event risk management manual.* Dana Point, Cal: Alexander Berlonghi.

Berry, R. C., and Wong, G. M. (1986). *Law and business of the sports industries: Common issues in amateur and professional sports*, 2. Dover, Mass: Auburn House.

Birchall, H. (1992, January). The hostile sports fan. *Macleans*, p. 46.

Carlson, L. (1992). Spectator care: Learning from the super bowl. *The Physician and Sports Medicine*, 20(1): 141–143.

Chafetz, M. E. (1990, January/February). Managing alcohol in public facilities: Caveat manager. *Public Management*, pp. 20–21.

Champion, W. T. (1990). *Fundamentals of sport law*. Rochester, NY: The Lawyers Cooperative.

DeBenedette, V. (1988). Spectator violence at sport events: What keeps enthusiastic fans in bounds? *The Physician and Sportsmedicine*, 19(3):203–211.

Fenley, G. (1992, July). Wheel me out to the ball game. *Architectural Record*, pp. 140–142.

Gammon, C. (1989, April 24). Anger, then death: Tragedy struck British soccer as 94 fans were killed by an out-of-control crowd. *Sports Illustrated*, pp. 24–25.

Hudgins, H. C., Jr., and Vacca, R. S. (1979). *Law education: Contemporary issues and court decisions*. Charlottesville, Va: Michie Company.

Kirshenbaum, J. (1984, April 30). The road to L.A. (traffic congestion at the Olympics). *Sports Illustrated*, p. 14.

Leerhsen, C. (1988, May 16). When push comes to shove: Baseball faces a crisis in crowd control, fueled by beer and rowdies. *Newsweek*, pp. 72–73.

Leo, J. (1984, October). Take me out to the brawl game. *Sports Illustrated*, p. 87.

Lewis, J. (1992, June). Crowd control at concerts: Hazards of festival seating. *Trial*, pp. 71–72, 74–75.

Maloy, B. P. (1988). *Law in sport: Liability cases in management and administration*. Indianapolis, Ind: Benchmark Press.

Martinez, R. (1991). Catastrophes at sporting events. *The Physician and Sportsmedicine*, 19(11):40, 43–44.

Miller, A. W. (1989). Risk management. In G. Nygaard and T. Boone (Eds.). *Law for physical educators and coaches* (pp. 419–437). Columbus, Ohio: Publishing Horizons.

Miller Brewing Company. (1992). *Good times: A guide to responsible event planning*. Milwaukee, Wis: The Miller Brewing Company.

Miller, L. K. (1993). Crowd control. *Journal of Physical Education, Recreation and Dance*, 64(2):31–32, 64–65.

Neff, C. (1985, June). Can it happen in the US? *Sports Illustrated*, p. 87.

Newman, M., and Dao, J. (1992, December 27). A year after nine deaths, the scars endure at City College. *The New York Times*, p. 14.

Nygaard, G., and Boone, T. (1989). *Law for physical educators and coaches* (2nd ed.). Columbus, Ohio: Publishing Horizons.

Oshust, J. (1985). The law of public assembly facilities. In H. Appenzeller (Ed.), *Sports and law: Contemporary issues* (pp. 246–253). Charlottesville, Va: Michie Company.

Richter, S. T., and Murphy, D. T. (1989). The emergency medical system. In G. Nygaard and T. Boone (Eds.), *Law for physical educators and coaches* (pp. 315–361). Columbus, Ohio: Publishing Horizons.

Sharp, L. A. (1990). *Sport law*. Topeka, Kan: National Organization on Legal Problems of Education (Whole No. 40).

van der Smissen, B. (1990). *Legal liability and risk management for public and private entities*. Cincinnati: Anderson Publishing.

Wong, G. M. (1988). *Essentials of amateur sports law*. Dover, Mass: Auburn House.

Wong, G. M. (1994). *Essentials of amateur sports law*. (2nd ed.). Westport, Conn: Praeger.

Wong, G. M., and Ensor, R. J. (1985, May). Torts and tailgates. *Athletic Business*, pp. 46–49.

LEGAL CITATIONS

Allen v. Rutgers, The State University of New Jersey, 523 A. 2d 262 (NJ. Sup. Ct. 1987).

Bearman v. University of Notre Dame, 453 N.E. 2d 1196 (Ind. App. 3 Dist. 1983).

Bishop v. Fair Lanes Georgia Bowling, Inc., 803 F. 2d 1548 (11th Cir. 1986).

Bowes v. Cincinnati Riverfront Coliseum, 465 N.E. 2d 904 (Ohio App. 1983).

Chuy v. Philadelphia Eagles, 407 F. Supp. 717 (E.D. Pa. 1977).

Cimino v. Yale University, et al., 638 F. Supp. 952 (Ct. 1986).

Fernandez v. Miami Jai-Alai, 386 So. 2d 4 (Fla. App. 1980).

Gill v. Chicago Park District, 407 N.E. 2d 671 (Ill. App. 1980).

Rodgers v. Miami Dolphins, Ltd., 469 So. 2d 852 (Fla. App. 1975).

9

Marketing Sports Facilities

David K. Stotlar

Sports facilities contribute significantly to the economy of the United States. Sports facilities encompass a substantial part of the $50 billion per year sport industry (Associated Press, 1991; Comte and Stogel, 1990; Sandomir, 1988). From a broad perspective, spending categories can include spectators buying tickets, souvenirs, food, and parking. Spending by participants can also be included with attention to facility rental fees and memberships to private and commercial clubs. Any discussion of the economic contribution of the sports facility industry must be prefaced by a statement of which economic sectors are included.

Questions arise whether spending on concessions is really part of the sports facility market or of the food and beverage industry? Are souvenir sales part of general merchandise sales that just happen to occur at a sports facility? Because great variation exists in the classification of spending categories and industrial sectors, it is best to depend on statistics available from the U.S. Departments of Labor, Commerce, and Education, and the U.S. Census Bureau.

Regardless of the data employed, it is easy to see that sports facilities and their management are part of a multibillion-dollar industry. However, many sports facilities do not have marketing plans, which are the key to securing business. In a competitive market, the only facilities that survive are the ones that are effective in attracting events and clients (Buell, 1984). As a result, sports facility managers must be able to develop well-defined marketing plans. This chapter guides managers in planning and implementing a marketing program for their facilities. It does not attempt to cover mar-

keting of the programs that may occur within the facility. Although the process may be similar, all references here are to the task of attracting events to the sports facility.

PURPOSE OF A MARKETING PLAN

According to Cohen (1987), a marketing plan provides a road map for corporate development. Every facility was created for a specific reason—the accomplishment of specified objectives. While these differ for each facility, they do exist and the facility's manager is accountable for their achievement. The marketing plan stands as the tool to assist in the implementation of marketing and management strategy. Marketing plans also serve to communicate role specificity to new employees and to coordinate the assignment of responsibilities and tasks. Facility managers use marketing plans to identify problems, opportunities, and threats to efficient operation and to calculate the strategic use of human, financial, and physical resources. A well-developed marketing plan serves as a guide to performance of stated objectives.

Depending on the size of the facility and the capabilities of its staff, there are several ways to organize for market planning. For the largest sports facilities, the best approach to planning is typically through a committee of key executives (chief executive officer (CEO), vice presidents, event managers, and finance officers). This assures that top management is involved and that there is input from the frontline managers. However, some sports facilities may be so limited in staff resources that outside consultants must be hired. Once the

The marquee at Denver's McNichols Arena incorporates sponsors' signage and advertising for upcoming events.

COMPONENTS OF A MARKETING PLAN

marketing decision makers are organized, the marketing plan can be drafted.

The sports facility industry consists of two diverse segments, profit and nonprofit. The profit segment contains commercial facilities such as resorts, leisure/recreation enterprises, fitness and health clubs. The nonprofit segment includes primarily civic and academic (colleges and secondary schools) sports facilities. Since 1985 the line of demarcation between the two groups has almost disappeared. There is no longer a dichotomy between nonprofit and commercial sports facilities. Even civic and nonprofit sports facilities are tied to generation of revenue. Therefore, the failure of a facility to attract events and clients can bring about financial disaster for the facility's owner. This necessitates a marketing plan.

Cohen (1987) presents an approach to developing a marketing plan that is easily adaptable for both profit and nonprofit sport organizations. This conceptual model will be used as basic structure for the remainder of this chapter.

The Executive Summary

A successful marketing plan should begin with an executive summary. This section of the marketing plan presents an overview of the marketing plan and is often the most important aspect of the document. It sets the stage for the entire plan, and if it is not well conceived, other sections may never be read. Therefore, careful planning must be accorded to writing the executive summary. Also, many of the people who comprise the audience for the marketing plan do not have significant time to read an entire plan, and often make preliminary judgments based solely on the executive summary.

The executive summary should include an accurate and specific description of the facility being marketed, advantages it enjoys over its competitors, financial details, and projected profit or return on investment for the planned period. This section summarizes all sections of the marketing plan, so it is often the last part of the plan actually written (Cohen, 1987).

Analysis of Product and Service

The analysis of product and service examines characteristics of your product or service and determines precisely how they fit into an existing market. Probably the best start in examining products and services is to review the mission statement developed for the facility. It should explain the general purposes and objectives assigned to the facility.

Facility managers often use the terms *goods* and *services* to describe their purposes and objectives. For example, a civic sports arena provides the location and setup for a basketball tournament (services) and also sells sports merchandise at its on-site souvenir shop (goods). This situation also exists at athletic facilities of colleges and universities that offer sporting events for spectators, as well

as concessions and logo merchandise. Sports events do not clearly fall into the category of a product or a service. Mullin (1983) indicates that marketing a sport event is unique because the event is perishable; it has no shelf-life. If tickets to the event or seats in the arena are not sold, there is no tomorrow. Mullin (1983) also points out that, in sport, marketers have little control over the product. Facility managers often bring in events (e.g., a traveling circus, a monster truck competition) to fill the booking calendar, yet they have almost no control over the product.

Products and services are intermixed in sport facilities, yet characteristics relevant to marketing them need to be understood. Products are typically produced, distributed, and then purchased. For facility managers, there is no distribution: all clients (purchasers) hold their events at the facility.

Product Extensions

Sports facilities do not exist with a single product or service. The event is enhanced through various supplementary goods or services referred to as *product extensions*. Many sports facility managers have found that a substantial amount of money can be generated from such services as parking, concessions, and souvenirs. Spectators spend an average of $3.70 per game on food and beverages and as much as $20.00 on souvenirs (Howard and Crompton, 1995). This does not mean that the facility is in the food service or novelty industry, but rather that its use of product extensions gains additional revenues to those of the main event.

In the late 1980s, poor sales of product extensions led many municipalities and universities to hire outside companies to run the food-service aspect of their operations. In 1993, only about 32% of stadiums and arenas operated their own food and beverage operations. The remaining 68% contracted their operations to outside companies (Howard and Crompton, 1995). Some companies originally in the concession business began to see themselves in the business of sports arena management. As a result, the 1990s has produced a situation where concessions operators joined the major corporations in sports facility management.

Effectively marketing a facility requires a realization that success lies in identifying and meeting customers' needs, not just scheduling events that happen to come along. A thorough marketing plan will assist in identifying your customers and the products and services you do or can offer to meet their needs and desires.

The most appropriate method of determining your products and services is to define them in terms of consumers. McDonald, Sutton, and Milne (1995) developed an instrument they called TEAMQUAL to measure the factors most important to NBA spectators. Their results indicate that a variety of factors are important to the fans' enjoyment of the game. Their research found that several tangible aspects of the facility were important to fans, including the appearance of facility's personnel, the venue, and related equipment. The reliability of personnel, prompt service, and their willingness to assist customers were also significant. In addition, spectators were influenced by the knowledge level of a facility's personnel (McDonald et al., 1995). These factors, which facility managers can control, are useful in marketing efforts.

Marketing decisions are based on what has been traditionally referred to as the *marketing mix*, which consists of four basic elements—product, price, place, and promotion (the four *P*s). This framework, originally developed by Harvard professor Neil Borden, has been renamed, repackaged, and otherwise used in the profession for many years, but essentially remains constant (Lovelock and Weinberg, 1984). Stotlar (1993, p. 24) defines the four *P*s of marketing in the sports industry:

- *Product:* The nature of the sport product or service includes decisions as to product line(s), product extensions, and meeting both known and newly identified desires and needs within the designated group of customers.
- *Price:* A fair price allows your budget to break even or make a profit and also reflects the image you want to portray about your sport product or service. Considerations here include competitor's prices, available discounts, and market share.
- *Place:* The actual distribution of your sport product or service could include means of transporting goods to wholesale and retail outlets, or to the geographic location of your stadium or health club.
- *Promotion:* Getting your message about products and services to potential consumers can be attained through publicity, advertising, or other means of communication.

In the 1990s substantial attention has been focused on "relationship marketing," that is, using the marketing mix to establish an ongoing relationship with your customer. McDonald, Sutton, and Milne (1995) state that "consumers who are dissatisfied and feel that they are not receiving quality service will not renew their relationship with the professional sport franchise" (p. 14).

Situational Analysis

Analysis of the market for your product or service is the component of the marketing plan that incorporates the economic climate, demographics, demand trends, technological trends, analysis of competitors, and internal aspects of the organization (current status, special skills, etc.) (Cohen, 1987). This situation analysis provides you with facts and information necessary for planning an effective combination of the four *P*s in the marketing mix. No sports organization exists in a static environment; a constant state of change necessitates ongoing analysis. Recognizing and adapting to this change can make a difference in whether an organization can grow and prosper or is destined to die like the estimated 80% of new business ventures in the United States. In short, the best decisions are made when they are based on the best data.

Various economic environments affect the financial performance of sports facilities. Sports events are particularly vulnerable to changes in the economy because they are based on discretionary income. During strong economic cycles, the facility may be able to book high-priced events such as "Disney on Ice" and attract large crowds. However, during a recession these events may have limited engagements because of lower consumer turnout. It is essential for facility managers to keep an eye on economic forecasts and to use the information to make wise marketing decisions.

Because many sport facility operations are capital intensive, it is vitally important for the marketing plan to consider the interest rate for borrowed monies. The cost of financing is a critical factor in determining the ability of sports facilities to make a profit. As a result, any change in percentage points on a loan makes a difference of several thousand dollars in repayment schedules. Other information about capital acquisition is also important in the development of a marketing plan.

The availability of financing through property taxes, tax abatement provisions, tax exempt bonds, and lease-back arrangements must be investigated (Howard and Crompton, 1995).

As pointed out in Chapter 2, sport facilities are a labor-intensive business with the majority of their operating expenses arising from payroll costs and the associated benefit plans. Fluctuations in the minimum wage, worker's compensation, Social Security payments, and benefits drastically affect the cost of doing business.

The political environment also affects the marketing of a facility. Some sports facilities make their venues available to civic organizations. Private facility managers can base decisions on whatever factor they wish, but municipal facilities are governed by civil rights and public assembly laws. (What would or could you do if a radical political group wanted to rent your facility?) All of these factors must be considered in the marketing plan.

Federal tax law also plays an important part in marketing sports facilities. The 1986 Tax Reform Act seriously decreased the amount companies can deduct for the purchase of "sky boxes" and tickets, reducing it from 80 percent to 50 percent of the purchase price (Hackney, 1991; Howard and Crompton, 1995). The 1990s also brought a controversy forwarded by commercial sports facilities regarding the nonprofit status of YMCA fitness centers. The concern voiced by the private sector was that the nonprofit status of a YMCA amounted to unfair competition because the for-profit businesses had to pay taxes on their income but the nonprofit organizations were tax exempt.

Demographics of individual consumers (age, gender, marital status, lifestyle, occupation, and earned and discretionary income) are of less concern to the facility's manager than they are to clients such as promoters and organizers of events. The promoters and organizers must be attuned to specific characteristics of audiences that will be attracted to their productions. However, the facility's manager must know the demographic makeup of the local community in order to entice certain productions to the facility. The best source of information is the latest U.S. Census or data collected by a well-established market research bureau. Large cities often have an economic development office that can supply similar information.

Trends exist in every market. In the sport facilities market the demand is assessed through an exploration of available events and productions in comparison to similar facilities. For example, several trade shows in the sports field tour the country each year. They exist in fishing, hunting, skiing, fitness, and general sporting goods. Under these circumstances, competition to attract the show to your facility is extremely high. Plenty of other arenas and auditoriums are trying to attract the same events. In contrast, competition for an event such as the Super Bowl has fewer players (because of the seating requirements), but is fierce all the same.

Technological trends in sport facilities vary greatly. Sport facility owners have lost business because they were unable to meet the demands of the consumer. Televised sport events need adequate levels of lighting. If your facility cannot accommodate TV, you will in all likelihood lose that event. However, some facilities have developed advanced technologies as a plan to meet the demands of their specialized customers. Technological changes since 1980 have included portable outdoor field lighting, built-in TV hookups and accommodations for special effects and lighting. In addition, computer-assisted or automated ticket outlets may well put your facility in an advantageous position in the market. New and technological amenities may be needed to successfully market your sport facility.

Analysis of the Competition

Clearly determining competitors is a difficult task. Once identified, they should be studied. Do you compete for the same events (customers)? Would a tournament or event go to their facility if it were not coming to yours? See what the other sport facilities are doing; try to assess their strategy in the market place. Each of your competitors has a different position in the market; each has its particular strengths and weaknesses. All of these are important considerations in your marketing efforts.

Keeping an eye on the competition can assist your marketing process. One effective method is to frequent your competitors' territory. Go to their events, see what they are doing, watch their employees. Often you can get new ideas and inside information in casual conversations with event workers (Eby, 1987). You should also read the trade publications such as *Athletic Business Magazine* and *Amusement Business Magazine*. These publications provide considerable insight into frequent problems in facility management and marketing. They are also a valuable source of data on emerging trends in the industry.

The internal status of your sport facility is characterized by the chemistry that differentiates it from other facilities. The employees have special skills; the management, a certain vision and style. These unique assets can be classified as either strengths or weaknesses. In 1993 the University of Colorado lost an important event (Rolling Stones concert) because of its strict security practices. To some, this may be a strength, yet to one client, it was a weakness.

A true measurement of the skills of your staff is imperative. What kinds of attributes do your workers have? Is your sales force better than others in the industry? Maybe your facility has the advantage of longevity and a substantial percentage of your employees really knowing the business. On the other hand, some of your staff may not be performing on a par with the competition. In such cases a training program is well be worth the expense. The assessment of each of these components is an essential part of the marketing process. The implementation of marketing strategy will help you turn strengths into opportunities and prevent weaknesses from becoming opportunities for your competition.

Target Markets

A *target market* is the identification of the clients most likely to book your facility. An analysis of target markets considers market segmentation, marketing information systems, and research on consumer behavior (Stotlar, 1993). Sport facilities can direct their marketing efforts to either the individual consumer or to event owners who schedule the facilities for their sport events. Because of the nature of this book, only marketing to event owners is addressed.

Markets can also be measured in relation to their potential. Sport facilities have a restricted calendar, which allows for only 365 days of operation. Although in some instances, more than one event (basketball games) can occur during a single day, in other instances (ice show), it takes more than one day to set up the facility. Using the data collected in the situation analysis, forecasts can be made as to the growth of the market, the number of events that comprise the market, and the demand trends in this particular area.

Market Research

All sport manufacturers and many sport organizations conduct market research. This research is usually referred to as a Marketing Information System (MIS). Mullin (1983) indicates that marketing research is vital for all sports organizations because their fans, clients, participants, and consumers change rapidly. In addition, an MIS can enhance a sound quality-control system by providing valuable information to be used in designing facilities and services for the selected market. According to Levine (1987), conducting market research does not require a specialized business analyst, but could be as simple as conducting exit surveys with previous clients. As mentioned, several of these areas were researched by McDonald, Sutton, and Milne (1995). A variety of important questions can be addressed: What types of services in your facility attracted them? To what level were they satisfied with your facility? Were there problems with your staff, services, products, or facilities?

It is important to have accurate information available for marketing decisions. If one of your staff were to recommend that the parking lots be expanded and resurfaced because their poor condition had angered clients, MIS data could substantiate the claim. In all businesses, the quality of decisions reflects the quality of the information upon which they were based.

Sources of MIS data are typically identified as either primary or secondary. Primary research is research conducted directly with the event owners and operators using your facility (such as TEAMQUAL used by the NBA). Another way for sports facility managers to collect data is through automated records of all previous clients. As mentioned, business schools have taught the 80–20 principle for many years. In the facility management field, this may mean that 80 percent of bookings for the facility may be generated by 20 percent of the clients in the market. For example, when a stadium has as a primary tenant a major league baseball team that plays about 75 home games, it has one client that schedules a substantial percentage of the 365 days that events could be scheduled.

Sports facilities are also consumers in the sport industry and, therefore, every supplier to the facility should also be considered a potential consumer. For example, every facility purchases concessions goods, an industry that holds annual conventions. It might be good business to obtain information from your concession suppliers about bidding for upcoming trade shows in their industry. These suppliers undoubtedly have an interest in your success, and may even feel an obligation or loyalty to your facility (i.e., your account may be one of that 20 percent that accounts for 80 percent of their business).

Secondary research is not conducted directly by you. As stated earlier, there are market research bureaus and industry-specific magazines that produce volumes of facility-related research. Trade journals in the fitness industry are also valuable sources of information for facility marketing decisions.

Marketing Your Facility to Sponsors

Many facility managers sell stadium/arena advertising for an additional source of revenue. Facility managers must demonstrate to the potential sponsor that the audiences attracted to events held in the facility are ones the sponsor would like to reach. In market research for several major university football and basketball facilities, Stotlar and Johnson (1989) found demographic data to indicate that the distribution of age and income of the fans at collegiate football and basketball games matched the desires of sponsors very well.

Your job as the facility's manager is to identify businesses with both an interest and the ability to participate. According to Wilkinson (1986, p. 40), "the process of finding sponsors and then showing them how you can help them requires imagination and marketing effort." Not all businesses in a community have the ability to buy facility sponsorships and signage, and involvement with sports events is not the right partnership for everyone. Considerable controversy has emerged over the years about the association of tobacco and alcohol companies with sport. Some sport organizations, like the NCAA, have a policy against awarding a championship event to a facility with alcohol and tobacco signage.

Wilkinson (1988) recommends that facility managers begin by looking through the business pages of the telephone book, examining the ads in the newspaper, and simply taking a drive through the business district to spark your imagination in searching for possible clients. From that activity, you can generate a list of businesses and corporations that may have both an interest and the ability to join you in a sponsorship and signage program. Remember to consider the business relationships with the facility itself. There may be some natural relationships that would be strengthened through sponsorship and signage agreements from a direct tie between businesses. Many sports facilities have arranged for signage and scoreboard sponsorship from manufacturers of a soft drink. In exchange, part of the agreement gives the manufacturer exclusive rights to distribute its product in the facility.

Local businesses that are affiliated with national franchises and chains are also a good prospect. In this case, the local store may not have the financial ability to purchase your signage, but because of its franchise association, additional finances can be obtained from the corporate headquarters. For example, a national corporation with a locally owned fast-food restaurant may share the costs for stadium signage on a cooperative basis with its franchisor.

Corporate objectives in facility sponsorship can be divided into various categories such as sales objectives, image objectives, awareness objectives, and employee motivation objectives. Sales objectives include such areas as increasing the sales levels of certain brands or getting people to sample a product. Stadiums and arenas can provide an almost unlimited opportunity for product sampling. In this case, the number and demographics of people who come to your events provide the key to attracting the sponsor. Image objectives can also be enhanced through sport sponsorships. Because sport receives mainly positive media attention, many corporations believe sport sponsorships enhances their image with the public. Some CEOs believe that having their logos displayed in a sports arena gives the corporations special status in the community. The objective of increasing the morale of a corporation has also been teamed with sports sponsorships (Wilkinson, 1988). The recently constructed Coors Field in Denver created a feeling of connectedness between Coors employees and the Colorado Rockies baseball team.

Corporations are very interested in growth trends and spectator attendance at specific events.

Figure 9–1 Sponsors can be solicited for facility scoreboards.

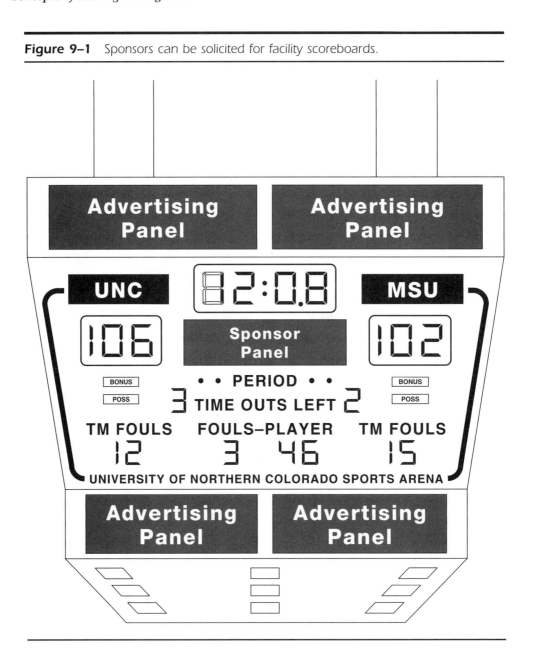

The strongest proposals have longitudinal data available for review by the sponsors. Heavily attended events and sports with rising popularity have proved enticing to many sponsors. Murphy (1986, p. 56) quotes a brewery official as saying, "When we evaluate possible event sponsorship, the questions we ask are, 'Is it our target audience? Is it reputable? Does it provide sampling opportunities?'"

Other criteria upon which companies make sponsorship decisions include current sponsors and mix of products; corporate relations with other sponsors; cooperation from the host facility for signage, access, and placement; the match between product image and event image; and the potential for VIP contacts.

Stadium and arena signage are generally reliable tools that can sell products and create positive images for corporations (Murphy, 1986). However, problems do occasionally arise. Stotlar and Johnson's (1989) research on stadium signage showed that in one venue, no one reported seeing a particular stadium sign and couldn't remember the corporation after they left the stadium. Would you tell the sponsor who purchased it? Ethical business practices mandate that you do. The sign's lack of visibility may have been due to decisions about size, color, or graphics, in which case, you might simply help the company make better use of the opportunity. If it chose not to renew, the sponsor might still refer a colleague based on your honesty and cooperation.

The quest for facility sponsors can be an exciting and rewarding one, but be assured that you must understand the needs and objectives of the sponsor and present information that will justify its involvement. A cardinal rule for facility managers in the sponsorship area is, "Don't promise more than you can deliver."

Marketing Objectives and Strategies

The marketing process must now shift from an analysis mode to an action stage. Specific objectives must be stated as a part of the marketing function. Marketing strategies must also be developed to accomplish those objectives. Probably the best way to present this material is through a detailed example. This allows you to see how the objectives are connected to strategies in a plan of action.

Scenario

A modern and attractive facility in an important market has recently been made better by improvements to parking areas and concessions services. The operating profit was $500,000 for the last fiscal year and was operated as a part of a large midwestern city's government. The facility is active with approximately 200 dates booked each year. The assessment of the facility's market potential indicates opportunities for more events. The city has a nonexclusive contract with Automated Ticket Services, a computerized ticket system, with which event owners using ATS deal with them directly. The box office is simply one more outlet on the ATS system. Concessions, parking, and novelty sales are assigned to independent contractors. These contracts stipulate in-

come to the facility from parking, concessions, and novelties.

In addition to the income from existing contracts, much can be done to increase revenue. The city is implicitly subsidizing many events with no formal policies expressing the goals underlying specific contract provisions. In addition, the city has not examined current costs and benefits to users and the public. The current management approach has been quite simple: stay within the annual budget and make the best of contracts in place. At this time, the facility is simply rented out for a fee. Users have been responsible for procuring and coordinating, on their own, all aspects of promotion, event staffing, and ticket sales.

Examples of Objectives and Strategies

OBJECTIVE: Increase event bookings by 10% over the previous year.

STRATEGY: Procure a manager who can develop and manage a campaign to increase awareness and benefits of the facility for target markets by either hiring a manager from outside the department who has experience in arena management or arranging for training of the current facility manager. Increase spending for trade advertising. Revise the current trade ad so it provides information of interest to promoters such as the versatility of the facility, the types of events that have succeeded, its ideal location and market characteristics, and the building seat count.

OBJECTIVE: Increase profit ratio.

STRATEGY: Manage the facility like a business venture rather than a city department. Track revenues and costs by event and department rather than tracking by budgeted line items.

OBJECTIVE: Examine current costs and benefits to users and the public.

STRATEGY: Detail income sources in terms of user fees, parking fees, and concessions. Detail costs of operating them. Put in place systems to track financial performance per event. This will allow cost benefit analysis for each event hosted in the facility.

OBJECTIVE: Generate additional revenues ($400,000 profit) from extended facility services.

STRATEGY: Move to "full-service concept." By providing and coordinating all services relating to product extensions, the facility can maximize income. This can be accomplished through in-house operation of concessions, box office, and parking services, sales of on-site advertising and promotions, the placement of advertising for event sponsors, and suite rental. Also consider providing all event management staff from part-time workforce, thus changing the personnel structure to reduce the number of full-time employees in favor of as-needed part-time employees or a city-run pool of casual labor. An additional benefit would be that the facility would exercise more control over each event.

OBJECTIVE: Increase sales force to attract new events.

STRATEGY: Establish a program of commissions to persons who bring in events and advertisers. Decentralize management decision making and the responsibly for negotiating deals with event sponsors and services.

OBJECTIVE: Attract advertisers for internal and external facility spaces.

STRATEGY: Contact and recruit potential advertisers/sponsors who match event demographics and concept. Research the facility and surrounding environment for additional ideas for on-site signage. Develop a rate card for facility advertising competitive with the local market. Develop professional sales presentations including a demographic survey of patrons. Have the marketing department of the facility designated as an advertising agency so that it can collect a 15 percent commission for local media buys placed for events by promoters.

OBJECTIVE: Increase public convenience for ticket purchases.

STRATEGY: Renegotiate the current ATS contract to provide the facility more control over event ticketing and ticket receipts. In exchange, ATS would be offered exclusive ticketing at the facility (except for events or tenants whose contracts stipulate otherwise). Install an ATS outlet at the facility box office and pay ATS 2 percent of gross ticket revenues as a fee for installation and maintenance with an additional ticket printing charge of 10 cents per ticket. The facility, which under the new contract would manage box-office operations through ATS, would charge promoters a fee equal to 13 percent of gross ticket revenues as a fee for managing ticket operations. ATS would still be responsible for the training of ticket sellers and ticket takers. Create a group sales position in the Marketing Department and charge promoters a 10 percent fee of group sales gross revenues.

Implementation and control is the essential last step of the marketing plan. Each objective must be assigned to a person(s) and be tied to a time frame for accomplishment. An effective facility manager must supervise start-up activities, administer public relations programs, oversee budget expenditures, and conduct cost analyses.

SUMMARY

This chapter is a guide for managers to plan and implement a marketing program for sport and entertainment facilities. As a part of the $50-billion-per-year industry, the sports facility business can benefit from well-designed and well-executed marketing plans. The essential components of a marketing plan for a sports facility include an executive summary, introduction, situation analysis, identification of target markets, marketing objectives, and effective strategies with specific methods for implementation. Particular attention is directed toward the task of attracting events to the sports facility. Therefore, without well-developed marketing plans, many sports facilities lack an important key to securing business. In today's market economy, only facility managers who are effective in attracting events and clients will survive.

QUESTIONS

1. What are the essential components of a sports facility marketing plan?
2. What is the difference between primary and secondary marketing research information? What are the sources for these data and how could they be used in marketing the facility?

ACTIVITIES

1. Examine a local newspaper for advertisements about upcoming sports events. Discuss in small groups the timing, placement, and content of these ads.

2. Investigate the possibilities of purchasing signage at an area sport arena or stadium. Discuss the availability of signage, price, and marketing materials.

SUGGESTED READINGS

Cohen, W. (1987). *Developing a winning marketing plan.* New York: John Wiley.

Kotler, P., and Andreasen, A. R. (1987). *Strategic marketing for nonprofit organizations*, (3rd ed.). Englewood Cliffs, NJ: Prentice-Hall.

Small Business Administration (1984). *Management Aid Number 2.020 Business Plan for Retailers*. Fort Worth: United States Government Printing Office.

REFERENCES

Associated Press (1991, August 30). *Sports business.* Associated Press wire service, Slug /9120 3114.

Buell, V. P. (1984). *Marketing management: A strategic planning approach*. New York: McGraw-Hill.

Cohen, W. (1987). *Developing a winning marketing plan.* New York: John Wiley and Sons.

Comte, E., and Stogel, C. (1990, January 1). Sports: A $63.1 billion industry. *The Sporting News*, pp. 60–61.

Eby, S. M. (1987). *Psssst! (Do You Want to Know a Secret?). Small Business Success*. Boston: Inc. Publishing.

Hackney, H. (1991, January 8). Sports Inc.: The IRS bowl. *Financial World*, pp. 42–43.

Howard, D. R., and Crompton, J. L. (1995). *Financing sport*. Morgantown, WVa: Fitness Information Technologies.

Levine, M. (1987, November). Improving your marketing game. *Athletic Business*, p. 16.

Lovelock, C., and Weinberg, C. (1984). *Marketing for public and nonprofit managers*. New York: John Wiley and Sons.

McDonald, M. A., Sutton, W. A., and Milne, G. R. (1995). TEAMQUAL: Measuring quality in professional team sports. *Sport Marketing Quarterly*, 4(2):9–15.

Mullin, B. J. (1983). Sport marketing, promotions and public relations. Amherst, Mass: National Sport Management, Inc.

Murphy, L. (1986, October). The controversy behind event marketing. *Sales and Marketing Management*, pp. 54–56.

Sandomir, R. (1988, November 14). The $50 Billion Sport Industry. *Sports Inc.*, pp. 14–23.

Simmons Market Research Bureau. (1986). *1986 Study of media and markets vol. 10 sports and leisure*. New York: Simmons Market Research Bureau.

Stotlar, D. K. (1993). *Successful Sport Marketing*. Dubuque, Iowa: Brown-Benchmark.

Stotlar, D. K., and Johnson, D. A. (1989). Assessing the impact and effectiveness of stadium advertising on sport spectators at division one institutions. *Journal of Sport Management*, 3(2):90–102.

Wilkinson, D. G. (1986). Sport Marketing Institute. Willowdale, Ontario: Sport Marketing Institute.

Wilkinson, D. G. (1988). Event Management and Marketing Institute. Willowdale, Ontario: Sport Marketing Institute.

PART II

Specific Areas and Special Groups

10

Sports Equipment and Ancillary Areas

Newton Wilkes, Marcia L. Walker, Todd Seidler

Two components that are often overlooked in the management of sports facilities are equipment and ancillary areas. In this chapter, managerial considerations related to equipment will be examined first, followed by a section on ancillary areas. To avoid confusion, the following definitions are provided: *Facilities* are the buildings used for some activity; *equipment* includes usable, nondisposable items that are added to a facility and are expected to be used over a period of years. It may be either fixed (backboards, scoreboards) or portable (uniforms, bats, balls, bleachers). *Supplies* are disposable and frequently replaced articles (athletic tape, marking pens).

Because sport is a major industry, sport equipment has become a multibillion-dollar business. As a result, sport administrators' responsibilities have expanded. Computerization is now a necessity. Monies awarded in lawsuits involving various aspects of sport products and equipment have grown to astronomical amounts. Innovative equipment has been developed. Even the administrative philosophy dealing with the acquisition, use, and maintenance of equipment is quite different.

THE ROLE OF EQUIPMENT IN SPORTS

The impact that sport has on our society and on the world is enormous. It exerts a powerful influence in several ways: sociologically, psychologically, politically, financially, and so on. Likewise, the amount and effect of the equipment that makes sport possible is virtually immeasurable.

Sociological Influences

George Bush used to keep his 45-year-old Rawlings Claw baseball glove in his desk drawer in the Oval Office. Oriole infielder René Gonzales kept his gamer in a bag that once contained Wonder Bread. No other piece of equipment, perhaps no other inanimate object, exerts the hold on us that the baseball glove does. Most anyone who has played the game remembers a favorite glove from his or her youth, the one he or she hung from the handlebars of a bicycle (Wulf and Kaplan, 1990).

How is sport sociological and what is the connection between sports equipment and society? Sport is sociological because "all sports involve humans interacting with other humans in a structured way" (Curry and Jiobu, 1984, p. 17).

In the United States, we are surrounded by sport. From a distance we see sport on television, in the movies, and in advertisements. As spectators, we watch our favorite teams compete, whether they are professional, collegiate, high school, club, or youth league. As participants, we are running, hitting, serving, throwing, spiking, sledding, riding, skating, hiking, or skiing.

It is difficult to imagine anyone in the United States who has not used some type of sports equipment at one time or another (riding a bicycle, playing tennis, taking a hike). Furthermore, in many situations sports equipment is not even used for

One type of ancillary area is the attractive entrance to the Hall of Fame at the James E. Wilson, Jr., Center for Intercollegiate Sports at Tulane University. (Courtesy of Sizeler Architects, New Orleans, Louisiana)

sports. For example, employees in many professions (nurses, orderlies, waitresses, waiters, fast-food workers, carpenters) have adopted tennis shoes as part of their standard uniforms because of the comfort they provide, and warm-up suits have become commonplace as everyday wear for many people. "As much as 70 percent of the over four billion dollars spent on sports clothing may be for nonsports use" (Curry and Jiobu, 1984, p. 3). *American Marketplace* (1990) reported that 9 percent of all women's shoes and 14 percent of all men's shoes are bought for athletic use.

A recent survey states that "sports is an element of American life so pervasive that virtually no individual is untouched by it. . . . (The) United States is a nation of sports fans . . . (and) sports participants" (Miller Lite Report on American Attitudes Toward Sports, cited in Coakley, 1990, p. 1).

What then is the connection between sports equipment and society? Most sports involve the use of some type of equipment as an essential part of the activity itself. Try to imagine ice skating without skates or playing golf without a club! Even sports that do not require tools to perform the activity (running, walking, swimming), do have uniforms or costumes, footwear, and other supplies.

Many similar sports use equipment that is quite different. Note the differences in these sports: water skiing, alpine skiing, and cross-country skiing; softball and baseball; field hockey and ice hockey. Some of these sports have similar names, yet each is unique, as may be observed based on the equipment.

Sporting equipment is found in every class and society in the world. For years the local, regional, and national sporting goods stores were the primary outlet for sports equipment and supplies. In recent years, however, there has been a proliferation of stores specializing in particular activities or recreational enterprises. Most cities have specialty shops with gear and uniforms for individual activities (running, tennis, golf, bicycling, archery, and dance); team sports (soccer, baseball, and football); outdoors, mountain, and wilderness activities (fishing, camping, backpacking, alpine skiing); water sports (canoeing, windsurfing, and rafting); aerobics, fitness, and exercise activities; and so forth.

For many people, the way one dresses to participate in a sport is as important as the utensils needed to play the sport. It is not enough to play well; one must "look the part" also. Sports reporters spend considerable time commenting on how the players are dressed, particularly in announcing womens' sports events (figure skating, tennis, gymnastics). Unfortunately, sometimes the emphasis has been placed in the wrong direction, enforcing the old idea that women had better look good, because they can't play good. Recently, there has been a positive change with the addition of more women's sports programs and expanded media coverage, however there is still a considerable lag behind the opportunities available for males in sport.

Some types of equipment have become associated with particular segments of society. For example, a stereotyped impression exists that blacks and basketballs go hand-in-hand. This is emphasized by Coakley: "It is no accident that blacks in the United States have excelled in sports requiring little expensive equipment and training. For example, basketballs are cheap and the best coaching is widely available in public school programs. Furthermore, outdoor basketball courts are cheap to build and cheap to maintain" (Coakley, 1990, p. 212).

In the same line of thinking, certain sports and sports equipment originally associated with the wealthy have become popular with the middle class (tennis, golf, bicycling). In the late 1800s and early 1900s, "bicycling was a particular favorite of many wealthy people" (Spears and Swanson, 1978, p. 147).

An example of the sociological emphasis, Coakley (1990, pp. 184–185) states that "discrimination was also obvious in the realm of facilities and equipment. Women were often given the old gym. . . . Other hand-me-downs included the old

swimming pool, old uniforms from the men's teams, and used equipment. When hand-me-downs were not available the women either had nothing or had to share facilities and equipment with the men."

To correct this widespread bias, Congress passed Title IX of the Educational Amendments in 1972. The purpose of Title IX is to prohibit sex discrimination in education programs that receive federal financial assistance. Title IX specifies eleven areas where males and females must receive equal treatment, one of which is the provision of sports equipment and supplies. A sport program is in compliance (in the area of equipment and supplies) if there exist equivalent amount, quality, suitability, maintenance, replacement, and availability.

Finally, one of the negative sociological influences connected with sports is the relationship between sports attire and gangs. Unfortunately, due to the popularity of sports apparel and the heroic images portrayed in advertising some drug dealers and gangs have adopted particular sport products as part of their identity.

" 'The Intervale gang uses all Adidas stuff, exclusively—hats, jackets, sweatpants, shoes,' says Bill Stewart III, a probation officer at the Dorchester District Court in Boston, one of the busiest criminal courts in the nation. 'They even have an Adidas handshake, copying the three stripes on the product. They extend three fingers when they shake hands' " (cited from Telander, 1990, p. 43).

These examples show a definite connection and point to ways that society influences sports and equipment and the impact that sports and equipment have on society.

Psychological Influences

Is there any connection between sports equipment and the psychology that is a part of games and activities? Consider the following: Teams that appear in attractive uniforms of the latest styles carrying the most innovative implements always draw attention. If it does nothing more than assist athletes with their self-esteem, then that is enough to make a difference to many players and coaches. Furthermore, many coaches use this approach not only to "psych up" their athletes, but also, to "psych out" their opponents.

Merkel (cited in *"Team Uniforms"*) states that "the psychological high that nice-looking uniforms give athletes may provide the winning edge. Winning isn't only based on the coach's strategies, but also how kids feel. If they look good, they feel good and if they feel good, they play good [sic]."

Unfortunately, there is a dark side to this element of wanting to look good. A serious problem exists in many cities where young people are attacking their peers over a pair of sneakers or other sports apparel. According to Telander (1990, p. 38): "In some cities muggings for sportswear are commonplace—Atlanta police, for instance, estimate they have handled more than 50 such robberies in the last four months." Chicago districts "have had about 50 reported incidents involving jackets and about a dozen involving gym shoes each month."

There have also been killings associated with the muggings. A 15-year-old boy from Anne Arundel County, Maryland, was strangled by his basketball buddy for his two-week-old $115 basketball shoes.

In another incident, a 14-year-old boy was shot to death in the hallway of his junior high school by someone who wanted his silky blue Georgetown jacket. In Houston, a 16-year-old boy was shot to death when he refused to turn over his Air Jordan hightops. One additional situation involved an 18-year-old Baltimore youth who "was robbed of his $40 sweatpants and then shot and killed" (Telander, 1990, p. 38).

These are merely a handful of the violent incidents occurring over possession of sports apparel. It is a sad commentary that, for some people, what one wears is more valuable than one's self.

Political Influences

What connection exists between politics and sports? In competition at all levels (including the Olympics), "athletes and coaches push rules to the limit and constantly seek new technology and technique" (Curry and Jiobu, 1984, p. 183).

Indeed, equipment is an issue worldwide. The type of equipment allowed for Olympic competition is strictly enforced for most sports. There are some exceptions, however. Presently there are no rules governing the size of tennis rackets being used in international competition. "Not until fairly recently did racket size become an issue. We expect that explicit rules will soon be made to regulate racket size and other technological changes" (Curry and Jiobu, 1984, p. 184).

Regulations regarding equipment in many sports are in question at the present time internationally. One example is whether skinsuits should be permitted in swim meets (Curry and Jiobu, 1984).

The types of equipment allowed in competition are major factors among teams of the National Football League (NFL), National Basketball Association (NBA), National Hockey League (NHL), National Collegiate Athletic Association (NCAA), and National Association of Intercollegiate Athletics (NAIA). In competition, everyone wants an edge for winning. All sports leagues have established strict rules to govern this issue, and continually enforce them to provide fair play.

Equipment is also used for recruiting purposes. Teams entice recruits with the best-looking uniforms, latest gadgets, most efficient machines, quality service, and supplies. Equipment is part of the package when deals are being negotiated.

Fitness and health clubs purchase and advertise the latest, most striking, finest quality exercise machines in order to attract customers. Because it is a highly competitive business, having the most expensive and the best equipment is imperative.

The latest craze is computerized fitness machines: treadmills, rowing machines, bicycles, stairclimbers, weight resistance, and strength training machines. Some machines even provide a printed report at the end of each session showing workout results.

Financial Influences

There was a time when only one type of tennis shoe was available for all types of sports. This is no longer the case—some sport shoe manufacturers make more than 150 models (Girard, 1988, October).

One example of this growth is in the fitness industry. According to the Sporting Goods Manufacturers Association's (SGMA) Sports Participation Index, "almost one in five Americans over the age of six participated in some form of fitness-related activity at least once a week in 1991. Three of the top four growth sports and recreation activities, based on frequent participation, are fitness-related—stair-climbing machines, cross-country ski machines and treadmills" (Schmid, July 1992, page

17). This translates to millions of Americans spending money on athletic equipment and clothing.

In the late 1980s and 1990s the annual sales of exercise equipment skyrocketed, increasing from $1.2 billion in 1987 to $2.05 billion in 1991. Much of this revenue was generated by sales of home exercise equipment (e.g., treadmills, exercise bicycles), and much of that equipment was purchased by people 45 years old and older ("Over-45 buyers," 1993).

It is estimated that there are 55 million walkers and 3,000 walking clubs in the United States. There are at least fifteen brands of walking shoes and 140 styles to accommodate these participants (LeUnes and Nation, 1989, p. 6). Such an enormous supply has been created to meet the consumers' demands for choices of style, fit, cost, and material, depending on specific use.

Exercise walking has yet to reach its peak. The sport is becoming specialized into fitness walkers, hiking and backpack walkers, race walkers, mall walkers, and so on. "The newest and fastest-growing group of enthusiasts are the mall walkers. Dozens of malls around the country have organized walking clubs, complete with T-shirts, social hours, and special incentive coupons provided by the mall proprietors" (Girard, 1988, December, p. 46). So much interest has developed that at least two major shoe manufacturers are developing a special mall walking shoe (Girard, 1988, December).

A completely different commercial enterprise that spends immense financial resources on equipment, uniforms, and other supplies is intercollegiate sports. This, of course, varies greatly among divisions (NCAA I–III, NAIA, NJCAA), conferences (Big 8, Midwest Collegiate Athletic, Big Sky), and levels of play (college, high school). Table 10–1 gives an example of the costs for intercollegiate football apparel.

Other types of sports associations and enterprises also spend enormous amounts on equipment. When the University of Kentucky developed a 3500 square-foot fitness center for the faculty and staff, they spent $400,000 of which more than half was spent on new equipment ("Kentucky takes," 1987). Another example is the renovation of Joliet (Illinois) Junior College's campus fitness center which cost "$152,000, with the exercise equipment accounting for about $91,000 of that amount" (Yost, cited in "Creatively financing," 1988, p. 34).

Administrative Philosophy

The philosophy of the administration determines the basic program offered by any sports organization. That philosophy, which includes policies and procedures, also governs the selection, care, and utilization of equipment within the program.

For example, if the program involves competitive sports and the philosophy is founded on "being number 1," then the tools must be adequate to make this possible. Such equipment should be of

Table 10–1   Sample cost of intercollegiate football apparel*

Item	Estimated cost of practice equipment	Estimated cost of game equipment
Shoes	$50.00	$50.00
T-Shirts	5.00	5.00
Pants	22.00	48.00
Jersey	15.00	90.00 for 2 ($45.00 each)
Socks	2.00	2.00
Supporter	2.00	2.00
Shoulder pads	125.00	**
Helmet	95.00	**
Hip, knee, thigh pads	11.00/set	**
Sweats	40.00/set	**
Subtotal	$367.00	$197.00
Total	$564.00	

*Costs based on average sporting goods prices.
**Same equipment as used in practice.

the highest quality and should accommodate the specific needs of individual athletes. Materials that are inappropriate, obsolete, poorly designed, worn, or damaged will diminish the performance of the individuals or teams. On the other hand, if the program is one with a recreational or leisure emphasis, and the philosophy is based on "equal opportunity for all participants," materials might be selected for durability and versatility rather than using a specific person's needs as the criterion.

Another point to emphasize is that sports and fitness facilities are designed to accommodate and use equipment. From the design stages throughout the planning process, it is essential to incorporate all aspects concerning equipment. For example, when developing a fitness club facility it is important to ask and answer many questions prior to building or renovating:

1. What is the purpose of the facility?
2. What types of equipment are necessary to fulfill that purpose?
3. How much equipment is needed to provide for the number of participants and for different activities and interests?
4. How much space is needed for the necessary equipment?
5. How can the facility be designed to provide adequate supervision for use of the equipment and protection against vandalism and theft?
6. How can the facility be designed to promote risk management and to eliminate liability factors?

SELECTING EQUIPMENT

It is essential that every program director know the equipment purchasing process thoroughly and be acquainted with the policies and procedures of that particular organization. The director should also be familiar with as many strategies, ideas, and techniques for purchasing and maintaining equipment as possible. Selection of equipment and supplies should provide an adequate amount of properly designed equipment to allow maximum learning and participation.

The first step in planning equipment purchases is to determine the needs of the program. The needs for one program may vary greatly from that of other programs. Equipment and supplies required for a public school athletic program are different from those needed for a private fitness facility. It is necessary to consider the scope, variety, and nature of the overall program. It is very important that the person responsible for purchasing supplies and equipment carefully study his or her situation and estimate its needs objectively and realistically. Some of the factors in a needs assessment include available space and facilities; desired activities; the safety and health of the participants; and the skill, age, sex, and number of participants.

Once the manager has evaluated the needs of the program, the next step is the selection process. Some aspects of the selection process that are not necessarily associated with the needs assessment include quality of the product, choice of a dealer, standardization of equipment, trends and styles, centralized purchasing, and ordering timeliness.

PROCURING EQUIPMENT

Procurement is the next step. The process begins with a request for purchase and ends with the payment of the invoice. This process usually begins after the budgeting and selection are complete. The primary goal of the procurement process is to obtain the desired, high-quality equipment and supplies, on time, and at the lowest possible cost.

There are two common methods for purchasing supplies and equipment—direct purchasing and bid purchasing. Each method has advantages and disadvantages. Most organizations use one or both of these methods depending on the situation. In direct purchasing, the individual manager or director is allowed to spend the money as he or she sees fit. It is then that person's responsibility to shop around and get the best value. For example, if the purchase is under a specific dollar amount, typically $100, equipment may be ordered directly. The advantages of this method are that the individual knows the limits of his or her budget and will usually shop around to find the best buys. This system also allows for quick, small mid-season replacements or other emergency purchases without going through a lot of paperwork.

Most large organizations require a competitive bid process to purchase budgeted items. In most of these organizations bidding is a well-defined and highly structured procedure. Basically, this process involves making a list of the items desired for purchase and allowing several wholesalers to submit on them. A contract is awarded to the lowest bidder who is reputable and can meet the terms of the purchase order. The primary advantages to competitive bidding for equipment are that it usually results in the lowest cost available to the purchasing organization and that it also produces a set of checks and balances to help ensure that the best interests of the organization are served. Disadvantages include the length of time it takes to get through the bid process and the fact that there are usually more people involved than in direct purchasing, which increases the chances of mistakes.

INVENTORY AND CONTROL

The organization's leader, whether department chairperson, athletic director, manager, owner, or other administrator, is ultimately accountable for all supplies, apparatus, and materials. The administrator must take the lead in establishing policies and appropriate guidelines. Creating an impractical or theoretical system is a waste of time and poor management. A useful inventory system is well organized and easy to operate. All of the staff should thoroughly understand and follow the system. State-of-the-art methods should be used and constantly revised to incorporate changes in curriculum, budget, purchasing, and so on.

Jensen (1983) states that "inventory involves keeping an amount of stock that is adequate to avoid frequent shortages and resultant small orders, yet not so large that it occupies an inordinate amount of storage space."

Accountability for equipment is based on properly securing it and maintaining accurate records of that stock. An excellent accountability system also saves money for the program by reducing the loss of equipment. Money saved in one area may then be used in another area or may make it possible to acquire additional items to build up the inventory.

A critical element of accountability that is often overlooked is the inspection upon receiving. Materials should be inspected upon delivery to ascertain if the amount is correct (compared to the purchase order) or if any damages occurred during shipment or handling. The shipment should also be inspected for proper sizes of items and quality of materials.

Immediate action should be taken for any problem or error that is discovered. Delay in action can make it difficult to hold the vendor responsible and, as a result, the purchaser may have to absorb the loss or damages. In addition, most items are ordered with a specific time frame in mind and an interruption will impede the schedule.

All records of the receiving transaction, including date of arrival, should be updated immediately and discrepancies or problems should be registered on the computer inventory or in the noncomputerized filing system. When this process is incomplete, the items should be coded and only then should they be placed in their proper storage areas. There needs to be an area in the equipment room specifically for receiving, recording, and coding materials.

It is important also to provide a specific area in the equipment room only for issuing equipment. This helps organize the area and prevent confusion and clutter. Equipment should be distributed to the users in an organized and standardized manner. Whether there is only one sport or many separate activities, the distribution should be the same. Therefore, it is necessary to design a distribution method appropriate for the particular programs and the types of equipment. The method should be simple, fast, and accurate.

One suggested system is to develop a bar code identification card to give every person using the equipment. In many settings, such as universities and private clubs, identification cards are required. It would be relatively simple to use the same card for issuing equipment.

Other common systems use identification (ID) cards with photos or plastic-laminated cards. Regardless of the system, the basic information to provide is individual identification, current membership status (expiration date), and a code number.

In situations such as intercollegiate athletics, for which equipment may be issued for an extended period of time (season, year), it is necessary to devise a different system. The ID card can be used to issue items, but it is not kept by the equipment manager. The individual's code and a list of the dispersed items are recorded. At the end of the season or some other set time, the individual again presents his or her ID and the returned items are cleared from the record. The individual is charged for items that are not returned, according to the record.

Compiling accurate records and systematically updating them is a vital function of the inventory process. It is not uncommon for administrators to spend 70 or 80 percent of their time on such transactions. Fortunately, computerization has sharply reduced the amount of time and effort spent on this monumental task. The most obvious benefit is that instead of compiling and maintaining handwritten records and accounts of the stock on hand, it is much faster to put all the information on a computer and simply input changes as they occur.

Computers also provide for the consolidation of information, which keeps records complete. Other assets of computerization in the sports equipment world include increasing work production, eliminating the redundancy of activities, improving reaction time by collating data quickly, providing a check-and-balance system and audit trail, and helping to cut expenses by using staff more efficiently, which may reduce employee costs (Andrus and Lane, 1989).

LEGAL CONCERNS

The sports manager must be aware of several legal concerns related to sports equipment. Two of those areas, product liability and protective equipment, are addressed here. One must also pay attention to federal laws that affect managers dealing with sports equipment. The application of Title IX of the Education Amendments of 1972, previously mentioned, and the Americans with Disabilities Act (ADA) must be examined. These laws are discussed more thoroughly in other parts of this text; however, managers must learn to apply these mandates in all areas, including sports equipment.

PRODUCT LIABILITY

"*Product liability* refers to the liability of a manufacturer, processor, seller, lessor, or anyone furnishing a product that causes injury to another. Liability is predicated on negligence, breach of warranty, or, most recently, strict liability" (Baley and Matthews, 1984, p. 68).

Manufacturers produce a product that is intended for specific purposes. If the consumer purchases the product and uses it in the specific manner for which it is intended, then the product should be safe to use. When a product is defective or is used for unintended purposes, an injury or loss can occur. Injuries and assessments of liability have caused many manufacturers to place warning labels in visible areas on their products. Most indicate that the label is not to be removed nor, as in the case of a football helmet, should the product be tampered with because this may void warranty or displace responsibility to the consumer for altering the product in the event of an injury. Product warning labels should signify dangers of a product even if it is used properly and safely (Horine, 1991). Manufacturers of football helmets, diving boards, gymnastics, fitness and exercise equipment have experienced increases in lawsuits.

Stotlar (1987) agrees, reporting that "manufacturers and purchasers of athletic equipment have in many cases been held to foresee all possible uses and misuses of the equipment and to warn users of the potential risks which accompany the use and misuse of the equipment in question." This trend has caused a weakening of the defense by assumption of risk (by adults and children) and strengthened the case for "one's voluntary exposure to a known danger" (Stotlar, 1987).

Ultimately, the user must be informed of the specific inherent dangers of a product before the user can be held liable. Otherwise, the user cannot be held accountable for all of the assumptions of risks.

PROTECTIVE EQUIPMENT

Many of the country's national associations, sporting goods manufacturers, and some insurance companies are advocating continued research to make sporting, recreational, and fitness equipment as safe as can reasonably be expected. The National Operating Committee on Standards for Athletic Equipment (NOCSAE), National Collegiate Athletic Association (NCAA), National Federation of State High School Associations (NFSHSA), National Youth Sports Coaches Association (NYSCA), National Athletic Training Association (NATA), National Strength and Conditioning Association (NSCA),

American Coaching Effectiveness Program (ACEP), Rawlings, Worth, Athletic Technology Inc. (ATI), Kenko, Wilson, and Riddell, to name several, continue to monitor, suggest, and initiate standards and regulations to provide safer protective equipment for athletic/recreational enthusiasts.

One group, the Athletic Equipment Managers Association (AEMA), has instituted a certification program to improve the knowledge and promote education of athletic equipment managers ("Equipment managers," 1990).

As Adrian (1990) notes, several certification bodies for various sports evaluate the specifications of protective equipment, materials, and playing surfaces. Some of the councils are the Hockey Equipment Certification Council (HECC), Eye Safety Certification Council (ESCC), NOCSAE, the Football Sports Equipment and Facilities Committee of the American Society for Testing Materials (ASTM), and the Consumer Products Safety Commission.

ANCILLARY AREAS

The term *ancillary* means subordinate or subservient. Thus, an ancillary area is thought of as having a lesser or auxillary function. While the definition may remain the same, the operational function of ancillary areas in sports facilities seems to have developed into a different philosophy in the mind of designers and managers alike. Some of the ancillary areas to consider are locker, shower, and dressing areas; equipment storage and issue areas; mechanical and audiovisual equipment areas; and reception, lounge, and concession areas.

Locker, Shower, Dressing Areas

Sports facility managers are ever vigilant to discover the treasured method that would forever ensure a beautiful, aromatic, spotlessly clean and dry locker room, dressing, and shower area. As we all too well realize, no facility area will remain spotlessly clean forever with just a single effort. There must be a planned, constant attention to maintenance of the facility's ancillary areas to make a positive impression.

Although many ideas relative to the design and location of locker rooms, lockers, showers, and dressing areas look good on paper, some are adequate in theory only (Cohen, 1993), and after short periods of use the flaws are revealed. Turner and Hauser (1994), enumerate ten guidelines that may prove beneficial in the design and supervision of the dressing and shower areas:

1. Design locker rooms for visual openness and safe traffic flow.
2. Floors and walls need careful planning in terms of drainage, and nonslip and nonabrasive surfaces.
3. Ventilation systems must be able to handle the moisture produced in locker rooms, and attention must be given to the planning of wet and dry areas.
4. Careful attention to the placement of electrical switches, outlets, blow dryers, and lights can add a safe element to your locker room.
5. Plumbing needs careful thought and planning in relation to stability, access, pressure, and hot water needs.
6. Cleanliness and ease of maintenance of the locker room are extremely important for health and safety.
7. Glass items, including windows, should be kept to a minimum.
8. Benches in a locker room need careful attention as to type, placement, stability, and safety.
9. The types of lockers, how locker doors open, and the types of locker tops and bases are important safety factors in locker-room design.
10. Planning for amenities and emergencies can create a safer and healthier locker room.

Equipment Storage and Issue Areas

Management of equipment storage and issue areas requires consistent efforts. Not only should all equipment be inspected and maintained on a regular and documented schedule, but the storage and issue areas must be of sufficient size and design to eliminate clutter as well as provide enough space to move around unimpeded.

While there are no specific space requirements for every ancillary area, Walker (1989) recommends that ancillary (support) space average 20 to 22 percent of the activity space. Plans must be accurate and detailed and consider the exact purpose(s) of the area, in order to project the required space dimensions and the costs. Horine (1991) suggests that maintenance costs can be reduced and security improved if there is an equipment manager.

Because design configurations are mainly based on the purposes of the facility, there is apparently no single pattern that will meet all requirements. It should be noted, however, that there are a few basic features that might be incorporated into any equipment storage and issue area. Walker and Seidler (1993) offer the following hints for successful locker-room management:

1. Locate the equipment storage and issue area near locker rooms and activity areas, and adjacent to a corridor.
2. Provide double-wide, high doors for easy transportation of equipment into and out of the storage areas.
3. Make certain that doors (including facings), hinges, and locks provide adequate security.
4. Windows, if any, should be small enough and located at a height to prevent unwanted entry into the storage and issue area.

The entrance to the facility should be inviting. (Courtesy of Barker Rinker Seacat and Partners Architects, Denver, Colorado)

5. Keys to the area should be accounted for and issued on a limited basis.
6. The equipment storage area should be designed to allow various types of storage compartments and the hanging of equipment from walls and ceiling.

Railey and Tschauner (1993) offer an additional hint: control air temperature and humidity to avoid adversely affecting the life expectancy of your equipment. Air control will also provide measures of comfort to facility operators and users.

Turner (1987) states that audiovisual (AV) equipment should be an integral part of any facility design and planning. Technology is an important feature of today's society and extremely useful in many ancillary areas and main facility areas. Audiovisual and computer usage can prove beneficial to instruction, security, inventory, cost, climate, and motivation of employees and patrons. Examples of audiovisual equipment are camcorders, television sets, VCRs, tape recorders, stereos, and headsets.

Because electronic equipment can be sensitive to temperature, especially heat, it is important that the storage area include proper ventilation and insulation. Flynn (cited in Walker and Seidler, 1993, p. 89) recommends that the AV storage area be accessible, well-protected, and secure. Readily available should be a cart that can transport equipment safely and easily to lessen accidental damage.

Service Areas

Facilities for which profits or customer satisfaction are paramount often provide amenities for functional considerations and ambience to promote each patron's return to the facility. Such service areas are the reception area, lounges, and health bars.

Relative to the reception area, there should be a staff member who possesses quality personal relations skills and knowledge of the facility. Further, it should be equipped with the appropriate machinery to provide required services. For example, furniture should reflect proper decor; a good telephone and intercom system should be installed; a computer, typewriter, fax and a calculator with tape should be available (Horine, 1991, p. 273). It would also be helpful to locate the reception area

A well-secured area for equipment storage and issue

where supervision can be easy (Railey and Tschauner, 1993, p. 255).

This area may be the primary control and management area of the facility. There may need to be some type of foyer outside the activity area to help maintain floor quality and to provide an area in which to sell tickets.

The purpose or initial desires for the lounge health bar areas will dictate whether they will be concession ventures or complete food and beverage services. Is the purpose for customers to enjoy relaxation and refreshments during their activity periods? Is the goal to attract a lunch and/or dinner clientele? Is the main purpose to generate a profit? Keep in mind that revenues can be generated also from vending machines.

Whatever the reasons, particular aspects must be contemplated. Railey and Tschauner (1993) offer the following suggestions:

1. Install plenty of water fountains because they produce little or no litter and help deter dehydration.
2. It should be inconvenient to carry food and drinks from the lounge and health bar areas into exercise and workout areas. Litter and liability may be increased.
3. These ancillary areas encourage socialization and relaxation, while promoting increased profits.
4. Hire a consultant to help with operational concerns and important decisions.

An additional suggestion is to provide double entry doors in the lounge area to facilitate catering and movement of large items.

Cohen (1991) emphasizes that, "it's tough to lose money in concessions—but are you making enough?" In order to enhance profits, Cohen recommends streamlining to offer only the most popular items. It appears that too many choices confuse customers and many do not make decisions on a timely basis. Most patrons simply do not want to waste time waiting to be served.

Mechanical Equipment Area

Aspects to consider when designing the area that houses mechanical heating and cooling systems are as follows: (1) locate the room away from areas where noise becomes a distractor; (2) design doorways to allow bulky equipment easier access in and out of area in case of breakdowns or necessary replacement; (3) the construct of flooring, walls, and ceiling should be of materials that provide a proper control of internal atmosphere, security, and safety to equipment and employees; and, (4) regularly scheduled maintenance of the mechanical equipment area should be relatively convenient.

The mechanical equipment area must have the HVAC system. In addition, aquatic areas must have a secure room for chemical filtration, and ice arenas must provide for the storage of ice maintenance equipment.

SUMMARY

The management of sports equipment is a critical part of the manager's job. The manager must not only understand the selection and procurement process, but also must be knowledgeable about computerization applications, accountability techniques, and legal requirements and standards in the field. It is a complex task that is essential to a manager's success.

It is important that ancillary areas be given sufficient consideration as to design, function or purpose, space requirements, safety features, maintenance, types of materials, and amenities. This chapter offers some suggestions to manage and operate ancillary facility areas prudently.

Proper supervision and informed employees are key to successful management and operation of ancillary areas. It is important to remember that even though no single design pattern meets all requirements, architects and planners should adhere to sound principles of construction and traffic flow. In the process of designing the facility and deciding on appropriate materials, it is critical to consider safety, legal ramifications, maintenance, and access.

Various areas draw patrons to a facility for activity, but few have the impact on relaxation and ambience that well-designed and maintained ancillary areas do. An impression of a facility is directly related to its ancillary areas as well as its amenities.

QUESTIONS

1. What are the steps one should follow to acquire sports equipment for a facility?
2. What are the safety and legal concerns regarding sports equipment?
3. What are the ancillary areas?
4. What is the role that equipment plays in sports?

ACTIVITIES

1. Select a specific program such as a youth sports program. Develop a plan that includes the types of sports that will be played, the equipment needed to play those sports, and the process one must go through to acquire the equipment.
2. Survey or visit local sports equipment businesses to acquire knowledge of new equipment and determine its proper use.
3. Develop an inventory system that would be practical for a high school physical education program (or any other specific program).

SUGGESTED READINGS

Ammons, J. (1990). Locker purchasing tips. *Athletic Business* 14(7).

Barnard, A. (1992). Locker room logistics. *Athletic Business* 16(3).

Berg, R. (1992). Dirty laundry, done dirt cheap. *Athletic Business* 16(10).

Brown, S. C. (January 1987). Security considerations, predesigning them into your campers recreation facility. *JOPERD.*

Cohen, A. (1991). Down in front. *Athletic Business* 15(7).

Cohen, A. (1994). Locker room layouts. *Athletic Business* 18(1).

Facility Planning. (1989). New looks in locker rooms. *Athletic Business* 13(4).

Holdman, M. (1990). Fine-tuning the laundry. *Athletic Business* 14(10).

Lizarrage, A. (1991). Clean up your act. *Athletic Business* 15(12).

McArthur, S. (1992). Don't throw in the towel. *Athletic Business* 16(7).

Meagher, J. W. (1990). 43 steps to a successful facility. *Athletic Business* 14(8).

Olson, J. F. (January 1987). Operational considerations, private and public sector activity and recreational programs. *JOPERD.*

Schmid, S. (1990). Livable locker rooms. *Athletic Business* 14(7).

Schmid, S. (1990). Lockers to fit every need. *Athletic Business* 14(12).

Seidler, A. H. (January 1987). Maintenance, the most underrated aspect. *JOPERD.*

Shannon, J. L. (January 1987). A look to the future. *JOPERD.*

Strauf, D. L. (1994). Storage solutions. *Athletic Management* 6(6).

Thornton, J. (1988). Getting more for less in locker room design. *Athletic Business* 12(12).

REFERENCES

Adrian, M. (1990, summer). Covering the risk. *Training and Conditioning*, pp. 11–13

And in the beginning, our football heroes. (1990, June 21). *Scholastic Coach*, pp. 68–69.

Andrus, S., and Lane, S. A. (1989, March). Computerizing the athletic department. *College Athletic Management*, pp. 30–34.

Baley, J. A., and Mathews, D. L. (1984). *Law and liability in athletics, physical education, and recreation*, (2nd ed.). Dubuque, Iowa: Wm. C. Brown.

Coakley, J. J. (1990). *Sport in society*, St. Louis: Mosby.

Cohen, A. (1991). Concessions come of age. *Athletic Business* 15(5).

Cohen, A. (1993). Locker rooms: What works, what doesn't. *Athletic Business* 17(3).

Creatively financing fitness centers. (1988, April). *Athletic Business*, pp. 32, 38.

Curry, T. J., and Jiobu, R. M. (1984). *Sports—a social perspective*, Englewood Cliffs, NJ: Prentice Hall.

Equipment managers can be certified. (1990, October 22). *NCAA News*, p. 16.

Girard, L. (1988, October 24). L. A.'s mystique on your feet. *Sports inc.*, pp. 44–45.

Girard, L. (1988, December 12). Walking with the cardiac set. *Sports inc.*, p. 46.

Harris, H. A. (cited in Zeigler, E. F.) (1988). *A history of sport and physical education to 1900*. Champaign, Ill: Stipes.

Horine, L. (1991). *Administration of physical education and sport programs*. (2nd ed.). pp. 89–114. Dubuque, Iowa: Wm. C. Brown.

Jensen, C. R. (1988). *Administrative management of physical education and athletic programs*, (pp. 352–356). Philadelphia: Lea and Febiger.

Kentucky takes care of its own. (1987, October). *Athletic Business*, p. 15.

LeUnes, A. D., and Nation, J. R. (1989). *Sport psychology: An introduction*, (pp. 6, 414). Chicago: Nelson-Hall.

Over-45 buyers likely to fuel exercise equipment boom. (1993, August 3). *Rocky Mountain News.*

Railey, J. H., and Tschauner, P. R. (1993). *Managing physical education, fitness, and sports programs*, (2nd ed.). Mountain View, Cal: Mayfield.

Schmid, S. (Ed.). (1992). Industry Briefings. *Athletic Business*, p. 17.

SGMA recreation market report 1989. (Available from Sporting Goods Manufacturers Association, 200 Castlewood Drive, North Palm Beach, FL 33408).

Spears, B., and Swanson, R. A. (1978). *History of sport and physical activity in the United States.* Dubuque: Wm. C. Brown.

Stotlar, D. K. (1987, January). Athletic equipment, product liability gone awry. *Journal of Physical Education, Recreation, and Dance*, pp. 27–29.

Team uniforms: Choosing the perfect fit. (1987, January). *Athletic Business*, pp. 52–53.

Telander, R. (1990, May 14). Senseless. *Sports Illustrated*, pp. 36–38, 43–44, 46, 49.

Turner, E. T. (1987, January). Facility design and trends, innovations. *Journal of Physical Education, Recreation, and Dance*, pp. 34–35.

Turner, E., and Hauser, D. (1994). Safe and sanitary. *Athletic Business* 18.

Vanderzwaag, H. J. (1984). *Sports management in schools and colleges*, New York: Wiley.

Walker, M. L. (1989) A space analysis of physical activity and ancillary areas in selected small colleges and universities. Unpublished doctoral dissertation, The University of New Mexico, Albuquerque.

Walker, M. L., and Seidler, T. (1993). *Sports equipment management*. Boston: Jones and Bartlett.

Wulf, S., and Kaplan, J. (1990, May 7). Glove story. *Sports Illustrated*, pp. 66, 82.

11

Fitness and Health-Related Areas

Frank B. Ashley, III, Shannon Courtney, Virginia L. Hicks

HEALTH AND FITNESS CLUBS

According to the International Health, Racquet and Sportsclub Association (IHRSA), in 1993 more than 18 million adults nationwide were members of a health/fitness club. Nine million adults enroll in health/fitness clubs annually. The club industry has changed dramatically since 1975, but experts agree that it is nowhere near its maturation. The club business is still in its adolescence and much can be learned about the future of the business by looking at its past (Winters, 1994). First came the "sweat-box gyms" where the "real men" worked out with barbells clanging. There were very few machines, no aerobic equipment, and no women. Women worked out in fitness clubs or figure salons which promoted "no sweat" exercises and passive exercise machines (Gandolfo, 1993).

The idea of practical preventive medicine brought about aerobic exercises such as jogging, running, and eventually aerobic dance. Aerobic exercise machines (rowers, treadmills, and stair climbers) brought the aerobics movement indoors. Sweat-box gyms began to add weight machines, cardiovascular machines, and female members. Country clubs began converting racquetball and tennis courts into weight rooms, and installing aerobic floors, and the fitness boom was on. Along with this change in exercise equipment, the change in the diversity of club memberships was another challenge that accompanied the evolution of the club business. Primarily in recent years the target market of the health/fitness club was the young, single, male adult. Today's lifelong market includes, kids, young adults, baby boomers, and the 50 and older crowd. A big change for today's managers is the amount of focus being placed on business and management (Loyle, 1994; Faust and Caro, 1993).

Management

The success of managing a club in the competitive business world depends on how you plan and operate your club. Knowing yourself and the conditions of business help build your vision into a system for success. The manager must be able to set goals and determine the method to meet these goals. The clubs that successfully perform these functions are the ones that will prosper. Managers must realize that every club operates as an interaction of four basic subsystems: customers, operations, people, and money (Faust and Caro, 1993).

Customers

The customers, or members, are the starting and ending point of every health/fitness club. Decisions have to be made about how to identify target populations and then how to serve these prospective members. Managers should realize that today's members are more knowledgeable about fitness and healthful lifestyles and this fact forces management to provide more services and programs than ever.

Operations

The needs and desires of the members have to be addressed by the club. They include facilities, equipment, policies, programs, and everything the manager plans, implements, maintains, and operates. Managers can expect a continuation of the improvement in equipment and facilities with greater tailoring to meet market and member needs.

Staff

Employees are a critical resource because your business is only as good as your employees, especially in a service business. Club managers in the future will have some of their biggest challenges dealing with staff, particularly in hiring and training employees.

Money

A manager's ability to spend the club's monetary resources effectively will increase the focus on the Management Information System and accounting system. Cost/benefit analyses are beginning to replace intuition and momentary infatuations with new hardware and exciting concepts. Money is a precious resource and is often scarce.

Hiring

Hiring is one of the most challenging aspects of health/fitness club management. Employees are a critical resource in service businesses and poor hiring decisions can cost clubs in more ways than they can imagine. Hiring the wrong person can result in high turnover costs, which include the direct costs of ads, interviews, and training. There could eventually be a cost in terms of diminishing member service or canceled memberships. Clubs need to hire individuals who have good interpersonal skills and can establish a rapport with members. As the manager, you must make sure that front-desk and on-floor trainers and instructors know members, greet them by name, and ask about their workouts. Although it is helpful to hire individuals knowledgeable about fitness, preference should be for qualified applicants with good interpersonal skills. Most managers realize that proper technique of exercise can easily be taught but "people" skills must be developed over time (Sudy, 1993).

Once an employee has been hired, the manager must focus on employment development and team building. To improve efficiency and enhance customer service, policies and programs must be implemented to encourage a positive "team" atmosphere. One way to accomplish this is by continually advocating the philosophy set forth in your mission statement. This statement should be incorporated into all aspects of your employees' daily operations, clearly visible where it will serve as a constant reminder to all employees of your club's focus and goals. Another important step in team building is to develop a sense of loyalty among employees in your club. Employees need to know that you will support them during difficult situations. This may mean standing behind an employee when encountering a difficult member. Finally, successful managers in the fitness business must try to make the work environment as enjoyable as possible without risking professionalism. Employees who are happy at work and who enjoy their jobs are productive, efficient, and oriented to customer service. In the club you must attempt to maintain a positive upbeat atmosphere (Sudy, 1993).

Attracting and Retaining Members

Members are the lifeblood of the club industry. Clubs are constantly in the business of attracting new members with various marketing, promotional, and sales techniques. With the large number of health and fitness clubs in the United States today, attracting new members may not be enough to keep membership rates at their peak. It is tremendously important for clubs to keep current members. According to IHRSA, approximately 38 percent of club members quit within their first year and average health club membership is 2.6 years for multipurpose clubs and 2.4 years for fitness-only clubs (IHRSA, 1994). Reducing membership dropout is an ongoing challenge for club managers.

Experts in the fitness industry maintain that the campaign to keep members should begin the day a person joins your club, and should continue for the duration of his or her membership. Most clubs focus on new members during the first four to six weeks of their membership but these individuals should be given a year's worth of guidance. In order to retain your members, you must first understand why members drop out. Typical reasons cited include: (1) They join to transform their bodies overnight and when it doesn't happen they quit; (2) They discover the club does not meet their expectations (equipment poorly maintained, long waits for certain equipment, or feeling like they just do not belong); and (3) They lose motivation.

You must realize that members do not just join a club, they join a lifestyle and you must create an enjoyable experience for them (Winters, 1994).

Several fundamental managerial strategies play a critical role in keeping members happy. The first strategy is to have quality programming. Programming is a way of marketing to the people who already have purchased memberships. It should be all inclusive and each program needs a specific marketing plan and good budget to be successful. You cannot just post a sign-up sheet and expect people to show up on their own. Another strategy entails using the personal touch by calling members regularly to see how they are doing or to ask why they have not been working out. A third strategy to retain club members is the development of a positive atmosphere. This can be done by running special events such as one-day nutritional seminars and socials like a holiday party. Club maintenance plays a critical role in creating an environment that attracts and keeps members. Locker rooms and shower areas have to be hospital-clean and equipment should not be in need of repair. You should also ask the maintenance staff what they are hearing in the locker rooms. A suggestion box at the front desk is an excellent way to find out about members' concerns and complaints. All problems should be addressed and resolved as quickly as possible.

Another important factor in building a positive atmosphere is selling T-Shirts, caps, and other items with your club's logo. The more people identify with your club, the more they are likely to stick with it (Winters, 1994). A key element in these management strategies is simply staying informed.

Club managers must also realize that the cost of recruiting a new member is six times greater than the cost of retaining one. It is not realistic to believe that you are going to retain all of your members, but if you can retain 5 percent to 10 percent of those who may otherwise drop out, then you have done a good job. Even if they cannot be retained forever, you can make the average membership last a little longer, which means more profit per member (Winters, 1994).

Besides retaining current members, managers are frequently charged with keeping membership numbers high through the development of new targets for marketing club memberships. The hottest markets today and probably for the future are people older than 40 and seniors. Research shows that by the year 2000 more than 35 million people in the United States will be 65 years or older (IHRSA, 1994). When targeting the 40+ market, it is important to note that some health clubs' marketing, advertising, and programming practices work better than others to attract and retain them. If you are trying to tap into this market, there are six questions to be answered:

1. Are your ads attracting older customers? Older models should be used and ads should include photos that reinforce older peoples' sense of vitality and independence. Credibility and safety are also very important, therefore ads should include information on the credentials of fitness directors and instructors.

2. Are your club's membership sales efforts appropriate for this market? High-pressure sales techniques do not work and flexible membership plans should be offered.

3. Will your club's culture make mature members comfortable? The culture of the club can make or break your efforts to draw this population. Older members do not want to be intimidated or feel invisible to the staff. There should be no slinky leotards and muscle shirts in ads or the club.

4. Can your club cater to the social needs of the members? Older members have more time on their hands and may spend it in the club and it is necessary for the club to accommodate their social needs.

5. How important is staff involvement? Staff should have special training in designing programs for deconditioned exercisers and working with seniors. Most groups that grant certification also offer training.

6. Do your fitness programs really help older members achieve desired results (Loyle, 1994)?

Liability for Fitness Facility Management

Managers in the club and fitness environment are faced with substantially greater safety demands than managers of any other sport facility. Therefore, a risk management plan is essential to controlling the cost of injuries in your club. Development of risk management plans includes identifying and analyzing risks, selecting appropriate techniques to reduce these risks, implementing the techniques, and evaluating the results. Areas that should be evaluated for danger include the facility, equipment, staff, and supervision of members (Jacobs, 1994).

Facility

The manager's first consideration in evaluating a facility is determining whether your facility is up to date with current codes and innovations. It is recommended that clubs provide a minimum of 100 square feet per participant, in order to provide a safe environment. With the competition for membership dollars, many clubs are overlooking the need to limit their membership accordingly. There should be ample space around equipment to ensure safe participation by members. Overcrowding simply amplifies problems.

Equipment

Quality should be the manager's most important factor in selecting and purchasing fitness equipment. You should also ensure that installation of all equipment is done by a competent professional, regular maintenance is scheduled for all equipment, and all work is documented. As mentioned, proper spacing of exercise equipment stations must be planned to allow users to move from one station to another without bumping into other members during their exercises. All electrical cords should be secured so members will not trip. In addition, cables should be checked regularly for breakage or fraying, and timing devices and temperature settings on the Jacuzzi, steam room, and saunas must be in proper working order and checked often. The final step is to ensure that all members are properly trained in the use of all equipment.

Staff

Staff training and development is an ongoing management responsibility. In today's club business, emphasis is being placed on instructor certification and up-to-date training in cardiopulmonary resuscitation (CPR) and first aid. Monthly staff meetings should be held to deal exclusively with the promotion of safety and to train staff to handle emergencies.

Maintaining confidentiality is another important requirement for all staff members. Members often provide personal information they expect to be held in confidence. The only law that specifi-

cally requires that certain information be kept confidential is the Americans with Disabilities Act, and it is limited to medical records and conditions. For managers of health clubs, it is always wise to insist on practices that maintain client confidentiality, decreasing the likelihood of litigation concerning privacy.

Supervision

Proper management can address the lack of adequate supervision that is a frequent claim in litigation against fitness clubs. The current standards indicate that fitness facility managers must provide "continuous" supervision of all fitness areas during operating hours. Proper supervision dictates an obligation to instruct members in proper and safe use of equipment and to stop misuse of equipment. The level of supervision depends on the risk of the activity. Financial considerations should never be a reason to deviate from acceptable standards of use and caution.

Computers in the Fitness Club

More than 70 percent of health/fitness clubs use microcomputers and club management software (Anderson, 1994). Club management software can increase efficiency if you select and use the programs according to your facility's needs. The right club software package combined with proper use can result in more satisfied members, increased sales, reduced collection efforts, lower staff cost, and a healthier bottom line. Several options exist for the club manager. You can hire external consultants to write custom software for your operation, which would be a good choice if you have specific needs and a large budget. Costs for custom systems start around $10,000 to $15,000. If your club has unusual features and programs, this may be the best choice. However, several very extensive commercial software programs are available for club management. Their software features include payroll, inventory control, locker management, membership data, reservations, membership identification, rentals, user management, and word processing. To ensure that the system does not have more features than are reasonably needed, you should develop a list of priorities that includes the features essential to your club (Anderson, 1994).

Software vendors can provide a list of facilities similar to yours, for which they have supplied club management systems Visiting these facilities allows you to see which software programs comparable clubs are using and how satisfied they are with the product. Facility managers can provide insights into the software's strengths and weaknesses, and also give hands-on training demonstrations. Your decision should not be based solely on initial set-up cost, but on customization, training, and lifetime cost of using software (hardware, support, upgrades). Vendor support is vital and while a few software vendors offer 24-hour live support, others provide limited hours of live support with extended coverage available by paging the support department. The key is to make sure your vendor provides the support coverage needed by your club. Criteria used to make a decision on what type of system suits your needs include quality of software, features, ease of use, lifetime costs, vendor stability, geographic location, and user support and training. You should prioritize your criteria and then make a decision based on a thorough analysis (Anderson, 1994).

Specialized Club Areas

Locker Rooms

Although equipment, courts, and pools frequently get more attention as glamorous attractions, the often forgotten locker room can impact the way members perceive various clubs. Health club managers depend greatly on the thoughts and feelings of current and prospective members regarding their facilities. In this regard, locker rooms in health/fitness clubs should be spacious with visual openness and safe traffic flow. The decor of locker rooms should be appropriate to the club including framed posters, plants, flowers, bookcases, lighting, colors, and background music. Soft colors in a warm spectrum of light are especially popular in locker rooms of the 1990s. An "open design" locker room can be patrolled easily, which helps prevent theft and vandalism.

Cleanliness and ease of maintenance are extremely important features for locker-room health and safety. Cleaning must be done daily and it should be a top priority for the entire staff. The ventilation system in locker rooms must be able to handle the moisture produced and attention must be given to the planning of separate wet and dry areas. Adequate air circulation and ventilation keeps areas dry and helps clothes, towels, and foot gear dry quickly.

Attending to members' need for privacy is another key concern of club managers. A trend today is the planning of "family locker areas" where mothers and sons or fathers and daughters can share a stall with private shower and dressing area. This can be facilitated by partitioning locker rooms or creating unisex changing rooms for families with small children. All of these strategies may not be feasible given budget constraints, type of club, and fees being charged. A manager of a health/fitness club must realize that one of the biggest mistakes is not paying enough attention to the locker room, and the key is to listen to members needs.

Pro Shops

According to an IHRSA poll, 81 percent of clubs surveyed indicated they had a pro shop and average annual revenue was reported to be $25,000. Therefore, the majority of health and fitness center managers are buying into the theory that pro shops can generate significant revenue. While this data is encouraging, managers must make a determined effort to emphasize the pro shop as part of daily operations. Today's pro shops have become increasingly sophisticated with wide product selection, innovative merchandising, and highly personal services. They offer items that department stores, discounters and mail-order shops do not carry. Regardless of your club's size, the pro shop can capitalize on the status associated with the health club business. The most successful clubs average $10,000 to $15,000 per month in merchandise and sportswear sales (IHRSA, 1994).

Your pro shop should also carry supplies for the activities programmed at the facility. If you want members to buy at your club rather than a local retailer, you have to show that you are serious about having the merchandise. If only limited merchandise is offered, the customer will not see you as a serious source, but if you have a good stock level, members will more likely come in and browse. Because people want to be associated with their clubs, service is the key to a successful pro shop. Personalizing service and maintaining competitive pricing will give you a big advantage over retailers (Lustigman, 1994).

The majority of pro shops (83 percent) are owned and operated by the fitness center, but some fitness centers decide to avoid financial risk and obligations by leasing the operations to a local retailer. If you believe that volume will not be big enough to justify the expense, another option may be kiosks. These carts are very similar to those found in malls and they can be leased or purchased. The carts can display a wide range of fitness apparel, products, and accessories in the club and they can be locked at night for security (Lustigman, 1994).

Salons

Health/fitness club members like to look as good as they feel, therefore a number of clubs are adding beauty salons to their facilities. Fewer than 12 percent of IHRSA clubs operate on-site salons (IHRSA, 1994; Monahan, 1994). Some clubs enter the beauty business because of the revenue and others enter just to increase member services. Before going into the salon business, there is a need for thorough research. Important considerations include determining necessary structural changes such as increasing the exhaust system to handle fumes and scents from equipment and beauty products. Equipment for the salon depends on services offered, which range from haircuts and coloring to full spa treatments (hair styling, facials, manicures) (Monahan, 1994).

Success of a salon depends on how well it is managed. Some clubs maintain management of the salon and hair stylists and other staff; others rent chairs to stylists who provide their own supplies and keep profits after paying monthly rent. The trend is to turn the whole operation over to a leaseholder which gives the salon a ready-made customer base and the club a whole new pool of potential members. With a comfortable space and good operator on board, most owners say that club-based salons carry little risk and can have a positive effect on membership (Monahan, 1994).

Nutrition Programs and Snack Bars

Nutrition is a key component in the overall fitness equation, and it has gradually moved into the health/fitness club environment. Many fitness centers offer computerized testing, dietary counseling, classes, and even concessions. Nutrition-based concessions have been marginally profitable and require a large amount of square footage (about 1000 sq. ft.). If your club has the space, nutritional concessions may round out the club's offerings to promote a healthy lifestyle. However, even if space is available for a nutrition concession, there remains the question of whether you could get more money in rent from doing something else with that space (IHRSA, 1994; Tiersten, 1989).

When studying the pros, cons, and feasibility of a nutritional concession, the considerations are similar to those for adding a salon or pro shop. You must first decide if it is going to be leased out or be managed by the club. The preferred method of health and fitness club managers is to lease the space to a vendor who would pay rent to the club.

ATHLETIC TRAINING AND SPORTS MEDICINE FACILITIES

The main focus of this section is the design of an athletic training facility or physical therapy/sports medicine clinic. A physical therapy clinic differs from an athletic training facility in that it does not include first aid and taping sections, and deals with fewer numbers of patients or athletes at one time.

Most athletic training facilities have been around for many years, but have failed to expand with the increase in the number of intercollegiate athletic teams, as well as the changes in functional rehabilitative techniques that require a great deal of space. Whether you are remodeling or building a facility, the following suggestions may be helpful.

Before planning the size and location of your training room or sports medicine center, you need to determine whom you are going to be treating.

Lounges and health bars are becoming very popular.

Will this facility serve both male and female athletes? Will nonathletic students and faculty be allowed to use the facility? What types of equipment are needed, and what types of treatment and rehabilitative services are to be provided? Once you have answered these questions and estimate of the number of athletes you will serve, you can begin working with your architect on the size of your athletic training or sports medicine facility.

Location and Space

An athletic training facility, centrally located to the athletic fields and gymnasiums, provides quick assistance to injured athletes. The facility should be accessible to both men's and women's locker rooms with separate and private entrances. The primary entrance from the outside or main building should be large enough to provide access to a wheelchair or gurney with two people assisting an injured athlete.

Athletic training facilities and sports medicine clinics associated with a health service may provide X rays, a pharmacy, and referrals to physicians. Facilities not connected with the health services on campus should have a prearranged protocol with an X ray, a pharmacy, and medical referrals through the (team) physician treating the patient.

Training Room and Staff Office

The size of the training or sports medicine facility depends on the space available and the budget. To estimate the square footage for an athletic training facility, Ray (1994) suggests the following formula:

$$\frac{\text{number of athletes at peak hour}}{20 \text{ per table per day}} \times 100 = \frac{\text{total square}}{\text{footage}}$$

It is suggested that an adequate facility has 1000 to 1200 square feet, but less than 1000 square feet is not realistic. For example, the University of Northern Colorado's Athletic Training Room has approximately 1100 square feet, which is considered an average size. Large universities and college training facilities can be up to 10,000 square feet (Dethlefs, 1993).

The preferred design of the training room varies with each trainer but a consensus seems to be for an L-shape (see Figure 11–1) with a centrally located office to allow for supervision of the taping, hydrotherapy, and treatment/rehabilitation areas (Dethlefs, 1993).

The office should have windows or glass to allow monitoring activities or private conversations. Shades on the office windows can give the privacy of an examination room if a separate room is not available. The office should be off limits to athletes. Personal athletic files, medication, insurance information, and educational material kept in the office should not be accessible to athletes. Medications should be kept in a locked medicine cabinet in the office accessible only to the head trainer or team physicians.

Telephones should be located in the office and in the larger training rooms, and one phone may be placed in the rehabilitation and treatment area for staff use only. Most sports medicine clinics have a few offices each with a clear view of the rehabilitation room, and most provide a phone in the room for patients to use.

Taping and First Aid Area

The taping area is one of the busiest places in the training room. It is used not only for taping but also for the administration of first aid for minor injuries such as lacerations, abrasions, and blisters. Your first aid area should consist of a sink with an eye wash and soap dispenser on the wall. Cabinets and drawers placed below and above the countertop provide ample storage space and easy access to bandages, gauze, disposable latex gloves, wraps, and topical ointments.

Taping tables should be near or parallel to the first aid counter so the trainer can give quick first aid treatment without having to walk to a different area. A space or waiting area behind the tables allows athletes to enter and exit without interfering with the trainer. Some taping tables have an extended counter that allows athletes to be taped from either side. This counter should be approximately 36 inches high for the trainer's comfort. Like the first aid counter, taping tables should have a surface such as vinyl or formica that can be cleaned easily.

Small quantities of taping supplies can be stored underneath the taping table. Your bulk supply of tape should be stored in a separate cool, dry area. A large closet to hold padding and bracing material should be near the taping area. Thus, you

Figure 11–1 An L-shaped athletic training center

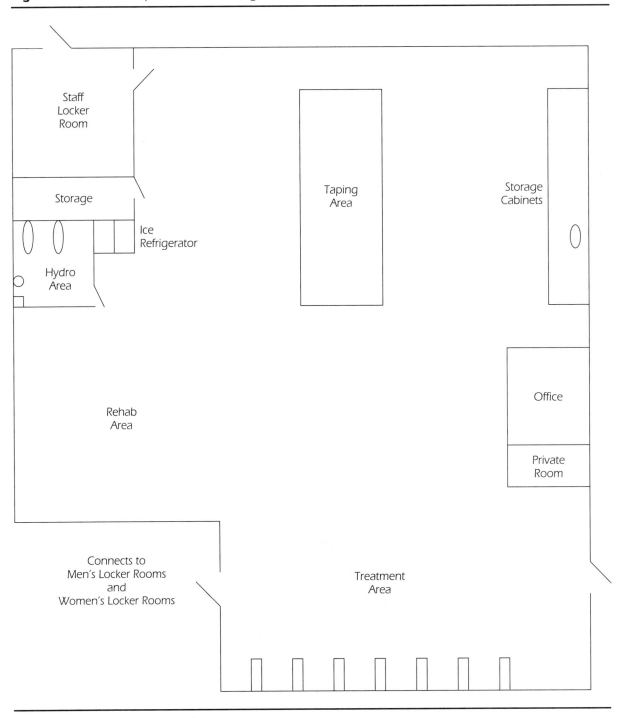

have easy access to a knee brace or protective padding for an injury, but most of the time such materials are stored out of the way.

Frequently used floor surfaces are vinyl and carpet, however they can be stained easily by adherents or ointments. Rubber carpet runners provide some protection, are easily cleaned, and can be replaced when worn out (Ray, 1994).

Hydrotherapy Area

The size of the hydrotherapy area varies according to the number of whirlpools, ice baths, and extremity tanks, and, in some facilities, swim tanks or swimming pools. An ice machine and freezer may also be in this area. A surrounding wall or a separate room to enclose the hydrotherapy area will control the noise and splashing water.

The surface of the floor should be a nonslip material and the floor should slope slightly toward the drain to prevent standing water (Ray, 1994). It is essential to have a proper plumbing system with hot and cold running water as well as adequate drainage, and the ability to expand.

Extra caution should be taken in the hydrotherapy area due to the risk of electrical shock. This area should be clearly visible from the staff office to allow supervision of athletes or patients entering a hydrotherapy tank. The controls for the whirlpools and extremity tanks should not be accessible from the water. On/off controls should be located on the wall away from tanks or outside the hydrotherapy area.

An adequate number of outlets should be placed throughout the area and allow connection of one whirlpool per outlet. Outlets should be placed 4 to 5 feet above the floor, with spring covers, and contain ground-fault interrupters that would shut off the electricity with an electrical surge of 5 miliamps or more (Dethlefs, 1993). The ground-fault interrupter should be checked and tested on a regular basis and updated every year. These inspections should be documented and kept as a part of the facility's risk management plan.

Rehabilitation and Treatment Area

The main area in the training room or sports medicine clinic is the rehabilitation and treatment area, which should be visible from the staff office. This area should not be congested and should provide a large open space for treatments and the use of modalities such as muscle stimulators, ultrasound, and a hydroculator. Isokinetic testing equipment requires a large space and is often located in a different room. Extremity weights and a variety of functional exercise equipment such as sport cords,

Hydrotherapy area

Treatment and functional rehabilitation area

fitter, and physio balls may also be located in this area for therapeutic exercise.

Rehabilitation tables or plinths should be approximately 30 inches apart to allow for a modality, a three-shelved cart, and space for athletes and trainers to move between them. The treatment tables should be adjustable to heights comfortable for trainers, clinicians, and elevation of an extremity. The number of treatment tables depends on the number of athletes you treat (see prior formula).

Outlets should be placed between tables and located 4 to 5 feet above the floor to keep cords off the floor. These outlets should also contain ground-fault interrupters.

If your exercise area is combined with your treatment area, all weights, bikes, and functional therapeutic exercise equipment should be located on one side of the room away from the modality and treatment tables. Many training facilities have separate areas or rooms for large exercise equipment and weights, which allows for more space with less supervision in the treatment area.

The rehabilitation area should be carpeted to allow for good traction when performing functional exercises. The area should be easily cleaned and also provide a nice atmosphere. The walls in the rehabilitation and treatment area, as well as the entire facility, should be of material in which hooks or bolts can be installed for cabinets or equipment.

Many athletic training facilities and clinics have a large walk-in closet in this area for storage. Storage space under the treatment tables or in the cabinets above the tables does not take up additional space.

Lighting

Good lighting is necessary in your athletic training facility or sports medicine clinic. Nonglaring lights should be set high in the ceiling so they do not interfere with tall athletes or athletes who may need to stand on the tables. Illumination should be 30 foot candles, 4 feet above the floor (Arnheim and Prentice, 1993). Windows or skylights are an excellent source of light, and add to a pleasant atmosphere. It is important that a nonglaring fixture be used for the patient's comfort while he or she is lying on the table.

Universal Precautions

Blood and bodily fluids are a concern for the physical therapist and more so for the athletic trainer. Precautions should be taken to protect against bloodborne pathogens. Latex gloves should be readily available throughout the training room and sports medicine clinic, and especially at the first aid counter where most bleeding or oozing wounds are treated. In a physical therapy clinic, debridement (removal of dead skin) and treatment of open wounds requires clinicians to wear latex gloves, masks, and gowns for their protection.

Biohazard containers must be placed in the facility. These containers are easily recognizable by their bright red or orange color and must be carefully marked as biohazard containers. All soiled materials such as gloves, gauze, and bandages must be discarded into these containers. Biohazard containers should be accessible and away from high-traffic patterns, but close to the treatment area.

FITNESS LABORATORIES

The fitness laboratory, also called the human performance laboratory or exercise physiology laboratory, is an essential component of a health/fitness facility at a college or university. Both educational and research opportunities are available for university students and staff and for local community members. Individuals or groups can use the fitness laboratory and learn first-hand to understand the "hows, whats, and whys" of physical activity.

Students and staff from such disciplines as exercise science, health promotion, nursing, nutrition, physical education, physical therapy, and others can enhance their classroom learning through hands-on experience. Conducting both field and technical fitness assessments for cardiorespiratory endurance, flexibility, muscular strength, muscular endurance, and body composition can be a daily occurrence for students working in a fitness lab. In addition to fitness assessments, analysis of blood lipids, measurement of pulmonary function and blood pressure, and nutritional assessments can be completed in the fitness laboratory.

The fitness laboratory also provides an opportunity to link members of the campus and members of the community. Both can be scheduled to use the fitness laboratory to accomplish numerous goals and objectives related to health and fitness. In addition, participants in an employee wellness program could benefit from a fitness laboratory. A student of nutrition, for example, could gain experience consulting a participant in cardiac rehabilitation about results of a cholesterol count.

A well-equipped fitness laboratory in a dependable facility can be the vehicle for participants to understand exercise physiology in a real-life way. The size of the fitness laboratory can range from one room with minimal equipment to a spacious complex filled with state-of-the-art equipment, but regardless of the size or sophistication of the equipment, personnel is the key.

Personnel

The success of a fitness laboratory depends on the professional personnel working there. They must be knowledgeable, conscientious, and concerned about each and every person who comes to the laboratory for testing or consultation. The fitness laboratory staff must be trained in proper use of the equipment and must demonstrate reliability and consistency with their assessments. Also, the staff must encompass the ability to train new students who are preparing to work in the fitness laboratory. Excellent communication skills are also crucial because sensitivity to an individual's needs can make all the difference to his or her success. Testing and recording results requires staff who are reliable and exhibit the perseverance to write necessary reports.

The minimum requirement for working in a fitness laboratory is a degree from an accredited four-year college or university in health or a fitness-related field such as exercise science, exercise physiology, health promotion, physical education, and exercise technology. A degree in a medical field such as physical therapy and nursing is also appropriate. The preferred requirement is an advanced degree at the masters or doctorate level, especially for the director of the fitness laboratory. In addition, all personnel administering fitness tests must be certified in cardiopulmonary resuscitation.

It is also important for personnel to carefully refer to *Guidelines for Exercise Testing and Prescription* by American College of Sports Medicine (ACSM, 1991). A physician is required for some graded exercise tests. A cardiologist, for example, must oversee the "maximum stress test." Special training is also required for medical tests such as blood screens.

Professional certification from a nationally recognized organization such as the American College of Sports Medicine (ACSM) is strongly suggested. Hiring a program director, health fitness director, health fitness instructor, and exercise specialist as described by the ACSM is highly recommended.

Finally, every member of a fitness laboratory staff should be prepared:

- to assess and prescribe an exercise program that enhances physical fitness by adhering to the recommendations of ACSM.
- to prescribe a personalized exercise program taking into account each participant's demographic factors, blood lipid profile, medical history, motivational level, physical condition, physical fitness evaluation, lifestyle, interests, and readiness to change.
- to prescribe the appropriate exercise keeping in mind mode, intensity, frequency, duration, and rate of progression.
- to have a basic understanding of the five components of wellness: emotional, social, intellectual, spiritual, and physical (including nutrition).

Facility and Environment

A safe environment with accessibility to everyone is the best possible scenario for a fitness laboratory. Although ramps for wheelchairs are in place at many facilities, everyone, regardless of individual challenge, should have the same opportunity to participate in the various assessments. Many assessments have been effectively modified to accommodate different physical challenges. For example, an arm ergometer can be used to test a participant's cardio-respiratory endurance if the participant is unable to use a treadmill or cycle ergometer; a hoist can be used to lower someone into the hydrostatic tank to assess body composition if the participant is unable to walk; and appropriate written information or an interpreter can be provided for the client if he or she is unable to hear or does not understand English.

The ACSM's book, *Health/Fitness Facility Standards and Guidelines* (1992), contains thorough information on environmental and safety guidelines for a laboratory in terms of temperature, humidity, air circulation, light levels, and space allocations. In short, ACSM recommends 120 to 180 square feet for fitness testing with good air circulation (6 to 8 exchanges per hour), appropriate temperature (68° to 72° Fahrenheit), and a humidity reading of more than 60 percent. Also, sterilization policies are imperative for the fitness laboratory.

These kinds of regulations must be addressed to meet the standards set forth by the Occupational Safety and Health Administration (OSHA), the Federal Drug Administration (FDA), and the Environmental Protection Agency (EPA). Additional standards must be met in laboratories dealing with hazardous secretions and nonflammable gas such as helium.

Equipment and Safety

Equipment in a fitness laboratory must be reliable and in good working order. The correct test protocol must be selected for the specific population. Experienced staff must be aware of various testing protocols for a variety of populations. Only then can participants in the fitness laboratory get the results they deserve and an insurance of their safety. (See Appendix C-1 for a thorough list of equipment needs.)

Appropriate screening of personnel is important to guarantee both safety and security. All government regulations must be followed diligently. Confidentiality of all records is crucial and numerous forms must be completed before any participant should be tested in the fitness laboratory. Forms that must be completed and on file include informed consent, medical history questionnaire, medical clearance, lifestyle evaluation, and if needed an accident/injury form. (See Appendices C-2 to C-4 for samples.) Additional information such as Health Risk Appraisals can also be helpful.

Operation protocol, procedure manuals, emergency procedures, and testing instructions for all equipment must be readily available to staff. The staff must be thoroughly familiar with cleaning and maintenance of all equipment and machinery and a strict schedule must be followed. The *Guidelines for Exercise Testing and Prescription* (ACSM, 1991) must also be followed. Job descriptions and evaluation forms should also be available and administrators should be well trained in their effective and responsible use. Procedures for emergencies must be thoroughly understood by the entire staff and frequent practice drills are beneficial.

SUMMARY

Managing a fitness club has special challenges and rewards. The tasks of marketing and customer service are always foremost in the manager's mind. Successfully operating the club depends on the provision and management of club programs, facilities, equipment, and staff.

When designing or renovating an athletic training facility or sports medicine clinic, safety and traffic patterns need careful consideration. The athletic trainer or clinic director should work closely with the architect on the specific design and size of each area. It is also important to consider possible expansions. Rehabilitation of athletic or work-related injuries is constantly expanding and improving, as should treatment facilities.

Organization is the key to a well-designed fitness facility with smooth operations. To ensure the efficient flow of people in a fitness laboratory, scheduling is critical. Policies and procedures must be followed and evaluations should be ongoing in order to provide a positive atmosphere for learning, for research, and for growth. Proper maintenance and upkeep of all equipment is also extremely important. Successful programming of the fitness laboratory provides a healthful environment. A well-trained, cooperative staff, who keep abreast of the latest information pertaining to exercise physiology and health promotion provides an environment of continuous improvement.

QUESTIONS

1. What major strategies do managers use to satisfy clients of a health club or fitness center?

2. What are the dangers and areas of increased liability associated with management of a fitness facility?

3. What are the critical elements to include in an athletic training facility?

4. What requirements are necessary for a person to work in a fitness laboratory?

5. Which agencies determine the standards for health and fitness laboratories?

6. What are the primary services provided by an athletic training or sports medicine facility?

7. Describe the precautions that must be taken when working in an athletic training or sports medicine facility.

8. What types of fitness assessments can be conducted in fitness laboratories?

9. Explain the difference between the *minimum* requirement and the *preferred* requirement for working in a fitness laboratory.

ACTIVITIES

1. Shelly Byrd is an athletic trainer for the Jordess Fitness Center. She must set policies to help manage the center. Determine the types of policies needed and develop a sample of one type of policy.

2. You have been hired as a consultant to assist in designing a fitness laboratory. Define your organization and draw a fitness laboratory that meets the needs of your organization.

3. Visit a local health club and conduct a risk management survey. Discuss the changes that are needed.

SUGGESTED READINGS

Adams, G. M. (1994). *Exercise physiology laboratory manual* (2nd ed.). Dubuque, Iowa: W.C. Brown and Benchmark.

American Association of Cardiovascular and Pulmonary Rehabilitation. (1995). *Guidelines for cardiac rehabilitation programs* (2nd ed.). Champaign, Ill: Human Kinetics.

Coast, J. R., Crouse, S. F., and Jessup, G. (1995). *Exercise physiology videolabs*. Dubuque, Iowa: W.C. Brown and Benchmark.

Heyward, V. H., and Stolarczyk, L. M. (1996). *Applied body composition assessment*. Champaign, Ill: Human Kinetics.

MacDougall, J. D., Wenger, H. A., and Green, H. J. (1991). *Physiological testing of the high-performance athlete* (2nd ed.). Champaign, Ill: Human Kinetics.

Rowland, T. W. (1993). *Pediatric laboratory exercise testing clinical guidelines*. Champaign, Ill: Human Kinetics.

REFERENCES

American College of Sports Medicine. (1991). *Guidelines for exercise testing and prescription*, (5th ed.). Philadelphia: Williams and Wilkins.

American College of Sports Medicine. (1993). *Resource manual for guidelines for exercise testing and prescription*, (2nd ed.). Philadelphia: Lea and Febiger.

American College of Sports Medicine. (1992). *Health/fitness facility standards and guidelines*, Champaign, Ill: Human Kinetics.

Anderson, T. (1994). Integrated club management software. *Club Industry*, 10(11):24–25.

Arnheim, D. D., and Prentice, W. E. (1993). *Principles of athletic training*, (8th ed.) Chicago: Brown and Benchmark.

Dethlefs, D. (1993, December). Facility planning: Training basics, *Athletic Business*.

Fahey, T. D. (1986). *Athletic training principals and practice*. Palo Alto, Cal: Mayfield.

Faust, G., and Caro, R. (1993). Managing clubs in the mid-90s. *Fitness Management*, 9(3):33–38.

Forseth, E. A. (1986, spring). Consideration in planning small college athletic training facilities. *Athletic Training*, pp. 22–26.

Gandolfo, C. (1993). Industry change? *Fitness Management*, 9(3):40–42.

Hafen, B. Q., and Hoeger, W. W. K. (1994). *Wellness: Guidelines for a healthy lifestyle*. Englewood, Colo: Morton.

Heyward, V. H. (1991). *Advanced fitness assessment and exercise prescription*, (2nd ed.). Champaign, Ill: Human Kinetics.

IHRSA. (1994). *Profiles of success*. Boston: International Health, Racquet and Sportclub Association.

Jacobs, P. (1994). Brace yourself. *Club Industry*, 10(1): 17–22.

Lohman, T. G. (1992). *Advances in body composition assessment* (monograph no. 3). Champaign, Ill: Human Kinetics.

Lohman, T. G., Roche, A. F., Martorell, R. (1988). *Anthropometric standardization reference manual*. Champaign, Ill: Human Kinetics.

Loyle, D. (1994). Taking aim at the 40-plus market. *Club Industry*, 10(11):17–21.

Lustigman, A. (1994). Sweat shops. *Club Industry*, (1): 24–30.

McArdle, W. D., Katch, F. I., Katch, V. L. (1994). *Essentials of exercise physiology*. Philadelphia: Lea and Febiger.

Michlovitz, S. L. (1990). *Thermal agents in rehabilitation*, (2nd ed.). Philadelphia: F. A. Davis.

Monahan, J. (1994). Looking good. *Club Industry*, 10(4): 14–17.

Porter, M. M., Porter, J. W. (1981, winter). Electrical safety in the training room. *Athletic Training*, pp. 263–264.

Powell, J. W. (1983, June). Safety in the athletic training room. *Journal of Physical Education, Recreation and Dance*, pp. 50–55.

Ray, R. (1994). *Management strategies in athletic training*. Champaign, Ill: Human Kinetics.

Sol, N., and Foster, C. (Eds.) (1992). *ACSM's health fitness facility standards and guidelines*. Champaign, Ill: Human Kinetics.

Sudy, M. (1993). Cutting your risk in hiring. *Fitness Management*, 9(11):40–42.

Tiersten, S. (1989). Should you offer nutrition programs? *Fitness Management*, 5(2):25–30.

Winters, C. (1994). The art of keeping members. *Club Industry*, 10(2):18–23.

12

Aquatic Facilities

Alison Osinski

The manager responsible for the day-to-day operation and upkeep of an aquatic facility should be knowledgeable in all areas of pool management and maintenance. Introductory training and certification courses in pool chemistry, maintenance, and operation are offered regularly throughout the United States by several nationally recognized agencies including the National Swimming Pool Foundation, the National Recreation and Park Association, Aquatic Associates, the YMCA of the USA, and the National Spa and Pool Institute. Many states require by code that pool managers be certified or licensed in order to legally operate a pool within the boundaries of the state.

DAY-TO-DAY OPERATIONS

Bathing Codes

All of the U.S. states, except Mississippi and Kansas, have compiled "bathing codes" that comprise health and safety, administrative, building, general industry safety orders, and education codes pertaining to pools. County and municipal bathing codes have also been enacted in some areas. Bathing codes are distributed free, or available at a nominal charge, to pool owners, builders, operators, and technicians from state and county boards of health. Many states also adopt by reference other building, plumbing, and electrical codes, and recommended industry guidelines. Regulations may govern things such as application and permit requirements, equipment specifications, acceptable water quality parameters, lifeguard qualifications and supervision requirements, chemical storage, handling and dispensing methods, signage requirements, and record-keeping procedures.

Some states' codes are more comprehensive than others, and more up-to-date with trends and common and acceptable practices of the aquatic industry. Codes are not uniform across the states or even within a single state. When conflicts arise, the strictest code should be followed.

In most states, violations of a bathing code are misdemeanors, punishable by fines. Most bathing codes give state and local health officials the authority to enforce standards of design and operation at public, semipublic, and special-use pools, and to close down an aquatic facility if it poses a threat to the public health.

Pool Equipment

The aquatic facility's manager should be familiar with all the components, equipment, and materials of the pool. He or she should know the correct sizing and installation of the equipment, as well as the daily, seasonal, and preventive maintenance required to keep the hundreds of pieces of equipment in a typical pool operating properly for the life expectancy of the equipment. Whether the piece of equipment is an inexpensive effluent pressure gauge or a sophisticated and expensive accouterment such as a moveable pool floor, the aquatic facility's manager should know its proper operation.

Chemicals

Pool managers should thoroughly understand chemical adjustments and the mechanical operation of the equipment that makes the water physically, bacteriologically, and chemically safe for human immersion. The manager should have a suitable grasp of the process of water circulation, basic hydraulics, filtration, back washing and filter cleaning, wastewater discharge, vacuuming, and the use of specialty chemicals such as clarifiers, sequestering and chelating agents, enzymes, defoamers, and algaecides.

It is essential to be familiar with sanitizers and oxidizers, including chlorine, bromine, and non-halogen products, as well as ozone generators and alternative sanitizing technologies, chlorine stabilizers, superchlorination, and the use of nonchlorine oxidizers. The aquatic facility manager should comprehend the importance of water balance or mineral-saturation control through adjustment of pH, total alkalinity, calcium hardness, total dissolved solids, and water temperature.

The pH level is determined by the concentration of hydrogen ions in a specific volume of water. The result is a measure of the acidity or alka-

Indiana University Natatorium represents a modern aquatic facility. (Courtesy of architects Browning Day Mullins Dierdorf, Indianapolis, Indiana)

linity of the water. In most aquatic facilities, the pH range (typically 7.2–8.0) is specified by code. Keeping the pool water within ideal pH ranges increases bathers' comfort, and prevents damage to the pool and related equipment.

Total alkalinity is a measure of the ability of water to resist changes in pH. Alkaline minerals in the water occur primarily in bicarbonate form in swimming pools but also as sodium, calcium, magnesium and potassium carbonates, and hydroxides. The acceptable range is 80 to 150 ppm with an ideal range of 100 to 120 ppm. Low total alkalinity causes an inability to maintain a good pH level and can contribute to corrosion of pipes and staining of pool walls. High total alkalinity will cause overstabilization of water pH and high acid demands, and may result in formation of bicarbonate scale or a cloudy white precipitate.

All products dissolved in the water, including chemicals, bathers' waste products, pollution, and windborne debris contribute to the buildup of total dissolved solids (TDS). As TDS increases, sanitizer effectiveness as measured by oxidation reduction potential (ORP) is reduced, algae growth increases, the water becomes cloudy, and scaling increases. In addition, natural corrosion and staining increase. When TDS exceeds 1500 ppm, drain and refill the pool.

Water Temperature

Appropriate water temperatures vary depending on several factors. These factors include (1) region of the country, (2) primary use, (3) primary programming, and (4) age of participants. Typical temperatures for aquatic facilities are as follows:

- 104°F in spas (maximum temperature),
- 86° to 94°F in therapy pools, 83° to 86°F in multipurpose pools, and
- 78° to 82°F in competitive pools.

Pool operators should also note that calcium is less soluble in warm water than in cold water.

HVAC Systems

A basic understanding of heating, ventilating, and air conditioning (HVAC) systems (Figure 12–1) and pool heaters, and their required performance standards is critical. Pool managers must ensure that the ambient air quality is not harmful to the health

of either the staff or bathers who spend an extended amount of time in the natatorium.

Air Quality

The air quality in a natatorium is typically assessed by measuring several factors including temperature, humidity, noise, lighting, and level of odor and contaminants. The ambient air temperature should be comfortable and be maintained at two to seven degrees higher than water temperature. Low relative humidity is recommended. In the summer humidity levels of 50 percent to 60 percent are standard. In the winter, or when outside temperatures dip below 45°F, a level of 35 percent to 50 percent is best.

Poor air quality in the natatorium may cause *sick building syndrome*, a situation in which occupants display symptoms of illness that last two or more weeks and subside or disappear when the person leaves the facility for a period of time. Symptoms most often reported by occupants include drowsiness, headaches, irritability, chills, forgetfulness, and reduced productivity. Many people have also reported an increase in allergic responses, hypersensitive diseases, viral and bacterial infections. While the exact cause of sick building syndrome is not known, authorities often cite airborne pollutants and inadequate ventilation. Carcinogenic trihalomethanes (THM) exposure and chloroform inhalation have also been identified in some cases. Other contributors are a poor air flow in the natatorium, inadequate oxidation of organic contaminants, endotoxin inhalation, and lack of preventive maintenance and corrective service or repair on HVAC units.

Heat Loss

Pool managers should be familiar with energy-efficient and cost-saving methods of pool operation. Heat loss is a significant problem in pool operations (Figure 12–2). Radiation (heat lost to the surrounding cold still air) and evaporation (heat lost to water dissipation) are primary factors. Conduction (heat lost through contact with a cold object) occurs primarily through pool walls. Convection also causes heat loss by moving air or water. Other factors affecting heat loss include the temperature difference between air and water, the pool surface area, the relative humidity, air

Figure 12–1 HVAC systems (Courtesy of Aquatic Consulting Services)

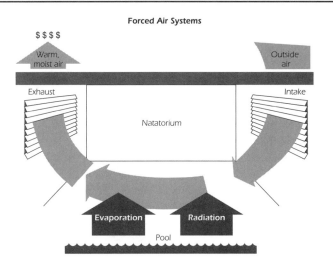

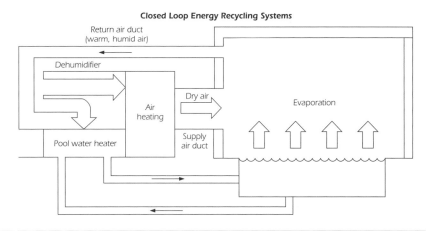

velocity, and the geographic location of the facility.

Managerial concerns about heat loss should be addressed through a comprehensive energy management plan. Use of pool covers is one of the most effective ways to reduce pool heating costs. Covering the pool can reduce heating costs from 50 to 70 percent. The use of pool covers can also prevent dirt and debris from entering the pool, reduce maintenance time and costs, decrease chemical consumption, reduce need to ventilate indoor pools and pretreat outside air, and slow rusting and deterioration of structural components. Additional procedures to manage energy include establishing specific energy-reduction goals, conducting peri-

odic energy audits, and training pool personnel in effective energy management techniques.

Safe Pool Management

The aquatic facility's manager should fully understand the proper procedures to safely handle, store, transport and dispense chemicals into the pool, and make sure that all employees of the facility who may come into contact with hazardous chemicals are trained in use of personal protective gear, chemical containment, and clean-up procedures for spills, evacuations, and chemical emergency and first aid procedures (see Table 12–1).

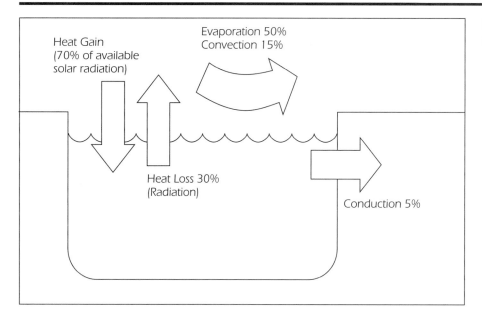

Figure 12–2
Causes of heat loss

To analyze and maintain the quality of water in the pool and air in the natatorium, the manager should be capable of using various instruments such as color comparritor, titration, or turbidometric test kits and reagents; dip-and-read strips, electronic test instruments, light meters, thermometers and hygrometers, and volumetric pumps. He or she should be able to read flowmeters, pH/ORP controllers, and pressure and vacuum gauges and then determine the necessary steps to keep the equipment in proper operating order. He or she should know how to prevent common water problems like algae, discoloration, mineral staining, foaming, and irritating odors, or water conditions that lead to skin rashes, eye irritation, or bather's discomfort.

Pool Problems

The manager should know how to identify and solve a water or air problem if it does take place. To identify a pool problem, managers should initially test and analyze the air and water. Be sure to check pressure gauges and flowmeters and eliminate the possibilities one by one. Next, identify and take steps to minimize or correct the problem. In formulating a chemical safety management program managers should develop standard operating procedures, review Material Safety Data Sheets (MSDS) and properly label all hazardous materials. Employee training and retraining programs should also be established. Be sure to develop an emer-

Table 12–1 *Safe management of chemicals*

- You can prevent accidents and releases of hazardous materials into the environment.
- Make a complete inventory of hazardous materials (quantity, where, how stored).
- Identify hazards.
- Determine what can go wrong by using the "What if...?" hazard analysis method.
- Assess the likelihood of accidents.
- Evaluate potential consequences of accidents.
- Establish a preventive maintenance program.
- Clean up chemical spills immediately.
- Notify your supervisor of all chemical spills.
- Wear appropriate protective gear when handling chemicals and cleaning up spills.
- Put spilled chemicals in isolated overpacks; do not put them back into their original containers.
- Label chemical salvage drums.
- Dispose of chemicals in an approved manner.
- Don't throw spilled chemicals into a dumpster.
- Call fire department or hazardous materials team for spills over 100 pounds.

gency response plan, practice the procedures, and document and investigate all accidents. The manager should know ideal chemical levels, be able to read and comprehend a daily chemical log, and know whether proper chemical adjustments are being made.

Measurements and Calculations

The aquatic facility's manager should be capable of taking measurements and performing calculations required of the job. Such practical applications might include determining breakpoint, bather capacity, volume, turnover and flowrate, amount of water loss, velocity of water moving through the circulation pipes, total dynamic head, and adequate filter size (see Table 12–2). Although requirements for turnover time vary by state, the general recommendations are as follows:

- 30 minutes in spas
- 60 minutes in wading pools
- 2 hours in flumes, splash pools, heavily used swim school pools, warm-water therapy pools
- 6 to 8 hours in swimming pools

LAWS AND REGULATIONS

All aquatic facility managers should be familiar with applicable state, federal, and local health and safety, building, hazardous materials, electrical, and fire codes that apply to pool design or operation and be aware of industry guidelines regarding common and acceptable standards in the aquatic industry. The following are some of the laws and regulations with which the facility manager should be familiar:

- State and local bathing codes (Health and Safety Code, Administrative Code, General Industry Safety Orders, State Building Code, Education Code, etc.)
- National Sanitation Foundation, Standard 50
- National Electrical Code, Article 680: Swimming Pools, Fountains, and Similar Installations
- OSHA 29 CFR 1910.1200: Hazard Communication Standard
- U.S. EPA SARA Title III: The Emergency Planning and Community Right-to-Know Act
- Uniform Fire Code, Article 80: Hazardous Materials

- U.S. EPA: Pesticide Worker Safety Regulations
- U.S. EPA Clean Water Act
- OSHA 29 CFR 1910.1030: Occupational Exposure to Bloodborne Pathogens
- PL 101-336: The Americans with Disabilities Act
- OSHA CFR 1910.146: Confined Spaces Regulation
- American Public Health Association: "Public Swimming Pools: Recommended Regulations for Design and Construction, Operation and Maintenance"
- Centers for Disease Control: "Suggested Health and Safety Guidelines for . . ."
- IAPMO Uniform Swimming Pool, Spa, and Hot Tub Code
- National Spa and Pool Institute (NSPI) Standards 1 through 7
- World Waterpark Association: "Considerations for Operating Safety"
- National Swimming Pool Foundation (NSPF): "Design Compendium"

The federal government passed the Americans with Disabilities Act (ADA) to ensure that people with disabilities have access to all facilities. Compliance with the law requires that all individuals have access to the facility (be able to get into the natatorium), have access to the goods and services provided in the facility (be able to get into and out of the swimming pool), and have access to auxillary facilities (be able to use the locker rooms). Pool modification for ADA compliance might include wet ramps, dry ramps, zero-depth entry, locker-room amenities, and wider decks.

Table 12–2 The relationship of flow rate and the turnover time of water

---

Flow Rate

    360,000 *gallons of water*
÷   360 *minutes required for turnover*
=   1,000 *gallons per minute (gpm)*

Turnover Time

    360,000 *gallons of water*
÷   1,000 *gpm (flow rate)*
=   360 *minutes or 6 hours*

RISK MANAGEMENT

Reports and Checklists

Successful pool management also includes development of maintenance schedules, logs, checklists, and report forms, along with inspecting and evaluating facilities, equipment, programs, policies and practices. An extensive set of checklists is provided in Appendix B. These documents can be of great value in the assessment of risks inherent in a program or facility, and can help eliminate or minimize risks. For example, by posting meaningful signage, installing alarm systems and effective barriers, purchasing quality rescue equipment, providing adequate illumination, complying with hazardous materials regulations, instigating safe electrical practices around the pool, and informing patrons of the hazards and health risks associated with warm water immersion, the pool manager can promote safety awareness and minimize the frequency and severity of participants' injuries. Collectively, these efforts lessen the probability of lawsuits as a result of negligence.

Some of the common reasons for aquatic lawsuits include injuries due to hidden hazards, inadequate supervision, inadequate facility maintenance, and inadequate, inaccessible, or improperly maintained rescue equipment, and signage that does not provide meaningful warning. Injuries inflicted by other patrons, failure to prohibit swimming under dangerous conditions, and product liability are also major concerns. As stated, the unsafe handling, storage, or dispensing of chemicals also poses a substantial risk. With regard to personnel, the lack of qualifications, certification, attentiveness, and training have also led to legal problems.

Certification Courses

Once the risk management tasks have been identified and the information has been collected, it can be used to determine policy or programming changes, improvements in the way the facility is operated, and equipment or facility maintenance or replacement. It is critically important for aquatics managers to keep current in this constantly changing field by attending professional meetings and conferences, and by reading trade publications and professional aquatic journals. Many states provide or require courses to certify pool operators. Certification courses cover not only operation and procedures, but provide information on new trends in the industry.

Trends

Some of the more recent pool designs include a trend away from single, multipurpose pools. Multiple pool facilities, pools built as part of community centers, and special-use pools designed for fitness, competition, therapy, diving, and recreational swimming are the most popular. Leisure pools and shallower pools are also influencing aquatic construction. Many pools include features involving moving water and create a pleasing environment with lighting, plants, and graphics. Accessibility is always a concern and awareness has been heightened by ADA laws. The use of automation and computer-assisted management has dramatically increased in recent years.

Another general trend is the increase in community leisure pools. Community leisure facilities are being designed for both swimming and nonswimming activities. Although the majority of Americans cannot swim, most people enjoy being in and around the water. Good pool design and innovative programming allows even nonswimmers to participate in and enjoy some aquatic activities. Therefore, leisure pools are replacing the traditional rectangular or L-shaped community pools because traditional pools are less likely than leisure pools to generate revenue in excess of expenditures.

SUMMARY

A pool manager's responsibilities are many and varied. For an aquatic facility to operate effectively, the pool manager must schedule the facility for maximum use, properly staff the facility to provide adequate supervision, prevent financial losses by generating revenue in excess of expenditures, and avoid overexerting the staff or straining pool systems when demands are heavy.

The facility's manager is responsible for the total operation and management of his or her pool. Staff screening, selection, training, scheduling, auditing, and evaluating are all part of managing a pool. The manager is responsible for developing clearly defined job responsibilities, recruiting, hiring and firing employees, conducting pre-employment orientation and regularly scheduled in-service training. Managers must also develop pool supervision guidelines and rotation schedules, plan for emergencies, and implement emergency procedures. In the area of personnel management, evaluations of job performance and formal auditing procedures are key factors in the successful operation of the pool. Managers must develop, review, and update rules and enforcement procedures such as lifeguard or staff manuals, operating manuals and procedures, maintenance schedules, chemical safety procedures, safety literature and posters, inventory forms, and record-keeping procedures. In conclusion, aquatic facility management is both challenging and rewarding.

QUESTIONS

1. What types of codes pertain to pool management?
2. What are the risks associated with managing an aquatics facility?
3. How do you achieve and maintain water balance?
4. What are the recommended water temperatures for different types of pools—multipurpose? therapy? competition?
5. What is sick building syndrome?
6. What is the required turnover time for various pools—wading? spa? therapy? flume? swimming schools? public pools?

ACTIVITIES

1. Write a risk management policy for a natatorium.
2. Interview an aquatic facility manager regarding his or her requirements for hiring and training staff.
3. Visit different types of aquatic facilities and observe the safety practices.
4. Conduct a safety audit of a swimming pool.
5. Make a list of specific aquatic programs you (the manager) would like to offer and then design a natatorium to meet those needs.

SUGGESTED READINGS

Centers for Disease Control. (1983). *Swimming pools: Safety and disease control through proper design and operation.* Atlanta: CDC, Center for Environmental Health.

Clayton, R. D., and Thomas, D. G. (1989). *Professional aquatic management.* (2nd ed.). Champaign, Ill: Human Kinetics.

Flynn, R. B. (1993). Facility planning for physical education, recreation, and athletics. Reston, Va: American Alliance for Health, Physical Education, Recreation, and Dance.

Gabrielsen, M. A. (Ed.) (1987). *Swimming pools: A guide to their planning, design and operation,* (4th ed.). Champaign, Ill: Human Kinetics.

Johnson, R. (1989). *YMCA pool operations manual.* Champaign, Ill: Human Kinetics.

Mitchell, P. K. (1988). *The proper management of pool and spa water.* Marietta, Ga: Hydrotech Chemical Corporation.

National Swimming Pool Foundation. (1989). *Pool-spa operators handbook.* San Antonio, Tex: NSPF.

Osinski, A. (1996): Swimming pool design, maintenance, management and operation (software). San Antonio, Tex: National Swimming Pool Foundation.

Osinski, A. (1994, February). Compendium of codes. *Aqua,* 19(2):49–55.

Parks, J. B., and Zanger, B. (Eds.) (1990). *Sport and fitness management: Career strategies and professional content.* Champaign, Ill: Human Kinetics.

Taylor, C. (1989). *Everything you always wanted to know about pool care: But didn't know where to ask.* Chino, Cal: Service Industry Publications.

Van Rossen, D. (1992). *Aquatic manager's handbook.* Springfield, Ore: Aquatic Resources and Programs.

Warren, R., and Rea, P. (1989). *Management of aquatic recreation resources.* Columbus, Ohio: Publishing Horizons.

Williams, K. (1992). *The aquatic facility operator manual.* Hoffman Estates, Ill: National Recreation & Park Association, National Aquatic Section.

REFERENCE

Osinski, A. (1996). *Swimming pool design, maintenance, management and operation.* [Software]. San Antonio, Tex: National Swimming Pool Foundation.

13

Indoor Sports and Activity Areas

Kathryn Malpass, Ed Turner, Greg Waggoner

This chapter addresses five areas for indoor sports and activities: large court space, small court space, weight areas, dance studios and aerobics areas, and mat rooms.

LARGE COURT AREAS

Large indoor court space usually consists of areas to play basketball, badminton, volleyball, and tennis. Many large court areas double as concert space, graduation space, and other nonsport meeting space. Therefore, large court space is multipurpose space that calls for careful planning, design, and scheduling.

General Space Planning

Large courts are often located in open areas of facilities. Large court areas can therefore be either sport-specific or multipurpose facilities. Multipurpose large court space may be used for nonsport activities such as concerts, graduations, convocations, and conventions. With today's skyrocketing construction costs, multipurpose large court areas are more prevalent than single-purpose facilities. When large court areas are used for multiple activities, some type of separation among the court areas is needed. The separation can take the form of motorized key-controlled solid panels or drop nets. The solid-panel system gives better acoustical and visual isolation than netting. Solid-panel systems are more costly than drop netting. If a solid-panel system is employed, it should have ample doorways to allow easy traffic flow to and from

each separated area. Solid-panel systems should also be rebound surfaces and they should be relatively maintenance free. Drop nets come in three nylon or plastic forms, either solid, mesh, or a combination of solid and mesh. Drop nets should also be motorized and key operated. Drop nets are less expensive than solid panel dividers, however they give less acoustical and visual isolation for divided areas of large courts.

In addition to facilitating teaching and using space well, both systems promote safety. The dividers stop objects hit, kicked, and thrown in one activity area from entering another activity area. The dividers also contain balls and other objects within a given space so that users do not have to constantly chase the objects over the whole of the large multipurpose area.

Whether area dividers are solid wall panels or drop nets, careful planning is required for them to be effective. Not only do dividers need to be planned for safety, isolation, and containment, but also for transition of both space and court users. Ample openings must be provided for egress and access and for good traffic flow. Dividers must not overlap onto the various activity areas that the dividers are separating. These dividers must allow for traffic flow within and around the large court space.

The court floor linings for multipurpose areas need careful consideration. Lines will overlap and this cannot be prevented. The court layout and lining should be planned in such a way as to keep overlapping to a minimum.

The least planned area in any facility is storage space. Large court areas are no exception.

Chaska Community Center in St. Paul, Minnesota, uses this large court space for a variety of activities. (Courtesy of Barker Rinker Seacat and Partners Architects, Denver, Colorado)

Storage areas need to be strategically placed in each activity area of large court space. The storage areas must be large enough to hold all equipment employed in that area as well as maintenance equipment. Doors to storage areas must be wide enough to allow easy movement of equipment. There should be no door thresholds on the floors that would impede the rolling of heavy equipment in and out of the storage areas. Storage areas should be built flush with walls for considerations of safety and maintenance. All storage areas must be secured with a good locking system. They need to be cool and dry and equipped with shelves, racks, bins, hooks, sinks, and troughs as appropriate.

A multipurpose gymnasium has floor markings for net dividers for different sports. (Courtesy of Greeley Recreation Center, Greeley, Colorado)

General Programs

Because large court areas provide vast amounts of space, many different activities are held in such areas. Teaching classes, intramurals and recreational play, athletics, concerts, graduations, convocations, and conventions are some of the common activities. This varied and heavy use of large court areas calls for careful scheduling. It is suggested that a "non-attached" facility manager be in charge of scheduling. Not being affiliated with any group that might want to use the large court area, this manager is neutral and therefore bases scheduling on the needs of all facility users. In many large court facilities, classes occupy the facility from 8 A.M. to 2 P.M. Monday through Friday, athletics use the large court areas from 3 P.M. to 7 P.M. Monday through Friday, and recreational users have the facility from 7 P.M. to midnight except on athletic game nights. Weekends are usually reserved for recreational use, except for athletic games and other special programs. Many times nets, seats, platforms, tables, backstops, and backdrops must be removed or put in place between activities in large court areas. If this is the case, the manager must schedule the time and the personnel to change the facility for its next use.

Floor surfaces vary in large court areas, usually from wood to synthetics. In either case, if a large population of spectators are going to be on the floor area for seating or traffic flow, the manager must schedule ample time to cover the floor and to place chairs, tables, and booths on the floor. A large plastic cover works well to protect floors in this situation. Putting floor covers in place or removing them takes a number of personnel and quite a large amount of time. If refreshments are served, the plastic floor covering will need to be cleaned after its use, before it can be stored.

Maintenance and cleaning personnel need flexible schedules in order to accommodate the odd hours of large court use. Some personnel need to work the shift from 8 A.M. to 4 P.M., some from 4 P.M. to midnight, and some from midnight to 8 A.M. This staggered schedule provides time for housekeeping and special cleanup chores when the large court area is not in use. If a large gathering uses a multipurpose large court late at night during the week, all maintenance and housekeeping needs to be completed during the early morning hours of the next day in order to have the area prepared for use at 8 A.M.

A multipurpose facility needs special storage areas for housing large numbers of chairs, dollies, floor covers, standards and backboards, and maintenance equipment. Wood floors need to be dry mopped twice each day to remove grit and other unwanted debris. Wood floors need a light sanding and a new protective coating once every year. Long-term care for a wood floor means sanding to bare wood, repainting lines and total resurfacing once every seven to ten years. Maintenance of synthetic floors is different from that of wood floors and can vary from synthetic surface to synthetic surface. Normally, synthetic floors need daily wet and dry mopping. Synthetic floors also need to be stripped and resealed at least once a month, more often depending on amount of use.

If large court areas are to serve several purposes, careful attention must be given to placement of electrical outlets, lighting, ventilation, and acoustics. If concerts are to be held, staging must be available along with overhead lighting, sound systems, and electrical hookups. Concerts and large-scale spectator events also require clearly marked aisles, seat numbers, and access/egress pathways to meet emergency standards.

A crisis management plan must be in effect if large numbers of individuals are using large court areas. This plan must be coordinated with staff, security personnel, local officials, and emergency personnel. The crisis management plan should be practiced at least every six months to ensure that all parties are coordinated and that any given crisis can be appropriately handled. Appropriate signage must be placed throughout large court areas to impart information regarding access/egress, seating areas, rules and regulations, directions, floor plans, and emergency information. Careful planning for size, information, placement, and maintenance yields signs that are articulate, visible, and helpful to all.

With large crowds in large court areas, security is very important. Ample trained security personnel and ushers need to be employed to control and direct the crowd. These personnel need training, prior to their first working session, that includes crisis management, handling emergencies, crowd control, plans to help disabled people to and from their seats, and any other special needs that call for preplanning.

Basketball, Volleyball, Tennis, and Badminton Courts

The court lines for large courts need to allow for ease of traffic flow between and around the court areas. Nets should not impede traffic on the perimeter. Because large court areas often overlap, colored lines distinguish courts for different games. No one court should take priority; the use of pastel colors helps keep all lines visible to the same degree.

Floors of basketball courts can be either wood or synthetic. Most players prefer wood floors. Volleyball and badminton floors should be wood for teaching and competitive purposes. Synthetic floors for recreational badminton and volleyball are acceptable. Indoor tennis courts need to be synthetic because wood floors allow the ball to bounce too quickly and this deters from the users' success.

Standards for volleyball, tennis, and badminton floors should be the floor-mounted, telescoping type or the self-standing socketed floor plate mounted type so they never need to be moved. In both of these systems there are no bases on the standards. The standards mount directly to and are supported by the floor. The lack of bases promotes safety because there is no base for users to step on or fall into. Volleyball standards should have padding to prevent injuries from severe impacts. All socket floor supports must be flush with the floor surface and have a spring-loaded closure that is also flush. For volleyball competition, an official's stand must be provided. The official's stand must be easily moveable, stable, and padded. Court layouts and standard mounts for volleyball, tennis, and badminton should provide adequate tension on the nets. Volleyball nets need to be easily adjustable for men's and women's heights.

Lighting is an important consideration for badminton, tennis, and volleyball areas. The lights must be bright enough to see, yet not have so many lights in a grouping that players lose the shuttlecock, tennis ball, or volleyball in the intensity of the lights. Light fixtures need to be at least as high as the lowest ceiling obstruction. This nonobstructive distance should be a minimum of 24 feet. Indirect lighting works well for badminton, tennis, and volleyball. The ceiling color is also important so the participants can clearly visually follow the shuttlecock, tennis ball, or volleyball. Bright white is not an acceptable ceiling color because many shuttlecocks and volleyballs are white and would blend with a white ceiling. Off-white or light pastel colors work well on badminton and volleyball courts. Lighting for all of the areas should be between 50 and 70 foot-candles.

Basketball backboards and standards should be telescoping, moveable, and collapsible for ease of storage. Backboards should be glass. The basketball standards should attach to flush mounted floor plates. Lighting for basketball must be bright enough for good visual acuity and for television coverage.

All large court areas must have electrical outlets for scoreboards, timers, and the news media. Scoreboards should be able to accommodate basketball, tennis, badminton, and volleyball. The scoreboards should be placed so that spectators and players, from all four of these sports, can easily see them. All lighting control boxes should be located for convenient access.

Spectator seating and viewing must be planned for each of these special-use large court areas. Seating should be easily electronically moved since each court area is of a different size and spectators like to be as close as possible to each event. All seating should have clear sight lines to the specific large court area being used at the time. Ample provisions must be made for announcing, score tables, media tables, seating for special guests and sport participants. The tables and seating should be located 8 feet to 10 feet from the sidelines to add to the margin of safety for participants. Computer hook-ups and electronic media outlets must be provided in these areas. If videotaping, radio broadcasting, or live TV broadcasting is to be done, special areas must be provided for cameras, spotters, and announcers.

Careful consideration must be given to locker-room locations and sizes to handle the participants and officials for all four of the large court areas that have been discussed. Storage areas must also be in close proximity and carefully planned to handle the equipment for these four large court areas. Last, if food and novelty items are to be sold, the concession areas must be safe and convenient to each large court area. Ample trash receptacles should be placed in the concession areas, in the court areas, and outside. Adequate and well-placed trash receptacles help in cleanup and maintenance.

SMALL COURT AREAS

Small court areas for racquetball, handball, and squash are very expensive to build and usually used by small numbers of participants, at a given time, compared to other specialized areas. For these reasons, careful planning in design and scheduling is very important for small court areas.

Racquetball, Handball, and Squash

Design and Location

Racquetball and handball are compatible and can be played on the same court (40 ft. × 20 ft. × 20 ft.). The sport of squash, however, is played on a different sized court. To compound this, there are both Canadian-sized squash courts and American-sized squash courts. Also the game of American squash doubles is played in a different sized court (45 ft. × 25 ft. × 20 ft.) than squash singles (32 ft. × 18 1/2 ft. × 16 ft.). Because squash courts vary in size, they must be constructed separately from racquetball-handball courts.

Small court areas can be constructed of portland cement walls, panel system walls, or tempered glass walls. Portland cement walled courts were the first to be used, but panel wall systems, along with glass wall system, are the state of the art. Portland cement walls and panel walls are cheaper to install than glass walls. The plastic coated fiberboard, panel system gives good ball rebounding action and is easily maintained. Panel

Racquetball courts

wall systems vary in cost depending on the thickness of the panels. Portland cement walls require more long-term maintenance than either panel or glass wall systems. All small courts should be designed with a back glass wall for both instructional and observational use. At least one court should have a glass side wall with tiered seating directly outside this wall for both instructional and tournament viewing. All small courts should have a hard maplewood floor. Wood floors also vary in cost depending on the type of floor system.

For instructional purposes a minimum of eight courts should be built, to allow for a class size of sixteen to twenty students. Fewer than eight courts makes for very small classes. Courts should be built in banks of four or more, which are all placed in one location of the facility. Small courts of the same type should not be located in different areas of a facility because it creates a time management problem for instructional use. Instructors should not be spending time walking across large spaces in order to teach another portion of their class because courts are separate and spread out.

All small courts should also have a gallery or balcony for viewing from above the court as well as seating on the floor level of the court. This multi-level viewing aids instruction. Courts should also have a small storage box, flush to the wall, for valuables and extra balls. These boxes are usually on a side wall, near the rear of the court, and usually measure about 12 in. by 8 in. by 6 in. Each small court should also be equipped with a two-way public address system for both instructional and management purposes.

Lighting in small courts can be of many types with metal halide being the best at this time. All lights must be flush with the ceiling and be accessible for maintenance. Because each small court is a room in itself, it becomes a maintenance nightmare if the work crew has to maneuver hydraulic lifts in and out of each court. Access to lights from a crawl space above works nicely.

Air vents and acoustical treatments must be placed in the ceiling in the rear ten feet of the court, the only area of the ceiling that is not used in racquetball and handball. Squash does not use the ceiling. Ventilation must be sufficient to maintain adequate circulation of air and remove water vapor. Moisture on the walls or floor makes playing in small courts hazardous. All surfaces of small court areas must be flush and careful planning must be given to all seams, doors, lights, vents, and storage areas.

Storage areas for equipment and maintenance must be built close to the small court area. Separate storage areas for users' coats, rain and snow gear, and books should be built in the small court area. Refrigerated water fountains also should be located in the small court area of a facility.

Scheduling

Small courts are scheduled for classes, tournaments, competitions, recreation, maintenance, and other activities. Priorities for scheduling courts depends on the philosophy of the facility. In some facilities, class use is the priority; in other facilities, tournaments and recreational use may have the first priority. In any case, careful consideration must be given to scheduling blocks of time for each activity in small courts. Maintenance should be scheduled at "off" times or at times when there is a very low user demand.

Small court areas are sometimes used for wallyball, fitness activities, and rebounding activities. If activities other than racquetball, handball, and squash will be played on small courts, they must be able to physically withstand the impacts of the other activities. For instance, volleyballs hitting the ceiling, lights, and vents can do major damage to courts not designed for this use. If wallyball is to be played, net attachments must be set into walls. Rebounding activities such as tennis, soccer, or volleyball must be assessed individually to determine if courts can withstand the impact of the balls in each of these sports.

Tournaments, both in-house and out-of-house, may be planned for small court areas. In-house tournaments can be played at any time during the week and should be scheduled according to competitors' schedules and facility usage. Out-of-house tournaments are normally scheduled on Fridays, Saturdays, and Sundays so that more individuals from other geographic locations and worksites can travel to and compete in them. Special considerations as to management, maintenance, and staffing must be made for out-of-house tournaments. Additional provisions for marketing, security, refreshments, parking, novelty sales, and registration must be made. If a small court is physically isolated from other portions of the facility, it is much easier to play for out-of-house tournaments than if it is integrated with the rest of the facility.

A manager may wish to designate one (or more) of the small courts as a challenge court, which would require separate scheduling. Challenge courts allow for continuous play and a sign-up schedule needs to be posted by their doors. This schedule should be updated once or twice per day.

Risk and Liability

Small court areas should be checked routinely for cleanliness and proper functioning. Dirt or moisture on the floor creates slippery surfaces. Moistures on the walls makes the ball move too quickly and burned-out lights in small courts decreases visual acuity. Any of these items could lead to injury and possible litigation. If small court areas are used heavily, each court should be checked every four hours.

The floor surface of small court areas needs constant surveillance. Once the surface coating becomes too worn, small courts become dangerously slippery. Floor coatings need to be maintained and resurfaced on a regular schedule in order to prevent slippage. The amount of court usage dictates its resurfacing schedule.

Protective eyewear should be required on all small courts for players of racquetball, handball, and squash. No exceptions should be made to this policy. Signs indicating mandatory protective eyewear should be posted at the door to each court. Supervisors should also make random checks to ensure all small court users are wearing eye protection.

Various ways of scheduling allow fair use of small courts:

- Sign-up sheets posted at each court the day before its use
- Call-in reservations, usually taken one day in advance
- First-come, first-served during times of low use
- Time limits, often one hour, during peak times

Equipment on a rental or sign-out basis should be checked for condition before it is given to a user. Racquets need to be checked for cracks, warpage, and grips. Protective lenses should be checked for cleanliness and clearness. Individuals playing on small courts should be required to wear appropriate clothing and footwear. Back walls of glass make supervision and risk management much easier than do solid walled courts.

Balconies or galleries above courts can be an open invitation to injury. Enclosing the gallery with polycarbonate sheeting or tempered glass avoids problems. If the gallery is open, stray balls may be hit into this area. Signs should be posted to indicate this danger to gallery members. A fence-like railing or wall should enclose the gallery to prevent individuals from falling into the court area. This barrier should be at least 4 feet high.

Thoughts for the Future

At least one small court should be equipped with four built in-video cameras. These cameras, mounted in the walls about 18 feet high near each of the four corners, are remote controlled and can tape activity on the court by the push of a button. Some courts also have a built-in 52-inch video monitor and a deck for immediate replay of action that has been recorded. All equipment should be flush with the balls and protected from impact by clear polycarbonate sheeting.

This special small court could also have a clear tempered-glass window on the lower lefthand corner of the front wall for frontal viewing and frontal videotaping. This window is placed at a sitting height so the viewer behind the glass can be seated comfortably in a chair.

The weight training area at the East Boulder Recreation Center in Boulder, Colorado (Courtesy of Barker Rinker Seacat and Partners Architects, Denver, Colorado)

WEIGHT AREAS

Design and Location

Because of increased litigation and rapid changes in weight equipment, planning and design of weight areas is of paramount importance.

Weight areas normally come in two forms: a room enclosed by walls and secured with a door and open areas. The open weight area not surrounded by walls needs special supervision and some means to isolate the area when not in use.

The type of weight lifting dictates the space for a weight area. The weight area may be for power lifting, bodybuilding, or conditioning, or it may contain machine or free weights. Many weight areas are combination lifting areas.

The size and shape of the weight area depends on the types of activities in the area, the number and types of machines and free weights in the area, and the number of peak-time users. Because machine weights occupy large spaces, the more machine weights, the larger the area needs to be. Free weights occupy much less space than machine weights. If powerlifting is the focus of a weight area, large platformed areas allow heavy free weights to be lifted and dropped safely without damage to the floor.

The minimum size of a weight area is 3500 square feet, which gives ample space for a variety of machine weights and free weights. Weight areas can be any shape. If weight areas are in a room, they will probably be rectangular. Open weight areas can be designed in any shape.

Whenever possible, the weight area should be the lowest level of the building because of the large amount of weight to be supported by the weight area floor and the sound from dropped weights.

Weight areas can be very noisy so they need careful placement in relation to "quiet" areas. Placing weight areas on the perimeter of the building can reduce the noise in a facility. Good acoustical treatment also helps contain sound, especially when it is on floors, ceilings, and walls. Walls should be treated internally (insulation) and externally to absorb sound that escapes the weight area. Open weight areas can also use acoustical clouds suspended over the area.

Weight area floors may be covered by either a rubberized synthetic or indoor-outdoor carpeting. Both materials work well. Poured, rolled, or interlocking tile rubberized surfaces are initially more expensive to install than indoor-outdoor carpeting. The rubberized surfaces are also more costly to maintain, but last longer than indoor-outdoor carpeting. Indoor-outdoor carpet is good acoustical material and is available in many bright colors. It must be vacuumed daily and steam cleaned at least once a month. Without platforms to absorb the impact of heavy weights dropped in powerlifting, indoor-outdoor carpeting tears up quickly. Integrated rubber pads give extra protection at high stress areas where dumbbells and other free weights may be dropped and near benches where flys and pullovers are done.

Mirrors are an important factor in weight area design. Mirrors should be on adjacent walls and 18 inches above floor level. The 18-inch space is for padding so that weights do not roll against mirrors and so that maintenance machines do not hit the mirrors. Mirrors break easily and should be placed with an eye to preventing breakage. Mirrors on the ceiling above lifting areas may also be installed.

Heavy and long workouts with weights cause people to perspire profusely. To deal with odors, special attention must be given to ventilation of weight areas to remove airborne moisture and recirculate air quickly.

Windows in weight areas should open to help air circulation. Many large windows and natural light coming into the weight area can brighten the space. Weight areas are one of the few activity spaces in sports facilities that are compatible with windows.

Scheduling

Weight areas serve a various clientele so scheduling must accommodate instructional use, competitive use, athletic use, recreational use, and maintenance. Except for maintenance, which should be done in "off" hours, the schedule depends on the facility's priorities. Block schedules works well for weight areas. For example, the block from 8 A.M. to 2 P.M. may be for instruction. This is the instructional block of the schedule; other lifting priorities can also be scheduled in blocks of time.

Weight areas need supervision so staff must be scheduled to supervise the weight area whenever it is open. The supervisors should be knowledgeable about weight training and well-trained in safety use and handling of all equipment in weight areas.

If the weight area is large and heavily used, more than one trained supervisor at a time is needed.

Risk and Liability

Constant supervision in weight areas reduces the risk of accidents. Knowledgeable and well-trained supervisors should be constantly moving from location to location within the weight area to give instructions and monitor activity, including safety precautions.

Supervisors should also check all machines and free weights for damage and record inspections on check sheets provided for this purpose.

Weight areas should have distinct marked patterns for traffic flow and specifically designated lifting areas. The patterns and lifting areas may be enhanced by different colors of floor surfacing. Adequate space must be allocated for each machine weight and for free weight lifting. Lifting areas should be spread out so that one free weight lifter never has to lift over another. Collars should be required on all bar free weights at all times.

Supervisors should not allow food or beverages in weight areas because spillage increases maintenance and decreases safety. With ample storage racks for all free weights, weights should never be allowed to remain on the floor. Dumbbell racks, barbell racks, and plate racks must be provided.

Built-in storage space for gloves, straps, and other items should be provided. Storage for maintenance equipment in weight areas helps keep them cleaned and maintained. A trained staff member should check all machine weights daily. This inspection includes overall appearance, cables, pullies, stack weights, grips, and handles. If a weight machine needs maintenance or repair, it should be completed immediately or the machine should be disabled and labeled with signs clearly indicating it should not be used. Ample trash receptacles must be placed in weight areas.

Safety and supervision of lifting techniques is needed more in free weight areas than in machine weight areas because free weight lifting is more dangerous than machine weight lifting. Weight areas must be secured when not in use. An enclosed weight room must be abled to be locked. An open weight area can be cordoned off with rope or plastic chain with numerous attached signs indicating the weight area is closed. If the weight area is open, it needs visual monitoring at all times so a facility supervisor can ensure that no one enters the area and lifts. If the weight area is in an enclosed room, an emergency phone should be in the room in a conspicuous place with emergency numbers near it.

Thoughts for the Future

Weight areas of the future will be both indoor and outdoor facilities. The outdoor area will be an extension of the indoor weight area similar to today's outdoor decks for indoor swimming pools. The idea is to be able to lift in the sun and warm weather. Access to the outdoor weight-lifting deck area must be from within the indoor area. The deck must have an outdoor, applicable, floor surface in order to withstand changes of weather.

Electronic technology will be the norm for new weight areas. A built-in large-screen television monitor and videotape equipment including mounted cameras will be in all weight areas. High-quality stereo systems designed specifically for use in weight areas will also be available for all facilities.

DANCE STUDIOS AND AEROBICS AREAS

With the growing trend in group exercise classes, an indoor sports facility should include at least one area to be used exclusively for dance exercise. Each group exercise program should be evaluated as to the projected number of participants especially during prime usage hours. The exercise room should be large enough to accommodate the needs of the program.

Program Requirements

Consideration should be given to the number of participants who will be allowed to exercise in the room at any given time, the desired instructor-to-participant ratios, and the type of activity in the room. For example, will the room be used for step classes or will locomotor movements such as leaping and skipping be included in aerobic dance combinations? A 3000-square-foot room may be able to handle as many as eighty participants in the step class but only thirty participants for dance combinations which include the locomotor movements found in traditional aerobics and dance. In general, a minimum of 36 square feet per participant is recommended for step-type classes (Patton et al., 1989), and 100 square feet per participant for other types of dance exercise (Turner, 1993).

The larger number of participants who use the facility during peak hours, the more important access becomes to the design. In general, an exercise studio should have at least two doors, opening into a lobby or large hallway that is capable of handling large numbers of individuals. This facilitates participants' clearing the studio quickly so that a following class may enter without delay. At least two water fountains should be located in the hallway nearby for participants to fill their water bottles.

In many cases, the facility design should include two or more exercise studios, which may be entirely separate rooms or one room divided by a folding wall. The design should reflect all possible uses of the room, such as the need for a large activity space during certain hours, smaller spaces for variety in programming, and the possibility of using the room for meeting space.

Storage

The studio should include storage areas for exercise equipment such as steps, mats, and individual dumbbells on racks that are easily accessible to participants. If locker rooms are inadequate or inconvenient, participants may bring their gear bags to class with them. Space for participants' belongings can be provided on top of the storage units along one wall of the studio.

Secure storage should also be provided for sound equipment used by the instructor. This equipment should be convenient to the location from which the instructor will lead exercises. Ample room should be provided for tape decks, compact disc (CD) players, amplifiers, video recorder, camera, and the storage of tapes, CDs, and videos. A shelf where the instructor can secure personal belongings should also be included.

Sound Systems

Speakers and large-screen televisions should be either suspended from the ceiling or mounted high off the floor on corner shelves. There should be enough speakers to fill the room evenly with sound. An adequate sound system includes a wireless microphone attachment so the instructor can move freely around the room. The system should provide separate volume controls for music and the instructor's microphone. It is always wise to consult an acoustical specialist before purchasing a sound system.

It is very important that the room have good acoustical properties. If the participants are unable to understand the instructor's directions due to poor acoustics, the instructor will have to yell louder, often resulting in voice strain and injury. Walls, ceilings, and some floor surfaces may improve acoustic properties and reduce echoes. The reverberation of sound should not last longer than two seconds if participants are to clearly hear directions. Keeping the music level no higher than 90 decibels also reduces voice strain for instructors. An ideal and motivating volume for exercise classes can be achieved at 85 decibels, even lower for background music often used with stretching classes (Niestemski, 1993). A trained sound specialist can assist with identifying decibel levels in the exercise studio.

Workout Environment

Participants enjoy their workouts more if the room is bright and open. Walls should be light in color. Windows that provide natural light add a pleasant atmosphere for the studio. Skylights and windows placed near vaulted ceilings add a feeling of spaciousness to the room. Placing windows on the north side of the building cuts down on glaring sunlight, which can be distracting (Turner, 1993). The room should be well lit regardless of whether windows are an option. Incandescent lighting is preferred over fluorescent. Dimmers on the lights provide options for instructors, especially for floor work and relaxation classes.

Managers of facilities should evaluate the needs of their programs as to whether the inside wall of the studio should have a glass wall or windows. Glass creates a sense of openness for the room, yet may make some participants uncomfortable. One option is to provide segmentation in the windowed wall with columns or deep dividers to cut down on viewing angles from the hallway. Placement of the exercise studio away from the lobby and weight training areas also provides a sense of privacy for participants.

Full-length mirrors should be placed on at least two adjoining walls so that movement can be analyzed effectively. The mirrors should be installed flush to the wall and at least 12 inches from the floor. Ballet barres can be installed in front of the mirrors and should extend six to eight inches from the wall. A general guideline to determine how much barre space is required is five feet per participant (Turner, 1993).

The exercise studio does not have to be rectangular; in fact, many new designs have curved walls creating a pie-shaped room. The instructor leads from the narrow section, with participants who prefer the back of the class filling the wider portion of the room. If the program includes classes with a high instructor-to-participant ratio, a raised platform is recommended, facilitating both supervision by the instructor and viewing for participants. Although some types of exercise classes lend themselves to platforms, most dance aerobics do not. If the room is used by traditional dance as well as exercise classes, it might be better to eliminate the raised platform, resulting in additional floor space.

Appropriate temperature and humidity controls are especially important considerations for the exercise studio. The body heat of exercisers increases the cooling load up to three times that of a normal room. Physiologically we know that skin temperature is related to the surrounding air temperature. As a person exercises, the skin's temperature increases as a result of the body's heat production. When the skin's temperature reaches the air temperature at approximately 92° F, heat loss through convection and radiation gradually end. Sweating then becomes the only way the body can cool itself. Stoll and Beller (1989) found that wiping sweat with a towel or allowing sweat to drop off the body does not actually cool the body.

As the relative humidity reaches 100 percent, the air is saturated with water vapor and cannot accept any from the skin. Without a cooling effect, the body's temperature rises rapidly, and if allowed to continue can lead to death, which occurs at 105 to 108° F. The opposite extreme of too dry an environment is not beneficial for an aerobic training effect, due to the increase and severe loads placed upon the cardiac system in trying to cool the body. It is therefore important to find a happy medium where training can occur comfortably and the body can absorb perspiration ef-

Aerobics classes require considerable space. (Courtesy of Barker Rinker Seacat and Partners Architects, Denver, Colorado)

ficiently. The recommended temperature for the exercise studio is 60 to 70°F (Francis, 1987) with the humidity setting between 50 and 60 percent (Patton et al., 1989).

Ventilation in the exercise room can be improved with ceiling fans or a good blower system. A 3000-square-foot room requires between six and ten ceiling fans. The ceiling should be at least 16 feet tall if ceiling fans are used. Higher ceilings of a minimum of 24 feet are recommended for rooms hosting modern dance and ballet (Turner, 1993). The taller the ceiling, the better chances for adequate air circulation. These fans and blower may add noise to the room, and should be as silent as possible to avoid interfering with the quality of sound in the room.

Floor Surfaces

The most important factor to consider when designing an exercise studio is the type of surface on the floor. Current research shows that injuries in aerobics and dance most frequently occur in the legs and feet, especially when exercising on a nonresilient surface. Resiliency is the floor's ability to absorb shock that would normally be transmitted back into the participant's feet, legs, and back (Stoll and Beller, 1989). An unyielding surface like concrete does not absorb shock effectively, creating more stress to the body.

Research studies have not been able to agree conclusively that any one type of flooring is best in exercise studios. The problem is that in order to test the floor, other variables such as the type of shoe, kind of activity, and the intensity of the exercise must be controlled. Much of the data that has been gathered cannot be interpreted due to these variables.

Experts do agree on four important qualities in flooring for exercise studios:

- Shock absorption to absorb vertical movements,
- Stability to control lateral movements,
- Traction to permit free movement, and
- Resiliency so the surface springs back into shape (Ryan, 1988).

Finding a balance of the four qualities has been the challenge, however. One of the best shock-absorbing floorings is a thick sponge pad. Regular foam develops dips in it after prolonged use, but the new synthetics are specially designed to hold their shape. One especially promising surface is a microcell foam, which is available at one quarter the cost of wood. The product comes in interlocking sections that can be moved if necessary. However, problems may occur with any interlocking surface due to the breakdown of edges of the sections, sometimes resulting in participants tripping or turning an ankle.

These types of synthetic floors are usually soft enough that individual mats are not necessary for floor exercises. But problems with instability have occurred with individuals working out on wrestling mats. The foot sinks into the padding, causing the participant to trip or sprain an ankle. Cleaning also presents a unique problem; bacteria may grow if the surface is texturized and is not thoroughly scrubbed with a chemical cleaner.

Although the quality of polyurethane surfaces has improved drastically in the last ten years, these surfaces are not resilient enough for dance exercise because they are usually poured directly over concrete. Maintenance of these surfaces continues to be plagued with cracking and peeling of coatings. The life cycle of these surfaces is also much shorter than wood floors.

Carpet is relatively easy to install and the new sport varieties have special shock-absorption backings. It should be used with a foam cushioning and never applied directly over concrete. Carpet should have a very tight, dense nap and one that is anti-static, and mildew- and strain-resistant (Ryan, 1988). Because carpet is soft, individual mats are often unnecessary for floor exercises. It comes in a variety of colors, and is good acoustically because sound does not bounce off it. Carpet is versatile and works well in multipurpose rooms. But carpet may cause some participants to have skin reactions as the result of the chemicals applied to make it antifungal. These treatments help to stop the carpet from absorbing sweat and humidity, which causes the carpet to mold and smell. Carpet has potential to stain, discolor, stretch, and retain odors, requiring regular cleaning. It has an expected life span of only two to four years depending on the usage. Sometimes carpet can catch the foot, causing the participant to trip. Free movements like pivots and glides are restricted by the carpet as well.

Historically, suspended wood floors have been preferred by dancers. Suspended wood floors provide shock absorption, the ability for lateral movements, spring and freedom to pivot and twirl. Wood is asthetically pleasing yet provides flexibility in multipurpose rooms that may also serve as meeting areas. But the wood floor built on one layer of sleepers such as that of a racquetball court is generally not resilient enough for high-energy dance exercise. Too much humidity can cause the wood floor to warp as well. Participants need floor mats

due to the hard surface. Some acoustical problems may also occur because sound can echo off the wood surface.

The newer suspended wood floors have become specialized to the various sport activities, so that a floor fits the activity space for which it is intended. The dance exercise floor should be installed so that the grain of the wood is all going in the same direction. The applied finish should allow gliding without being slippery (Turner, 1993). Wood flooring should never be damp mopped and water-based waxes should not be used because they can dull the finish and permanently damage the floor (Ferguson, 1989). A wood floor that is properly maintained should last from 30 to 50 years (Seals and Cooper, 1991).

Current research shows that the type of subfloor is a more important factor than the top layer of the floor. Three types of subfloor constructions are recommended:

- *Suspension floor*: Plywood, foam rubber, or other synthetic material is placed in various patterns, with the finished floor floating on it.
- *Spring floor*: Coiled metal springs are covered by a plywood subfloor, with the finished floor resting on the plywood.
- *Padded floor*: Padded materials such as foam or other synthetics are laid over a plywood or concrete surface, covered with the finished floor (Stoll and Beller, 1989).

Cost is a determining factor when selecting a floor surface. The least expensive alternative is the padded floor, with the suspended and spring floors costing significantly more. The policy of some facilities of restricting the types of exercise programs to low-impact because of a low-quality floor is simply unacceptable, however.

Price alone should not control the buying decision. It is the unfortunate facility owner who selects the most economical floor without taking the time to make an educated decision on the best surface for the money. The overall cost of a floor surface should not only be evaluated for initial expense but also for maintenance, life cycle, and replacement costs.

The cost of surfacing the floor is one of the most expensive investments in an indoor sport facility. It should be selected early in the planning process, before other less critical expenses are determined. A realistic budget will hold up under last-minute budget cuts, and quality floor surfaces help to bring in and retain participants. Flooring is an investment that deserves appropriate time in the facility designing process. A floor surface is relatively permanent; once installed, floors are seldom, if ever, changed.

A good way to evaluate floor surfaces is to visit locations where they are installed and speak with the owners, instructors, and participants to determine if they are happy with the floor surface (Ryan, 1988). How many injuries in their programs can be attributed to the floor surface? A surface with good shock absorption can take a low, bouncing jump for a few minutes in 20- to 30-second intervals without any jarring sensation to the body. In swiveling and pivoting actions to test for floor traction, the shoe should be the same type normally used for exercise, should not stick or slide, but should rotate easily (Klinger et al., 1986).

It is the sport professional's legal and ethical duty to provide the safest surface a program can afford. Important questions to ask when selecting a surface include:

- Does this surface reduce the risk of injury to participants?
- How does this surface serve the functions and activities of participants?
- What is the long-term cost of this surface?
- What do similar facilities use as their surfaces? Any complaints?
- Will this surface be an asset to the facility in marketing memberships?

MAT ROOMS

Mat rooms in sports and recreation facilities can be multipurpose rooms if care is taken in the design and management of the facility. Three specific activities are common to mat rooms: gymnastics, wrestling, and martial arts. Wrestling is actually a martial art, however, it will be addressed separately for the purpose of this discussion. Each activity requires similar needs in facility design, equipment, and management; however, each activity also has unique needs in equipment design and management. A sports and recreation facility's planner is wise to identify the primary activity of the target populations of the facility. The mat room's characteristics can then reflect that activity.

Gymnastics

The main area for gymnastics will accommodate many activities at the same time. The floor exercise is conducted on a mat (42 ft. × 42 ft.). Other gymnastics activities include the balance beam, uneven and even parallel bars, rings, high bar, pummel horse, and vault. Each of these activities require apparatus and approach and landing area of considerable size. The vault requires a minimum of 100 feet for approach, apparatus, and landing. This span is also required for tumbling trampolines. Due to the apparatus and activities of gymnastics, the main activity room must be a minimum of 42 feet by 100 feet, however, an ideal gymnastics room may be as large as 120 feet by 90 feet (Flynn, 1985, p. 45).

The ceiling of a gymnastics room should be at least 23 feet high to allow room for people on the high bar, rings, and trampoline (Flynn, 1985, p. 45). These participants must have more than enough space to perform their stunts without fear of the ceiling. A ceiling of this height can accommodate various apparatus, as well.

The floor of the gymnastics room should be of hard wood. If there is little use planned for the room other than gymnastics, floors constructed of vinyl products rather than hard wood may be less expensive and easier to maintain. All floor plates should have reinforcement around them and be recessed and flush (Flynn, 1985, p. 45). The floor exercise mats should have a spring floor underneath, which serves two primary purposes: it decreases injuries of participants by absorbing the impact and it provides for more spring and enhances the participants' ability to perform stunts. A makeshift spring floor can be constructed of tennis balls inserted in socks and stapled to plywood.

Many gymnastics rooms have landing pits beneath apparatus such as the high bar or rings. The pits should at least span the full width of the apparatus supports and run at least 15 feet behind and in front of the apparatus to provide the landing area. The pit should be at least 36 inches deep and filled with chunks of foam rubber of varying sizes. The corner and ledges of the pit should be padded.

The walls of the gymnastics facility should be made of acoustical block to decrease noise. At least two walls next to the floor exercise area and the balance beam should have full-length mirrors to allow participants to observe their performances. A dance bar may run the length of the room at waist height along the mirrors. At least one drinking fountain should be set into the wall. If windows are in this facility, they should be small and placed high or made of translucent block. Because sun rays in the room can inhibit participants' performances, indirect sunlight is desirable.

Individuals entering from outside the building should have to travel through a foyer or hallway to reach the entrance of the gymnastics room so that outdoor dirt and mud is not tracked directly into the room. The area around the entrance of the main gymnastics room should be free from activity and provide room for storage cubicles for participants and spectator seating.

The gymnastics area should be adjacent to the main gymnasium, locker rooms, and the athletic training room for good traffic flow. Double doors, or an overhead garage door, at least 8 feet high should link the gymnastics rooms with the main gymnasium so that apparatus can be moved from the room to the main gym for meets. It is dangerous and logistically difficult to move apparatus or mats up or down flights of stairs or around corners.

Storage considerations are important to a gymnastics facility. A storage room directly off the main room with double doors, or an overhead garage door, is necessary. This room should be large enough to store apparatus, chalk boxes, landing mats, spring boards, and the like.

A coach's office with dimensions of at least 12 feet by 12 feet is necessary for organizational and administrative needs. This office should be adjacent to the main room and have a window for two-way observation. This room should also have an emergency phone and allow privacy for leader-participant dialogue. An additional video lounge adjacent to the gymnastics room and the coach's office can allow for "technique" sessions. Either the coach's office or the video lounge can house a sound system in a gymnastics facility for floor exercise routines.

A custodial closet with room for janitorial supplies should be located adjacent to the main gymnastics room. It is important to keep the facility clean and sanitary, especially since bare feet are common in gymnastics.

The heating, ventilation, and air condition (HVAC) considerations for this facility include a warm, dry climate with good air exchange. A room too cold invites injuries and a room too hot causes fatigue. The recommended temperature is 72°F.

Wrestling

A wrestling room must accommodate a minimum of two full-sized (42 ft. × 42 ft.) wrestling mats so its dimensions have to be a minimum of 42 feet by 84 feet. A room of this size accommodates approximately forty wrestlers fairly comfortably. The area necessary for participants varies according to the size and calibre of the participants. A 3528-square-foot area gives forty wrestlers an average of just over 88 square feet per participant. This is the recommended minimum area for technique and drilling purposes for secondary- and higher-caliber participants. The recommended area per participant engaging in "live" wrestling is 175 square feet. If that much space is not available, there will have to be fewer participants at one time.

Participants should have as much room as possible; many wrestling practice injuries occur as a result of participants falling on one another. The mat sections should always be taped firmly together to prevent wrestlers from falling on unprotected areas or tripping and injuring themselves. Some facility managers keep a mat stored in the main gymnasium that is used for home meets and not for daily practice. This practice substantially reduces wear and tear on wrestling mats and prolongs their life spans.

A wrestling room should be free of posts, pillars, ledges, and benches. Windows must be placed at least 6 feet high and should not allow direct sunlight into the room. Direct sunlight can inhibit participants' performances and over time the ultraviolet rays of the sun can damage the wrestling mats.

The floor of a wrestling area should be of hard wood. Concrete floors do not allow enough cushion for the participants and they allow the mats to sweat, which can cause damage and create a sanitary problem. Fake floors of particle board or plywood can be installed to alleviate this problem, but they add to the noise. All of the walls, as well as any obstructions that cannot be removed, in a wrestling facility should be padded from the floor up to at least 6 feet. The walls above the padding can accommodate ranking boards, records, bulletin boards, a Hall of Fame, and apparatus. For hydration, a drinking fountain should be set into the wall.

The wrestling room can have a high ceiling to accommodate climbing ropes, an important apparatus for the sport. However, a low ceiling of approximately 12 feet is usual to minimize noise and hold heat.

In addition to climbing ropes, many wrestling rooms have anchored chin-up bars, peg boards, and similar apparatus. The room should be large enough to have an area designated for stationary bikes, takedown machines, jumping rope, and similar activities. Ideally, an area adjacent to the wrestling area accommodates cable weight machines and dumbbells for circuit training. Such an area can be separated from the main activity room by a wall only 5 or 6 feet high.

The entrance to the wrestling area should be free of activity and accommodate spectators. Somewhere near the entrance, an area should have hooks for participants to hang sweats, headgear, jump ropes, and so on.

A storage area adjacent to the wrestling room is important for supplies such as landing mats, stationary bikes, and clocks. Ideally, this area is large enough to store a spare wrestling mat, which requires space of at least 42 feet by 10 feet and should have double doors, or an overhead garage door, at least 8 feet high.

A custodial closet should be adjacent to the wrestling room to store janitorial supplies. Due to the nature of the wrestling (sweat, blood, and bodily contact), cleanliness is extremely important. Solutions to clean these mats daily must neutralize the Hepatitis B virus and Human Immunodeficiency Virus (HIV) and sanitize, yet not be abrasive or irritating to the skin. Solutions with ammonia are suitable. Policies in place must be consistent with removal protocols for biohazardous wastes. Individuals should clean their own blood using neutralizing solutions, rubber gloves, and disposable towels, which must be discarded in a container for biohazardous waste. All of these supplies should be available for participants.

A coach's office with dimensions of at least 12 feet by 12 feet is necessary for organizational and administrative tasks. It should be adjacent to the main room and have a window for two-way observation. This room should contain an emergency phone and allow privacy for leader-participant dialogue. An additional video lounge adjacent to the wrestling room and the coach's office can allow for "technique" sessions. Either the coach's office or the video lounge can accommodate a sound system, which can augment a workout session.

The heating, ventilating, and air conditioning considerations for the wrestling room include a warm dry climate with good air exchange. If the room is cold, it will invite injuries for two primary reasons: the athletes will have a difficult time stretching their muscles and the mats will be too hard, inviting injury upon landing. Once a group of participants begins activity, the room temperature and humidity rises, and as a result, good air exchange is important. Good air exchange is also necessary in order to minimize bacterial and fungal growths that are commonly associated with skin diseases in the sport of wrestling. Auxiliary heaters are necessary in the event that a coach or participant wishes to substantially raise the temperature of the room for a short period of time.

A foyer or hallway acts as a dirt and mud barrier between the entrance to the building and the entrance to the wrestling room. The wrestling room needs to be near the athletic training room, the locker rooms, and the main gymnasium. Some wrestling areas have their own locker rooms adjacent to the facility, which is complete with a sauna or steambath.

It is vital for the wrestling room to be on the same level as and close to the main gymnasium. Ideally, a set of double doors, or an overhead garage door, connects these two areas so that wrestling mats can be moved. Having personnel carrying mats up or down flights of stairs, around corners, and through narrow doorways is dangerous and not practical. This is especially important if a competition mat is not stored in the main gymnasium.

Martial Arts

A martial arts room is commonly called a "dojo," the Japanese word for gymnasium. Because martial arts come in many styles and forms, some are best facilitated by a gymnasium and some are best facilitated by a mat room or wrestling room. Art forms such as Karate or Tae-kwon-do require hardwood floors or short carpet. Art forms such as Judo or Aikido require mats. A standard judo mat is harder and offers a rougher surface than a standard wrestling mat.

Beyond the floor or surface, martial arts require a blend of the gymnastics room and the wrestling room. The total dimensions and space needs, including storage, office, custodial, and HVAC, are similar to those for wrestling and gymnastics. The entrance to the dojo should allow room for spectators and storage cubicles for the participants. Many dojos have a "ceremonial gate" to the activity area.

Anchored bars hanging from a ceiling of approximately 12 feet can accommodate heavy bags and other apparatus to punch or kick to meet many needs of the martial arts participant. For hydration, a drinking fountain should be set into the wall.

The storage needs are similar to those for wrestling and include space for heavy bags and sparring equipment. Again, sanitation is important here due to bare feet, blood, sweat, and bodily contact. Protocols for handling biohazardous wastes must be followed here as well.

SUMMARY

The diversity of both sport and nonsport use of large court facilities creates a unique challenge for planning, scheduling, and maintenance. Back-to-back scheduling of large court space can create housekeeping, security, and scheduling nightmares for a facility's manager. Knowing the variables to consider, however, can help a manager succeed in planning and operating a large court or multipurpose area.

The design of small court space for racquetball and handball is identical. Squash courts are of a different size than racquetball and handball courts, and singles and doubles courts are of different dimensions, too. The high cost of these courts requires careful planning and outfitting to accommodate safe and efficient use of space.

The major decision in designing space for a weight area is whether the space is to be open or closed. This decision formulates the use and security policies for the facility. Size of the weight area is determined by the types of lifting, the types of equipment, and the numbers of users. Weight areas need to be safe and must be secured when not supervised.

Wise planners recognize the importance of a quality dance exercise area to the success of an indoor sports facility. Fitness consumers are becoming more aware of their purchasing power and choose to exercise at the safest and most accessi-

ble locations. Group exercise classes can be a lucrative source of income for the sports facility. It is worth the time, money, and effort to provide well-equipped and managed dance exercise and aerobics areas.

The dimensions of mat rooms depend on the kinds of activity and the specific equipment they are to accommodate.

Lighting in mat rooms should be adequate, and include protective covering for safety, and should not distract participants. Fifty footcandles on task is recommended for mat rooms (Flynn, 1985, p. 28). Mat rooms can be designated or they can be multipurpose depending on the facility's plan. When dealing with elite participants engaging in an activity, it is best to design a facility specific to that activity. A mat room usually serves particular activity, however, most mat rooms accommodate other activities to some extent. For example, a gymnastics room with mirrors, a dance bar, and a sound system combined with a martial arts room with a hardwood floor can accommodate dance, as well. Once the activities are identified, a mat room can be designed to meet the needs of those activities and accommodate the participants.

QUESTIONS

1. In what ways can a manager use the available large court space for activities offered at the same time?
2. What are the different dimensions for small court sports? Why do they differ?
3. What is the difference between open or closed space used in weight area?
4. What are the recommended floor surfaces for the various indoor sports areas?
5. How do mat rooms differ for gymnastics, wrestling, and martial arts?
6. What are the safety requirements for adventure activity and rock climbing areas?

ACTIVITIES

1. In groups of three or four, visit an indoor sporting event. Each group should have a specific area of management to observe. Consult with each other and then write a group synopsis on the positive and negative aspects of the management. Specific managerial areas can be security, admissions, crowd control, parking, marketing, promotions, and ease of operation in

relation to facility design. Report findings to the class for both information and feedback.

2. A local fitness facility built eight racquetball courts and placed glass doors on the rear paneled wall of each court. The glass door was to be used for instructional purposes and for official viewing in sanctioned tournament play. Unfortunately for this facility, a glass door located in the center of a paneled back wall did not allow an instructor or an official to see into the two back corners. Therefore, sanctioned tournaments cannot be held and instruction is difficult because the instructor can view only a portion of the court. How could this facility have been designed to prevent these difficulties?

SELECTED READINGS

Colten, A. (1994, October). Weighting game. *Athletic Business*, 18:61–65.

Horine, L. (1995). *Administration of physical education and sport programs*. Dubuque, Iowa: Brown and Benchmark.

Miller, S. (1993, August). How to buy variable resistance equipment. *Club Industry*, 9:49–51.

Railey, J., and Tschauner, P. (1993). *Managing physical education fitness and sports programs*. Mountain View, Cal: Mayfield.

Strauf, D. (1994). Storage solutions. *Athletic Management*, 6:34–40.

Turner, E. (1987, January). Facility design, trends, and innovations. *JPERD*, 58:34–35.

Wallen, S. (1994). The challenge of around-the-clock hospital cleaning. *Cleaning Management*, 31:24–27.

REFERENCES

Albohm, M. (1987). Musculoskeletal injuries. In N. Van Gelder and S. Marks. (Eds.). *Aerobic Dance-Exercise Instructor Manual*, p. 282. San Diego, Cal: International Dance-Exercise Association (IDEA) Foundation.

Architectural Showcase. (1990). *Athletic Business*, 14(6): 43, 61–62, 65.

Architectural Showcase. (1992). *Athletic Business*, 16(6): 79.

Architectural Showcase. (1993). *Athletic Business*, 17(6): 75, 90, 102.

Berg, R. (1994). Floored: Maple flooring manufacturers say time and money are on their side. *Athletic Business*, 18(4):9.

Ellison, T. (1992). Sport floor dynamics. *Athletic Business*, 16(4):54–60.

Ferguson, M. (1989). Great strides in flooring. *Athletic Business*, 13(11):60–62.

Flynn, R. B. (1985). *Planning facilities for athletics, physical education, and recreation*. Reston, Va: The Athletic Institute and American Alliance for Health, Physical Education, Recreation, and Dance.

Francis, L. (1987). Teaching dance exercise. In N. Van Gelder and S. Marks (Eds.), *Aerobic Dance-Exercise Instructor Manual*, p. 254. San Diego, Cal: International Dance-Exercise Association (IDEA) Foundation.

Klinger, A., Adrian, M., and Tyner-Wilson, M. (1986). *The complete encyclopedia of aerobics: A guide for the aerobics teacher*, pp. 272–273. Ithaca, NY: Mouvement Publications.

Niestemski, S. (1993). Taking control of voice injury. *Fitness Management*, 9(8):40–41.

Patton, R., Grantham, W., Gerson, R., and Gettman, L. (1989). *Developing and managing health/fitness facilities*, pp. 134–136. Champaign, Ill: Human Kinetics.

Ryan, P. (1988). Aerobic floors. *Dance Exercise Today*, 6(4):42–45.

Seals, J., and Cooper, J. (1991). High performing hardwood. *Athletic Business*, 15(3):45–47.

Sport surface improvements. (1989). *Athletic Business*, 13(7):31–35.

Stoll, S., and Beller, J. (1989). *The professional's guide to teaching aerobics*, pp. 94–98, 150. Englewood Cliffs, NJ: Prentice Hall.

Turner, E. (1993). Indoor facilities. In R. Flynn, (Ed.). *Facility planning for physical education, recreation, and athletics*, pp. 37–39. Reston, Va: American Alliance for Health, Physical Education, Recreation, and Dance.

14

Outdoor Sport and Adventure Activity Areas

Jeff Steffen, Scott Hall

OUTDOOR SPORTS AREAS

Outdoor sports areas consist primarily of playing fields for activities such as football, soccer, lacrosse, baseball, softball and similar activities. It is very important when designing, scheduling, and using these facilities to keep safety as the utmost concern. The setup of these fields should provide adequate room between fields so that accidents from balls and participants do not occur. Boundary fencing, walls and light posts should be well padded and not be close to the playing area if possible. Spectators' areas and team benches should also be in safe positions.

Playing Fields and Surfaces

Playing fields can be made of grass, prescription natural turf, or synthetic turf. Each of these surfaces has advantages depending on the use intended for the area. According to Mendel (1992), "perhaps the most scrutinized and argued issue in the comparison between natural and synthetic turf is that of safety."

The traditional grass field provides a low-cost, safe surface for most activities. Only simple maintenance such as mowing, watering, and periodic aeration and fertilization are necessary to keep the area in shape. Although inexpensive, grass surfaces can suffer great damage if overused or used in saturated or soggy conditions. Such damage can be permanent and render a playing field unuseable.

A prescription-type athletic turf is a surface that has taken the positive aspects of a traditional grass playing field and improved on it. This system employs a complex drainage system under the actual grass to drain excess moisture. As a result, the grass grows stronger and more resilient thus allowing for greater usage of the playing surface. This type of surface, however, is expensive—installing the drains and sub-base layers can cost as much as $200,000 for a traditional football or soccer field. Like the traditional grass surface, this type of surface requires routine maintenance procedures. Although a prescription-design turf can be quite expensive, it may be a sound choice for a stadium or practice area that is in constant use.

Another surface for outdoor playing areas is artificial or synthetic turf, which is installed by paving the actual playing area with asphalt and covering it with a closed-cell foam pad. The turf "carpet" is then installed over the pad. Although artificial turf is the most durable and most maintenance-free surface, it also has a high incidence of injury and a large initial installation cost.

Artificial turf allows activities at greater speeds because players and balls move faster. This surface has been blamed for an increased number of injuries, mainly in the sport of football, as a result of increased traction and colliding with the hard playing surface.

Artificial turf is necessary in indoor stadiums, for obvious reasons, but can be an effective choice for extremely wet or harsh climates or high traffic areas. Artificial turf should not be considered for a

Folsum Stadium at the University of Colorado at Boulder (Courtesy of architects Sink Combs Dethlefs, Denver, Colorado)

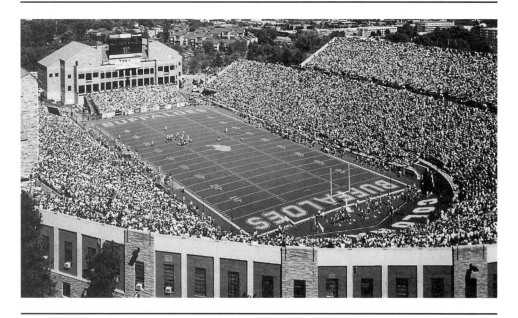

football or track and field if throwing events are to be conducted in the stadium. At the 1992 U.S. Olympic Track and Field Trials in New Orleans' Tad Gormley Stadium, a special raised landing surface of foam and mesh, covered by a layer of turf, had to be installed above the primary artificial turf playing field to protect it from the impact of implements in the throwing events. Artificial turf was

This stadium in Kings Island, Ohio, is the home of the ATP tennis championships. (Courtesy of architects Browning Day Mullins Dierdorf, Indianapolis, Indiana)

chosen for the playing field of Tad Gormley Stadium because it was to be used extensively for high school football and soccer games following the completion of the U.S. Olympic Track and Field Trials. Due to the large expense and trouble (not to mention the destruction of the protective turf covering) of protecting the turf, all track and field meets held at this site since 1992 have conducted the throwing events outside the stadium. One year later in the 1993 NCAA Division I Championship meet, this presented still another problem because the javelin event was held in dangerous conditions after dark.

An ironic example of the use of artificial turf involves the New Jersey Meadowlands, home of the NFL's Giants and Jets teams. Artificial turf continues to be used there not because it provides the best surface on which to play football, but rather because it withstands the punishment it receives from the large crowds that attend numerous rock concerts in the facility on a regular basis.

There are many choices concerning the playing surfaces of outdoor sport areas. For example, "the World Cup doesn't do artificial turf, and the international soccer community has high expectations for the surfaces its teams perform on" (Berg, 1993). Before any decision, the needs of the programs and safety of the participants should be carefully observed and weighed.

Track and Field Areas

A well-planned track and field facility is essential in order to conduct a safe and well-organized com-

The track and field complex at Macalester College in St. Paul, Minnesota, is a well-maintained athletic field. (Courtesy of architects Toltz, King, Duvall, Anderson and Associates, St. Paul, Minnesota; photographer John Geib)

petition. When designing and constructing a track and field facility, it is important to work with a contractor who is a member of the U.S. Track Builders Association. This ensures that the design will meet all of the technical specifications required by such organizations as the National Collegiate Athletic Association (NCAA) and International Amateur Athletic Federation (IAAF). Another benefit of working with an experienced track builder is that the contractor can construct the best track for the available budget.

The facility should be designed to give the athletes the opportunity for optimal performance. Multiple jump and throw areas and the ability to run the sprint events in both directions is important both for performance and for handling large numbers of competitors. A common finish line for all running events prevents confusion by both spectators and officials and eliminates needless delays between races. An adequate and safe warm-up area should be near the competition area to reduce the number of athletes in the competition area and make it safer. A special location should be assigned in the bleachers or alongside the warm-up area for team seating.

Auxiliary facilities such as concessions and a first aid or trainer's area should be planned for the comfort of both spectators and competitors. Telephones are important in case of emergency and a public telephone is helpful. Cellular telephones are common equipment among athletic trainers and emergency medical staff. Concession areas can serve spectators while also providing significant revenue. Periodic announcements by the management can assure the public's awareness and the success in both areas.

To help in preparing the competition facility, a manager who understands the complexities of each event should be selected to see that the facility meets all regulations. He or she should check all equipment (pits, standards, hurdles, etc.) to see that everything is in proper working order. Another role of the manager is to serve as a troubleshooter by anticipating problems and taking action to prevent or correct them. Such action includes setting up flags or barricades to prevent individuals from entering unsafe areas such as the throwing sectors or from crossing the track. Some facilities have added safety fencing (snow or chain link) in strategic places to protect un-

suspecting track runners from being hit by errant or misdirected implements. Protective cages are now mandatory in the discus and hammer events.

Working with the meet director, the facility's manager should estimate the number of contestants in each event and develop a workable schedule. For small meets, sample meet schedules are listed in high school and collegiate rule books. In large invitational meets, the schedule should be determined by the meet director and his or her committee based on such factors as the number of participants and the ability of the facility to handle these athletes safely.

To aid in the organization and conduct of the meet, it is very helpful to enlist volunteer track and field officials. They can do a variety of tasks such as timing and judging, conducting the field events or setting up, moving, or breaking down equipment such as pits and hurdles. Local running and track enthusiasts, school boosters, and parents are also candidates for this group. A complete list of official assignments and their responsibilities is in any track and field coaching or rule book, which are also very helpful in developing a plan or checklist to manage a well-organized meet.

Thoughtful design, proper planning, and the enthusiastic work of officials and support staff lead to an atmosphere conducive to top track and field performances.

Adjacent Areas

To ensure that outdoor sport areas are complete, be certain permanent or portable facilities are available to serve as locker and dressing rooms, public rest rooms, and equipment storage areas. These facilities should be adequate in size and should be located near the playing fields or track facility.

ADVENTURE ACTIVITY AND ROCK-CLIMBING AREAS

The management of adventure activity and rock-climbing areas incorporates many of the concepts presented in Chapters 2 through 10. This section presents issues specifically for management of ropes courses and indoor climbing walls.

Ropes Courses

The management of a ropes course requires a rigorous risk management plan, which begins with annual safety inspections by a reputable ropes course builder. Standards such as those developed by the Association for Challenge Course Technology (ACCT) should be followed for the safety of participants. The manager of the facility should conduct monthly physical inspection of anchors, belay cables, and poles/trees.

Equipment used on a ropes course requires specialized care and storage. Ropes and harnesses require storage in a cool dry place. Care should be taken not to allow ropes and harnesses to be exposed to petroleum products. Keeping ropes clean and limiting exposure to the sun's ultraviolet rays increases the length of their program use. Cordage breaking strength should be a minimum of 5500 pounds. Regardless, ropes should be inspected before each use to check for weak spots or excessive wear. Ropes showing weak spots or excessive wear should be retired from the program immediately. Rope logs are useful to document hours of use. Other equipment such as helmets, carabiners, and belay devices should be inspected monthly.

Security and access are two additional management concerns. Often courses are constructed in areas that are not visible to the public. Fences increase security but can detract from the users' experiences. A common strategy is to restrict access to high elements by requiring the use of a 12-foot ladder or detachable climbing rungs.

Recognized experts in the field provide valuable training in management of and instruction for ropes courses. Properly managed and supervised, a ropes course can serve a wide variety of clientele from elementary students to senior citizens; with modifications, the course can be made accessible to people with physical challenges or disabilities.

Indoor Climbing Walls

With the advent of sport climbing came a surge of popularity in indoor climbing walls. Indoor climbing facilities range from bouldering walls 8 feet high to walls with a variety of surfaces and angles that are 18 to 40 feet high. Regardless of the height, proper management assures a safe experience for the participants. A reputable builder should conduct annual safety inspections of the climbing facility. Procedures for care of ropes, helmets, and harnesses are the same as those mentioned in the previous section. Items of particular concern for indoor wall include belay certification procedures, equipment check-out, supervision, and security.

Standardizing belay certification procedures assures continuity in a program. An example of policies and procedures for the climbing sequence are presented in Figure 14–1.

A sports climbing group created by the Outdoor Recreation Coalition of America (ORCA) provides information in three major areas:

1. *Risk awareness*—specific risk management guidelines for both retailer and manufacturer of sport climbing facilities
2. *Guidelines and standards for manufacturers and testing distribution*—a framework for the con-

There has been a surge in popularity of indoor climbing walls.

Figure 14–1 Indoor climbing wall safety policies

Although there is a wide variety of climbing styles and procedures, The University of Northern Colorado (UNC) has adopted the following safety policies to standardize use of its climbing wall. By adhering to these policies, an internal consistency exists assuring things are done the "right way," and a predictable and safe climbing environment will be established in which both staff and students may safely learn and enjoy themselves.

1. The climbing wall is not to be used without a trained UNC staff member present for the duration of use.

2. All climbers must wear helmets while on the wall. Helmets are to be properly fitted using an adjustable strap and worn flat on the head.

3. No one is to climb on the wall without the use of a belay. The belay system (rope, pulley, and quick link) must be checked by a staff member before it is used. All belayers must be UNC adventure program approved and a backup belayer must be used at all times! Belayers are to give their full attention to the climber while the backup belayer monitors the belayer and keeps the working area of the belayer clear of obstacles and people.

4. Sit harnesses are used to safely support climbers while climbing and give a secure clipping-in point for belaying. Nine-millimeter rope will be used to construct a Studebacher sit harness with the proper finishing knots. Completed harnesses are to be checked by a staff member before being used to climb or belay. Harnesses should be checked by climbers and belayers after each use for proper tightness and that all knots are still secure.

5. Only UNC locking carabiners are to be used to connect ropes to climber and belayer. All carabiners are to be locked so that they screw down.

6. Climbers are to clip into the end of the rope that runs closest to the wall over the pulley. This end of the rope should be finished with a bowline on a bight and a safety knot.

7. The following safety check proceeds every climb: The belayer checks the climber's harness, knots, and that the climber is clipped in correctly. The climber then checks the belayer's harnesses, knots, and that the belay devices are clipped in correctly. The backup belayer then checks both the climber's and belayer's harnesses, knots, and rope connections. Any problems should be corrected before climbing. If there is a disagreement on a problem, ask a staff member to make a final check.

    A. Verbal commands are to be used by the climber and belayer to communicate the start and finish of the climb. The following communication must be used verbatim before the start of every climb:

        CLIMBER: "On belay?"
        BELAYER: "Belay on."
        CLIMBER: "Climbing."
        BELAYER: "Climb away."

    B. At the end of the climb, when the climber has returned to the ground, the following communication should take place signaling that the climber no longer needs a belay:

        CLIMBER: "Off belay."
        BELAYER: "Belay off."

    C. Other commands can be used by the climber to let the belayer know of the climber's intentions and what is expected of the belayer. The following is a list of climber commands and appropriate responses by the belayer:

        CLIMBER: "Tension," or "Up ropes."
        BELAYER ACTION: Take available slack out of rope.
        CLIMBER: "Slack."
        BELAYER ACTION: Give climber rope to lessen tension of rope (usually about 4 to 8 inches for each request).
        CLIMBER: "Down climb."
        BELAYER ACTION: Watch climber and give slack as climber needs it.
        CLIMBER: "Rest."
        BELAYED ACTION: Hold climber in present position until climber gives further directions.

Figure 14–1 (continued)

CLIMBER: "Falling!!!"
BELAYER ACTION: Go immediately to breaking position.

    D. It is often helpful for the belayer to give a verbal response to the climber's request. This can be as simple as "thank you, OK, and got you."

  8. All jewelry should be removed to avoid injuries and interferences while climbing.

  9. Clothing should be comfortable and allow a full range of movement. Large belt buckles and shoes with cleated bottoms should be avoided. Care should be taken to tuck in shirttails and other loose material that could be caught in belay devices.

  10. UNC staff members give regular safety inspections to climbing equipment and climbing wall, but each climber has a responsibility to point out possible safety problems to a UNC staff member.

The safety guidelines for the UNC indoor climbing wall are written with your safety in mind. By disregarding them or skipping a step, you greatly increase your chances of an accident that could injure yourself or another. By taking the time to follow the above guidelines you are insuring your own safety and the continuation of this program.

I have read and understood the complete safety policy and procedures regarding the indoor climbing wall. If not, I will ask for further explanation from a staff member so that I clearly understand each policy and what is expected of me.

Name (please print) _____

Signature _____ Date _____

SOURCE: Jeff Steffen, University of Northern Colorado.

sistent use of equipment from production to consumer

3. *Insurance and legal resources*—ORCA has developed a list of insurance providers and attorneys who are familiar with the industry.

Supervision and security of indoor walls begins with the employment of trained climbing instructors to assure participants receive the most professional level of instruction. Security of the wall can be as simple as a locked door to the facility or more complicated as removing lower holds to 12 feet (access only with a ladder) or some sort of device covering the lower 12 feet of the wall (i.e., curtain or wood panels).

SUMMARY

A brief description of outdoor sports areas is provided. The different types of playing fields, types of surfaces, and auxiliary facilities are addressed.

Because only the basics are explored here, potential sport managers are encouraged to consult in-depth resources and experts for further information about specific areas.

Management of adventure activities and rock-climbing areas requires specific technological knowledge to ensure the safety of participants. As this movement continues to grow, administrators will be forced to consult outside agencies or hire specific technicians to stay abreast of standards and requirements in the field.

QUESTIONS

1. What are the primary concerns when designing and scheduling outdoor facilities?
2. What are the most common surfaces of playing fields?
3. A well-planned track and field facility can provide many advantages when staging a competition. What are the important factors in the design of a quality track and field facility?

ACTIVITY

Choose an outdoor activity, outline your program's needs, and design a facility to meet them.

SUGGESTED READINGS

Doherty, K. (1980). *Track and field omnibook.* Los Altos, Cal: Tasnews Press.

Gambettam, V. (Ed.) (1989). *The athletic congress's track and field coaching manual.* Champaign, Ill: Leisure Press.

Lockrell, D. (1991). *The wilderness educator.* Merrillville, Ind: ICS Books.

Webster, S. (1989). *Ropes course safety manual, an instructor's guide to high and low elements.* Dubuque, Iowa: Kendall/Hunt.

REFERENCES

Berg, R. (1993, May). High-tech turf. *Athletic Business,* p. 47.

Mendel, B. (1992, May). The turf debate resurfaces. *Athletic Management,* p. 23.

15

Facilities for Seniors

Wendy Busch

The uniqueness of managing operations in a sports facility designed for use by senior citizens goes beyond the barrier-free guidelines set forth in the Americans with Disabilities Act (ADA) and must consider all of the needs of the population it serves. Addressing those needs at the inception of facility design is ideal, however, existing facilities can be renovated to create a user-friendly atmosphere for these clients. A well-designed sport and activity area for seniors can be good sales and marketing tools, especially with the aging of the currently active population.

The most critical management elements to consider when addressing exercise facilities for seniors include the staff and its experience level, appropriate programming and, of course, the actual exercise facility. The age-related declines of the human sensorium are complex and usually present in multiples. How well a facility's physical accommodations for age-related changes are planned and integrated is a basic concern for designers, the staff, and ultimately the members. The type of community and the activity level of the residents also determine appropriate management, from staff and operations to medical evacuation plans.

STAFFING

The most critical decision is the selection of qualified staff who have experience working with older adults and who are familiar with the special needs of the older population. The staff not only has responsibility for the safety of participants but should also be active in creating policies and procedures for them. Experienced personnel have the knowledge and ability to adapt programs and the skill to recommend changes when necessary.

The staff may also be responsible for the selection of appropriate exercise equipment for lease or purchase. Some older individuals are not physically capable of using the same equipment that younger people use in their regular exercise regimens. Maintenance logs of the equipment in the exercise facility must remain current and the staff should consider this duty a very important part of their domain. Aside from the legal aspect of record keeping, a daily inspection of the equipment ensures the machines are in safe, good working order.

PROGRAMMING

Regular exercise programs that address the specific needs of the older population must be developed. Sport and fitness programs for seniors must concentrate on building strength and maintaining skills for the Activities of Daily Living (ADL). The simple action of turning a door knob when suffering from advanced osteo- or rheumatoid arthritis is a painful challenge. Aside from arthritis, many seniors suffer from a variety of age-related conditions, many of which can be managed with appropriate exercise. An example of such a condition relates to the balance and gait difficulties often apparent in older individuals. A lessening of overall body strength can combine with changes in the vestibular and visual systems and create a predis-

Many seniors actively engage in exercise programs to stay fit and healthy. (Courtesy of College of Health and Human Sciences, University of Northern Colorado, Greeley, Colorado)

position for falling. Falling is often the major consideration when elderly individuals use your facility. An individual who is predisposed to falling may offset weaknesses by developing strength, coordination, and flexibility through appropriate exercises. A proper exercise prescription for individuals or groups should address the physical and the psychosocial needs of older individuals. Management of such a program should be under the direction of staff members experienced with aging populations.

DESIGN

A well-designed facility to serve seniors should have enhancements beyond barrier-free design. An easily accessible exercise area is the most obvious planning challenge for sport and fitness facilities. What is not obvious are the enhancements designers must create when initially drafting or renovating an existing facility to accommodate age-related physical deficiencies. These accommodations include considerations for lighting, flooring, wall coverings, acoustics, and heating and air conditioning.

Lighting

Older individuals may have experienced changes that impact several aspects of vision. These changes can affect not only a person's visual acuity, but also the ability to perceive certain colors, light-to-dark

adaptation, and interference from glare. The area must be well lighted with a combination of natural and high-intensity discharge lights (HIDs). The light should be two to three times brighter than what would be selected for a younger population. The safety of transition zones adjacent to the exercise areas must not be overlooked. Seniors may have a longer light-to-dark adaptation time, so hallways must be well lighted. Glare creates problems for seniors and must not be induced while increasing light levels (Brown, 1987; Patton et al., 1989).

Colors

The yellowing of the cornea and presence of changes in the crystalline lens of the eye cause a shift in the visual spectrum, creating a decrease in sensitivity to blues, greens, and mauves. An individual with an age-related color shift will see reds, oranges, and yellows (longer wavelength colors) more easily. This knowledge can be useful when selecting colors of floors or designating specific areas for weights or equipment. Contrasting colors are a good designator for a carpet border or accenting the area where the wall and floor meet.

Visual Acuity

Older individuals may wear bi- or trifocal corrective lenses that change the ability of the eye to focus smoothly. This affects a person's ability to handle changes in floor levels or transition zones; appropriate modifications can denote changes in flooring type or elevation. Signage is another important consideration; all signs in an exercise or strength and conditioning area must be in large, bold print, especially signs concerning heart rates and proper use of machines. Wall clocks should have faces large enough for seniors to view easily when taking heart rates during exercise class. All other facility signage (informational, directional, and emergency) should also be designed with seniors in mind.

Flooring

An age-related change in nerve transmission in the central and peripheral nervous system creates an overall decrease of kinesthetic awareness. Older individuals may experience additional challenges if decrements in balance, gait, and vision are present. The choice of flooring and floor coverings is critical for safety as well as esthetics. When selecting flooring and floor coverings, it is important to consider ambulatory individuals as well as wheelchair users, therefore, a proper energy return factor is necessary. The floor covering must not impede wheelchairs, be easily maintained, not have a shiny or slippery surface (which could contribute to glare or falling), and should not create acoustical problems in the area. When selecting colors, it is important to consider the age-related perceptual changes that occur in color vision. Floor covering can be designed to designate the proximity of walls, ramps, or exits using this knowledge. Seniors like warm colors because they can "see" them and the colors should reflect this preference (Brown, 1987).

Wall Covering

The wall coverings should neither be too busy nor too boring. The older eye tires easily with a "busy" background. Floor-to-ceiling mirrors enable the participants of an exercise or strength class to correct faulty biomechanics. The reflection of more light without glare is also an advantage of mirrors (Savage, 1987).

Acoustics

Age-related changes of hearing include a rising sound threshold and a decline in the ability to dis-criminate a particular sound from background noise. In a proper sound system, speakers may best be placed by an acoustical engineer. An acoustical engineer has the expertise to compensate for background sound generated by fans or air conditioners. As with other considerations, it is important to "get it right the first time." Costs can be high if incorrect choices are made initially; modifying mistakes can be expensive (Pelton, 1987; Patton et al., 1989).

Climate

Older people have a diminished ability of thermal regulation and are at a greater risk of hyper- or hypothermia than younger individuals. To compensate for this age-related change an exercise area for seniors should have adequate ventilation, heating, and air conditioning. If fans are necessary, it is important that they not become sound generators by creating background noise, which is bothersome for individuals with hearing loss.

STRENGTH AND WEIGHT TRAINING AREAS

Strength and conditioning should be a major component of any sport and fitness facility and it is especially important for the senior population (Evans and Rosenberg, 1991). Ideally, hand weights and machines should be in separate areas. If limited space does not permit separate areas, the border area or a section of an exercise room can be designated for weights and machines. If a strength and conditioning area is also in a general exercise area, conflicts must be managed through scheduling or limiting class size in both sections. These areas should be bright, open, free of barriers and accessible to wheelchairs. Floor-to-ceiling mirrors are necessary for seniors to monitor their performances and techniques when lifting or using machines. A single colored, durable carpet that contrasts visually with weights and equipment is an ideal floor covering and preferred over rubberized mats, which typically have an uneven surface. An improper surface can create a hazard for seniors with gait, balance, or vision difficulties (Hutton, 1991). Lighting and wall coverings should be appropriate for the strength and conditioning area according to the specific principles stated above.

Weight room signage is important to demonstrate and remind exercisers of proper techniques for using machines and weights. Encouraging and reminding clients to wear proper clothing when using certain machines is important because seniors may not know of the need for proper footwear when using a treadmill, for example. Brightly colored posters with large print and large pictures displayed in the appropriate areas can also be beneficial.

EQUIPMENT

Seniors may or may not have physical challenges that make exercise difficult. The selection of equipment for a senior exercise area should assume that the majority of users has some form of age-related impairment due to arthritis, Parkinson's disease, obesity, or balance and gait difficulties. The equipment should be easy to use and easily accessed by seniors. As an example, the recent evolution of the recumbent bicycle provides an efficient workout and back support and is easily mounted and dismounted. Other senior-friendly improvements in equipment are motorized treadmills that are pre-programmed for a 0 M.P.H. start and 0% incline, including progressive warm-ups and cool-downs. The new generation of aerobic trainers has an improved capability to measure a user's heart rate and the next generation of equipment will enable the user to have an individually prescribed exercise program loaded into the equipment's on-board computer. This is beneficial for heart rehabilitation patients and other users monitoring for special needs. The initial cost of a machine and its maintenance must be weighed against the benefits for the facility and the people participating in fitness programs.

Weights are very important to maintain and build strength, especially in frail or previously sedentary individuals (Cress, 1993). Free weights can be used by the majority of this population, including wheelchair users and those participating in chair exercises. Cuff-type free weights are useful for individuals who have arthritis in their hands or who are unable to grasp a handle. Weight benches should support the back and enable the user full range of motion during the weight portion of the workout. Finally, the weight and equipment area of an exercise facility for seniors should be super-vised by an individual who has experience working with seniors.

EMERGENCIES

Although all established emergency procedures should be in place, managers must develop plans to meet the specific needs of seniors. This includes general evacuation procedures and protocols for medical and general emergencies. Ideally, areas used by seniors have direct access to the street or parking area to accommodate emergency vehicles. If this is not possible, consideration for the best location must be written into evacuation and emergency plans.

It is wise to have a direct emergency telephone line in the area, as well as specialized emergency equipment. If a direct line is not possible, 911 signage should be prominently displayed on or near the phone. In addition, personal breathing masks for performing CPR should be easily accessible to staff throughout the facility. A standard location (i.e., at a fire extinguisher) ensures the staff's ability to react quickly while protecting themselves against communicable or infectious diseases. A portable oxygen bottle is an excellent addition to an emergency equipment list. Oxygen kept in an exercise area can be used by your staff or emergency personnel. In a population of older participants, heat disease, hypertension, and other profound diseases is considerably higher than in a younger population.

SUMMARY

Clearly, appropriate design and management considerations benefit all populations and ages. Nowhere is this more apparent than with the elderly. Properly designed sport and exercise facilities can enhance an elderly person's quality of life by maintaining skills (ADLs) and slowing age-related declines. The positive effects of exercise go beyond physical capabilities and extend into the psychosocial realm. This is truly an important consideration for seniors, who, as a group, have a high incidence of isolation and depression. Sport and fitness areas for seniors should address physical age-related changes and make accommodations for individuals with a multiplicity of challenges. The facility should be user-friendly and incorporate the right combination of staff, equipment and physical surroundings, and age-appropriate programs. As our population ages, the number of facilities that cater to seniors is increasing and becoming more competitive. The aging population of "baby-boomers" is creating a demand for well-managed and properly designed facilities with high levels of quality and sophistication. Additionally, the caliber of exercise activities and sport-related programs has become a critical factor in the selection of a facility. Designers and managers of sports facilities have a unique opportunity to create a successful business and concomitantly enhance the quality of life for the senior population.

QUESTIONS

1. What are the unique aspects of managing operations for senior citizens?
2. How are population trends affecting sports facility development?
3. Which characteristics describe a sports facility designed primarily for senior citizens?
4. How is programming for the older population different from programming for children, students, and young adults?

ACTIVITIES

1. Develop a checklist of criteria to determine if a facility is user-friendly for senior citizens. Visit facilities and assess them using the checklist. Defend your position.
2. How would you resolve the following managerial challenges? Defend your position.
   A. A group of senior citizens wants the swimming pool temperature to be warmer and the competitive swimmers are arguing for cooler temperatures.
   B. A committee to decorate the new community recreation center, for all ages, is split on choices of colors. One group wants bright colors in patterns and textures; another wants neutral tones of beige and gray.
   C. The finance committee has to make some decisions about investing a certain amount in one of the following: better central air conditioning, skylights with electronic shades, a staff member for seniors, the latest computerized treadmill.

SUGGESTED READINGS

Hall, K. B. (1991). Designing fitness trails for seniors. *Parks and Recreation*, 26(8): 28–31.

Hooyman, N., and Kiyak, A. (1996). *Social gerontology.* Needham Heights, Mass: Simon and Schuster.

Penner, D. (1990). *Elder fit: A health and fitness guide for older adults.* Reston, Va: AAHPERD Publications.

Swaringen, J., and Raynor, M. (Eds.) (1990). *Senior games planning guide.* Raleigh, NC: North Carolina Senior Games.

REFERENCES

Brown, W. J. (1987). From Churchill to china dishes. *National Association for Senior Living Industries (NASLI) News*, 3(4):1, 19, 29.

Cress, M. E. (1993). Age-related changes: A scientific basis for exercise programming. *Topics in Geriatric Rehabilitation*, 8(3):22–36.

Evans, W., and Rosenberg, I. H. (1992). *Biomarkers.* New York: Simon and Schuster.

Hutton, T. (1991, November/December). Falls. *APDAP News Transmitter.*

Patton, R. W., Grantham, W. C., Gerson, R. F., and Gettman, L. R. (1989). *Developing and managing health/fitness facilities.* Champaign, Ill: Human Kinetics.

Pelton, H. K. (1987). Have you heard of the acoustical environment of a retirement center? *National Association for Senior Living Industries (NASLI) News*, 3(4):9, 21, 30.

Savage, C. (1987). Color your projects with research. *National Association for Senior Living Industries (NASLI) News*, 3(4):7, 29.

16

Facilities for Impaired Persons

Todd Seidler

Recreational and competitive sports are undergoing tremendous change. To stay abreast of these changes, facility and program managers must remain aware of technological advances in facilities and equipment, the latest management techniques, trends in program popularity, and identifying and attracting new user groups, among others. This chapter focuses on one potentially huge group of participants that has traditionally been overlooked by many activity and sports providers, that is, people with disabilities.

According to Wyeth (1989), more than 46 million people in the United States have a significant disability. Approximately 75 percent of these people are between the ages of 16 and 64. In the past, people with disabilities were often told, directly or indirectly, that they should be inactive and not participate in sports and recreational activities. Fortunately this attitude has been changing over the last several years. Doctors, therapists, and disabled people have recognized the fact that participating in these activities is at least as beneficial for people with disabilities as it is for people who do not have disabilities. This enlightened attitude has brought a steady increase in the number of people with disabilities who desire to participate in activity programs. This often overlooked group represents a mostly untapped resource of potential participants. In order to attract and provide facilities and programs for people with disabilities, facility and program managers must understand the basic accommodations that are required.

BASIC CONCEPTS

Facility managers must remain aware of constantly changing legal requirements that affect facility operations. First and foremost, facility managers and program directors have a legal duty to provide safe facilities, equipment, and programs for all participants. A proactive risk management program is now necessary and must be executed on a continuing basis (see Chapter 6). The Occupational Safety and Health Administration (OSHA) established guidelines for safety in construction, equipment, and maintenance in 1970. Two years later Title IX of the Educational Amendment Act was enacted to end discrimination on the basis of sex in educational settings. The Architectural Barriers Act of 1968 and Section 504 of the Rehabilitation Act of 1973 require that federally assisted facilities meet stringent accessibility requirements. Public Law 94-142 provides for free and appropriate education for children with disabilities in the least restrictive environment, while Public Law 95-606, the Amateur Sports Act, mandates that the United States Olympic Committee ensure competitive sports opportunities for athletes with disabilities (Sherrill, 1986).

Perhaps the most sweeping and important legislation that impacts facility and program managers is the Americans with Disabilities Act (ADA) of 1990. The ADA (Public Law 101-336) is a comprehensive civil rights legislation that is strong, clear, and enforceable and mandates full accommodation for people with disabilities. The ADA defines *disability* as a physical or mental impairment that substantially limits one or more of an individual's major activities of daily living such as walking, hearing, speaking, seeing, learning, and performing manual tasks.

One of the primary purposes of the ADA is to ensure that facilities and organizations that provide public accommodations are usable by all people. It requires that any recreation or sports provider make "reasonable accommodations," for participants who have disabilities. It does not require separate facilities for people with disabilities. The intent is to give people at all levels of ability access to facilities and programs at the same time and, when possible, interacting with each other. The ADA influences the design of facilities, equipment, and programs and is having a widespread effect on recreational and sports opportunities.

It is not possible nor is it the intent of this chapter to give specific details of planning accessible facilities. At the present time, understanding the specifics of the Americans with Disabilities Act Accessibility Guidelines (ADAAG) may be somewhat difficult and confusing. They are written in mostly broad terms and are very subject to interpretation. Several unofficial documents claim to provide accurate, specific information on the ADA but they do not carry official or legal authority. The Architectural Transportation Barriers Compliance Board, also known as the Access Board, has recognized the need for more specific guidelines in order to remove much of the guesswork for sports and recreation professionals. These guidelines should make compliance with and enforcement of the ADA much simpler.

PLANNING FOR ACCESSIBILITY

The requirements mandated by the ADA for existing facilities are different from those of new facilities or those undergoing a major renovation. For new construction or a major renovation, the guidelines are fairly straightforward: It is necessary to comply with all of the requirements of the ADA.

For existing facilities, compliance is less clear. The ADA mandates that all architectural and communication barriers limiting people with disabilities be removed. This rule, however, only applies when removal is "readily achievable," which is de-

fined as removal that is easy to accomplish and can be carried out with little difficulty or expense. Thus, expensive building or renovation is not always required. An organization can provide accessibility to programs by any of several other methods. They include acquiring a different facility, moving a program to an accessible facility, and providing services at alternative sites (through renting, leasing, trade-outs, etc.). Because every situation is different, each case is evaluated on its merits. The facility's manager must use his or her best judgment about how to proceed.

Making a facility accessible and inviting to people with disabilities begins in the parking lot. Sometimes just getting in the front door and to the front counter is half the battle. It is important to provide reserved, accessible parking spaces, drop-off areas, appropriate curb cuts, and if necessary, a low-slope ramp to the front door. Participants with physical disabilities should not have to use a side or rear entrance. They should be able to use the same entrance and facilities as their friends, companions, or relatives who accompany them. At the main entrance, an extra wide electrically operated door allows easy access to the facility itself. An accessible, inviting facility has a section of the business counter that is lower than normal in order to make it comfortable for a person in a wheelchair or a short person to ask questions or fill out paperwork. This also makes it more inviting and user-friendly for children.

When planning a facility's accessibility it is important to keep in mind the different types of limitations people have. A common mistake is to assume that "accessibility" means a facility is accessible to someone in a wheelchair. Participants or staff may have or encounter a range of limitations. Disabled people use power wheelchairs, manual wheelchairs, crutches, walkers, or prostheses or may be able to walk with some level of assistance. Some speech, hearing, and mental impairments are not readily observable. Visual impairments range from minimal to total blindness. Participants may be partially or completely deaf. Still others have limited physical strength or a mental impairment.

It is helpful to visualize a person with one of the disabilities listed above and imagine that person on a visit to the facility being planned. From the parking lot to the main entrance, all through the facility, and then back to the parking lot. What are the barriers and what is the best way to eliminate them? Different limitations require different kinds of accommodations, so it is necessary to go through this process to look at the facility from several perspectives. It can be very enlightening to recruit several people with different disabilities to assist in the planning of the facility.

It is much easier and less expensive to plan a new facility to accommodate those with disabilities than it is to remodel an existing one. When planning the construction of a new facility or the renovation of an existing facility, it is recommended that someone with insight into the specific needs of people with disabilities be on the planning committee. Professional consultants are available who specialize in planning recreational or sports facilities to meet or surpass the guidelines set forth by the ADA. In addition to having at least one disabled person on the planning committee, it is wise to have one or several review the plans before the construction documents are drawn. As with any other area of concern in the planning process, it is essential for the committee to do its homework and learn all that it can about accessibility.

STAFF AWARENESS

A high level of customer service is an essential element of well-managed facilities and programs. In order to provide good service to people with disabilities, staff members must first develop an awareness of the basic disabilities and the common problems these individuals face. It is usually not accurate to assume that staff members know how to provide a high level of customer service to all patrons. Formal training programs for all staff dealing with the public is usually necessary. First and foremost, all customers should be treated with dignity, courtesy, and respect. People with disabilities want to be treated like any other patron.

Staff training can be provided in a number of ways. Consultants can be brought in to run in-service workshops or clinics on disabilities and accommodating them. Some companies sponsor a disability awareness day with great success. Arranging for one or several people with disabili-

ties to use the facility and then give careful feedback on their treatment to staff members can also be an effective training tool.

It is important to make all clients feel welcome. Some common responses to people with physical disabilities include talking to their companions as if the person with the disability weren't there ("I asked the question, tell me"), talking louder than normal to someone with a visual impairment ("I don't see very well but I can hear you just fine") and talking to a person with a physical disability as if he or she had a mental impairment ("I'm an adult. Don't talk down to me").

Common sense will guide some actions but many of the things the staff should know about courtesy and service to people who have disabilities are not always realized by staff members. For example, whenever possible, staff should sit, squat, or kneel when dealing with a person in a wheelchair. It is more polite to talk to someone eye-to-eye rather than look down on him or her. On occasion a physically disabled client has a problem with a urine-leg bag. If a spill occurs, someone familiar with procedures to dispose of infectious materials should be available. Also, when talking to someone with a severe visual impairment, staff members should introduce themselves each time so the customer knows who they are. Also, when giving directions, explain them. It does not do much good to point or say "over there."

Programs and facilities for able-bodied and people with disabilities should be integrated whenever possible. The ideal situation allows a disabled patron the choice of participating in an activity open to all or taking part only with those of similar abilities. The important thing to realize is that customer service, for all customers, is an essential facet of our business and effective training will ensure that we provide the best for all users.

COMPETITIVE SPORTS

Sports for people with mental impairments are different from sports for people with physical disabilities. Special Olympics is designed to allow those with mental retardation, specifically, to have a chance to participate in activities. The emphasis is on participation, not winning. On the other hand, sports programs for athletes with physical disabilities are designed for competition.

One area of sports programming that is growing rapidly is competitive sports for those with physical disabilities. These sporting events are occurring from the local "grass roots" level all the way up to world-class competitions. The ultimate event occurs every four years when the Paralympics are held in conjunction with the International Olympics. In fact, the Paralympics and the International Olympics use the same venues and facilities, which are designed with the needs of all athletes in mind.

We must get away from the perception that people with disabilities are helpless or cannot do much. This attitude is mainly born out of ignorance and sympathy. One only has to attend one of these sporting events to see just how "able" those with disabilities really are. Athletes with physical impairments are classified to ensure fairness and an equitable starting point from which to compete. Just as athletes without disabilities are categorized by gender, age, weight, and so forth, athletes with disabilities are classified by functional ability. Through this system of classification, even athletes experiencing severe functional limitations, (e.g., muscular dystrophy, osteogenesis imperficta, quadriplegia, cerebral palsy, amputation, and spinal cord injury) are able to participate in sports and compete against athletes with similar abilities.

Along with the traditional competitive sports, some have been adapted to accommodate the different abilities of athletes with disabilities. Examples include wheelchair basketball, sit volleyball, three-track, mono-, and sit skiing, boccia, and tandem events for athletes with visual impairments. Other events such as goal ball, slalom (wheelchair obstacle course), and field events (club throw, high toss, soft discus, and others) have been created specifically to meet the abilities of certain groups of athletes.

Competitive sports for athletes with physical disabilities are quickly increasing in numbers and can open up a variety of opportunities for the sports programmer to attract new participants.

SUMMARY

The job of managing facilities related to sports and activity programs is increasingly complex. With budgets being reduced, customers' priorities constantly changing, innovations in technology, and many other factors affecting the job, it is more difficult to stay up with new methods to increase productivity. Not many professions demand such knowledge in so many diverse areas. In most organizations, there is a constant search for new methods of marketing programs and attracting clientele. The community

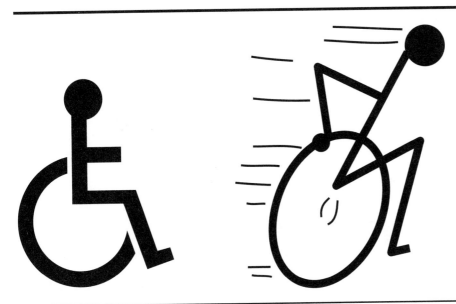

Figure 16–1
"Speedy" is the active version of the international symbol for accessibility.

of people with disabilities represents a vast pool of potential customers. In order to attract this group, many stereotypes must be suspended and a new awareness developed. One example of action to change the stereotypes is the development of "Speedy," an alternative to the international symbol of accessibility. Speedy shows movement, unlike the old, passive graphic (Figure 16–1).

Simply meeting a basic minimum standard can comply with the ADA, but human decency and customer service require us to go beyond. Sports and recreation facilities and programs should not be just accessible, but should be inviting and friendly for everyone.

QUESTIONS

1. Where can a facility manager go for specific information on the ADA?
2. What is meant by "readily achievable"?
3. How do you define *disability*? Does your definition differ from (how?) or match the ADA's definition?
4. What is the fundamental difference in philosophy between Special Olympics and sports for athletes with physical disabilities?
5. Why is it important for all staff members to be familiar with the needs of all patrons?

ACTIVITIES

1. To get a real feel for the problems of facility accessibility it is helpful to get first-hand experience. If you are not in one already, get in a wheelchair.
   A. Spend a couple of hours going through a sports or recreational facility in the wheelchair without standing or using your legs or feet for any reason. No cheating!! Go through the entire facility—locker rooms, rest rooms, showers, parking lot, weight room, lobbies, racquetball courts, gyms, offices, and so on. Try using telephones, drinking fountains, emergency exits, customer service counters, equipment check-out counters, and any other general facilities or services you encounter.
   B. Now, imagine how difficult your tour would be with limited or no use of your arms (quadriplegia).
   C. Make a list of the difficulties and obstacles you encountered and suggestions for reducing or eliminating them.
2. Repeat your tour while simulating a different disability. Try it on crutches, using hands clenched into fists, or no hands. Using a blindfold, try to navigate the fa-

cility with minimal or no assistance. For safety reasons, and to avoid total frustration, do this with another person.

3. Report your experiences in class and compare results.
4. Contact one of the Disabled Sports Organizations (DSOs), national or local, and get as much information about that organization as you can. In a classroom setting, different students can be responsible for obtaining information from each of the DSOs. This information can then be shared in class.

SUGGESTED READINGS

Architectural and Transportation Barriers Compliance Board (1991). Accessibility guidelines for buildings and facilities; Transportation facilities; Amendment to final guidelines. (36 CFR Part 1191) *Federal Register*, 56(173):45500–45527.

Berg, R. (1991). Rights of passage. *Athletic Business*, 15(11).

Department of Justice (1991). Nondiscrimination on the basis of disability by public accommodations and in commercial facilities: Final rule. (28 CFR Part 36) *Federal Register*, 56(144):35544–35691.

Miller, D. A. (1990). Designing rec facilities for multiple populations. *Athletic Business*, 14(10).

Munson, A. L., and Comodeca, J. A. (1993). The act of inclusion. *Athletic Management*, V(4).

Nesbitt, J. A. (1986). *The International directory of recreation-oriented assistive device sources*. Marina Del Ray, Cal: Lifeboat Press.

Paciorek, M., and Jones, J. (1989). Sports and recreation for the disabled: A resource manual. Indianapolis, Ind: Benchmark.

Public Law 101-336 (1990, July 26). *Americans with Disabilities Act of 1990*. Washington, DC: U.S. Government Printing Office.

Staff. (1992). Open wide. Facility managers and the ADA. *Athletic Business*, 16(6).

The Americans with Disabilities Act Accessibility Guidelines for Buildings and Facilities (ADAAG) and the Uniform Federal Accessibility Standards (UFAS) can be obtained free of charge by calling the Architectural & Transportation Barriers Compliance Board (ATBCB) at (800) 872-2253.

REFERENCES

Bosco, P. (1994). The ADA: today, tomorrow and tomorrow? *Buildings*, 88(2).

Cohen, A. (1993). Help wanted? Help found. *Athletic Business*, 17(10).

Flynn, R. (1993). *Planning facilities for physical educa-

tion, recreation and athletics. Reston Va: American Alliance for Health, Physical Education, Recreation and Dance.

Krotee, M. L., and Blair, P. F. (1991). International dimensions of HPERD, sport, and aging. *Journal of Physical Education, Recreation and Dance,* 50(5).

Reiner, L. S. (1994). The ADA challenge. *Athletic Business,* 18(8).

Seidler, T. L., Turner, E. T., and Horine, L. (1993). Promoting active lifestyles through facilities and equipment. *Journal of Physical Education, Recreation and Dance,* 64(2).

Sherrill, C. (1986). *Adapted physical education and recreation,* Dubuque, Iowa: Wm C. Brown.

Wyeth, D. O. (1989). Breaking barriers and changing attitudes. *Journal of Osteopathic Medicine,* 3(4):5–10.

APPENDIX A

Samples of Legal Documents

A-1

Summons Before the Circuit Court

Jane Doe	Plaintiff	)
		)
VS		) Case No. CV123-456CC
		)
REGIONAL MEDICAL CENTER	Defendant	)
		)

The State of Missouri to: REGIONAL MEDICAL CENTER
PLEASE SERVE:

_____

_____

_____

Pleading to the Petition, a copy of which is attached hereto, and to serve a copy of your pleadings upon

_____

Attorney for PLAINTIFF, all within 30 days after service of this summons upon you, exclusive of the day of service. If you fail to do so, judgment by default will be taken against you for the relief demanded in the Petition. PLAINTIFF'S INTERROGATORIES TO DEFENDANT; PLAINTIFF'S REQUEST FOR PRODUCTION OF DOCUMENTS TO DEFENDANT REGIONAL MEDICAL CENTER

Dated: May 15, 19XX   _____, CIRCUIT CLERK
Fee Enclosed: $00.00   by _____, Deputy Clerk

RETURN OF SERVICE OF SUMMONS

I hereby certify that I have served the within Summons by: (check one)
_____ delivering a copy of the Summons and Petition to the Defendant(s) _____

_____

_____ leaving a copy of the Summons and Petition at the dwelling place or usual abode of the Defendant(s) with _____ a person of the Defendant's family over the age of 15 years.
_____ making a due and diligent search and failing to find the within-named _____

_____ (for service on a corporation) delivering a copy of the Summons and the Petition to: (include name, title and address) _____

SERVED IN _____ _____ ON THIS _____ DAY OF _____, 19XX.
    (county)   (state)

Sheriff's Fees:
Summons $ _____
Non-Est $ _____   _____
Mileage $ _____   Sheriff of _____ County,
Total $ _____   By _____
Page No.   _____   Deputy Sheriff
                                                            Attorney Notified: _____

A-2

Petition in Damages in the Circuit Court

Jane Doe, Plaintiff,

VS

REGIONAL MEDICAL
CENTER, Defendant.

)
)
)
)
)
)
)
)
)
)
)
)
)

Case No. CV123-456CC

Count I

As and for her cause of action against Defendant, Regional Medical Center, for personal injuries, Plaintiff states:

1. Plaintiff is a resident of the County of _____, State of _____.

2. Defendant Regional Medical Center is a Corporation and can be served by serving _____ _____ at Defendant's business office located at _____.

3. The tortious acts herein complained of occurred in whole or substantial part in _____ County, state of _____.

4. At all times concerned herein, Defendant occupied and controlled the business premises located at _____.

5. At all times concerned herein, Defendant transacted business with the general public at the relevant location as an exercise facility, offering various exercise classes for the general public.

6. Defendant owed a duty to the general public, and the Plaintiff, in particular, to keep Defendant's premises safe and without hazard.

7. At all times concerned herein, Defendant was a public business open to provide services to the invited public and Plaintiff, in particular, and as such Plaintiff was a business invitee of the premises.

8. On or about September 21, 19XX, Plaintiff was at the premises of Defendant located at _____ _____, and fell, violently and forcefully striking the floor and causing the injuries hereinafter described.

9. The floor on which Plaintiff fell was a dangerous, unsafe condition to Defendant's patrons in general and Plaintiff in particular.

10. The injuries of Plaintiff as below described were a direct and proximate result of the Defendant's negligence in one, more or all of the following particulars, to wit:

    a. The Defendant negligently failed and omitted to provide any warnings of the dangerousness of the condition of the floor;

    b. The Defendant knew or in the exercise of ordinary care should have known that said floor was in an unsafe condition and that patrons and invitees such as Plaintiff would be caused to fall;

c. The Defendant negligently failed to perform supervision and ordinary maintenance to see that the floor of its facility was properly maintained and in a safe condition;

d. The Defendant negligently failed to inspect the area of Plaintiff's fall;

e. The Defendant negligently designed and constructed the floor where Plaintiff fell in such a way and with such materials as to create an unsafe condition.

11. As a direct and proximate result of the aforesaid negligence of the Defendant, Regional Medical Center, Plaintiff has sustained the following injuries: all the bones, organs, muscles, tendons, tissues, nerves, veins, arteries, ligaments, circulation, membranes, discs, cartilages, and joints of her body were fractured, broken, ruptured, punctured, compressed, dislocated, separated, bruised, contused, narrowed, abrased, lacerated, burned, cut, torn, wrenched, swollen, ulcerated, strained, sprained, inflamed and infected; she has incurred and will continue to incur expenses as and for physicians and medical expenses; there has been a complete loss of enjoyment and the fruits of enjoyment of life, all to her damage. Further, that the Plaintiff Jane Doe has suffered a loss of income and impairment of ability to earn an income as a result of this occurrence and injuries are permanent and will in the future be impairing, limiting and painful.

12. WHEREFORE, Plaintiff Jane Doe prays for judgment against Defendant, Regional Medical Center, in such sum that is fair and reasonable, for her costs herein incurred, and for prejudgment interest from the date of the accident, or as otherwise provided by law.

Count II

As and for her cause of action against Defendent, Regional Medical Center, for personal injuries, Plaintiff states:

13. Plaintiff realleges and incorporates the above and foregoing paragraphs one through twelve inclusive, as if fully set forth herein *in haec verba*.

14. At the above-mentioned time and place, Plaintiff attended an exercise class conducted by Defendant.

15. At said time, Plaintiff weighed approximately two hundred and ten pounds, was five feet four inches tall, and was fifty-two years old.

16. The accident aforesaid and injuries and damages hereinafter described were the direct and approxi-

mate result of the negligence, carelessness, faults and omissions of the Defendant in one, more or all of the following particulars, to wit:

a. Defendant and its employees negligently failed to take a medical history from Plaintiff to evaluate her risk factors;

b. Defendant and its employees negligently failed to require Plaintiff to undergo a physical examination before beginning physical activity;

c. Defendant and its employees negligently failed to instruct Plaintiff in the proper way to perform the exercises that she was to be involved with;

d. Defendant and its employees negligently failed to instruct Plaintiff in the proper way to monitor her vital signs;

e. Defendant and its employees negligently failed to instruct Plaintiff in the proper wearing apparel for the exercises to be conducted;

f. Defendant and its employees negligently failed to provide Plaintiff with adequate warm-up activities before starting the exercises;

g. Defendant negligently failed to provide a trained professional to lead and conduct the class;

h. Defendant and its employees negligently failed to evaluate Plaintiff's risk factors in order to determine the type and level of activity that she should have been involved in;

i. Defendant negligently failed to advise Plaintiff in the proper way to exercise safely;

j. Defendant negligently failed to provide adequate warnings and instructions concerning the risks and dangers of the exercise program that Plaintiff was participating in.

17. As a direct and proximate result of the aforesaid negligence of Defendant, Regional Medical Center, Plaintiff has sustained the following injuries: all the bones, organs, muscles, tendons, tissues, nerves, veins, arteries, ligaments, circulation, membranes, discs, cartilages, and joints of her body were fractured, broken, ruptured, punctured, compressed, dislocated, separated, bruised, contused, narrowed, abrased, lacerated, burned, cut, torn, wrenched, swollen, ulcerated, strained, sprained, inflamed and infected; she has incurred and will continue to incur expenses as and for physicians and medical expenses; there has been a complete loss of enjoyment and the fruits of enjoyment of life, all to her damage. Further, that the Plaintiff Jane Doe has suffered a loss of income and impairment of ability to earn an income as a result of this occurrence; all of the aforesaid injuries were caused by said occurrence and are permanent and will in the future be impairing, limiting and painful.

WHEREFORE, Plaintiff prays for judgment against Defendant, Regional Medical Center, in such sum that is fair and reasonable, for her costs herein incurred, and for prejudgment interest from the date of the accident, or as otherwise provided by law.

Count III

As and for her cause of action against Defendant, Regional Medical Center, for personal injuries, Plaintiff states:

18. Plaintiff realleges and incorporates the above and foregoing paragraphs one through seventeen, as if fully set forth herein *in haec verba.*

19. Defendant expressly warranted to Plaintiff that Defendant's trained experts would advise her on how to safely exercise.

20. Further, Defendant expressly warranted that Defendant's trained fitness professionals would determine the exercise program best suited to Plaintiff's needs.

21. Such representations by the Defendant were made to induce Plaintiff to participate in exercise programs offered by Defendant and were a material factor in Plaintiff's decision to participate in said programs.

22. In participating in the exercise program, Plaintiff relied on the skill and judgment of Defendant and its employees and the express warranties described above.

23. Defendant's trained experts did not advise Plaintiff on how to safely begin an exercise program, nor did Defendant's trained fitness professionals determine the exercise program best suited to Plaintiff's needs.

24. By reason of the failure of Defendant to provide said expert advice and trained fitness professionals, Defendant did thereby breach its express warranties.

25. As a direct and proximate result of the aforesaid breach of Defendant, Regional Medical Center, Plaintiff was caused to fall and has sustained the following injuries: all the bones, organs, muscles, tendons, tissues, nerves, veins, arteries, ligaments, circulation, membranes, discs, cartilages, and joints of her body were fractured, broken, ruptured, punctured, compressed, dislocated, separated, bruised, contused, narrowed, abrased, lacerated, burned, cut, torn, wrenched, swollen, ulcerated, strained, sprained, inflamed and infected; she has incurred and will continue to incur expenses as and for physicians and medical expenses; there has been a complete loss of enjoyment and the fruits of enjoyment of life, all to her damage. Further, that the Plaintiff Jane Doe has suffered a loss of income

and impairment of ability to earn an income as a result of this occurrence and injuries are permanent and will in the future be impairing, limiting and painful.

WHEREFORE, Plaintiff prays for judgment against Defendant, Regional Medical Center, in such sum that is fair and reasonable, for her costs herein incurred, and for prejudgment interest from the date of the accident, or as otherwise provided by law.

Count IV

As and for her cause of action against Defendant, Regional Medical Center, for personal injuries, Plaintiff states:

26. Plaintiff realleges and incorporates the above and foregoing paragraphs one through twenty-five, as if fully set forth herein *in haec verba.*

27. Defendant implicitly warranted to Plaintiff that Defendant's trained experts would advise her on how to safely exercise.

28. Further, Defendant implicitly warranted that Defendant's trained fitness professionals would determine the exercise program best suited to Plaintiff's needs.

29. Such representations by the Defendant were made to induce Plaintiff to participate in exercise programs offered by Defendant and were a material factor in Plaintiff's decision to participate in said programs.

30. In participating in the exercise program, Plaintiff relied on the skill and judgment of Defendant and its employees and the implied warranties described above.

31. Defendant's trained experts did not advise Plaintiff on how to safely begin an exercise program, nor did Defendant's trained fitness professionals determine the exercise program best suited to Plaintiff's needs.

32. By reason of the failure of Defendant to provide said expert advice and trained professionals, Defendant did thereby breach its implied warranties.

33. As a direct and proximate result of the aforesaid breach of Defendant, Regional Medical Center, Plaintiff was caused to fall and has sustained the following injuries: all the bones, organs, muscles, tendons, tissues, nerves, veins, arteries, ligaments, circulation, membranes, discs, cartilages, and joints of her body were fractured, broken, ruptured, punctured, compressed, dislocated, separated, bruised, contused, narrowed, abrased, lacerated, burned, cut, torn, wrenched, swollen, ulcerated, strained, sprained, inflamed and infected; she has incurred and will continue to incur expenses as and for physicians and medical expenses; there has been a complete loss of enjoyment and the fruits of enjoyment of life, all to her damage. Further, that the Plaintiff, Jane Doe has suffered a loss of income as a result of this occurrence; all the aforesaid injuries were caused by said occurrence and are permanent and will in the future be impairing, limiting and painful.

WHEREFORE, Plaintiff prays for judgment against Defendant, Regional Medical Center, in such sum that is fair and reasonable, for her costs herein incurred, and for prejudgment interest from the date of the accident, or as otherwise provided by law.

_____

ATTORNEYS FOR PLAINTIFFS

A-3

Acknowledgment, Assumption, Consent, Waiver, Release Form

I acknowledge the risks inherent in the activities that I am about to enter and for this facility and location where the activities take place. All of these risks have been carefully explained to and are understood by me.

I hereby assume those risks. I hereby acknowledge that I will be voluntarily engaging in an activity or activities involving a risk of harm to me and others. I know and fully understand the risk of harm, and I hereby accept that risk.

I voluntarily assume the known and appreciated risks involved.

I knowingly and voluntarily accept these risks of harm. I understand and appreciate the risks involved and accept those risks as an inherent condition of the various activities in which I will be engaged.

I hereby consent to these activities and to the risks inherent therein.

I have also been advised of my right to, and, in fact, urged to have a complete physical examination, including but not limited to a stress test and blood workup. Further, I acknowledge that I have been advised to have a physical examination at least annually and not to embark on any strenuous exercise program without a complete physical examination. Any medical information that I wish to have brought to the attention of instructors and operators of this program are attached to this form, initialled and dated by me, and hereby incorporated by reference. I hereby waive any claims against anyone involved in performing this contract for any disease, illness or injury that would have been preventable by the disclosure of a physical examination. I hereby waive any and all claims against the other party or parties to this contract.

I understand and expressly assume all dangers of these activities, the facility, and location. I waive all claims arising out of the activities and from the location and facility, whether caused by negligence, breach of contract, or otherwise, and whether for bodily injury, property damage, or loss or otherwise.

To the maximum extent permitted by law, I hereby release all other parties, their employees and agents, from any liability for any of their actions or inactions.

I hereby expressly and without reservation intend to and, in fact, do accept total responsibility for my actions or inactions which result in damages of any kind to me or to anyone else involved.

In consideration of being allowed to participate, I hereby agree to indemnify and hold harmless those other persons involved with me in this activity and program.

I fully intend that this agreement shall bind me, my heirs, distributees, assigns, and anyone claiming any interest through me. My rights have been fully explained to me, and I hereby enter into this agreement to induce the other party or parties to enter into it and to provide the goods or services to me as contemplated by our various agreements.

Enrollee   Date

Witness   Date

A-4

Risk Management Survey for a Health, Fitness, Sports, Recreation, and Athletic Facility

Facility name: _____

Address: _____

_____

Person(s) interviewed: _____

Person completing this survey: _____

Date: _____

The only purpose of this publication is to provide information relevant to the subject property. It is published with the understanding that Rabinoff Consulting Services, Inc., is not engaged in rendering legal, medical, or other professional services by reason of the publication of this work.

This facility survey document is to be used as a risk management instrument and is not a legal evaluation. It is to be used solely for documentation of the concepts of risk management and should not be construed as legal advice for a legal defense. It represents solely the opinions and observations of the person completing the checklist. If legal, medical, or other expert assistance is required, the services of such competent professional persons should be sought.

TABLE OF CONTENTS

I. Instructions to Person Completing This Checklist

The information in this document is confidential and is shared only with the staff of this facility.

This checklist is intended to be simple, while being as comprehensive as possible in the time given to complete it. The items are written so one may simply check "yes," or "no," or "not available" ("N/A").

Some sections are followed by space for comments, in which further explanations are to be written and keyed to the appropriate number and/or letter for the applicable section. Additional or general comments can be recorded at the end of the document in the space provided.

This checklist must be *signed and dated* by the person completing this survey.

Signature: _____

Date: _____

II. General Information

Full corporate name _____

Company owner or operator, name, and title _____

_____

Years in this type of business _____

Manager's experience and background _____

_____

Person(s) responsible for making and implementing business decisions (hiring, supervising, training) _____

_____

Number of members _____ Minimum age _____

Types of memberships available: Individual _____

Family _____ Corporate _____ Other _____

Describe: _____

New member orientation? Yes _____ No _____

Describe: _____

Number of full-time employees _____

Minimum age required _____

Number of part-time employees _____

Minimum age required _____

Annual gross receipts $_____, if available

Days and hours of operation?

    M–F   _____ A.M. _____ P.M.

    Saturday _____ A.M. _____ P.M.

    Sunday _____ A.M. _____ P.M.

Which of the following items are offered at this facility?

_____ Aerobic classes How many per day? _____

_____ Free weights (including barbells and dumbbells) Square footage of area _____

_____ Cardiovascular machines How many? _____ Specify type: _____

_____ Sauna _____ Steam room

_____ Showers _____ Hot tub

_____ Locker rooms _____ Cold plunge

_____ Whirlpool

_____ Body toning machines How many? _____

_____ Tanning beds How many? _____

_____ Racquetball or handball courts How many? _____

_____ Tennis courts Number indoor _____ Number outdoor _____

_____ Basketball courts Number indoor _____ Number outdoor _____

_____ Jogging track Indoor _____ Outdoor _____

_____ Swimming pool(s) Indoor _____ Outdoor _____ What is the depth? Shallow _____ ft. Deep _____ ft.

_____ Child care offered

_____ Masseuse/Masseur

_____ Beauty salon

_____ Dance studio

_____ Gymnastics

_____ Trampolines

_____ Martial arts

_____ Pro shop

_____ Restaurant

_____ Bar or lounge

_____ Alcoholic beverages (sold or permitted)

_____ Nutrition center or food supplements (sold)

_____ Special events (e.g., camps, adventure excursions, dances, picnics, etc.)

Specify: _____

Do you sublease space to others? Yes _____

No _____ If yes, please describe: _____

III. Screening for Physical Activity Readiness

	YES	NO	N/A
A. Profile on medical history			
1. Physical Activity Readiness form?	_____	_____	_____
2. Health questionnaire?	_____	_____	_____
3. Physician release required for special participants?	_____	_____	_____
4. Records maintained with health screening information?	_____	_____	_____
B. Any consent, waiver, release, assumption-of-risk forms used?	_____	_____	_____
Specify: _____			
C. Qualified staff to do exercise screening tests?	_____	_____	_____
D. Testing equipment properly maintained?	_____	_____	_____
E. Emergency procedure in place for testing?	_____	_____	_____
F. Program and membership information includes:			
1. Description of services?	_____	_____	_____
2. Hazards and risks?	_____	_____	_____
3. Disclaimer?	_____	_____	_____
4. Minor consent (parent or guardian)?	_____	_____	_____

5. Membership
   agreement? _____ _____ _____
6. Guests? _____ _____ _____

G. Percentage of participants over
   50 years of age _____
H. Orientation for new
   members _____ _____ _____
Comments: _____

IV. Emergency Plan

	YES	NO	N/A
A. Procedures in place for emergencies, including a written emergency evacuation plan?	_____	_____	_____
B. At least one CPR-certified person on duty during operating hours?	_____	_____	_____
C. Emergency telephone numbers (e.g., police, fire, EMS) posted by each telephone?	_____	_____	_____
D. Staff trained in emergency procedures?	_____	_____	_____
E. The expected response time less than 15 minutes?	_____	_____	_____
F. A manager on duty at all times?	_____	_____	_____
G. Emergency equipment and supplies accessible (fire extinguishers, stretchers, sprinkler)?	_____	_____	_____
H. First aid kit available and well stocked?	_____	_____	_____

I. Practice, Drills, and Education

1. Drills documented?	_____	_____	_____
2. Mock drills varied to match the most common and most serious potential emergencies the specific facility might encounter?	_____	_____	_____
3. All shift personnel involved in drills and emergency training?	_____	_____	_____
4. Staff reviews actual facility incidents that involve injured patrons?	_____	_____	_____
5. Emergency education or training given to staff?	_____	_____	_____

J. Documentation of accidents/incidents (e.g., form completed)? _____ _____ _____
Comments: _____
_____

V. Subleasing

	YES	NO	N/A
A. Contracts executed with all independent contractors?	_____	_____	_____
B. Subcontractors managed and supervised?	_____	_____	_____
C. Subcontractors required to carry liability insurance?	_____	_____	_____
D. Space leased or rented by outside organizations for meetings?	_____	_____	_____

Comments: _____
_____

VI. Staffing and Personnel

A. Academic course work, degrees, or certification required for any staff? Yes _____ No _____
Specify: _____
_____

B. Experience required for any staff? Yes _____
No _____ Specify: _____
_____

C. Background and employment records of all prospective employees checked prior to hiring?
Yes _____ No _____ Specify: _____
_____

D. Special staff preparation and requirements:			
1. Nutritionist?	_____	_____	_____
2. Physical therapist?	_____	_____	_____
3. Athletic trainer?	_____	_____	_____
4. Personal trainer?	_____	_____	_____
5. Health promotion and/or special populations staff?	_____	_____	_____
6. Massage therapist?	_____	_____	_____
7. Babysitting or child care?	_____	_____	_____

Comments: _____
_____

VII. Facility Checklist

A. General

	YES	NO	N/A
1. Floor free of debris, standing liquid, and undamaged?	_____	_____	_____

2. Entries & exits visible, marked, and unobstructed? _____ _____ _____
3. At least 2 entries & exits? _____ _____ _____
4. Floor coverings properly secured? _____ _____ _____
5. Partitions functioning and undamaged? _____ _____ _____
6. "No Smoking" signs visible and undamaged in hallways? _____ _____ _____
7. Storage areas properly secured? _____ _____ _____
8. Smoking areas specified? _____ _____ _____
9. Flammable or combustible materials properly stored? _____ _____ _____
   List and describe controls for these materials:
   _____
10. Emergency power available? _____ _____ _____
    Specify: _____
11. Housekeeping satisfactory? _____ _____ _____
Comments: _____
_____

B. Handball, Racquetball, Squash Courts

	YES	NO	N/A
1. Entries & exits visible, marked, unobstructed?			
2. Walls clean, free of debris, and undamaged?			
3. Walls smooth and undamaged?			
4. Floors smooth (no cracks or warps)?			
5. Lights functioning?			
6. Eyeguard and safety rule signage visible, undamaged, and enforced?			
7. Light switches undamaged and functioning?			
8. Doors flush with walls?			
9. Doors in good condition?			
10. Movable walls?			
11. Viewing window?			

Comments: _____
_____

C. Auxiliary Courts (e.g., basketball, volleyball, badminton)

	YES	NO	N/A
1. Entries & exits visible, marked, and and unobstructed?			
2. Signs visible and undamaged (safety, no smoking, exit)?			
3. Floor free of debris and standing liquid?			
4. Floors smooth (no cracks or warps)?			

Comments: _____
_____

D. Aerobic Area

	YES	NO	N/A
1. Separate classes for different levels?			
2. Safety or warning signage?			
3. Visible clocks?			
4. Flooring made of shock-absorbent material?			
5. Floors clean, free of debris, and undamaged?			
6. Mirrors secured and unbroken?			
7. Mats, aerobic steps, and other equipment stored properly?			
8. Instructor certification(s) and training required?			
9. Instructor covered by facility's insurance?			
10. Class size enforced, based on space restriction?			

Comments: _____
_____

E. Cardiovascular or Circuit Training Area

	YES	NO	N/A
1. Signage (warning signs) visible and undamaged?			
2. Climate controlled?			
3. Nonslip flooring and drip mats?			

4. Restrictions for using area (age, handicapped, etc.)? _____ _____ _____

5. Housekeeping, infection controlled? _____ _____ _____

6. Machine and equipment maintenanced and documented? _____ _____ _____

7. Area supervised? _____ _____ _____

Comments: _____

_____

F. Weight Training Area

	YES	NO	N/A

1. Space allocation allows easy access to equipment? _____ _____ _____

2. Signage
   (a) Instructional signs visible and undamaged? _____ _____ _____
       (1) Signs emphasizing safety? _____ _____ _____
       (2) Safety, spotting, warning, and acknowledgement of assumption-of-risk signs? _____ _____ _____
   (b) Entries & exits visible, marked, and unobstructed? _____ _____ _____

3. Proper environment for weight training _____ _____ _____
   (a) Air exchanges and ventilation adequate? _____ _____ _____
   (b) Lights functioning properly? _____ _____ _____
   (c) Sufficient ceiling space for overhead lifts? _____ _____ _____

4. Flooring
   (a) Nonslip _____ _____ _____
   (b) Shock-absorbing? _____ _____ _____
   (c) Easily cleaned, repaired, and replaced? _____ _____ _____
   (d) Free of debris? _____ _____ _____

5. Wall Covering
   (a) Mirror(s) _____ _____ _____
       (1) Positioned higher than largest weight plates? _____ _____ _____
       (2) Secured and unbroken? _____ _____ _____
       (3) Positioned away from activity? _____ _____ _____
       (4) Above and away from dumbbell rack? _____ _____ _____
       (5) Easily cleaned and replaced? _____ _____ _____
       (6) Cracked or distorted mirrors replaced quickly? _____ _____ _____
   (b) Walls free of protruding objects? _____ _____ _____

6. Weight training equipment maintenance and service
   (a) Manufacturer-suggested maintenance program? _____ _____ _____
   (b) Manufacturer's guidelines for repair used? _____ _____ _____
   (c) Service contracts used? _____ _____ _____

7. Weight training equipment
   (a) Weight stacks protected by shields? _____ _____ _____
   (b) Collars and clips _____ _____ _____
       (1) Properly stored? _____ _____ _____
       (2) In proper working order? _____ _____ _____
       (3) Free of corrosion? _____ _____ _____
   (c) Do sitting or lying resistance machines have correct body position illustrations and instructions? _____ _____ _____
   (d) Weight storage, dumbbell racks adequately positioned, easily accessible? _____ _____ _____
   (e) Benches
       (1) Braced firmly? _____ _____ _____
       (2) Surfaces cleaned & disinfected regularly? _____ _____ _____
   (f) Warning signs visible and undamaged on equipment? _____ _____ _____
   (g) Staff in-service training conducted on equipment, using manufacturers' manuals? _____ _____ _____
   (h) Weight machines, weight racks, anchor points securely anchored to wall or floor, where required? _____ _____ _____

(i) Weight machines, squat racks have properly functioning safety stops? _____ _____ _____

(j) Weight machines, weight racks, and pulley mechanisms? _____ _____ _____

    (1) Cables not broken or frayed? _____ _____ _____

    (2) Lubricated? _____ _____ _____

    (3) No undue metal stress? _____ _____ _____

    (4) Free of corrosion? _____ _____ _____

    (5) Nonslip material on pedals? _____ _____ _____

    (6) Nonslip rubber grips onmachines? _____ _____ _____

8. Inventory of resistance training machines

    (a) Weight stacks? _____ _____ _____

    (b) Hydraulic? _____ _____ _____

    (c) Free weight machines, no chains or cables? _____ _____ _____

    (d) Computerized or electronic? _____ _____ _____

    (e) Other: Specify: _____

9. Adequate supervision by qualified staff? _____ _____ _____

10. New member orientation given? _____ _____ _____

Comments: _____

H. Playing Fields

	YES	NO	N/A
1. Fields clear of debris?	_____	_____	_____
2. Fences in good condition and of adequate height?	_____	_____	_____
3. Playing surface in good condition?	_____	_____	_____
4. Baseball dugouts in good condition?	_____	_____	_____
5. Backstops in good condition?	_____	_____	_____
6. Storage area free of debris, organized, equipment stored, doors locked?	_____	_____	_____

Comments: _____

I. Running Track

	YES	NO	N/A
1. Indoor _____ Outdoor _____			
2. Proper signage (directional, safety, other)?	_____	_____	_____
3. Surface inspected regularly?	_____	_____	_____
4. Proper surface? Describe: _____	_____	_____	_____
5. Adequate lighting?	_____	_____	_____
6. Proper drainage, if outside?	_____	_____	_____

Comments: _____

G. Tennis Courts

	YES	NO	N/A
1. Playing surfaces free of debris and undamaged?	_____	_____	_____
2. Tennis court nets in good condition?	_____	_____	_____
3. Windscreens in good condition?	_____	_____	_____
4. Fences and gates in good condition?	_____	_____	_____
5. Proper lighting & lights protected?	_____	_____	_____
6. Warning signs posted?	_____	_____	_____
7. Snow, ice, water removal adequate?	_____	_____	_____
8. Equipment securely stored?	_____	_____	_____
9. Necessary padding?	_____	_____	_____

Comments: _____

J. Pool

	YES	NO	N/A
1. Pool area monitored?	_____	_____	_____
2. Pool area highly visible?	_____	_____	_____
3. Entries & exits visible, marked, and unobstructed?	_____	_____	_____
4. Adequate number of exits?	_____	_____	_____
5. Walkways undamaged, properly drained, free of debris and standing liquid?	_____	_____	_____
6. Walkways slip-resistant?	_____	_____	_____
7. Emergency telephone or alarm?	_____	_____	_____
(a) Emergency phone numbers posted?	_____	_____	_____
8. Ceiling and pool lights covered and functioning?	_____	_____	_____

9. Signs (exit, no smoking, number of users, no diving, regulation and safety rules) visible and legible? (No diving in depth less than 9 feet or less than 25 feet of forward clearance) _____ _____ _____

10. Pool(s) vacuumed daily or as needed? _____ _____ _____

11. Water quality tested and water analysis log posted daily? _____ _____ _____

12. Algae not visible in pool? Water not discolored from algae bloom? _____ _____ _____

13. Water level acceptable? _____ _____ _____

14. Water depths are plainly marked at or above the water surface on the vertical wall of of the pool and on the edge of the deck? _____ _____ _____

15. Ground fault circuit interrupters on all electrical outlets? _____ _____ _____

16. Light switches proper and functioning? _____ _____ _____

17. Adequate ventilation (no unpleasant, discernible odors or fumes)? _____ _____ _____

18. Diving board? _____ _____ _____
    Height _____
    (a) Slip-resistant surface? _____ _____ _____

19. Drains maintained and working properly? _____ _____ _____

20. Ladders secured and undamaged? _____ _____ _____

21. Chemicals
    (a) Stored properly? _____ _____ _____
    (b) Labels legible? _____ _____ _____
    (c) Labels show appropriate warnings? _____ _____ _____
    (d) Correctly dispensed into pool? _____ _____ _____
    (e) Employees trained in storage and use of hazardous chemicals? _____ _____ _____

22. Storage area free of debris and uncluttered? _____ _____ _____

23. Emergency equipment
    (a) Ring buoy (1 each side)? _____ _____ _____
    (b) Extension poles (1 each side)? _____ _____ _____
    (c) Shepherd's crook? _____ _____ _____

    (d) First aid kit well stocked and easily accessible? _____ _____ _____

24. Deck and floors leading to pool slip-resistant? _____ _____ _____

25. Decks clean, sanitized at least twice weekly and free of algae? _____ _____ _____

26. Lifeguards _____ _____ _____
    (a) Possess appropriate certification? _____ _____ _____
        Type(s)? _____
    (b) Qualified in emergency procedures & rescue? _____ _____ _____
    (c) Properly dressed & identifiable? _____ _____ _____
    (d) Adequate number and positioning? _____ _____ _____
    (e) Given frequent relief breaks and rotated? _____ _____ _____

27. If no lifeguard on duty, is there a surveillance camera scanning pool area? _____ _____ _____

Comments: _____
_____

K. Hot Tub

	YES	NO	N/A
1. Age restriction?	_____	_____	_____
2. Temperature regulation?	_____	_____	_____
3. Timers functioning?	_____	_____	_____
4. Chemicals correctly used?	_____	_____	_____
5. List of warnings visible and undamaged?	_____	_____	_____
6. Emergency phone?	_____	_____	_____
7. Proper supervision?	_____	_____	_____

Comments: _____
_____

L. Sauna

	YES	NO	N/A
1. Age restriction?	_____	_____	_____
2. Automatic temperature regulator shuts off heat when maximum temperature is reached?	_____	_____	_____
3. Timers functioning?	_____	_____	_____
4. List of warnings visible and undamaged?	_____	_____	_____

5. Emergency phone, panic button, or alarm easily accessible? _____ _____ _____
6. No locking or latching doors? _____ _____ _____
7. Proper supervision? _____ _____ _____
8. Proper maintenance? _____ _____ _____
9. Sauna heater secured (users can't touch)? _____ _____ _____
10. Area clean and free of debris? _____ _____ _____
12. Doors open out? _____ _____ _____
13. Window in door? _____ _____ _____
Comments: _____

M. Steam Room

	YES	NO	N/A
1. Age restriction?	_____	_____	_____
2. Automatic temperature regulator shuts off steam when maximum temperature is reached?	_____	_____	_____
3. Timers functioning?	_____	_____	_____
4. List of warnings visible and undamaged?	_____	_____	_____
5. Emergency phone, panic button, or alarm easily accessible?	_____	_____	_____
6. No locking or latching doors?	_____	_____	_____
7. Proper supervision?	_____	_____	_____
8. Proper maintenance?	_____	_____	_____
9. Steam head secured (users can't touch)?	_____	_____	_____
10. Area clean and free of debris?	_____	_____	_____
11. Door opens out?	_____	_____	_____
12. Window in door?	_____	_____	_____

Comments: _____

N. Therapeutic Whirlpool (Not to be confused with hot tub)

	YES	NO	N/A
1. Emergency procedures posted?	_____	_____	_____
2. Timers functioning?	_____	_____	_____
3. Daily inspection and water testing?	_____	_____	_____

4. Proper surface (nonslip)? _____ _____ _____
5. Area free of debris and standing liquid? _____ _____ _____
6. Warning signs? _____ _____ _____
7. Inspection log? _____ _____ _____
8. Supervised? _____ _____ _____
9. Emergency phone or alarm? _____ _____ _____
Comments: _____

O. Tanning

	YES	NO	N/A
1. Tanning beds in enclosed private area?	_____	_____	_____
2. Emergency procedures and warnings visible and undamaged?	_____	_____	_____
3. Beds disinfected between uses?	_____	_____	_____
4. Maintenance plan in place (e.g., check bulbs for leakage)?	_____	_____	_____
5. Strict adherence to manufacturer's suggestions for use of equipment?	_____	_____	_____
6. Eye protection provided and required?	_____	_____	_____
7. Waivers signed before use?	_____	_____	_____
8. Timer coin operated?	_____	_____	_____

Token _____ Other _____
Comments: _____

P. Dressing Areas, Locker and Shower Rooms

	YES	NO	N/A
1. Hallway and locker floors			
(a) Nonskid surfaces?	_____	_____	_____
(b) Free of debris?	_____	_____	_____
(c) Proper drainage?	_____	_____	_____
2. Electrical			
(a) Ground fault interrupters on outlets?	_____	_____	_____
(b) Emergency power system?	_____	_____	_____
3. Lockers			
(a) Free of corrosion?	_____	_____	_____
(b) Free of rough or jagged edges?	_____	_____	_____

(c) Secured to floor or
immovable? _____ _____ _____
4. Showers
   (a) Easy temperature
      control? _____ _____ _____
   (b) Nonskid floors? _____ _____ _____
   (c) Signs noting caution? _____ _____ _____
5. Locker room maintenance
   adequate (sinks, floors,
   mirrors, toilets, urinals
   sanitized)? _____ _____ _____
6. No dripping water or
   leaks? _____ _____ _____
7. Benches, tables, chairs
   secured? _____ _____ _____
8. Adequate space in locker
   rooms? _____ _____ _____
Comments: _____
_____

Q. Restaurant, Bar, Lounge, Snack Bar

	YES	NO	N/A
1. Alcohol served or permitted?	_____	_____	_____
2. Employees trained in serving alcohol?	_____	_____	_____
3. Facility meets health inspection standards and permits up to date?	_____	_____	_____
4. Cooking surfaces and kitchen have automatic fire protection system?	_____	_____	_____
5. Area clean, free of debris and grease accumulation?	_____	_____	_____
6. Proper refrigeration?	_____	_____	_____
7. Glass containers?	_____	_____	_____
8. Pest control?	_____	_____	_____

Comments: _____
_____

R. Off-Premise Activities: Camps, Adventures, Excursions, Special Events

	YES	NO	N/A
1. Properly supervised?	_____	_____	_____
2. Insurance checked in advance and proof of coverage furnished by carrier?	_____	_____	_____
3. Proper waiver and similar forms signed by participants?	_____	_____	_____

Specify: _____

4. Risks properly explained? _____ _____ _____
5. Adequate transportation? _____ _____ _____
6. Transportation
   insurance? _____ _____ _____
7. Warning signs
   properly posted? _____ _____ _____
Comments: _____
_____

S. Pro Shop

	YES	NO	N/A
1. Subcontracted?	_____	_____	_____
2. Insured?	_____	_____	_____
3. Reputable, insured vendors?	_____	_____	_____
4. Proper labels and warnings on products?	_____	_____	_____
5. Proper security?	_____	_____	_____

Comments: _____
_____

T. Beauty Salon, Masseuse/Masseur

	YES	NO	N/A
1. Subcontracted?	_____	_____	_____
2. Insured?	_____	_____	_____
3. Licensed personnel (if required by state)?	_____	_____	_____
4. Proper security?	_____	_____	_____

Comments: _____
_____

U. Nutrition Center, Food Supplements, Nutrition Advice

	YES	NO	N/A
1. Instructors qualified (i.e., licensed nutritionist on staff)?	_____	_____	_____
2. Diets recommended?	_____	_____	_____

Comments: _____

V. Child Care Center

	YES	NO	N/A
1. Staff-to-child ratio?	_____		
2. Staff requirements for employment?	_____	_____	_____
3. In-service training?	_____	_____	_____
4. Emergency care training provided to staff (Pediatric Medic First Aid, PEDS, or Red Cross equivalent certification)	_____	_____	_____
5. Adequate space?	_____	_____	_____
6. Rules posted?	_____	_____	_____

(a) Language (simple)? ___ ___ ___
(b) Pictures? ___ ___ ___
(c) At children's eye
level? ___ ___ ___
7. Flooring
(a) Stain-resistant? ___ ___ ___
(b) Nonslip? ___ ___ ___
Specify type of floor: _____
8. Wall covering
(a) Stain-resistant? ___ ___ ___
(b) Washable? ___ ___ ___
9. Communication to front
desk or appropriate
personnel? ___ ___ ___
Describe: _____
10. Security and records
(a) All children clearly
visible? ___ ___ ___
(b) Restricted exit
(escapable in case
of fire or emergency)? ___ ___ ___
(c) Child registration
(sign-in and sign-out)? ___ ___ ___
(d) Parental releases for
all children? ___ ___ ___
(e) Continuous super-
vision? ___ ___ ___
(f) Children's immun-
ization records
and medical histories
on file? ___ ___ ___
(g) Accident/incident
records maintained? ___ ___ ___
11. Housekeeping
(a) Daily clean-up? ___ ___ ___
(b) Proper sanitation? ___ ___ ___
12. Equipment and Activities
(a) Sinks and toilets at
appropriate heights? ___ ___ ___
(b) Refrigeration? ___ ___ ___
(c) Tables for changing
diapers? ___ ___ ___
(d) Washable mats? ___ ___ ___
(e) Safe toys and games? ___ ___ ___
(g) Exercise equipment? ___ ___ ___
Comments: _____
_____

W. *Martial Arts, Gymnastics*

	YES	NO	N/A
1. Is the program for competition training?	___	___	___
2. Is the program for instructional purposes?	___	___	___
3. Does your facility host competitions?	___	___	___
4. Qualified and/or certified instructors? Specify: _____	___	___	___
5. Proper acknowledgment of assumption-of-risk, waivers, consent forms executed by students or parents?	___	___	___
6. Proper floor covering (e.g., resilient, extra carpet padding)?	___	___	___
7. Proper signage (contact rules, etc.)?	___	___	___
8. Class size enforced, based on space restriction? What is it? _____	___	___	___
9. Subcontractors?	___	___	___
10. Safety equipment required? Specify: _____	___	___	___

Comments: _____
_____

VIII. Suggestions and Recommendations

_____
_____
_____
_____
_____
_____
_____
_____

SOURCE: Rabinoff Consulting Services, Inc., Littleton, Colorado. Used with permission.

APPENDIX B

Aquatics Resources

B-1

Pool Inspection Checklist

POOL INSPECTION CHECKLIST

Pool: _____

Inspection Date: _____

Address: _____

City, State, Zip: _____

Phone: _____

Aquatic Director: _____

Executive Director: _____

Pool 1: _____

Pool 2: _____

POOL 1   POOL 2

_____   _____   1. A six-inch black disk or the main drain grates are clearly visible from any point on the deck. Water is crystal clear and has less than 0.5 NTUs.

_____   _____   2. Multiple main drain grates, or antivortex drain covers are provided.

         _____   _____   2 or more drains

         _____   _____   Antivortex drain covers if single drain is installed

         _____   _____   Plumbed with a T design to prevent suction entrapment

         _____   _____   Installed less than 15 feet from the pool walls and no more than 30 feet apart

         _____   _____   Grate area 4× the area of the drain pipe

         Pipe diameter = _____ inches

         Pipe area = _____ in.^{2}

         Grate area _____ in. × _____ in. = _____ in.^{2}

         _____   _____   Grates removable only with the use of tools

         _____   _____   Not in line with diving boards

_____   _____   3. The pool is vacuumed daily or as needed. No settled debris is visible.
Vacuum type: _____

_____   _____   4. The circulation system is properly plumbed to provide uniform distribution of water throughout the pool and prevent hazards.

	Pool 1	Pool 2
Inlet type	_____	_____
Inlet number	_____	_____
Inlet location	_____	_____

_____ _____ 5. Sodium fluorescein dye tests or ribbon tests convey a uniform circulation pattern and absence of dead spots.

_____ _____ 6. A hydrostatic relief valve has been installed on in-ground pools in areas where the ground freezes or where high groundwater tables may pose a problem.

_____ _____ 7. Algae is not visible in the pool. The water is not discolored from an algae bloom.

_____ _____ 8. Coping stones and tile lines are not chipped, cracked, or loose.

_____ _____ 9. The pool shell is finished in a smooth but slip-resistant, easily cleaned, watertight surface material, white or off-white in color. There are no cracks in the shell except structural expansion joints.

	Pool 1	Pool 2
Pool construction material	_____	_____
Surface material	_____	_____
Surface color	_____	_____

_____ _____ 10. The presence of minerals or dissolved metals has not caused surface staining or water discoloration.

_____ _____ 11. Correct water level is maintained to allow removal of floating debris and the continuous overflow of water into the pool gutters or skimmers.

Perimeter Overflow System		
	Pool 1	Pool 2
Skimmers (number)	_____	_____
Gutters (type*)	_____	_____

*prefabricated, water-to-waste, fully or partially recessed, rim flow, roll-out

_____ _____ 12. Skimmer weirs, equalizer lines, skimmer baskets, deck covers, and flow-adjustment or antivortex control plates are all present and in good repair.

_____ _____ 13. Movable floors are fully operational, and can be adjusted to any desired depth.

Reinforced concrete floor (AFW)	_____
Stainless-steel scissor-jack floor with PVC planking (AFW-KBE Kaiser)	_____
Glass-fiber reinforced polyester floor operated by a cable system and hydraulic mechanism (Recreonics)	_____
Number of stainless-steel hydraulic cylinders	_____
A movable floor is installed over the entire pool	_____
A movable floor is installed over a portion of the pool, and is used in conjunction with trailing ramp, rolling bulkheads, vertical wall that can be raised and lowered, or stainless-steel removable fence	_____

_____ _____ The slotted PVC edge strip is securely fastened to the concrete floor with stainless-steel sheet metal screws and can withstand the forces created when the floor is moved up and down through the water column. Slots are $1/8$ inch or less in width.

_____ _____ The floor travels at speeds not exceeding 1 foot per minute.

_____ _____ The floor can be raised flush with the pool deck and is handicapped accessible.

_____ _____ The floor can be raised above deck level for vacuuming or access below.

_____ _____ Manholes are built into floor for inspection below.

_____ _____ The water-soluble lubricant or hydraulic fluid level is checked weekly.

_____ _____ Sacrificial anodes installed to protect the stainless-steel hydraulic cylinders from corrosion are inspected and replaced yearly.

_____ _____ If multiple hydraulic cylinders are installed, the cylinders operate in unison. The floor is perfectly level when in a raised position. Tile is not separating from the concrete floor because of torque resulting from uneven cylinder operation.

_____ _____ The variable depth gauge reflects true depth.

_____ _____ Permanent depth markings installed on the pool deck and vertical pool wall indicate that depth varies.

_____ _____ 14. Movable rolling bulkheads, rollers, and grating are in good repair. Bulkhead chambers are inflated with compressed air to achieve adequate buoyancy and are being moved properly to prevent back injuries to staff, wear on rollers, and scratching of gutters. If starting blocks are installed on the bulkheads, the bulkheads are capable of supporting the anticipated maximum weight of swimmers, officials, starting blocks, and timing equipment during a competitive event.

Number of bulkheads	_____
Dimensions (length and width) of bulkheads	_____
Possible course lengths	_____
Frequency of movement	_____

_____ _____ 15. A current license or permit to operate a public pool is posted in a conspicuous place in the facility.

_____ _____ 16. Adequate storage space has been provided for wet, dry, and secure storage of equipment. Decks are uncluttered. They are not used for storage of teaching or maintenance equipment.

_____ _____ 17. Pool equipment is being properly used.

_____ _____ 18. The pools, when not in use, are covered with insulating pool blankets.

_____ _____ 19. Safety covers that meet strict performance standards set by the American Society for Testing and Materials in ASTM standard F1346-91 (formerly ES-13) are installed to prevent access to pool or spa water. The covers

_____ _____ have a continuous connection between the pool and deck. They are installed in a track, rail, or guides, or otherwise locked or secured into the deck.

_____ _____ are capable of supporting a load of 400 lb. per square feet.

_____ _____ bear an identification label indicating the name of manufacturer and installer, and compliance with ASTM safety cover standards.

_____ _____ are provided with automatic auxiliary pumps or designed in a way that prevents accumulation of standing water on top of the cover.

_____ _____ 20. Emergency exit doors are unlocked, and crash bars are operational. An alarm sounds when an emergency door is opened.

_____ _____ 21. Infrared or light-beam alarms have been installed to detect unauthorized entry to the pool deck.

_____ _____ 22. Pool alarms have been installed to warn of unauthorized entry to the pool area. Types of alarms are:

_____ _____ underwater electronic sensors and medallions

_____ _____ pressure wave tubes

_____ _____ floating surface wave motion devices

_____ _____ sonar devices

_____ _____ 23. Windows and hinged or sliding doors leading directly to the pool have latching devices installed out of the reach of small children, at least 40 and preferably 60 inches above the floor.

_____ _____ 24. If no physical barrier is installed between a dwelling and the pool, a resettable alarm is installed on all sliding doors and windows that open to the pool area.

_____ _____ 25. Barriers and fences are installed and maintained in compliance with local codes and industry recommendations in order to lessen unauthorized entry to the pool area and prevent young children from gaining access to the pool (thereby reducing the likelihood of pediatric submersion accidents).

Fence height: _____

_____ _____ The facility is fenced.

_____ _____ A barrier is installed between a dwelling and the pool.

_____ _____ Perimeter fences do not block the view of the pool.

_____ _____ If plants and shrubs are used on the outside of the fence as an additional barrier, they do not obstruct the vision of the pool from the dwelling.

_____ _____ The fence does not have external footholds or handholds or horizontal members to make it easy to climb.

_____ _____ The fence is installed in such a way to prevent other objects, building walls, or permanent structures from being used to climb into the pool area.

_____ _____ Walls or solid barriers constructed of cement block or brick, if installed, do not contain indentations or protrusions closer than 45 inches apart.

_____ _____ With chain-link fences less than 6 feet in height, wire mesh, slats, barbed wire, or other means approved by local building officials is used to prevent the openings in the fence from being used as a climbing surface.

_____ _____ The size of holes in the chain-link fence do not exceed $1^{3}/_{4}$ ($2^{1}/_{4}$) inches.

_____ _____ There is less than 2 inches of space between the bottom of the barrier and the ground or pool deck.

_____ _____ There are no holes or spaces in the fence where children could slip through.

_____ _____ Vertical members in the barrier are not more than 4 inches apart. A block or sphere 4 inches in diameter cannot pass through.

_____ _____ On ornamental iron fences, the distance between the tops of horizontal members is not greater than 45 inches apart.

_____ _____ A removable baby-barrier fence constructed of coated nylon mesh is available to provide additional security.

_____ _____ Gates in the fence open outward away from the pool.

_____ _____ Gates are at least as high as the required height of the fence.

_____ _____ Access gates can be locked when the pool is not in use or not supervised. A key-operated lock, keypad, or key-card system, which is integral to the gate, is installed.

_____ _____ The locking mechanism is mounted on the inside of the gate, and at least 4 feet off the ground, and more than 6 inches below the top of the gate.

_____ _____ To prevent access to the latch from the exterior of the gate, the latch is protected by a rigid webbing, shield, or plate installed to either side, below, and above the latch to the top of the gate. The shield does not have openings greater than $^{1}/_{4}$ inch in diameter.

_____ _____ The gate closer is adjusted to allow the gate to self-close and positively self-latch from any open position.

_____ _____ 26. All lights are operational, and installed in compliance with the current (1993) National Electrical Code, Article 680.

_____ _____ 27. The pool area is well lit and sufficient overhead and/or pool lighting is provided. Illumination at the water surface is at least 100 lumens per square foot for indoor pools and 60 lumens per square foot for outdoor pools.

Nighttime illumination level: _____ foot-candles

Daytime illumination level: _____ foot-candles

	Pool 1	Pool 2
Bulb type	————	————
Wet or dry niche	————	————
Number of underwater lights	————	————
Wattage of each pool light	————	————
Type of deck lighting	————	————
Number of deck lights	————	————
Wattage of each deck light	————	————

———— ———— 28. A security lighting system is installed in the natatorium. Lights are tested on a regular basis.

———— ———— 29. Glare from natural lighting does not interfere with the ability to see below the surface of the water.
Orientation of pool (direction): _____

———— ———— 30. Glare from artificial lighting does not interfere with the ability to see below the surface of the water.
Placement and location of lights: _____
_____

———— ———— 31. Ground fault circuit interrupters (GFCI) have been installed on all electrical outlets in the pool, locker rooms, and other wet areas of the facility.

———— ———— 32. The deck and all floors leading to the pool are slip resistant and meet minimum friction coefficients (0.6–0.7).
Deck surface material: _____

———— ———— 33. Deck mats, raised-grid interlocking tiles, or antibactericide runners, if used, are removed daily for cleaning and disinfection.

———— ———— 34. Decks are clean, disinfected at least twice weekly, and algae free.
Number of hose bibs: _____
Hose bib location: _____
Backflow prevention: _____

———— ———— 35. Decks on all four sides of the pool are a minimum of 8 feet wide. A minimum of 12 feet of unobstructed deck space is provided where diving boards or starting blocks are installed. At least 10 feet of deck space separates the swimming pool from the wading pool, spa, or other pool in the same natatorium.

	Pool 1	Pool 2
Minimum deck width	————	————
Area of deck	————	————

———— ———— 36. Decks are sloped properly to drain, and do not collect pools of standing water.
Number of deck drains: _____
Maximum distance between drains: _____
Coved wall bases present: _____

———— ———— 37. All ladders, backstroke flag stanchions, guard chairs, rails and treads, deck plates, and other deck equipment are tightly secured.

———— ———— 38. When stanchions, starting blocks, or other pieces of deck equipment are removed, anchor sockets are capped.

———— ———— 39. The fresh-water fill spout is located so as not to be a tripping hazard. An air gap of at least 6 inches has been provided between the spout and the pool as a means of backflow protection.
Water supply source: _____
Drought restrictions: _____

Fill pipe diameter: _____

Height above surface: _____

_____ _____ 40. A drinking fountain has been provided in the pool enclosure.

_____ _____ 41. Backstroke flags and support stanchions are placed 15 feet (USS short course, NCAA, NFSHSA) or 16 feet 5 inches (USS long course, FINA) from each pool edge.

_____ _____ 42. Underwater observation windows are mounted flush with the pool wall. Hardware securing the window frame to the pool wall does not protrude or otherwise pose a hazard to bathers.

_____ _____ 43. Spectator seating areas are physically separated from the pool deck.

_____ _____ 44. Electrical wiring does not pass directly over the pool.

_____ _____ 45. Towel and equipment hooks are installed on the walls in a way that does not present a hazard to bathers.

_____ _____ 46. Swim lanes are a minimum of 7 and preferably 10 feet wide.

    _____ _____ 1.0 to 1.5 feet of additional open water installed outside first and last lanes.

    _____ _____ Lane markers are 10 or 12 inches wide.

    _____ _____ Ceramic tile lane markers have a minimum coefficient of dynamic friction of 0.6.

    _____ _____ Lane markers terminate 6 feet 7 inches from each end wall.

    _____ _____ Lane lines terminate in a cross line 3 feet 4 inches long and either 10 or 12 inches wide.

_____ _____ 47. Targets have been provided and are in alignment with swim lanes.

_____ _____ 48. Floating lane lines are secured to the pool with recessed hooks. Lines are stored on a reel, and the lane line reel is covered and stored off deck.

_____ _____ 49. The competitive timing system and scoreboard are fully operational. Allowances in course length were made for space taken up in a swim lane by the touch pads.

_____ _____ 50. Acoustical treatment has been considered in the design of the natatorium. Reverberation time and background noise do not make it difficult to carry on long-distance conversations, hear instructions, or listen to information over loudspeakers.

_____ _____ 51. An adequate means of egress from the pool is provided.

_____ _____ 52. The pool is handicapped accessible and in compliance with the ADA and barrier-free design requirements.

_____ _____ 53. Rescue equipment including rescue tubes, ring buoys, extension poles, and shepherd's crooks are all in good repair and immediately available for use.

_____ _____ 54. Elevated lifeguard chairs are placed at appropriate locations around the pool deck. Lifeguard chairs and towers are in good repair and of a safe design. The design of the elevated platform and guardrails conforms with OSHA requirements as described in 29 CFR 1910.23.

_____ _____ 55. The first aid kit is well stocked and instantly accessible. (Minimum: 24-unit first aid kit.) A first aid room is provided.

_____ _____ 56. A backboard, rigid cervical collars, head immobilizer, and straps are in good repair and immediately available for use. Guards are trained and practiced in current spinal management techniques.

_____ _____ 57. An emergency telephone is located on the pool deck.

_____ _____ 58. Emergency phone numbers are posted. Directions to the facility and other pertinent information to be conveyed to the 911 operator are posted next to the phone.

_____ _____ 59. A closure policy has been developed in case of lightning and severe weather. Evacuation procedures have been planned. A lightning detector has been purchased.

_____ _____ 60. Pool rules, methods of enforcement, safety literature, and meaningful warning signs are posted.

_____ _____ 61. Pool capacity (bather load) signs are posted. Capacity limits are not exceeded.

Method of determining bather load: _____

Maximum bather load: _____

_____ _____ 62. Depth markings are plainly and conspicuous at or above the water surface on the vertical wall of the pool and on the edge of the deck. Markings conform to local and state codes as to size, color, and spacing. Depth is marked to indicate feet and inches. Numbers other than those indicating depth have been removed.

_____ _____ 63. Depth or drop-off lines and/or buoyed lifelines are correctly positioned in the pool to indicate sudden changes in slope.

———— ———— 64. A contour depth chart is posted next to the pool to help swimmers judge the depth and shape of the pool.
Slope ratio (shallow) ——————

———— ———— 65. Steps, treads, ramps, ledges, or other protrusion into the pool are marked with a color-constrasting coating or tile on both the top and vertical rise.

———— ———— 66. Water slides or flumes are structurally sound, properly installed, and adequately maintained.

———— ———— 67. Diving is not permitted into areas of the pool less than 9 feet deep or where there is less than 25 feet of forward clearance.

———— ———— 68. Starting blocks are located in water at least 9 feet deep. Warning labels are affixed. Blocks are removed from the deck except during competition or training for competition. Use of starting blocks is prohibited unless swimmers are under the direct supervision of an instructor or coach.

———— ———— 69. Diving board surfaces are slip resistant. All nuts, bolts, hinges, fulcrums, rail mounting devices, band fasteners, and guardrails have been properly maintained and are in good condition.

———— ———— 70. One- and 3-meter diving boards are located in water at least 12 feet 6 inches and 13 feet 2 inches deep respectively, and are positioned in accordance with state and local codes, recommendations of national certifying agencies, and common and acceptable standards of the aquatic industry.

	Pool 1	Pool 2
1-meter diving boards (number)	————	————
3-meter diving boards (number)	————	————
Jump board	————	————
Platforms (height)	————	————
Sparge system in diving well	————	————
Guardrails	————	————
Leading edge of guardrails extends past the deck edge	————	————
Protective netting	————	————
Type of boards	————	————
Fulcrum assemblies and footwheels (type and adjustable distance)	————	————
Type of standards	————	————
Treads (number and spacing)	————	————
Ladder handrail spacing	————	————
Main drains are at least 5 feet off center from board midpoints	————	————
Distance between boards	————	————
Distance between board and side wall	————	————
Depth of water directly below board	————	————
Depth 6 feet forward of the board	————	————
Depth 12 feet forward of the board	————	————
Depth 18 feet forward of the board	————	————
Shock-absorbing surface material installed below stands	————	————
Overhead clearance	————	————

———— ———— 71. The pool manager or operator is certified by a nationally recognized agency, and is knowledgable in all aspects of pool operation, water chemistry, and maintenance.

———— ———— 72. Pool water is tested at least once every two hours and analyzed at least one hour prior to use by the public.

———— ———— 73. Test kits are properly stored and reagents fresh.
Brand(s) of test kits: _____

———— ———— 74. Levels of water quality and all chemicals are in acceptable ranges.

———— ———— 75. A system of regular testing, recording of findings, and chemical adjustment of pool water has been implemented. A daily pool water analysis log is posted. Capability of testing:

☐ ORP   ☐ FAC
☐ TAC   ☐ CAC
☐ Cyanuric acid   ☐ pH
☐ Acid/base demand   ☐ Total alkalinity
☐ Calcium hardness   ☐ TDS
☐ Iron   ☐ Copper
☐ Nitrates   ☐ Water temperature
☐ Air temperature   ☐ Relative humidity
☐ Saturation index   ☐ TAB

———— ———— 76. Bacteriological water analysis is performed on a regular basis by an independent laboratory as required by code.

———— ———— 77. Detailed maintenance checklists for daily opening and closing procedures, and seasonal and long-term maintenance are maintained, completed daily, and available for inspection.
———— ———— daily checklists
———— ———— preventive maintenance checklists
———— ———— seasonal checklists

———— ———— 78. Trash containers are covered and emptied as needed.

———— ———— 79. Markings and graffiti have been removed.

———— ———— 80. Water temperature is maintained at acceptable levels and is appropriate for the primary activities in the pool.
Water temperature: P1 _____°F   P2 _____°F

———— ———— 81. Ambient air temperature is comfortable and at 3 to 7 degrees higher than water temperature.
Air temperature _____°F

———— ———— 82. Air quality is monitored. No unpleasant odors or irritating fumes are discernible.
———— ———— ppm of chlorine gas present in the air
———— ———— ppm of ozone present in the air
———— ———— ppm of carbon dioxide present in the air

———— ———— 83. Low humidity levels (50–60% summer, 30–50% winter) are maintained.
Type of air handling system: _____
Humidity level (%): _____

———— ———— 84. Fresh air is introduced to the pool area at a rate of 0.5 cfm per square foot of pool and deck area, in compliance with ASHRAE Standard 62-1989 "Ventilation for Acceptable Indoor Air Quality."
Location of air supply inlets and returns: _____
Air circulation pattern in the natatorium: _____

———— ———— 85. Upon visual inspection, the ceiling over the pool does not show signs of deterioration.

———— ———— 86. A safety orientation is provided to new members or guests before they are permitted to use the pool.

———— ———— 87. At least two certified lifeguards are at the pool during all times of operation, at least one of whom is positioned in an elevated guardchair and has no duties to perform other than the close supervision of participants in water contact activities.

———— ———— 88. Lifeguards are at least 18 years old, medically fit, have good eyesight, and are physically able to meet the demands of the job.

———— ———— 89. Lifeguards and aquatic instructors possess current certifications appropriate to their jobs, have adequate training for the facility, are qualified and practiced in emergency procedures and other aspects of their jobs, including use of rescue equipment.
Frequency of in-service training: _____
Date and topic of last training session: _____

_____ _____ 90. Lifeguards are properly dressed and readily identified by patrons.

☐ Uniform ☐ Hat or visor
☐ Sunglasses ☐ Protected from the sun
☐ Whistle ☐ Rescue tube
☐ Protective equipment

_____ _____ 91. Lifeguards are alert, rotated to different positions at least once every 40 minutes, and are given frequent relief breaks away from surveillance duties.

_____ _____ 92. The number of guards and supervisory personnel is adequate for the activities being conducted, age and skill level of participants, the size and shape of the facility, and environmental conditions that might limit their ability to provide necessary supervision.
Number and locations of guards on duty: _____ _____
_____

_____ _____ 93. Supervision is provided in accordance with the "10/20 Rule."
Average scan time over 3 minutes _____ seconds
Auditing procedures:

☐ Stop watch ☐ Videotaping
☐ Hunsucker dolls ☐ Red ball drills
☐ Hand paddle drills ☐ Simulated emergencies
☐ Mannequins ☐ Independent auditors
☐ Other: _____

_____ _____ 94. Contractors have indemnified the agency and listed the agency as a separate insured. Facility rental charges include the cost of providing lifeguards and facility supervisors. Staff have been trained in special emergency procedures for situations that might arise during programs operated by contractors.

_____ _____ 95. The doors leading to the equipment and chemical rooms are locked and only accessible to authorized personnel.

_____ _____ 96. Appropriate signage and warnings are affixed to the outside doors of the equipment and chemical rooms.

_____ _____ 97. The pool chemical room has at least 2 exits, and does not open onto the pool deck or to other heavily traveled areas.

_____ _____ 98. The surge chamber is properly sized to hold 1 gallon of water for each square foot of pool water surface area.

_____ _____ A guardrail is installed around the surge chamber hatch.
_____ _____ Surge tank volume is _____ gallons. Type:

☐ surge chamber ☐ balancing tank
☐ surge trench ☐ in-pool surge capacity
☐ vacuum filter tank

_____ _____ 99. The hair/lint strainer is clean. Additional baskets and gaskets or O-rings are provided.
_____ _____ 100. Pressurized filter tanks and hair and lint traps are properly sealed.
_____ _____ 101. The centrifugal force pump is properly secured to its base, located so as to avoid cavitation, and is operating quietly.
_____ _____ 102. The pump is self-priming or located so as to eliminate the need for priming.
_____ _____ 103. The recirculation pump is properly sized according to the manufacturer's pump curve.

	Pool 1	Pool 2
Influent pressure (psi) $\times$ 2.31 = feet of head	_____	_____
Vacuum reading (Hg) $\times$ 1.13 = feet of water	_____	_____
Feet of head + feet of water = TDH	_____	_____
Minimum flowrate (gpm)	_____	_____
Pump horsepower (hp)	_____	_____

_____ _____ 104. The flowmeter is operational, accurate, and properly located on a return line at operator eye level.

	Pool 1	Pool 2
Meter type	_____	_____
Straight length of pipe prior to the flowmeter is > 4 times the pipe diameter	_____	_____
Straight length of pipe after the flowmeter is >10 times the pipe diameter	_____	_____
Pipe diameter	_____	_____

_____ _____ 105. Rate of circulation meets minimum turnover requirements and accommodates peak bather loads.

	Pool 1	Pool 2
Volume (gallons)	_____	_____
Required flowrate (gpm)	_____	_____
Actual flowrate (gpm)	_____	_____
Required turnover (hrs)	_____	_____
Actual turnover (hrs)	_____	_____

_____ _____ 106. Pipes are not leaking, are properly supported, and do not show external signs of calcification, corrosion, or deterioration. Pipe type:

☐ PVC 40 ☐ copper
☐ CPVC 80 ☐ stainless steel
☐ cast iron ☐ galvanized steel

_____ _____ 107. Valves and piping on multifilter systems isolate individual filter tanks for maintenance or repair.

_____ _____ 108. Pipes are sized to carry water efficiently through the circulation system. Maximum velocity permitted: discharge pipe 10 fps, suction pipe 8 fps

	Flowrate (gpm)	Pipe diameter (in.)	Pipe area (in.^{2})	$(0.32 \times gpm)$ ÷ pipe area
Pool 1				
Suction	_____	_____	_____	_____
Discharge	_____	_____	_____	_____
Pool 2				
Suction	_____	_____	_____	_____
Discharge	_____	_____	_____	_____

_____ _____ 109. Air pressure relief valves have been installed on all pressure filter tanks.
Manual _____ Automatic _____

_____ _____ 110. The filter tanks are positioned to allow accessibility and proper air circulation.

_____ _____ 111. Total filter surface area meets recommended design flow rates.

	Pool 1	Pool 2
Filter type*	_____	_____
Filter brand	_____	_____
Filter model	_____	_____
Design flow rate (gpm/ft^2)	_____	_____
Required filter size (ft^2)	_____	_____
Recommended filter size (ft^2) (25% oversized)	_____	_____
Filter area per tank (ft^2)	_____	_____
Number of tanks	_____	_____
Total filter surface area (ft^2)	_____	_____
Properly sized	_____	_____

*Filter types: rapid sand, pressure D.E., vacuum sand, vacuum D.E., high rate sand, regenerative D.E., cartridge

_____ _____ 112. Diatomaceous earth, chemicals, or discharged pool water are neutralized, separated, settled, or otherwise disposed of in accordance with the Clean Water Act, U.S. EPA 40 CFR 122.26: Storm Water Discharge, and local regulations.

_____ _____ 113. A clean sight glass or visual outfall of at least 3 feet has been provided.

_____ _____ 114. A sump pit or backwash holding tank has been installed and has been sized to prevent water discharged during the backwash process from flooding the filter room.

_____ _____ 115. Adequate drainage has been provided in the pump room.

_____ _____ 116. Filter media or elements are clean. No channeling, mud ball formation, or bridging is evident.

_____ _____ 117. All influent and effluent pressure gauges and vacuum gauges are operational and accurate.

	Pool 1	Pool 2
Vacuum (Hg)	_____	_____
Influent pressure (psi)	_____	_____
Effluent pressure (psi)	_____	_____

_____ _____ 118. The pool auxiliary rooms are clean, and maintained in a safe and acceptable manner, well lit, and ventilated.

Cleanliness: _____
Ventilation: _____
Temperature: _____
Relative humidity: _____
Illumination: _____

_____ _____ 119. Diagrams and operating instructions are posted in the pump rooms. Operating manuals have been obtained from the manufacturers.

_____ _____ 120. All piping, filters, and components of the mechanical operating system are labeled, tagged, or color coded.

_____ _____ 121. Pool chemicals and other flammable materials are stored a safe distance from the heater.

_____ _____ 122. Adequate clearances have been established between the heater and the equipment room walls.
Distance to wall: _____

_____ _____ 123. The heater is installed on a level, noncombustible base.

_____ _____ 124. The heater is properly sized and maintained.

	Pool 1	Pool 2
Type of heater	_____	_____
Heater size (BTU)	_____	_____
Intermittent ignition or pilot light	_____	_____
Temp. maintenance or intermittent heat	_____	_____
Fossil fuel	_____	_____
Pool surface area (ft²)	_____	_____
Maximum temperature rise	_____	_____
Required heater output (BTU/hr)	_____	_____
Output ÷ heater efficiency = input	_____	_____
Properly sized*	_____	_____

*Temperature maintenance—commercial pools: _____ ft² (pool surface area) × 15 (constant that represents the BTUs required to raise water temperature one degree per square foot of water surface area) × _____ (desired increase in water temperature over ambient air temperature) ÷ _____% (E rating) = _____ BTUs input

_____ _____ 125. Safety devices on the heater prevent improper operation and eliminate the possibility of patrons being accidentally burned by excessively high water temperatures.

        _____ _____ High-temperature limit switch

        _____ _____ Thermostat

        _____ _____ Low-voltage fireman's switch (if a timer is installed)

        _____ _____ Check valves between the filter and heater, and between the heater and chemical injection equipment

_____ _____ 126. The heater is downstream of the pump and filter and upstream of chemical injection equipment.

_____ _____ 127. A copper, stainless-steel, or CPCV heat sink has been installed between the heater and piping.

_____ _____ 128. Compensation has been made for variables that reduce heater efficiency.

        _____ _____ Heater size increased by 4% for each 1,000 feet in altitude

        _____ _____ Wind breaks erected near outdoor installations

        _____ _____ Properly vented to ensure combustion and adequate exhaustion

        _____ _____ Heater is close to the pool to minimize heat loss

_____ _____ 129. An active solar heating system has been installed and is operating effectively.

    Type: _____ open loop (water)

            _____ closed loop (antifreeze)

    Panels: _____ flat plate _____ flexible plastic

             _____ glazed _____ unglazed

    Collector location _____

_____ _____ 130. UFC Standard No. 79-3 hazard identification signs are posted.

_____ _____ 131. MSDS sheets are posted for all chemicals stored on the premises. MSDS stations and a master file have been created.

_____ _____ 132. Chemicals are correctly dispensed into the pool. Injection:

    ☐ peristaltic pump ☐ gas chlorinator

    ☐ piston pump ☐ brominator

    ☐ diaphragm pump ☐ erosion feeder

    ☐ slurry pot ☐ hand feeding

_____ _____ 133. Empty or used containers for chemicals are rinsed and disposed of in accordance with manufacturers' recommendations.

_____ _____ 134. A clearance of 36 inches has been established in front of and to the sides of electrical panels. The area is identified by paint and/or physical hazard tape in compliance with NEC and OSHA requirements. The designated area is clear of obstructions.

_____ _____ 135. Automated chemical controllers are calibrated and operating properly.

	Pool 1	Pool 2
Controller brand	_____	_____
Model	_____	_____
Paper print-out	_____	_____
Automatic probe cleaner	_____	_____
Conversion charts are not needed to obtain ORP readings from ppm values	_____	_____
Data-voice communications, remote and local log-on, data downloading and programming	_____	_____

_____ _____ 136. Chemicals are stored, contained, labeled, transported, and handled in compliance with safe chemical storage practices.

	Pool 1	Pool 2
Primary bactericide	_____	_____
Alternative sanitizer-oxidizer	_____	_____
pH adjustment chemical	_____	_____

Chemical inventory

- ☐ gas chlorine
- ☐ sodium hypochlorite
- ☐ calcium hypochlorite
- ☐ lithium hypochlorite
- ☐ trichloro-s-triazinetrione
- ☐ sodium dichloro-s-triazinetrione
- ☐ sodium bromide
- ☐ bromo-chloro-dimethylhydantoin
- ☐ oxygen
- ☐ polymeric biguanide
- ☐ potassium peroxymonosulfate
- ☐ sodium carbonate
- ☐ sodium hydroxide
- ☐ sodium sesquicarbonate
- ☐ muriatic acid
- ☐ carbon dioxide
- ☐ sodium bisulfate

- ☐ sodium bicarbonate
- ☐ calcium chloride dihydrate
- ☐ sodium hexametaphosphate
- ☐ sequestering agent
- ☐ chelating agent
- ☐ clarifier
- ☐ aluminum sulfate
- ☐ enzymes
- ☐ test reagents
- ☐ filter cleaners
- ☐ diatomaceous earth
- ☐ sodium fluorescein
- ☐ crystal violet
- ☐ algaecides
- ☐ defoamer
- ☐ other: _____
- ☐ other: _____

_____ _____ 137. Equipment for containing and cleaning up chemical spills is available. Containment dikes, overpacks, and chemical clean-up gear has been provided.

_____ _____ 138. Emergency fresh-water drench showers and eyewashes are available for all persons required to handle chemicals. (ANSI Standard Z358.1-1981, and CA General Industry Safety Orders)

_____ _____ 139. Personal safety gear, such as goggles, full face shields, splash guard aprons, neoprene gloves, boots, respirators, gas masks, SCBAs, disposable latex gloves, and one-way CPR pocket masks are available, and staff members have been instructed in their use.

_____ _____ 140. The facility is in compliance with all state bathing codes. [Health and safety, building, general industry safety, and administrative codes that pertain to the design, construction, maintenance, and operation of pools in the state.]

_____ _____ 141. The facility is in compliance with the Uniform Fire Code, Article 80: "Hazardous Materials."

_____ _____ 142. The facility is in compliance with the EPA SARA Title III: "Emergency Planning and Community Right-to-Know Act."

_____ _____ 143. The facility is in compliance with the EPA or Dept. of Agriculture's Pesticide Safety Training requirements.

_____ _____ 144. The facility is in compliance with OSHA's "Hazard Communication Standard."

_____ _____ 145. The facility is in compliance with the state's Safe Drinking Water and Toxic Enforcement Act. [For example: CA Proposition 65, NV Proposition 11, GA Safe Drinking Water Act, NH Groundwater Protection Act, MA House Bill 5109 . . . , or the U.S. EPA Clean Water Act]

_____ _____ 146. In compliance with the state education code (for example, CA Education Code §10911.5) all public recreation employees having direct contact with minors have submitted a set of fingerprints to the Department of Justice. A criminal record summary has been furnished and is maintained by the employer in a secure file separate from personnel files.

_____ _____ 147. The facility is in compliance with the OSHA "Occupational Exposure to Bloodborne Pathogens" requirements.

_____ _____ 148. The facility is in compliance with the OSHA "Confined Spaces" Regulation [29 CFR 1910.146] requiring that before an employee enters a confined space, internal atmosphere of the confined space is tested with a dosimeter for oxygen level, flammable gasses and vapors, and toxic air contaminants (hydrogen sulfide and carbon monoxide).

     _____ _____ Lifeline and retrieval system provided

     _____ _____ Dosimeter

     _____ _____ Harness

     _____ _____ Floor sign

     _____ _____ Annual inspections to ensure proper operation of rescue and recovery winch

     _____ _____ Ventilation blower to provide steady, fresh air to confined spaces and reduce levels of contaminants

     _____ _____ Permit system & controlled entry authorization procedures

     _____ _____ Personnel training for operations in confined spaces

_____ _____ 149. Fire extinguishers are charged and located throughout the facility.

_____ _____ 150. Locker rooms are adequately sized to provide patrons with a desired level of privacy.

	Square Footage	Anticipated No. of Users	Ratio
Men's locker room	_____	_____	_____
Women's locker room	_____	_____	_____
Boy's locker room	_____	_____	_____
Girl's locker room	_____	_____	_____
Staff locker room	_____	_____	_____
Family changing room	_____	_____	_____

_____ _____ 151. Lockers are provided in adequate numbers to provide storage for anticipated bather loads.

	Tier Design	No. of Lockers
Men's locker room	_____	_____
Women's locker room	_____	_____
Boy's locker room	_____	_____
Girl's locker room	_____	_____
Staff locker room	_____	_____
Family changing room	_____	_____

_____ _____ 152. Provisions have been made for the storage of patrons' valuables.

_____ _____ 153. The locker rooms are adequately illuminated and ventilated.

	Illumination	Temperature	Rel. Humidity
Men's	_____	_____	_____
Women's	_____	_____	_____
Boy's	_____	_____	_____
Girl's	_____	_____	_____
Staff	_____	_____	_____
Family	_____	_____	_____

_____ _____ 154. Locker-room maintenance is completed as needed. Sink basins, floors, mirrors, toilet bowls, and urinals are cleaned and disinfected.

_____ _____ 155. The locker-room plumbing has been checked for dripping water or leaks. Showers, faucets, and toilets are working and in good repair.

	Group	Private	Semiprivate	Disabled
Men's	_____	_____	_____	_____
Women's	_____	_____	_____	_____
Boy's	_____	_____	_____	_____
Girl's	_____	_____	_____	_____
Staff	_____	_____	_____	_____
Family	_____	_____	_____	_____

_____ _____ 156. Toilet paper, towels, soap, and other amenities are available and containers filled. Amenities:

☐ toilet paper   ☐ paper towels
☐ soap   ☐ suit dryers
☐ hair dryers   ☐ scales
☐ diaper changing table ☐ baby seats in stalls
☐ hand dryers   ☐ plastic bags for wet suits
☐ towel warmer

_____ _____ 157. A diaper-changing area, sanitary bed liners, and a disposal can for soiled diapers has been provided.
　　　　　_____ Men's locker room
　　　　　_____ Women's locker room
　　　　　_____ Family changing room

_____ _____ 158. The suit dryer is operational and in good repair.
　　　　　_____ Men's locker room
　　　　　_____ Women's locker room
　　　　　_____ Boy's locker room
　　　　　_____ Girl's locker room
　　　　　_____ Staff locker room
　　　　　_____ Family changing room

_____ _____ 159. Benches, chairs, and tables are secure and in good repair.

_____ _____ 160. The locker rooms are aesthetically pleasing, and provide a comfortable and pleasant environment.

_____ _____ 161. The spa (15-minute) timer is operational and located so it cannot be reached by a bather sitting in the spa.

_____ _____ 162. An emergency shut-off switch for the spa's pump is installed on the spa deck. The switch is clearly labeled.

_____ _____ 163. Sauna (30-minute) timers are suitably located on the outside of the rooms, and operational.

_____ _____ 164. Steam room (30-minute) timers are suitably located on the outside of the rooms, and operational.

_____ _____ 165. Signs are posted instructing bathers on the proper use of saunas, steam rooms, and spas, and warning bathers of the hazards associated with their use.

_____ _____ 166. The sauna is satisfactorily maintained, and is cleaned and disinfected daily.

_____ _____ 167. A protective wooden railing has been installed around the sauna heater.

_____ _____ 168. The steam room is satisfactorily maintained and is cleaned and disinfected daily.

_____ _____ 169. A safeguard has been installed to prevent bathers from accidentally coming into contact with the steam head.

_____ _____ 170. The steam generator is properly sized for the steam room. (1 bhp or 33,478 BTU or 10 kw per 400 ft^3)
Steam generator size _____
Room dimensions: area _____ ft^3

_____ _____ 171. Doors to the sauna and steam room open out. A window has been installed in the door. No locking or latching devices are present.

_____ _____ 172. Subdued lighting, a clock, thermometer, hygrometer, and emergency alarms have been installed in the steam room and sauna, and are operating properly.

_____ _____ 173. A temperature regulator has been installed to automatically shut off the heat or steam in the sauna or steam room when maximum temperature has been reached.

_____ _____ 174. An adequate number of nearby parking spaces have been provided in anticipation of maximum bather loads.

_____ _____ 175. Measures are taken to prevent infestation by roaches and other pests.

_____ _____ 176. A lockout-tagout kit is available for use by employees. Staff members have been taught that before maintenance or service work is performed, equipment must be "locked out" and tagged, and the lock and tag can only be removed by the employee who put them there [29 CFR 1910.147, OSHA Lockout/Tagout Standard].

Attach diagrams of each pool and pump room.

B-2

Water Analyses

POOL WATER

Pool _____ Date _____

_____ ORP
_____ FAC
_____ TAC
_____ CAC
_____ Cyanuric acid
_____ pH
_____ Acid/base demand
_____ Total alkalinity
_____ Calcium hardness
_____ Total dissolved solids
_____ Iron
_____ Copper
_____ Nitrates
_____ Water level
_____ Clarity
_____ Air temperature
_____ Water temperature
_____ Flow rate
_____ Turnover
_____ Pressure differential
        _____ Influent pressure
        _____ Effluent pressure
_____ Saturation index
_____ Humidity
_____ Discernible odor
_____ Measurable chlorine (or other) gas
present in air
_____ Bacteriological water quality analysis
performed

SOURCE WATER

Water Source _____ Date _____
Drought restrictions _____ Yes _____ No
Water utility company _____
Water sample gathered from _____

_____ ORP
_____ FAC
_____ TAC
_____ CAC
_____ pH
_____ Acid/base demand
_____ Total alkalinity
_____ Calcium hardness
_____ Total dissolved solids
_____ Iron
_____ Copper
_____ Nitrates
_____ Nitrites
_____ Water temperature
_____ Saturation index
_____ Discernible odor or taste

B-3

Pool Measurements

	POOL 1	POOL 2		POOL 1	POOL 2
Pool shape	_____	_____	Natatorium volume	_____	_____
Location	_____	_____	Illumination level (daytime)	_____	_____
Pool length	_____	_____	Illumination level (nighttime)	_____	_____
Pool width	_____	_____	S deck width	_____	_____
Minimum depth	_____	_____	E deck width	_____	_____
Maximum depth at main drain	_____	_____	N deck width	_____	_____
Pool area < 5′ deep	_____	_____	W deck width	_____	_____
Pool area > 5′ deep	_____	_____	Perimeter overflow system	_____	_____
Water surface area	_____	_____	Lane lines: number and width	_____	_____
Maximum bather capacity	_____	_____	Slope ratio (shallow)	_____	_____
Volume	_____	_____	Slope ratio (deep)	_____	_____
Weight of water in the pool	_____	_____	Required flow rate	_____	_____
Year built/renovated	_____	_____	Actual flow rate recorded	_____	_____
Orientation of the pool	_____	_____	Turnover required	_____	_____
Deck length	_____	_____	Actual turnover time	_____	_____
Deck width	_____	_____	Filter size and design flow rate	_____	_____
Pool deck area (− pool area)	_____	_____	Number and location of inlets	_____	_____
Spectator gallery dimensions	_____	_____	Number of main drains	_____	_____
Spectator gallery area	_____	_____	Means of egress	_____	_____
Natatorium area	_____	_____	Sauna	_____	_____
Ceiling height	_____	_____	Steam room	_____	_____
Deck to ceiling beams	_____	_____	Water feature	_____	_____

B-4

Daily Swimming Pool Chemical Log

Pool _____ Date _____

TIME	FAC	pH	Water Temp.	Air Temp.	Bather Load	Chemicals Added
Opening	_____	_____	_____	_____	_____	_____
	_____	_____	_____	_____	_____	_____
	_____	_____	_____	_____	_____	_____
	_____	_____	_____	_____	_____	_____
	_____	_____	_____	_____	_____	_____
	_____	_____	_____	_____	_____	_____
	_____	_____	_____	_____	_____	_____
	_____	_____	_____	_____	_____	_____
	_____	_____	_____	_____	_____	_____
	_____	_____	_____	_____	_____	_____
	_____	_____	_____	_____	_____	_____
	_____	_____	_____	_____	_____	_____
	_____	_____	_____	_____	_____	_____
	_____	_____	_____	_____	_____	_____
	_____	_____	_____	_____	_____	_____
Closing	_____	_____	_____	_____	_____	_____

ORP	_____	Iron	_____	Flow rate	_____
TAC	_____	Copper	_____	Turnover	_____
CAC	_____	Nitrates	_____	Influent pressure	_____
Cyanuric acid	_____	TDS	_____	Effluent pressure	_____
Total alkalinity	_____	Water level	_____	Pressure differential	_____
Calcium hardness	_____	Water clarity	_____	Saturation index	_____

B-5

_____ 1. Start seasonal opening procedures at least one month prior to the scheduled opening day.

_____ 2. Conduct a complete inventory.

_____ 3. Check for winter damage and vandalism.

_____ 4. Make sure that chemical and maintenance contracts are in effect.

_____ 5. Check to see that repairs and/or renovations scheduled during the off-season were completed.

_____ 6. Hire the pool staff. Plan preseason training programs.

_____ 7. Order staff uniforms. Purchase sunscreen products and personal protective gear.

_____ 8. Replace worn or missing rescue equipment.

_____ 9. Restock the first aid kit.

_____ 10. Prepare all record forms and logs. Revise the staff, policy, and operating manuals.

_____ 11. Pump any accumulated water and debris off the top of the winterizing pool cover.

_____ 12. Remove the winter pool cover. Clean and store it for the season.

_____ 13. Turn on the water supply.

_____ 14. Have the phone company restart service.

_____ 15. Empty all debris from the pool. Do not try to pump out dead or decaying leaves and animals.

_____ 16. Drain the pool with a trash pump.

_____ 17. Pump remaining liquid from the pool using a sump pump with auto shutoff.

_____ 18. Rinse down the pool using a high-pressure nozzle and hose. Flush out the gutters or skimmers.

_____ 19. Sandblast, acid wash, chlorine wash, recoat, repaint, replaster, fiberglass, patch liner tears, or otherwise prepare the pool surface.

_____ 20. Paint or touch up depth markings, drop-off lines, lane lines and targets, step edges, and graphics before refilling the pool.

_____ 21. Clean all pool and deck equipment.

_____ 22. Remove the winterizing plugs and expansion blocks. Uncap the inlets.

_____ 23. Lubricate all metal parts and hardware.

_____ 24. Replace gutter drain grates, bolts, gaskets, inlets, and plugs.

_____ 25. Check for proper operation of the hydrostatic relief valve.

_____ 26. Bolt the main drain grates to the pool bottom.

_____ 27. Clean and replace skimmer baskets, weirs, and lids.

_____ 28. Reassemble circulation pipes, the pump, and motor. Drain antifreeze from all piping and flush with fresh water.

_____ 29. Pressure test all circulation lines to make sure the pipes have not broken during the off-season. Repair broken pipes before leaks develop.

_____ 30. Service and reinstall flowmeters, pressure and vacuum gauges, thermometers, and hygrometers.

_____ 31. Reinstall the hair and lint skimmer basket. Replace gaskets or O-rings. Make sure the lid seals tightly.

_____ 32. Replace cracked or chipped tile.

_____ 33. Replace broken or burnt-out pool lights, lenses, and seals. Lubricate, tighten bolts, and reinsert in the pool wall.

_____ 34. Check that all ground wires are connected.

_____ 35. Service the heater, replace elements, turn on the gas and relight the pilot, or check electrical connections.

_____ 36. Clean the filter media or elements. Repair or replace filter elements or cartridges if necessary. Close and replug the filter tank.

_____ 37. Test the manual air pressure relief valves on pressurized filter tanks.

_____ 38. Drain and clean the surge chamber. Check that valves, overflow, and water level devices are in operating order.

_____ 39. Have the maintenance and start-up chemicals delivered.

_____ 40. Reinstall the chlorinator, controllers, and other chemical feed pumps.

_____ 41. Begin filling the pool with water 7 to 10 days prior to the anticipated opening day.

_____ 42. Start circulating and filtering the water as soon as possible after the water level covers the inlets. Remember to shut off the skimmer lines to prevent air from entering the system.

_____ 43. Superchlorinate or use a nonchlorine shock product to oxidize organic contaminants out of the water and prevent an algae bloom.

_____ 44. Add sequestering or chelating agents to prevent mineral staining.

_____ 45. Add a clarifier so suspended particles will flocculate and either settle or filter out of the water.

_____ 46. Balance the water.

_____ 47. If planning to stabilize the chlorine, gradually add cyanuric acid.

_____ 48. Restock the test kit with fresh reagents. Calibrate testing instruments.

_____ 49. Vacuum the pool and backwash as needed until the water clears.

_____ 50. Conduct a dye test to check inlet operation and locate circulation "dead spots" in the pool.

_____ 51. Turn on the water heater and begin to raise the water temperature to desired levels.

_____ 52. Cover the pool with a solar or insulating pool blanket to help prevent heat loss and reduce energy costs.

_____ 53. Reinstall ladders, rails, guard chairs, backstroke flags, stanchions, slides, and diving boards.

_____ 54. Replace handles on hose bibs and fill spouts.

_____ 55. Clean and disinfect the decks. Inspect for cracks or deterioration. Resurface if necessary.

_____ 56. Clean and arrange the deck furniture.

_____ 57. Repaint, "spruce up," and clean the pool building, locker rooms, and auxiliary areas.

_____ 58. Replace vandalized or missing signs. Check that all signage required by code is posted.

_____ 59. Stock supplies.

_____ 60. Continue regular maintenance of grounds.

_____ 61. Conduct a preopening inspection and safety audit of the facility.

_____ 62. Run mandatory preseason training sessions for the pool staff.

B-6

Pool Winterizing Checklist

_____ 1. Adjust the chemical balance of the pool water to recommended levels.

_____ 2. Superchlorinate.

_____ 3. Add an algaecide to prevent algae growth.

_____ 4. Add sequestering or chelating agents to prevent mineral staining and scale buildup.

_____ 5. Clean and vacuum the pool because debris left in the water will consume chlorine during the off-season.

_____ 6. Empty and store skimmer baskets and hair and lint traps for the winter.

_____ 7. Backwash the filter thoroughly.

_____ 8. Clean the filter media or elements.

_____ 9. Drain sand filters. Remove cartridges or D.E. filter elements, inspect for tears or excessive wear, and store for the winter.

_____ 10. Lower the water level to below the skimmers and return lines. If necessary, remove the remaining water from the recirculation lines using an air compressor or industrial tank vacuum cleaner.

_____ 11. Open all pump room valves and loosen the lid from the hair and lint skimmer. However, if the filter is below pool water level, close the valves leading from the pool to the filter.

_____ 12. Grease all plugs and threads.

_____ 13. Add a nontoxic antifreeze such as propylene glycol (1 part antifreeze diluted in 2 parts water) to the pipes to prevent bursting. Do not use automotive antifreeze.

_____ 14. Plug the skimmer or gutter lines. Winterize with antifreeze and expansion blocks. Secure the skimmer lids to the deck to prevent their loss.

_____ 15. Plug vacuum and return lines, and the main drain.

_____ 16. The hydrostatic relief valve is operational.

_____ 17. Drain and protect pumps. If a pump and motor will be exposed to severe weather disconnect, lubricate, perform seasonal maintenance on the pump, and store. Add antifreeze to protect pumps and seals from residual water after draining.

_____ 18. Clean surge pits or balancing tanks.

_____ 19. If underwater wet niche lights are exposed to the elements, remove them from their niches and lower them to the bottom of the pool.

_____ 20. Disconnect all fuses and open circuit breakers.

_____ 21. Drain the pool water heater. Grease the drain plugs and store for the winter.

_____ 22. Turn off the heater gas supply, gas valves, and pilot lights.

_____ 23. Install the winter safety cover.

_____ 24. Return unopened chemicals and empty storage containers to the distributor.

_____ 25. Properly store opened chemicals in tightly sealed containers in a well-ventilated room. Dispose of test reagents, sanitizers, and other chemicals that will lose potency over the winter.

_____ 26. Disconnect, clean, and store the chlorinator, controllers, and other chemical feed pumps. Store controller electrodes in liquid.

_____ 27. Clean and protect pressure gauges, flowmeters, thermometers, and hygrometers.

_____ 28. Store all deck furniture (chairs, lounges, tables, umbrellas, etc.). Identify and set aside all furniture in need of repair.

_____ 29. Remove deck equipment, hardware, and nonpermanent objects such as ladders, rails, slides, guard chairs, starting blocks, drinking fountains, handicapped lifts, portable ramps, clocks, weirs, and safety equipment—to prevent vandalism. Store in a clearly marked, identifiable, weather-protected location. Cap all exposed deck sockets.

_____ 30. Remove the diving boards. Store the boards indoors, upside down, and flat so they will not warp.

_____ 31. Open hose bibs and fill spouts.

_____ 32. Turn off the water supply to restroom showers, sinks, and toilets. Drain the pipes and add antifreeze. Remove shower heads and drinking fountain handles.

_____ 33. Have the phone company disconnect the pool telephone and discontinue service for the winter.

_____ 34. Install an alarm system on the pool deck.

_____ 35. Inventory supplies and equipment. Make suggestions for preventive maintenance and repair, upgrading, and equipment purchases.

Daily Locker Room
Maintenance Checklist

Facility _____ Date _____

The person who completes the task must initial the space next to it.

_____ 1. Trash containers emptied

_____ 2. Litter, debris, clothes, or misplaced articles picked up

_____ 3. Area checked for unpleasant odors, algae, mold, or mildew

_____ 4. Mirrors cleaned

_____ 5. Toilet bowls and urinals cleaned and disinfected

_____ 6. Sink basins cleaned

_____ 7. Toilet paper and towels available

_____ 8. Soap and other amenities available and containers filled

_____ 9. Suit dryer operational and in good repair

_____ 10. Hair dryers operational

_____ 11. Diaper changing area clean; sanitary bed liners available

_____ 12. Marks and graffiti removed

_____ 13. All lights operational; burnt-out lightbulbs replaced

_____ 14. Floor drains cleaned

_____ 15. Floors swept, rinsed, and disinfected

_____ 16. Walls and ceilings cleaned

_____ 17. Nonslip flooring or mats removed for rinsing and disinfection

_____ 18. Lockers opened and checked for items left behind by bathers. Interior and exterior of lockers cleaned and disinfected

_____ 19. Showers, faucets, and toilets working and in good repair

_____ 20. Plumbing checked for dripping water or leaks

_____ 21. Benches or seating secure and in good repair

B-8

Daily Pool Maintenance Checklist

Pool _____ Date _____

The person who actually completes the task must initial the space next to it.

Opening

_____ 1. Inspect the grounds, safety equipment, the pool itself, deck, bathhouse, office area, pump and chemical rooms, and auxiliary areas for broken or malfunctioning equipment, minor maintenance needs, or vandalism that may have occurred since the previous day.

_____ 2. Record the chemical readings. Add chemicals if needed.

_____ 3. Turn off the pool and deck lights, and security alarms. Turn on the bathhouse and office lights.

_____ 4. Vacuum the pool. Clean the vacuum.

_____ 5. Clean the hair and lint strainer.

_____ 6. Backwash the filters if needed.

_____ 7. Scrub off the scum line.

_____ 8. Empty and clean the skimmer baskets or gutters.

_____ 9. Sweep, rinse, and disinfect the decks. Clean the deck drains.

_____ 10. Wash down and arrange the deck furniture.

_____ 11. Insert new garbage bags and put the garbage cans back out on the deck.

_____ 12. List all maintenance jobs to be done during the day. Report repair needs to the proper supervisor.

_____ 13. Clean up the guard room, pool office, first aid room, pump room, chemical room, storage rooms, and bathhouse.

_____ 14. Perform preventive maintenance scheduled for the day.

_____ 15. Unlock the entrance doors to the pool immediately before opening to the public.

Closing

_____ 1. Pick up the refuse and debris on the deck.

_____ 2. Straighten or put away deck furniture.

_____ 3. Empty the garbage cans, rinse and store off the deck.

_____ 5. Take the final chemical readings. Make chemical adjustments. Superchlorinate if necessary.

_____ 6. Turn on the deck, security and pool lights.

_____ 7. Clean the locker rooms or bathhouse.

_____ 9. Make sure that all running water on deck and in the bathhouse is turned off.

_____ 10. Compile a list of maintenance jobs or repairs that need to be done prior to re-opening.

_____ 11. Check all areas of the facility to make sure all patrons have left the premises.

_____ 12. Lock all doors and gates.

_____ 13. Turn on the security alarm system to warn of unauthorized entry onto the premises overnight.

All maintenance duties have been satisfactorily completed.

Maintenance Supervisor _____

B-9

Pool Emergency Response Plan

Examine the accident scene and make sure it is safe to proceed with the rescue.

Primary Rescuer

1. Signal the emergency to notify staff that you are leaving your designated post to provide rescue assistance.
2. Enter the water (if necessary), and approach the injured victim.
3. Perform the rescue and manage the situation within 20 seconds.
4. Bring the injured patron to the prearranged point on the deck, or if the patron is not in physical danger and cannot be moved, bring the first aid equipment to the victim.
5. Provide emergency first aid treatment until relieved by paramedical or medical authorities.

Additional Rescuers

1. Notify emergency (EMS) and supervisory personnel that an accident has occurred and request assistance.
2. Send someone to meet the emergency vehicle and direct EMTs to the accident.
3. Clear the pool and move all patrons away from the impact zone.
4. Provide crowd control.
5. Direct relatives or friends of the victim away from the accident site; provide comfort and assurance that the victim is being properly cared for.

6. Bring first aid kits or other rescue equipment to the prearranged point on the pool deck.
7. Remove hazards that might hinder the rescue attempt.
8. Identify the victim and if the injured patron is a minor notify parents.
9. Gather as much information as possible about what happened so that emergency personnel can pass the information on to the hospital emergency room staff after transporting the victim for medical care.
10. Find out to which hospital the victim is being taken.
11. Immediately after the incident, conduct a thorough investigation into the incident, gather additional information about the accident, staff involvement, and condition of the facility at the time of the accident.
12. Ask witnesses to write by hand (in their own words), sign, and date an account of what happened and what they observed.
13. Complete an accident report.
14. Contact the facility's insurance carrier or attorney.
15. Designate one individual to provide information to patrons and the media.

Remember: Always check for possible spinal injury before making a water rescue.
Treat life-threatening emergencies first.

- Nonbreathing and cardiac emergencies
- Severe bleeding
- Poisoning

B-10

Aquatic Accident Report

Name of injured party			Address	
Phone number	Sex	Age	Class or activity in which enrolled	
Date of accident			Time of accident	
Where did the accident occur?				
What was the injured party doing when he/she was injured?				
What piece of equipment, if any, was involved?				
Name and location of supervisor(s) at the time of the accident				
What part of the body was injured?			Type of injury sustained	
First aid administered				
Did the injured party seek medical assistance?			Was EMS called?	
Describe what happened:				

Yes   No

☐   ☐   Were blood products or bodily fluids present?
☐   ☐   Were universal precautions taken? What protective gear was worn by the employee?
☐   ☐   Did an exposure incident occur? Employee's name:

Witness 1 (Name, address, phone, signature)		
Witness 2 (Name, address, phone, signature)		
Witness 3 (Name, address, phone, signature)		
Signature of person filling out report	Position	Date

Certification Courses

The following courses and certificates are offered by the following agencies.

Aquatic Facility Operator (AFO)
National Recreation and Park Association
650 W. Higgins Road
Hoffman Estates, IL 60195
(312) 843-7529

Certified Aquatic Manager (CAM)
Aquatic Associates
1608 Harbor Drive
Springfield, OR 97477
(503) 746-2286

Certified Pool-Spa Operator (CPO)
National Swimming Pool Foundation
10803 Gulfdale, Suite 300
San Antonio, TX 78216
(210) 525-1227

Pool Operator On Location (POOL)
YMCA of the USA
101 N. Wacker Drive
Chicago, IL 60606
(312) 977-0031

Tech 1, Tech 2, NSPI Certified
NSPI Certificate Program
National Spa and Pool Institute
2111 Eisenhower Ave.
Alexandria, VA 22314
(703) 838-0083

Sources of Codes, Regulations, and Guidelines

Copies of codes, regulations, and guidelines that apply to operating a pool are available from the following agencies.

Americans with Disabilities Act (ADA)

U.S. Senate Subcommittee on Disability Policy
113 Senate Hart Office Building
Washington, DC 20510

U.S. Government Printing Office
Superintendent of Documents
Mail Stop SSOP
Washington, DC 20402-9328

Architectural and Transportation Barriers Compliance Board (ATBCB)
1111 18th Street NW Suite 501
Washington, DC 20036

Equal Employment Opportunity Commission (EEOC)
1801 L Street, NW
Washington, DC 20507

Department of Transportation
400 Seventh Street SW
Washington, DC 20590

Federal Communications Commission
1919 M Street NW
Washington, DC 20554

U.S. Department of Justice
Civil Rights Division
P.O. Box 66118
Washington, DC 20035

"Chlorine Safety at Nonresidential Swimming Pools"

The Chlorine Institute
2001 L Street NW
Washington, DC 20036

The Emergency Planning and Community Right-To-Know Act of 1986 (U.S. EPA SARA Title III)

U.S. Environmental Protection Agency
Washington, DC 20460

Hazard Communication Standard (OSHA 29 CFR 1910.1200)

Occupational Exposure to Bloodborne Pathogens (OSHA 29 CFR 1910.1030)

OSHA Publication Office
200 Constitution Ave., NW, Room N-3101
Washington, DC 20210

National Electrical Code

National Fire Protection Association
Batterymarch Park
Quincy, MA 02269

NSPI Standards

"ANSI/NSPI-1: American National Standard for Public Swimming Pools"
"ANSI/NSPI-2: Standard for Public Spas"
"ANSI/NSPI-3: Standard for Permanently Installed Residential Spas"
"ANSI/NSPI-4: Standard for Aboveground Swimming Pools"
"NSPI-5: Standard for Residential Swimming Pools"
"ANSI/NSPI-6: Standard for Residential Portable Spas"
"NSPI-7: Workmanship Standards"

"Official Swimming Pool Design Compendium" (NSPF)

National Swimming Pool Foundation
10803 Gulfdale, Suite 300
San Antonio, TX 78216

Pesticide Safety Training Regulations, U.S.A.

U.S. Environmental Protection
   Agency
Washington, DC 20460

Pesticide Safety Training Regulations, California

State of California Environmental
   Protection Agency
Department of Pesticide Regulation
1220 N Street
P.O. Box 942871
Sacramento, CA 94271-0001

"Public Swimming Pools: Recommendations for Design and Construction, Operation and Maintenance"

American Public Health Association
   (APHA)
1015 15th Street NW
Washington, DC 20005

"Suggested Health and Safety Guidelines for Public Spas and Hot Tubs"

"Suggested Health and Safety Guidelines for Recreational Water Slide Flumes"

"Swimming Pools: Safety and Design Control through Proper Design and Operation"

Centers for Disease Control
U.S. Department of Health and Human Services
1600 Clifton Road
Atlanta, GA 30333

Uniform Fire Code

Western Fire Chiefs Association, ICBO
5360 S. Workman Mill Road
Whittier, CA 90601

"WWA Considerations for Operating Safety"

World Waterpark Association
P.O. Box 14826
Lenexa, KS 66214

APPENDIX C

Fitness Laboratory Resources

C-1

Equipment for a Fitness Laboratory

Essentials

Emergency defibrillator
Emergency crash cart
Spine board
First aid kit
Cleaning supplies
Clock
Stethoscope and sphygmomanometer
Padded mat
Red bags for disposal of biohazardous
  materials
Drinking fountain
Restroom
Curtains or dividers
Sterilization material

Stature, Recumbent, Length, Weight, Segment Length, Body Breadth, Circumference

Balanced scale
Stadiometer
Movable anthropometer
Platform weight
Sliding anthropometric caliper
Standard anthropometer with extension rods
Spreading caliper

Body Composition

Underwater weighing tank, chair, scale, and thermometer
Residual lung volume measured by helium dilution, nitrogen washout, or oxygen dilution technique
Anthropometrical tape measure
Surgical marking pen

Skeletal anthropometer
Lange skinfold calipers
Bioelectrical impedance analyzer
Near-infrared interactance

Cardiorespiratory Fitness

Cycle ergometer
Treadmill
Arm ergometer
Bench
Stop watch
Metronome
12-Lead ECG (A lead is a pair of electrodes placed on the body and connected to an ECG recorder.)
ECG monitoring system
O_2 and CO_2 analyzers
Access to a quarter-mile track
Borg's perceived exertion chart
Portable heart rate monitor

Muscular Strength and Endurance

Static and dynamic testing
  Cable tensiometer
  Handgrip dynamometer
  Back and leg dynamometer
  Constant-resistance and variable-resistance exercise machines
Isokinetic testing
  Electromechanical and hydraulic devices (Cybex II, Orthotron, Omnitron)
Omnikinetic testing
  Omnitron total power for measuring isokinetic strength, endurance, and power
  Omnitron dynamometers
Pull-up bar and modified pull-up bar

Flexibility

Sit-and-reach box
Yardstock
Goniometer
Flexometer

Pulmonary Volumes and Capacities

Portable spirometer
Open-circuit method (Most widely used technique; subject breathes ambient air.)
Closed-circuit method (Subject breathes and re-breathes from a prefilled container of oxygen.)
Indirect calorimetry
Portable spirometry
Douglas bag technique
Computerized instrumentation (collection, analysis, and output of physiologic and metabolic data)

Extra

Antistatic carpet	Measuring wheel	Copy machine
Computer	Appropriate software	Refrigerator
Locked file cabinets	Overhead projector	Phone
Slide projector	Conference table	Video system
Screen	Calculators	Chairs
Tape player		Towels

Dream List

Blood analyzer (cholesterol, glucose, triglycerides)
Lactate analyzer
Swim flume
Load cell (hydrostatic weighing)
Altitude chamber
Dual energy X-ray absorptiometry (DEXA)
Total body water analyzer
Rowing ergometer
Skiing ergometer

Health Questionnaires

MEDICAL

Please print.

Name: _____

Date: _____ ID No.:_____

Phone no.: (home) (_____)_____

(work) (_____)_____

Address: (home) _____ Zip _____

(work _____ Zip _____

Age: _____ Ethnicity: _____

Physical injuries: _____

Limitations: _____

Contact in case of emergency: _____

_____ Phone: _____

Have you ever been diagnosed as having any cardio-vascular abnormalities? Yes _____ No _____

If yes, what was diagnosed and when? _____

_____

Have you ever had any of the following cardiovascular problems?

Myocardial infarction	☐	Bypass surgery	☐
Arrhythmias	☐	Heart murmur	☐
Chest	☐	Palpitations	☐
Valve problems	☐	Chest pressure	☐
Shortness of breath	☐	Heart attack	☐

Do you currently have respiratory (breathing) ailments?

Asthma	☐	COPD	☐
Common cold	☐	Emphysema	☐
Bronchitis	☐		

Have you had any of the following:

Rheumatic fever	☐	High blood pressure	☐
Kidney/liver disease	☐	Obesity	☐
Diabetes	☐	High cholesterol	☐

Does anyone in your family have any of the conditions listed above? If yes, please list family member and problem: _____

_____

_____

Is your mother living? Yes _____ No _____

Age at death: _____ Cause: _____

Is your father living? Yes _____ No _____

Age at death: _____ Cause: _____

Are you on any medications now? Yes _____ No _____

If yes, please list: _____

_____

_____

Do you have allergies? Yes _____ No _____ If yes, please list: _____

_____

_____

Have you been seen by a physician in the past year? Yes _____ No _____

Have you ever experienced any adverse effects during or after exercise (such as fainting, vomiting, shock, palpitations, hyperventilation)? Yes _____ No _____ If yes, what? _____

_____

_____

_____

LIFESTYLE

Do you use tobacco? Yes _____ No _____

If yes, type? _____

How many years? _____ How much per day? _____

If No: Have you ever used tobacco? Yes _____

No _____

If Yes, How many years did you use tobacco? _____

Amount per day? _____

No. of years since you quit? _____

How often do you drink the following?

Coffee:	___ oz./day
Tea:	___ oz./day
Caffeinated cola:	___ oz./day
Hard liquor:	___ oz./day
Wine:	___ oz./day
Beer:	___ oz./day

What do you do for physical activity? _____
How often do you exercise? _____ days per week/month;
How long each session? _____ minutes
Estimate your intensity level: Circle one or list your
target exercise heart rate: Easy, Medium, Hard or
THR = _____ per minute
Please describe your knowledge of exercise and fitness.
Circle one: Good, Fair, Poor
What is your occupation? _____
   Inactive work (e.g., desk job) _____
   Light work (e.g., light carpentry) _____
   Heavy work (e.g., heavy carpentry, farming,
     lifting) _____

Which do you eat regularly?

Breakfast	☐	Midafternoon snack	☐
Midmorning snack	☐	Dinner	☐
Lunch	☐	After-dinner snack	☐

How often do you eat out each week? _____ times
   Current weight: _____
   What would you like to weigh? _____
What weight loss method(s) have you tried? _____
_____

How long does it usually take you to eat a meal?
_____ minutes
Do you eat while doing other activities? (watching TV,
reading, etc.) _____
When you snack, how many times per week do you eat
the following:

Cookies, cake,	_____	Cheese &
pie		crackers _____
Soft drinks	_____	Candy _____
Fruit	_____	Doughnuts _____
Milk	_____	Potato chips, etc. _____
(skim, low		Fried bread _____
fat, whole)		Ice cream _____
Veggies	_____	
Other (identify)	_____	

How often do you eat fried foods?
_____ times a week
Do you salt your food at the table?
Yes _____ No _____
Please describe your knowledge of nutrition?
Circle one: Good, Fair, Poor
How would you characterize your life? Circle one:
Highly stressful, Moderately stressful, Minimally
stressful

Please check if you would like information about:
_____ Muscular strength and endurance
_____ Flexibility
_____ Cardiovascular fitness
_____ Percentage of body fat
_____ Diet and eating habits
_____ Management of stress
_____ How to quit smoking or drinking
_____ How to rehabilitate after an injury

PHYSICAL ACTIVITY READINESS

For most people, physical activity should not pose a problem or hazard. This questionnaire (PAR-Q) has been designed to identify the small number of adults for whom physical activity might be inappropriate or who should have medical advice concerning the type of activity most suitable for them.

YES NO

☐ ☐ 1. Has your doctor ever said that you have a heart condition *and* that you should only do physical activity recommended by a doctor?

☐ ☐ 2. Do you feel pain in your chest when you do physical activity?

☐ ☐ 3. In the past month, have you had chest pain when not doing physical activity?

☐ ☐ 4. Do you lose your balance because of dizziness or do you ever lose consciousness?

☐ ☐ 5. Do you have a bone or joint problem that could be made worse by a change in your physical activity?

☐ ☐ 6. Is your doctor currently prescribing drugs (for example, water pills) for your blood pressure or heart condition?

☐ ☐ 7. Do you know of *any other reason* that you should not do physical activity?

Comments: _____

Client's Name: _____ Date: _____
Client's Signature: _____
Wellness Consultant: _____

SOURCE: PAR-Q is based on the ACSM's Guidelines, Fig 2-1, 5th ed. 1995.

C-3

Informed Consent Forms

FITNESS TESTING

The purpose of these tests is to determine your level of fitness so that you can plan your exercise program based on your strong and weak areas.

Station I	Orientation—Informed consent for fitness testing
	Health and Lifestyle History, and Physical Activity Readiness, blood pressure
Station II	Flexibility (modified sit and reach)
	Muscular strength (grip dynamometer)
	Muscular endurance (sit-ups)
Station III	Percentage of body fat (skinfolds)
Station IV	Height and weight
	Waist and hip circumference
Station V	Cardiovascular test (one-mile walk test)
Station VI	Check out and computer entry
Station VII	Consultation on results

The risks in undergoing these tests are minimal. You may experience some muscle soreness following the muscular endurance test, a slight pinch during the body fat test, and soreness from the walk test but this will be minimized by adequate warm-up and cool-down periods.

The benefits to you include a personal assessment of your aerobic fitness, muscular endurance and strength, percentage of body fat, and low-back flexibility. Suggestions for an exercise program specifically designed for your level of fitness will be given in a post-test interview when you will be given your test results.

Your participation is completely voluntary and all records will be kept strictly confidential.

The nature, demands, risks, and benefits of the fitness test have been explained to me and I understand what my participation involves. I understand that I am free to ask questions at any time and that I can withdraw from the test at any time. I consent to participate in this fitness testing.

Signature of participant _____
Date _____
Signature of witness _____

PHYSIOLOGICAL ASSESSMENTS

I agree to voluntarily engage in one or more of the following tests to assess cardiovascular function and/or various components of my physical fitness.

I understand that the laboratory technicians have had much experience with this type of testing. They will explain the testing procedures and answer my questions. My records will be confidential. Privacy will be provided.

The tests will be completed in _____ Human Performance Laboratory. The director of the lab, _____, will supervise the collection of data.

If I decide to participate, I am free to withdraw my consent and to stop participation at any time with no penalty to me.

As a participant, I will receive extensive information about my physical fitness. I will be given a copy of this consent form.

Please read the descriptions of the tests and sign at the end if you give your consent.

Bioelectrical Impedance (BIA)
You will be lying on a bed with electrodes placed on your right ankle and right wrist. A low-level (harmless) electrical current will pass through your body. You will not experience discomfort; this assessment is very safe.

Near-Infrared Interactance (NIR)
There will be a minimum of two measurements taken at the chest and thigh. The two sites will be marked with a surgical marking pen; the marks can be washed off. A light probe will be placed firmly against the skin. An infrared light beam (harmless) will be passed into the site. Percentage of body fat will be estimated by measuring

how much of the light is absorbed and reflected by the muscle and fat layers under your skin.

Hydrostatic Weighing (HW)

With your bathing suit on, you will sit on a chair in a tank of water. After we make sure you understand what we want you to do, you will blow out as much air as you can from your lungs (exhale) while you slowly duck under the water for 3 to 5 seconds. A reading will be made as soon as possible while you are under water and you will be told when to come up. It should take only 3 to 5 seconds. You may have some discomfort if you are afraid of being under the water. You can lift your head above the water at any time.

Pulmonary Function

This test measures the air left in your lungs after you try as hard as you can to blow all the air out of your lungs. You will be asked to breathe through your mouth into a machine called a spirometer. The part that goes into your mouth (the mouthpiece) will be cleaned and sterilized (harmful germs will be killed). Your nose will be blocked. You will be asked to blow all the air that you can from your lungs into the machine. Helium (a harmless gas) will be added to the air you breathe to help measure the air left in your lungs. The mouthpiece and the noseclip (plug) may cause some discomfort.

Skinfold Technique

Skinfolds will be taken at three of the following seven sites: chest, side, back of arm, back, stomach, hip, and thigh. A minimum of three measurements will be taken at each of the selected skinfold sites. During the skinfold testing, you may experience a slight pinching from the caliper used to measure the skin and fat fold.

Total Body Water

Total body water will be measured using the deuterium dilution technique. This method involves the oral ingestion of a known quantity of deuterium oxide ($\frac{1}{2}$ tsp) and the collection of saliva samples ($\frac{1}{2}$ tsp). This method is safe, fast, and accurate.

DEXA

You will lie very still on your back on a padded table for 15 to 20 minutes while an X-ray scanner makes a complete scan from your head to your feet. The amount of radiation from the X-ray scan is very small—about 1/20th of a dental X ray. There may be some discomfort in lying still during the test.

Graded Exercise Stress Test

This test includes performance on a treadmill or cycle ergometer. A protocol such as the Bruce protocol will be used and the workload will be increased periodically during the test. You will continue exercising during the test until you reach the predetermined submax heart rate or to the point you are fatigued or feel discomfort or other symptoms that dictate the termination of the test. During the test there is a possibility of abnormal changes with fainting, abnormal heart beat, changes in blood pressure, and, in rare instances, a heart attack. During the test you will be closely monitored by trained professionals and every attempt will be made for your safety. There will be close observation of the cardiac function, which will be monitored continuously by ECG readings. Oxygen consumption may be measured during the graded exercise test. This will require exercising with a noseclamp and using a mouthpiece. Realize you may terminate the test at any time and this test is voluntary on your part.

Freedom of Consent

You are making a decision whether to participate. Your signature indicates that you have decided to participate. This signature indicates that you understand this document.

Date _____ Subject No. _____

Signature _____

Witness _____

C-4

Report of an Accident or Injury

Date of accident or injury _____
Time of incident _____
Participant's name _____
Home phone _____
Address _____
Work phone _____
Address _____
Description of accident _____
_____
_____
_____

Action taken by the staff member(s) _____
_____
_____

Witnesses (include phone numbers and addresses) ____
_____
_____
_____
Staff person reporting _____
Date _____
Director's name _____
Date _____

File this accident/injury report in the participant's file and give a copy to the Director.

APPENDIX D

Professional Agencies
and Resources

D-1

Agencies and Organizations

ADVENTURE

Association for Challenge Course Technology (ACCT)
P.O. Box 970
Purcellville, VA 22132

Association for Experiential Education (AEE)
2885 Aurora Ave., Suite 28
Boulder, CO 80303-2252
(303) 440-8844

Colorado Outward Bound School (COB)
945 Pennsylvania Street
Denver, CO 80203
(303) 837-0880

National Outdoor Leadership School (NOLS)
286 Main Street
Lander, WY 82520-3128
(307) 332-6973

Outdoor Recreation Coalition of America Climbing
    Sports Group (ORCA)
P.O. Box 88126
Seattle, WA 98138-0126

Project Adventure, Inc. (PA)
P.O. Box 100
Hamilton, MA 01936
(508) 468-7981

Wilderness Education Association (WEA)
Colorado State University
Ft. Collins, CO 80521
(970) 223-6252

AQUATIC

American National Red Cross
17th & D Streets NW
Washington, DC 20006
(202) 639-3886

Ellis and Associates
3506 Spruce Park Circle
Kingwood, TX 77345
(713) 360-0606
(713) 360-0869 (FAX)

Royal Life Saving Society
191 Church Street
Toronto, Ontario M5B 1Y7
Canada
(416) 364-3881

United States Lifesaving Association
    (USLA)
P.O. Box 366
Huntington Beach, CA 92648
(500) FOR-USLA

YMCA of the USA
110 N. Wacker Drive
Chicago, IL 60606
(312) 269-0503

YWCA of the USA
726 Broadway
New York, NY 10003
(800) YWCA-US1
(212) 614-2858

SPORTS FOR THE DISABLED

Members of the United States Olympic Committee

American Athletic Association of the Deaf (AAAD)
3607 Washington Blvd., Suite 4
Ogden, UT 84403-1737
(801) 393-8710

Dwarf Athletic Association of America (DAAA)
418 Willow Way
Lewisville, TX 75067
(214) 817-8299

United States Cerebral Palsy Athletic Association (USCPAA)
200 Harrison Ave.
Newport, RI 02840
(401) 848-2460

Disabled Sports USA (DSUSA)
451 Hungerford Drive, Suite 100
Rockville, MD 20850
(301) 217-0960

Special Olympics (SO)
1325 G Street, Suite 500
Washington, D.C. 20005-3104
(202) 628-3630

United States Association for Blind Athletes (USABA)
33 North Institute
Brown Hall, Suite 015
Colorado Springs, CO 80903
(719) 630-0422

Wheelchair Sports, USA (WSUSA)
3595 E. Fountain Blvd., Suite L-1
Colorado Springs, CO 80910
(719) 574-1150

Emerging Group, not a member)

U.S. Les Autres Sports Association (USLASA)
1475 W. Gray, Suite 166
Houston, TX 77019
(713) 521-3737

Resources

For more information about ADA requirements affecting specific areas, contact the following agencies.

Public Services and Public Accommodations

Office on the Americans with
  Disabilities Act
Civil Rights Division
U.S. Department of Justice
P.O. Box 66118
Washington, D.C. 20035-6118

(202) 514-0301 (Voice)
(202) 514-0381 (TDD)
(202) 514-0383 (TDD)

Employment

Equal Employment Opportunity
  Commission
1801 L Street NW
Washington, DC 20507

(202) 663-4900 (Voice)
800-800-3302 (TDD)
(202 663-4494 (TDD for 202 area code)

Transportation

Department of Transportation
400 Seventh Street SW
Washington, DC 20590

(202) 366-9305 (Voice)
(202) 755-7687 (TDD)

Accessible Design in Construction and Alterations

Architectural and Transportation
  Barriers Compliance Board
1111 18th Street NW
Suite 501
Washington, DC 20036

800-USA-ABLE (Voice)
800-USA-ABLE (TDD)

Telecommunications

Federal Communications
  Commission
1919 M Street NW
Washington, DC 20554

(202) 632-7260 (Voice)
(202) 632-6999 (TDD)

Source: The Americans with Disabilities Act Questions and Answers Booklet, July 1991. Washington, DC: U.S. Government Printing Office.

INDEX

Downsizing

by Ralph R. Roberts

Downsizing For Dummies®

Contents at a Glance

Table of Contents

Introduction

D o you feel crowded by clutter? Are you a prisoner of your possessions? Has your pursuit of the American Dream become a nightmare, leaving you feeling disenchanted and deep in debt? Do you yearn for a simpler life with a healthier work-life balance — less toil and turmoil and more living? Have your children moved out, leaving you in a house that's far too big and with an emptiness you need to fill? Are you worried about leaving your loved ones with a big mess when you're no longer around to help clean it up? Are you having to downsize your parents, who should have scaled back years ago but kept putting it off until they can no longer do it themselves?

If you answered "yes" to any of those questions, you need to *downsize* (yourself or someone else) — shed possessions and perhaps move to a smaller home to make life less cluttered, more affordable, and more manageable; free your mind; and focus on what really matters at this stage in your life.

If you're like most people, you're dreading the prospect of downsizing. The process can be very stressful and overwhelming, but like most major life changes, it can open the door to new possibilities that you may never have imagined. In fact, it can be the first step on the path to a totally new life. Even so, it's no less a challenge, and you're probably thinking that you could really use some help right now — guidance from people who have been through the process and have firsthand experience.

Welcome to *Downsizing For Dummies*. We've been through the downsizing process several times, not only downsizing ourselves recently but also our parents and grandparents. We've observed and felt the emotional conflicts and pain of having to part with treasured possessions, leave the family home, and transition to a new lifestyle. We've done the hard work of researching locations, finding the perfect living situation for ourselves and our loved ones, building a new home (when we decided to downsize), sorting, packing, moving, and all the many tasks those processes entail. In this book, we share the collective wisdom we gained through our experience to make your downsizing journey as smooth and successful as possible.

About This Book

Downsizing For Dummies is a guide to living a richer, fuller life with less stuff, lower bills, and fewer worries. It's a guide for envisioning and transitioning to a life with fewer possessions that's better suited to your current needs and desires. After all, downsizing isn't restricted to retirees who need to shed their possessions and move to a smaller home. Downsizing can benefit anyone. It's all about using your personal, professional, and financial assets most efficiently to live the life of your dreams, whether your dream life revolves around family, travel, leisure, adventure, comfort and security, work, or all of the above, regardless of your age.

In *Downsizing For Dummies*, we lead you step-by-step through the process, from deciding whether downsizing is right for you (or a loved one) to executing a successful move and transitioning to a new life. Along the way, we guide you through the process of envisioning your future lifestyle; choosing a location; getting other people to help; planning and managing your finances and your estate; digitizing photos and important documents; sorting, selling, giving away, and disposing of your possessions; and buying (or building) and selling a home. With this book and your own creativity, talent, intelligence, and energy, you'll be able to envision a richer, fuller, more manageable future and successfully transition yourself or your loved one to that new life.

We wrote this book so that you can approach it in either of two ways: You can flip to any chapter for a quick, stand-alone mini course on a specific downsizing topic, or you can read it from cover to cover. You may not need all the information and guidance that's packed into this book. For example, if you've already decided to downsize and have a clear vision of your future life, you can skip Chapters 2 and 3 and head directly to Chapter 4 to start crafting your downsizing plan and setting the stage for a successful transition. Likewise, if you've already engaged in estate planning with your attorney and financial advisor, you can skip Chapter 7. We don't want you to have to read any more than necessary — you have enough on your mind.

Foolish Assumptions

Every book, article, screenplay, blog post, and other written document makes assumptions about the audience, the purpose for writing the piece, the scope of the material to be covered, and the appropriate tone. As we began to develop the concept for this book, we made the following foolish assumptions:

>> **You're downsizing your personal possessions, not a business.** Downsizing is a hot topic both in families and for businesses. This book is not about

downsizing a business to reduce overhead. It's about downsizing a household to make it more affordable and manageable and free up resources to pursue other opportunities in life.

>> **You're not necessarily an older retired person.** Although most people seeking help with downsizing are older retirees (or their children), people of any age can benefit from downsizing, depending on their circumstances and the life they envision for themselves. For example, we know young children and teenagers who are in dire need of some downsizing in their bedrooms.

>> **You're committed to improving your life or the life of a loved one.** We assume that you're feeling some level of dissatisfaction with your life or the living situation of a loved one. It's just not working, and you need to do something about it. We wrote this book to help people overcome a major challenge in their life: a living situation that's no longer sustainable, perhaps because of financial strain, concerns about a loved one's safety and security, a strong desire for a different and better life, or some other reason.

>> **You're overwhelmed by the prospect of downsizing and don't know where to start.** The thought of downsizing can trigger the fight-flight-or-freeze response. Right now, we assume you feel like the proverbial deer in the headlights — frozen in place, unable to move, because downsizing seems so daunting. We've broken down the process for you and provided the guidance and assurance you need to tackle what can be an overwhelming task with confidence.

Icons Used in This Book

Throughout this book, we've sprinkled icons in the margins to cue you in on different types of information that call out for your attention. Here are the icons you'll see and a brief description of each.

REMEMBER

We want you to remember everything you read in this book, but if you can't quite do that, remember the important points we flag with this icon.

TIP

Tips provide insider insight from behind the scenes. When you're looking for a better, faster, cheaper way to do something, check out the tips.

WARNING

"Whoa!" This icon appears when you need to be extra vigilant or seek professional help before moving forward.

Beyond the Book

In addition to the priceless information and guidance you'll find in the pages of this book, you can access the *Downsizing For Dummies* Cheat Sheet online. Just go to www.dummies.com, and enter "Downsizing For Dummies Cheat Sheet" in the search box.

The Cheat Sheet includes downsizing pros and cons, relocation factors to consider, seven ways to get a loved one on board with downsizing, guidance on how to budget for your post-downsizing lifestyle, and decluttering basics.

Where to Go from Here

You should be walking to the cashier and handing them this book! But . . . after that, *Downsizing For Dummies* presents the guidance you need in the sequence that follows the downsizing process itself, starting with envisioning your future life (post downsizing) and wrapping up with executing the transition to that new life. However, you may take a different approach, or you may already be in the early stages of downsizing and finished with some of the required tasks, so feel free to skip around.

We recommend starting with Chapter 1, which covers the downsizing process in a nutshell. Reading this chapter first gives you the mental framework for understanding the rest of the topics and how they fit into a cohesive downsizing strategy.

If you're still on the fence about whether downsizing is right for you or a loved one, head to Chapter 2, where we help you make that determination. You may also want to check out Chapter 3 for inspiration, especially if you're having trouble envisioning and planning for the future. Chapters 4 and 5 can come in handy to ensure that you have a solid downsizing plan in place and many hands on deck to execute it before diving in.

Downsizing also involves getting a handle on your finances and becoming a master of using all your assets efficiently to finance your lifestyle. When you're ready to take control of your finances, check out the chapters in Part 2.

If you find yourself wondering, "What am I going to do with all this stuff?!" turn to Part 3, where we provide guidance on sorting your possessions, digitizing photos and documents, and selling, storing, giving away, and disposing of your belongings. Here's where you do all the heavy lifting.

If your downsizing dream involves living a nomadic existence, you can pretty much skip the chapters in Part 4, but if you need housing, you can find guidance here related to buying or building a home, selling your existing home, packing your belongings, and coordinating a successful move.

In Part 5, "The Part of Tens," we provide some bonus material, including ten good reasons to downsize, ten tips for less stressful downsizing, ten ways to reduce your living expenses, and ten ways to supplement your income.

That's all the direction we're going to provide. Where you go from here is pretty much up to you, but we encourage you to dive in whatever starting point you choose. This is the rest of your life we're talking about.

1
Getting Started with Downsizing

Get a quick primer on downsizing, so you can begin to envision the possibilities and get a feel for what it involves, regardless of whether you're moving or downsizing in place.

Weigh the pros and cons of downsizing to find out whether it's the right choice for you or an aging relative and discover your *why* for downsizing, so you'll have a purpose in place to drive the process.

Paint the big picture of your downsized life — how you'll be living when you're free from all the stuff that has been tying you down and distracting you from what really matters in your life.

Devise your downsizing plan so all the pieces are in place to ensure success and clarify in your mind what needs to be done and how you're going to do it.

Recruit friends and family members to pitch in.

Arrange the professional assistance you need to ensure a smooth and successful process that's not too overwhelming for you.

IN THIS CHAPTER

» Answering the five key downsizing questions

» Opening your eyes to new lifestyle opportunities

» Laying the groundwork for successful downsizing

» Optimizing the use of your existing assets

» Letting go of everything that's weighing you down

» Selling your current home and exploring new living arrangements

Chapter **1**

Downsizing in a Nutshell

Much of what we acquire in life isn't worth dragging into the next leg of our journey. Travel light. You will be better equipped to travel far.

— GINA GREENLEE

Anytime you approach a new topic or task, it can seem overwhelming, especially in the case of something like downsizing, because there's not only so much you need to *know* but also so much you need to *do* and often so *little* time to do it. You need to figure out where you're going to live, how you're going to live for the next decade or two or three, and when you're going to make the transition. You need to get rid of a bunch of stuff, some of which you may be very emotionally attached to. You need a financial plan in place to be sure that your money lasts for as long as you do. You need to sell your home and buy or rent a new place. You need to keep all your loved ones posted. Downsizing gets complicated and overwhelming in a hurry.

To make downsizing less complex and burdensome, you can benefit from having a general understanding of the overall process — a conceptual framework on which to hang all the details. In this chapter, we provide you with that framework. Think of it as the downsized version of *Downsizing For Dummies*. Here, we introduce you to the most important information and guidance you need to execute a successful downsizing mission and redirect you to chapters in the book where you can find additional coverage of each topic.

Downsizing: Who, What, When, Where, and Why?

In a way, downsizing can be boiled down to answering five questions: *Who? What? When? Where?* and *Why?* Who's downsizing? What are you keeping and getting rid of? When are you planning to make the transition? Where are you going to live? and Why are you downsizing? Answer those five questions, and you'll have the clarity you need to move forward with conviction. If you struggle with any of those questions, maybe you're just not ready to downsize.

In this section, we provide guidance on how to answer each of these key questions.

Who?

Who's downsizing? may be the most complicated of the five questions and the most difficult to answer, especially if more than one person is involved in the process. Answering this question involves identifying both the people doing the downsizing and the people being downsized. Often, these are the same people; for example, we downsized ourselves from a 7,000-square-foot home to a condo less than half that size. However, the people being downsized and those doing the downsizing can be different — for example, adult children downsizing their ailing parents from their family home to an assisted living facility. See Chapter 5 for more about getting others involved.

Answering the question of who's downsizing also may require a deeper dive into personalities and circumstances. If you're downsizing yourself or yourself and a partner, you need to explore who you are at this stage of your life, evaluate your current living situation, and consider your vision for the future. To find out whether you're a good candidate for downsizing, answer the following questions:

>> **Do I have a strong desire to stay where I am or am I willing to consider moving?** If you love where you're currently living, you may decide to downsize in place — reducing your possessions while remaining in your home. You may

also be able to convert a portion of your home into an independent living space for yourself and rent out the rest. On the other hand, if you're open to the idea of moving, why not check out your options?

>> **How long can I continue living here comfortably and safely?** Consider your finances and health and your desire to continue to maintain your current residence. Can you afford it in terms of money, time, and energy? Do you want to invest the effort in caring for a larger home than you currently need?

>> **Would downsizing help or hinder my ability to live a richer, fuller life?** Think about what you find enjoyable and fulfilling. Can you do more of it by downsizing or by staying where you are? For example, if you enjoy spending time with family but they rarely visit anymore, would you be able to spend more time with family if you moved closer to them or were freer to travel?

>> **By downsizing, what do I have to gain and lose?** Make a list of downsizing pros and cons. On one half of the page, write a list of everything that excites you about the prospect of downsizing. On the other half, write down everything that makes you reluctant to downsize or afraid of it. For example, will a smaller place mean having less yard for gardening? Will it mean having to leave friends and neighbors?

>> **Will you and your partner get along in closer quarters?** In a smaller living space, you may feel more cramped and have less privacy, which can strain a relationship. Then again, less space may encourage you to spend more time outside your home, which can enrich your relationship.

See Chapter 2 for additional guidance on deciding whether downsizing is right for you or a loved one.

The question *Who?* also applies to the people you want in your life. Some downsizers are drawn to family and old friends and colleagues, while others want to meet new people and develop fresh relationships. Some people value their solitude and would rather spend their time communing with nature or reading good books.

What?

The question *What?* also applies to what you want out of your life. What do you value most — health, safety, security, travel, adventure, learning, relationships? What's on your bucket list? Your values, dreams, and desires serve as guideposts leading you in the direction you need to travel.

On a smaller scale, the question *What?* applies to what you're keeping and what you're getting rid of, along with the type of lifestyle and living arrangements you're considering. A house, apartment, condominium, RV, multigenerational home, or over-55 community? Alone or with partner or a roommate or two or three?

When?

When? is a key question. The best answer to this question for most people is *as soon as possible,* but we need to qualify that answer by advising you to plan carefully. Don't rush into downsizing, but don't put it off too long, because long delays can narrow your options. Some people kick the can down the road for so long that eventually they lose all control over the decision-making process. Family members or others outside the family must step in, in which case you have little to no control over the outcome.

In some cases, your decision of when to downsize is easy. It's linked to some other major life change, such as retirement, the death of a spouse, job loss, or divorce. You may suffer a reduction in income that forces your hand, and that's okay. Recognizing that you need to downsize to reduce your living expenses when you're struggling to keep up can help you steer clear of an even more devastating financial loss, such as foreclosure or bankruptcy.

Where?

If moving is part of your downsizing plan, the question *Where?* becomes crucial, especially if part of the reason you're downsizing is to reduce your living expenses, to travel more, or to live somewhere you've always wanted to be.

To make a well-informed decision about where you want to move, consider the following factors:

>> Affordability

>> Climate

>> Surroundings

>> Proximity to family and friends

>> Cultural and social opportunities

>> Convenience

>> Safety (crime stats)

>> Job/career opportunities

See Chapter 3 for more about choosing a downsizing destination.

Why?

Perhaps the most interesting question related to downsizing is *Why?* Here's a list of potential benefits of downsizing that may help you answer that question for yourself:

>> **Less stress.** Downsizing can alleviate a major source of stress: financial worry. It can also reduce stress in other ways; for example, living in an environment that's free of clutter can be much more relaxing and peaceful. In addition, you may find that you have more time and mental energy to commit to leisure and recreation.

>> **Less clutter.** Downsizing involves reducing your possessions and getting organized, which makes your remaining possessions easier to manage. You remove items that you no longer need from your life, which lightens your load and provides you with a greater sense of freedom.

>> **More time to focus on what matters to you.** If you're working to support a lifestyle that's not bringing you the satisfaction and fulfillment you desire, downsizing may help. When you're not trying to keep up with the Joneses, you may find that you have more time and money to spend on what you truly value, such as relationships, travel, reading, and other hobbies and interests.

>> **Improved health and fitness.** Less stress alone translates to improved health and fitness, but add to that the extra time, focus, and money you'll have to invest in meal prep and exercise, and you'll be well on your way to achieving your health and fitness goals.

>> **Enhanced creativity.** People tend to be more creative when they're relaxed and their minds aren't cluttered with never-ending to-do lists. Ridding yourself of possessions and scaling down your responsibilities gives your mind the freedom to be creative in all areas of your life — career/business, relationships, finances, spiritual development, recreation, and more.

>> **Less burden on loved ones.** Downsizing can alleviate the burden on loved ones who may worry about your health and safety and your ability to maintain a large home full of belongings. Also, by downsizing while you're still physically and mentally capable of doing it yourself, you leave your heirs with less clutter and fewer complications to deal with when you pass. This can be a huge stress reliever for you, too.

REMEMBER

While you're entertaining the question of *Why downsize?* you may also ask yourself, *Why not downsize?* What do you have to lose by downsizing, and how much does that matter to you? Some people have valid reasons to resist downsizing; for example, downsizing sometimes results in lost freedom and self-determination or having to accept the reality of your own physical or mental decline. Discussing both the potential benefits and the drawbacks of downsizing is important for coming to terms with a major life change.

Envisioning Your Future

Downsizing is a creative process — you're reinventing yourself. Every invention begins as a thought, or a mental image. Engage your imagination to envision your downsized future by answering the following questions:

>> How do you see yourself living for the next 5, 10, 15, or 20 years?

>> How do you look and feel physically, mentally, and emotionally?

>> Where are you living — in terms of both your geographical location and your living arrangements (for example, house, condo, apartment, RV, assisted living facility)?

>> What are you doing — traveling the world, taking a cruise, building a business, playing golf, binge-watching *Game of Thrones* (again)?

>> Who are you with — your life partner, family members, old friends, new friends, caregivers?

TIP

Create a *vision board* (collage) that reflects your future life in pictures and words. See Chapter 3 for more details about clarifying your downsizing vision.

Navigating a Major Lifestyle Transition

Downsizing can mean anything from scaling back to choosing a completely different lifestyle. If you're merely shedding possessions and opting to live a simpler life, you can safely skip this section — you'll be living the same life on a smaller scale. However, if you're planning a major overhaul — for example, from fully employed to fully retired or from a settled life to a nomadic one — you may struggle with the transition. The ideal life you romanticized for years, and perhaps decades, may not meet your expectations. The reality can be very different from the fantasy — for better or worse. What's important is that you're prepared, mentally and emotionally, for the change.

Here are a few suggestions for establishing the right mindset for downsizing:

» **Accept the inevitable.** If you feel that factors outside your control (for example, loss of income or declining health) are forcing you or compelling you to downsize, don't fight it — go with the flow. By accepting the inevitable and playing a more active role in the process, you'll have more control over the outcome.

» **Acknowledge the past, accept the present, and plan for the future.** People often get stuck in the past, either because they loved that period of their lives or because something traumatic occurred that they can't get over. Take some time to acknowledge the past while realizing that it's over and then let it go. Accept your present situation for what it is instead of denying it or wishing it was different. Then, start planning for your future — the only thing you have the power to change.

» **Acknowledge your emotions.** Whether you're eager and enthusiastic about downsizing or angry, frustrated, and afraid, recognize how you feel about the situation. If you tamp down your negative emotions instead of acknowledging them and expressing them in an appropriate way, they'll find expression in counterproductive ways. When you're open and honest about them, you can begin to deal more effectively with the source of those emotions — for example, if you're afraid because your future is uncertain, you can start planning for your future so that it's less uncertain.

» **Research your options.** You're already researching downsizing by reading this book, but dig deeper into specific downsizing options, such as geographical locations and living arrangements. You can do a great deal of research on the internet, but you may also want to spend time visiting different relocation destinations and housing options.

REMEMBER

If you're thinking *no* to downsizing, maybe you just don't know enough to say *yes*. Seeing the life you could be living by downsizing may be all you need to change your mind and attitude toward it. If you're downsizing a reluctant parent or trying to get your life partner on board, look for ways to share what you know and enable them to sample the life they could be living.

» **Talk to peers who've already downsized.** You can learn a great deal from people who've been through the process, including mistakes to avoid and tips for easing the transition. They may have done much of the research for you and have some excellent recommendations.

» **Remind yourself *why* you're downsizing.** Losing motivation and getting discouraged, especially early in the process, is common, so keep your eyes on the prize by reminding yourself why you're doing it.

Getting All Your Ducks in a Row

To a great extent, successful downsizing relies on careful planning. Of course, even with the perfect plan, you're likely to encounter unexpected challenges. We know a couple who planned impeccably and still had to downsize three times before they finally found the right fit. However, a well-laid plan can help you avoid many of the most serious and unpleasant surprises and recover more easily from those that are unavoidable.

In this section, we touch on the basics of downsizing planning, which we cover in greater depth in Chapter 4.

Choosing a lifestyle and housing

Downsizing, like any project, begins with the process of setting a goal. In this case, the goal revolves around lifestyle and housing — where and how you're going to live during the next stage of your life. In the following sections, we break down this goal into three factors:

>> Lifestyle

>> Location

>> Housing

Considering different lifestyle options

Lifestyles are difficult to pin down because of the sheer number of options and the fact that different lifestyles often overlap and intersect, but here's a short list to get you thinking about the lifestyle you envision:

>> Active versus sedentary

>> Activist (campaigning/working for political or social change)

>> Agrarian (living off the land)

>> Aquatic (swimming, fishing, water sports)

>> Communal versus independent

>> Conventional versus Bohemian (unconventional, artistic, adventurous)

>> Entrepreneurial (innovative, business-oriented)

>> Minimalist (living with very few possessions)

>> Settled versus nomadic

>> Traditional (living in small groups, hunting, gathering, herding, farming)

>> Urban/suburban

TIP

Imagine what you'll be doing most days, where you'll be doing it, and with whom. Your vision reflects your lifestyle. If you're hanging out in coffee shops, visiting museums, and dining out with friends and family members, for example, you're probably going to to want to live in a more urban setting. If you're tending a garden and feeding chickens, you're leaning toward a more rural/agrarian lifestyle. If you're crisscrossing the country in an RV, you're more nomadic.

Choosing a location

If you're planning a nomadic lifestyle or opting to downsize in place (without moving anywhere), choosing a downsizing destination is moot. Otherwise, location can be a huge factor in your downsizing decision.

Start by choosing a general location, such as a country or a state, and then narrow your choices to more specific areas. See the earlier section "Where?" for a list of factors to consider when choosing a downsizing destination.

Exploring your housing options

Although you can downsize in place (without moving), downsizing often involves moving to a smaller place — usually one that's more affordable and easier to care for. Housing options vary considerably, as reflected in the following list:

>> Apartment

>> Assisted living facility

>> Condominium (condo for short)

>> Existing home (usually a single-level ranch-style home for downsizers)

>> Modular home (built off-site and placed on a lot)

>> Multigenerational home (moving in with your adult children)

>> New construction (single-family home or condo)

>> Retirement community (typically for people over 55 or 60)

>> RV

>> Skilled nursing facility

>> Tiny home

>> Townhouse, duplex, or triplex (two or three homes that share a wall but have separate entrances)

TIP

When your goal is affordable housing, consider not only the rent or mortgage payment but also any amenities a housing option offers, such as a pool, hot tub, walking trails, parks, fishing ponds, gym, social activities, and meal plans. These amenities can save you a considerable amount of money on travel, recreation, and entertainment.

Establishing your timeline

When you have a downsizing goal in mind, set a deadline — the date you'd like to be downsized. Are you looking to be downsized next week, two months from now, or more like three years from now? It's never too early to start planning.

After setting a deadline, break down your goal into realistic milestones, so you have a timeline for getting everything done. You may want to set milestones for the following activities:

>> Meet with a financial advisor to evaluate my finances.

>> Meet with an attorney to plan my estate.

>> Find a new place to live.

>> Sort my belongings.

>> Organize my photos and documents.

>> Sell stuff.

>> Pack.

>> Sell my home.

>> Move into my new home.

REMEMBER

Your timeline and milestones are unique to you. For example, if you're planning a more nomadic lifestyle, your timeline may include travel plans, such as getting a passport, arranging transportation, and reserving places to stay. If you're downsizing in place, obviously, you don't need to sell your home, find a new home, pack, or move.

Creating to-do lists

Create a to-do list for each milestone to break them down even further. For example, if you're planning a garage or estate sale, you may have the following to-do list:

>> Set dates and times.

>> Get change.

>> Get shopping bags and boxes.

>> Advertise.

>> Place street signs.

>> Organize and arrange items for sale.

>> Mark prices.

If you're preparing to meet with your financial advisor, your to-do list may be a list of information and documents your financial advisor needs, along with questions and concerns you want to discuss.

Drafting a budget

Regardless of where and how you choose to live, it needs to be affordable, so take the following steps to draft a budget:

1. **Total your monthly income from all sources, such as the following:**

   - Income from work or business

   - Social security payments

   - Pensions/annuities

   - Investment income

   - Reverse mortgage payments

2. **Total your anticipated monthly expenses, such as the following:**

   - Housing (rent or mortgage, insurance, property taxes)

   - Utilities (gas, electricity, water, trash, phone, television, internet)

   - Groceries/meals

   - Recreation/entertainment (concert tickets, sporting events, vacations, hobbies)

   - Transportation (vehicle payment, insurance, fuel, maintenance and repair; public transportation; or ride-sharing services such as Uber and Lyft)

   - Medical (insurance premiums and out-of-pocket costs)

   - Clothing and shoes

   - Personal care and miscellaneous personal expenses (toiletries, cosmetics, gym memberships, dietary supplements, home décor and furnishings, gifts, and so on)

3. **Subtract your monthly expenses from your monthly income and hope the result is positive.**

   If it's negative, you need to trim your expenses and come up with other sources of income.

See Chapter 6 for more about budgeting and finances related to downsizing.

Protecting and Leveraging Your Assets

Unless you're filthy rich, your finances are going to limit your downsizing options. Taking steps to protect and leverage your assets can help you stretch your money and have more available to leave to your heirs (if you so desire). Here are a few specific ways to protect and leverage your assets:

» Meet with an accountant who specializes in taxes to explore tax strategies designed to help you keep more of your money.

» Consult an attorney who specializes in estate planning and asset protection to ensure that you're properly cared for if you're ever unable to care for yourself and that your money and property is passed to your designated beneficiaries when you die in a way that holds inheritance taxes to a minimum.

» Meet with your financial planner to discuss strategies for investing money and drawing income out of your investment accounts in ways that minimize the tax impact.

» Consult your financial planner and accountant to discuss ways to cash out the equity in your home if you need additional money to cover expenses — for example, a traditional mortgage, reverse mortgage, or home equity line of credit.

See Part 2 for more about protecting and leveraging your assets.

Decluttering Basics

Downsizing is all about getting rid of material possessions that are weighing you down and holding you back from living a rich, fulfilling life that's less physically, mentally, and emotionally exhausting. It's not rocket science. However, you do need a titanium backbone to eliminate items you're psychologically or emotionally attached to.

Focus more on what to keep and less on what to get rid of. If you keep only the things that are going to add value to your life, all you'll have left is a huge pile of stuff you can safely get rid of. When you're more focused on what to get rid of, you'll end up convincing yourself to keep many more items. You really need to keep your blinders on and focus exclusively on what to keep.

In Chapter 9, we encourage you to sort items into the following categories:

» **Keep:** These are the essentials that will stay with you when you transition to your newly downsized life.

» **Store:** This category is for items you can't part with but won't fit in your downsized living space or lifestyle.

» **Sell:** You may be able to sell many of your possessions online or off-line (for example, in a garage sale or estate sale) to earn some extra cash to finance your new lifestyle. Be prepared, however, to have to sell most items at a deep discount.

» **Give away:** One of the easiest ways to shed possessions is to give them away to family members, friends, and other people you know, especially if you're getting rid of items that have significant sentimental value or items you want to keep in the family.

» **Donate:** Several nonprofit organizations, such as Goodwill, the Salvation Army, and veterans groups, accept donations of gently used household items. Some organizations may even pick up your donations for free.

» **Toss:** Whatever's left, you can push out to the curb or toss into a dumpster for disposal. (See Chapter 14 for details.)

These categories aren't etched in stone. When we downsized, we weren't interested in selling anything or paying for a self-storage unit, which eliminated two of the categories — Sell and Store. We decided what we wanted to keep, we let family members and friends take what they wanted, we donated most of our remaining belongings, and we threw the rest in the trash.

As Stephen Covey advises in his book *The 7 Habits of Highly Effective People,* "Start with the end in mind." Imagine your downsized life and keep only the things you'll be using in that life. If you're downsizing from a 3,000-square-foot home to something more in the range of 900 square feet, for example, or driving off into the sunset in an RV, you're obviously going to need to take a small fraction of your current belongings along for the ride.

Moving Out and Moving On

Unless you're downsizing in place, the process involves moving out of one home into another or living as a nomad, traveling from one place to the next. Whatever you decide, you can be sure of one thing: You're about to make some very big decisions. In this section, we highlight some of the major factors to consider. See Part 4 for additional details, along with guidance for navigating a successful transition, packing, and moving.

Addressing your changing priorities

Over the years, your choice of home was probably driven, at least in part, by a growing family and accumulating wealth. You needed more space to house your family and possessions. When you're downsizing, especially if you're nearing a certain age or experiencing physical or cognitive challenges, your priorities change. Whether you're buying an existing home or building a new home from scratch, you must consider features that may not have crossed your mind in the past, such as the following:

>> Proximity to caregivers and to everything you need with convenient and affordable transportation (so you don't have to drive anywhere)

>> Single-level home (so you don't have to climb stairs)

>> Step-free entrance

>> Wider doorways (to allow access for a walker or wheelchair)

>> Patio versus a large yard (so you have less outdoor maintenance)

>> More efficient use of vertical space (because you have less square footage)

>> Lever handles (instead of knobs) on doors and cabinets

>> Nonslip flooring

>> Shower with no-step entry, grab bars, and adjustable showerhead

>> Raised or adjustable-height toilet

>> Automatic or rocker light switches

>> Hands-free faucets or faucets with lever handles

>> Lower cabinets or cabinets with pull-down shelves

>> Multilevel or adjustable countertops

>> Availability of assistance, such as meal preparation, housekeeping, and nursing

Selling your home

Regardless of whether you're planning to buy a new home or move to a rental unit, or you have some other living arrangements in mind, you'll need to sell your existing home. As you plan to sell, remember the following key points:

REMEMBER

>> List your home with a top-selling Realtor in your area. You'll earn enough extra by listing with a top-selling Realtor to more than cover the commission.

Realtors specialize as seller's agents or buyer's agents. Choose a seller's agent — you want someone in your corner who can sell your home fast for top dollar. (Some real estate teams have both buyer's and seller's agents, enabling you to buy and sell through a single group.)

>> Follow your Realtor's recommendations to make repairs and updates to your home to bring it up to market value, but don't over-improve the property. In other words, don't invest more than you can ever hope to recoup from the sale. Buyers aren't looking for million-dollar homes in neighborhoods where most of the properties are selling for $400,000 or less.

>> If you're expecting a profit of more than $250,000 (or more than $500,000 for a couple) from the sale, consult your accountant to discuss the tax implications.

>> If your area is experiencing a housing market slump, consider postponing the sale until the market recovers. However, if you don't expect the market to recover anytime soon, you may be wise to accelerate the sale. A good Realtor can help you make the best decision.

>> In a sizzling housing market, consider buying a new home before selling, so you don't end up selling with no place to move into. In a down market, you may be better off selling first, so you don't get stuck with two mortgage payments.

See Chapter 16 for more about selling a home.

Buying a new home

When you're in the market for a smaller home, take your time to find exactly what you're looking for. Imagine that your new home will be the last home you'll ever own. Does it have the potential to serve your current and future needs?

Work closely with a Realtor (a buyer's agent) to explore your options. Develop a comprehensive list of everything you're looking for, but be open to suggestions from your Realtor, who may bring up factors you haven't considered. Provide as much information and insight as possible, including the following:

» Price range

» Size (square feet)

» Number of bedrooms and bathrooms

» Style

» Location

» Amenities (pool, clubhouse, gym, social activities, and so on)

» Whether you'll need assistance (meals, housekeeping, nursing)

» Your current situation, including why you're downsizing

» Whether you plan to pay cash or finance the purchase

See Chapter 15 for more about finding the right home for you and Chapter 16 for guidance on how to navigate the purchase.

Exploring other living arrangements

When you're downsizing, owning a traditional home or condo isn't the only option. You may want to consider other living arrangements, such as the following:

» Couch surfing — a series of brief stays with friends and family members

» Traveling and living in a van, bus, or RV

» Living on a boat/houseboat

» Living in an alternative structure, such as a tiny home, treehouse, shipping container, or *yurt* (portable round tent) — don't knock it until you've explored these options

» Living in a commune — a property shared by people with similar interests and goals

» Sharing a home with friends or family members

TIP

Worldwide Opportunities on Organic Farms (WWOOF) makes it possible to volunteer on organic farms around the world in exchange for shelter, food, and sometimes pay. Visit wwoof.net for more info.

Our Downsizing Experience

When we decided to downsize, we were living in a 7,300-square-foot home with four bedrooms, four full bathrooms, two half bathrooms, and a three-car garage (see Figure 1-1). When our children were living with us, having all that room made sense.

FIGURE 1-1:
The front of the home we downsized from.

We were also at a stage in our lives when we entertained frequently. Our home on Tara was a great party house. It had partially covered walkouts from the main floor and the basement, as shown in Figure 1-2, which allowed our parties to spill outdoors. We enjoyed hosting homecoming gatherings, prom parties, birthday celebrations, and relatively large holiday get-togethers.

In 2017, our daughter, Kaleigh, earned her bachelor's degree and secured a full-time teaching position. She moved out in December 2017. Our son, Kyle, graduated high school in May 2011 and started college the following fall at Albion College. After leaving for college, he spent very little time at home, and after earning his master's degree from Michigan State, he moved to Arizona.

And just like that, we were empty nesters.

Our large home, which had been the neighborhood hub of activity, was suddenly silent. Three of the four bedrooms were almost permanently vacant, and we rarely used all but one of the bathrooms. We were heating and cooling and insuring and maintaining all that square footage. We obviously needed to downsize.

FIGURE 1-2:
The back of the home we downsized from.

At the same time, we were facing a major transition in our lives — from being very involved parents to being a couple again. We needed to figure out how we were going to live the next stage of our lives together.

Fortunately, we knew what we wanted: more quality time together. And we knew what we enjoyed: shopping, dining out, movies, plays, concerts, sports events, cultural celebrations, and the great outdoors. We wanted a smaller place that either of us could manage on our own, a place with walking paths and convenient access to our doctors, our favorite stores (Trader Joe's and Whole Foods), and everything we enjoyed.

Finding the right location and the perfect lot was probably the biggest challenge for us. We spent every weekend exploring our options — driving through areas we liked around Detroit, Michigan, looking for real estate signs and developments — and eventually decided to build in a new development we discovered in Rochester Hills, north of Detroit, near Oakland University. We chose a lot and worked closely with the builder, Robertson Brothers, to build our *forever home* — the home we plan to live in for the rest of our lives (see Figure 1-3).

FIGURE 1-3:
The front of the
home we
downsized to.

At about 3,000 square feet, our new home on Weston is less than half the square footage of our home on Tara. Following our builder's advice, we had to carefully budget that available square footage.

In close consultation with our builder, we eliminated the standard offerings and chose to convert our lower level into a gym (mostly). We decided to allocate a large chunk of the available square footage to the master bedroom, master bathroom, and gym. This didn't mean we had to scale back the living room or kitchen, however.

We added lights and electrical outlets — can't ever have too many of those. We insulated and heated our garage. One of the first things we did after closing on the property was to have our carpenters and painters complete that space. We also set aside space for our wine closet (something we enjoy) and made more effective use of vertical space, especially for storage.

Our new home has a master bedroom, a guest bedroom, three full bathrooms, a den that can be converted into a third bedroom, and a lower-level office that can be used as another bedroom (what it was originally designed for).

Even with the added storage space, we needed to shed more than half of our possessions. We spent months sorting through everything, deciding what to keep and what to get rid of. We ended up giving away most of our belongings to friends and family members, donating items to charity, and keeping only what truly added value to our lives.

Perhaps what we miss most are the walkouts at the Tara home, but we now have a small porch off the back of the Weston home that's perfect for just the two of us (see Figure 1-4).

FIGURE 1-4:
A cozy back porch.

TIP

If you're going to build a new home, clear your calendar and focus solely on the construction — don't plan any vacations for the foreseeable future. Plan the construction as carefully as you'd plan a trip across the country or around the world. When you're done moving into your new place, you can resume your normal life and travel as much as you like.

We were fortunate in a way. We built our condo during the COVID-19 pandemic. Travel and live entertainment weren't options then, so we could devote our time and energy and ideas to making our construction project a success.

We loved our home on Tara, and we still have fond memories of the 30 years we lived there, but we don't miss it. Downsizing was a relief. As soon as we moved into our condo on Weston, we felt that a huge burden had been lifted. We're content in our forever home and eager to explore and enjoy our new surroundings and get to know our new neighbors.

IN THIS CHAPTER

» Coming up with a good reason to downsize

» Examining the potential benefits and drawbacks of downsizing

» Gathering your thoughts about your current living situation

» Taking the family's pulse

» Deciding what's best for your aging parents

» Addressing a major issue — whether to sell the family home

Chapter **2**

Deciding Whether Downsizing Is Right for You (or Your Parents)

When you make the right decision, it doesn't really matter what anyone else thinks.

— CAROLINE KENNEDY

Possibly the biggest decision you need to make at this point in your downsizing journey is whether it's right for you. It may be, but then again it may not be. You may be better off with the status quo. You may even be better off *upsizing* — perhaps the topic for our next book.

The point is, in the process of making this life-changing decision, you have many factors to consider, including whether you're satisfied with your current living arrangements, how you want to live the next stage of your life, whether downsizing will be worth the time and effort, how much you really care about leaving surviving family members with a big mess after you die, and so on.

We can't make the decision for you, but in this chapter, we present reasons that people commonly have for downsizing, along with important considerations to inform your decision. We want you to start your downsizing journey with your eyes wide open and end it with no regrets. We don't want you telling people ten years down the road that you should never have listened to those *Downsizing For Dummies* authors.

Recognizing Common Reasons People Downsize

We look at downsizing not solely as scaling back your material possessions but as more of a lifestyle decision. How do you want to live the next 10–20 years of your life? How do you envision your future?

As you get older, your values change. You begin to realize that you really can't take it with you — when you die, you'll leave behind all the material possessions you accumulated over the course of your life. What's most valuable is internal: your health, character, reputation, memories, accomplishments, and experiences.

The challenge you face now is figuring out how to use your resources most effectively to optimize what you value most. For example, if what you value most is the time you spend with your children and grandchildren, you may want to upsize to a living arrangement that's attractive to them and conducive to visits. On the other hand, if your bucket list is full of trips to exotic lands, selling your home and shedding most of your possessions so you can travel light and have more money for traveling in comfort may be the best choice.

When deciding whether downsizing is right for you, looking at common reasons other people downsize can often help you discover your own reasons. Here are some reasons to consider:

>> You're reaching a point at which you can no longer afford the life you've been living. For example, you're on a fixed income, but the cost of insurance, property taxes, groceries, gas, and more has continued to rise.

>> You have too much stuff. Clutter can trigger depression and anxiety and make finding what you really need difficult.

>> Your current lifestyle is preventing you from pursuing your dreams, so you want to steer your resources in a different direction.

>> You have more belongings than you're able or willing to maintain.

>> Your primary goal is to relocate to your dream location, and you simply want to make the move a little easier.

>> You want to free up some money to invest for a more comfortable retirement.

>> You want to travel more and spend little (or no) time at home, so you want to lighten your load.

>> You have health issues and need to transition to a place where you can get more assistance — not necessarily moving to an assisted living facility or a nursing home, but maybe moving in with a friend or family member.

>> You don't want to leave your loved ones with a huge, complicated mess to sort out after you die.

AN UPSIZING NIGHTMARE

Kathleen's parents raised three children, including her, in a 900-square-foot house. Imagine! After the kids left the nest, their parents were left wondering, "What next?" They included their children in their decision to downsize, but they ultimately decided to "upsize" to a larger home! They had worked their whole lives, saved their pennies, and wanted to live a great life in a great home. Their neighborhood was going through a rebirth. The families they had come to know had all moved on. They became fish out of water as young families moved in.

They upsized to a home that was four times larger than the home they raised their family in. It had two floors and a walkout leading to a lake — it was a massive move up! They had accumulated a lot of stuff and inherited some things from their own parents, and soon this home became a warehouse cluttered with possessions.

As they grew older, the situation became a major source of stress for the entire family. When it came time for them to downsize, they fought like Muhammad Ali to stay. They had accumulated so much stuff that over the years, letting go of anything became a major ordeal. Their children spent months decluttering the home to sell it.

Now, we want to ensure that this doesn't happen to our children or to you and your children, or their children, or their children's children. Our hope is that this book alleviates some of the pain of downsizing and prevents much of the pain from any reluctance to do so.

Weighing the Pros and Cons of Downsizing

Most decisions involve trade-offs, and downsizing definitely has advantages and disadvantages — some obvious and others you're not likely to discover until you do it. Downsizing is a very personal journey that can take months to fully execute, or even longer if you decide to build a new home. Before you hop on board, carefully consider the pros and cons.

REMEMBER

When facing the decision of whether to downsize, consider not only the pros and cons of downsizing but the pros and cons of *not* downsizing. If you choose not to downsize, what are the likely consequences of that choice? Who will suffer those consequences — you, your children, the state?

Potential benefits of downsizing

Downsizing offers a long list of potential benefits — too many to cover in a short section of one chapter — but here are the highlights:

>> Less home to clean, maintain, heat, cool, and insure

>> Lower utility bills

>> Smaller house payments

>> Less debt/more money in your pocket

>> Fewer possessions to organize and maintain, making it easier to find things and less likely you'll misplace them

>> Increased freedom and more money to do what you want

>> Less anxiety-inducing clutter, resulting in clarity of mind and better sleep

>> A fresh start

>> A chance to escape from any unpleasant neighbors

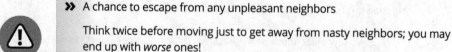

Think twice before moving just to get away from nasty neighbors; you may end up with *worse* ones!

WARNING

>> More time to spend with friends and family

>> Improved family dynamic — downsizing can often force family members to spend more time together in communal areas (which can have a positive or negative effect on the family dynamic)

>> A more manageable life, especially if you're downsizing to a living situation in which you can get the help you need (assuming you need help)

Potential downsizing drawbacks

You can't shed belongings and move without experiencing some pain. Here are some of the possible downsides of downsizing:

>> **Difficult choices:** You'll need to make some difficult decisions about what to keep and what to let go — not exactly *Sophie's Choice* difficult, but challenging nevertheless.

>> **Loss of convenience:** For example, if you have a workout room, downsizing may mean you'll need to hit the local gym instead. You may also need to trim your collection of power tools, kitchen appliances, and personal spa equipment. *What?! No paraffin wax machine?! No bubbling foot spa?!*

>> **Less room for storage:** You never really appreciate how valuable storage space is until you have less of it.

>> **Cost:** Moving can be expensive. Even if you're downsizing your living space, you may have expenses related to buying and selling a home, moving, and furnishing the new place.

>> **Less room for entertaining:** You may need to cut down on your dinner parties, scale them back, or eat out more . . . *yes!*

>> **Cramped living space:** You and your partner may feel as though you're always on top of each other — and not in a good way.

>> **Loss of the familiar:** You'll be taking on something new and unfamiliar. It's like starting over for some people, which can feel as though you're closing a chapter of your life and leaving memories behind.

>> **Loss of friends:** If you have close relationships with neighbors, moving can make you feel as though you're breaking off close friendships.

>> **Change in routine:** You'll need to establish a new routine in a new place. If you're downsizing to an assisted living arrangement, you may also be looking at a loss of independence and freedom.

>> **Loss of status:** You may feel as though you just dropped down a few rungs on the ladder of success.

>> **Disappointment:** You may feel disappointed if the reality of downsizing doesn't quite live up to the ideal you romanticized.

WARNING

If your first attempt at downsizing doesn't work out and leaves you feeling disappointed, it's not the end of the world. You can always try something different. However, downsizing mistakes may be costly; you can end up paying more in agent commissions and closing costs, not to mention moving costs — so do it right the first time.

Analyzing Your Situation and Mindset

When you're deciding whether to downsize, you need to do a *gut check* — honestly evaluate your situation and your mindset. Your situation may be that all your children have moved out and you have far more home than you need; or your expenses are rising and you're afraid of running out of money before the grim reaper pays a visit; or you're bored and you want to finally pursue your dream of joining Cirque du Soleil. You need to evaluate where you are and where you want to be when you're deciding whether to downsize.

Likewise, you need to look inside yourself to get a sense of what you really think and feel about downsizing. What's your vision for the next 10–20 years of your life? What will you be giving up? What do you expect to get in return? Are you looking forward with confidence and excitement or fear and trepidation? If you don't have a solid plan that you're fairly certain will make you happier, you run the risk of being disappointed and getting discouraged, so take some time to analyze both your situation and your mindset.

Examining your situation

In the first section of this chapter, we presented a list of common reasons people downsize, but what's most important is *your* reason. To discover your *why* (or *why not*) for downsizing, examine your current situation by answering the following questions:

>> **Is your situation such that you have no choice but to downsize?** For some people, downsizing isn't a choice. Financial strain, health conditions, or pressure from family members may compel you to downsize, regardless of whether you want to.

TIP

Even if you're being compelled to downsize by forces outside your control, taking the initiative and being proactive can give you more control over the outcome. Don't just throw up your hands in despair; be an active participant as much as you're able.

>> **Are you leading the life *you* want to live?** If you feel as though you're a victim of circumstance or you're living passively and simply reacting to decisions that other people make, you may want to downsize to start living your life with intention — living your dream instead of enabling others to live theirs. Sometimes, having a big house and lots of possessions can be like wearing a ball and chain.

>> **Are you lonely?** You may be able to improve your social life by downsizing and moving to a community where you're more likely to meet compatible individuals — for example, an over-55 community with lots of social activities. (In Rochester Hills, we don't call them senior centers; we call them OPCs — older people's centers!)

>> **Is your home too much for you to clean and maintain?** If your home is falling into disrepair, or your housekeeping is starting to slip and you can't afford to hire out the work, it can be a sign that you're ready to downsize.

>> **Are you burning through your savings?** Ideally, you want to die without a penny in savings, meaning you enjoyed your money while you lived. But perhaps you want to leave some money behind for your survivors. Whatever the case, examine your finances carefully to make sure you're not burning through your savings too quickly (see Chapter 6 for guidance). If you are, downsizing may be the solution.

>> **Do you have more house than you need?** If you have rooms that you never use, you may be a good candidate for downsizing. Or you can lease those rooms to generate additional income.

>> **Do you need to unlock the equity in your home to finance your dreams?** If you have significant *equity* in your home (you can sell it for much more than you owe on it), you may want to sell your home to cash out your chips and use the proceeds to support the lifestyle you envision for yourself. Of course, other options are available for unlocking the equity in your home, such as refinancing or opening a home equity line of credit (HELOC). (See Chapter 8 for different ways to use your home to generate income.)

>> **If you were to die today, would you leave a total mess for your loved ones to deal with? Do you care?** Many people downsize to ease the burden on their loved ones, in which case moving to a more manageable home, shedding possessions, and organizing documents become top priorities. However, if you've already done a fantastic job of organizing everything and living simply, downsizing may be unnecessary.

>> **Do you need assistance with medical or personal care?** If your health is declining or you simply need a little more help than in the past, downsizing can be an opportunity to move into housing where you can get the help you need.

>> **Are you and your partner on the same page?** If you have a partner and one of you wants to downsize while the other doesn't, that can be a deal breaker. (See the later section "Making sure you're on the same page as your spouse (or siblings)" for details.)

WHEN YOUR "WHY" IS OBVIOUS

Your *why* for downsizing doesn't need to be complicated. It can be something simple, such as "I want to slash my living expenses and work less so I have more time and money to pursue my interests."

When our son, Kyle, was in college, he had a very simple reason for wanting to downsize from a dormitory to a fraternity. The reason he gave us was that it would save *us* money. Yes, we raised a clever young man. He knew exactly what to say to convince us that his choice was a wise one.

But his true reason was even simpler than that: "I just want to get out of the dorms!" Your *why* for downsizing can be just as simple and straightforward. Maybe you're tired of owning a home and caring for it and you want to move to a condo with a grounds crew to mow the lawn and trim the bushes, or maybe you want to spend your retirement years cruising the oceans. Simple is okay.

REMEMBER

Knowing your *why* for downsizing is important not only for deciding whether it's right for you but also for motivating you as you move forward and guiding subsequent decisions, such as these:

>> Your choice of lifestyle

>> Your dream location

>> Your timeline

>> The resources you'll need to execute your plan

Keeping your reason for downsizing in mind and taking an honest look at the full scope of your situation will help you devise an effective and efficient plan.

Taking stock of your thoughts and feelings

Downsizing can be physically, mentally, and emotionally draining, so you want to go into it with the right mindset. If you're feeling forced to do it or filled with fear or dread, those negative feelings will sap your motivation and energy and can result in a less desirable outcome.

To take stock of your thoughts and feelings, answer the following questions:

>> **What do you dread most about downsizing?** Most people dread the time and effort it will take, while others are more put off by the idea of having to

give up things they're emotionally attached to. By knowing what you dread most, you can start thinking about how to make it less dreadful — for example, by getting others to help or by keeping only the things you're most emotionally attached to.

» **What's the biggest perk you're expecting from downsizing?** For example, you may be able to retire earlier, have more time to pursue your interests and have fun, or move to a place you've always wanted to live.

TIP

To maximize your motivation and energy, keep your eyes on the prize — the freedom, independence, and peace of mind you'll gain when you have fewer possessions to worry about.

» **Are you downsizing because you want to or because you're being "forced" to?** Downsizing because you want to can boost your motivation and energy. Feeling forced to downsize can have an equally negative effect. Focusing on the potential benefits, especially if you're feeling compelled to downsize, can help you establish a more positive attitude.

» **Are you afraid you'll get rid of something you'll want or need later?** Chances are good that if you haven't used or looked at something in 5 years, you probably won't in the next 10–20 years.

» **Are you worried that others will think less of you if you own less?** Downsizing is about what *you* think and the life *you* want. Don't concern yourself with society's norms or what others think or expect from you. You have one life, and you need to live it fully.

» **What does "enough" look like to you?** Advertising ensures that we never feel as though we have enough. We're constantly being enticed to want what we don't have. Take a different approach. Think about the least you need in order to live the life you envision for yourself and think less in terms of possessions and more in terms of adventures, experiences, personal fulfillment, and people.

REMEMBER

If you are married or have a life partner, you'll have to be on the same page every step of the way. Downsizing is stressful, so work toward developing a positive mind-set and a common goal. If either of you feels overwhelmed, encourage each other.

Considering Your Loved Ones

The bigger your family, the more complicated the decision about whether to downsize becomes, because more people will be impacted by your decision. You certainly want to involve your partner (if you have one) in the decision-making process, but you may want to consult your children, grandchildren, and close friends as well.

In this section, we present the option of involving other people in your decision to downsize, and we guide you through the process.

Making sure you're on the same page as your spouse (or siblings)

Assuming you've had long-term relationships, you're well aware of the importance of communication, especially when you're making a life-changing decision that's likely to affect someone else. If you're thinking about downsizing, you definitely need to involve your partner in the decision, unless, of course, you plan to downsize out of the relationship. (Hey, it happens.) And if you're planning to downsize your parents (they are shrinking, after all), you'll probably want to consult with them and any siblings you have.

The bottom line: Everyone who will be involved in the downsizing decision and activities needs to be on the same page. Downsizing is stressful, and any dissension will make it even more so.

REMEMBER

When communicating with loved ones, be open and honest. Commit to full transparency, so everyone has all the information and insight they need to form honest opinions and make well-considered decisions. Here are a few suggestions for communicating effectively with your spouse, siblings, and other loved ones involved in the process:

>> **Share both your thoughts and your feelings.** Are you reluctant? Eager? Angry? However you feel about downsizing, get it out there so your emotions can be addressed. If you don't, you're at an increased risk of feeling regret, bitterness, and resentment later. Encourage everyone to express their thoughts and feelings.

>> **Hold meetings specifically to discuss downsizing.** Scheduled meetings will keep the discussion focused on downsizing and reduce distractions. Limit each meeting to no longer than one hour.

>> **Come to meetings prepared with notes and take notes during the meeting.** Coming prepared with notes or a list of topics you want to discuss and share helps keep the meeting on track and ensure that all your concerns are addressed. Encourage others to come prepared as well. The more prepared everyone is, the more productive your discussions will be.

>> **Focus your first meeting on the big picture — whether everyone thinks downsizing is a good idea and your visions for the future.** In later meetings, you can go into more detail about how you'll downsize, who's going to be involved in the process, and who gets what (see estate planning, discussed in Chapter 7).

By the time we left, the neighborhood we lived in for 30 years was completely different from the neighborhood we knew and loved when we were raising our children. The neighborhood we now live in feels more familiar to us. Instead of *Back to the Future*, our relocation was more like Forward to the Past.

Listening to your kids' opinions

When you're thinking about downsizing, consider bringing your children into the loop. We say *consider* because you may have good reasons not to involve them in your downsizing decisions. Some children can be too controlling, too selfish, too lazy, too busy, or just not interested. If they want to participate, and you want them to, then we encourage you to involve your kids in the festivities. Just as parents are affected by their children's decisions, children can be affected by what their parents decide. And in some cases, downsizing involves a role reversal, with children caring for their parents and making decisions for them. In certain situations, grandchildren may be calling the shots.

Whoever's affected by or involved in the downsizing should be included from the get-go. Start by involving them in the decision about whether to downsize. Present them with a list of pros and cons, instructing them to hold off on expressing their opinions until they've had time to think about it. Then, schedule a meeting to be held several days or a couple weeks later to get everyone's input. Delaying the discussion elicits more thoughtful feedback and deeper insights.

Ultimately, parents need to learn to work with their children, and children need to learn to work with their parents to ensure a smooth operation. Children can be thoughtful and offer great insights if that's what you expect from them and hold them to.

Every person is different, so we can't tell you specifically how to communicate with each of your children most effectively, but we can offer some insight into what you can expect from them in different situations — for example, children who are still living with you versus those who've moved out, and adult children versus younger children. In the following sections, we discuss those differences.

Whether you're a parent, child, or grandchild, be honest, open, and assertive. Don't just roll over and do what other people tell you to do. Be open to negotiating, and don't let your concerns and interests be ignored or discounted.

Parents, beware. Don't make the common mistake of teaming up with the weakest link in the family just to get your way. You want the most competent of your children to be involved, even if that child is a little more assertive than the others.

Holding firm with adult children who still live with you

If you have adult children still living with you, you're in the most challenging scenario, because your downsizing will disrupt their lives. *No more free food, housing, Wi-Fi, laundry service?! And where am I going to put all my stuff?!*

Well, this may be a golden opportunity to get your freeloading fledgling to move out and move on without having to serve an eviction notice. The conversation can be difficult, but hold firm. Sometimes, the only way to live the dream of becoming an empty nester is to fly the coop yourself. Ultimately, you need to do what's best for you and your partner, and in the long run, forcing independence on children is what's best for them, too — it's a necessary step on their journey to interdependence.

Considering younger children who live with you

As for younger children who live with you, you're well advised to consider their needs and plans with greater empathy. For example, you may want to postpone any decision to downsize until after your children graduate high school. And if a child plans to attend college and stay closer to home (or even continue living at home and commute to college), you may want to delay your decision even longer.

Of course, your children may be all in on downsizing and even moving. Maybe they're struggling to fit in at school, or they share your dream of managing a coconut plantation in the Philippines. The only way you'll know is to start discussing your dreams and preferences as a family.

Involving adult children who don't live with you

If you're close with your adult children, including them in your discussions and decisions is likely to come naturally. If they're distant physically or you rarely communicate, they probably won't be involved, regardless of whether you want them to be. Here are a few guidelines for gauging your adult children's level of involvement:

>> If your adult children live near you and spend time with you, get them involved. Remain in close contact throughout the process, share your thoughts, and listen to their opinions.

>> If they live far away or you rarely see them for other reasons, consider whether trying to get them involved is worth the time and effort.

>> Share financial information, such as your budget — water, gas, electricity, taxes, maintenance — to the degree you feel comfortable and believe your adult children are responsible enough to know.

>> Set parameters on acceptable involvement and feedback. For example, you may want your children to accompany you as you check out properties, they may kick the tires with you, and you may want them to express their opinions, but you may draw the line at them telling you what to do. (If you have a child who's a know-it-all, you're familiar with our cautionary language.)

Letting close friends and neighbors in on it

If you have close friends and neighbors who will be impacted by your downsizing decision, and who will be supportive whatever you choose, consider drawing them into your discussion circle. They may have unique insights to share or feelings about you that you weren't aware of.

You may realize, through your discussions, that you don't want to live without them nearby, or maybe they'll decide to downsize and join you on your adventure! Perhaps you'll decide to move in together, buy a duplex, or arrange for side-by-side condos. When we moved, we tried to recruit our neighbors to move with us!

Making the Tough Call for an Aging Loved One

Persuading aging loved ones to downsize can be a monumental challenge. Parents generally don't appreciate their children telling them how to live their lives any more than children appreciate their parents telling them how to live theirs. In addition, if your parents have lived in their current home for a considerable time, they're probably attached to it financially, emotionally, and in terms of comfort and convenience.

Here are a few suggestions on how to be more persuasive:

>> Don't pitch it as downsizing. Pitch it instead as a better living arrangement for this stage of their lives. Not downsizing, but *life-sizing* — making their life more manageable and enjoyable.

>> Work with your parents to create a comprehensive list of everything they want/need in a new home, such as a single level, ramps, a walk-in bath/shower, and so on.

>> Discuss their needs regarding location, so they'll have easy access to friends, shopping, medical care, public transportation, parks, work (if they still work), and so on. (See Chapter 3 for more about location considerations.)

>> Make a list of items in their current home that they can't live without, so they know you're being sensitive to their concerns. Assure them that certain belongings they want to keep in the family will be saved.

>> Take your parents on tours of different places that you think may appeal to them. They may not know just how nice some of these places are.

>> Most important, establish an atmosphere of open and honest communication. The more you talk about it, the more they'll warm up to the idea and accept the inevitable . . . or the louder they'll yell at you. In either case, the feedback is valuable.

WARNING

Don't assume that you know what's best for your parents. You may or may not. Listen carefully to what they say and ask questions until you fully understand their needs and preferences. Even if you're ultimately unable to address all their concerns, you'll achieve a better outcome by engaging them in thoughtful discussion. However, if your best attempts fall short, be prepared to make a tough decision that your parents may never come to terms with.

A TOUGH CALL

When your parents' health begins to fail, you may need to make a tough decision that they will never accept but that's best for them and the rest of the family. Kathleen and her sister had to make such a decision for their ailing parents — yes, the same people we introduced in an earlier sidebar who upsized after their kids moved out.

After having the conversation that their parents weren't ready to hear, Kathleen and her sister took them for a drive (no, not the *Throw Momma from the Train* kind of drive). The first stop was the doctor's office, where their longtime doctor called their attention to the mobility challenges in their current home. Kathleen and her sister both broke down crying. The doctor turned to their parents and said, "Look at what this is doing to your daughters." It was an emotional moment for everyone, but Mom and Dad still didn't want to face the facts.

The next stop was an excellent assisted care facility, where Kathleen and her sister had scheduled a tour and lunch was served. Their mom kept her eyes closed the entire time. Their dad probably would have gone along with the plan, but as long as his wife resisted, he wouldn't budge, so their children's heartache endured. Their mom eventually passed away, leaving their father no choice but to move into an assisted living facility.

Who can blame Kathleen's parents? Nobody wants to lose their freedom and independence. When someone is placed in a facility, they often feel trapped. They have no way out. As their children, we may need to make difficult decisions that our parents don't like, but we can do it with empathy. They're giving up a great deal — in some cases, their lifelong dreams. You can only hope that they will begin to realize the gravity of the situation and have empathy for their loved ones as well.

Settling a Major Dilemma: To Sell or Not to Sell Your Home

One of the big decisions that comes with downsizing is whether to sell the family home. In some cases, the decision is a no-brainer: You need to cash out the equity in the home to finance your new life, or you simply want to get rid of it, and nobody else in the family wants it. In other cases, you may feel pressured by family members, or even by relatives who are long since dead, to keep the property in the family.

As you mull over this important decision, keep the following considerations and options in mind:

>> You can cash out equity in the property in ways other than selling it. For example, you can mortgage it, take out a HELOC, or arrange a reverse mortgage. (See Chapter 8 for details.)

>> You may be able to lease the property to full-time or part-time residents, something that has become increasingly easy through services like Airbnb and Vrbo. You can even use these services to lease a portion of your home while you still live there.

>> You can sell interests in the property to other family members so that you share ownership of it. You can even arrange it so you're acting as the bank, collecting monthly payments.

>> If maintenance is the reason you want to sell, you can hire a property management company to maintain the home and arrange for regular cleanings.

>> For homeowners whose health is deteriorating, home health care may be a viable alternative to selling their home and moving to an assisted care facility.

GETTING CREATIVE

Twin sisters faced a difficult dilemma. Their mother wasn't acting like herself anymore. She became a hoarder, filling her home with things she would never use. Every time she went shopping, she would buy five or six of everything.

Her doctor ran some tests that showed she was suffering from Alzheimer's disease. When the sisters started looking into selling their mother's home, they were advised not to. Moving would be counterproductive to her condition, and she wanted to avoid losing money on the sale of the home. So, one of the twins sold her condo and moved in with their mother to provide care and cleaning.

Through this arrangement, they were able to keep the family home while providing the care and attention their mother needed. Unfortunately, freeing up a family member to care for an ailing loved one isn't always an option.

IN THIS CHAPTER

» Approaching downsizing as an opportunity to reinvent your life

» Deciding where to live the next stage of your life

» Weighing the option of living a nomadic lifestyle

» Digging up details about potential destinations

» Sampling a place or lifestyle before making the leap

Chapter **3**

Envisioning Your Future: Lifestyle and Location

Mentally, I have to get my body and mind in the right place before I start the routine, but once into the zone, it's like I turn on a switch. I envision myself doing the same thing for the Olympic Games.

— SIMONE BILES, U.S. GYMNAST

Are you starting to look around your living space and wondering where in the world all the clutter came from? Do you find you have rooms in your home you never go into? If you're feeling somewhat burdened and tied down by owning too much stuff and occupying too much space, it's time to think about downsizing.

But downsizing isn't necessarily limited to getting rid of a bunch of belongings and moving to a smaller place to make your life more manageable. It can be an exciting opportunity to reinvent yourself, move to a new location, and adopt an entirely different lifestyle.

Maybe for you, the American dream turned out to be a nightmare. Climbing corporate and social ladders, owning a big house in a great neighborhood, raising children, and trying to keep up with the Joneses just didn't bring you the joy and fulfillment you were hoping for, or it did for a while, but now you're ready for your next adventure. These days, you have more freedom to explore life in a new way, and a life of less (as in fewer material goods) may be the perfect solution to free you up for other adventures. This is your chance to determine what the rest of your life will look like, and what your priorities will be.

In this chapter, we provide the encouragement, inspiration, and guidance to dream big in the context of downsizing. We also advise you to consider all the factors that go into making one of the biggest decisions of your life, so you'll get it right the first time. A major mistake some people make when downsizing is to invest significant resources into a poor choice they don't have the means to escape when they come to realize their error. By following our guidance in this chapter and taking the time to think about what you really want, you'll have a much better chance of avoiding that trap.

Building Your Vision

A fortunate few have a clear vision for their future. They can close their eyes and imagine, engaging all their senses, the life they desire — the location where they want to end up, their living quarters, the people around them, the activities they're involved in, the food and beverages they're consuming, and more. Most people, however, struggle to answer one of life's simplest, yet most challenging, questions: *What do you want?* Even after mulling over that question for months or years, they may still have only a fuzzy idea, at best.

Before you downsize, we encourage you to honestly answer some important questions: *What do you want? How do you want to live the rest of your life? How do you want to live the next 10–20 years of your life?* and *What do you want to be when you grow up?* (It's never too late to answer that last question.)

In the following sections, we present a few different approaches to building your vision of your future life.

Complete our lifestyle questionnaire

Here's a lifestyle questionnaire we created to start you thinking about what's important to you and engaging your imagination in the process. These may seem like heavy questions to start with, but they are the key themes you should keep in your mind when deciding what the next phase of life will look like and focus on. Simply write your answers on a separate piece of paper (you'll probably need a pad of paper):

>> When are you happiest?

>> Are you holding onto any emotional baggage — regrets, disappointments, bitterness, resentment? Now is a good time to let all that go and replace it with gratitude.

>> What will people say about you at your funeral? Now is the time to start living the stories you want them to tell about you.

>> What would you do if you had only six months to live?

>> What's your reason/purpose for living? What motivates you to wake up in the morning eager to face the day?

>> What's holding you back? Who or what is standing in the way of the life you want or need to transition to?

>> What do you hope to accomplish? What legacy do you wish to leave behind?

>> Who will play a key role in your future life? Think in terms of friends, family members, colleagues, and so on. If you don't have anyone in mind, that's okay.

>> Are you envisioning permanent housing or a more nomadic lifestyle that involves lots of travel and adventure?

>> Will you be working? If so, is it paid or volunteer work? Full-time or temporary? Describe the type of work you want to do. Are you running your own business or working for someone else? Do you need to live near your place of employment, or can you work remotely?

>> What do you envision yourself doing in your free time? List activities you'd like to participate in, such as specific hobbies, swimming, biking, walking, working out, fishing, playing golf or tennis, learning/playing a musical instrument, attending concerts, dancing, visiting museums, boating, traveling, learning a foreign language.

>> What are you thinking in terms of location and climate? Hot and dry? Temperate? Seasonal? Inland or coastal? Mountains, plains, or forest? Domestic or foreign? Will you migrate, living in a cooler area over the summer and wintering in a warmer area?

>> Will you need assistance? If yes, what level of assistance? For example, do you need a health-care worker 24/7, a daily check-in, a few hours a week, or only on-demand care? Maybe all you need are cleaning services, help with preparing meals, and transportation.

> » What types of services do you need or desire nearby? Medical facilities? Shopping? Restaurants? A gym? A library? Museums? Theaters? Golf courses? Cultural events? A church, synagogue, or mosque? Or are you envisioning living in a remote location, perhaps off the grid?

REMEMBER

Living for others is okay if it gives your life purpose and meaning, but prioritizing yourself is fine too, even if it makes you feel a little selfish. If you don't focus more on your own personal happiness, you may become resentful doing too much for other people. You'll be doing everyone the most good if you're enjoying your life.

List your must-haves, nice-to-haves, and please-no's

One way to figure out what you want in life is to create three lists: one for must-haves, another for nice-to-haves, and a third for what you want to avoid. This approach is especially helpful if you have to negotiate with a partner or additional family members to address everyone's interests and concerns. Here, we describe the three lists:

> » **Must-haves:** List everything you can't or won't live without. Your list may include location, house size (style, square footage, types and number of rooms), furnishings, access to shopping and entertainment venues, ease of movement through the home, assistance, proximity to family, and so on. It's likely to be a long list, but include only those things you won't compromise on.

> » **Nice-to-haves:** List everything you'd like to have but you're willing to negotiate. For example, maybe you'd like to have a pool, but it's not a deal breaker. You can include the same types of things as on your must-haves list, but these aren't nonnegotiable.

> » **Please-no's:** Make a list of everything you consider unacceptable. Many people, for example, refuse to live in communities that have covenants restricting what they can do to their homes. You may have certain locations or property types (a condo, for example) that you'd never consider.

TIP

If you're downsizing with a partner or other family members, work together as a group to create three master lists instead of having each person create three lists of their own. You can negotiate as you create your master lists.

Build a vision board

A *vision board* is a collage of pictures, motivational phrases, and other items that reflect a person's dreams, ambitions, and anything else that truly matters. You can cut pictures and text out of magazines and mailers, use your own photos, or copy and print ideas and images you find online. What you choose to include on your vision board is entirely up to you, but here's a list to spark your imagination:

>> Photos depicting the location you want to live in

>> A photo of your dream home or a blueprint of its floor plan

>> Pictures of rooms that inspire you to downsize

>> Pictures of people you'd like to have in your life

>> Inspirational quotations or phrases, such as "Less is more" and "Make life fantastic!"

>> Pictures or phrases that represent your personal, professional, or financial goals

>> Lists of your downsizing priorities, such as your list of must-haves from the previous section

>> Photos of people engaged in activities in which you want to participate

>> Photos of places you'd like to travel to

TIP

If you're downsizing with other family members, hang your vision board in a central location to remind everyone of your shared vision and to encourage everyone to contribute to the board. Your vision board can be as neat and tidy or as cluttered as you all agree to.

REMEMBER

There's no right or wrong way to create a vision board. We prefer the old-school approach using a poster board, glue, and magazine clippings, but many people go digital, using social media platforms such as Pinterest or Instagram to create online vision boards. You can even copy and paste images into a Word or Google doc or use a graphics program such as Photoshop.

Gather more details in vision folders

A vision board is a big-picture document; it's not suitable for collecting and storing details. So we recommend supplementing it with *vision folders*. You can create a vision folder for each aspect of your downsizing project, such as the following:

>> Location

>> Housing

>> Health care

>> Transportation

- » Budget/expenses
- » Employment/business opportunities
- » Activities/entertainment
- » Amenities
- » Shopping and restaurants
- » Belongings to keep
- » Belongings to hand down
- » Belongings to get rid of

After labeling your folders, you can start to stuff them with documents, brochures, photos, lists, advertisements, and other items relevant to each folder. You can then consult specific folders over the course of your downsizing, depending on the stage of the process. For example, when you're ready to start sorting your many possessions, you can consult your Belongings folders to determine their fate.

OUR VISION BOARDS AND FOLDERS

When we started to discuss the possibility of downsizing, we created several vision boards. We added pictures and wrote potential locations on massive poster boards and created vision folders. Our downsizing goal was focused primarily on housing; our aim was to simplify our lives, not make a significant change in lifestyle.

Our vision boards and folders reflected our goal. We had folders for mortgage, location, floor plans, flooring, window treatments, furnishings, and so on. We were interested in new construction, so we had quite a collection of folders. Throughout the process, we could pull a relevant folder to review our options; for example, when the time came to choose window treatments, we pulled that folder to check out our options.

We also kept track of furniture and furnishings we planned to keep, along with notes about whether any pieces needed to be reconditioned, such as our old coffee table. We took a photo of our bed in our old home, printed it, and wrote its dimensions on the photo, so we could envision how it would fit in our new bedroom. Now that may seem a little on the obsessive-compulsive side to you, but all these details came in handy during discussions with our builder.

Choosing a Location: Factors to Consider

Where will you live? On its surface, that question may appear easy to answer, until you start digging into all the factors you need to consider to formulate a thoughtful response: climate, terrain, cost of living, proximity to loved ones, and so on. You may even contemplate a nomadic lifestyle — wandering from place to place instead of settling down.

In this section, we present some of the key factors to consider when choosing a location or opting for a nomadic lifestyle.

Settled or nomadic

Traditionally, people settle in one location that acts as their home base, even if they travel frequently. Many have two properties — a primary residence and a vacation home, or a winter and a summer residence. Another option is to live a nomadic existence, traveling from place to place without staying in one location for more than a few months to a couple years.

If you're thinking about becoming a nomad, consider the pros and cons.

Pros

Living a nomadic existence, you can look forward to the following potential benefits:

» Freedom

» Low cost of living

» Flexible working conditions

» Frequent travel

» Unlimited opportunities to meet new people

Cons

Living a nomadic existence isn't the romantic ideal it can seem to be. Expect the following drawbacks:

» Physical discomfort

» Poor and/or unreliable phone/internet service

» Little to no support network

- » Reduced privacy and security

- » Uncertainty and the anxiety that accompanies it

- » Loneliness if you start missing friends and family

- » Exhaustion, because living on the road can be draining

EMBRACING THE NOMADIC LIFESTYLE

Downsizing doesn't necessarily mean moving to a smaller residence. It may constitute living a nomadic lifestyle. When Tracey, the woman who cleaned our house for many years, downsized, she took to the road in a 1966 camper.

Tracey is a single mom. Over the years, she worked hard to support herself and her son. Vacations were few and far between and usually involved camping with her son's Boy Scout troop, often in a leaky tent. After her son graduated high school and headed off to college in the fall of 2018, Tracey put most of her belongings in storage, leased her house to a local postal worker, hitched her camper to her van, loaded up her five dogs, and headed south toward sunshine and warm breezes.

You won't find Tracey with her nose stuck in a book. She loves her freedom, solitude, and the great outdoors, kayaking, boating, riding her bike, walking her dogs — no lawn to mow, no home to maintain, no commitments or appointments.

Unfortunately, Tracey ran into a few snags. She didn't know that she had to reserve a campsite a year or two in advance. The snowbirds who migrate biannually between the northern and southern states had claimed all the best spots a year or two before she headed south. Finding available campsites became a major challenge. When she finally found a vacancy, it was often only for a few days, so she would skip from one campground to the next, unhooking the camper and then hooking it back up with each stop. Skipping from one campground to the next, she traveled the Carolinas, Texas, and Florida.

A little more than halfway into her adventure, her tenants stopped paying rent. She had to return to Michigan to deal with the situation, not knowing what condition her home would be in — fingers crossed, no broken pipes! She came back to find thousands of dollars in damage. She made the repairs and hit the road again in December 2019. Soon after, COVID struck, forcing her to return home in February.

Tracey is continuously tweaking her downsizing plan. This time, she's planning to sell her house and travel until the housing market crashes again, at which time she'll probably buy another house — something small in or near the Florida Keys. She figures she'll save about $900 a month not having a house — no mortgage, homeowner's insurance, electricity, gas, water, maintenance, and so on. She also dreams of eventually getting a 40- to 50-foot sloop and living on it in a harbor along the Florida coast.

As for the problem she had securing campsites, Tracey discovered a solution. One summer, she landed a gig as a camp host, greeting campers, fielding their questions, dealing with common issues, and overseeing the grounds — no pay, but she was able to stay at the campground over the summer for free. She had an opportunity to do that again in the summer of 2022.

Here's Tracey's advice for anyone considering the nomadic life:

- Separate your feelings and memories from "things" — your house, pictures, trinkets, and so on.

- Be prepared to sacrifice the comfort of a home.

- Be sure your camper, tent, or other shelter is appropriate for the environments you plan to live in.

- Pack the bare minimum, no duplicates.

- Test the lifestyle before going all in. Try it for three months. You'll need to pay for storage, but it'll be cheaper than having to buy new stuff if you decide later that living as a nomad isn't for you. This downsizing option is drastic — on average, it involves letting go of 80–90 percent of your belongings.

- Map your planned route.

- Reserve campsites along your planned route at least one year before hitting the road.

- Check the rules at each campground. Rules may apply to the age of your camper, the number of dogs permitted, electric and water hookups, wastewater disposal, and so on.

- Create a plan B. If your best laid plans fail, what are you going to do?

- Use a bank that has branches in the locations where you plan to travel.

- Use a virtual mailbox service to handle your snail mail and packages. Such a service can weed out junk mail, deposit checks, scan and send mail electronically, and forward documents and packages.

Foreign or domestic

One of the big questions you face if your downsizing plan involves a move is whether to relocate abroad or within your home country. Either way, you may be able to reduce your cost of living to create a more affordable lifestyle.

In the following sections, we present the potential advantages and disadvantages of each option.

Foreign

More and more people in the U.S. are choosing to relocate to foreign countries to stretch their incomes or experience a life filled with more play and adventure and less work. Foreign destinations may have a lower cost of living overall thanks to lower taxes, lower housing prices, reduced health-care and pharmaceutical costs, lower food prices, and so on.

REMEMBER

Approximately 25 percent of the U.S. population think they need at least $1 million in savings to retire comfortably. Although that assumption may be valid for those who continue living in the U.S., it's not the case for those who live abroad in countries where life is more affordable. For example, according to some estimates, you can live well in some areas of Mexico for about $12,000 per year. If you're getting $1,000 a month or more in social security payments, that income alone can cover your living expenses.

When choosing a foreign destination, consider the following key factors:

>> Climate

>> Affordability

>> Quality health care

>> Languages spoken

>> Safety/security (crime rates)

>> Rules and regulations for relocating there (countries often require proof of income, assets, and health insurance to ensure that you won't be a financial burden)

TIP

For a list of top retirement destinations, check out the World Economic Forum's top 10 list at www.weforum.org/agenda/2022/02/best-places-to-retire-list. Here are the top five on that list:

>> Panama

>> Costa Rica

>> Mexico

>> Portugal

>> Colombia

Domestic

Even if you choose to remain in your home country, certain areas may have a lower cost of living than others. For example, in the U.S., some states, counties, and towns/cities are more affordable than others based primarily on their popularity and tax rates. Property tax rates can vary considerably, and some states don't levy a state income tax.

If you're relocating domestically in the U.S. as part of your downsizing plan, check out *U.S. News and World Report*'s top 10 retirement destinations at money.usnews.com/money/retirement/articles/the-best-places-to-retire. We can save you some time — of the top 10, eight are in Florida. Notably *not* listed is America's number-one retirement community: The Villages in central Florida. It also happens to be the world's capital of Viagra sales.

If you're looking to move to a state with no state income tax, check out AARP's "9 States That Don't Have an Income Tax" at www.aarp.org/money/taxes/info-2020/states-without-an-income-tax.html. Yes, Florida is on that list, too!

Terrain

Terrain refers to the surface features of an area of land, such as desert, mountain, valley, oceanfront, riverside, forest, and so on. Each has its pros and cons.

The prime consideration is affordability. Waterfront property is probably the most expensive, comparatively speaking, but even some desert areas, such as Phoenix, Arizona, can be very expensive. You can also expect to pay a premium for living anywhere with awesome views, such as some mountain locations.

Climate

Climate is a huge consideration. It determines not only what your heating and cooling bills will look like but also how comfortable you'll be and how much you'll be able to enjoy the outdoors.

Most people prefer a comfortable temperature year-round without excessive precipitation, which is why, in the U.S., the southwest and southeast coastal areas are so popular (except during hurricane season). Most people consider San Diego, California, ideal: 12 inches of rain, no snow, sunny about 266 days of the year, 7 comfortable months when the average high is in the range of 70–85 degrees Fahrenheit, only about 13 days when the average high is over 90 degrees, and only a few months where the nighttime low drops to 45–50 degrees.

Phoenix, Arizona, has both desert and mountain terrains, so residents can head up into the mountains in midsummer for relief. You can be in the arid desert one day and the cool mountains the next, and even get caught in a blizzard in a few hours' drive.

REMEMBER

Choosing not to relocate when downsizing is perfectly acceptable. We like the climate and terrain where we live in Michigan. We have everything: four seasons; plenty of greenery; easy access to lakes and streams; proximity to friends, family, doctors, entertainment, shopping, and our favorite sports venues; and everything else we value. If you're generally happy at your current location, stay as close to it as possible.

Size/population

Downsizing doesn't apply to the size of the town or city you live in. You can downsize your home while upsizing from a small town to a big city. When deciding where you're going to live, you basically have the following three options with respect to size and population density:

>> **Urban:** In urban areas, you can expect high population density, lots of traffic, homes close together, more cultural diversity, more to do, a greater selection of stores and restaurants, better public transportation, more job opportunities, more public services, more opportunities for social interaction, and potentially more crime and pollution.

>> **Suburban:** In the suburbs, you have many of the benefits of city living (due to proximity to a city) without some of the drawbacks. Schools are generally better (see the later section "School system" to understand why schools matter), crime and pollution are less of a problem, traffic may be less congested, and homes are usually spaced a little farther apart. However, you usually pay a premium in terms of housing prices and property taxes.

>> **Rural:** Rural areas are in the country, closer to nature, and have lower population densities. As a result, benefits include a more relaxed lifestyle, greater privacy, cleaner air, less crime, more peace and quiet, less traffic and congestion, greater affordability, and good schools. Drawbacks of rural living are mostly related to a lack of convenient access to everything urban areas offer: stores, restaurants, sports and entertainment venues, public transportation, public services, cultural offerings, and so on.

Clear distinctions between urban, suburban, and rural areas are tough to pin down, but about 52 percent of the population of the U.S. reports living in a suburban area versus 27 percent urban and 21 percent rural.

Affordability

Affordability is a key consideration, especially if you're retiring and will have a fixed income. In fact, affordability is one of the primary factors that drives people to downsize. To determine how affordable any given option is, you need to crunch the numbers. Examine your current income and savings in light of estimated expenses, which are likely to include the following:

>> Mortgage or rent

>> Homeowner's or renter's insurance

>> Property taxes

>> State and local income and sales taxes

>> Utilities (gas, electricity, water, sewer, trash disposal, phone, television, and internet service)

>> Homeowner association fees

>> Transportation, which may include a car payment, auto insurance, fuel costs, and maintenance and repair fees

>> Health insurance

>> Life insurance

>> Groceries, toiletries, and other necessities

>> Memberships

>> Entertainment

>> Dining

WARNING

Don't get sucked into trying to keep up with the Joneses. Create a life that's affordable for *you*. One of the biggest financial mistakes people make is overextending themselves. They often end up in bankruptcy and foreclosure and have a difficult time recovering their financial footing. By living within your means, you can avoid financial setbacks while reducing your anxiety overall.

Employment opportunities

Employment may or may not be a consideration for you. If you're retiring for good and plan to live off your savings, pension, and social security benefits, employment is a nonissue. Likewise, if you can work remotely, your place of employment won't factor into your decision. However, if you need (or want) to work, and you need to be on-site, consider the employment opportunities in and near the areas on your relocation list.

BUSIER IN RETIREMENT (DOING WHAT YOU LOVE)

When Kathleen's father was planning to retire, he was worried that he'd have nothing to do. In retirement, he never stopped. He was busy with outdoor activities — gardening, senior citizens outings, and more. He never passed up an opportunity to do something or go somewhere. He was always ready to go! He could finally enjoy his grandchildren and attend all their sporting events. He was probably busier in retirement than he was when he was working full-time.

As the door is closing on your career, another door is opening to your retirement years. There's no shortage of work or play to be had, so if you want to work, you can find plenty of opportunities — both volunteer and paid positions. You can even start your own business if you're so inclined.

My cousin John drives a hearse for funeral homes — they'll give him as much work as he can handle. A friend of ours works for Door Dash, delivering carryout food orders. The gig economy is alive and growing, providing unlimited opportunities just about anywhere you decide to live.

Health care

Regardless of whether you're downsizing, health care can weigh heavily on nearly every major life decision, especially if you or your partner or children have existing health issues. Here are a few tips for dealing with concerns about health insurance and treatment:

» If you're retiring and relocating, consider moving close to a hospital system in case anything happens to you or your partner. Or at least move close to your doctors or to transportation that can get you to a nearby hospital.

When we were relocating, we wanted to be near Henry Ford Health, a leading health-care and medical-services provider in the Southwest Detroit region. It's the group that we're comfortable with. We try to schedule our appointments around noon, so we can have lunch together at one of Detroit's top restaurants.

» If you're moving a long distance (such as to a different state), ask your physician for a referral and schedule an initial consultation with your new doctor, to prevent any disruption to any medications you're taking or treatments you're undergoing.

» If you're turning 65, at which point you become eligible for Medicare, contact your insurance agent to discuss your options or check out *Medicare For Dummies*, 4th Edition, by Patricia Barry.

>> Before choosing a place to live, ask your insurance agent to advise you on how the move will impact your premiums. Health insurance premiums are based, in part, on your age and zip code. Moving to a different zip code can impact not only the rates your doctors charge but also your health insurance premiums.

>> If you plan to live or travel to a foreign country, contact your insurance agent to obtain a suitable traveler's health insurance policy. Medicare generally doesn't provide coverage outside the U.S., but some Medicare Advantage plans do.

If you're turning 65 and planning to relocate or already outside the country, hold off on signing up for Medicare until you're situated. Medicare is tied to social security, and you can't change any Medicare information until you change it with the Social Security Administration (SSA). You'll probably be better off delaying registration until after you've settled down and changed your address with the SSA. Otherwise, anticipate major hassles.

Proximity to friends and family

Family members and close friends constitute your support network, so don't overlook their importance in any decision to relocate. Whether you're relying on others, or they're relying on you, moving far away can leave you (and them) feel-ing isolated and scrambling to find help when crises arise.

Ultimately, you need to do what's best for yourself, which may involve staying close to your current location or embarking on a major relocation. Others can then decide whether being near you is a priority for them. Our son has moved to five different states over the course of less than a decade, while we've remained in the same area. Now that he's ready to settle down, he wants to be near family and many of the close friends he grew up with, so he's decided to return home to Michigan! Sometimes, you just get lucky when you stay in your hometown and your family comes back to roost.

Activities, entertainment, and restaurants

If you're planning a relocation, consider moving closer to what you enjoy, such as the following:

>> Walking trails or bike paths

>> Parks

>> Restaurants, coffee shops, bars

>> Shopping

- >> A farmers' market or fresh produce stand
- >> A college or university
- >> A concert venue
- >> A racetrack or sports stadium where your favorite team plays

Getting around

Do you like to walk? Do you enjoy exploring the place you live? Do you like to engage in a variety of activities outside your home and beyond the confines of your neighborhood? Then walkability and transportation may be two key considerations, especially if you don't drive or don't like to drive.

Walkability

Walkability is a measure of how walker-friendly an area is. It's gauged by the presence or absence of quality sidewalks (or footpaths) and pedestrian crossings, traffic and road conditions, safety, accessibility to businesses and services, and so on. To get a feel for an area's walkability, visit the area in the morning, the middle of the day, and the evening, and walk around.

Also, consider *where* you like to walk. Do you prefer walking in the country with little or no foot traffic, in the woods, or in an urban setting? Do you like fresh air and nature or walking through the business district, where you can stop at a diner for a cup of coffee or a bite to eat? Where you like to walk can have a big influence over where you want to live — a more rural or urban area.

DON'T UNDERESTIMATE CONVENIENCE

When we started to discuss downsizing, we realized just how inconvenient our current location was. Everything was hard to get to. When choosing a new location, we wanted easy access to everything we enjoy. Now, we can step out the door in any direction and immediately be on a bike and walking path. At our previous home, the nearest path was a half mile away.

We live near major highways, a 30-minute drive from downtown Detroit. We have easy access to indoor and outdoor malls, coffee shops, bars, restaurants (including two fabulous sushi bars), and stores (Whole Foods and Trader Joe's being two of our favorites). The college campus nearby provides affordable entertainment in the form of theater productions, indoor and outdoor concerts, and fascinating presentations open to the public.

Transportation

Transportation can be any combination of riding a bicycle, driving a car, taking a train or bus, calling a taxi, or using Uber or Lyft. Some communities also have vans or shuttles that seniors can ride for free or at a reduced cost. In larger metropolitan areas, you can even rent an electric car, bike, or scooter to get around.

When you're considering where you want to settle, give some thought to how you're going to get around and access the businesses, services, events, and other offerings you'll need and want.

TIP

If you're an avid bicyclist, think about where you're going to park or store your bike and perform minor repairs. In our community, people with bikes need to get approval, before moving in, to put in bike stands, where they can park their bikes and pump up their tires.

Crime rates

Before moving to any area, check out its crime rates, which you can do online at sites such as www.city-data.com and www.crimemapping.com. You can also call the local police station or sheriff's office (call the nonemergency number, *not* 911) and ask to speak with the community resource officer. Or visit the area, introduce yourself to some of the residents, and ask them to weigh in on how safe the neighborhood is.

Public amenities and cultural centers

Some residential communities offer a broad array of amenities that most individuals or couples couldn't afford on their own, such as a clubhouse, pool, hot tub, gym, golf course, tennis courts, fishing ponds, and more. They may also organize a variety of events and activities, such as concerts, dances, pickleball tournaments, yoga, and crafts. In some communities, these amenities are available only to residents and their guests, typically for a monthly amenities fee. In others, outsiders can join but are usually required to pay a much higher monthly or annual fee.

REMEMBER

You may pay more for a property in a residential community that offers amenities, but they can make your life more enjoyable and even save you money on things you would otherwise pay for separately, such as green fees and gym memberships.

Towns and cities are often too large and diverse to offer anything like what you can get in a residential community, but you can find other amenities spread across the town or city, such as the following:

>> Libraries

>> Community centers

>> Museums

>> Theaters

>> Concert venues

>> Sports venues

>> Churches, synagogues, mosques, and other religious organizations

School system

Whenever you're buying a property, buy into an area with a quality school system, even if you're an empty nester. The quality of the school system has a significant impact on resale value. In fact, when we were looking to relocate, the school system was one of the top three factors we considered: affordability, price, and school system. We considered an addition that had some nice homes in it, but it wasn't in the right school system, so we crossed it off our list.

WARNING

Be careful about buying into a senior living center because they're generally located in some of the lower-ranking school districts. Land is cheaper in lower-ranking school districts, which is a key reason senior living centers tend to be built in these areas.

Existing property or new construction

If you're downsizing to a smaller home, one of the big decisions you need to make is whether to buy an existing home or have one built (new construction). Here, we help you weigh the pros and cons.

TIP

If you're looking to buy a newly constructed home in a subdivision, get in as early as possible. Builders often offer lower prices to kick-start the development, enabling you to get your foot in the door at the lowest price.

Pros

Benefits of new construction include the following:

>> Floor plans are generally more open with bigger, brighter rooms, and you may have the option to customize the floor plan.

>> If you buy before the home is finished, you may have the option to choose colors, window dressings, light fixtures, and other custom features.

>> Newly constructed homes tend to be more energy-efficient.

» A newly constructed home is more likely to have smart-home features built in, such as a programmable thermostat.

» New homes may be healthier, due to the use of construction materials that have low or zero volatile organic compounds.

» Maintenance costs are likely to be lower because everything's new.

Cons

Here are some of the potential drawbacks of new construction to consider:

» New construction typically costs more.

» You'll probably be waiting six months to more than a year for your home to be built.

» New housing additions typically sprout up in remote locations, resulting in longer commutes. In urban areas, new construction is generally limited to high-rise condos or smaller homes on smaller lots, providing less outdoor space.

» In new housing additions, mature trees are generally scarce, so don't expect much shade — at least for a few years.

GETTING THE INSIDE TRACK

Kathleen and I were looking at high rises, new construction, old construction — nothing was entirely off the table. We spent every weekend driving through areas and down streets that we liked around Detroit, Michigan. We looked for real estate signs and developments.

One weekend we were driving around Rochester Hills, north of Detroit, near Oakland University. It's a beautiful area with a Whole Foods, a Trader Joe's, a broad offering of activities tied to the university, and much more — nearly everything on our downsizing wish list.

Off of Walton, north on Brewster, on the left side of the street, we noticed a sign — "Coming Soon! Robertson Brothers, Single Family Homes!" — along with a phone number to call, so I did. The salesperson didn't tell me much — only that he didn't have permission to share any information until they had a model to show.

I'm not a very patient person, so I called around to other Robertson Brothers sites for information. Crickets. I then decided to go to Rochester Hills' municipal offices and visit

(continued)

(continued)

the building department. The person behind the counter was Maureen Gentry. We got into a conversation because my dad's mom's maiden name was Gentry. I told her I wanted to see what was being built by Robertson Brothers on the site we had visited. Because of the Freedom of Information Act, she had to share that with me. I was able to get all the plans that were filed with Rochester Hills. I took pictures of lots, site plans, units, square footage, and more.

Every week, we texted, emailed, called, and communicated with the salespeople, so they knew we were very interested. Around Halloween 2020, they started taking reservations at their headquarters in West Bloomfield. When we went to put our reservation in, there were ten other couples there to put a deposit down for a site at the development. We wanted site 21, and so did another couple. They drew names to see who would get it between the two of us, and we didn't win. Turns out, we got our next choice, site 19, and we ended up with the very best site in the development, we think! The rest is history, and we're now living in our forever (downsized) home!

Opting for a Nomadic Existence

Making the decision to live a nomadic existence requires answering many more detailed questions, such as these:

>> Where will you go (country/region)?

>> Where will you live when you get there?

>> How will you afford to live there? (Will you be living off retirement benefits or savings or working, and if you're working, how will you secure work?)

>> How long will you stay there?

>> What will you need when you get there?

>> What will you do with all your belongings?

>> How will you stay in touch with family and friends — phone, internet service, carrier pigeon?

>> Where will you go for medical care, and how will you pay for it?

>> Who can you call for help?

To find guidance for answering these questions and transitioning to a nomadic lifestyle, we encourage you to check out *Digital Nomads For Dummies*, by Kristin Wilson.

Researching Locations

Before you move anywhere, do your homework to find out whether the place you're considering checks all your boxes. Here are some valuable sources for gathering information about specific locations:

>> City-Data (www.city-data.com) is an excellent resource for researching U.S. cities. Select a state and city to view a large collection of data, including population and income data, median house/condo value, crime rates, climate info, lists of schools in the area, points of interest, and more.

>> Use the Cost of Living Calculator at BestPlaces.net (www.bestplaces.net/cost-of-living) to compare the overall price of goods and services between different locations in the U.S. For an international cost of living comparison, visit www.expatistan.com/cost-of-living.

>> Use social media, such as Facebook and Instagram, to connect with people who live in locations you're considering and pump them for information. Ask about housing, health care, shopping, cost of living, what they do for fun, their favorite restaurants, the quality of area schools, crime, which neighborhoods are popular, and so on.

>> Consult a real estate agent in the area and provide a list of what you're looking for. Pump them for information about the area, too. In the U.S., you can find qualified real estate agents on Realtor.com (www.realtor.com/realestateagents).

TIP

Contact a top agent — not necessarily one who sells high-end real estate, but an agent who moves the most homes in the area. Production is a good gauge of how motivated an agent is to help clients. See Chapter 16 for more about finding and buying a home.

>> If you're considering relocating to a different country, search the web for "relocate to" or "retire in" followed by the location you're interested in — for example, "relocate to Costa Rica." The search results are likely to include links to relocation services that specialize in that area, along with other informative websites and blogs.

Test-Driving a Location or Lifestyle

Before you make an offer on a house or sign a lease for an apartment in the location you think you want to live, we strongly encourage you to try before you buy. Arrange for a short-term rental (at least a couple weeks to a few months) and move to the area on a trial basis. Short-term rentals are more easily accessible than ever through services such as Airbnb (`www.airbnb.com`) and Vrbo (`www.vrbo.com`). Of course, if you have friends or relatives in the area, you may be able to stay for free or swap homes for a couple weeks or months.

REMEMBER

For the full experience, you really need to live in a place for at least a year. Winter can differ distinctly from summer. Some areas have alternating dry and rainy seasons. In some locations, a town can seem alive and vibrant over the course of two weeks and then return to being Sleepy Town the rest of the year. We're not recommending that you test-drive a location for an entire year, but during the limited time you're there, talk to the locals to find out what life is like the rest of the year.

TIP

Consider approaching your research as a two-step process: First, visit the top three to top five areas you're considering and test them out. Then, do a deeper dive to dig up details about cost of living, housing, jobs, and more. Or, perhaps best of all, do your research while you're test-driving the area. Use the opportunity of being on location to scope out neighborhoods and communities.

NO FRESH PRODUCE?!

Greg and Kathy Woods moved from Michigan to Florida and soon discovered that they could no longer indulge in one of their simple pleasures — eating fresh fruit and vegetables from a local produce stand or farmers' market. It was all supermarkets. They missed having easy access to fresh produce, and if you've ever experienced the difference between a garden tomato and one grown in a greenhouse, you can imagine their disappointment.

Had they spent a few weeks in that location before buying a house there, they could have avoided this common mistake.

Whenever you relocate, you can expect to encounter some disappointments. You need to make some trade-offs, but you want to know, before you go all in, what those trade-offs will be. With a temporary relocation, you can take a place for a test-drive and kick the tires before investing a great deal of time, money, and effort.

IN THIS CHAPTER

» Getting your head in the game

» Reaching consensus on the desired goal

» Separating wants from needs

» Taking stock of your resources — financial and otherwise

» Drafting your overall game plan

Chapter **4**

Laying the Groundwork

Before anything else, preparation is the key to success.
— ALEXANDER GRAHAM BELL

Some people put more time and effort into planning a vacation than they do planning to downsize. As a result, they spend far more time, money, and energy than they need to; they feel flustered throughout the entire downsizing experience; and they increase their risk of feeling disappointed by the outcome. They may even end up somewhere they don't want to be with insufficient resources to correct course.

When you're getting ready to downsize, pretend you're planning an Alaskan cruise for 2,500 passengers. You need to prepare the itinerary; line up a ship; hire a captain, and crew; stock the ship with food, beverages, and other supplies; schedule activities and entertainment; and more. And even with the most careful planning, you're likely to encounter some unexpected surprises. You might run out of lobster or bump into an iceberg or two.

Downsizing isn't quite as extreme as executing an ocean voyage, but its success relies almost as much on careful planning. In this chapter, we guide you through the process of laying the groundwork for downsizing, so you'll be better prepared to embark on your journey.

Developing a Positive Mindset

If you're excited about downsizing, this isn't the section for you. You already have the positive mindset needed to overcome the emotional challenges of downsizing. If, on the other hand, you're down on downsizing, you need to get your head in the game.

Maybe you feel like you're being forced to downsize by a control freak relative or circumstances beyond your control. If that's the case, you have three choices:

>> Fight to the death to stay put.

>> Fight a losing battle and be miserable.

>> Embrace downsizing as an opportunity and look forward to the potential benefits and opportunities.

You see where we're going with this — even if you don't want to downsize, we strongly encourage you to go into it with a positive attitude, *especially* if it's inevitable.

REMEMBER

Most people who are forced to downsize are more resistant to the force than to the downsizing. Nobody, especially in the United States of America, likes to be forced to do *anything*. Nobody likes to have their freedom and control taken away. However, the more you're actively and enthusiastically engaged in the process, the more freedom and control you have — and the better the outcome. Our grandparents all fought against our urging them to downsize, and the one regret they all shared after doing it was that they hadn't done it sooner. Kathleen's mom, on the other hand, chose to stay put.

Here are a few ways to nurture a more positive mindset about downsizing:

>> **Research downsizing.** The more you know, the less you'll "no." Chances are, if you're reluctant to downsize, you don't know enough about it. Fear of the unknown is probably driving your thoughts. Reading this book is a good start, but we also encourage you to talk to other people who've downsized and research your downsizing options. Talk to your friends, coworkers, people at church, and so on about their experiences.

>> **Sample your new life.** One way to become more acclimated to the idea of downsizing is to visit your destination location and check it out. You may enjoy it more than you expect. Even if you don't, the visit will equip you with more knowledge on which to base your downsizing and relocation decisions.

>> **Hang out with positive people.** Positive thinking is contagious, so consult people who are enthusiastic about *life* and about downsizing. Negative

thinking is also contagious, so avoid the Debbie and Danny Downers of the world, who can fill your head with all sorts of negative thoughts and catastrophic scenarios.

>> **Center yourself.** Practice yoga, qigong, or tai chi, meditate, pray. All of these disciplines center your mind on the present, which is especially helpful if you're prone to worrying about the future — what hasn't happened yet and therefore isn't part of your reality.

>> **Just do it.** Downsizing is like a fitness program — getting fit can be overwhelming, but walking a mile a day isn't too hard, and once you get started, progress flows naturally. You just need to overcome the inertia of getting started. Downsize one room or one closet of your home to start building momentum.

REMEMBER

Be careful around well-intentioned friends and family members who unintentionally cause you to question or doubt your decisions. They may say something like, "Why would you move from this house? It's so beautiful!" They're not living your life. *You* are.

Consulting with Family Members (or Not)

Downsizing, especially when it involves a major relocation, is a family decision, but it need not involve *everyone* in the family. The decision is primarily up to the people doing the downsizing — the individual or couple or their caregivers. You may want to involve other family members in the decision or just keep them in the loop — letting them know what you're doing without asking for their advice. But you may not. Some family members may not be helpful, and their attempts to "help" can even be counterproductive.

In this section, we guide you through the process of teaming up with your partner (if you have one), figuring out how much family involvement you want or need, and getting everyone moving in the same direction — in other words, we offer some guidance on how to herd cats.

Teaming up with your partner

If you're in a long-term relationship and downsizing together, you're aware of the importance of having a shared vision. As Abraham Lincoln famously warned, "A house divided against itself cannot stand." If your idea of downsizing involves relocating to a cabin on a lake in Minnesota, and your partner dreams of moving to an apartment near downtown Austin, Texas, to enjoy the nightlife, you probably won't be downsizing anytime soon . . . maybe not until *after* the breakup.

Before you involve anyone else in your downsizing decisions, you and your partner need to get on the same page. Here are a few suggestions that may help:

>> **Commit to full transparency.** Communicate openly about your needs and desires. Use the word "know" instead of "no," as in the statement "You don't know enough to say no." Don't say no without giving the other person's position ample consideration; you likely don't know enough about it. In other words, instead of rejecting an idea outright, ask your partner to tell you more about it, so you'll understand what's being proposed.

>> **Leave the past behind.** If you're having to downsize as a result of a financial setback in the past, you can't do anything about that. It's over. You can build a better future, however. Play the hand you've been dealt instead of stewing over it.

>> **Solve — don't blame.** Most disagreements are over problems that need to be solved. Brainstorm a list of solutions, discuss each solution's pros and cons, and choose the most promising one.

>> **Listen twice as much as you speak.** Hear your partner out and ask questions until you fully understand before formulating your opinion.

>> **Research your options together.** If you want to look at different housing options and living arrangements but your partner doesn't, you have a serious problem. You must do it together. It's mentally draining, but you both need to examine your options and decide together what's best.

REMEMBER

If you're the one dragging your feet while your partner is doing all the work, shame on you. Don't blame your partner if the outcome isn't what you expected. Better yet, use this trumpet blast as your wake-up call to play an equal part in your future together. Downsizing requires unity and teamwork.

We were fortunate to be able to work together. What works best for us is using the word "know" over "no." If Kathleen expresses an idea Ralph initially disagrees with, he just says something like, "Tell me more." Usually, when he understands her reasoning and has a sense of how she feels, his "no" changes to a "yes" or "maybe." But even if we ultimately disagree, at least we have a deeper understanding of each other and a sense that we're being heard and our opinions are respected.

Deciding how much input you want and from whom

Assuming that you and your partner (if applicable) are of one mind on downsizing, you may not need to include anyone else in your decision or even keep anyone else in the loop, but doing so may be to your benefit, especially if your decision is going to impact them in some way.

For example, if your daughter relies on you to watch her children (your grandchildren) and you're moving 600 miles away, you may want to give her a heads-up. Likewise, if your downsizing plans involve living close to loved ones who provide the help *you* need, including them in planning meetings would be prudent. You can't always rely on other people, especially if you exclude them from the decision-making process.

Here are some guidelines to help you decide which people to include in your downsizing plans, which ones to exclude, and the level of involvement you want them to have:

>> Loop in anyone who's likely to be significantly impacted by your downsizing decisions, unless you think they'll throw a wrench in the works.

>> Engage others in your decision-making process if they will play a significant role in your future — helping you move, visiting you, driving you to appointments, providing in-home care of any kind. They need to feel included.

>> Seek advice from anyone you know who's been there, done that — people who've downsized successfully and seem happy in their current situation.

>> Think twice about consulting anyone who's opinionated or bossy — anyone who's likely to nitpick your decisions or cause you to doubt your own judgment. If you're just seeking advice on what color to paint a wall, that's fine, but if someone is questioning (or worse, criticizing) your decision to downsize, that's not helpful.

>> Be prepared for additional complexity depending on your family dynamic. Some people have two or three families from previous marriages, and adult children from different families may try or need to be involved in the downsizing process. Some family members can be helpful, whereas others may try to insert themselves uninvited to protect interests they have or think they have.

>> To solicit additional advice, feedback, and support, consider posting about your downsizing adventure on your social media accounts.

WARNING

Post on social media only if you're skilled at filtering or ignoring comments. You may receive a great deal of helpful advice and emotional support, but you can also get information and advice that's counterproductive or discouraging.

We kept everybody in the loop on our downsizing plans and progress, and we received a great deal of helpful information and support. Every Friday night, we visited our plot of land — at first, just some dirt — and posted about our trips to the spot (our "picnics") on Facebook. We received only positive feedback. We would get advice from family members and friends over the course of the week and put it into action over the weekend.

Whenever you buy or sell real estate, all your friends and family members suddenly become real estate experts. The same is true when you have a baby — everyone knows best how to care for and raise that baby, and it's usually at odds with what you think is best. Some of the information may be very helpful; some, not so much. You have to sort it out for yourself and decide what to accept and what to ignore.

SERIAL DOWNSIZERS

Courtland Munroe was a successful midwestern physician. He and his wife, Mary Lou, had four children, and they raised them in a big house, a really BIG HOUSE (4,500 square feet), in Illinois. After their children moved out, Courtland and Mary Lou decided to downsize. They wanted something more manageable and easier to maintain. They discussed options with their kids — A, B, and C — to get their input before deciding what they thought would be best.

First, they downsized to a 2,300-square-foot home in an enormous over-55 community south of Ocala, Florida, called The Villages. The community has its own newspaper, bank, restaurants, doctors, financial advisors, real estate agents, outdoor concerts, and so on. In a relatively short time, the population at The Villages increased from 40,000 to 150,000. The development has enough land to support double the current population. But the community just grew too big, too fast for the Munroe's tastes.

Their second downsize was to a 1,900-square-foot home at Waterman Village — a multi-stage living facility for seniors near Orlando. At the time, it cost $240,000 to move in and $3,900 a month in rent, which included meals, utilities (except electricity), maintenance, and once-a-week maid service. They downsized a third time, while remaining at Waterman Village, to a 1,700-square-foot unit.

Here are their words of advice:

- When you think you've gotten rid of enough, do another pass. Don't keep moving things that you should've gotten rid of the first time.

- If you haven't used something in 20 years, you won't.

- Your treasures may not be treasures to your children. Give them what's special to them, keep what's special to you, and get rid of the rest of your personal treasures.

- Make sure you have one of everything you need — especially tools.

Getting everyone else on the same page

Major life decisions can rattle families and stir up all sorts of conflict and chaos over what's best or what's right, especially when siblings are making decisions that impact the fate of parents with failing health. Getting everyone moving in the same direction is crucial, but it can be very challenging. Many of the suggestions presented in the previous two sections can help — open, honest communication and mutual respect are keys to success. Here are a few additional suggestions for reaching consensus:

>> Gather everyone together at the same time to discuss what you're all thinking and feeling. You can use a video communications app, such as Zoom, to include anyone who can't be physically present. Make it fun. Schedule a meeting followed by a family dinner.

>> Focus the discussion on the issues at hand. Don't let the conversation wander off into exchanging anecdotes about the past or, worse, dredging up past incidents that caused bad feelings among family members.

>> If you're downsizing parents with failing health, keep everyone informed about their condition. Otherwise, siblings who aren't seeing your parents regularly may think everything's okay when it's not. Keep a journal and update siblings regularly.

>> Parents, consider keeping your children informed about your finances, downsizing plans, and any estate planning you're engaged in (see Chapter 7). Engaging in ongoing discussions can be less disruptive than having a big discussion in the middle of a crisis or leaving it up to your children when you're unable to help.

REMEMBER

If possible, avoid excluding any of your adult children from the conversation. If you're downsizing your parents and you have siblings, be sure your brothers and sisters are included in any discussions. Consider how you would feel if you were left out of family meetings, conversations, and decisions.

>> Look for win-win solutions. With compromise, someone always feels that they're the loser, having to give up something. Thinking about solutions more creatively can often benefit everyone.

WARNING

Be careful about handling sensitive issues via text. If it works for you and your family, great. But texting often leads to misunderstandings that quickly spiral out of control. Phone and in-person communications are less prone to escalation.

When he was growing up, our son was close with a great family. The parents (we'll refer to them as the Lockhorns) have two daughters our son's age and two older children. Now, they're empty nesters. Their children have all moved out — they're married or on the path to marriage — and they have a huge home to themselves. You can almost hear echoes where there once was laughter.

To anyone looking at their situation from the outside, the Lockhorns obviously need to downsize, but they can't get on the same page about when or how to do it. In her eyes, all they need is a couple dumpsters and a free weekend. He wants to stay put.

Standoffs like these occur more often than you may think, and finding common ground to break the stalemate can be a huge challenge. It usually requires open, honest dialogue in an atmosphere of mutual love and respect. If you're in a situation like this, we encourage you to start that conversation now.

Tabulating Your Net Worth and Monthly Income

Planning for any major life change requires knowing what you have to work with in terms of financial resources. Examine your net worth and monthly income by doing the following calculations:

>> **Net worth:** To calculate your net worth, add the value of everything you own and subtract the total of what you owe, such as mortgage loan balances and credit card debt. Knowing your net worth is important whenever you're applying for a loan. It serves as a good indicator of how much house you can afford and how much money you'll qualify to borrow. (Your Beanie Babies and Longaberger baskets don't count!)

>> **Monthly income:** Total the amount of money you plan to receive and draw each month to cover your expenses. Depending on how, when, and why you're downsizing, you may receive income from the following sources:

- Employment or business income

- Savings

- Social security income

- Pension income

- Personal retirement savings, such as individual retirement accounts (IRAs) and 401(k)s

- Rents (from property you own and lease)

- Royalties

- Other investment income

TIP

If you haven't done so already, create a My Social Security account at www.ssa.gov/myaccount. You can then log in to obtain valuable information, such as your estimated monthly social security payments when you decide to start claiming your benefits.

REMEMBER

Your net worth can help you gauge your overall financial health. During your working years, your net worth should be rising. After you retire, it may start to decline, which is okay, as long as you don't outlive your savings. Monitor your net worth, checking it at least once a year to ensure you're meeting your financial goals and not heading toward insolvency.

MONEY IN THE BANK

If you're relocating, ideally, you want enough cash in the bank to cover the down payment on your new home, along with closing costs, moving costs, and something extra for unforeseen expenses. Having enough money in the bank enables you to buy a new place without worrying about having to sell your existing home first.

We sold some investments, so we had the cash in the bank that we needed for the down payment, closing costs, and extras for our condo. Because we're over the age of 59½, we could also sell certain retirement assets (Roth IRAs) without having to pay taxes or penalties. At the same time, we obtained a home equity line of credit (for a $300 fee), which we could draw from to cover unexpected expenses. (With a home equity line of credit, you pay interest only on the amount of money you draw.) We didn't draw any equity, but the line of credit gave us some breathing room.

We were able to sell and close on our house a week or two before we closed on our condo, but even if we hadn't sold our house so quickly, we would have been able to move forward with the purchase of the condo.

REMEMBER

If you struggle with personal finances, consult a financial advisor or a family member skilled in money management for advice on handling the financial aspects of downsizing and retirement (if applicable). Some people are too embarrassed about their financial situation to share it with others, but being honest and open about it with someone who knows how to manage finances is the best way to get some control over your future.

Distinguishing between Essentials and Extras

Face it, you don't need much to live. A bedroom, bathroom, and kitchen would do the trick for most individuals or couples. An efficiency apartment. A tiny home. A camper. So, distinguishing between wants and needs usually comes down to prioritizing within a fixed budget.

You know your net worth and monthly income (discussed in the previous section). You're now ready to examine what you need and what you want in light of what you can afford. Here's what to do:

1. **Make two lists — one for essentials and the other for extras.**

   Consider labeling one "What I/We *Need*" and the other "What I/We *Want*."

2. **List everything you need on your essentials list.**

   This list includes all the nonnegotiables, such as housing (mortgage/rent), electricity, gas, water, sewer, taxes, food, clothing, health care, transportation, internet, phone, household maintenance, and so on.

3. **List everything you want (but don't need) on your extras list.**

   This list includes dining out, entertainment, hobbies, gifts, travel (unless it's already on your essentials list), and so on.

4. **Put the items on your extras list in order of priority.**

5. **Assign a dollar value to each item on each list.**

6. **Adjust items on your lists so that their total cost is within your means.**

   Adjustments may include changing dollar amounts, reprioritizing items, and removing low-priority items from your extras list.

The goal of this exercise is to start you thinking about what you really need to live and the lifestyle you can afford. In the next section, we encourage you to draft a budget that provides a more detailed accounting.

Drawing Up Preliminary Plans

Planning for downsizing is like planning a vacation. You come up with your big idea — your vision — and then you break it down into tasks that bring your vision to fruition.

In the case of a vacation, your vision is usually a vacation type or destination. You want to go hiking in the mountains or relax on a beach. You then create plans around that vision. Your plan must cover how you're going to get to your destination and travel when you get there, what you need to pack, how you're going to pay for stuff when you get there, and so on.

With downsizing, your vision usually includes location, housing, and lifestyle (see Chapter 3). To bring your vision to fruition, you need to draw up a budget and a to-do list, create a packing list, schedule activities, and delegate tasks. In this section, we lead you through that process.

Drafting a budget

Unless you're independently wealthy, successful downsizing relies a great deal on your ability to manage a budget. Think of downsizing as a business. You have start-up costs and operational costs, so create a budget for each to identify costs and pinpoint where you'll get the money to cover those costs.

In this section, we take a big-picture look at budgeting. See Chapter 6 for details on handling your finances.

Start-up costs

Start-up costs are those that apply to making the transition, such as the following:

>> Cost of preparing your existing home to sell it (if that's what you've decided to do)

>> Down payment on a new home (if you'll be buying a new home)

>> Moving/storage costs

>> Cost of new furniture and furnishings

To cover these start-up costs, you'll probably rely mostly on savings and the sale of existing assets, not on monthly income. For example, the down payment will come from savings or from the sale of your existing residence. You'll have to come up with a chunk of change from your savings or a separate short-term loan to cover the cost of preparing your home for sale and moving and storing (if necessary) your belongings. As for the cost of furniture and furnishings for your new place, you can pay for those out of the proceeds from the sale of your home, from savings, or by purchasing them on credit (making the payments part of your operational costs).

REMEMBER

During your transition, you may have double the expenses for a time — two house payments, for example, while you're waiting to close the sale of your existing residence. Be sure that you have enough cash or credit (such as a home equity line of credit) to cover the additional costs.

Operational costs

Operational costs are monthly expenses, which include the following:

>> Mortgage/rent

>> Home repairs/maintenance

>> Homeowner's insurance

>> Utilities (electricity, gas, water, sewer, trash)

>> Phone and internet service

>> Auto and auto insurance

>> Health insurance and out-of-pocket medical and dental expenses

>> Groceries

>> Clothing

>> Toiletries

>> Pet care

>> Dining out

>> Entertainment (movies, concerts, plays)

>> Travel, vacations

>> Gifts

WARNING

Regardless of whether you're downsizing into retirement or merely to scale back, don't create a budget that has you living from paycheck to paycheck. Factor in a buffer to cover unexpected expenses and situations. Some couples draft a budget that enables them to live on one income, so that if anything happens to one of them, the other can carry them through at least for a few months.

People have devised all sorts of clever methods for budgeting. One of the simplest is to calculate your fixed expenses — the cost of all essentials — and then pay yourself a monthly allowance you can use to buy anything you want — dinner out, Super Bowl tickets, mani-pedis, whatever. If you're a couple, you may want to divide your monthly allowance between the two of you.

REMEMBER

Software, including smartphone apps, is readily available to help with creating and managing budgets. You can use a basic spreadsheet program such as Excel, a personal finance program such as Quicken, or a personal finance app such as Mint. We recommend using a personal finance program or app, because it can automatically track and categorize your spending to help you stay on budget.

Creating a packing list

Regardless of whether you're moving from one home to another or taking your show on the road as a nomad, you need to figure out what you're taking with you. We get into the nitty-gritty of sorting belongings in Part 3 of this book, but we encourage you to start thinking now about what you'll be keeping and what you'll be getting rid of.

TIP

Create a separate list for each room in the house and divide each list in two — one side for items you plan to keep, and the other for items you know you're going to get rid of. Focus on large items, such as furniture, kitchen appliances, cars, boats, and large power tools. You can deal with the smaller items as you sort your belongings in Part 3.

Making a to-do list

Perhaps the most important step to laying the groundwork for downsizing is creating a *to-do list* — a comprehensive list of everything that needs to be done to move you from point A to point B, from your current living situation to your new life.

Everyone's downsizing to-do list is unique. Lists vary based on the person's (or couple's) current situation, downsizing goals, and what has already been done. For example, someone who's downsizing from a large home to a small condo will have a very different to-do list from someone who's getting rid of nearly all their personal possessions, buying a camper, and hitting the road. Here's a sample to inspire you to start creating your own to-do list:

1. **Choose a location and lifestyle.**

2. **Have a meeting of the minds with my loved ones to ensure that we're all in agreement.**

3. **Get prequalified for a mortgage loan (unless you're paying in cash, not taking out a mortgage loan).**

4. **Connect with a great real estate agent.**

5. **Research existing homes or new construction.**

6. **Downsize belongings by half.**

7. **Place existing home on the market.**

8. **Make an offer on an existing home or new construction.**

9. **Pack.**

10. **Move.**

After you have a general list, you can break down the process even further by creating separate lists for each step. For example, you can break down Step 3 into researching lenders and loan rates, choosing a lender, and providing the required paperwork. You can break down Step 7 into lining up contractors to address any repairs and maintenance issues, and meeting with your real estate agent. For Step 9, you can break it down room by room.

TIP

Follow Stephen R. Covey's advice from his book *The 7 Habits of Highly Effective People* to "start with the end in mind." As you create your list, envision the day you'll be transitioning to your new downsized life. Then, list all the steps you must take to reach that point.

Scheduling activities

With your to-do list (from the previous section) in hand, start scheduling activities. For some items on your list, you can simply choose a deadline — a date by which the task will be completed. For other items on the list, you may schedule a date and time. What's important is that every item on the list has a point in time when it will be completed. As the old saying goes, "A goal without a deadline is merely a wish." And wishes often go unfulfilled when they're neglected. Without goals, you'd never score in soccer, football, hockey, or lacrosse.

REMEMBER

With new construction, schedule time to visit the building site frequently to monitor progress, ask questions, and communicate any concerns you have. Builders don't catch everything. And regardless of whether you're buying an existing home or building a new home, schedule time to meet the five neighbors on each side of you and the ten across the street. In real estate, this is known as the *5, 5, 10 rule*. If you're really interested in what's going on in the area, knock on some doors to find out.

SCHEDULING FOR NEW CONSTRUCTION

If your downsizing plans include building a new home, expect a long to-do list and a packed schedule. Our to-do list included the following:

- Choose appliances
- Choose blinds
- Choose flooring
- Choose room colors (paint)
- Choose cabinets
- Visit the building site
- Meet the neighbors

Throughout the process, we needed to schedule meetings with the builder to modify the floor plan to better fit our furniture. The cabinet supplier needed to know room dimensions for the cabinets and countertops, and the builder needed to know the dimensions of our bed, living room furniture, and large kitchen appliances to fine-tune the floor plan.

In addition to scheduling meetings with the builder and suppliers, we scheduled some time for entertainment and started referring to this time as our Friday night picnics. We would visit our lot and picnic on the lawn. We met the family across the street and shared lemonade. During several of our Friday night picnics, we would tour nearby business districts and eat out at the local restaurants. Adding some fun to the work was a great stress reliever.

TIP

If you're buying furniture, appliances, or flooring, schedule time to visit the design center in each store and speak with the professionals on staff to get advice. You can usually walk around on your own to check out what's available and even measure items to see how they'll fit, but you may want to get professional advice when you're picking out styles and colors.

Delegating duties

With a to-do list and a schedule, you know *what* needs to be done and *when*. Now, you just need to know *who* is in charge of each task — who's accountable for completing each task or ensuring it's completed by the scheduled date and time?

TEAMING UP WITH YOUR PARTNER

We downsized as a team. We didn't divvy up tasks as many couples choose to do because we work well together and we both have flexible schedules. It wasn't as if one of us was working a day job and needed the other to do all the heavy lifting, so we were able to attend all scheduled meetings together, visit the building site together, and make all the decisions together.

If you're downsizing with a partner and one of you is working 60 hours a week, you may not have the luxury of doing everything together. Instead, you'll need to find your comfort level and communicate clearly.

Downsizing is very hands-on, especially if you're building a new home. It's a huge step. You're moving to what, in many cases, is your last home. You're setting the stage for the next 10–20 years of your life. You don't want to place the burden of making decisions that impact both your lives on just one of you. This may be your last major life decision . . . not to put any pressure on you.

If you're taking care of everything on your own, delegating the work and responsibilities isn't an issue, but if you're relying on others to contribute, assign each task to one or more individuals. Provide each person (professional or not) with a personalized to-do list along with deadlines and let them work out the details. Keep in touch to monitor their progress and ask whether they need help or guidance but let them handle the details. Don't try to micromanage the process — micromanaging hurts morale.

IN THIS CHAPTER

» **Making downsizing a family affair**

» **Recruiting friends to pitch in**

» **Outsourcing to professionals to ease your burden**

» **Keeping everyone motivated**

» **Helping your parents or other loved ones downsize**

Chapter **5**

Rallying the Troops

Many hands make light work.

— PROVERB

D ownsizing can be a major operation involving both tasks that require the ability to perform manual labor — sorting, packing, and hauling belongings from one place to another — and tasks that require particular expertise — estate planning, budgeting/financial management, examining legal contracts, selling an existing home, finding (or building) a new home, and so on.

If you're one of those people who believes that to do it right, you have to do it yourself (or if yours is a relatively simple downsize), you may decide to fly solo, perhaps relying only on your partner to pick up the slack. If, however, you're looking at a last-move-of-your-life transition, we strongly encourage you to consider making downsizing a team effort. Recruiting the right people to help — family members, friends, and professionals — can expedite the process, help you make better-informed decisions, and ease your burden so that you can focus on higher-level tasks, such as planning, scheduling, and coordinating. With the help of a great team, you're likely to achieve a better downsizing outcome.

In this chapter, we lead you through the process of identifying the type of help and helpers you need and coordinating their efforts.

Tapping Your Family for Help

The strength of a family, like the strength of an army, lies in its loyalty to each other.

— MARIO PUZO

Family is usually the go-to source for help when you really need it. Family members are typically willing to help as long as someone tells them what to do. However, some family members are better equipped to provide the help you need, and you may not want the help you're likely to get from others.

In this section, we sort out the type of help family members are often great at providing from the type of "help" you don't want.

REMEMBER

When approaching family members and friends for help, don't make them feel obligated. After identifying the ones you want on your downsizing team, feel them out by talking about your plans. You can usually tell from the way they react whether they're interested in helping. They may offer to help outright, or they may respond with a heavy sigh, saying something like, "I'd hate to be you" — a sure sign that they're not at all interested in helping you.

TIP

If you have any family members with pickup trucks, stay close to them — they just may come in handy!

Knowing the type of help family members can provide

Family members typically fall into the manual labor category. They're generally useful for providing the following assistance:

>> Gathering boxes, bags, tape, and other packing supplies

>> Sorting and packing

>> Cleaning

>> Preparing meals

>> Scheduling, delegating, and coordinating tasks (see the later section "Delegating and Coordinating with Team Members" for details)

>> Deciding what to keep in the family and what to get rid of, which is perhaps the most difficult task of all (see Chapter 9 for details)

>> Running errands, such as driving items to charity organizations and the local trash dump.

For example, maybe your daughter can clear out closets and bedrooms, your brother can clean the garage, and your nieces and nephews can label boxes, while you consult with family members to decide who gets what.

REMEMBER

While family members are often relegated to packing, lifting, and moving, some may be highly skilled professionals who can help with estate planning, buying and selling real estate, financial planning, or other downsizing tasks. Don't overlook family members for professional tasks. For more about getting professional help, check out the section "Hiring Professionals" later in this chapter.

Recognizing the type of help you don't want

Family — you gotta love 'em, but you don't have to involve every family member in your downsizing adventure. Some family members may not be qualified to provide the help you need or desire. Here are the types to cross off your roster:

>> Control freaks, who think they know better than you how to live *your* life

>> Yes-men or yes-women, who tell you what they think you want to hear instead of what they really think

>> Lazy people, like the armchair quarterback who will sit in the recliner and watch while everyone else does all the work (they'll demotivate your crew)

>> Crazy makers, whose lack of focus or frenetic energy makes you anxious

>> Careless klutzes, who will break your belongings and leave you with a bigger mess than when they started

WARNING

Downsizing makes everyone an expert, even if they aren't, so be prepared to filter the advice and "help" you're being offered. You don't want know-it-alls, nor do you want people simply mirroring you. You need people in your corner who think about the things you tend to overlook and ask, "Have you considered this? Have you considered that?"

Getting a Little Help from Your Friends

Friends can help the same way family members typically do — sorting, packing, and hauling. However, your friends can generally do more for you with respect to offering advice.

As your friends, they're probably also your peers — they're about the same age as you, grew up during the same era, and are in the same socioeconomic bracket.

They get you — they know your interests and lifestyle preferences — so they can probably serve as a better source than family members for advice on downsizing, especially if they've already been through the process.

Friends can be especially useful in the following ways:

>> Providing suggestions for locations and lifestyle options

>> Serving as a sounding board for your thoughts and ideas

>> Referring you to reputable and reliable businesses and professionals

>> Marketing your home through their personal and professional network

>> Providing support and encouragement throughout the process

>> Holding you accountable to meet your downsizing goals

Depending on how close you are with your friends, they may decide to join you on your downsizing adventure!

Hiring Professionals

Professionals are the people you hire to perform the tasks that you're unable or unwilling to do or that they can do better. We're big fans of hiring professionals. Why? Although you pay a premium for professional help, that premium covers the following benefits:

>> Higher-quality work, meaning better outcomes

>> Faster results

>> Reduced chance of costly mistakes

>> Warranties, in some cases

>> Peace of mind, and less stress

In the following sections, we introduce the professionals who often play a role in downsizing and explain how they can help ease the burden (and your mind) while empowering you to achieve a better outcome.

TIP

Before hiring anyone, always get at least three quotes, check references from current and past customers/clients, and interview the top candidates for the job.

A financial advisor

Downsizing is all about managing your finances to cover the cost of the lifestyle you desire and can afford and, if you're downsizing into retirement, making sure you don't outlive your savings. A knowledgeable and skilled financial advisor can help you with the financial aspects of downsizing in the following ways:

>> Offering strategies to minimize your tax burden so you have more money to work with, including how to draw money from your retirement accounts so you pay the least amount of tax possible

>> Recommending investment options with the right risk-reward profile for you

>> Assisting with estate planning to ensure that your heirs receive more of your assets and the government receives less

>> Assisting you in developing a budget that enables you to live within your means without having to make too many sacrifices

REMEMBER

Finances play a large role in downsizing, so be sure you have a qualified financial advisor in your corner to help you build and manage your wealth. A good financial advisor can save you multiples of what you pay for their services.

A certified public accountant

In addition to a financial manager (see the previous section), who's in charge of your big financial picture, consider hiring a certified public accountant (CPA) to provide more specific financial advice. Having a CPA is especially helpful if your finances are complex (for example, you're self-employed or a large part of your income is from investments) and if you plan to finance the purchase of your next home. Your CPA can ensure that you show enough income on paper to qualify for the mortgage amount you're seeking.

For example, we receive a significant portion of our income from a variety of investments, so we don't have pay stubs from jobs to prove that we have sufficient income to cover monthly mortgage payments. To enable us to secure a mortgage loan, our CPA wrote up a clarification to show that while our income alone might not qualify us, our income plus positive cash flow from our investments would. The more complicated your financial situation is, the more likely you're going to want a CPA.

Attorneys

TIP

We use the plural, *attorneys*, here, because we recommend that you work with attorneys who specialize in different areas of law. General-practice attorneys do it all, but they often spend more time on research and they charge by the hour (often by fractions of the hour), so you end up paying more for a lower level of expertise. Here are the types of attorneys you may find most helpful when downsizing:

>> **Real estate attorney:** Whenever you're closing on the sale or purchase of a property, have a real estate attorney review the closing papers, preferably before the scheduled closing, and take your attorney to the closing to handle any surprises.

>> **Condo/HOA lawyer:** If you're buying a condo or buying into an addition that has a homeowner association (HOA), have an attorney look over the condo/HOA agreements before you sign them.

>> **Trust/estate lawyer:** You'll need an attorney's help with putting all your assets into a trust so they don't end up in probate when you die. Probate is a costly hassle for heirs. (See Chapter 7 for details.)

REMEMBER

According to LegalJobs.io, lawyers specialize in 26 different areas. When you're in the market for a lawyer, choose the one who's best suited for the specific issue you need resolved.

MEET OUR LAWYERS

When we decided to downsize from our home to a condominium, we used two lawyers:

- **An estate attorney to put all our assets into a trust.** Our attorney added the condo to the trust as soon as we closed on it.

- **An attorney who specializes in condo/HOA documents.** He reviewed the master deed, bylaws, and all the other documents prior to closing.

Because we've been in real estate our entire lives, we didn't use an attorney for the closing, but unless you have specialized training in this area, you should have an attorney at the closing when you're buying any real estate. We hired a title company to look over the paperwork, which gave us another set of eyes on the legal documents.

Appraisers

One of the big challenges of downsizing is being sure that you're getting a fair price for whatever you're selling — whether it's your family home or a Picasso you found while cleaning out your attic. When you have anything of value to sell, we strongly recommend that you consult an appraiser first.

As with attorneys, be sure to hire an appraiser who specializes in the type of appraisal you need, such as the following:

>> **Real estate appraiser** for homes and land

>> **Insurance appraiser** to ensure adequate coverage for any loss or damage of personal property

>> **Estate appraiser** to determine the value of property and ensure equitable distribution

>> **Business appraiser** to estimate the value of a business for a merger, acquisition, or succession planning

TIP

If your downsizing plan involves selling your home, get an appraisal to maximize your price. Don't settle for the comparative market analysis from a real estate agent. Despite being in real estate all our lives and knowing the property values in our area, we still order appraisals whenever we're second-guessing ourselves, to be sure that we're getting a professional opinion from someone who doesn't have a vested interest in the outcome. An appraiser can ensure that you're not overpaying or underselling.

During the writing of this book, the housing market was so hot that you could list your home for nearly any price, and you'd get it.

TIP

When you're building your A-Team, start with one professional you trust and network through that person to find other qualified professionals. For example, start with a top-notch financial advisor and ask for referrals to attorneys, accountants, and others, so you're not simply rolling the dice when choosing people to add to your team.

Real estate agents

When downsizing, you're typically selling one home and buying another, so you probably need two agents.

>> A *buyer's agent* represents the person buying the property. They show homes that match their clients' criteria; help clients evaluate properties; keep them

informed about market conditions; help their clients prepare, submit, and negotiate offers; and arrange the closing They often act as a liaison between their clients and loan officers, who help buyers arrange financing.

>> A *seller's agent* represents the person selling the property and has a *fiduciary responsibility* to the seller, meaning the agent is required to act in the best interests of the seller. The seller's agent markets the property, works with buyer's agents to arrange showings, and advises the seller on all offers that come in — accepting, rejecting, and countering them. The seller's agent also facilitates the closing and deals with any other post-sale issues.

REMEMBER

We recommend that you use a seller's agent to sell your property and a buyer's agent to find and buy your new home. If you're buying in different markets — for example, selling in New York and buying in Arizona — having a separate agent in each location is an absolute necessity. But even if you're buying and selling a home in the same vicinity, you should seriously consider using a separate buyer's and seller's agent.

You can use a dual agent to represent you in both transactions, but if you were getting brain and heart surgery, would you use the same surgeon for both? Of course not! You would want a specialist for each. In the same way, choose a specialist when buying and selling real estate.

TIP

Ask around to find out who's the top-performing agent in the market you're interested in. The best agent doesn't charge any more than the worst agent. Choose an agent with a solid track record. Avoid newbies — let other customers break them in. Using a seasoned agent may even save you some money.

A bank, mortgage company, or loan officer

Many people downsize to reduce their debt and expenses. They don't even want to think about taking out *another* loan. However, downsizing often involves taking out a loan or engaging in some creative financing maneuvers that a bank, mortgage company, or loan officer can help facilitate and even advise on.

For example, even if you'll have enough money in the bank after selling your existing home to buy a new home, you may want to take out a mortgage to free up money for something else, such as travel. Or you may want to take out a reverse mortgage to help with cash flow. Having a loan professional on your team can make it easier to execute your financial plan.

TIP

If you don't have an ongoing relationship with a loan officer you trust, consider borrowing money through a local credit union, if one is available to you. Credit unions are owned by their members and offer rates that are tough to beat. The bankers aren't knocking on doors to drum up business or driving fancy cars.

They're more like order takers who follow the system: "Here's the rate; here's the cost." It's very transparent.

Your other option is to deal with a loan officer at a commercial bank or a mortgage company. In our real estate business, we use a few loan officers consistently — people who are on top of it, doing it every day, and have efficient systems and technology in place. One loan officer we work with has an entire mortgage team. She doesn't charge any more than anyone else because she can make up her costs with the volume of business she does. What's key is that you have a loan officer on your team who can make the process go as smoothly as possible.

A title company

If you're buying or selling a home, work with your real estate agent to choose a reliable, reputable title company — one that has a strong reputation for smooth closings. The title company ensures that the deed to the property is accurate and complete so the legal owner of the property doesn't encounter any nasty surprises later (for example, the true deed holder showing up to claim the property). The title company also issues a title insurance policy to protect against nasty surprises.

REMEMBER

Even if you buy a newly constructed home, you need a title insurance policy. As the construction on your new home is nearing completion, visit your title company to order a title insurance policy.

A home inspector or builder

If you're buying an existing home, contact your village, city, township, or county office to arrange a certificate of occupancy inspection on the property. This is the best type of inspection money can buy, because you get a team of inspectors that specialize in all areas of home construction: a builder, an electrician, a plumber, an HVAC specialist, and so on. It's much better than hiring a "home inspector" you don't know.

Second best is to have someone you know in home construction inspect the property for you: a licensed builder, roofer, plumber, or electrician. We had a window contractor (a friend who's a builder) check our condo for everything that was outside our scope of knowledge. Even if you're knowledgeable, always have another set of eyes look at a property before you close on it; they're likely to see something you overlooked.

Downsizing pros

One of the easiest ways to downsize is to outsource the project, or parts of it, to downsizing professionals, such as the following:

TIP

>> Downsizing specialist (such as a Senior Move Manager), who can handle everything, including developing a moving plan, sorting belongings, overseeing the sale of unwanted items, hiring a real estate agent, arranging for storage, packing, shipping, unpacking, and so on

To find a qualified Senior Move Manager, search the National Association of Specialty & Senior Move Managers directory at www.nasmm.org/find-a-move-manager.

>> Professional organizer

>> Auctioneer

>> Estate sale specialist

Movers

If you have burly relatives with big trucks and trailers willing to move you, more power to you. Otherwise, consider hiring a moving company. You'll pay more for professionals than for a move-it-yourself crew, but you may save money in the long run in terms of less damage to your belongings, the place you're moving from, and the place you're moving to; less risk of injury; less worry; and more time and energy to focus on higher-level tasks, such as sorting and organizing.

TIP

To save money, you can pack and label everything yourself and have the movers transport it.

WARNING

Don't store boxes in a home you're trying to sell — they're not appealing and can detract from the home's perceived value. Move your boxes to storage instead. Some moving companies have their own storage facilities and may offer storage for less than what you would pay separately for that service.

An interior designer

If you're downsizing to a different home, you want to make it yours, and you're not skilled at interior decorating, consider hiring a professional designer. You may hire a designer for only one or two rooms or for the entire home. Here's what an interior designer can do for you:

MOVING? HIRE A PRO!

If you have the money, we strongly recommend hiring a reputable, reliable moving company. The movers we hired performed an initial assessment. They inspected every inch of the house and garage and figured out almost to the box the number needed for our clothing and everything in our kitchen cabinets. They eyeballed big, bulky items, including thousands of pounds of weights and exercise equipment, to determine ahead of time the best strategy for moving them. They really had to know what they were doing to move some of our belongings safely and without damaging anything.

One summer day, the company sent two people to pack up all our crystal, china, serving dishes, seasonal items, books, small appliances, and most of what we had in the garage. By moving day, they had everything packed and labeled, and had all the logistics worked out for carrying things from the house and garage to the trucks without damaging anything. They packed the trucks so efficiently that you'd have a tough time slipping a piece of paper between any two items!

>> Arrange your belongings in the new space for optimum comfort, movement, and aesthetics.

>> Help you choose colors and patterns.

>> Help you choose furniture, appliances, flooring, window dressings, and décor that are consistent with the look and feel you desire and within your budget.

When we were in the market for window treatments, we were surprised to discover *power blinds* — window blinds that you can open and close with a remote control! Interior designers know what's in and what's on its way out and can introduce you to possibilities you may never have discovered on your own.

REMEMBER

Order early. Supply chain disruptions, primarily due to the COVID-19 pandemic, have resulted in significant delays in the delivery of furniture, appliances, and home furnishings. You may be waiting months to a year or longer to receive items if you don't order early.

Health-care professionals

Depending on your situation and your reason for downsizing, you may benefit from having your doctor or other treatment providers on your team. Health-care professionals can provide valuable advice to inform your decisions about accessibility and mobility issues, the level of care you or your partner requires and will require, and lifestyle factors that can help you improve and maintain your health as you age. For example, having to climb stairs may not be a big deal now, but ten years from now, it may be. According to one study, one in four adults age 65 and older fall each year, with most falls occurring in the home.

TIP

If you never want to move again, create a plan for *aging in place*, meaning choosing a location or facility that provides increasing access to the care you need as you grow older and perhaps require more assistance. You may choose to move to a facility that offers different levels of care, from independent living to assisted living, or opt for relying more on family members in the future or hiring homecare professionals if they become necessary.

Delegating and Coordinating with Team Members

As you rally your troops for your downsizing project, your primary focus becomes delegating and coordinating everyone's efforts. You'll start to lose people if you're disorganized or fail to communicate clearly what they need to do and when it needs to be done. We discuss scheduling tasks and delegating duties in detail in Chapter 4, but you may also benefit from creating a list of everyone on your team, along with notes about what you need them to do and dates by which you need them to complete their tasks. Some people on your team may appreciate having a detailed to-do list spelling out exactly what you need them to do and when.

Of course, not everyone on your team needs a detailed to-do list. For your real estate agent, you may pencil in a date for starting your search for an agent, a deadline for choosing an agent, and a target date for selling or buying a property. If you hire an auctioneer, you may set a date for the auctioneer to visit and evaluate what you'll be auctioning off and another date for the auction.

REMEMBER

Handing someone a detailed to-do list may strike you as a level of micromanagement that doesn't fit your style, but people tend to perform better when you tell them exactly what to do and when you need it done. If you're disorganized and people are standing around doing nothing or bumping into one another, they're not going to stick around very long.

Motivating Your Crew

Keeping your crew motivated and on task can be a huge challenge, especially if you have some reluctant volunteers. Here are a few tips for making downsizing more fun, exciting, and productive:

» Throw a downsizing party. Invite everyone you know to come shopping, giving them first dibs on your best stuff.

» Be positive. Mood is contagious. If you set a positive mood, everyone will be happier and more productive.

» Play upbeat music to get everyone in the groove.

» Schedule downsizing activities around lunch or dinner, with the meal following the work. You can even schedule a decluttering weekend, alternating work with fun activities and outings.

» Provide snacks and drinks and take breaks every hour or so if you're working through the day.

» Tackle one room or space at a time to stay on task. If you have many helpers, assign one or two people to each space.

» Host a decluttering party with prize drawings (for belongings you want to get rid of). To add to the fun, give each guest one opportunity to "steal" an item from someone else.

» Throw an unpacking party at the new place with a celebration dinner to follow.

» Introduce a challenge — for example, the first person or team to pack/unpack their assigned room gets to choose the restaurant. Or have a race — the person or team that downsizes the most in an hour wins first pick of whatever you decide to get rid of.

REMEMBER

The best ways to motivate people are to be organized and to communicate clearly. People will generally do what they're told, don't like other people wasting their time, and won't take the initiative. You need to tell your helpers what needs to be done and how you want it done, so they won't have to think too much about it.

Helping a Loved One Downsize

Ideally, you're the one downsizing and calling the shots, but that's not always the case. Sometimes, loved ones, usually parents or grandparents, need to downsize and are unable or unwilling to do it themselves. They may even insist on staying put in a house that has become too much for them and poses an increasing risk to their health and safety.

How do you help people who refuse to admit they need help? How do you convince someone to move when they're adamant about staying put? How do you make decisions about what's best for someone when you're 99.9 percent sure they'll hold it against you for the rest of their life?

Well, we can't guarantee that we have all the answers, but we can offer some guidance on how to handle reluctant downsizers diplomatically and effectively and make the process more efficient, regardless of whether your loved one is excited or reluctant about the prospect of downsizing.

Just talk about it

Nearly every change begins with an idea and a conversation, not with a decision or a command (tough love), so regardless of how your loved ones feel about downsizing, starting with a conversation is best. Assume that whatever your loved ones want is what's best for them, as long as it's not placing their health and safety at too much risk. Remember that life is inherently risky, so "too much" is a matter of how much risk and worry your loved ones and you can tolerate.

Introduce the topic lightly with a more exploratory tone. For example, you may ask your parents, "Have you given any thought to downsizing?" Or you may offer an observation to one of your parents, such as "I noticed that Mom seems to be having trouble recalling where she's put things." The goal is to start a conversation; you don't need to know where it's headed. You just want to get your loved ones thinking and talking about what they're dealing with. You want to increase their awareness of what you perceive as a looming problem that will eventually need to be resolved.

WARNING

Avoid the temptation to pressure or coerce someone into downsizing before they're ready. Any pressure is likely to be counterproductive, causing your loved ones to dig in their heels.

Having these discussions with parents is tough because you're all experiencing a role reversal. As you were growing up, your parents were telling you what was best for you and what you should do. Now, you're finding yourself in a position in which you feel a need to tell them what's best for them and what *they* need to do. Sometimes, taking a more collaborative approach can help with this challenging transition. For example, you may suggest, "Last weekend, I went through a bunch of stuff I had in storage and got rid of more than half of it. If you'd like, I can help you do some reorganizing next weekend. Maybe we'll find some cool stuff!"

Ease the transition

If your loved ones have been living in the same home in the same neighborhood in the same town or city for a long, long time, you may have two factors working against you: their comfort and their fear of the unknown. Moving to an unfamiliar home in an unfamiliar area full of strangers may strike them as both scary and unnecessary. Here are a few ways to ease the transition:

TIP

>> Working together, create a pros and cons list for their current living situation and alternative living arrangements. Do your homework, so you have at least a few alternatives to offer and information about them.

"No" means "know." When loved ones say "no" to downsizing, they're often saying they don't "know" enough to say "yes." Your job is to find out their reasons for not downsizing so you can chip away at every objection they may have. Creating a list of pros and cons is a good way to find out why your loved ones are saying "no" and to provide the information and insight they need to say "yes."

>> Frame downsizing as an opportunity to free up capital for a more comfortable and enjoyable future instead of as a solution to a problem (the problem being that your loved ones are getting older and may be increasingly less capable of caring for themselves).

>> Help them review their finances (see Chapter 6) to show them what they can afford. They may think they can't afford a certain lifestyle they would like when they really can afford it. Having a financial advisor involved in this discussion can be beneficial.

>> Team up with your loved ones to create a wish list of everything they would like in a new living arrangement so they can have more input in the choices.

>> Start the decluttering process early, even before you have a new home or lifestyle lined up. The fewer belongings you have to deal with later, the smoother the transition will be.

>> Take your loved ones on tours of different homes, housing additions, communities, and facilities. They may not be aware of what's available.

>> Choose a home/living arrangement that's similar to the one they currently have. In other words, arrange for a move to something that's not dramatically different from what they have now but is far more manageable.

>> Make wherever they live more like home. Be sure they have their most memorable belongings. Hang their favorite photos on the wall or print photo albums to place on end tables or a coffee table or upload them to a digital photo frame.

CLASSROOM CONDO

Builders are coming up with all sorts of creative ideas for developing housing units, especially for seniors. Here in Michigan, we have a developer who buys old schools no longer in use and develops them into condos. You can have a condo the size of a classroom, and the entire building is wheelchair accessible.

We heard about one of these when it was in an early stage of development, and we took Kathleen's grandma to look at it. She loved it and was happy there till the day she died.

Sometimes you need to think outside the box and offer creative solutions to persuade someone to make the change. It's not always easy, but it can be fun and rewarding!

Start downsizing the least-used areas

Most of the "junk" you're going to get rid of as you downsize your loved ones is stored in the least-used areas of the home — the basement, attic, crawl space, shed, or garage — so start there. Getting started is half the battle, and you can build momentum on your growing sense of accomplishment because you'll be getting rid of a boatload of belongings. Then you can move to the closets, shelves, cabinets, and filing cabinets. It's pretty much downhill from there — furniture and appliances. (See Part 3 for more about decluttering.)

Provide emotional support

Downsizing can be very emotional. We're talking major life changes here, especially if your loved ones stand to lose some freedom and independence. Here are a few practical ways to provide emotional support:

>> Show empathy. Listen to your loved ones and validate their feelings. They may be grieving a loss. Admit that the change is difficult. Don't argue with their feelings.

>> Let your loved ones make as many of the decisions as is reasonable. Offer your opinion, guidance, and support, but let them call the shots. Of course, if they're making choices that you have good reason to believe are not in their long-term best interests, you may need to be more assertive with your opinions.

>> Ask questions until you fully understand what your loved ones want before offering your opinions or input. As a rule of thumb, listen twice as much as you speak.

» Listen when your loved ones want to tell stories about precious belongings, even if you've heard those stories a hundred times already. You may even ask them about certain items you come across while decluttering, such as "Where did you get this?" or "Who gave this to you?"

» Check in with your loved ones during the process to make sure they're dealing with it okay. Ask how they're feeling and give 'em a hug every now and then.

» Set aside any items your loved ones are having trouble giving up and decide what to do with them later in the process, so you can continue to progress toward your goal. Return to these things later, when you have the time and space to deal with their emotional attachment in a more patient and understanding way.

Make it fun

You're probably busy. You work 40+ hours a week. You have your own nuclear family to care for. You coach Little League. You probably don't have a lot of extra time and energy to devote to family members who need to downsize and are dragging their feet. Given the fact that you're reading this book, you're probably also highly efficient, and you want to get this done and over in a weekend, maybe two. So, you approach downsizing as a military operation — "Pack 'em up, and move 'em out!"

Authoritative may not be the best management style for easing emotional strain and boosting productivity. It's more likely to leave everyone in a state of shock. Instead, make your downsizing operation pleasant and fun, as explained in the earlier section "Motivating Your Crew."

Protecting and Leveraging Your Assets

Manage the financial aspects of downsizing to get the most out of your money and avoid outliving your nest egg.

Discover ways to reduce expenses and create new income streams when you're living on a fixed income.

Get up to speed on estate planning to protect your assets and interests and those of your heirs when you're unable to do so yourself.

Explore various methods of cashing out the equity in your home to help finance your post-downsizing lifestyle.

IN THIS CHAPTER

» Figuring out how much money you have to work with

» Examining your monthly income and expenses

» Stretching your dollars when you're on a fixed income

» Discovering tips and tricks for slashing expenses

» Creating new income streams

Chapter **6**

Getting a Handle on Your Finances

Wealth is the ability to fully experience life.

— HENRY DAVID THOREAU

Money gets a bad rap. The root of all evil? Hogwash! Greed may be the root of all evil, but not money. Can't buy happiness? Maybe, but it can sure buy comfort, peace of mind, awesome adventures, sumptuous dinners out, and extravagant parties. More to the point of this book, money can turn downsizing from a cold, cramped tent camp into a cozy cottage on the beach. Money is the means for making your downsizing dreams your new reality, so you need to get a handle on it and manage it wisely.

In this chapter, we bring you up to speed on the basics of money management, so you know how much money you have to work with — in cash (savings), equity (anything of value you can sell), and debt (other people's money) — and what your monthly budget is likely to look like (income minus expenses). We also offer some tips and tricks on the two key financial topics of how to spend less and earn more when money gets tight.

As you crunch the numbers, you'll begin to shape your vision of what's possible. You may find that you need to scale back your downsizing dreams a bit, or you may be pleasantly surprised to discover that you can afford a much more ambitious future than you initially resigned yourself to!

Calculating Your Net Worth

Net worth is the amount of money you would have if you sold all your stuff and paid off all your debts. Officially, the equation goes like this:

Net worth = Assets – Liabilities

We like to think of it more like this:

Net worth = Own – Owe

A strong positive net worth indicates that you

» Own more than you owe

» Can afford to pay off all your loans at any time by liquidating assets

» Probably know more about net worth than you realize

REMEMBER

Listing *everything you own* is a major piece of this work; so is listing *everything you owe*. Only with this approach can you really see where you stand financially and start working toward where you want to be.

To calculate your net worth, take the following steps:

1. **List everything of value you own.**

   Include your cash savings, retirement/investment accounts, the money stuffed in your mattress, your house, cars, boats, jewelry, tools, electronics, private island . . . whatever you can withdraw from an account or sell for cash.

2. **Write a reasonable estimate of each item's value next to it.**

3. **Total the value of all the items to determine the value of what you own.**

4. **List all your loans.**

   Include the first and second mortgage on your home, your car loans, boat loans, any construction loans, credit cards, any personal loans, and so on.

5. **Write the current balance next to each loan.**

6. **Total the balances to determine what you owe.**

7. **Subtract what you owe (Step 6) from the value of what you own (Step 3).**

   The remaining amount is your net worth.

TIP

Use a personal finance program, such as Quicken, or a spreadsheet program to monitor your net worth. Your net worth is a great gauge for measuring your financial progress. It should rise over the course of your early years leading up to retirement. From that point, if it tapers off over the course of your retirement years, that's okay, as long as you don't run out of money before your ticker stops ticking.

Your net worth is like a report card reflecting your performance in the realm of personal financial management. Knowing your net worth can come in very handy as you formulate and execute your downsizing plans. With net worth in hand, you're better equipped to do the following:

» Determine how much money you have available to support your downsized life.

» Prove to banks that you're creditworthy, so you can qualify for loans at competitive interest rates.

» Facilitate estate planning by helping to determine the equitable distribution of your wealth to your heirs.

» Budget effectively — you can quickly and easily recognize when you're burning through your savings too fast, or whether you have extra to spend or invest.

REMEMBER

A large positive net worth can help you borrow money at competitive interest rates. A low or even a negative net worth can limit your downsizing options significantly, but it's not necessarily catastrophic, assuming you have a strong cash flow (more income than expenses) or you can come up with a brilliant idea to make money. A good credit score (670–739) is also essential for qualifying for a loan, so if your score is below 700 work toward improving it. You can find smartphone apps, such as the Experian app, for tracking and improving your credit score. A great score is anything over 800. Generally, the people most in need of money can't borrow it, while people who have plenty of money can borrow as much as they want!

FINDING CASH UNDER THE FLOORBOARDS

Over the course of Ralph's career in real estate, he has invested in foreclosure properties and even helped many homeowners avoid foreclosure. His resident foreclosure attorney tells the story of a friend who purchased a run-down property from someone who apparently wasn't fully aware of his net worth or how to use it to give himself a better life.

"The house was out in the country, and the broker had listed it as 'In Need of TLC,' which is a broker's way of saying that the house is a piece of junk.

"The owner was an old man, and nobody could tell whether he failed to maintain the property because he didn't care or couldn't afford to. My friend, the buyer, actually dealt more with the man's daughter. She was helping her father sell the house, so he could move in with her family just down the road. The father's memory was fading, and he required a little extra attention. Well, the father didn't exactly think so, but he was going along with the plan anyway.

"When the day came for my friend to move in and start repairing the house, he discovered something a little odd. The old man was sitting in the living room. My friend called the daughter and then sat down next to her father. The old man told him some stories that only old men know, and when the daughter arrived, she was apologetic. My friend said there was no need to apologize — they had just been talking. The daughter said, 'I know Dad can tell some tall tales sometimes — he claims he's a millionaire, but look around you. . . . Is this how millionaires live?' The two left the house and went to the daughter's place.

"A few hours later, the old man rushed into the house my friend was rehabbing, carrying a crowbar and shouting, 'Why didn't someone tell me we were moving? I forgot all my stuff!' The daughter was fairly close behind him and didn't know what to make of it.

"The old man went straight to the backroom, threw an old beat-up rug out of the way, dug his gnarly finger into a hole in the pine floorboard, and pulled it up. He then took his crowbar and started prying up more of the floorboards, revealing more and more of his 'stuff.' Underneath that floor was more than $2 million worth of rare coins, gold items, paper money, bonds, stock certificates, and collectible rare guns.

"The old man literally wheelbarrowed all his 'stuff' out of the house and into his beat-up 40-year-old pickup truck. The daughter stood there with a more dazed look on her face than my friend had.

"My friend actually called me while it was all going on and said, 'You'll never believe this, but that old man I thought was a little crazy . . . turns out, he's a millionaire! He buried it all in the floor. He's wheelbarrowing it all out of the house right now!' As it turns out, he lived through the Great Depression and didn't trust banks, so he just kept all his valuable items right where he knew they'd be safe — under the floor of his falling-down farmhouse."

Don't let this happen to you or one of your loved ones. Take stock of your net worth and put it toward building a better life for you and your family!

Gauging Your Cash Flow

Cash flow is a measure of the amount of money passing through an entity, like you and your partner or family. To calculate it, you simply subtract expenses from income:

Cash flow = Income – Expenses

For budgeting purposes, you typically calculate cash flow on a monthly basis, because you're usually dealing with monthly bills — utility bills, mortgage payments, credit card bills, and so on. However, monitoring your annual cash flow is also essential — especially for determining whether your spending is sustainable over the long haul.

Knowing your monthly cash flow enables you to do the following more easily:

>> Budget, or make adjustments to ensure a positive cash flow.

>> Qualify for loans and other types of credit — lenders need to see that you have sufficient income to cover your monthly payments.

>> Make well-informed downsizing choices related to location, housing, and lifestyle.

Your annual cash flow helps shed light on your long-term solvency. It may show that you're blowing too much money and having to draw from your savings at an unsustainable rate or reveal that you can afford to spend more.

REMEMBER

In your early years, you want to see a positive cash flow, meaning you're earning more than you're spending each month. In your later years, a negative cash flow may not be a concern, assuming you have assets you can cash out to make up the difference (as explained in the previous section).

In the following sections, we lead you through the process of totaling your income and expenses and using those figures to calculate your cash flow. We also introduce the topic of using debt as a means to address cash flow issues.

Tabulating your monthly and annual income

Imagine cash flow as a river. Its current is a factor of how much money is flowing in and how much is flowing out. In this section, we explain how to calculate the amount of money flowing into your accounts monthly and yearly.

First, identify potential sources of income, which may include one or more of the following:

>> Employment income (salary or hourly pay) from a traditional job, which is typically reported to you at the end of the year on a W-2 form

>> Business or self-employment income, which may be reported to you at the end of the year on forms 1099-MISC (miscellaneous) or 1099-NEC (nonemployee compensation)

>> Gig income from moonlighting or side jobs, which may be reported to you at the end of the year on forms 1099-MISC or 1099-NEC

>> Social security retirement/disability benefits, reported at the end of the year on form SSA-1099

>> Monthly pension or annuity checks, reported at the end of the year on forms 1099-R

>> Distributions or dividends from retirement accounts, such as 401(k)s, traditional individual retirement accounts (IRAs), Roth IRAs, and non-retirement investment accounts, also reported at the end of the year on forms 1099-R

>> Dividends and capital gains from non-retirement investment accounts, reported at the end of the year on forms 1099-B or 1099-DIV (dividends)

>> Monthly interest you draw from savings accounts or certificates of deposit, reported at the end of the year on forms 1099-INT (interest)

>> Unemployment compensation, reported at the end of the year on form 1099-G (government)

>> Income from any partnerships, reported at the end of the year on form K-1.

REMEMBER

For cash flow calculations, work with net income figures (the amount of money you receive from various income sources *after* taxes) or, if you use gross income figures, be sure to subtract taxes as an expense in the next section.

TIP

To calculate monthly income from a salaried position, divide your annual salary by 12 months. To calculate your annual income from an hourly job, multiply your hourly rate by the number of hours you work each week and multiply the result by 52 weeks (or however many weeks you work at the job over the course of a year). Divide that number by 12 to get your gross monthly income.

TIP

Regardless of how young you are, visit the Social Security Administration (SSA) website and create an account at `https://www.ssa.gov` (see Figure 6-1) You can then sign in to your account to see how retiring at different age milestones impacts your monthly retirement checks. The site has additional useful information and tools to help you plan for retirement.

TRADITIONAL VERSUS ROTH IRA

The difference between a traditional and a Roth IRA is this: With a traditional IRA, you don't pay taxes on the money you invest, but you pay taxes when you withdraw the money; and if you withdraw money before reaching the age of 59½, you owe a 10 percent penalty on the amount withdrawn. With a Roth IRA, you pay taxes on the money before investing it, and you withdraw it tax-free. A traditional IRA is considered a tax-deferred investment.

As of 2022, you're allowed to contribute up to $6,000 tax-free into IRAs annually (a traditional or Roth IRA or a combination of the two). That cap increases to $7,000 if you're over the age of 50.

With a traditional IRA, you deduct the amount you contribute from your reported annual income, so you don't pay income taxes on that amount. As a result, you have more money to invest, and more money to grow over the life of that investment.

With a Roth IRA, on the other hand, you aren't permitted to deduct your contributions from your income, so you end up paying taxes on those contributions before investing them.

When you reach the age of 59½, you can withdraw from the Roth IRA without having to pay taxes on those amounts. You can withdraw money from a traditional IRA at the age of 59½ without paying a 10 percent penalty, but those withdrawals are subject to income tax.

Who created the Roth IRA? William Roth — the author of the Taxpayer Relief Act of 1997.

FIGURE 6-1:
Open an
account on the
SSA website.

Estimating your monthly and annual expenses

In terms of cash flow, expenses are the money flowing out of your accounts. Start by listing all your expenses — fixed and variable. *Fixed expenses* are about the same every month, such as your phone and cable bills. *Variable expenses* are those that change from month to month, such as groceries and recreation costs. Here are several common spending categories to get you started:

>> Auto — monthly payment, license/registration fees, insurance, service/maintenance, fuel

>> Clothing

>> Dining out

>> Education

>> Entertainment/recreation — cable/satellite TV, subscriptions to streaming services, concerts, plays, bowling, golf

>> Gifts

>> Groceries

>> Home maintenance and repair

>> Household supplies — toiletries, laundry supplies, dishwasher detergent, cleaning supplies, tools

>> Insurance — homeowner's or renter's insurance, auto insurance

>> Medical/dental — insurance premiums, prescription medications, out-of-pocket costs

>> Mortgage payment or rent

>> Pets — food, supplies, veterinary care, boarding fees

>> Property taxes and homeowner association fees

>> Personal care — hair, nails, massage, gym membership

>> Travel

>> Utilities — electricity, gas, water, sewer, trash, internet service, phone service

REMEMBER

You may need to finagle the dollar values a little to convert annual or semiannual expenses, such as homeowner's insurance and property taxes, into monthly bills. For example, if you pay property taxes in spring and fall, calculate the total and divide by 12 to convert them into a monthly expense, and set aside that money each month to cover property taxes when that bill arrives.

After you determine your monthly expenses, simply multiply the total by 12 to calculate your annual expenses.

TIP

Here are a few tips for managing your expenses:

>> Use a personal finance management program, such as Quicken, Mint, or YNAB, to record and categorize every income and expense transaction.

>> Consider using your credit or debit card or other e-payment method to pay for *everything,* so you can more easily track your expenses. Using a credit card may also enable you to earn cash back or other rewards.

WARNING

If you tend to overspend with credit/debit cards and e-payment methods, you may be better off using them exclusively for your auto pay accounts and using cash for everything else.

>> Give yourself an allowance for discretionary spending — for example, $500 a month to spend on whatever you want. Having money set aside for discretionary spending also provides a safety net for unpleasant surprises, such as auto repairs or having to replace a major appliance. If the unpleasant surprise doesn't materialize, then here comes a fun and unexpected vacation!

>> *Cap your monthly expenses.* When you have a pretty clear idea of how much money you spend each month just to live, raise the total a little to give yourself some fun money and a little breathing room, and cap it at that amount. (Some people go so far as to calculate their monthly expenses and then double the amount to give them some extra cushion.) As soon as you hit your limit for the month, stop spending.

>> See the later section "Exploring ways to trim expenses" for more specific tips.

Calculating your cash flow

When you know your total monthly and annual income and expenses, calculating cash flow is easy. Just subtract your total expenses from your total income.

If you end up with a negative number, reflecting negative cash flow, you have some work to do. You need to boost your income, reduce your expenses, or do both. Boosting income may require little more than working with your financial advisor to draw more money from your retirement accounts or cash out equity you've built up in your home or other physical assets. You can also boost income by developing other income streams (see the later section "Exploring ways to generate additional income" for some ideas).

Reducing expenses requires tightening your belt — allocating less money for discretionary spending. See the later section "Exploring ways to trim expenses" for ideas.

REMEMBER

Monitor both your monthly and annual cash flows, so you'll have both a short-term and long-term gauge of how you're doing financially. If your annual cash flow is negative, you'll need to make adjustments to your monthly cash flow to get back on track.

Leveraging the power of debt to help finance your dreams

The reason we look at both net worth and cash flow is because you can use the two in tandem to access the money you need to downsize to the life you desire. If you're cash poor but equity rich, you can cash out the equity by selling items of value or borrowing against them to increase your cash flow. And if you suddenly discover or unlock another source of income, you can use that to increase your net worth.

REMEMBER

While cash flow is like a river, net worth is like a reservoir. You can draw from that reservoir when you don't have enough cash flowing in to cover expenses and replenish the reservoir as necessary whenever the opportunity presents itself (you experience a windfall profit, you earn some income on the side, or certain expenses drop off your ledger, as happens when adult children graduate from college and move on).

Accounting for Medical Insurance and Health-care Costs

If you're young and fit as a fiddle, you may pay little, if any, attention to medical insurance and health-care costs. You're simply rolling the dice and hoping you don't get sick or injured. On the other hand, if you're over 60, and certainly if you're over 65, you'll need to account for the costs of medical insurance, doctor visits, and medications. All these expenses can take a big chunk out of your monthly budget.

If you're gainfully employed, have a health insurance plan through your employer, and see doctors regularly, you can use your financial records to budget for these expenses. If you don't have health insurance, we recommend that you consult with an insurance agent who specializes in medical insurance, especially if you're in a special situation, such as traveling abroad, or if you're a U.S. citizen who'll be turning 65 and signing up for Medicare. Specialized plans may include *travel insurance* (to cover accidents or illness when you're on a trip), *medical stop-loss insurance* (to handle catastrophic claims), and *supplemental insurance* (to cover what a standard plan doesn't).

Because many people downsize as part of their retirement plan, we asked our friend and insurance agent Jane Saigh to weigh in on the topic of health insurance. She offered the following considerations:

» If you're retiring/downsizing before age 65, you may be able to continue to receive coverage under your employer's health-care plan thanks to the Consolidated Omnibus Budget Reconciliation Act of 1985 (more commonly known as COBRA), but this can be expensive.

» If you haven't reached the age of 65, you may be better off shopping for an individual plan. You can consult a health insurance rep or shop for a plan online at Healthcare.gov.

» If you're healthy and fit, a short-term plan may be a good solution. Again, we recommend that you consult an agent who specializes in health insurance. Plans vary by state.

» If you're healthy and fit, consider a high-deductible plan to cover large, unexpected health-care bills. You can then contribute money to a health savings account (HSA) to cover out-of-pocket costs while claiming a tax deduction for those contributions. If you don't use the money in your HSA, you can roll it over into a retirement account, such as an IRA, when you turn 65.

If you're a U.S. citizen nearing the age of 65, the time has come to start thinking about Medicare coverage. Here are the basics you need to know about Medicare:

>> Medicare pricing is determined by zip code, so you must declare an address. If you don't have an address, consider using a virtual mail service, such as iPostal1.com.

>> Medicare Part A is covered by payroll taxes, assuming you've earned about 40 credits or quarters (about 10 years of work and contributions into the system). Medicare Part A generally covers the following expenses:

- Inpatient care in a hospital

- Skilled nursing facility care

- Nursing home care (inpatient care in a skilled nursing facility that's not custodial or long-term care)

- Hospice care

- Home health care

>> Medicare Part B currently costs $170.10 per month (or higher depending on your income), which is automatically deducted from your monthly social security payments, or you can have three months' worth of premiums deducted quarterly from a bank account of your choosing. Medicare Part B generally covers the following expenses:

- Clinical research

- Ambulance services

- Durable medical equipment

- Mental health care (inpatient, outpatient, and partial hospitalization)

- Limited outpatient prescription medications

>> Medicare Parts A and B are automatic, but you can add to them as shown in Figure 6-2. You have three options:

- Stick with your original Medicare plan, Parts A and B, which will cover about 80 percent of all your health-care costs.

- Add Medicare supplemental insurance and/or Medicare Part D (drug coverage). If you don't add Medicare Part D, you're subject to a penalty — yes, you need to pay for drug coverage regardless of whether you take medications.

- Choose a Medicare Advantage plan, consisting of Medicare Part C, which combines Parts A and B with prescription drug coverage, or, if prescription drug coverage isn't included, you can add Part D.

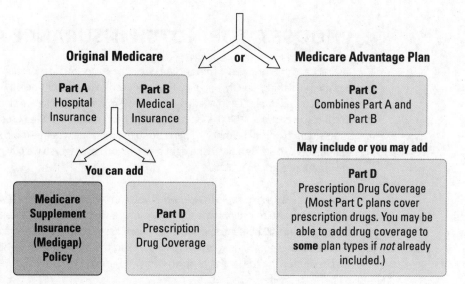

Original Medicare or **Medicare Advantage Plan**

Part A	Part B
Hospital Insurance	Medical Insurance

Part C
Combines Part A and Part B

May include or you may add

You can add

Medicare Supplement Insurance (Medigap) Policy

Part D
Prescription Drug Coverage

Part D
Prescription Drug Coverage
(Most Part C plans cover prescription drugs. You may be able to add drug coverage to **some** plan types if *not* already included.)

FIGURE 6-2:
You can add to basic Medicare coverage or opt for a Medicare Advantage plan.

WARNING

If you're healthy and fit and think you'll try to save a little money by not enrolling in Medicare, think again. You may save a little money at first, but if you decide to sign up later, the late–enrollment penalties are stiff.

>> If you're not eligible for premium-free Part A and don't buy it when you're first eligible, your monthly premium may increase by 10 percent.

>> If you don't sign up for Part B, your monthly premium can rise 10 percent for each full 12-month period that you could've had Part B but didn't sign up for it. And this isn't a one-time late fee — you'll be subject to the penalty for as long as you have Part B (like the rest of your life).

>> The penalty for not signing up for Part D when you're first eligible is calculated by multiplying 1 percent of the national base beneficiary premium ($33.37 in 2022) by the number of full uncovered months you didn't have Part D or creditable coverage. The penalty stays with you for the remainder of your Part D coverage.

TIP

For more about Medicare, check out *Medicare For Dummies*, 4th Edition, by Patricia Barry (Wiley).

CHOOSE A TOP-NOTCH INSURANCE AGENT

Insurance agents are paid a commission when they sign you up for a plan. You don't pay them anything directly, and a quality agent can save you considerable money. Just recently, for example, Ralph needed a new CPAP machine to help him sleep. The machine costs about $1,200. Medicare paid 80 percent, and our Blue Cross Medicare supplement covered the other 20 percent, so the machine was free (no cost to us). Jane (our agent) also set us up with the right prescription coverage, so we pay next to nothing for our prescription meds.

Your agent may also be able to help when you run into problems. As we were downsizing, we were also transitioning from private insurance to Medicare. Certain bills weren't being covered 100 percent, and some bills were being generated for an account that didn't exist anymore. Jane was able to help us sort out these glitches in the system as we confronted the challenges of downsizing.

Planning to Live on a Fixed Income

When you're in the workforce, your income generally rises at least a little faster than inflation, so you can keep up with the rising costs of everything from utility bills to groceries. When you're living on a fixed income, however, inflation is likely to outstrip any cost-of-living adjustments you receive from the SSA or your pension plan.

Living on a fixed income is all about budgeting — having a solid grasp of your income and expenses, as explained in the earlier section "Gauging Your Cash Flow." However, four factors make budgeting on a fixed income especially challenging:

>> Monthly bills, such as gas, electric, water, and sewer, can fluctuate.

>> Annual and semiannual bills are easy to overlook when you're creating a monthly budget.

>> Unexpected bills, such as auto or home repair bills or a heating bill for an unseasonably cold winter month, may take a big chunk out of your budget.

TIP

You may be able to take the sting out of large auto or home repair bills by buying a vehicle warranty and home warranty, but those are additional expenses. For more predictable home heating and cooling bills, consider getting on a budget with your gas and electric companies.

>> Discretionary spending can be difficult to track and even more challenging to rein in, which is why we recommend giving yourself a monthly allowance.

Living on a fixed income can be a challenge, but downsizing is actually one of the best solutions for overcoming this challenge. Downsizing enables you to slash your expenses, so you can live within your means and have more money to spend on what you enjoy. In the following sections, we provide additional guidance on how to live on a fixed income — by reducing expenses and finding or creating additional sources of income.

REMEMBER

As you get older, consult with your financial advisor to reevaluate your investment options. Generally, you want to gradually transition from riskier to safer investments — for example, from growth stocks to those that pay dividends or from stocks and bonds to an annuity that pays you the same amount each month regardless of how the underlying investments are performing.

Exploring ways to trim expenses

One of the big reasons most people downsize is to cut their living expenses. A smaller house is generally accompanied by a smaller mortgage, lower homeowner's insurance premiums, lower utility bills, lower maintenance and repair costs, and lower property taxes. If you move to a location with great public transportation or within walking distance of everywhere you need to be, you may even be able to shed a car or two, along with the costs of licenses and registrations, vehicle insurance, fuel, repairs, and maintenance.

In this section, we look at ways to trim expenses on top of the big cuts we just mentioned.

REMEMBER

Look beyond your monthly bills to how they're calculated. For example, we moved into a condo in an area where the sewer bill is tied directly to the water bill, and the lion's share of that bill is for sewage treatment. The way the municipality looks at it, the more water you use, the more waste you're sending down the sewer pipes to the waste management facility. Makes sense, but the water we use for our lawn doesn't go down the sewer. We should have gotten a dedicated irrigation water meter installed beside our regular water meter when our condo was built.

Cap your expenses by category

One way to cut spending is to cap monthly spending for each category — for example, $500 for groceries, $200 for dining out, $100 for gifts, $300 for travel. You don't spend beyond the cap in any given month, and you set aside any surplus in each category to offset overages or unexpected bills in other months.

Some people practice this approach by using a separate envelope for each category. When they receive money, they place the budgeted amount of cash into its respective envelope and pay bills and expenses out of those envelopes. Technology provides more efficient methods through personal finance software, credit/debit cards, and e-payment methods. Now, you can have every transaction tracked and sent to your personal finance software, so you can see exactly what you're spending every month in each category in real time.

REMEMBER

Small expenses add up. That $5 coffee you treat yourself to every day costs you $150 each month and more than $1,800 a year! Look for these low-hanging fruits as you search for expenses to cut. Cigarettes, booze, and fast food are a few other no-brainers to cut, and the cuts will improve your health, possibly leading to lower doctor bills and insurance premiums.

Negotiate with service providers

If your cable, satellite, or phone bill is too high, you may be able to negotiate with service providers to reduce your monthly charges. You probably won't have any luck with your gas or electric company (because the government controls the rates) or with the water, sewage, or trash companies. Call your cable, satellite, or phone provider or visit their website to see whether they're offering more affordable plans or can do anything to help bring down the cost.

Of course, you're likely to have better luck if you have an alternative. Threatening to switch to a competitor (assuming you're willing to do that if your current provider calls your bluff) can be a very effective tactic. Simply call your current provider, and let them know that you're struggling to pay the bill, and if they can't lower your bill, you'll be forced to switch to a competitor's plan. You may even explain that you'd really like to stay with them, and you're willing to do so if they can match the price the competitor is offering. (Here's a secret: When they tell you they can't, they mean they won't. Usually, a supervisor can push through any deal they're willing to offer.)

WARNING

Be careful about negotiating yourself into a higher bill. Every time we call our cable company to switch to a lower-cost plan, we end up with a higher bill the following month. We're willing to put up with slightly slower internet and fewer channels, and we get *that*, but we also get a higher bill. Go figure.

Tap into government programs

Depending on your age, income, any disabilities, and other factors, you may be able to trim your expenses with help from various government programs. For example, Cook County (Chicago, Illinois) offers a property tax exemption for homeowners who are 65 or older. It provides property tax savings by reducing the equalized assessed value of the eligible property. If you qualify as low income, the U.S. government's Low Income Home Energy Assistance Program offers help with heating and cooling bills, weatherization costs, and even water and sewer bills.

BUNDLES OF BUNDLES

Everything is a bundle these days — cable, internet, phone, cell phone. We canceled our landline, and because it was part of a bundle, our bill went *up!* To reduce our cost, we added a business line through Google Voice. The phone cost a couple hundred dollars, but it always works, and it eliminated our monthly phone bill. When we moved to our new house, we plugged in our Google phone, and it instantly recognized us and carried the number to the new location.

One day, we noticed a charge of $200 on our credit card for a satellite radio service for our car. We called to see about reducing the monthly charge and discovered that the rates they quote on their website and over the phone are quite different — they're higher when you call. We ended up keeping the package we had.

The point of this story is that negotiating with service providers can be very confusing, frustrating, and discouraging. To be successful, you need patience, persistence, and knowledge (do your homework). You may even need to cancel a service and do without it for a while until the provider comes to its senses and offers you a special deal to come back. This is the one thing you can count on 100 percent — the provider will *always* offer a better deal after you cancel service.

REMEMBER

Programs are available at the federal, state, and local levels to help people who need assistance covering their living expenses, so if you or a loved one is struggling to pay their bills and can't manage to do so by cutting discretionary spending, search for programs online, either through a general search engine or on the websites of applicable governing bodies, such as www.usa.gov.

Many government agencies and charitable organizations offer assistance programs. Pharmaceutical companies also offer programs to help pay for prescription medications. You just need to be aware of them, and the internet is a great place to start your search. Kathleen's grandpa was in the military at a time when a lot of people got frostbite. If you were in the service during this time, you could apply for a $10K compensatory "gift" — recipients were never required to pay it back. Unfortunately, Kathleen's grandpa was rejected because he had too much money in the bank.

Optimize your health

Inflation on health-care costs generally runs about two times higher than inflation on nearly everything else. As we were writing this book, HealthView Services projected health-care inflation would remain at 12 percent through 2022 and into 2023. In other words, it pays to be healthy now more than ever before. In addition, good health enables you to remain in the workforce longer, earning and contributing, which, for many people, enhances their quality of life. In fact, just being healthy enhances your quality of life.

Everyone on our writing team has had experience with various doctors, trainers, and other health and fitness experts, and we've distilled their collective advice into the following seven guidelines for getting and staying healthy and fit:

>> **Lay off the bad stuff.** Avoid nicotine, alcohol, marijuana, caffeine, illegal drugs, processed (junk) foods, fast foods, sweets (including sweet beverages), and trans fats (like those in most fried foods and chips).

>> **Eat mostly whole foods and mostly plants.** Whole foods are those that haven't been processed, such as everything in the produce section of your grocery store (fresh veggies and fruits), nuts, seeds, beans, whole grains, fish, meat, and eggs. As they say in natural medicine circles, "You can pay the farmer now or pay the pharmacist later."

>> **Drink enough water.** Your body needs water to stay hydrated and to detox. In general, men need about 16 cups of water/fluids daily and women need about 12 cups daily, but needs vary individually. Your urine should be clear to light yellow. If it's intense yellow or orange, you're not drinking enough water.

>> **Get off your butt.** A combination of cardiovascular and weight or resistance training for at least 30 minutes most days is best, but all physical activity is better for you than sitting or lying around. If you don't like gym exercise, take long walks, garden, practice yoga, play pickleball — just do something that puts your body in motion!

>> **Sleep 7–8 hours per night.** Your body detoxes, repairs any damage, and replenishes its energy supplies as you sleep. Sleep quality is also important, so be sure you're getting restful, restorative sleep. If you're tired shortly after waking up, consult your doctor for help.

>> **Silence the stress.** Stress kills, so avoid it as much as possible, and develop stress management skills to deal more effectively with unavoidable sources of stress. Maintain an active social life with happy, positive, self-fulfilled people. Dance, sing, laugh, have fun!

>> **Consult a doctor who practices functional, integrative medicine.** Conventional doctors are skilled at treating acute illnesses, such as infections and broken bones, and prescribing medications to alleviate symptoms. They're not as skilled at diagnosing and treating chronic illnesses, identifying the underlying cause of illnesses, or optimizing health. Visit the Institute for Functional Medicine website at www.ifm.org for more about the advantages of functional and integrative health care and to find a functional medicine clinic near you. If you've been dealing with a chronic medical condition, and you're not feeling 100 percent, consulting a functional and integrative practitioner is even more important.

Ask and barter

Most people have more possessions than they know what to do with. You can probably furnish your entire home with other people's surplus and without paying a dime for anything — and you can probably get some high-quality furnishings and appliances! Just post a request for what you need on social media and pass the word around your circle of family and friends.

To extend your reach, you can post what you're looking for online on places like Facebook Marketplace, Craigslist, and Freecycle.org. Facebook Marketplace and Craigslist are also great for buying gently used items at a discount.

REMEMBER

Get creative. We have a friend who doesn't have a car, but his condo has a garage. He lets his neighbor park in his garage in exchange for being able to use the neighbor's car occasionally.

Take advantage of freebies

Your community may be a great source for free entertainment, services, and other offerings. Search online to see whether your municipality or county has a community foundation or visitors center and look into what's available. Here are a few freebies that may be available in your community:

>> Library for books, videos, and music CDs, and educational opportunities that are open to the public

>> Community center for a free or low-cost gym and recreational activities

>> Local colleges or universities for free plays, presentations, concerts, and sports events

>> Scholarships and grants for educational or training opportunities

>> Museums

>> Parks and trails

>> Aquatic centers

Exploring ways to generate additional income

What do you do when you discover that your expenses are exceeding your income? You get to work finding or creating sources of supplemental income. In this section, we explore a few common ways people generate additional income after retiring or scaling back their workweek and discovering that they're struggling to make ends meet.

Get a job

The labor market is tight as we write this book. Businesses in nearly every industry are struggling to find workers, and you can usually work as much or as little as you want. Here are just a few ideas to open your mind to the possibilities:

>> If you have teaching experience, you can find work teaching part-time, substitute teaching, working as a classroom aide, or monitoring study halls.

>> If you have experience in law enforcement, consider working in security for businesses, including sports and entertainment venues.

>> If you've been in construction all your life, you can find plenty of work as a handyperson.

>> More and more grocery stores are hiring people to shop for their online customers and prepare orders for pickup and delivery.

>> Many businesses need part-time or full-time drivers. You can drive a shuttle for a motel, a car rental company, or a senior center; deliver auto parts to mechanics; or drive a bus. We know a retired police captain who drives a hearse for local funeral homes.

>> Motels and resorts need a variety of staff to keep everything clean and well-stocked and serve customers.

TIP

Try to find a position in which you can use your experience and expertise to negotiate higher pay. Nothing is wrong with general labor, but if you have a particular skill, you'll earn more doing that.

WARNING

If you're receiving social security retirement benefits before your full retirement age (FRA) and you earn more than the earnings limit ($19,560 annually in 2022), your payments will be reduced by $1 for every $2 you earn over the limit. In the year you reach FRA, your benefit is reduced by $1 for every $3 you earn above $50,520 (in 2022). After you reach FRA, you can earn as much as you like without having your benefits reduced.

Start a side hustle

A *side hustle* is additional employment that generates supplemental income outside your full-time job. They're usually part-time or self-employment gigs. Here are a few examples to open your mind to what's possible:

>> If you have experience as a teacher, you can tutor or create and sell study guides and worksheets online or to publishers. You may also find work writing questions for exams and test prep books.

>> If you have specialized knowledge and experience in business, manufacturing, computers, electronics, or another field, you may be able to find lucrative work as a consultant.

>> Turn a hobby into a cottage industry. For example, if you like to sew, offer your services as a seamstress. If you're skilled at maintaining and fixing small engines, you can offer that service or buy used lawn mowers, chain saws, and snowblowers to fix up and resell.

TIP

If you've had a hobby, such as collecting coins, stamps, paintings, or antiques, those items could be valuable. Now may be the perfect time to downsize your collection to generate the cash you need to pursue your dreams.

>> Uber, Lyft, DoorDash, Grubhub, and other companies are always in need of drivers. You make your own hours, get paid, and even collect tips!

>> If you have a large following on social media, consider becoming an influencer and getting paid for your product recommendations and for running ads on your website or blog.

>> Take surveys online through sites such as InboxDollars (`www.inboxdollars.com`), Swagbucks (`www.swagbucks.com/g/paid-surveys`), and MyPoints (`www.mypoints.com/paid-surveys`).

>> Serve as a mock juror on sites such as OnlineVerdict (`www.onlineverdict.com`), where you can be part of a legal focus group for attorneys who are preparing for trial.

>> Test websites through services such as Userfeel (`https://www.userfeel.com/`) and TryMyUI (`www.trymyui.com`).

REMEMBER

Side hustles can generate substantial income. Working just eight hours a week for $40 an hour can generate an additional $1,280 for the month.

Take on a roommate

If you have an extra room or two in your home or apartment, consider taking on a roommate. You may be able to cover your entire month's rent or your mortgage payment and then some by leasing part of your space. As a result, you can dial down your living expenses considerably. Just imagine having a mortgage of $1,500 a month and leasing one room for $900 — you cut your housing expense by 60 percent! You may even be able to persuade your roomie to pitch in for utilities — gas, electric, internet, water, sewage, trash, and renter's insurance.

REMEMBER

Taking on a roommate can be a great way to save money and set aside more for your future when you're planning to downsize but aren't quite ready to pull the trigger. You can continue living in your large home as you declutter and set the stage for downsizing.

LIVIN' LARGE

In 1975, after Ralph graduated high school, he bought a three-bedroom house with his graduation money. He paid $9,000 for it and put $900 down. His monthly mortgage payment, including property taxes and insurance, was $115 a month. There were two bedrooms on the first floor and one upstairs.

As soon as Ralph closed on the house, he rented rooms to some high-school buddies, charging each $30 a week. That amounted to $240 a month. Ralph was living upstairs for free and earning an extra $125! If you own more home than you need, you can rent out part of it, live there for free, *and* earn extra money on the side.

WARNING

Be selective when choosing people to rent to. If you're thinking, "How bad can it be?" watch the Netflix series *Worst Roommate Ever*. It's all about sociopathic and sometimes violent roommates who "turn the lives of their unsuspecting roommates into real-life nightmares." We're not trying to scare you off from taking on a roommate; just be sure to vet the person properly before letting them in your home — check identification and references and order a background check from a site such as PeopleFinders.com. Consult your attorney to draw up a renter's agreement that protects you and your property. Be sure it has an escape clause that enables you to back out of the agreement if the situation isn't working out for you. It should also include a clause that allows you to visit the portion of the property you're renting out without advanced notice, so you can see whether your roomie is trashing the place.

- » Preparing your will

- » Granting someone your power of attorney

- » Having a say in your medical care and end-of-life plan

- » Organizing your important documents in one place

- » Transitioning your business to new owners

- » Deciding whether life insurance is right for you

Chapter 7

Planning Your Estate

Always plan ahead. It wasn't raining when Noah built the ark.
— RICHARD CUSHING

The title of this chapter is "Ugh!"-worthy. Estate planning is an onerous task that forces you to confront your own mortality when you're probably at the pinnacle of enjoying your life. Who *wants* to do that?

The only silver lining in this dark cloud is that by arranging for your eventual demise, you'll have shed yourself of a significant burden: any worry or concern about what will happen to you, your loved ones, and your stuff when you're unable to make decisions for yourself and you ultimately pass from this Earth. You certainly don't want everything you worked so hard to build over the course of your long life to fall into the wrong hands — those of lawyers and government institutions — and you definitely want to be sure that someone you totally trust is making medical and end-of-life decisions for you when you're unable to.

In this chapter, we guide you through the process of planning your estate so that you maintain some degree of control over your situation and protect your assets in the event of incapacitating illness or death. Our hope is that by the end of this process, you'll be able to breathe a big sigh of relief and pop the cork on a bottle of champagne to celebrate the liberation of your mind from one of life's major concerns: asset protection.

REMEMBER

When should you start planning your estate? The sooner the better. Tragic events are unpredictable and emotional. Having a plan in place for an untimely death or disability can alleviate the burden on loved ones. It also lifts the burden of concern from you knowing that you won't be leaving a legal mess for your loved ones to sort out. And as soon as your plan is complete, the heavy lifting is done; you simply need to review and update your plan once a year or so.

Getting up to Speed on Estate Planning Basics

Your *estate* comprises everything of value you own: bank accounts, investment accounts, real estate, vehicles, jewelry, guns, businesses, and so on. *Estate planning* is the process of developing a strategy for the organization and distribution of assets in the event of incapacitation or death. You plan your estate to do the following:

» Ensure that assets are distributed according to your wishes.

» Reduce conflict and stress among loved ones who may disagree over what you would've wanted.

» Minimize taxes and legal expenses.

» Ease the burden on family members.

» Ensure that people you trust will care for any dependent children when you can't.

» Ensure that you're properly cared for if you become incapacitated.

» Potentially reduce medical bills by positioning yourself as being entirely dependent on Medicare, so you have more money to leave to your loved ones. Consult an estate attorney or insurance professional who specializes in Medicare coverage for guidance on how to position yourself in this way. The overall goal is to make yourself look asset-poor so that Medicare foots the bill for your long-term health care instead of requiring you to hand over all your assets to offset the costs.

>> Alleviate worries about what will happen to your assets, loved ones, and business when you die or if you become incapacitated.

An estate plan should include the following essential documents:

>> Your last will and testament (a simple or joint will, as explained in the next section, "Step 1: Preparing Your Will(s)")

>> Power of attorney to give the executor of your will the legal rights to act according to the provisions in your will

>> Your living will and/or advance health-care directive

>> A business-succession plan (if you own one or more businesses) to specify what happens to the business if you die or become incapacitated

>> Your end-of-life plan (for example, cremation or burial, party plans, and so on)

A major goal of estate planning is to keep assets from having to go through *probate* — the legal process for determining the validity of a will and distributing the property of someone who has died.

In the following sections, we guide you through a basic step-by-step process for planning your estate, and we provide you with a comprehensive checklist to ensure that you haven't overlooked anything important.

REMEMBER

Estate planning ranges from simple to highly complex. If you have only a few heirs and a dozen or so valuable assets (bank and investment accounts, a home, cars), you can do it yourself, and this chapter may be all you need. If you've been married more than once, have children from other marriages or relationships, own businesses and have business partners, have a dozen or more bank and investment accounts, and so on, this chapter serves as a good introduction, but you'll need more guidance.

Step 1: Preparing Your Will(s)

A *will* is a legal document that informs loved ones and the courts what you want to happen if you die or become incapacitated. Four types of wills are commonly used for different purposes:

>> A *simple will* (sometimes referred to as a *last will and testament*) is used to specify who gets what when you die and who you want to take care of your dependent children, assuming you have dependent children.

>> A *joint will* is signed by two or more people (usually spouses) in favor of the other person inheriting everything.

>> A *living will* designates an individual to make medical decisions for you if sickness or injury leaves you unable to make those decisions yourself. A living will helps reduce the emotion and panic loved ones already feel when tragedy strikes.

>> A *testamentary trust will* places some or all assets into a trust for the beneficiaries and names a trustee to handle the trust. It's generally added later in life when more assets are available but add it as soon as you have any significant assets, because a sudden passing is always possible. The more valuable the assets, the more important it is to have them held in a trust.

Everyone should have a living will and either a simple will or a joint will (for couples). These are perhaps the most important documents in your estate plan, and you should have them in place regardless of your age. In the following sections, we provide guidance on how to write these different types of wills.

WARNING

Just having a will won't keep your assets out of probate. You need to combine it with a trust or use other tactics, such as naming beneficiaries to your accounts, to bypass probate. See the later section "Step 2: Keeping Your Valuable Assets Out of Probate" for details.

Several approaches to writing a will of any type are at your disposal, including:

REMEMBER

>> **Hire a local attorney.** This option is the one we recommend because it gives you the best chance of ensuring that your interests are protected and the legal language is appropriate for your jurisdiction.

An attorney may cost several hundred dollars, but you'll save money and aggravation by having your will done properly and professionally. The other options we present in this list are for those without a lot of assets who want some assurance that the belongings they treasure will reach the right people.

>> **Use will preparation software.** Search the web for "will preparation software," and you'll find plenty of options, including Nolo's Quicken WillMaker (www.willmaker.com), U.S. Legal Wills (www.uslegalwills.com), and Trust & Will (trustandwill.com).

>> **Start with a form or template.** You can also find plenty of free and low-cost forms or templates for writing a will online. Search for "will fill-in-the-blank form" for links to various online resources.

>> **Do it yourself.** With the guidelines we provide in the following sections, you can cobble together a basic will that may serve your purposes. However, we still recommend that you have a lawyer review it, notarize it, and store it for you in case anyone disputes its authenticity later.

Also, check out *Wills and Trusts Kit For Dummies* by Aaron Larson.

REMEMBER

However you choose to prepare your will, be sure to file it with your local probate court. If you change your will later, be sure to file the revised version.

Writing a simple will

A *simple will* is a legal document that describes in some detail how you want your money, home, and other valuable assets distributed and who you want to take care of your dependent children after you die. Everyone who owns anything of value — real estate, cars, jewelry, stocks, bonds, pets, and so on — or who has dependent children should have a simple or joint will. Why? Here are two good reasons:

>> If you die without a will, you have no guarantee that your wishes, even if known by your loved ones, will be carried out.

>> Without a will, your heirs will suffer the consequences of higher legal and court costs, delays, and hassles, along with possible emotional conflict if they can't easily agree upon an equitable distribution of assets. Money can bring the evil out in people. Without a will, your entire family may end up not talking with one another ever again after your death.

REMEMBER

A will tells the executor your name and what you want to happen with your stuff, but it doesn't prevent your heirs from having to go through probate. You must combine your will with a strategy for keeping your valuable assets out of probate, a topic we discuss in the later section "Step 2: Keeping Your Valuable Assets Out of Probate."

As you're writing your own will or gathering information to meet with your lawyer, be sure to include the following details:

>> The name of the person you want to serve as the executor of the will. The executor has the following duties:

- Locates the will and files it with the local probate court if you haven't done so already. (Filing it yourself is best.)

- Notifies banks, credit card companies, and government agencies of your death.

- Makes any probate decisions.

- Represents the estate in court.

- Sets up a bank account for funds coming into the estate and funds used to pay any bills.

- Files an inventory of assets with the court.

- Ensures that property is properly maintained until it can be distributed or sold.

- Pays the estate's debt and taxes.

- Distributes assets.

- Disposes of any remaining property.

>> A comprehensive list of assets, including bank and investment accounts, homes, cars, boats, jewelry, and whole life insurance policies. Be sure to update this list annually and whenever you acquire or dispose of a significant asset.

>> A list of beneficiaries, their contact information, and details about who gets what.

>> The name(s) and contact information of guardian(s) who have agreed to care for any dependent children you have.

>> The name(s) and contact information for anyone you want to write out of your will — people who may have a legal claim to your property who you don't want contesting the will.

After completing your will, be sure to have it signed and notarized. Provide a copy to the executor of your will and to your lawyer. If you don't want the executor to see your will until after your death, have your lawyer keep it and give your executor your lawyer's contact information and your lawyer your executor's contact information.

REMEMBER

Wills aren't written in stone. You can always review and revise your will. Just be sure to destroy all copies of any earlier versions.

Writing a joint will

A *joint will* (sometimes referred to as a *mirror will*) is very similar to a simple will, in that it designates an executor, names the beneficiaries, lists assets, and explains who gets what. However, a joint will is used mostly for couples (spouses or life partners). A joint will typically states that the surviving partner inherits all the assets, but it also includes details about what happens to those assets when the surviving partner dies. For example, our joint will would state that if Kathleen dies, then Ralph gets everything, and if Ralph dies, then Kathleen gets everything, but if we both die, then our children inherit our assets.

REMEMBER

A key characteristic of a joint will is that after one partner dies, the surviving partner can't alter the will, even if that partner has a change of heart about how assets are distributed. This can be good or bad, depending on your perspective.

For example, suppose that you and your spouse have three children, and you want to be absolutely sure that when you both pass away, your children benefit from the wealth you worked so hard together to build. You pass away, and your spouse remarries. You don't want your spouse to write any of the children out of the will. On the other hand, suppose your spouse passes away, and one of your children becomes a drug addict. You don't want your drug addict son to get a pile of money because that may kill him, but with a joint will, you can't change anything to keep him from getting the money when you die.

If you're writing your own joint will, follow the same guidelines for writing a simple will explained in the previous section but add a clause at the beginning stating something like the following:

> This will is made pursuant to an agreement between us, by which it is mutually agreed that we would execute a joint and mutual will, leaving to the survivor all property, real and personal, of the party first to die, and on the death of the survivor, leaving all of their property to our children equally.

Writing a living will

A *living will* gives you some control over medical decisions when you're unable to make those decisions for yourself. You can write a living will yourself or with the help of an attorney, or by filling out a form or using specialized software. Just be sure that your living will contains the following details:

>> The names and contact information of the primary and secondary people you trust to make medical decisions for you when you're unable to do it.

>> The types of medical treatment that are permissible and those that are prohibited — for example, whether you can be put on a ventilator.

>> Whether you should receive any life-prolonging treatments, such as CPR, blood transfusions, dialysis, intravenous drugs, oxygen, or surgery.

>> Whether, when deemed permanently unconscious, you should be hooked up to a feeding tube.

>> Whether you should be given palliative care, such as morphine, to alleviate suffering.

In addition to, or instead of, a living will, you can make your wishes known by filling out and signing an advance medical directive. Many doctor offices can provide the form you need to fill out. See the later section "Step 4: Ensuring You Have Some Control Over Medical Decisions" for additional guidance.

Knowing when to use a testamentary trust will

A *testamentary trust will* enables you to place assets in a trust with certain conditions in place (such as the minimum age that an heir will start receiving distributions from the trust). It can be a great solution for ensuring that children and grandchildren don't receive too much money when they're too young to appreciate it or too much money at one time when they're not responsible enough to spend it wisely. A testamentary trust can be a very valuable tool for reducing taxes on the money placed in the trust and distributed from it.

When preparing your testamentary trust will, be sure to include the following details:

>> The names and contact information for all beneficiaries who will receive assets from the trust, along with details about who gets what and when they get it.

>> The name and contact information of the person you designate to act as testamentary trustee. Choose someone you trust totally.

>> A detailed list of your assets that should be placed in the trust.

REMEMBER

A testamentary trust will is used in conjunction with your last will and testament. It doesn't become effective until you die — the trustee you name sets up the trust after you die. See the next section, "Step 2: Keeping Your Valuable Assets Out of Probate," for more about trusts.

Step 2: Keeping Your Valuable Assets Out of Probate

One of the main purposes of estate planning is to prevent your valuable assets from ending up in *probate*, where the court decides who gets what, delays prevent your loved ones from being able to move on, and taxes and legal fees can take a chunk out of what your heirs inherit. To keep property out of probate, you basically have two approaches from which to choose: with a trust or without one. (A *trust* is a written document that enables a third party, the trustee, to manage your assets, according to your wishes or best interests, if you're ever unable to do so for yourself — usually as a result of death or disability.) In the following sections, we explore these two approaches, starting with the easy one first.

WARNING

For your trust to be active, you need to transfer your assets into the trust. If you have a trust with no assets in it, when you die, it's like you had no trust at all.

Steering clear of probate without a trust

You don't necessarily need to place all your assets into a trust to protect them from probate. You can transfer your assets more directly to your heirs in three ways:

» Name beneficiaries for all your accounts — bank accounts, investment/brokerage accounts, traditional and Roth individual retirement accounts (IRAs), 401(k)s, pensions, and 403(b) plans. Then, all your beneficiaries need to do is contact the financial institution and provide a death certificate and details on where they want the money transferred.

» Name beneficiaries for any vehicles you own. In many states in the U.S., you can register for a transfer on death certificate (TOD) for any vehicle that requires a title of ownership. Whoever inherits the vehicle can then take the TOD, title, and their identification to the Bureau of Motor Vehicles (BMV) to have the title transferred to their name (outside the probate process). You may even be able to get a TOD certificate for a car you're buying on credit; in that case, your heir will need to pay the balance on the loan to obtain the title.

» File a transfer on death deed (TODD) with the Register of Deeds office in any county where you own real estate. With a TODD in place, your heir simply needs to visit the Register of Deeds office with your death certificate and the required identification to have the property's deed transferred over to their name.

WARNING

If you're thinking about simply adding your heirs' names to a deed, carefully reconsider. Adding someone to an existing deed makes them an owner, which gives them some control over the property and perhaps more control over your life than you may want them to have. And because they didn't pay you anything in return, the value you provided may be subject to a gift tax.

They may also pay more capital gains tax on the property when they sell it later. If they receive the property at the time of your death (via a TODD), the cost basis of the home is its value when they took possession (not when you bought the home). If you add their names to the deed now, the cost basis is what you paid for it. Cost basis matters because that's how the profit on a home is calculated when it's sold:

Profit = Sales price – Cost basis

The larger the cost basis, the smaller the profit, and the lower the capital gains tax. For example, suppose you bought a house for $150,000 in 2000. You place your only child's name on the lease. You die 30 years later, and your daughter immediately sells it for $450,000. Because she didn't live in it for at least two years before selling it, her profit subject to capital gains tax is $300,000. Had you deeded her the property with a TODD, the cost basis of the home would have been $450,000, her profit $0, and her capital gains tax $0.

WARNING

Many people also use a *quitclaim deed* to transfer ownership of property. Using a quitclaim deed, you can sign ownership over to a loved one or multiple loved ones, but you'd better trust them to do what's right. If they file the quitclaim deed before you die, they can take possession of your house and kick you out. Also, all signatories to the quitclaim deed become equal owners, which can cause problems, as described in the nearby sidebar "Brotherly love." The moral of all this cautionary language is this: Don't legally transfer your property to others until you absolutely need to (for example, upon your death).

BROTHERLY LOVE

Ralph has been involved in real estate and probate for the past 40 years. Recently, he received a call from an old acquaintance whose parents had just passed away. Prior to their death, they signed a quitclaim deed, leaving their home to their four boys. The youngest was living at the home and had been taking care of their parents. Before their death, the parents told the brothers that the youngest would get the home when they died.

As soon as their parents passed away, the three older boys decided that they deserved equal shares of the home, which caused a huge blowout. Money often brings out the worst in people. Two of the older brothers relinquished their claim to the house, but one persists in pursuing his claim, so the situation remains unresolved. The two brothers who agree that the house rightfully belongs to the youngest will likely go to court, along with the youngest brother, to file a motion in an attempt to overrule the brother who's still contesting ownership.

The moral of this story is that you need to be specific and put everything in writing. Don't leave any loose ends. Don't leave anything open to interpretation. Document your wishes in writing, being very specific about the outcomes you desire. If the parents had placed their property in a trust and indicated in a joint will that the youngest son was to inherit the property, this entire mess could have been avoided. But as soon as they deeded their home to all four sons, they set the stage for future family conflicts.

Be sure your heirs have all the information they need to locate your assets and key documents. All this work you're doing to put all the pieces in place will do your heirs little good if they don't know where to find the information they need. You'll end up making everybody's life harder rather than easier.

Using a trust to protect your assets

A more formal way to protect your assets from probate is to create a trust and place all your assets in the trust. Combining a trust with a will clarifies how you want your assets to be distributed upon your death, making probate unnecessary.

Using a trust to protect your assets is a two-step process: You create the trust, and then you transfer all your assets to it, as explained in the next two sections.

Types of trusts

Before delving into the process of creating a trust and populating it with assets, you should understand that not all trusts are created equal. First, they differ depending on whether they're revocable or irrevocable.

» A *revocable trust* can be modified or canceled at any time by the creator (grantor).

» An *irrevocable trust* can be modified or canceled only with the permission of the beneficiaries.

In addition, trusts differ depending on their purpose. In fact, at least 13 different types of trusts are available. Here, we list some of the more common types:

» A *testamentary trust* enables you to set limitations and conditions on when and how beneficiaries can access assets. For example, you can specify that your child can take out $40,000 per year to cover college expenses, starting at the age of 18 and ending at the age of 22.

» A *special needs trust* enables you to provide money to support living expenses and medical care for a dependent with special needs.

» A *qualified terminable interest property (QTIP) trust* enables you to divide assets among your beneficiaries at different times. A QTIP trust is typically used to enable a spouse to draw assets from the trust over the course of their lifetime without accessing the full principal amount of the assets, so the remaining assets are available for the couple's children upon the death of the surviving spouse.

» With a *blind trust,* the trustees keep the details of the trust and how assets will be distributed secret to reduce the chance of any conflicts among beneficiaries or between the trustees and the beneficiaries. Politicians often hold their investments in blind trusts to avoid conflicts of interest.

» A *spendthrift trust* enables you to prevent heirs from squandering their inheritance. For example, you can set up the trust to pay out a certain percentage of the assets to your heirs over an extended period or allow them to receive income earned by the assets without being able to cash out the assets earning that income.

» A *charitable trust* distributes assets to one or more charities or nonprofit organizations upon the grantor's death. This type of trust is often used to avoid or reduce estate taxes or gift taxes.

» A *generation-skipping trust* enables you to bequeath your assets to your grandchildren instead of your children, which is sometimes useful for avoiding or reducing estate taxes. This type of trust also enables you to give your children access to the income generated by the assets.

REMEMBER

You can have more than one trust, and a trust can be more than one type; for example, you can have a blind testamentary trust or a blind spendthrift trust.

Creating a trust

We strongly recommend that you consult a lawyer who has expertise in estate law or probate to ensure that your trust meets all your goals and is worded in the appropriate legalese. If you're a do-it-yourselfer or are just curious about the process, here it is:

1. **Create a trust document that includes the following information:**

- The name of the trust, which may simply be your last name followed by "Family Trust" — for example, "The Roberts Family Trust"

- Your name, address, phone number, and email address as the grantor (also known as the settlor or trustor)

- The name, address, phone number, and email address of the trustee in charge of managing the trust and of the successor trustee (your backup option)

- A comprehensive list of assets held in the trust

- A list of the trust beneficiaries, along with details of who gets what and when and their contact information — address, phone number, email address

2. **Sign the trust document and have it notarized.**

3. **Open a bank account for the trust.**

   This step is especially important if you're creating a trust that pays out money to beneficiaries over time. For the name of the account, use the trustee's name followed by "as Trustee of the John Doe Family Trust."

4. **File your trust and will with your local probate court, so it doesn't get lost or misplaced.**

   Filing your trust involves signing it, having it notarized, and taking it to your local probate court to have your documents recorded. If you amend your will or trust, be sure to file the revised versions with the court.

Placing your assets in the trust

After creating a trust, you're ready to start placing assets into it. This step requires changing your name as the owner of each asset to the name of the trust. For example, you'd contact your bank and request that the names on your accounts be changed from "John Doe" to "Trustee of the John Doe Family Trust."

The process differs depending on the asset type and how you hold ownership of it. For example, you need to go to the BMV to change the name on the title for any vehicle you own. Likewise, you change the name on the deed to your home by filing a quitclaim deed at your county's Register of Deeds office. As long as you're using the quitclaim deed to transfer ownership to the trust, you retain possession and control of your home for as long as you're alive and of sound mind and body.

Deciding how to take title when buying property

Whenever you buy real estate, you have the choice of specifying how you want ownership of the property structured — how you *take title* of the property. Taking title is a little off topic here, but if buying a home is a part of your downsizing plans, you should know your options. How you choose to take title can impact how protected your home is from creditors and how easily the property passes to your heirs. The overall goal is to take title in a way that enables you to live in the home for as long as you desire and pass it along to your heirs as unencumbered as possible. Here are your options for taking title:

>> **Sole and separate:** You or your spouse or life partner (not both of you) own the property. With this option, titles of most homes are in one person's name. In some states, you may be able to buy and sell property without your spouse's signature. In other states, you may be permitted to buy property without your spouse's signature but sell it only with your spouse's signature.

If you're married and own a property sole and separate from your spouse, and you die, this option may leave your surviving spouse with a major headache, along with legal costs and delays, especially if you didn't leave a will. However, owning a property sole and separate may be useful if your spouse is engaged in financially risky behavior that may place your home at an increased risk to creditors.

>> **Joint tenancy:** Joint tenancy is usually the default option for couples who want to share equal rights to the property during their lives and each have their rights of ownership pass to the surviving spouse through the right of survivorship (bypassing probate). Both parties are also equally responsible for the property, so if one owner borrows against the property, both owners are responsible for paying back the loan.

If you're buying a property with a spouse or life partner, you probably want to take title as joint tenancy — your mortgage lender may require it. If you're buying a property with someone other than a spouse or life partner, taking title as tenants in common may be the better choice.

>> **Tenants in common:** Two or more people hold title to the property in equal or unequal portions, but all owners have the right to occupy and use the entire property. For example, if you own 33.3 percent of a property, you can occupy the property and use the kitchen, living room, den, deck, and pool, but when the time comes to sell, you receive only 33.3 percent of the profits. You can sell your share separately, according to the terms set forth in your initial agreement with the other owners, and you can borrow against the value of your share of the property. This option has several disadvantages:

- If you die, the other owners receive your share — none of your share passes to your heirs.

- All owners share the liability for any debts on the property — for example, if one owner doesn't pay their share of the property taxes, the other owners are responsible for paying them.

- Any liens on the property by any owner must be cleared before the property can be sold.

>> **Community property:** Everyone listed as an owner owns the property equally and in its entirety, meaning the portion you own isn't protected against any lawsuit or collections actions taken against any of the other owners. Another owner of the property can take a mortgage loan out on it, and if they default on that loan, the lender can foreclose on the property. This option is available only in Arizona, California, Idaho, Louisiana, Nevada, New Mexico, Texas, Washington, and Wisconsin.

HOW WE TOOK TITLE

How you hold title is important, but sometimes you have to do what your lender requires — at least until after you close on your property. Traditionally, when you purchase a property with your spouse, the lender requires that you take title as a joint tenancy, with both your names on the title. They don't want to deal with anything odd, such as taking title in the name of your trust. If you try to add a trust to the transaction, you may end up having your loan request denied.

Under the direction of our estate-planning attorney, we closed on our condo with both our names on the title. Then our attorney transferred the deed to our trust. By placing the property in our trust, we're allowed to enjoy it for as long as we live, and it passes to the surviving partner when one of us dies, but as soon as both of us are gone, the property passes to our children.

We also have the option of breaking the trust if we ever decide to sell the condo.

>> **Community property with right of survivorship:** This option is the same as the community property option, but when one owner dies, their share of the property is passed along to the surviving owners. This option is available only in Arizona, California, Nevada, Texas, and Wisconsin.

Step 3: Creating a Power of Attorney

Power of attorney (POA) is a legal document granting another person authorization to act on your behalf in legal, financial, medical, or other personal or business matters. As part of your estate planning, you should grant POA to a trusted friend or loved one to act on your behalf whenever you're unable or unavailable to do so — for example, if you have an accident or develop an illness that leaves you physically or mentally incapacitated. That person then acts as your *attorney-in-fact* with a fiduciary responsibility to do what's in your best interests.

POAs differ in scope, trigger/duration, and type:

>> **General versus limited:** A *general POA* gives the attorney-in-fact broad powers to handle personal and business financial transactions, settle claims, employ professional help, and more; it's most appropriate for someone who's going to be out of the country and out of touch for a considerable time, such

as a husband or wife who's serving overseas in the military. A *limited POA* can restrict that authority to certain matters (such as financial or medical) or to specific transactions (such as closing on the sale of a home).

» **Durable, nondurable, or springable:** A *durable POA* remains in effect when you're incapacitated and unable to make decisions and act on your own behalf. It's mostly used for people who are incapacitated by illness or accident. A *nondurable POA* is better for temporary use — for example, when you're going to be traveling for a few months and need someone to take care of your finances while you're away. A *springable POA* is one that's triggered by a particular event, such as your doctor declaring you incompetent.

» **POA type:** POAs can be used for different situations and purposes. For example, a *medical POA* assigns someone to make medical decisions for you when you can't do it for yourself. A *military POA* assigns someone to take care of your financial and legal affairs when you're deployed.

To create a POA, you can hire a lawyer, use an online legal service (such as `LegalZoom.com`), or do it yourself using a template or form available online. Regardless of the method you use, be sure to follow these steps:

1. **Choose one or more people you fully trust to act as your attorney(s)-in-fact.**

    They don't need to be attorneys, but you may want them to consult your attorney, financial advisor, accountant, doctors, and so on when making key decisions.

2. **Write your POA agreement and have your attorney review it or hire an attorney to write the agreement for you.**

REMEMBER

    We strongly recommend hiring a lawyer to prepare your POA. You want to be sure it complies with your state's laws and grants the powers you need your attorney(s)-in-fact to have without granting them too much power.

3. **Have your POA notarized and provide a copy to your attorney(s)-in-fact and your attorney.**

4. **Keep your attorney(s)-in-fact in the loop as much as you're able.**

    They should be informed of any changes in your life that may impact the decisions and actions they're taking on your behalf.

Step 4: Ensuring You Have Some Control over Medical Decisions

We sincerely hope that you're never in a situation in which you're unable to make medical decisions for yourself, but being prepared for the worst is your best chance to have some control over the outcome. To give yourself some control over the medical treatment you receive when you're unable to make decisions for yourself, take the following precautions:

>> Write a living will detailing the type of medical treatments you wish and don't wish to receive under various conditions. See the earlier section "Writing a living will" for details.

>> Create a medical POA assigning a primary and secondary attorney-in-fact to make medical decisions for you when you're unable to do it for yourself, as explained in the previous section.

>> File an advance medical directive with each of your doctors. Your doctors will provide the forms they need you to fill out. (You also need to file this directive with the hospital.)

REMEMBER

An advance medical directive or living will doesn't do you any good if you just place it in a folder and file it away in a cabinet. Distribute copies to all your doctors and to loved ones, especially to the person you put in charge of calling the shots when you're lying in the hospital.

Step 5: Planning Your Business Succession

If you own a business, you should start thinking about what will happen to it when you're gone. You need to have a business succession strategy in place as part of your estate plan.

Business succession planning can be very involved and often requires close coordination between existing and new owners and management. Entire books are dedicated to the subject, including *Business Succession Planning For Dummies*, by Arnold Dahlke. Here, we walk you through the process, so you have a high-level view of what's involved:

1. **Decide what you want to happen to the business when you're gone or when you end your active participation in it.**

For example, do you want to sell it or pass it along to someone in your family?

2. **Estimate the value of your business.**

   An accurate business valuation can help you determine a fair price for your business, if you choose to sell it, and will help you understand the tax implications of your ownership transfer options. Conducting a business valuation is beyond the scope of this book, but you can find several methods and tools online for conducting a business valuation. We recommend hiring an accountant with experience in this area.

3. **Evaluate the legal and tax implications of the transfer of ownership.**

   Whether you plan to sell the business, give it away, or transfer ownership to a family member, partner, or someone else, consult with your business attorney, accountant, and financial advisor to find out what's involved and determine the best approach.

4. **Identify mission-critical roles in your organization, including your own role, along with other key positions that would be difficult to fill.**

   If you leave the business, who's going to fill your role? Others are likely to look for the exits when you leave — who are they and what roles do they play in your organization?

5. **Develop a list of qualifications for each position that's likely to be vacated when you leave the business.**

6. **Develop a plan for filling the vacancies.**

   Your plan may include the following:

   - A list of existing personnel who are qualified to fill the vacancies at least temporarily

   - Recruitment plans for finding additional candidates to fill the vacancies

   - Development of policies and procedures to help train candidates

   - Training programs to prepare new hires for their positions

7. **Execute your plan for transferring the business to the new owner(s).**

Step 6: Buying Life Insurance (or Not)

Life insurance is most useful when you're working to support your dependents and want to provide them with a safety net in the event that you die unexpectedly. They can then use that money to cover your funeral expenses and their living expenses until they transition to life without you. It can also be used to finance the education of dependent children and to fund your trust, if you set one up. If you have dependents, we encourage you to consult with your financial advisor and an insurance agent to figure out how much life insurance you need.

Life insurance can also be a useful part of your estate plan even if you no longer have dependents. Your heirs can use the proceeds from a life insurance policy to pay your funeral expenses, any income tax due on the disposition of assets, the balance on any loans, and so on without having to sell assets. Generally, the less you have in assets, the more you need life insurance for the protection of your family's needs after you're gone. You generally have two choices:

>> **Term life insurance** protects you for a limited number of years and has no cash value. It's the more affordable of the two options.

>> **Whole life insurance** provides lifelong protection (as long as you continue to pay the premiums) and accrues a cash value that you can borrow against or withdraw when you're still alive.

REMEMBER

If you don't have dependents, you can probably do without life insurance, especially if you have one or more retirement accounts and your heirs are listed as the beneficiaries. When you die, they can use whatever money is left in your retirement accounts to pay any taxes and claims against the estate. The money will also help them buy some time to arrange for the sale of other assets, such as your home. Take the money you would've spent on a life insurance policy and put it into a retirement account, such as a traditional or Roth IRA.

Step 7: Documenting Your End-of-Life Plan

Your *end-of-life plan* details the management of your funeral and remains. As you develop your end-of-life plan, be sure it includes the following:

>> Your funeral or memorial service arrangements

TIP

To ease the burden on your family, consider planning your own funeral or memorial service with a local mortuary. You can then include a simple directive in your last will and testament telling the executor of your will to contact that specific mortuary to set your plan in motion.

>> Whether you want to be buried, cremated, or have your body donated to science

>> Whether you want to be an organ donor

REMEMBER

If you want to be an organ donor, be sure to register online at www. organdonor.gov/sign-up or through your local BMV.

» Whether you want to publish a death notice or an obituary — you may even consider writing it yourself

» How to pay for the funeral arrangements

Step 8: Gathering and Organizing Essential Documents

Estate planning success is measured by how easy you make it for survivors to find everything they need to settle your estate. Keep all documents the executor of your will is going to need in a file folder, box, or designated section of your filing cabinet. Essential documents include the following:

» Marriage, divorce, and separation papers

» Your and, if you're married, your spouse's birth certificates

» If you have dependent children, their birth certificates or adoption papers

» Property deeds and titles

» Business and investment share certificates

» Your last will and testament, living will, and testamentary will (if applicable)

» Your advance medical directive

» Your POA

» Your business succession plan (if applicable)

» Usernames and passwords for all applicable email and online accounts

» Your trust document, assuming you created a trust

» Names and contact information for all your accounts and for your legal and financial advisors — bank and investment accounts, gas, electricity, cable, phone, water, your lawyer and accountant, and anything and anyone else your executor may need to know about

» Your life insurance policy

» Maps to any hidden treasures

» Your end-of-life plan

WARNING

Store your estate documents in a lockbox at your local bank or in a quality safe in your residence and provide your attorney and the executor of your will the details they need to access those documents. Also, create a backup digital copy of all your estate documents and store them in a secure folder in the cloud. No home can safely protect your documents from fires, hurricanes, earthquakes, floods, or theft.

Step 9: Completing an Estate Planning Checklist

Estate planning can be a very involved process with lots of moving pieces. To be sure you haven't overlooked something important, complete the following estate planning checklist:

- ❏ Your full name, address, phone number, social security number, and email address
- ❏ Your spouse's or life partner's full name, address, phone number, social security number, and email address
- ❏ The identity and location of any former spouse(s) (divorced or deceased)
- ❏ The names, addresses, phone numbers, social security numbers, and email addresses of all children and the identity of the other parent for each child
- ❏ The identity of any deceased children
- ❏ The names, addresses, and other identifying information for grandchildren, or other *shirttail relatives* (distant relatives or in-laws) or nonrelatives who may have a legal claim to your estate
- ❏ If you have dependent children, who will be named as guardian if the other parent is unable to act
- ❏ Names, addresses, phone numbers, and email addresses of all individuals who will serve as personal representatives of your estate, trustees of your trusts, and decision-making agents under general durable POAs and health POAs (at least one primary and one alternate)
- ❏ A copy of the deeds for all real estate
- ❏ Copies of the most recent monthly or quarterly statements for the following:
  - Checking and savings accounts
  - Certificates of deposit

- Money market funds

- Annuities

- Bonds

- Investment accounts

❏ Copies of the most recent monthly or quarterly statements and beneficiary designations for the following:

- Regular and Roth IRAs

- 401(k)s

- Pensions

- 403(b) plans

❏ Copies of operating agreements, bylaws, share certificates, buy-sell agreements, and the most recent entity-level tax returns (1120s, 1120Ss, and 1065s) for all closely held corporations, LLCs, and partnerships in which you and/or your spouse are members, shareholders, or partners

❏ Copies of all term life insurance binders showing the death benefit and designated beneficiaries

❏ Copies of life insurance policies with cash surrender values showing the cash value, death benefit, and designated beneficiaries

❏ Titles for all autos, trucks, boats, airplanes, and the like

❏ A detailed description of all personal property, especially jewelry, art, antiques, collections, and unique furniture, along with any statements of their appraised value

❏ Specific burial plans and ceremonial preferences

❏ Details about who gets what — names, contact info, specific dollar amounts or percentages, and descriptions of specific items

❏ Any age limitations specifying when heirs will be eligible to receive their inheritance, for example:

- All income beginning at age 21

- One-third of principal at age 24

- Half the balance at 27

- The entire balance at 30

- ❏ The name and contact info for the person who will administer the funds not distributed, if different from the people named as personal representatives and trustees

- ❏ Details about any trusts you've established

- ❏ Details about any of the heirs who require a special needs trust

- ❏ Details about any donations to charitable organizations during the life of the trust or upon your death

- ❏ Details about any college plans and college savings plans for children or grandchildren (for example, 529 plans)

- ❏ A comprehensive list of log-in information for online accounts, including social media accounts (all usernames and passwords)

- ❏ A business succession plan for each business you own

- ❏ Names and contact information for all key financial and legal advisors and services, including your

  - Certified public accountant

  - Financial advisor

  - Lawyer

  - Business partners

REMEMBER

If you have personal items you want others to have when you're no longer here, you have to spell this out. If it's jewelry, books, china, or mementos, say who you want it to go to. That will alleviate hard feelings among your loved ones when you're gone.

Having a trust means your loved ones won't have to deal with the probate courts. This is especially helpful when they're grieving. Your trust should specifically name who you want to be in charge of your estate. Choose wisely.

When you're getting your affairs in order, you need to find someone who specializes in trust and estate law. Not a general counsel. Not a criminal lawyer. You need state-specific legal counsel.

HANDLING AN ESTATE

Ralph managed an estate for Tom, a childhood friend who died in his 60s — way too young. Tom's mom passed away a decade before he did. Tom and his sister, who lives in Spain, had their mother sign quitclaim deeds to get her real estate assets transferred over to them, completely bypassing the probate process.

When Tom passed away, the real estate was placed in the sole possession of his sister. All she had to do was present a copy of his death certificate to the county recorder to become listed as the sole owner. She signed one property over to his girlfriend of 30 years and sold the other one.

Tom also had a collection of seven cars. Ralph thought those would have to go through probate, but Melissa Patterson, who is in the car business with her husband, was able to meet with the sister. She showed up to the meeting with six titles and a lease agreement for the seventh car, along with Tom's death certificate and Tom's sister, who was fine with the girlfriend having the cars. She left the meeting with titles for the six cars he had owned.

When Ralph found out about the gun collection, he called a friend to find out what to do with them. He's the one who told Ralph to take them to the police station. He also warned, "If one of those guns is stolen, you're going to have a fun afternoon." Ultimately, Ralph sold the guns, and the money from the sale went to the estate.

Chapter **8**

Using Your Home to Generate Income

If you do not find a way to make money while you sleep, you will work until you die.

— WARREN BUFFETT

Your home can be a money pit or a cash-generating machine. Often, it's both. You pour money into it with mortgage payments, maintenance, repairs, renovations, property taxes, insurance, homeowner association (HOA) fees, and utilities, but you can use that same property to generate income. You can lease all or a portion of the property, charge for parking or storage, run a bed and breakfast, generate and sell solar or wind energy, grow and sell produce, launch a home-based business, or cash out the equity as your home increases in value over time.

As a downsizer, you may choose or be compelled to become more entrepreneurial as you scale down your possessions and reduce your 9-to-5 workload, especially if you're struggling to support yourself on a fixed income. You need to find other sources of income, and one source that's packed with potential is the home you live in.

In this chapter, we reveal several ways to turn your home into a cash-generating machine to help finance your newly downsized life.

REMEMBER

You're not restricted to only one option presented in this chapter. You can mix and match options to use your home to generate income in different ways.

Leasing Your Home (or a Part of It)

As a homeowner, you have something other people need: living space, parking space, storage space, perhaps even a vacation rental. You can lease any extra space you have to generate additional income. Here are a few options to consider:

>> Lease one or more rooms you're not using in your home (or your basement), essentially taking on a roommate. Several online services can help you find a suitable roommate, including Roomster (www.roomster.com) and Roommates.com (www.roommates.com).

WARNING

Before leasing your home or any part of it, consult your insurance agent to see if any coverage needs to be added to your homeowner's policy to protect yourself from any liabilities.

>> Transform a section of your home into a rental suite or build a separate rental suite if regulations in your area permit it.

>> Lease your entire home as you downsize to something smaller, using the rent you collect as another income stream.

>> Start your own bed and breakfast or become an Airbnb host.

>> Lease your garage for parking space or storage. If you have garage or other parking space available, you can list it online on sites such as Spacer (www.spacer.com).

>> Rent out your pool, something that has become a big business thanks to the stay-at-home mentality during the COVID-19 pandemic. You can list your pool for rent online at Swimply (swimply.com).

WARNING

List your pool for rent through a company that's insured and bonded; don't do this on your own. If something bad were to happen to one of your guests, you could be held responsible.

>> Host events, such as weddings, showers, and graduations (if you have a large enough space).

>> Lease a portion of your lot to someone who wants to erect a tiny home on it. Okay — this one's a little out there, but it gives you a sense of what's possible.

In this section, we reveal what's involved in being a landlord and suggest ways to make it easier.

If you're downsizing, don't assume that you need to sell your big house to move to a smaller one. You may be better off leasing that big house and using a portion of your rental income to make the mortgage payments on your smaller home. You may get a better return on your real estate investment than anything you can hope for in the stock market. However, you need to consider some of the concerns and hassles you're likely to encounter, such as finding good tenants, collecting rent, and dealing with bad tenants.

Taking on the role of landlord

Whenever you lease property you own, you become a landlord and take on the following responsibilities:

>> Finding, screening, and contracting with prospective tenants

>> Providing tenants with safe and habitable living space

>> Maintaining and repairing the property on a timely basis

>> Collecting rent, giving tenants sufficient notice before raising the rent, and evicting tenants who don't pay the rent

>> Notifying tenants before entering the premises

>> Returning security deposits promptly when tenants move out, assuming they met their obligations

The key to being a successful landlord is finding the right tenants. We own multiple rental properties and use software called Buildium (www.buildium.com) to manage them. Buildium includes a feature for screening prospective tenants through TransUnion, one of the three major credit reporting agencies.

However, even if you perform your due diligence and are a great judge of character, you can overlook key details about a prospective tenant's financial, personal, and family situation. Try to get as much information as you can but realize that all the available information may not be enough. In other words, hope for the best but plan for the worst.

Buildium provides a credit report and background check and will advise you on whether to reject applicants. If it doesn't turn up anything negative, it'll present you with a list of your top applicants. You'll still need to meet with applicants to do your final screening, but thanks to Buildium, you'll have the background information you need to make a well-informed decision.

You can't totally a trust a previous landlord's positive review of prospective tenants. If those tenants are slow payers or are in the process of being evicted, their current landlord or property management company is highly motivated to get rid of them and may tell you that they're great tenants when they're really tenants from hell. You definitely need to contact previous landlords, but take what they say with a grain of salt.

If your prospective renters are a family, try to schedule a time for the whole family to visit the rental property to see whether they're all going to like living there. You can also do a surprise visit to check in with them a week or so after they move in, so you can get a feel for how they're treating your property — it's probably the best your property is ever going to look again.

As seasoned landlords, we offer the following words of advice:

>> Set your rents a little below the top of the scale to retain good tenants.

>> Keep up on maintenance and repairs. You wouldn't live in a home that's in poor condition, so it's not right to expect someone else to live in a run-down property.

>> Adhere closely to your municipality's rental ordinances. Many municipalities require that rental properties be inspected and registered with them (for a fee).

>> Avoid leasing to friends or family members. You don't want to risk your relationships over any disagreements about rent or how the property is being managed and maintained.

>> Be prepared to deal with unexpected situations, such as tenant illness, death, and divorce. When you become a landlord, you're playing a part in people's lives, and life can get messy. Be firm but flexible, patient, and understanding.

Using a property management company

If the idea of being a landlord is the only thing standing in the way of your decision to lease your property, consider outsourcing those onerous responsibilities to a property management company. For a fee, the property management company handles the following tasks:

>> Markets vacancies.

>> Screens tenants and signs leases.

>> Collects rents.

>> Fields calls from tenants.

>> Oversees maintenance and repairs.

>> Collaborates with law enforcement to handle evictions when necessary.

REMEMBER

Contact a few property management companies in your area to find out about the services they offer and their cost. Ask for and check references — talk to property owners who use the property management companies you're considering to find out how reliable and reputable they are.

Running your own bed and breakfast

If you own a property with extra rooms and don't necessarily want to move out of it, consider turning it into a *bed and breakfast (B&B)* — essentially a cross between a hotel and a private residence. Thanks to online services such as Airbnb (`www.airbnb.com`), more and more people are transforming unused bedrooms into B&B rentals.

Before you list your home as a B&B, consider the following factors:

>> **Your personality:** Are you a people person? If you're not a people person, you probably won't like running a B&B. You'll be sharing your living space with others and will be called on to attend to their needs. You must be friendly and accommodating.

>> **Your freedom:** You need to be available to answer phone calls and see to the needs of your guests. If you're a homebody, perfect! If, on the other hand, you cherish your freedom and don't like having your day interrupted, this probably isn't the gig for you, unless you can afford to hire an assistant.

>> **Your location:** Do you live in a popular location? If you're near a waterfront, a large city, or a place that has many popular attractions — concerts, sporting events, conventions, museums, historic sites, and so on — you won't have any trouble marketing your property. However, if you live in Podunk, U.S.A., you'll struggle to find anyone who's interested.

REMEMBER

Another option is to lease your entire home as a vacation rental, which you can do on sites like Airbnb and Vrbo (`www.vrbo.com`). While Airbnb allows property owners to lease out individual rooms in their homes, Vrbo makes listings exclusive to entire properties — an entire home, apartment, or cottage, for example.

Selling Your Home

The most obvious way to use your home to generate income is to sell it, assuming you can sell it for more than you owe on it. One of the big perks attached to selling a primary residence is that up to $250,000 of the profit is tax-free at the federal level for an individual homeowner and up to $500,000 is tax-free for a couple. The only catch is that you must have lived in the home for at least two of the past five years.

REMEMBER

Calculating the profit on the sale of a home can be a very involved process. It's not a simple matter of subtracting what you paid for the property from what you sold it for. To calculate your profit, take the following steps:

1. **Start with your original investment in the property — how much you paid for it at closing (your cash basis in the property).**

   Your *cash basis* is the purchase price plus certain expenses that you paid at closing, such as settlement fees, title insurance, and property taxes owed by the previous owner.

2. **Add the cost of additions and major improvements.**

   Don't include the cost of maintenance and repairs or anything else that doesn't add value to the property. Examples of additions and major improvements include adding a family room, building a second story on a one-story home, and constructing a garage on the property.

3. **Subtract any amount allowable for depreciation (if you used part of your home for a business or as rental property) and losses due to damages or theft that weren't covered by insurance.**

4. **Subtract the result from the amount you sold the property for.**

5. **Subtract your agent's commission and any other expenses related to the sale of the home.**

   The resulting amount is your profit or loss — more specifically, your *capital gain* or *capital loss*.

TIP

If you decide to sell your home, list it through one of the top real estate agents in your area — the person who sells the most homes. Don't even think about listing it yourself (for sale by owner) to avoid the cost of paying agent commissions. In addition to saving you the time, effort, and headaches of listing and selling your own home, a top agent can help you avoid making costly mistakes, such as getting your property tied up on contract with an unqualified buyer. A great agent can also sell your home faster and for significantly more money than you'll get by selling it yourself. Even after paying the 6–7 percent agent commission, you're likely to come out ahead.

TIMING IS EVERYTHING

When we decided to downsize, we wanted to sell our home, but not right away. We didn't want to have to move twice — for example, from our home to an apartment and then from the apartment to our forever home. We were fortunate because we didn't need to sell our home to finance the purchase of our new home. We had a $100,000 line of credit we could draw from along with a vacant rental property that we owned free and clear.

Instead of selling our primary residence, we sold our rental property, which provided us with sufficient cash for a down payment on our new home. That cash, plus the $100,000 line of credit, gave us the capital we needed to move forward on our new home comfortably. Because we were building a home, we needed to have cash available to cover the *draws* — the payments due when the builders complete a certain stage in the process.

After we moved, we listed our old home for sale.

Everyone's situation is different. Carefully examine your goals in light of the resources you have available to meet those goals and discuss your options with your financial advisor or accountant. You may be better off selling your existing home before buying a new home, or vice versa, depending on the market and on your specific situation.

WARNING

Don't list your home for sale if you're planning to refinance your mortgage to cash out equity in the home. Refinance first and then list your home for sale. Nobody's going to refinance a home that's being sold.

Borrowing Against Your Home to Cash Out Equity

As you pay off the mortgage on your home and it increases in value, you build up equity in the property. *Equity* is the difference between your property's market value and what you owe on it. In other words, if you sold the property and used the proceeds from the sale to pay off your mortgage, equity is the amount of cash you'd receive at closing.

You can cash out the equity in your property in various ways, including the following:

» Sell the property and pay off your mortgage.

» Refinance your mortgage for a higher amount and pay off the existing mortgage.

» Take out another, separate mortgage on the property, leaving the existing mortgage in place (commonly referred to as a second or third mortgage).

» Take out a reverse mortgage, explained in the next section.

If you refinance or take out a separate mortgage, you basically have two options:

» **Home equity loan:** With a *home equity loan,* you get a lump sum of cash all at once, and you immediately start to accrue interest on that total amount. It's just like your first mortgage.

» **Home equity line of credit (HELOC):** With a *HELOC,* you're approved to borrow up to a certain maximum, but you start accruing interest only on the amount of money you actually borrow. A HELOC is generally best for financing new construction projects, repairs, and renovations, because you pay these bills out of the line of credit as they come in.

TIP

Every homeowner who has a mortgage and some equity built up in their home should have a HELOC as a safety net. A HELOC can buy you some valuable time if you ever experience a financial setback, such as a large unanticipated medical bill. You can draw money from the HELOC and then pay it back. Having a HELOC in place can help you avoid foreclosure when you don't have sufficient cash flow to cover your mortgage payments.

We often warn homeowners, *Don't use your home as an ATM.* Some homeowners refinance their homes over and over as mortgage rates drop and their homes appreciate to cash out equity to pay bills and buy whatever they want and really can't afford — new cars, new boats, big-screen TVs, and so on. They cash out all the equity in their homes and then don't have any left when they really need it.

However, when you're downsizing or trying to stretch your income over the course of your retirement, you can use the equity you've built up in your property strategically to meet your downsizing goals. Most lenders allow you to cash out up to 80 percent of the equity in a property.

Here are some ways to use the equity in your property to meet your downsizing goals:

>> Cover your down payment on your new downsized home.

>> Use a portion of it as your *earnest money deposit (EMD)* on your new downsized home. When you make an offer on a home, you typically put up 1–3 percent of the purchase price as an EMD to demonstrate your good faith in following through on the deal. The money is held in an escrow account and applied to the down payment at closing. If you back out of the deal for no good reason, the seller keeps the money (ouch!).

>> Cover draws on new construction. Draws are made during the completion of a newly constructed home. For example, money may be drawn to reserve the lot, upon completion of the basement, when the roof is done, and so on. When the home is completed to your satisfaction, you then pay the builder the balance you owe.

>> Use it to cover your living expenses or pay for whatever you want. Again, we normally discourage cashing out the equity in your home to cover living expenses, but if you're retired and have a plan in place that enables you to cash out some or all of the equity in your home without losing it in foreclosure, it's worth considering.

Of course, if you used your home as an ATM and already cashed out all the equity you built up in it, you ruined your opportunity to use that equity now to improve your life post downsizing, when you really can use it.

Making the Most of a Reverse Mortgage

If you're 62 or older with some equity built up in your home, consider using a *reverse mortgage* to free up some of that equity. Like a traditional mortgage, you're borrowing money and using your home as collateral to secure the loan, but unlike a traditional mortgage, you have no monthly mortgage payment, and you're allowed to continue living in the home for as long as you own it. Interest and fees are added to the *principal* (loan balance). When you sell the home or pass away, the balance is paid off at closing.

To determine whether a reverse mortgage is right for you, consider the following pros and cons:

Pros

>> You can stay in your home for as long as you own it (and are alive, obviously). You keep the title to your home.

>> You have various options for receiving the money, such as the following:

- Line of credit to draw money as needed

- Monthly payments

- Lump-sum distribution

- Any combination of those options

>> Neither you nor your heirs will ever be personally liable for paying more than the home is sold for. In other words, you can't get *upside down* (owing more than the home is worth) like you can with a traditional mortgage.

>> You can use the money to pay off any existing mortgage on the home.

>> Qualifying is simplified — lenders don't require a minimum credit score and generally don't require proof of income.

>> You have no monthly mortgage payments — but you still need to pay your homeowner's insurance premiums, property taxes, and HOA fees.

>> Your heirs inherit the home and receive any equity that's left in the property after the loan balance is paid off. Your heirs can choose to pay off the loan balance or refinance if they want to keep the property.

>> Proceeds from the loan are not taxable.

>> The interest rate may be lower than that of traditional mortgages and home equity loans.

Cons

>> You must reside in the home. You can't lease your home to someone else.

>> Fees may be higher than those for a conventional mortgage. Fees include the loan origination fee and Federal Housing Administration (FHA) mortgage insurance. Your mortgage insurance premiums help fund FHA reserves, which are used to pay back lenders when borrowers fail to repay their loans.

>> The loan balance (principal) increases over time, meaning the value the home contributes to your estate (and your heirs' inheritance) may decrease over time.

>> Although the money you receive isn't considered income for tax purposes, it may impact your ability to qualify for other needs-based government programs, such as Medicaid or supplemental security income benefits. Be sure to discuss this possibility with a government benefits specialist to ensure that your eligibility won't be compromised.

The most common type of reverse mortgage, *a home equity conversion mortgage (HECM)*, is backed by the FHA. To qualify for an HECM, you must meet the following requirements:

>> Be at least 62 years old.

>> Own your home outright or have paid down a considerable amount on the mortgage.

>> Live in the home as your principal residence.

>> Not be delinquent on any federal debt.

>> Stay current on property taxes, homeowner's insurance, and HOA fees.

>> Sit through an information session presented by an approved HECM counselor.

WARNING

The biggest risk involved in a reverse mortgage is the possibility of losing your home in foreclosure if you don't pay your property taxes, homeowner's insurance, or the fees associated with the reverse mortgage. As long as you stay current on those bills, however, your home ownership is protected. Nobody can take your home solely because you owe more on it than it's worth.

So, is a reverse mortgage right for you? Here are a few factors that can make a reverse mortgage an attractive solution:

>> You're struggling with cash-flow issues (more flowing out than flowing in). You've tried everything in terms of reining in your budget, and you're still tight on cash.

>> You've built up significant equity in your home — you paid off your first mortgage (or a significant portion of the principal balance), your home has increased considerably in value, or both.

>> You plan to stay in your home for a long time — at least long enough to recoup the loan origination fee and any other up-front costs of the loan.

>> You have, and will continue to have, sufficient funds to cover your homeowner's insurance, property taxes, and HOA fees, along with your other living expenses. (Perhaps the reverse mortgage will provide the money you need to cover these expenses.)

>> You're in your 70s, 80s, or 90s. Although you can qualify when you reach the age of 62, the older you are, the bigger the benefit — the more money you get to spend and the less time you have to spend it.

>> You don't have heirs or aren't concerned about leaving the property (or the equity you have in it) to them.

WARNING

Con artists are constantly on the prowl for victims and often focus their efforts on affluent older people, including homeowners who have considerable equity built up in their homes. Be sure to work with an FHA-approved lender to apply for an HECM loan. Start with your bank, but be sure to compare rates and fees as you would when applying for any loan.

TIP

Look for a lender that specializes in reverse mortgages. It doesn't matter whether the lender is a bank, credit union, or mortgage company or is located in another state, but you want a lender who knows reverse mortgages inside and out, and can provide quality service and the information and guidance you need to make well-informed decisions.

3

Decluttering: Sell It, Give It Away, or Trash It

Get up to speed on decluttering basics — general guidelines that apply to every room in the house.

Declutter one room at a time — tips for decluttering bedrooms, bathrooms, kitchens, living rooms, offices, laundry rooms, garages, sheds, and more.

Sort items into six categories: keep, store, sell, give away, donate, and toss.

Downsize your photo, video, and document collections by dumping most of them and digitizing the memorable and important ones.

Sell your belongings for top dollar at an estate sale, a garage/yard sale, or online.

Explore your storage options for items that don't fit in your new downsized life but you don't want to get rid of yet.

Give your belongings away when you can't or don't want to sell them or store them.

Explore different ways to discard anything you can't get rid of, including toxic and potentially harmful items you can't just toss in the trash.

Chapter 9

Sorting Your Belongings

If your stuff isn't serving you, it won't be serving you any better packed away in a box somewhere.

— MELISSA CAMARA WILKINS

A major part of downsizing — perhaps the biggest challenge of all — involves eliminating a good chunk of the possessions you accumulated over the years and organizing the rest. Recently, our coauthor's daughter downsized from a 3,000-square-foot home to one half that size. For the first two weeks after she moved, she couldn't pull her car into the garage because it was packed with furniture and other belongings that wouldn't fit inside the new house. Her first order of business — having a garage sale to get rid of it all. Had she decluttered before moving, she would've avoided moving all that stuff. And she moved it twice — from the home she sold to a storage unit and from there to her new home. Moral of the story: Declutter *first* and have the garage sale *first*.

One of the goals of downsizing is to lighten your load — to unshackle yourself from the ball and chain restricting your freedom and your ability to live a richer, fuller life with less worry. No, we're not talking about your spouse; we're referring to that other ball and chain: the home that's larger than you need packed with twice or three times the belongings you'll ever use. Yes, it's high time you declutter, and the first step is to sort your belongings. (For more on the art of decluttering, check out *Decluttering For Dummies*, by Jane Stoller.)

In this chapter, we deliver the guidance and motivation you need to begin decluttering your life. We start by covering decluttering basics and then lead you room by room through the process with the ultimate goal of creating six easy-to-manage stacks:

>> Keep

>> Store

>> Sell

>> Donate

>> Give away

>> Toss

With six convenient stacks, you'll be well on your way to meeting your downsizing goal, addressing each stack in turn.

Mastering Decluttering Basics

Decluttering is deceptively difficult. It sure sounds easy — all you're doing is getting rid of some belongings and organizing what's left. However, most people underestimate just how much they need to get rid of. As a result, they end up moving or storing much of what they don't need, which defeats the very purpose of downsizing.

To avoid this common mistake, master the following downsizing basics:

TIP

>> **Start with the end in mind.** This is one of Stephen Covey's seven habits of highly effective people, but it's especially relevant to downsizing. Before packing anything to move to your new place, be sure you know where you're going to put it.

Think about downsizing in terms of a percentage or fraction. If you're moving to a place that's a third the size of your current home, set a goal of getting rid of at least two-thirds of your belongings.

>> **Take inventory of what you have.** One of the first things a moving company does is a walk-through of your home to estimate the number of trucks and movers needed. Start with the big items — furniture and large

appliances — and measure carefully for fit. Decide whether to keep what you have or buy new. After furniture and appliances, move on to smaller items. An accurate inventory helps you determine how many moving boxes you need and starts you thinking about what you'll keep and what you'll get rid of.

>> **Set a reasonable deadline.** Downsizing takes time, but set a deadline to motivate yourself. A goal without a deadline is a pipe dream.

>> **Divide and conquer.** After setting a reasonable deadline, set even more reasonable milestones. For example, you can set a separate deadline for each room or set interim deadlines — 25, 50, and 75 percent completion dates. You can also divide and conquer by delegating some of the work among friends and family members who have volunteered to help.

>> **Take out the trash.** Eliminating trash is a no-brainer — an easy way to declutter without having to spend much time and effort deciding what to get rid of. For example, have you ever gone through your spice cabinet and simply cleared out spices that you *never* use and *will never* use? How 'bout disposing of medications that are beyond their expiration date? All easy-peasy.

>> **Start with small, easy downsizing projects.** Ease into downsizing by starting with a cabinet, closet, or small room. Getting started is often the biggest obstacle. By tackling small projects, you build momentum, motivation, and confidence to tackle bigger jobs, such as the kitchen.

>> **Eliminate duplicates.** If you have two or three or four of the same item, save all but one. You're not downsizing to Noah's Ark, where you need two of every animal.

>> **Digitize photo prints and paper documents.** Eliminate as much of the paper you store as possible by eliminating the ones you no longer want or need and digitizing the rest. See Chapter 10 for details.

>> **Don't rely on storage.** Strive to get rid of as much as possible without having to rent a storage unit for the overflow. You're downsizing to reduce your expenses and free yourself from the burden of having too many possessions, so what sense does it make to downsize and rent one or more storage units to keep things you don't have room for?

REMEMBER

Storage is a crutch to avoid making difficult decisions.

TEMPORARY STORAGE

When we discussed storage, it was never in relation to renting a storage unit. Our concerns were limited to where we were going to store items between moving them out of our existing home and moving them into our new home. Our move wasn't a smooth, continuous process; it happened in stages, and items came from different sources. Our new furniture came from one supplier, appliances were delivered from another, and many items were moved from our existing home.

Over the course of the first 30 days, something was happening every day. The movers packed up our belongings over several days, but we didn't move out of the house right away. We put everything in a moving truck and then stayed in a hotel for a week to give the contractors a running start to add finishing touches to our new home. Our hotel was only about four miles from our new home.

A week after we moved out (the week of Thanksgiving 2021), the truck arrived at our new condo with the mother lode — bedroom furniture, clothes, lamps, end tables, and more. At this point, everything came together — and we started to make the new condo our home.

We both work from home, so we had to ensure that our offices were set up as soon as possible. We ran into an obstacle moving Ralph's office desk: The frame wouldn't fit through the door! We had to reverse-engineer the desk. A family friend, a welder, cut it apart, moved it (in pieces) into the condo, and welded it back together. That desk will never be leaving!

Stop Cluttering

One of the keys to decluttering is to stop cluttering. As personal finance guru Dave Ramsey has written, "We buy things we don't need with money we don't have to impress people we don't like." Now that you're downsizing, the time has come to stop doing that. Put a moratorium on buying anything new until you're living in your newly downsized home. And after you transition to your downsized existence, reconsider every purchase.

To determine whether you really need something, ask yourself the following questions:

>> **Why do I want to buy this?** Are you buying it for yourself or because you think it will please someone else?

» **Do I really need this? Can I live without it? How often will I use it in the future?** If you're not going to use it often, is it something you can borrow?

» **Do I already have one of these?** Are you thinking of buying an item simply because you've misplaced the one you have?

» **How much value will this add to my life?** Is the cost, care, and storage you'll invest in the item more than the utility or joy it will bring into your life?

REMEMBER

As the old saying goes, "When you find yourself in a hole, stop digging." If you're thinking of downsizing, stop buying stuff. In the process of downsizing, you may discover that you already own it.

Decluttering One Room at a Time

According to a Chinese proverb, "A journey of a thousand miles begins with a single step." Likewise, the long process of decluttering starts with a single room — and usually with a single drawer of a single cabinet in that room.

REMEMBER

Decluttering a large home can be an overwhelming task, especially if you or others in your household are pack rats. We encourage you to approach this task room by room to make it more manageable. In the following sections, we offer guidance on a room-by-room basis.

Bedrooms

Assuming that your bedrooms contain only typical bedroom items, decluttering is fairly straightforward: You're dealing mostly with clothing and bedding. However, if your bedrooms are packed with books, videos, a TV set, a stereo system, plants, and other items, each bedroom can be like a microcosm of your entire home (without the kitchen and bathroom, of course). Start with the common items/areas found in a bedroom: nightstands, dressers, vanity, and closet.

Nightstands

Nightstands are clutter magnets, especially when they have not only a top but one or more shelves or drawers. You have your bare essentials: lamp, alarm clock, book, headphones, paper and pen, glass of water, coaster, reading glasses. And then you have all the extras: sleep mask, CPAP machine, candles, hand cream, body lotion, USB plugs and cables, knickknacks, lubricants... we'll just stop at that — we really don't want to know.

Sort all the little stuff (not the lamp or alarm clock, for example) into two piles — what to keep and what to get rid of — pack everything you want to keep into the smallest box possible, and label it "Nightstand."

REMEMBER

The more clutter you have on surfaces, the more time you spend cleaning. Every item and every horizontal surface collect dust. You must dust every item, move it to clean the surface, and then move it back. As you downsize, strive to keep all horizontal surfaces (tabletops, counters, and shelves) as barren as possible. Trim your knickknack collection down to a point at which your favorites will fit in a small curio cabinet and get rid of the rest.

Dressers

Dressers are notorious for becoming cluttered over time — the top and all the drawers. Decluttering the top is like decluttering a nightstand. The drawers pose another challenge. If the drawers are so packed that you need to push clothes down to open or close them, you have a problem. If they're stuffed with clothes you haven't worn in six months, there's hope.

Drawer by drawer, remove everything and sort it into two stacks: what to keep and what to get rid of. Fold everything you're keeping so items can be stored vertically instead of stacked on top of one another. Then, place them back in their designated drawer — for example, sock drawer, underwear drawer, T-shirt drawer, and so on.

REMEMBER

The good news about dressers is, you can pretty much move them as is to your downsized abode, assuming you're going to keep them.

Vanity

If you have a *vanity* (dressing table) in your bedroom or in a walk-in closet, chances are good that it's cluttered with a variety of beauty items: mirrors, combs, brushes, makeup, lotions, creams, earrings, hair ties, curling iron, hair straightener, and more. It may even contain photos, cards and letters, knickknacks, and a variety of other items.

In this case, forgo the drawer-by-drawer approach, because items tend to get mixed up in a vanity. If you have a large table, set everything out on the table and sort it by type. Get rid of anything you haven't used in the past few months and don't plan to use in the next few months, along with any duplicate items.

The final step — returning items to the vanity — is the most important. Don't just dump everything back into the drawers. Obtain drawer organizers or dividers to keep all the items you carefully sorted separate. You can also buy cosmetic and jewelry storage cases for the top of your vanity to increase your storage space vertically and place commonly used items in easy reach.

Start thinking about how you can declutter in terms of the container shapes and sizes you'll need when you're ready to sort all your belongings.

Closet

Closets are sort of like mini storage units for rooms. Nearly every room has one. Each bedroom has a closet. Most homes have one near the front door. Your kitchen has one (it's called a pantry). You may even have a linen closet in your laundry room or in a hallway.

The best approach for decluttering any closet is to empty it first. Lay out everything so you know what you're dealing with. Then create two stacks: one for keepers and one for everything you're going to get rid of — mostly anything you haven't used over the past year or so. Sort everything you're going to keep and then pack it (if you're moving soon) or return it to the closet.

All sorts of new closet cabinets and organizers are now available to maximize storage space while keeping everything in convenient reach. We encourage you to explore your options before returning items to your closet. When your closet is empty is the perfect time to install new shelving, rods, and organizers. We downsized to less than half the closet space, but with the help of the Lazy Lee system, we were able to maintain a respectable wardrobe and have everything within easy reach (see Figures 9-1 and 9-2).

FIGURE 9-1:
Before downsizing, we had a traditional walk-in closet.

FIGURE 9-2:
After downsizing:
Optimized
storage with
everything in easy
reach.

Bathrooms

Bathrooms start their lives as simple spaces — toilet, tub/shower, sink(s), medicine cabinet, and some sort of storage below the sink(s). Then, you need somewhere to hang your towels, so you install shelves for clean towels and hangers or hooks for towels in use. Maybe you even install hooks on the bathroom door. As your needs grow, you bring in another cabinet or install more shelving and hooks. Soon, you can barely move without bumping into something or knocking something over.

Here are a few suggestions for decluttering your bathroom:

>> **Review your towel collection.** Get rid of any towels and washrags you don't use. Animal shelters are a great place to donate towels and linens.

>> **Properly dispose of old medications and any meds you're not going to use.** Check the expiration dates and contact a local pharmacy to find out where to take your old medications for disposal.

>> **Thin the herd of shampoos, conditioners, creams, lotions, and medicinal ointments.** Combine partially used products when possible and dump anything you haven't used for more than a year and don't plan to use in the foreseeable future.

» **Clean out all drawers.** Empty the drawers onto a large table, sort everything by kind (hair care, dental hygiene, makeup, and so on), install drawer organizers, and return to the drawers all items you decide to keep while maintaining the groupings you created when you sorted.

Kitchen

A good sign that your kitchen needs decluttering is that you're using more than two-thirds of your cabinet or counter space. A good goal to work toward is to clear about 90 percent of your counter space and organize your cabinets so that you don't have to dig through everything to find what you're looking for. Here are a few recommendations:

» **Reduce your pot/pan collection.** Unless you're a master chef, you shouldn't need a 10-piece cookware set. You can usually get by with a small, medium, and large pot and a large frying pan.

» **Reduce your storage container collection.** Ten to 15 medium-large stackable storage containers should do the trick. Pitch any containers that don't have a matching lid.

» **Thin your herd of cups, glasses, and dishware.** If you're like most people, you have a collection that greatly exceeds the needs of three to four households.

» **Clear your countertops.** Having nothing more than a coffeemaker and maybe a toaster on your countertops is ideal. Clear off anything you don't use at least once a week. If you have a dishwasher, you can do without having a dish drainer on your counter, or you can buy a dish drainer that fits inside one of your sinks. Evict any non-kitchen items — mail, pens, paper, keys, and so forth.

» **Use drawer dividers to organize utensils, knives, and small gadgets.** Don't just dump items back into a drawer.

» **Dump any food or spices that are over six months old.** When you return items to your pantry, group them by type — cereals, pastas, canned foods, condiments, baking supplies, and so on.

» **Minimize your cookbook collection.** Store your favorite recipes on your computer or smartphone and simply look up recipes online when you want to cook something new. If you're old school, keep a few of your favorite cookbooks!

TIP

We're big fans of the lazy Susan for maximizing storage space. When we were building our condo, we made full use of the Lazy Lee storage system for our closets and kitchen pantry (see Figure 9-3).

FIGURE 9-3:
Our Lazy Lee doubles the storage capacity of a typical pantry.

Living room

Technology has done much of the heavy lifting in decluttering living rooms. An entertainment system now consists basically of a flat-screen smart TV with a soundbar, and you no longer need storage for DVDs or videotapes — you can stream whatever you want to watch. However, living rooms can still become cluttered with books, magazines, knickknacks, remote controls, game controllers, and other items. Here are a few suggestions for reducing the clutter:

» Donate books you'll never touch to the local library and toss old magazines into the recycle bin.

» Keep a few of your favorite belongings on display and hide everything else that's sitting on shelves, tables, and other surfaces, including photos, knickknacks, and candles.

» Store remote controls, video game controllers, device chargers, and other electronics in a separate box or basket in a drawer or under an end table.

TIP

If you're in the market for a new coffee table or ottoman, look for one that includes storage. While you don't want to enable any pack rat tendencies you may have by providing yourself more storage space, small furniture with built-in storage can replace the storage you're losing by downsizing to a smaller space.

Office

Whether you have a bona fide office or just a desk and a filing cabinet set up somewhere in your home, here are a few suggestions for downsizing and organizing your files and office supplies:

>> **Eliminate anything that's not office-y.** Anything that belongs in a kitchen, closet, gym, playroom, or knickknack cabinet needs to go. Your office should be all business, free from distractions.

>> **Clear the bookshelves.** Start by removing anything that's not a book — office supplies, photographs, medications, nutritional supplements, old tech (hardware and software), CDs and DVDs, and so on. You can combine some items with similar items from other areas of your home or place them in clear or labeled storage boxes for easy as-needed access. And, of course, you can dispose of anything you haven't touched in a year.

>> **Dump old files and folders.** Consider using the following three-pile system:

• **Shred:** Junk mail, receipts (except those you need for warranties, proof of purchase, or taxes), bank and investment statements that are more than two months old, last year's pay stubs, maintenance and repair records for cars or homes you no longer own, documents for organizations you no longer belong to, expired service contracts, expired warranties, your deceased pet's vet records

• **Scan:** Tax returns older than three years; receipts and credit card statements needed for warranties, proof of purchase, and noncash charitable donations; annual bank and brokerage statements; pension documents; social security statements

• **Store:** Birth certificates; passports; marriage certificates; divorce certificates; death certificates; social security cards; titles and deeds to cars and real estate assets; estate documents (wills, trusts, life insurance policies, powers of attorney, advance medical directives, and end-of-life documents); loan and mortgage documents (including paid-in-full statements for every loan you've ever had); military service records; medical records; your three most recent tax returns

Store difficult-to-replace documents, such as your birth certificate, passport, titles, deeds, and social security cards in a lockbox or a home safe that's rated for temperatures above 450 degrees for 60 minutes.

>> **Get organized.** After getting rid of as much excess as possible, organize the rest. Buy drawer dividers to organize everything in your desk and use boxes or a filing cabinet to organize all the folders, documents, and office supplies you decide to keep. Your goal is to make sure everything is easy to move and find, and fits in a designated space in your new destination.

TIP

Consider using clear boxes to store folders and supplies, so you can quickly and easily see what each box contains.

Laundry room

Laundry rooms are often much larger than they need to be and end up being used as auxiliary closet space. Downsizing your laundry room possessions depends on what you have stored in it. Here are a few general suggestions:

>> Tighten the caps on all laundry and cleaning products and place them in a plastic box or in a plastic bag inside a cardboard box in case they leak in transit. You're better off moving these items yourself instead of placing them inside the moving truck. (Take this opportunity to combine products, such as two half bottles of the same stain remover.)

>> If your laundry room doubles as a linen closet, sort your towels and bedding and get rid of anything you haven't used in the past six months and have no plans of using in the next six months.

TIP

If you're moving soon, you can use the towels and bedding to wrap fragile items or pack them in boxes or trash bags for your move.

>> Throw away any hangers you no longer use (you know the ones), and sort the remaining hangers by size and type.

>> If you store anything else in your laundry room, use this opportunity to find a more logical place for it.

REMEMBER

As our builder advised, downsizing your laundry room "gives you the square footage where you need it most." All you really need is room for a washer and dryer, a folding table, and a little space for supplies. Figures 9-4 and 9-5 show our original and downsized laundry rooms.

FIGURE 9-4:
Before downsizing: Our original laundry room.

FIGURE 9-5:
After downsizing: The bare essentials but still plenty of storage.

Garage/shed

Decluttering a garage or shed can be a monumental task. You may have some heavy-duty equipment and tools, such as a riding mower, push mower, power washer, log splitter, shop vac, and so on, along with a collection of smaller tools, hardware, gardening equipment and supplies, sports gear, and more.

We recommend starting your garage or shed declutter on a Saturday, so you can spill over to Sunday, if necessary. Choose a weekend that won't be too hot, too cold, or wet. We also recommend that you start by emptying your garage or shed completely, so you can see everything you have, sort it more easily, and clean your garage or shed while it's empty. Having a clean, empty space will gently discourage you from putting anything back into it that you don't absolutely need.

TIP

Before placing anything back into your garage or shed, designate various zones for storage — for example, designate one area for gardening tools and supplies, another for sports gear, another for power tools, and so on. Visit your local hardware store to check out products for organizing garages and sheds, such as toolboxes, shelves/racks, cabinets, workbenches, and wall organizers. Take the opportunity to not only downsize but also get organized.

We downsized from a two-car to a one-car garage and had storage built into the new garage to make better use of the vertical space (see Figures 9-6 and 9-7).

FIGURE 9-6:
Our two-car garage was spacious.

OUR DECLUTTERING JOURNEY

The first room we decided to downsize was Kathleen's office. We chose it because it's one of the smallest rooms in our former home. We were following our own advice: Start with the easiest room first.

Kathleen tackled the cabinets, which contained a large collection of school supplies from when our children were young. We gave most of that away — binders, paper, colored pencils — and dumped whatever nobody wanted. As Kathleen worked on the cabinets, Ralph focused on the bookshelves, packing up books we hadn't touched in years. Together, we looked through pictures we had framed, wrapped them in paper, and packed them in boxes for the move. We sorted files and set aside more than half for the shredder.

Our decluttering was more like prepacking. We were just doing the first pass before the movers came to finish the job. Paying movers to pack items we would later get rid of just didn't make sense. Our goal was to avoid as much packing as possible. That first room was more challenging than we had anticipated, but we felt great when it was done.

We built on our initial success by tackling the second-floor loft. We went through all the books, pictures, seasonal items, and so on. We were dealing with many of the same types of items we pitched and packed from Kathleen's office, which helped us maintain our momentum.

(continued)

(continued)

Third on our list was the living room, which had built-in cabinets packed with china, silverware, holiday decorations, and collectibles. We went through all of it, setting aside only the items we wanted to keep. As for the rest, we showed family members what we had and let them take whatever they wanted. We donated the leftovers.

With our confidence at its peak, we decided to tackle the kitchen, which was a huge undertaking. We knew that our condo had about half the cabinet space. Fortunately, we had a lot of room for improvement. As we emptied our cabinets, we discovered *three* waffle makers! Who needs *three* waffle makers? Apparently, we thought we did at some point in our lives.

As we decluttered, we encountered only a few surprises — items we thought we had gotten rid of but hadn't. Other than that, we knew where most everything was and had it cataloged and categorized appropriately.

All in all, it was a great relief. We now have less to organize, less to clean, more time to do what we love to do, and less stress from not having to look at, think about, and navigate around all that stuff. These are just a few of the many benefits of decluttering.

Sorting Your Stuff into Six Categories

Every downsizing expert has a system for sorting items. Some recommend a four-box system: keep, trash, donate, and sell. Others narrow it down to two: keep and get rid of. We recommend that you sort items into the following six categories:

>> Keep

>> Store

>> Sell

>> Give away

>> Donate

>> Toss

REMEMBER

Use any system that works best for you. If having six stacks of items seems too complicated, feel free to opt for a simpler method. We like our method because it provided us with a separate category for items we wanted to offer to family members first. It also provides an option for people who have excess stuff they want to put in storage instead of getting rid of entirely. When we downsized, we were committed to not putting anything in storage, and we didn't sell anything, so we used only four of the six categories we recommend.

You may want to add one more category to the list: overnight essentials or personal necessities. If you're planning to stay at a motel or somewhere else between the time you move out of your old place and move into your new place, be sure to pack a bag with all the clothes, toiletries, and other items you'll need when you're between homes. We made the mistake of boxing up several items we needed, including nail polish and razors, and had to buy replacements for the time we were between homes.

Keep

The keep category is for everything you plan to move with you and put to good use, such as the following:

>> Your bed and dressers

>> Living room furniture

>> Your main TV

>> Cookware and dinnerware you'll use regularly

>> Clothing you'll wear at least once a year

The guideline for getting rid of clothing is this: If it doesn't fit or you haven't worn it in the past year, get rid of it.

>> Bedding (one or two sets per bed at most)

>> Framed photos and other keepsakes

>> Essential documents

>> The family jewels

Keeping may involve rearranging. When we were discussing plans with our builder, we stressed the importance of building storage into the design so we had room to keep items with sentimental value. We're not able to display everything the way we did in the old house. Some items that were previously on display are now in cabinets.

Store

Whether you're planning to rent a self-storage unit or store items in the basement, attic, garage, or shed of your new home, assign those items to the store category.

Reserve storage for items that you'll probably use once or twice a year. If you can't imagine using something or even looking at it for several years, you should probably get rid of it, regardless of how attached you are to it emotionally.

Don't store items merely because you're struggling to make the tough call to get rid of them. If it can't pay rent, then you're providing free housing to something that's not offering you anything of value in return.

Sell

The only way some people will get rid of anything is if they can sell it for what they think it's worth. Unfortunately, most people won't buy anything you own for what *you* think it's worth. Whether they're shopping online or at a garage sale or an estate sale, they're looking for deep discounts, which is one reason that some people, like us, never sell anything.

If you have some valuable items and want to recoup your investment in them, set them aside and skip to Chapter 11 to find out more about selling them for top dollar.

Often what stands in the way of people getting rid of stuff is that they can't bear the idea of losing money on it. Selling a $350 juicer for $20 hardly seems worth the trouble, so you pack it up and move it to your new house, and there it sits gathering dust. Try to get past the idea of what you paid for something and think about what you *will* pay for it in terms of moving it, storing it, and thinking about it in the future. Cut your losses and sell it for whatever you can get for it, or just give it away.

DISAPPOINTING PROFITS

We got rid of a ton of belongings without selling a thing. We didn't even attempt a garage sale, estate sale, or auction, because we had seen the disappointment on the faces of people who had tried those options and failed.

Our neighbors across the street tried to sell their belongings and received little money in return. According to them, it just wasn't worth the effort and the hassle. Likewise, after hosting a three-day estate sale for their parents, Kathleen and her two siblings didn't earn nearly as much as they thought they would.

If you have a large collection of valuable items and plenty of time to kill, and you enjoy selling, then by all means, gather the things you want to sell and head to Chapter 11. However, don't go into it thinking you're going to make a killing.

Give away

One of the easiest ways to get rid of anything, especially large, bulky items, is to offer it free for the taking. All you need to do is take photos and post them to your social media accounts or send a group email or text to all your friends, family members, coworkers, and colleagues letting them know what you're getting rid of. Even if nobody you know wants it, someone usually knows someone who does.

We posted photos on Facebook to get rid of both a baby grand piano and a pool table — neither of which is easy to move. Pianos are expensive when you're in the market to buy one, but they seem to be a dime a dozen when you're trying to get rid of one. A family friend took both items and has made great use of them! We also had a large collection of board games. A high school friend took several of them for his vacation home in Northern Michigan. Our dining room table ended up at the home of a former employee.

WARNING

Don't coerce your children into taking things they really don't want just because you lack the courage to make the tough call to get rid of them. Your children may be adults, but you still need to set a good example by demonstrating your commitment to downsizing and your ability to make tough decisions. Besides, you don't want to saddle your adult children with a burden you no longer want to carry yourself.

Donate

One of the easiest ways to get rid of household items is to donate them to a charitable organization: Goodwill, The Salvation Army, a veterans organization, a local church, a local shelter, or some other philanthropic organization that accepts clothes and household items. With some organizations, you can get rid of everything you want to donate simply by boxing it up and making a single phone call!

TIP

Our go-to charity is Vietnam Veterans of America (VVA). Its Pickup Please program features the most convenient donation pickup services in the U.S. Simply pack your donations in boxes or bags clearly marked "VVA" and schedule a pickup 24 hours in advance online at `pickupplease.org`, informing them where the items will be. You can donate just about anything, including the following items:

- » Clothing, including shoes and accessories
- » Jewelry
- » Cookware, dinnerware, glassware
- » Books, DVDs, CDs, videotapes
- » Stereos, radios, small electronics

>> Bicycles

>> Tools

We called a local number to schedule a pickup. After they picked up a load, we scheduled them again. We had a place in our garage near the door where we put the donations. They came between 8 a.m. and 5 p.m. and hauled it all off.

Unfortunately, because of COVID, VVA suspended their pickups for several months. We just kept plugging away, adding to the collection in our garage. When they resumed their pickups, they cleared out everything!

Toss

You're down to the last category, which contains all the stuff that didn't make the cut in any of the other categories. These are the items that belong in the dumpster, such as the following:

>> Old food storage containers

>> Anything that's broken and not worth fixing

>> Clothing that nobody would be caught dead in

>> Personal items that nobody wants

>> Food items and spices past their expiration date

GIVE IT AWAY OR BURN IT

Parents often hold on to items their entire lives under the mistaken belief that their children will eventually want those items. Then the parents pass away, leaving their children with the huge burden of dealing with a houseful of things nobody wants.

A cousin who recently passed left his four children a house packed with stuff. It could have been featured on an episode of *Hoarders.* Two of his children live out of state, and none of the children has the time or desire to sort through the contents of that house. At the funeral the cousin's son voiced his vote for what to do with everything: "Give it away or burn it!"

Don't think that you're doing your children a favor by hanging on to things they'll cherish. Make the tough decision: Keep it for yourself or get rid of it. It's that simple.

Chapter **10**

Digitizing Photos, Videos, and Documentation

Don't just modernize and digitize your business, but also yourself.

— POOJA AGNIHOTRI

The most precious items we own are those that are irreplaceable. When people evacuate their homes to escape fire, flood, or storms, they load up their family members, pets, photos, videos, and essential documents — driver's licenses, birth certificates, social security cards, and passports. Their home and nearly everything else in it can be replaced. Photos and videos are recorded memories of events that can never be revisited, and documents that prove your identity can be very difficult to replace.

If you're like most people, over the course of your life, you've accumulated a vast collection of irreplaceable and difficult-to-replace photos, videos, and documentation, and you've probably spent little time organizing them. You may have a few photo albums, but chances are good that the better part of your collection is stuffed in envelopes in filing cabinets or in boxes in an attic or basement where nobody looks at them.

Dumping or shredding these items is out of the question. You want to preserve them for yourself and for future generations, but you don't want to keep lugging them around with you for the rest of your life and then pass the burden on to your heirs.

The solution? Digitization. Scale back your collection to the best of the best, scan them to create digital copies, frame a few originals, and shred the rest. In this chapter, we lead you through the process.

Exploring Your Digital Storage Options

When you're digitizing photos, videos, and documentation, the first decision you face is where to store the digitized files. Fortunately, in this 21st century, you have plenty of options — internal and external hard drives, thumb drives, cloud storage, and social media — and they're all relatively inexpensive. In this section, we lead you through the process of evaluating your options.

As you explore your options, consider the following six factors:

>> **Capacity:** Digital photos and videos consume a great deal of storage space. Does the storage solution you're considering provide enough space for your current and future needs? Are you going to end up with a bunch of discs or USB flash drives (also known as thumb drives) that you'll have to store and manage?

>> **Reliability:** Some storage devices are more reliable than others, but any device can fail, so be sure you have a backup strategy in place. Most cloud-based storage options automatically create backups to prevent data loss.

>> **Security:** Security concerns vary. If you're storing digital items locally on a computer or external hard drive, you need to consider the possibility that the device may be stolen. If you're storing documents that contain sensitive information in the cloud, you need to be more concerned about online security — ensuring that you use a secure username and password and enable two-factor authentication, for example.

Two-factor authentication grants users access only after they verify their identity in two ways — for example, by entering their username and password and then entering a code texted to their cell phone. Enable two-factor authentication whenever the option is offered.

REMEMBER

>> **Accessibility:** Accessibility involves making your photos, videos, and other documents easily available to you and others you want to be able to access them. Obviously, storing digital items in the cloud makes them far more easily accessible than if they're stored on a local computer, external drive, or thumb drive.

» **Flexibility:** Some storage solutions are better than others at providing options for turning photos into gifts and keepsakes. For example, you can store your photos and videos in the cloud and easily turn photos into albums, coffee mugs, framed photos, T-shirts, puzzles, and more.

» **Affordability:** Storage costs vary, but storage is relatively inexpensive, regardless of whether you choose to store items online or off-line. Think of costs more in terms of time — how much time will you spend copying and backing up files if you store them locally versus online?

Internal drives

Internal hard drives and *solid-state drives (SSDs)* are the fastest, most convenient method for storing files, especially if you're digitizing items yourself. These drives live on your device — your desktop, laptop, or tablet — and store your device's operating system, application software, and data.

Potential drawbacks of storing your digital photos, videos, and documents on an internal drive include the following:

» Even if you have gobs of storage, space is limited, and the more data you store on your device's internal hard drives, the less space you have for the operating system and applications. If the drive gets too crowded, system performance can suffer.

» Internal drives occasionally crash and fail, so you need to be sure to back up everything regularly.

» If your device is lost or stolen, you also lose its precious cargo (unless, of course, it's backed up). If you have any sensitive information on your computer (such as your name, address, or social security number), you may become an easier target for identity theft and other fraudulent activity.

» If you want to share your photos, videos, and documents with others, you need to email copies or upload them to the cloud, which involves another step in the process.

External drives

To avoid overcrowding on your device's internal drives, you can connect to one or more *external drives* to store all your scanned photos, videos, and documents. External drives are fast and affordable and won't bog down your device's operating system or applications. Most connect via USB or Wi-Fi and provide one or more terabytes (TB) of storage. One TB enables you to store about

>> 250,000 photos taken with a 12-megapixel camera

>> 250 two-hour movies in high definition (HD)

>> 6.5 million pages of documents stored as Microsoft Office files, PDFs, or presentations (approximately the contents of 1,300 filing cabinets)

When choosing an external drive, consider the following features:

>> **Connectivity:** Most USB drives connect via a USB port, but some are wireless, connecting via Wi-Fi, which eliminates at least one cable.

>> **Storage capacity:** Consider at least 1TB and possibly more if you have a lot of photos and videos.

>> **Hard drive vs. SSD:** An SSD has no moving parts, so it's generally faster and more durable than a hard drive, though it probably costs a little more.

>> **Durability:** If you plan to travel with it, look for an external drive that's built for road warriors. We use a LaCie Rugged external drive, and it works wonders. It's small, light, fast, easy to set up and use, and dust-, drop-, and water-resistant.

>> **Size/weight:** Most external drives are light and can fit in the palm of your hand. *Thumb drives* (*flash drives*) are tiny (smaller than your average thumb), but they're easy to lose or misplace and they have significantly less storage capacity than most full-size external drives.

TIP

Consider using a thumb drive to distribute small collections of photos and videos to loved ones. They're relatively inexpensive and very portable.

Cloud storage

Cloud storage is all the rage, and for good reason — it's fast, easy, convenient, and virtually unlimited. The only drawback is that if you need more than about 10–15 gigabytes (GB) of storage, you'll be paying a monthly or annual fee, which, over the long haul, can end up costing far more than an external drive.

REMEMBER

Regardless of whether you store your files locally or in the cloud, you should at least use the cloud for backups, so you can recover your precious data if your primary storage device is lost, stolen, or damaged.

Here are a few popular cloud storage providers to consider:

>> Google Photos (photos.google.com) is a great option if you have an Android phone. You can add your digitized photos to the photos you've taken with

your phone so you have everything in one place and can continue to add to your collection. You can also edit photos right inside the app.

>> Apple iCloud (www.icloud.com/iclouddrive) may be the best option if you have an iPhone or other Apple devices, for the same reason that Google Photos is probably best for Android users. iCloud is designed to fully integrate with your iPhone, making it easy to sync all data on your phone with your iCloud account.

>> Amazon Photos (www.amazon.com) may be the best option if you already have an Amazon Prime account. Amazon Prime members have unlimited full-resolution storage for photos and 5GB for videos. (To access Amazon Photos, log in to your Amazon account, open the All menu, and choose Amazon Photos.) Amazon Photos also makes it easy to convert your photos into prints, custom photo albums, and gifts such as throw pillows and refrigerator magnets.

>> Microsoft OneDrive (onedrive.live.com) is a good choice if you already have access to it through an existing Microsoft account. For example, if you subscribe to Microsoft 365 Personal, you get up to 1TB of storage.

>> Flickr (www.flickr.com) enables you to upload, organize, and edit your photos online and order prints, photo albums, and other products personalized with your photos.

>> Dropbox (www.dropbox.com) is great for general purpose cloud storage, but it doesn't have any built-in photo or video enhancement, editing, or photo-specific organizational tools.

>> Box (www.box.com) is similar to Dropbox. It's a good general purpose cloud storage option but doesn't offer any of the bells and whistles for managing and editing photos and videos that you'll find with the other cloud storage solutions in this list.

As you compare cloud storage options for photos, videos, and scanned documents, consider the following factors:

>> **Whether cloud storage is included with a service or product you already have.** You may have access to some cloud storage through your cellular provider, a Microsoft Office subscription, your Amazon Prime membership, Google, or Apple. Why pay for storage when you already have it?

>> **Whether the cloud storage solution has features for organizing, enhancing, and editing photos and videos.** For example, Google Photos enables you to browse photos by people, places, and things that matter to you; enhance and edit photos; and share them with loved ones via email, text, or social media platforms.

>> **Whether you can order prints, albums, coffee mugs, and other photo keepsakes and gifts through the cloud storage provider.** On Amazon, for example, you can easily convert your photos into prints, wall décor, calendars, and gifts without the added step of having to upload them again.

TIP

If you store data on your device and in the cloud, enable *syncing* or *automatic back-ups* so that you don't have to manually copy files to the cloud or create backups. Check your computer's help system and your cloud provider's documentation to find out how to set up automatic backups or syncing.

Social media storage

Many people these days rely on their smartphones and social media to store all their photos and videos — posting their most memorable photos and videos to their accounts on Facebook, Instagram, TikTok, and other social media platforms. You can take the same approach with your legacy photos and videos, digitizing them and then uploading them to your social media accounts for posterity.

WARNING

Don't rely solely on your smartphone or social media accounts for storing your photos and videos. Here's why:

>> If your phone is lost, stolen, or damaged, or if it crashes, you may lose all your irreplaceable data.

>> Social media doesn't offer the best tools for organizing photos and videos. You may have a vast collection online but be unable to find anything.

>> If your account is hacked or deleted for some reason or you accidentally violate the platform's terms and conditions, you may lose access to all your digitized photos and videos.

REMEMBER

If you take photos with your smartphone, be sure to set up your phone to back up all photos to the cloud. For example, if you have an Android phone, you can set it up to back up files to your Google account by taking the following steps:

1. **Tap the Settings icon.**

2. **Tap Google.**

3. **Tap Backup.**

4. **Tap Photos & Videos.**

5. **Make sure Backup & Sync is turned on.**

Photo processor storage

WARNING

If you're thinking of taking advantage of photo processors, such as Walgreens, CVS, and Snapfish, for free storage, reconsider. While these companies are great for turning photos into prints, photo albums, and other keepsakes and gifts, they may not be suitable for long-term storage.

Research a photo processor's terms of service carefully before trusting it with your family photos. Some companies will automatically delete photos after a certain amount of time if you haven't placed a recent order.

Eliminating Unnecessary Documents, Photos, and Videos

The first step in digitizing your photos, videos, and documents involves reducing your collection to the bare minimum. This step is the most time-consuming and challenging, but it will save you loads of time and aggravation later.

To make this task more manageable, break it down by item: documents, photos, and videos. In the following sections, we offer guidance on how to reduce your collections of each.

Downsizing your document collection

Documents generally fall into three categories: original documents you want to keep, important documents you want to scan, and documents you can shred.

Original documents to keep

Keep the originals of the following documents:

>> **Proof of identity:** Keep original birth certificates, passports, social security cards, and driver's licenses on file.

>> **Property documents:** Keep original deeds, appraisals, titles, and registrations on file.

>> **Marriage and divorce decrees and death certificates:** You never know when you may need these.

>> **Warranties and receipts:** Keep the originals of any warranties and receipts.

>> **User and maintenance guides:** Keep the user and maintenance guides for any tools and appliances you still own and discard the rest.

>> **Estate documents:** You should have originals of your last will and testament, trust documents, power of attorney documents, medical advance directive, living will, life insurance policies, and so on. See Chapter 7 for details.

>> **Proof of disability or military service:** You or your heirs may need the originals.

>> **Tax returns for the past six years:** If you get audited, the IRS probably isn't going to go much further back in time than the most recent six years.

REMEMBER

Store these documents in a safe-deposit box or a secure fireproof lockbox. If you're storing the documents in your home, find a very good hiding place and inform the person you named as the executor of your will where it is.

Documents to scan

As for important documents you want to keep for your records but don't need original copies of, you can scan them and then shred the originals so they're not taking up any space. Consider scanning and then shredding the following documents:

>> Tax returns older than six years

>> Receipts for any big-ticket items

>> Maintenance and repair records for vehicles you still own

>> Contracts that are still active

>> Pension documents

Documents to shred

The good news is, almost all documents these days are digital, including credit card and bank statements, so you can access them online whenever you need to or contact the source of the document to obtain a copy. Here's a short list of the documents that are safe to shred:

>> Credit card statements

>> Bank statements

- ❯❯ Brokerage statements

- ❯❯ Maintenance and repair records for vehicles you no longer own

- ❯❯ Old documents that aren't relevant anymore (probably most of the documents crowding your filing cabinet)

TIP

You can buy your own shredder to do the shredding yourself or hire a reputable firm to do it. If you choose to do it yourself, use a *cross-cut paper shredder*, which cuts paper into small pieces instead of strips, for improved security. If you hire a company to do it for you, make sure it's certified by the International Secure Information Governance & Management Association, or i-SIGMA (www.isigmaonline.org).

Deciding which photos to keep

Now the hard part — deciding which photos to keep. Here's a system that may help:

1. Set a goal.

Maybe you want to reduce your collection to a single box or cut it by 90 percent or end up with no more than 1,000 photos.

REMEMBER

You don't need to do it all at once. You can review photos over the course of a week, a month, or even a year. Just be sure to set a deadline to prevent the task from dragging on forever.

2. Remove and discard all poor-quality photos.

3. Remove and discard all photos that don't have someone you recognize in them.

For example, sort out photos of landscapes or places you've been that have no people in them.

4. Remove remaining photos from photo albums and label them on the back as best you can.

Keep them together in case you want to put them back into an album and so you'll have a general idea of the time period they're from when you start to digitize them.

5. Review all photos, discarding those you don't want to keep and sorting the ones you do want to keep by date as best as you can.

As you review photos, try to meet the goal you set in Step 1.

TIP

Consider keeping only three or four of your favorite photos from each event, vacation, and family gathering. You don't need a hundred photos of a single event to bring back your memories of it.

Paring down your video collection

Reducing a large video collection can be daunting, especially if you no longer have access to a device for playing videos or you lack the motivation to watch hours and hours of family videos. You need to either rely on any physical labels your tapes contain or have everything digitized and then edit it down.

TIP

We recommend digitizing your entire collection and then using video editing software to create the equivalent of a *highlights reel* — only the best clips from your entire collection. This approach can become very time-consuming if you have a large video collection, but after your collection is digitized, you can fast-forward through it to identify highlights. See the later section "Digitizing Your Video Collection" for details.

Scanning Photos and Documents

After sorting your photos and documents, you have two options: Scan them yourself or hire a service to scan them for you. Your choice pretty much boils down to cost (time and money). You can buy a photo/document scanner and feed your photos and documents into it, or you can hire a firm to do it. Cost varies depending on the level of service you prefer (for example, whether you're sending in a neat stack of items or dropping them off in boxes and albums).

In the following sections, we guide you through the basics of scanning photos and documents yourself and introduce you to some popular professional services that can handle the job for you.

Do it yourself

If you prefer the do-it-yourself option, you'll need a scanner. Although your all-in-one printer may be able to handle documents and a small collection of photos, a dedicated scanner is more suitable for scanning a large number of photos. When evaluating scanners, consider the following features:

>> **Speed:** A scanner's speed is measured in pages per minute (PPM).

>> **Support for documents, slides, and negatives:** Most photo scanners handle both photos and documents, but if you have slides or negatives, you'll need a scanner that can handle those as well.

>> **Auto feed:** You don't want to manually load photos one at a time. Some photo scanners allow you to load 30–40 photos at once.

>> **Connectivity:** Most scanners connect to a computer via a USB cable, but some support wireless connections such as Wi-Fi or Bluetooth.

>> **Resolution:** Look for a scanner that can scan at 1,200 dots per inch (dpi) or more in 24-bit color.

>> **Size:** Make sure the scanner can handle photos up to 8 x 10 inches.

>> **Two-sided option:** If your photos have notes written on the back, look for a scanner that can scan both sides.

>> **Software:** You'll want software that supports automatic photo enhancement and editing and uploads to popular cloud storage platforms such as Google Drive and Dropbox.

TIP

Consider borrowing or renting a scanner. Let all your friends and family members know that you're planning to scan your photo collection and ask whether anyone has a photo scanner they'd be willing to lend you. You're probably going to need the scanner just once. In some areas, you can rent a scanner; search the web for "rent a photo scanner" followed by your zip code to check for rental options near you.

The scanning process differs depending on the scanner and software you're using, but it usually involves loading photos, initiating the scan, and entering the following preferences:

>> **Storage location:** You can choose to store your digitized photos locally or in the cloud and specify the folder in which you want them stored. We recommend creating a separate folder for each year. If you have numerous photos in a given year, you may want to break them down into months.

>> **File name:** Consider naming your photos with the year, month, and event — for example, 1985_08_SumVac_01 for a photo taken in August 1985 during your summer vacation. In most cases, you enter a file name, and the scanning software will tack on a number or letter at the end — such as 01, 02, 03 or a, b, c — for each item/page you scan.

>> **Auto-enhancement:** If your scanner features auto-enhancement, you can turn it on or off. We recommend leaving it on unless you want to enhance photos manually to see if you can do a better job yourself. Some scanners will do two versions — an original and an enhanced version.

- » **Resolution:** Because you're scanning photos with the goal of getting rid of the originals, we recommend scanning them at 1200 dpi instead of a lower resolution such as 300 dpi or 600 dpi. You can always reduce the resolution later, but you can't increase it. However, the higher the resolution, the bigger the file, so if storage space is a concern, you may want to opt for 600 dpi.

- » **File format:** *TIFF* is best because it stores more detail; if you convert your photos into prints or other products later, TIFF will look best. *JPEG* is a compressed file format that's great for most purposes, such as sharing photos online; you can produce prints from JPEG files, but they won't look quite as good as prints produced from TIFFs.

- » **Photo/document:** Most scanners can scan photos or documents. Before you start scanning, you need to specify which one you're scanning.

- » **Advanced settings:** Some scanning software features additional settings, such as auto-rotation, curled photo correction (if the edges of your photos are curled), and reduced lines and streaks.

After entering your preferences, you click a button in the app or press a button on the scanner to start the scanning process.

TIP

Get your children and grandchildren involved! Kids love tech, and scanning family photos is a great way for them to contribute to preserving the family legacy. It also provides a golden opportunity to reminisce and chuckle as a family about some of the wonderful and even the slightly awkward events of the past (that time Uncle Bob wore a powder blue tux to the prom).

Hire it out

The easiest way to digitize photos and documents is to hire a company or individual to do it for you. All you do is box up your items, ship them off to the scanning service, and pay the fee. Most of these services can scan photos, slides, and negatives and transfer film and videotapes to DVDs. Here are a few of the more popular scanning services in the U.S.:

- » ScanMyPhotos (www.scanmyphotos.com)

- » DigMyPics (digmypics.com)

- » PhotoPanda (photopanda.org)

- » ScanCafe (www.scancafe.com)

Your local CVS (www.cvs.com/photo) or Walgreens (photo.walgreens.com) also offers photo and video transfer to DVDs or USB drives.

TIP

If you have damaged photos, you can find freelancers on Fiverr (www.fiverr.com) who can restore them for you and even convert old black-and-white photos into colorized versions.

Transforming Photos into Memorabilia

People collect piles of photos they rarely (if ever) look back at, which can be broken down into two issues: saving too many photos and never looking at them. To address both issues, turn your favorite photos into memorabilia and discard the rest. By *memorabilia*, we're referring to items such as the following:

» Framed photos or wall art (such as posters, collages, or photos printed on canvas or wood panels)

» Photo albums or books

» Digital photo frames that scroll through a collection of photos

» Calendars

» Pillows

» Photo cubes

» Coffee mugs, tumblers, wine glasses, or water bottles

» Coasters

You can order these items online through various businesses, including the following:

» Walgreens Photo (photo.walgreens.com)

» CVS Photo (www.cvs.com/photo)

» Shutterfly (www.shutterfly.com)

» Snapfish (www.snapfish.com)

» Amazon (www.amazon.com) — search for "photo gifts"

These items are a great solution if you're downsizing loved ones and want to surround them with memories while freeing them from the burden of managing a huge photo collection.

Digitizing Your Video Collection

Nowadays, nearly everyone records videos digitally using their smartphone, but that wasn't always the case. The home movie craze really got rolling in 1965 when Kodak released its Super 8 open-reel video camera. Since then, other video-recording formats have been introduced, including VHS, S-VHS, Betamax, VHS-C, S-VHS-C, Video8, Hi8, Digital8, DV, DVCAM, MiniDV, and DVC, along with modern camcorders that record directly to flash memory, hard drives, or mini DVDs.

If your family stayed true to the tradition of making home movies over several decades, chances are good that you have boxes of open-reel film, videotapes, and discs in a wide range of formats. Converting it all to digital format makes it much easier to watch, share, and edit, but how do you accomplish this feat? You have two options — do it yourself or hire a pro — as discussed in the following sections.

Do it yourself

If you have machines that can play video in the formats you have (for example, the camcorder used to record the video), you can buy a fairly small, inexpensive analog-to-digital converter and do the conversion yourself. If you have 8mm open-reel film, you'll need a separate 8mm and Super 8 reels-to-digital converter. If you have 16mm film, you're probably better off hiring a service to handle the conversion for you.

Reach out to everyone you know to see if anyone has the equipment you need or search the web for "video equipment rental near me." You'll use this equipment once, so we don't recommend buying it unless you're going to try to launch a side hustle as the neighborhood video digitizer, which isn't a bad idea for a retirement gig or to earn some extra spending money.

For converting analog video (from tapes) to digital video, you have two options in terms of equipment. One option is a video capture box with a preview screen, which makes the process very easy. For example, using the ClearClick Video to Digital Converter, the process goes like this:

1. **Connect your camcorder or videocassette player to the converter.**

   You use an RCA cable with a red, yellow, and white connector that connects the audio/video (AV) out ports on your player to the AV in ports on the converter.

2. **Plug your video player and the converter into a power source and turn them on.**

3. **Plug a USB flash drive into the converter's USB port.**

   Your digitized video will be stored on this drive.

4. **Press the Play button on your player and the Record button on the converter.**

   The converter starts converting the video to a digital format, such as AVI or JPEG, and stores it in one or more files on the flash drive.

5. **Wait for the video to end and then press the Stop button on each device.**

   ClearClick has an optional timer that can stop the conversion automatically after a specified number of minutes, so you can record video without having to monitor the process.

The other (more affordable) option is a product that includes a cable for connecting your video player to your computer and software that handles the conversion process. With analog-to-digital converters, such as the DigitNow USB 2.0 Video Capture Card Device Converter, your computer serves as the video capture box.

Hire a pro

Plenty of businesses specialize in converting old film and video in a variety of formats to digital format. Most of them transfer video to DVDs. Some are limited to videocassettes and don't accept 8mm or 16mm film. Others can handle 8mm and 16mm open-reel video as well. Here are some options to consider:

» Walmart (www.dvdwalmart.com/services-and-pricing/videotape-transfer) supports a number of video formats, including VHS, S-VHS, Betamax, VHS-C, S-VHS-C, Video8, Hi8, Digital8, DV, DVCAM, MiniDV, and DVC.

» Walgreens Photo (photo.walgreens.com/store/transfer-vhs-to-dvd) can transfer videocassettes, reels (8mm film), HD videos, photos, and slides to DVD.

» CVS Photo (www.cvs.com/photo) can digitize photos, slides, and negatives; 8mm, 16mm, and Super 8 film reels; and VHS, VHS-C, S-VHS, Hi8, Digital 8, and MiniDV, and transfer them to DVD or USB.

>> Kodak Digitizing (www.kodakdigitizing.com) can handle every format. You send in a box of 2, 10, 20, or 40 items for a fixed price (audiotapes, videotapes, film, photos, negatives, slides), and Kodak digitizes the items and returns them to you along with files on DVDs or USB flash drives (it's probably the most expensive of the four options we mention here).

WARNING

Compare prices closely when choosing a service. You don't want to trust your precious memories to a fly-by-night operation, but you shouldn't have to pay an exorbitant price to have your old tapes and films digitized. The quality of the end product probably won't vary enough from one provider to another to warrant a significantly higher price.

TIP

You may be able to find a freelancer to convert your videotapes and films to a digital format. Go to Fiverr at www.fiverr.com and search for "analog to digital video." Be sure to choose a freelancer who has plenty of positive ratings and few, if any, negative ratings. Also choose a reliable shipper and pack your items carefully before sending them.

IN THIS CHAPTER

» **Estimating the value of your valuables**

» **Checking out different sales methods**

» **Listing items for sale via websites and apps**

» **Organizing and executing an estate sale**

» **Going old school with a garage sale**

Chapter **11**

Selling Stuff You No Longer Want or Need

If you buy things you don't need, you will soon sell things you need.

— WARREN BUFFETT

I f you're like most people, the first thought that pops into your mind when you need to get rid of something is that you'll sell it and recoup some of your purchase price. If you have valuables — quality jewelry, paintings by famous artists, coin collections, or other collectibles — you may expect to do even better than that: You'd like to see a substantial return on your investment. In any event, you want to sell as many items as possible for the highest price you can get. You don't want to just give everything away.

When you decide to sell some things, you face two challenges: 1) setting a price and 2) choosing the best way to achieve your sales goal. For example, if your goal is to minimize the time and effort you put into selling stuff, you can outsource the task to a third party to handle everything for you. On the other hand, if your goal is to maximize your profit, you may choose instead to use a variety of marketing tools to put your items in front of the buyers who want them most.

In this chapter, we begin by offering guidance on how to determine how much your various belongings are worth. Then, we describe the most common ways downsizers sell their belongings — everything from auctioning them off, to hosting an estate or garage sale, to outsourcing the process to a third party. Finally, we take a deeper dive into the three most common approaches: garage sales, estate sales, and online listings.

REMEMBER

Getting the maximum price for anything requires knowing what it's worth and taking the time to market it properly. Don't overlook how much your time is worth to you. If you spend two 40-hour weeks generating a $1,000 profit, you're earning $12.50 per hour. If that's worth it to you, great. If it's not, you'd be better off giving your stuff away.

Finding Out How Much Something Is Worth

In 2000, a Fresno, California, resident, Rick Norsigian, bought a box of photo negatives at a garage sale for $45. A decade later, experts determined that the photos had been taken by famed American landscape photographer Ansel Adams and estimated the value of the negatives at $200 million. In 2007, a family from New York bought a bowl from the Northern Song Dynasty for $3. The Ding bowl, which dates to the 10th or 11th century, was sold to a London art dealer for $2.2 million.

How bad would you feel if you sold something worth millions of dollars, or even thousands of dollars, for mere pocket change? It happens more often than you may think, but far less frequently than most people hope. Still, people who know the value of antiques and collectibles sometimes capitalize on the seller's ignorance. The moral of the story: Sort through everything yourself and check the value of anything you think may be worth something. However, be realistic — most people think their antiques and collectibles are worth far more than anyone is willing to pay for them.

Here are a few ways to find out how much something is worth:

>> **Search eBay.** Log on to eBay (www.ebay.com), type a brief description of the item in the search box, tap the Search button, and scroll through the results.

REMEMBER

Be sure to compare apples to apples. In other words, compare the prices of items in the same condition as the item you have. Something in excellent condition is going to command a much higher price than a similar item in poor condition.

>> **Use a search engine.** Using a more general-purpose search engine like Google (www.google.com), Bing (www.bing.com), or DuckDuckGo (duckduckgo.com) expands your search beyond eBay. Above the search results, select the Shopping link to narrow your results to only items that are being sold or have been sold.

Google's image search is a great way to look things up when you don't know how to describe them in words. All you need to do is go to Google.com, click Images in the upper-right corner of the page, click the Search by Image icon (it looks like a camera), and use the resulting dialog box to upload a photo of the item. Your smartphone may be equipped with a similar feature that's accessible through its photo app.

>> **Search an online database or price guide.** Search online for databases or valuation websites that specialize in the type of item you're researching. For example, google "antiques database" or "collectibles database" or "collectibles price guide." Choose something promising from the list of search results and use the platform's search tool to look up your item. Here are a few databases/ price guides to get you started:

● Kovels (www.kovels.com)

● WorthPoint (www.worthpoint.com)

● World Collectors Net (www.worldcollectorsnet.com)

>> **Hire an appraiser.** Consult a local appraiser who's certified by the American Society of Appraisers (www.appraisers.org), the Appraisers Association of America (www.appraisersassociation.org), or the International Society of Appraisers (www.isa-appraisers.org). Each of these sites has a searchable member directory. Appraisers typically charge a flat fee or an hourly rate and can meet you at your home to go through all the items you think may be valuable.

If you have only a few items of value, consider posting them on an online valuation site, such as ValueMyStuff (www.valuemystuff.com), where appraisers can respond with their expert opinions for a small fee.

>> **Visit a local antique store or collectibles dealer.** You can take your item (or a photo of it) to a local antique store or collectibles dealer (such as a coin shop or a shop that deals in trading cards) and ask for their honest opinion about the item's value. A dealer may be able to sell the item for you on commission, getting you a higher price than you can get on your own.

Unlike an appraiser, who has an ethical responsibility to quote an accurate price, a dealer in antiques or collectibles may lowball you to acquire the item for far less than it's worth and then resell it.

>> **Consult an auctioneer.** Auctioneers have experience selling valuables and may employ their own appraisers. They may even host valuation or appraisal days, during which you can bring in items you think are valuable to have them appraised for free, sort of like on *Antiques Roadshow*.

>> **Visit your local library.** Your local library should have catalogs or price guides for popular collectibles, such as coins, stamps, and baseball cards, including the following:

- *A Guide Book of United States Coins*
- *Beckett Almanac of Baseball Cards and Collectibles*
- *Kovels' Antiques and Collectibles Price Guide*
- *Miller's Collectibles Handbook & Price Guide*
- *Scott Standard Postage Stamp Catalogue*
- *Standard Catalog of Vintage Baseball Cards*

OUR EXPERIENCE

As we checked the value of certain items online, we convinced ourselves not to sell them, either because the items were too valuable or because selling them wouldn't be worth the effort.

In the first case, we checked the value of a couple pieces of art we'd had in our possession for some time. We thought about posting them on Facebook for any family members or friends to take off our hands or trying to resell them. When we found out how much they're worth, we decided to keep them.

We were hosting a family gathering at Tara Drive (the house we were downsizing from) and were all together in the living room. We were looking at the paintings, trying to decide whether to keep them. (We can't recall what we paid for them.) Our nephew said, "If you don't want 'em, I'll take 'em!" We googled the artist's name, Roy Fairchild Woodard, and discovered the paintings were worth more than we thought — about $4,500 per painting — so we decided to keep them and make them work in our new condo.

We also had some collectibles — Longaberger baskets, Precious Moments figurines, a Lenox egg collection, Wallace silver-plate bells. We checked what similar items were listed for and had sold for on eBay, Facebook Marketplace, and other sites. None of the items was worth much, even if we had the original packaging and receipts. Packing up and shipping anything we sold wouldn't have been worth the trouble. We spread everything out in the living room and let family, friends, and our cleaning team take what they wanted.

TIP

If you're planning to sell an antique, don't touch it. Don't polish, clean, or refinish the metal or wood. Doing so may diminish the item's value. Copper, brass, bronze, and similar metals; certain stones; and certain woods develop a *patina* (a thin protective sheen) on their surface over time, which increases the value of the item.

Exploring Ways to Sell Your Belongings

Deciding where and how to sell your stuff is crucial to meeting your goals, including how much money you want to make, how fast you want to get rid of things, and how much effort you're willing to invest. In this section, we explain your options and offer guidance on choosing which options are best for you.

REMEMBER

You're not restricted to one option. You may, for example, choose to sell a few valuables through a local antique or collectibles dealer and sell the rest at a garage sale or estate sale.

Estate auction

An *auction* is a public sale in which items are sold to the highest bidders either individually or in *lots* (for example, a box of miscellaneous tools and hardware). While you can list items for auction online on sites such as eBay, we're talking about estate auctions, which occur off-line during a limited time period and sometimes online (or both). The auction may be held at an auction house or at an individual's or a couple's home.

An estate auction offers the following potential benefits:

>> The bidding process can drive up prices beyond what you're likely to get in a garage or estate sale.

>> You can host the auction off-site, at an auction house, instead of having people traipsing through your home or garage.

>> Depending on the auctioneer, you may be able to open the bidding to people in attendance as well as online bidders to gain exposure to more potential buyers.

>> The auction house manages the sale, making your job easy.

>> An auction occurs over a few hours on a single day, so you're not engaged in a long, drawn-out process.

An estate auction may not be an ideal solution. Consider the following potential drawbacks:

>> An auction is generally limited to a few hours on a single day, which may reduce attendance.

>> If you host the auction off-site, you need to move items from your home to the auction house.

>> The lead time for an auction can be longer than what's required for an estate or garage sale.

>> Buyers need to remove the items they purchase immediately, which may discourage bids on large items.

>> An auction house may charge a 10–15 percent commission or a flat fee of $1,000–$1,500 or more if you have only a limited number of items to sell.

Estate sale

An *estate sale* is a way to liquidate the contents of a home. It's often called a *tag sale* because items have individual price tags (as opposed to opening bids or no tags at all). Items in the home are usually kept in place — for example, the living room contains a TV, couch, coffee table, end tables, and entertainment center. Attendees wander through the home and peel the tags off the items they want (or pick up the items). When they're done shopping, they go to the cashier, who rings up their purchases, which the buyers then haul off — it's strictly cash-and-carry. Estate sales are similar to garage sales, but everything must go, and items are usually distributed throughout the home.

You can conduct an estate sale yourself or hire someone to do it for you. Deciding which option is best for you comes down to weighing the pros and cons of each option. Here are some factors to consider:

>> With the do-it-yourself option, you're in charge of everything: sorting and pricing items, advertising the sale, controlling the crowd, calculating and collecting payments, helping buyers load items, clearing out unsold items, and cleaning up the mess. For details, see the later section "Hosting an Estate Sale."

>> Professionals generally work on commission, so they're motivated to sell your stuff for top dollar. They're also more experienced than you are at sorting and pricing items, advertising the sale to increase interest, and contacting buyers they know will pay more for certain items. They may even sell some of the more valuable items to collectors and some of their other contacts before the first day of the sale.

>> Commissions can gobble up most of your proceeds. Professionals may charge a 40–50 percent commission (perhaps a smaller percentage if the total value of what you're selling is considerable). If the total value of everything you're selling is less than $10,000, the service may charge a minimum fee to cover its expenses.

REMEMBER

People who manage estate sales for a living often mark prices relatively high at the beginning of the sale and lower them over the course of the sale to clear out more items. They may also notify their contacts about things like bedroom and living room furniture, kitchen appliances, motor vehicles, and other higher-priced items to avoid getting a lot of lowball offers from bargain hunters. In other words, they're likely to do far more presales than you'd be able to do on your own.

WARNING

What the pros won't tell you is which items they can't sell. The pros we hired should have informed us that the piano Kathleen inherited from her parents was probably a no-go. Instead, we had to find out at the end of the sale, at which point we needed to scramble to get rid of it. We ended up rolling the piano out to the curb, where someone noticed it and hauled it off. Inside the piano bench, we left a heartfelt message written by Kathleen's brother, Mark, to the new owners (see Figure 11-1).

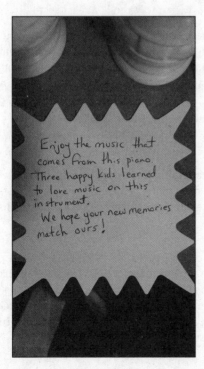

FIGURE 11-1:
Giving away a priceless item while sending goodwill into the world.

REMEMBER

If you're thinking about hiring a pro, talk to friends, neighbors, family members, and your estate attorney to gather references for reliable and reputable estate sales services in your area. Compare fees and contracts. For example, some services may charge separately for cleanup and charge extra if a dumpster is included, whereas another service may include those costs as part of the commission you pay.

Garage/yard sale

A garage or yard sale is very similar to an estate sale except for a few minor differences.

» A garage sale is usually restricted to the garage and driveway, so you're not going to have people entering your house. A yard sale spills out onto the lawn, but you still won't have people coming inside to shop.

» With a garage/yard sale, you're typically selling only a portion of your home's contents.

» An estate sale generally offers a wider selection of items. With a garage/yard sale, you're selling only unwanted household items, whereas in an estate sale, you're selling everything.

A garage sale is one of the best ways to get rid of things you no longer need or want without just giving them away, but don't expect to earn top dollar on the items you sell. Garage sales attract bargain hunters. If you set your prices high, you'll likely be packing up most of what didn't sell to put out for your next garage sale.

Online listing

One of the best ways to sell anything these days is to list it for sale online. The goal is to get your stuff in front of as many people as possible in the hopes that one of them is willing to pay the asking price. Here are a few online listing services to consider:

» **eBay:** eBay (www.ebay.com) is popular, so it's a great service for reaching prospective buyers. The two drawbacks are eBay fees and shipping costs. eBay charges an *insertion fee* when you create a listing and a *final value fee* (a percentage of the sale amount plus a flat fee) when your item sells — expect to pay about 15 percent of each sale. Shipping fees add to that cost, because buyers typically expect sellers to cover shipping.

TIP

To avoid covering the cost of shipping, you have a few options: Jack up the price, require that the buyer pay for shipping, or require that the buyer pick up the item in person.

>> **Facebook Marketplace:** Facebook Marketplace (`www.facebook.com/marketplace`) is great for selling or giving away stuff, because it's totally free — no charge for listing items and no sales commission. You pay shipping fees only if you agree to do so when you post the item. Buyers on Facebook Marketplace seem more willing to pay for shipping or to pick up items if they're nearby.

>> **Craigslist:** Craigslist (`craigslist.org`) is another great venue for downsizers because it's easy to post items and it's totally free.

>> **OfferUp:** OfferUp (`offerup.com`) is very similar to Facebook Marketplace and Craigslist in that it enables you to list and sell items locally and requires that you and the buyer arrange payment and delivery, but you may find it faster and easier to use. Through an app on your smartphone, you take a photo of what you want to list, add a description of the item, choose a category (for example, Electronics & Media, Home & Garden, or Vehicles), and tap a button to post it. You can list any item in about 30 seconds.

>> **Poshmark:** Poshmark (`poshmark.com`) is a social commerce marketplace for buying and selling new and secondhand fashion, household, and beauty products. If you're stylish, it's a great platform for building a community of followers who are eager to buy whatever you're wearing or using. It's less useful for downsizing unless you have a lot of great clothing to unload.

WARNING

The drawback with platforms like Facebook Marketplace, Craigslist, and OfferUp is that they don't provide the same level of anonymity and security as more commercial services like eBay do. With Facebook Marketplace and Craigslist, interested buyers contact you via phone, text, or email, and you arrange for payment and delivery, often in person. See the later section "Selling Your Belongings Online" for a list of precautions to follow to stay safe when selling items online.

Hiring someone to sell your stuff

Some people are great at organizing garage sales and estate sales, selling stuff online, and so on. They know how much things are selling for, they know where to list items to get the best prices, they're skilled at taking photos and composing product listings, they're naturals at haggling with prospective buyers, and they love doing it. Then there's the rest of us. If you're a member of the latter group, consider recruiting (or hiring) someone who's better equipped than you are to sell your belongings for you.

Here are a few ways to find suitable candidates:

» Ask everyone you know if they or someone they know is qualified and willing to work on commission.

» Contact local estate attorneys to find out who handles their estate sales.

» Search EstateSales.NET (`www.estatesales.net/companies`) for estate sale companies near you.

» Contact consignment shops in your area to find out whether they're willing and able to sell your items or know someone who can help.

Before signing a contract with someone to sell your belongings on your behalf, perform your due diligence by taking the following steps:

1. **Make a list of your top three candidates.**

2. **Obtain and check references.**

3. **Search the web for the company's or individual's name followed by "scam" or "review" to see if anything negative has been posted about them.**

4. **Search for the company on the Better Business Bureau's website (`www.bbb.org/search`) to see if any reviews have been posted or complaints filed about the company.**

5. **Visit a sale that the company or individual is handling to see them in action.**

6. **Review a copy of each candidate's contract.**

7. **Ask the following questions:**

   • **How much do you charge (commissions and other fees)?** The answer to this question is for comparison purposes with other firms.

   • **Is there a minimum charge, and if there is, how much is it?** Many firms charge a minimum to cover their expenses if the total value of your belongings isn't at least $10,000.

   • **What's your timeline from when I sign the contract to when your work is complete?** More important, can the firm meet *your* timeline?

   • **How long after the sale ends can I expect to receive payment?** You may need to wait several days to several weeks after the sale ends to receive your payment. Some firms may even continue to list items not sold during the initial sale, which can delay the final payment.

- **Do you have a certified appraiser on staff or accessible to you?** Ideally, you want a firm that uses an appraiser to verify the value of antiques, collectibles, and other valuables.

- **Do you charge, collect, and pay sales tax?** If your state or municipality charges tax on items sold in estate sales, you want to be sure the firm you hire collects and pays those taxes.

- **Are you insured?** If you're hiring a friend or family member to handle your sale, they're probably not going to be insured, but if you're hiring a firm, opt for an insured over an uninsured one.

- **Why should I hire you instead of [name of a leading competitor]?** This question is a good one to ask to identify possible issues with other firms that you hadn't considered.

- **How will my home be left after the sale?** Will it be empty, for example, and *broom clean* (free of clutter, dirt, and debris)?

REMEMBER

Outsourcing the task of selling your belongings may cost you a good chunk of your profit, but a skilled seller is likely to sell your items for more money than you can get for them, which takes some of the sting out of having to pay a sales commission. If you don't have the time, energy, strength, patience, or inclination to organize and advertise a sale and deal with buyers, we encourage you to outsource this task.

Selling Your Belongings Online

Selling your stuff online is often the easiest option with the lowest costs, especially if you're selling locally and your buyers are packing up and moving the items themselves. All you do is post your listings and collect the money.

TIP

Reserve your more valuable items for listing on eBay, where they'll have more exposure to collectors and dealers. List less valuable items that are more difficult and costly to ship on Facebook Marketplace, Craigslist, and OfferUp, where they'll get more exposure to local buyers willing to pick them up.

Every online platform is different, so we can't possibly give you detailed instructions for each one, but to show you just how simple it is, here's how to list something for sale on OfferUp:

1. **Run the OfferUp app on your smartphone.**

2. **Tap the Post icon at the bottom of the screen.**

3. **Tap Take Photo (see Figure 11-2).**

4. **Use your smartphone's camera to take one or more photos of the item and tap Done.**

5. **Type a title for the item and tap Next.**

6. **Enter additional details about the item and tap Next.**

7. **Type a price for the item and tap Next.**

8. **Specify your location and tap Post.**

Interested buyers contact you through the app, and you can arrange to meet them to complete the transaction at a mutually agreed upon location.

FIGURE 11-2:
OfferUp leads you through the process of listing your item for sale.

WARNING

Be careful out there, especially when you're selling locally and meeting people to finalize the sale. Follow these precautions:

>> Don't use your real email address. Communicate through the sales platform's messaging service to keep your email address private. You may even want to use a disposable email address for registering with the platform.

>> Meet in a public place and never go alone. Some police departments provide a designated area in their parking lots where online buyers and sellers can meet safely to complete their transactions.

>> Don't meet at your home or invite strangers into your home, especially when you're alone. Of course, if they need to come in to retrieve a sleeper sofa or refrigerator, you don't have much choice.

>> Don't share personal or financial information.

>> Take your cell phone with you, so you can call 911 in the event of an emergency.

>> Accept only cash payments and use a fake-money-detector pen to determine if any large bills are counterfeit. PayPal is another acceptable payment option. Don't accept cashier's checks or money orders because they're easy to counterfeit.

Hosting an Estate Sale

As we explain in the earlier section "Estate sale," you can hire a firm to conduct an estate sale on your behalf, but that option typically requires paying the firm 40 percent or more of the sales proceeds. If that idea doesn't appeal to you, consider hosting the estate sale yourself. You can divide it into the following three stages to make it more manageable:

>> Before (presale)

>> During (sale days)

>> After (post sale cleanup)

Before

Most of the work related to an estate sale is presale preparation. Here's what you need to do:

>> Recruit a couple assistants, especially for the days of the sale. Having one assistant to handle crowd control and another to help people load large items into their vehicles frees you up to work the cash register and haggle with shoppers over prices.

>> Search your home thoroughly to uncover all valuables you may have hidden or misplaced over the years. Search your attic, basement, crawl space, and shed; all cabinets and shelves; and behind, below, and above everything.

>> Remove or lock up all personal and sensitive items and anything you want to keep or pass along to family members or friends. People are going to enter your home like Viking invaders, so don't leave out anything you don't want them to see or think is for sale. Pay special attention to the following items:

- Diaries/journals

- Personal correspondence

- Financial and medical records (or anything with your name, address, account information, or social security number on it)

- Family photos

- Jewelry or precious metals or stones, such as diamonds

- Medications, alcohol, marijuana, and illicit drugs

- Sexually explicit material

- Firearms or other weapons

  Make sure any guns are unloaded and secured; have an expert check for you, if necessary.

REMEMBER

>> Consult an appraiser, if necessary, to check the value of any items you think may be worth something.

>> Sort and organize items for sale (see Chapter 9 for details). Empty cabinets and closets and set items out on tables or counters to make them easier to browse. You're essentially turning your home into a store, so group items in different sections — for example, all cookware and dinnerware in the kitchen, clothes racks in bedrooms, art along one wall.

REMEMBER

If the tables and racks you're using to display items are not for sale, mark them *Not for Sale*.

>> Price everything. You can get stickers online or wherever you usually purchase office supplies. Have SOLD stickers available to put on large items that people may buy and pick up later.

TIP

Consider selling some items, such as clothing, shoes, towels, and books at one low price (for example, $2 per book).

>> Set a date range and times for the sale — typically two or three days, including a weekend. Schedule sales for early mornings and afternoons.

>> Decide on payment methods you'll accept, such as cash and PayPal. Get change at your local bank — $10, $5, and $1 bills, along with several rolls of quarters. Also get rolls of dimes, nickels, and pennies if you're charging sales tax.

>> Start advertising the sale at least a couple weeks ahead. Here are a few ways to spread the word:

- Post about the sale on all your social media accounts.

- Email and text everyone you know.

- Post a classified ad in your local newspapers.

- Post about the sale on Craigslist and Facebook Marketplace.

- List your sale on estate sale websites such as EstateSales.NET and EstateSales.org.

- Post flyers around town with information about the sale. You may want to include photos of some of the items that are likely to attract the most attention.

- A few days prior to the sale, put up signs around the neighborhood in high-traffic areas to drive traffic to the sale location. On your signs, include the dates and times of the sale, the address, and arrows that clearly direct traffic to your location.

>> Have a system for managing foot traffic through your home. For example, as people start to show up for the sale, you may assign them numbers, so they don't have to wait in line for hours to get inside. When the sale opens, you can call the first five or so numbers and then call subsequent numbers as shoppers leave.

>> Have boxes and bags available for shoppers to pack up the items they purchase.

TIP

Most shoppers are going to show up on the first day. To increase traffic on subsequent days, consider offering steep discounts. For example, on day one, everyone pays full price; on day two, items are 25 percent off; and on day three, everything is 50 percent off.

During

During the sale, your responsibilities revolve mostly around crowd control and customer service. Specifically, you can expect to stay busy doing the following:

>> Assigning shoppers numbers as they arrive

>> Allowing a limited number of shoppers inside at any one time

TIP

›› Haggling with shoppers over prices

You can always hold firm on a price and take the shopper's contact information so you can sell them the item at a lower price if it doesn't sell by the end of the sale.

›› Monitoring shoppers to be sure they're paying for what they take

›› Working as a cashier, calculating prices, collecting money, and making change

After

After the sale, you're likely to have some items remaining, along with a mess to clean up. To wrap up, you'll probably need to attend to the following tasks:

›› Remove unsold items and arrange to have them picked up by a local non-profit or carted off in a dumpster.

›› If you allowed shoppers to buy items and pick them up later, or you agreed to deliver some items, follow through on your agreements.

›› Ship any items you agreed to ship (for example, if you sold things to remote buyers online or over the phone).

›› Clean your home or outsource that task to local house cleaners.

Conducting a Garage Sale

A garage sale is like a scaled-down version of an estate sale. It's usually much easier to prepare for and execute a garage sale, but the steps are generally the same as those for an estate sale, and you can break them down into the same three stages: before, during, and after. Review the previous section for details.

Here are a few additional tips for hosting a successful garage sale:

›› Have all your items arranged, priced, and displayed attractively by the night before the first day of your garage sale. Price everything in dollars and quarters, so calculating what a shopper owes will be easy.

TIP

Price items to sell. Don't price them high to leave room for haggling. Many people who attend garage sales don't like to haggle, so if you price items on the high side, you're likely to lose potential sales.

» Hide anything that's not for sale. You can place items you don't want to sell on shelves and hang sheets or tablecloths in front of them to indicate that they're off-limits.

» If you're selling any items that run on electricity or batteries, have an extension cord available and batteries on hand so shoppers can test the items.

» Expect shoppers to start showing up hours before your scheduled opening time. Whatever you do, don't be late.

» Have plenty of change available: $10, $5, and $1 bills, and quarters.

» Protect your cash. Don't leave it unattended.

» Advertise everywhere you can think of advertising online and off. Be sure to advertise on Craigslist and Facebook, and post photos of what you're selling, especially the good stuff.

» Plant some bright, eye-catching signs around the neighborhood the night before, with arrows that clearly point the way to your garage sale. Drive past the signs to see how effective they are in directing traffic.

» Play music during the garage sale. It'll make people feel more relaxed as they shop.

WARNING

Don't let anyone inside your home unaccompanied. Keep a pitcher of water and paper cups outside in case anyone needs a drink and direct them to a local store, restaurant, or gas station if they need to use the restroom.

If you're having a multifamily garage sale, have a system in place to keep track of who gets the money when an item sells. For example, you can color-code the stickers you use to price items or place a letter on each price tag — for example, J for Jan and D for Dan.

Chapter **12**

Giving Away Some Stuff

The only things we keep permanently are those we give away.

— WAITE PHILLIPS

Some items are so precious that you don't want to sell them even though you need to get rid of them; you want to find some way to keep them in the family. Or you may feel that some things aren't yours to dispose of, such as the stuff left behind by your adult children, who moved out years ago. People may be willing to take other items off your hands, but they aren't willing to pay for them. All these items fall into one category: possessions you may be able to give away (if you can find someone who wants them).

Unfortunately, because this category contains such a diverse collection of belongings, you need several strategies to deal with them. In this chapter, we present those strategies.

Returning Items to Your "Kids"

If you're a parent of adult children, they're probably using part of your home as a free self-storage unit. That was fine while they were living with you and as they transitioned to independent living, but now that they're gone and you're downsizing, the time has come for them to take responsibility for, and possession of, their belongings.

Set a deadline for them to retrieve their belongings and schedule a time for them to come over and help you sort through their stuff and pack it up. You shouldn't have to do the sorting and packing for them, but if you entrust the task solely to them, they may leave many of their possessions behind, so be present to ensure the job is completed to your satisfaction.

REMEMBER

Be clear about what will happen to their belongings if they don't clear them out by the deadline. At that point, it's your call — you can donate items, toss them into a dumpster, set them out at the curb, whatever.

At the same time, give your children the opportunity to take everything you collected and saved for them over the years, including the following:

>> School and sports team photos and yearbooks

>> Report cards, diplomas, certificates, awards, and other school papers

>> Trophies and plaques

>> Baby blankets, shoes, and clothing

>> Keepsakes

You may want to keep one or two of the most memorable items, but let your children decide what to do with the rest. For your own sake, don't ask them what they're going to do with any of it. Ignorance is bliss.

REMEMBER

If it's been sitting in your attic or basement for ten years and nobody has looked at it, you probably don't need it. When friends of ours moved, they forgot everything they'd stored in the attic — all those precious items they couldn't part with. If you're likely to forget about it when you move, that's a good sign you don't need it.

BABY BOXES

We had a container for each of our children, which we referred to as their "baby boxes." In each baby box, we kept what we thought was special — clothing, school papers, baby blankets, quilts, first pair of shoes, special knickknacks, certificates, and awards — and some things that were important to us that we thought would be important to our children later.

Having a box for each child simplifies the process of passing along their childhood "memories" without giving them an overwhelming collection of items to move and store. Just be sure they take that box when you're getting ready to downsize. We often hear stories about parents who continue to store and move their children's belongings. They'll say something like, "Yeah, we still have their stuff. They just never took it away."

Be sure they do.

Being Prepared for Disappointment

Chances are good that your children and other family members won't want some of the items you value and assume that they too will value. Your children are members of a different generation. What's important to you isn't necessarily what's important to them.

Unfortunately, when family members don't want keepsakes that you hold dear, their rejection of these things can feel as though they're rejecting *you*, which can hurt emotionally. Here are a few suggestions for avoiding and dealing with these difficult situations:

>> Remind yourself that you're getting rid of possessions because they no longer serve a purpose in *your* life and likewise may not serve a purpose in the lives of your loved ones.

>> Don't try to guilt someone into wanting something. All that does is instill negative feelings — guilt, resentment, and bitterness.

>> Sell it and spend the money on quality time with your loved ones.

>> Keep it yourself. If your child doesn't want something and you feel that attached to it, maybe it's a sign you should keep it. You may even want to make use of it; for example, instead of showcasing your fine china in a cabinet, use it. Regardless of whether you use it, you can simply hold onto it until you're ready to let it go.

REMEMBER

What holds sentimental value for you doesn't necessarily hold sentimental value for others. A family member not wanting something you treasure is not a reflection of how much they love you.

Deciding Which Family Member Gets the Family's Treasures

Some of your belongings may be in high demand. Everyone in the family wants the same special item, either because of its market value or its sentimental value. To prevent family squabbles over who gets what when you're gone or when you're unable to settle disagreements, consider the following approaches:

>> Give items now to the people you want to have them. Don't wait till you're gone. For example, we inherited the family china from Kathleen's parents, and we split it between our daughter and Kathleen's sister's daughter. We gave garage stuff to our daughter and her husband — shovels, tools, and so on. We gave other tools and equipment, such as snowblowers, to contractors who worked on our real estate projects.

>> Host a family auction using Monopoly money or dollar bills. Everyone attending the auction gets a certain amount of money and can bid on what they want.

>> Have a drawing for hotly contested items and allow family members to trade things at the end.

TIP

Create a list of any family treasures you decide to keep, along with the names of who gets what, and store the list with your last will and testament. In many states, you can include a *memorandum of tangible assets* with your will to assign property to specific individuals. Consult your lawyer to be sure that such a memorandum is legal in your jurisdiction; otherwise, you may need to include the list as a more formal part of your will.

REMEMBER

The old saying "You can't take it with you" has more than one meaning. Yes, it means that when you die, you can't take your physical possessions to the spiritual realm, but it also means that the place you're moving may not allow it.

SLOW MARKET FOR ANTIQUES AND CHINA

If you're a member of the baby boomer generation or older, accept the fact that the market for antiques, oriental rugs, designer china, and expensive silverware (except sterling silver) is pretty much gone. With the exception of rare pieces, most antiques are just considered old and aren't in high demand anymore.

In the old days, engaged couples would register at Macy's or Bloomingdale's for china, silverware, and everyday cups and glasses, but today's world is different. Young people shop at IKEA, Wayfair, and Target and are more likely to register online for games, camping equipment, and travel gear.

While we're not fans of cheaply made modern furniture, we applaud the younger generation for being more adventurous and in many ways more practical.

Offering Your Belongings to Family Members and Others

One way to give away belongings you no longer need or want is to find a good home for them — simply make them available to loved ones and anyone else who's willing to take them off your hands. Just be sure to follow the standard pecking order.

If you're clearing out your parents' home, for example, your siblings get first dibs. Likewise, if you're clearing out your own home and have items that belonged to your parents, you may want to offer them to your siblings first and then to your children.

After siblings and children, you can expand the offer to other family members and then to friends, colleagues, coworkers, and, finally, to complete strangers.

Here are a few sites where you can offer items for the taking:

>> Craigslist (craigslist.org)

>> Nextdoor (nextdoor.com)

>> trash nothing (trashnothing.com)

>> Freecycle (www.freecycle.org)

TIP

Take a photo of the item you're getting rid of and text it to the family member you want to have it, along with a brief message about why you're getting rid of it and why you think they may want it. Don't post it on a social media site such as Facebook or Instagram until you've exhausted the list of people you want to offer it to privately.

REMEMBER

Sometimes the best option for an item that many people in the family value is to sell it so loved ones won't fight over it. As long as it's yours to sell, you can make the tough call, take the hit from disgruntled family members, and move forward so you're not leaving behind an issue that divides your loved ones.

Donating Items to Nonprofits

Several nonprofit organizations are happy to take household items off your hands and sell them for you or pass them along to people who can put them to good use. In this section, we cover several of the most popular nonprofits that accept donated household items.

TIP

To find a charity that picks up donations of household items near you, visit Donation Town at donationtown.org, click Schedule a Donation Pick Up, enter your zip code, and click Find. If no charities in your area offer free pickup, the site presents a link you can click to find a list of drop-off locations.

Salvation Army

The Salvation Army (www.salvationarmyusa.org) sells donated goods through its local thrift stores and uses the proceeds specifically to fund its adult rehabilitation centers. These centers help people with drug and alcohol addiction overcome their addictions, develop work skills, and restore family ties.

The Salvation Army accepts a wide range of items, including the following:

>> Appliances (small and large)

>> Books

>> Cars, trucks, SUVs, boats, and campers

>> Clothing and shoes (men's, women's, and children's)

>> Electronics of all kinds, including computers and color TVs

- » Furniture of all kinds, including beds, mattresses, sofas, and sleeper sofas

- » Household goods of all kinds

- » Sporting equipment

- » Toys and games

Depending on where you live, the Salvation Army may provide free pickup or direct you to a drop-off location. To check out your options and schedule a free pickup (if available), visit satruck.org or call 800-728-7825.

Vietnam Veterans of America

Our go-to nonprofit organization for donating household items is Vietnam Veterans of America (VVA), which sponsors the Pickup Please program. All you do is schedule your pickup online at pickupplease.org, pack up your donations, label them, and put them out before the scheduled pickup time. VVA accepts the following items:

- » Small appliances, such as microwaves, blenders, toasters, and coffeemakers

- » Bicycles

- » Books

- » Clothing and accessories, including shoes, purses, belts, ties, and wallets

- » Electronics, including stereos, radios, game consoles, computers (desktop and laptop), monitors, DVD players, cameras, and typewriters

- » Small household furnishings, such as mirrors, nightstands, headboards, filing cabinets, and office chairs

- » Household items such as dishes, glasses, silverware, bedding, linens, pillows, draperies, curtains, rugs, comforters, home décor, baby items, art, and frames

- » Jewelry and cosmetics (unopened and unused)

- » Musical instruments

- » Sports and exercise equipment

- » Tools, lawn mowers, weed trimmers, and hand trucks (no items containing fuel)

- » Toys and games, including stuffed animals, board games, dolls, and action figures

VVA doesn't accept any of the following items:

>> Large appliances, such as washers, dryers, refrigerators, freezers, or dishwashers

>> Large furniture, such as sofas, sofa sleepers, box springs, or mattresses

>> Televisions

The only drawback with VVA is that its Pickup Please program is available only in certain areas in select states in the U.S.: California, Colorado, Connecticut, Delaware, Florida, Louisiana, Maryland, Michigan, New Jersey, New York, Oregon, Pennsylvania, and Virginia.

Donated items generate the majority of the funding that VVA needs to support local, state, and national programs for all U.S. veterans — not just those in a certain age group or who served in a particular war. VVA assists homeless and disabled vets and helps finance their medical care.

AMVETS

American Veterans, or AMVETS for short, operates thrift stores in 22 states, where they sell donations to fund their veterans assistance programs. AMVETS accepts the following items:

>> Small appliances (not large appliances such as refrigerators or ranges)

>> Bedding

>> Bicycles

>> Books

- Clothing and shoes (men's, women's, and children's)

- Curtains and drapes

- Electronics, including computers and flat-screen TVs that are less than five years old

- Furniture

- Housewares, including pots, pans, dishes, and kitchenware

- Jewelry

- Lamps

- Seasonal decorations

- Sports equipment and exercise equipment that's less than five years old

- Toys and games

If you live in Maryland, Washington, D.C., Northern Virginia, Delaware, Texas, or Oklahoma, you can schedule a pickup online at www.amvetspickup.org. If you live in another state, call 866-294-4488 to find out whether pickup service or drop-off boxes are available in your area.

Goodwill Industries

Goodwill Industries (www.goodwill.org) has more than 3,200 thrift stores around the U.S. and provides convenient drop-off sites, which makes it one of the more popular options for getting rid of household items. It also partners with Dell Reconnect to recycle and refurbish computers, which makes it one of the few options for getting rid of old computers. Proceeds from the sale of your items are used for employment training and job placement programs, especially for those who face barriers to employment.

Goodwill accepts the following items:

- Appliances

- Books

- Cars, trucks, SUVs, boats, and campers

- Clothing and shoes

- Collectibles

- Electronics

- Furniture

- » Housewares
- » Jewelry
- » Sporting equipment
- » Toys and games

To find a Goodwill donation center near you, visit `www.goodwill.org/donate/donate-stuff`.

Habitat for Humanity

Most people are aware that Habitat for Humanity builds homes for people in need. What they don't realize is that this same organization accepts gently used appliances, furniture, and household goods, which makes sense — the people who move into homes built by Habitat for Humanity need to furnish their homes as well. In many cases, the organization even provides free pickup for large items. To find a Habitat for Humanity ReStore near you, visit `www.habitat.org/restores/donate-goods`.

The Arc

The Arc is an organization dedicated to helping people with intellectual and development disabilities gain more control over how they live, learn, work, and play. Arc has several thrift stores across the country that sell donated household items to support their cause. The items they accept vary from one local chapter to the next but generally include the following (some chapters accept only cash donations):

- » Books
- » Cars
- » Clothing and shoes
- » Computers (excluding monitors)
- » Décor
- » Electronics (excluding televisions)
- » Furniture
- » Kitchen items
- » Toys

Contact your local chapter for details. To obtain contact information for your local chapter, visit thearc.org, select Find a Chapter from the main menu, select your state from the Find a Chapter drop-down list, and press the Submit button.

Local nonprofit groups

Several nonprofit groups in your area may accept donations of household items. Check into donating to the following organizations:

» Churches, especially those that host rummage sales or have their own thrift stores

» Shelters for victims of domestic abuse

» Local food banks, which may accept clothing and other items or have information about other local organizations that do

» Local libraries, for donating books

Pushing It to the Curb

If you live on a well-trafficked road, you can often get rid of gently used items simply by pushing them out to the curb (where you normally put out your trash). Over the years, some of our neighbors have disposed of toys, exercise equipment, furniture, and a host of other items this way.

TIP

After you place the items near the road, take a photo of them and post it on Craigslist (craigslist.org) or Nextdoor (nextdoor.com) along with your address to spread the word.

If the items aren't gone in a few days, you can call your trash company to arrange to have the items disposed of. Most trash companies will pick up smaller items but charge extra for larger items, such as mattresses and sofas. See Chapter 14 for more about disposing of items nobody wants.

Chapter **13**

Storing Stuff You Can't Part With

If you have to buy stuff to store your stuff, you might have too much stuff.

— COURTNEY CARVER

D ownsizing is all about shedding the burden of having too many belongings. It's not about finding or making more space to store your excess stuff. However, storing items may be unavoidable. For example, if you choose a nomadic lifestyle, you may have photos, keepsakes, and other belongings you're not ready to part with but you don't want to lug around with you while you're globetrotting. Or you may decide to live in a tiny home for a brief trial period, but you want to keep most of your belongings in case you change your mind — you don't want to have to replace all the items you just sold a couple months ago for pennies on the dollar.

When storing belongings is unavoidable, you need to know your options. In this chapter, we describe the most common storage options and help you decide which ones are best for you.

WARNING

Don't use the availability of storage as an excuse to avoid making tough decisions. You'll probably end up just kicking the can down the road. Recently, our coauthor, Joe, walked over to his next-door neighbor's house to check out their yard sale; they had just moved in about a year ago. They had loads of clothing, videos, toys, décor, and more. Joe asked, "Where did you get all the stuff?" His neighbor replied, "Most of this was in our storage unit." The obvious follow-up question, which Joe was polite enough not to ask, was "Why would you put a bunch of stuff in storage if you're only going to sell it a year later?" If you're thinking of moving a bunch of items to storage, ask yourself that question *before* renting a storage unit.

Reconsidering: Will You Really Ever Need This Item?

Even if you've already been through the sorting process in Chapter 9 and decided what you're going to get rid of, we encourage you to repeat the process with the items you're planning to move to storage. This time, be more aggressive when deciding what to get rid of. Go through your entire collection again and ask yourself the following questions for each item you plan to keep:

>> How frequently do I use it?

>> When was the last time I used it?

>> Will I ever really need it again?

>> Is it suitable for my new lifestyle or living space?

>> Will it improve my life more than it will detract from it?

>> How difficult/expensive would it be to replace if I find later that I can't live without it?

>> Is having it worth the cost of moving it and storing it?

REMEMBER

Keep your eyes on the prize — the goal is to reduce your possessions so you need no storage or less storage.

Exploring Your Storage Options

You've whittled down your belongings to the bare essentials, but you still have items that won't fit inside your new home or conform to your new lifestyle. Now what? In this section, we introduce you to several storage options and lead you through the process of evaluating them.

REMEMBER

As you review your various storage options, use the following criteria to evaluate them:

» Cost

» Convenience

» Security/privacy

» Protection from environmental factors such as extreme temperatures, moisture, sunlight, dirt/dust, or mold

Friends or relatives

Storing items with a friend or relative enables you to check all the boxes for the ideal storage solution, assuming you trust your friend or relative and they have suitable storage space. The big drawback is that you're shifting the storage burden from yourself to a loved one who may not appreciate it. We passed down our vinyl record collection to our son, Kyle, who convinced his aunt to store it for him, but it's not a long-term solution; he plans to reclaim the collection as soon as he's settled down.

Storing items with friends or family members can be an ideal solution if the person who's storing the item values it. For example, if you have a beautiful antique china cabinet that you think you'll never use again, but you don't want to get rid of it, a friend or family member who always loved it may be willing to put it to good use until you find a permanent home for it.

TIP

If you have a large or expanding family, consider passing around items instead of getting rid of them. Over the years, we've "loaned" high chairs, train sets, toys, play tables, and similar items to family members. Instead of being returned to us, they're usually passed along to other family members who need them, keeping them in circulation. Ultimately, most of these things will end up somewhere outside the family, but we'll never miss them, and in the meantime, we know they're being put to good use.

Portable storage containers

If you're moving out of your home but not moving into a new residence anytime soon, consider a portable storage unit. These containers are like small versions of the freight containers you see loaded on trains and semitrailers. A truck drops the container at your home, and you load it at your convenience. When you're done loading it, the truck returns to pick it up.

The container, now with your belongings in it, can then be dropped off at your new residence or taken to a safe, secure storage lot until you're ready to have it returned to you. You can even keep the container on your property, using it as a shed for extra storage space for as long as you need it, assuming your neighbors or your homeowner association doesn't have a problem with it.

To find out more about PODS, visit www.pods.com. Since PODS was founded in 1998, many other companies have started offering similar services, including the following:

>> U-Haul offers the U-Box (www.uhaul.com/UBox)

>> 1-800-PACK-RAT (www.1800packrat.com)

>> Zippy Shell (www.zippyshell.com)

Drop-off container services are more convenient than self-storage units (discussed in the next section), but they're also more expensive. In addition, depending on the laws and restrictions in your area, these portable storage containers may not be an option.

TIP

PODS are a great temporary on-site storage solution. We've used them several times in the past when we were rehabbing our kitchen, bathroom, and other areas of our home so our belongings would be out of the way but nearby.

Self-storage units

Self-storage facilities are popping up everywhere these days, providing people with plenty of affordable storage space for all their possessions. Self-storage units are usually leased by the month and available in different sizes, ranging from as small as 5 x 5 feet up to 10 x 25 feet. And if that's not enough space for you, you can rent multiple units.

Most facilities provide 24/7 self-service access. You receive a code or key to get through the gate and a code or key to unlock your unit. Many facilities require you to provide your own lock.

Here are a few potential drawbacks to consider:

>> Not all self-storage units are climate-controlled, so you need to think about whether any of the items you plan to store in your unit would be damaged by extreme temperatures or humidity.

>> If you pack your unit too tight, digging out specific items you need can be nearly impossible.

>> Some items, including hazardous materials, weapons, and perishables, are prohibited.

>> Pests can be a problem. For example, if your unit is next to a unit that contains items infested with roaches or bedbugs, your belongings may be exposed.

>> Many storage facilities have gates, locks, and 24/7 surveillance, but thieves can still break in and steal valuables.

WARNING

Don't use a storage container or self-storage unit to store money, precious metals or stones, or any other valuable items that are easy to carry off. These items should be stored in a safe or safety-deposit box as discussed in the later section "Protecting Your Valuables."

DO YOU REALLY WANT TO DO THIS?

When our house cleaner, Tracy, decided to live the life of a nomad, she rented a storage unit for some pieces of furniture she didn't want to give up — furniture that belonged to a family member.

She moved the furniture on a day that was far too hot. She struggled to get each item into her car. Then she struggled to get it out of her car to the storage building. Then she had to load it into an elevator for a ride up several stories and drag it down the hall to her unit. The storage unit was large enough to fit everything, but getting it to fit was a major feat.

Ask yourself, "Is this something I really want to do?" "Is the sentimental value of what I'm holding onto worth the cost of storage and the time, effort, and hassle of moving it over and over and over again?" "Is the item serving my needs or am I serving its needs?"

Maybe a certain item is worth the cost in money, time, and exertion, but as part of the downsizing process, you need to be making these determinations.

We were fortunate when we downsized. We're friends with someone in the moving business. When we told him we needed at least a week to move our belongings from our old home to the new condo, he offered to store everything in his climate-controlled warehouse. This gave us the time we needed to carefully place everything in the condo exactly where it fit best. Moving our belongings into the condo was like assembling a giant jigsaw puzzle — or more like a giant Jenga tower — with the placement of each piece affecting everything else. Together, we had to work out some complex logistics to get everything properly positioned in our new place.

Peer-to-peer storage options

While most people own more stuff than they have room to store, others have more storage space than they know what to do with, and a segment of that population rents out a portion of their excess space — typically a garage, warehouse, or even a barn. These *peer-to-peer storage* options may be more affordable than commercial storage options, and they provide you with a sense that you're giving your valued possessions a home instead of just packing them into a storage unit.

And wouldn't you know it, a website is available to connect people who need storage with people who have it. It's called StoreAtMyHouse (storeatmyhouse.com), and it bills itself as the Airbnb of peer-to-peer storage. You enter your location in the search box on the home page, and the site presents a list of peer-to-peer storage options within 50 miles of you. Another popular platform is Neighbor (www.neighbor.com), where you can find peer-to-peer storage options for all your belongings, as well as for cars, RVs, boats, trailers, and business inventory.

GETTING CREATIVE WITH STORAGE

Ray Confer is a real estate investor who leases residential units and their storage separately; for example, he leases three apartments in a house to three different renters and leases the garage to someone else for storage (unless he's using it to store items he owns). Another family friend leases out homes he owns while using the garages as storage units; he has three garages at three separate locations, each packed to the ceiling with stuff he thinks will be worth a fortune someday.

If you need extra space to store belongings that don't fit into your newly downsized home or apartment, you can probably find convenient peer-to-peer storage near you. On the other hand, if you have extra storage and are looking for ways to earn a little extra spending money, you can lease your storage to someone who needs it.

WARNING

Avoid storing valuables or any documents that contain sensitive information with strangers. Keep those items with you or store them with trusted friends or family members, or in a safe or safety-deposit box, as discussed in the next section.

Protecting Your Valuables

Money and other valuables attract thieves, so be selective about what you put in general-purpose storage. Friends, relatives, self-storage, storage containers, and peer-to-peer storage are suitable for furniture, appliances, décor, and other non-perishable household items, but consider more secure storage options for the following items:

>> Cash

>> Coins

>> Savings bonds

>> Stock and bond certificates

>> Precious metals, such as gold, silver, and platinum

>> Precious stones, such as diamonds and rubies

>> Expensive jewelry

>> Copies of any appraisals you have for your valuables

>> Season tickets to sporting events

- » Deeds to all real estate

- » Titles to all vehicles

- » Documents that prove your identity, including your birth certificate, passport, and social security card

- » Marriage certificate

- » Estate documents, including your last will and testament, trust documents, power of attorney documents, medical advance directives (including your living will), life insurance policies, and so on (see Chapter 7 for details)

- » Insurance policies and contact information needed to file a claim

Secure storage for the items on this list boil down to two options: a home safe or a safety-deposit box at a bank. In the following sections, we present the pros and cons of each option.

Home safes

Unless you've chosen a nomadic lifestyle, we recommend storing your valuables in a hidden home safe. About ten years ago, we stored our valuables in several small safes we hid throughout our home — the kind that were easy to carry out of the house and probably easy to bust open. We eventually replaced our multiple safes with a large hidden safe that we had professionally installed. It was so large, we decided not to move it to our condo.

Here are some of the benefits of having your own safe as opposed to using a safety-deposit box at a bank:

- » **Convenience:** You have access to the contents of your safe 24/7.

- » **Fire protection:** You can buy safes that protect the contents from fire damage. Older safety-deposit boxes may not provide fire protection.

- » **Cost:** Although a quality safe may cost more than a thousand dollars, it can pay for itself over the course of a few years; a bank may charge several hundred dollars a year for a 10-x-10-x-18-inch box.

- » **Size:** Safety-deposit boxes are usually about 18–24 inches long and vary in height and width — 3 x 5, 3 x 10, 5 x 10, and 10 x 10 inches being the most common. You can find much larger safes.

- » **Flexibility:** You can store anything you want in your safe, whereas a bank may have policies that prohibit storing certain items, such as cash, in their safety-deposit boxes.

>> **Control:** You have full control over what you're storing in your home safe (your bank isn't aware of what you're storing in there). You also control security around your safe, whereas you must trust a bank's security system to protect the contents of your safety-deposit box.

Here are some tips for buying, securing, and hiding a safe:

>> Buy a quality safe that's large enough for all your valuables.

>> Compare fire ratings and burglar ratings.

REMEMBER

A heavy safe provides additional protection because it's not easy for thieves to carry.

>> Hide the safe in a wall, floor, or cabinet and bolt it securely in place, if possible. A cabinet under a sink is usually a good option. You can also hide it under an old box.

WARNING

Don't hide your safe in the master bedroom or its closet or bathroom, or under the stairs. These are the first places a thief looks for valuables. The best places to hide a safe are the kitchen, pantry, and laundry room — places that thieves typically don't look for safes.

Safety-deposit boxes

If you're living a nomadic lifestyle and you don't have a trusted friend or relative who has room in their safe to store your valuables, a safety-deposit box may be your only option. You can store your valuables at a local bank while you trot the globe, fairly confident that your valuables are safe.

WARNING

Safety-deposit boxes are quickly becoming relics of a bygone era. You're going to continue to see them in movies and think that they're still an option for secure storage, but they're on their way out. Banks are becoming much more impersonal than they used to be. Some banks have only one teller. Many banks are exclusively online.

REMEMBER

Even if your local bank continues to offer safety-deposit boxes, they have the following drawbacks:

>> **Cost:** You'll pay an annual rental fee.

>> **Prerequisites:** You may be required to have an account at the bank.

>> **Protection from damage:** Your valuables may have little to no fire or flood protection.

>> **Security:** Banks still get robbed.

>> **Accessibility:** You can't get to your valuables when the bank is closed.

>> **Loss:** If you forget to pay your rent, the bank or the state can seize any assets stored in the box.

>> **Control:** What you can store in your safety-deposit box may be limited by the bank's policies.

Insuring Your Valuables

Downsizing usually involves reducing your insurance coverage, because you have less house and fewer belongings to cover. However, if you're storing items, you may need to add special coverage for the items you have in storage. Consult your insurance agent to find out whether you need to add coverage to your policy for any items you have in storage.

While you're at it, review your policy to see if you're paying to cover any valuables you've gotten rid of, such as the following:

>> Jewelry

>> Antiques

>> Collectibles

>> Cars

>> Expensive toys, such as boats, wave runners, and motorcycles

REMEMBER

Your monthly rent on your storage unit includes insurance for the building, but it doesn't insure your contents. Regardless of where you store your valuables, be sure you have them insured under your own policy. Also, make sure that any mover you hire carries insurance to cover possible loss or damage of your property.

Chapter **14**

Disposing of Your Remaining Belongings

You got rid of everything you could, and you're now looking at a pile of stuff that nobody wants — and it's too much to set out for your weekly trash-hauling service.

Now what?

The pile of stuff nobody wants may include items that belong in a landfill (such as old, worn-out furniture), items that can be recycled (such as steel and aluminum), and toxic items that need to be kept out of the environment altogether.

In this chapter, we lead you through the final step of downsizing your possessions: disposing of the remaining junk.

Recycling as Much as Possible

Some items don't belong in a landfill, such as the following:

» TVs (you usually have to pay a small fee to have TVs properly recycled)

» Refrigerators and freezers

>> Microwave ovens

>> Air conditioning units

>> Dehumidifiers

>> Dishwashers

>> Stoves and ovens

>> Washing machines and dryers

>> Water heaters

>> Scrap metal (steel, aluminum, copper, tin, zinc, and more)

WARNING

Certain items, such as refrigerators, televisions, and computers, contain substances that pose an environmental threat. Check local ordinances for rules and regulations that govern proper disposal of these items. Try searching the web for "electronic waste" followed by the name of your state.

TIP

Some people make a living out of picking up recyclable items and selling them to a local scrapyard. You may be able to obtain contact information for scrap haulers by calling a local scrapyard or recycling center.

Here are some other options to consider:

>> Appliance retailers may accept or pick up used appliances, especially if they participate in the U.S. Environmental Protection Agency's Responsible Appliance Disposal program.

>> Your electric company may accept or pick up used appliances. The company may even offer a credit for buying a newer, more energy-efficient model.

>> A used appliance dealer may take certain items off your hands to refurbish and resell or use for parts.

>> Your municipal waste management service may offer curbside pickup of old appliances to keep them out of its landfill.

REMEMBER

If you're getting rid of a refrigerator, freezer, or dehumidifier, some services may require the refrigerant and other substances to be removed first, which is not something most people have the equipment and expertise to do properly. Try to find a recycling service that takes care of it for you.

WARNING

If you're setting out a refrigerator or freezer for pickup, be sure to secure the door(s) shut or remove the doors entirely to prevent children from hiding or playing inside them and getting injured or worse.

TIP

Earth911.com can help you determine how and where to recycle, with the overall goal of wasting less and reducing the human impact on the environment. When you reach the website, select the How to Recycle link near the top to find out more.

Having Your Junk Hauled Off in Dumpster

Dumpsters are large waste containers that are dropped off empty and hauled off (usually to a landfill) or emptied into a garbage truck after being filled up. The smaller ones with lids, such as those commonly used at restaurants and retail stores, are referred to as *front-load dumpsters*. In the UK, Australia, and Ireland, they're referred to as *skips* or *skip bins*. Larger dumpsters without lids, such as those used at construction sites, are often referred to as *roll-off containers*. They're rolled off the back of a truck and then rolled back on when they're full.

Dumpsters come in these styles and sizes:

>> Front-load dumpsters can hold 2, 4, 6, or 8 cubic yards of waste.

>> Roll-off containers come in various sizes, including the following:

- 10 yards, which holds 10 cubic yards of waste

- 20 yards

- 30 yards

- 40 yards

Some roll-off containers have doors that enable you to carry items into the container instead of having to throw them over the top, which can be difficult with large, heavy items.

TIP

When placing items into your dumpster, imagine yourself playing Tetris or assembling a jigsaw puzzle. Carefully place the items so they take up as little space as possible. Throwing things over the sides can result in a lot of wasted space.

>> *Dumpster bags,* such as Bagster (www.thebagster.com), are reinforced plastic bags that can hold up to 3 cubic feet of waste. You buy the bags at a home improvement store such as Home Depot or Lowe's, or from an online retailer such as Amazon, fill them up, and then schedule a pickup. Before buying dumpster bags, contact the company to be sure they do pickups in your area. Also, read and follow the rules about where to place the bag and what you're allowed to put inside it.

OUR DUMPSTER

We had a dumpster sitting in our backyard for nearly three months while we sorted through our belongings, packed up what we wanted, and gave away a good portion of what we owned. Fortunately, a contractor who was working with us at the time had a spare dumpster he let us use.

Whenever we came across items we didn't want and nobody was willing to take off our hands, we pitched them into the dumpster. When it was full, we called the contractor who let us use the dumpster and paid the $300 dump fee. He hauled it off, dumped it, and returned it to us so we could start filling it right back up again.

If you have all your junk in a pile, you can figure out the size of the dumpster you need by taking the following steps:

1. **Measure the length, width, and height of the pile in feet.**

2. **Multiply the three numbers to get the number of cubic feet.**

3. **Divide the total cubic feet from Step 2 by 27 to determine the number of cubic yards.**

To find a company that offers dumpster services, start with your current residential trash removal service. If they don't provide dumpsters, they'll probably be able to refer you to a reputable local company. You can also search the web for something like "dumpster rental near" followed by your zip code.

TIP

Consider having a dumpster on your property as you sort through your belongings so you can pitch things into the dumpster during the process. Follow the *one-touch rule* — you want to handle an item only once.

WARNING

Your community may have restrictions on how long you're allowed to have a dumpster. If you belong to a homeowner association, be sure to read the covenant or contact someone on the board to check.

WARNING

Don't place any toxic or hazardous materials in a dumpster. What's classified as toxic or hazardous varies by country, state, county, and municipality, so check with the dumpster company if you have any questions. Here's a short list of items *not* to place in a dumpster:

>> Lead-acid, lithium-ion, or nickel-cadmium batteries (you can safely dispose of household alkaline batteries in the trash)

>> Asbestos

>> Toxic chemicals

>> Flammable liquids

Disposing of Toxic Items

Chances are good that you have some potentially harmful items and toxic substances you don't want to take with you and nobody else wants, such as the following:

>> Lead-acid, lithium-ion, or nickel-cadmium batteries (most modern alkaline batteries are disposable)

>> Paints (in most areas, you can open the container, let the paint dry out, and dispose of it in the trash)

>> Glues and solvents

>> Unused pesticides

>> Unused cleaning solutions

>> Fluorescent light bulbs (incandescent and halogen light bulbs can be placed in the regular trash)

>> Unused medications

>> Anything containing mercury (such as thermometers, thermostats, some batteries, and some light bulbs)

>> Motor oil

>> Antifreeze (used or unused)

Here are a few options to explore for safely getting rid of these items:

>> Some areas sponsor Tox Away Days for residents to drop off toxic or potentially hazardous items, including electronics.

>> A larger metropolitan area may have a ToxDrop site where residents can drop off toxic or potentially hazardous items on certain days of the week.

>> Auto supply stores are often required by law to accept used motor oil and engine coolant and used lead-acid batteries.

>> Home improvement stores may accept used lead-acid, lithium-ion, and nickel-cadmium batteries, along with fluorescent bulbs and used cell phones.

>> Local pharmacies may take back unused medications or refer you to a location where you can drop them off.

Hiring a Company to Haul Away Your Junk

If you don't like the idea of having to deal with a bunch of stuff that nobody, including you, wants, consider hiring a company that specializes in clearing out homes to do it for you. You should have no trouble finding a local company. Just search the web for "junk removal service" followed by your zip code or the name of your city or state.

Here are a few popular nationwide junk removal companies to consider:

>> 1-800-GOT-JUNK? (www.1800gotjunk.com), 800-468-JUNK (5865)

>> College H.U.N.K.S. Hauling Junk (www.collegehunkshaulingjunk.com), 833-626-1326

>> Junk King (www.junk-king.com), 888-888-JUNK (5865)

>> Fire Dawgs Junk Removal in Houston, Texas and several Indiana locations (firedawgsjunkremoval.com), 800-211-DAWG (3294)

REMEMBER

Shop for an eco-friendly, socially responsible junk removal service — one that will sort through your stuff, recycle as much as possible, and donate most of what they collect. You don't want your junk simply hauled off to the nearest landfill.

4

Moving Out and Moving In

Make a well-informed decision about where to live next, including whether to buy or rent, whether to build a new home or buy an existing one, and which options fit in your budget.

Navigate the process of selling your current home and buying your next home to maximize your return on both transactions.

Pack and label everything you're taking with you so unpacking at your destination isn't such a chore.

Execute a smooth and successful move, ensuring that nothing gets lost or damaged and your life is disrupted as little as possible.

Chapter **15**

Gimme Shelter: Choosing a Home

Buying real estate is not only the best way, the quickest way, the safest way, but the only way to become wealthy.

— MARSHALL FIELD

Unless you're opting for a nomadic lifestyle, you're going to need a place to live when you downsize — a home, condo, apartment, granny pod, or some other shelter. The good news is, you have more options than ever before. The bad news is, you have more options to consider than ever before. Which option is best for you depends on multiple factors, including your desired location, affordability, your health and fitness, how close you want to be to loved ones (and how close they want you to be to them), and more.

In this chapter, we introduce you to a broad range of options to increase your awareness of the possibilities and start you thinking about the pros and cons of each option. Our hope is that by the end of this chapter, you have a pretty clear idea of where you want to live and the type of living quarters that are the best fit for your desired lifestyle.

Finding Your Place in the World: Location, Location, Location

Location means something different to everyone, but when you look at property values, you realize that most people value nearly all the same things in a neighborhood:

>> Healthy environment (clean air and water)

>> Affordable cost of living

>> Attractive surroundings (landscape and development)

>> Low crime rates

>> Considerate neighbors

>> Good schools

>> Convenient access to shopping, restaurants, and things to do

>> Proximity to family members and friends

Answer the following questions to guide your search and narrow your options:

>> What's the climate like? If you don't want to be trudging through snow in the middle of winter, you can instantly rule out a variety of locations.

>> Are there family members or friends I want or need to live near?

>> Which locations would be most conducive to the lifestyle I envision living? (See Chapter 3 for lifestyle considerations.)

>> Of the locations I would consider, which are most affordable? Compare costs of living, taxes, travel costs, and other budget considerations.

>> Is the location easy to get around? Think in terms of traffic, availability of public transportation, airports, trains, and the ability to walk or ride a bike to get where you want to be.

>> Does the location facilitate my health and fitness? For example, if you have terrible seasonal allergies, you may want to move somewhere you can breathe more easily.

>> Will I feel safe there?

>> Where will I go for essentials (doctors, dentist, groceries), and how will I get there?

Before choosing a location, visit it. Better yet, rent a place in that location and spend a couple weeks pretending you live there.

REMEMBER

When you're buying into an area or building in an area, consider the value of the home not only now but in the future. Approach your home as an investment, not just a place to live.

Deciding Whether to Buy or Rent

When you're in need of a place to live, you always have the option of buying or renting. The following questions can guide you through the process of making the right choice:

>> **Can you afford to buy?** If you can afford to pay cash for a home or you have the income and creditworthiness to qualify for a mortgage loan, along with the financial resources to cover insurance, property taxes, homeowner association fees, and maintenance, buying is usually the better option, but that depends on your answer to the next question.

>> **Will you be staying put for at least three years?** If you're likely to move within three years, renting is probably better, because when you buy and sell quickly, you incur several expenses, including broker fees, mortgage origination fees, and title insurance, which take a few years to recoup. Additionally, if you sell within two years, you'll owe capital gains tax on any profit from the sale of the home.

>> **Does buying or renting offer greater value?** Basically, if you can rent something comparable for less than a monthly mortgage payment plus the cost of insurance, property taxes, homeowner association fees, and maintenance, renting may be an attractive option, especially if you don't expect property values to increase very much over the time you plan to own the property. In most cases, if you can pay cash or you have good credit, owning isn't much more expensive than renting (it may even cost less), *and* you have something to sell later for a profit.

>> **What would you prefer?** When you buy a home, you're on the hook for any maintenance and repairs. When you rent a place, you never have to worry about mowing the lawn; shoveling sidewalks; replacing the roof, furnace, or

hot water tank; recarpeting; or painting. You can come and go as you please. On the other hand, owning your own place gives you some additional privacy and freedom you may not have when you rent a place — such as having a backyard where your dog can roam free.

REMEMBER

Buying is a long-term commitment; renting isn't. If you've just lost your spouse or experienced some other traumatic event that's prompting you to move, consider a temporary living arrangement, such as renting or moving in with a relative, until you're through the grieving process and in a better position to develop a long-term plan. Don't make any major decisions about your future for a year or so — that will give you the time you need to grieve and get back to a position to make rational decisions, not emotional ones.

WARNING

Don't even think about buying until you've met all the following criteria:

>> You're debt-free or you have a manageable level of debt.

>> You have decent credit (generally a credit score of 680 or higher).

>> You have enough cash reserves to cover a down payment.

>> You have an emergency fund to cover at least three months of expenses.

>> You plan to stay put for several years.

>> Your mortgage (including insurance and property taxes) won't cost more than 28 percent of your monthly income.

Deciding Whether to Build or Buy

If you're going to buy something instead of rent, you have the choice of buying an existing property or building from scratch. Buying an existing property offers the following advantages:

>> **Convenience:** If you have cash or preapproval for a mortgage loan, you simply find the home you want, make an offer, and then close on the sale.

>> **Speed:** You can buy a home and move into it in a matter of weeks.

>> **Simplified financing:** When you buy an existing property, you have one loan that's typically at a fixed rate.

>> **Lower cost (maybe):** Assuming you can find the perfect place and it's in good condition, an existing home typically costs less than a new build. However, if the existing home needs substantial repairs and renovations to suit your needs, building may be the less costly option.

>> **More predictable cost:** When you buy a home, you know up front what the cost will be. When you're building, costs may change over the course of the project, and they usually go up, not down.

By contrast, building a home from scratch comes with the following advantages:

>> **Customization:** You can build the home you want instead of settling for what's available.

>> **Modernization:** A new home meets all the latest codes and standards for heating, cooling, ventilation, insulation, electricity, and plumbing, along with health and safety standards for building materials. Newly constructed homes are typically *greener* — more efficient in terms of energy and water use — which can also save you money.

>> **No maintenance or repair costs:** Since everything's new, and usually under warranty, you can look forward to at least a few years with little to no maintenance or repair costs.

>> **Possibly better resale value:** Most buyers prefer newer homes over older ones, so if you decide to sell your home later, you'll likely profit more from a home you built.

Unfortunately, while having a shiny new custom-built home to move into is an attractive proposition, new construction has several disadvantages, including the following:

>> You have to find a suitable lot on which to build the home, which can be quite a challenge.

>> You must find a reputable builder who's committed to quality construction.

>> Financing is complicated. You'll have a separate loan for the lot, a series of construction loans, and then a final mortgage loan at the end to consolidate the other loans.

Work with a lender that specializes in new construction loans to help simplify the process.

>> Your interest rate is less predictable. When interest rates are on the rise, you may be looking at having a much higher interest rate by the time your new home is finished than at the time construction began. Think about what your interest rate will be a year from when you break ground. (Of course, any decline in interest rates works in your favor.)

>> The cost may be less predictable. When you buy an existing home, you know the cost up front. However, when you're building, costs may change depending on the price of construction materials and labor.

WEIGHING THE COSTS OF BUILDING VS. BUYING

When we started looking for a new place, we found a condo we both really liked, but we immediately noticed certain aspects of it that wouldn't work. We would've needed to remodel the kitchen — the cooktop in particular was very small. We wanted to keep our bedroom furniture, so we needed a main bedroom that was big enough for all of it. We had to have at least one 16-foot wall in the main bedroom to fit our headboard and two oversized nightstands. We were saying things like "Let's move this" and "We'll have to redo the kitchen," which aren't things you say about your dream home.

Although we really liked the location and the condo overall, when we did the math, it didn't make the cut. It would've cost us $100,000 to $150,000 in repairs and renovations. We also didn't fall in love with any of the existing homes we looked at. We either didn't like a particular home at all or would've had to do pricey renovations to make it into what we wanted.

REMEMBER

When negotiating a building contract, if possible, opt for a lump-sum contract over a cost-plus contract. With a *lump-sum contract,* you pay the price you've been quoted. With a *cost-plus contract,* the price covers the builder's expenses plus a certain amount or percentage over that amount.

>> You need to communicate and collaborate closely with your builder to ensure you're getting what you want and the project stays on schedule.

WARNING

If you're building a new home, nail down all the details about what you want *before* construction begins. Every change you make during the process will cost you more money.

Estimating the Living Space You'll Need

When you decide to downsize, you need to estimate the living space you'll want or need to support your new lifestyle. According to some experts, the average person needs 100–400 square feet of space to feel comfortable in their living quarters, but that's a wide range and an arbitrary number. Some people need more like 1,000–2,000 square feet to feel comfortable.

You can take various approaches to estimating your desired living space, such as the following:

>> **Scale down by a percentage.** Do you want to downsize by a third, a half, or more? Take the square footage of your current residence, multiply by the percentage you want to downsize, and subtract that amount from your current square footage. For example, if you're living in a 2,400-square-foot home and want to downsize by one-third, multiply 2,400 by 0.33 to get 792, and then subtract that from 2,400: 2,400 – 792 = 1,608.

>> **Subtract rooms.** Suppose your current residence has three bedrooms (two of which you never use) and two full bathrooms (one of which you never use). You can probably easily downsize to a unit with two bedrooms and one bathroom, one bedroom and a bathroom, or even an efficiency apartment. Can you live without a basement or garage?

>> **Envision where you're going to put everything.** Think about where you're going to put everything you're taking with you — your bed, dressers, living room furniture, dining room table and chairs, kitchenware and appliances, office furniture, and so on. Draw a floor plan showing where everything will go and estimate how much space you'll need for everything to fit.

>> **Visit homes of various sizes.** Check out different-sized homes to see how they feel to you. If you feel cramped, you may have found your lower limit.

REMEMBER

Keep in mind that a home's floor plan can make it feel more or less spacious. You may feel more comfortable in less space depending on how the rooms are arranged.

In the following sections, we look more closely at what you should consider when determining the amount of living space you'll need.

Total square footage

Downsizing doesn't necessarily require you to live the rest of your life in cramped quarters. By shedding belongings and making more efficient use of existing space, you may feel *less* cramped in *less* space, especially if you move to an area and adopt a lifestyle that has you spending more time outside your home.

REMEMBER

Having a *great room*, which combines your kitchen, living room, and dining room into one large area, can make each of those areas feel larger while placing everything within convenient reach.

ENVISIONING THE SPACE WE NEEDED

At the grand opening of our subdivision, the founder said, "We put the square footage in all the right spots," meaning homes were designed to allocate more space where inhabitants would spend the most time — kitchen, living room, main bedroom, and bathroom.

As we were working with our builder on the design of our home, we tried to envision where our furniture and other belongings would fit and where we would be spending most of our time.

We wanted a nice size main bedroom along with a guest bedroom. We each needed an office, and we wanted a gym. We also wanted separate his and hers areas so we would each have our own space and wouldn't need to cross paths during the day.

During construction, we decided to expand the lower level to create a "his" space, which included the gym and Ralph's office. That left the entire main floor to Kathleen, including her office. We also decided to expand the garage — we added heat, cabinet storage, and a TV.

Over the course of the project, we had to compromise and work closely with our builder and the condo association. Some of what we wanted wasn't doable from a builder's perspective, and other items on our list wouldn't fly with the condo association. Don't be surprised if some of what you want can't be done.

Rooms and room sizes

One way to look at living space is to break it down by room and estimate the square footage for each:

» Kitchen: _____ square feet

» Living room: _____ square feet

» Dining room: _____ square feet

» Main bedroom: _____ square feet

» Second bedroom: _____ square feet

» Main bathroom: _____ square feet

» Second bathroom or half bath: _____ square feet

» Office: _____ square feet

MORE ROOMS IN LESS SPACE WITH ROBOTICS

Thanks to modern technology, architects and designers are developing ways that enable people to live more comfortably in less space. According to a recent article in *The Wall Street Journal*, you can now rent a 327 square-foot apartment with five rooms. Furniture can be tucked away in ceilings and floors and behind walls. "With the push of a button, a messy bedroom becomes a spotless living room."

Currently, these multipurpose robotic spaces are only for the rich and famous, but as the technology develops, they're likely to become more affordable, especially given the fact that they provide the amenities of a large home in a smaller package.

REMEMBER

Consider your current and future needs. You may need only one bedroom and one bathroom, but what if you have guests? Will you need a second bedroom for family members or friends who visit from out of town? Do you think you may need a bedroom for a live-in caregiver in the foreseeable future? Will you need a separate office, or can you carve out an area of your living room for office space?

Living room and dining room or office/den?

Most people who downsize move to a place without a formal dining room. They eat at the counter or at a table in the kitchen or great room (or on a tray in front of the TV), but if you're buying an existing home, it may come with a dining room. You don't necessarily need to use it as a dining room, however. You can use it as an office or den, or knock out a wall or two to expand your kitchen or living room.

WARNING

Be careful about removing walls. In some homes, certain walls support the upper floors or the roof or may have plumbing or electrical wires embedded in them. Before removing any wall, consult an expert — an architect or a builder.

Entertainment areas

By *entertainment areas*, we mean spaces used specifically for games, such as billiards, poker, or table tennis; a home theater; or a bar. Chances are, if you're downsizing, entertainment areas will be the first to go, but everyone's different — if you entertain frequently and need a wide-open space for your guests to hang out and have fun, your game room may be the biggest room in your house.

Entertainment areas don't need to be part of your traditional living space. They can be your garage, extra space above a garage, or a basement. You may also consider your living room or great room your entertainment area.

We expanded our garage capabilities by adding a heater and an insulated garage door so we can entertain in the winter. We also epoxied the floor to give the garage a more finished look and enable us to keep it cleaner. We want to be able to use the space year-round and not exclusively for indoor parking and storage.

Office space

With computers shrinking in size and books and paperwork going digital, office space can be anything from a converted den or bedroom, to a desk in the living room or kitchen, to a cubbyhole under a stairwell. Your "office" doesn't even need to be a permanent physical location — it can be a laptop or tablet computer that you can take anywhere with you.

When you're downsizing, look for opportunities to consolidate and create multi-purpose spaces; for example, a single room can serve as an office during the day and a guest bedroom at night and on weekends and holidays. Your living room can double as your game room. You can consolidate your kitchen and dining room.

In our previous home, Kathleen had a crafting station in one room and a separate office in another, which she had to consolidate into a single room in the new condo. When we were designing our condo, we took inventory of exactly what we needed to accommodate for those purposes in the design. We knew that Kathleen would need a room that would function as a combination den, office, and scrapbooking area, so we had cabinets built to serve the purpose of all three.

Outdoor living areas — porches, decks, balconies

Outdoor living areas are great, assuming you use them and they're easy to maintain. Otherwise, you can usually do without them or adjust to smaller versions. Our previous house had a very large two-level deck that was great for large parties and family gatherings. Now, we spend more time with friends and family out on the town at restaurants and other venues. All we really need is a small deck, so we can have coffee outside in the morning, get some fresh air, and read or eat our meals outside when the spirit moves us.

Outdoor living areas aren't essential, but they can significantly enhance your quality of life. Some people will spend entire days sitting on their front porch watching the world go by, while others will barely peek out a window. Some like to go outside but would rather sit at a coffee shop, visit a park, or walk around the neighborhood. Envision how you'll be spending your days and evenings and plan your living space accordingly. If you love spending autumn evenings conversing with friends around a fire, a deck or patio may feel like a necessity to you, but if you rarely step outside, allocate your space and resources to other living areas.

Pool or hot tub (or both)

Downsizing and maintaining a pool or hot tub may seem to be at cross-purposes, but we're talking about reinventing your life in the process of downsizing, so these luxuries are something to consider. Just keep in mind that both options require additional space and come with additional upkeep and expenses. People who downsize typically transition *away* from pools and hot tubs to shed the burden and save money.

Basement (or not)

Assuming the place you're downsizing to isn't on a floodplain, a finished basement is always a plus. It serves as storage space, provides easy access to mechanicals (heating, cooling, and ventilation system, hot water heater, water softener, and electrical panel), and may even be converted into extra living space — an extra bedroom, a bathroom, a game room, and so on — but only if you have ingress, egress windows. Nowhere in the country can you finish a basement without these windows. Some builders may be able to get a permit to build a basement without ingress, egress windows, but if they do get a special exemption, you may be stuck dealing with the consequences later.

If your basement has its own entrance and windows that let in a lot of natural light, all the better. You have a perfect place for some extra living space. You may even be able to rent out the space for some additional income. We use half our basement as a gym and the other half for mechanicals and storage.

POOL CLOSING

Friends of ours built a pool in their forever home so their grandchildren could come over and pop in and out of the pool at their leisure. Great idea, and it was a nice novelty until the grandkids lost interest. Our friends eventually got tired of maintaining a pool that nobody was using, so they filled it with concrete to give themselves a larger patio. This isn't the first built-in pool that's been filled with concrete.

If you do live on a floodplain, be careful about buying a place with a basement, make sure it has a reliable sump pump with backup power, and be sure to purchase flood insurance.

Garage/parking

If you own a vehicle, don't overlook the importance of having a parking space for it, preferably an attached garage. Second best is a detached garage. Third best is having your own driveway. If you have to park on the street, visit the area in the evening when everyone is home from work to see what the parking situation is. If you can't find a place to park, think twice about buying into the area.

In some housing additions, parking overnight on the street is illegal. Your vehicle may be ticketed or towed. If you visit a neighborhood at night and nobody's parking on the street, they're following either a written or an unwritten rule.

When we downsized, we decided right away to shed one of our vehicles. No way would we be able to fit two cars in our new garage. It's just too small. Besides, we can get by without a second car. For what we save in car payments, insurance, license, registration, maintenance, and fuel, we can afford to pay someone to drive us around when we need to be in different places or our car is in the shop.

Storage space

Even if you do an incredible job of reducing your possessions to the bare minimum, you'll need some storage space. You'll probably have at least several boxes of items you rarely use (or even look at) that you can't bring yourself to get rid of. Whether you're renting, buying, or building, think about where you're going to store those items. Does the place you're planning to rent, buy, or build have storage space built in — maybe a basement, attic, or closet under the stairs?

Storage space isn't all the same. Some storage space is organized, and some isn't. The best storage exhibits the following qualities:

>> **Efficiency:** You can store more in less space with efficient storage.

>> **Convenience:** Shelves and drawers that are designed to enable you to see everything and easily access it are better than storage in which items are buried or pushed to the back.

>> **Protection:** Quality storage protects your belongings from dust, moisture, and pests.

ORGANIZED STORAGE SPACE

When we were working with our builder to design our new condo, we made sure that organized storage space was built into the design. We gathered ideas for different cabinet designs and arrangements and storage systems and went through photos of our previous homes to come up with ideas for how to optimize our storage space and make the best use of vertical space. Storage is built in throughout the house, in the garage, and in the lower level.

As we moved into our condo, the garage became our staging area. All boxes passed through the garage on their way to their final resting place, so we could be sure that nothing we didn't specifically want inside entered the house.

Considering Mobility and Accessibility

As you shop for a place to call home, give some thought to *mobility* and *accessibility* factors — how you're going to come and go, move around inside the place, and reach everything you need. If you're healthy and fit at the moment, mobility and accessibility may not be significant concerns, but if you have a disability, are starting to feel the aches and pains of aging, or have a partner who struggles with mobility, don't overlook these challenges.

Whether you're renting, buying, or building, be sure that your future home features the following accommodations.

Throughout the home

>> At least one entryway without stairs or with a ramp

>> Wider doorways and hallways to accommodate wheelchair and walker access

>> Doors that are easy to open with lever door handles instead of traditional round ones (automatic, motorized door openers may also be available)

>> Stair-free design (everything on one level)

REMEMBER

If stairs are unavoidable, make sure they're in good repair and all stairwells have handrails. A chairlift can also be installed to help you navigate stairs.

>> Smooth flooring and thresholds to facilitate movement within rooms and from room to room

WARNING

Avoid high pile carpeting, area rugs, and any textured floor that may pose a trip hazard.

>> Nonskid mats or nonslip strips on any slick or slippery surfaces

>> Soft floors (no ceramic tile, for example) to prevent falls, reduce injuries from falls, and prevent glass and ceramic items from shattering

>> Closets with low, easy-to-reach shelves and rods.

TIP

Consider adding reinforcement between studs to ensure that all handrails have something solid to mount to.

Lighting

>> Adequate lighting during the day (use the brightest bulbs approved for each fixture) and night-lights at night

>> Convenient, easy-to-operate light switches or automatic switches

>> Glow-in-the-dark switches, if necessary

>> Convenient locations for flashlights throughout the home

>> Blackout shades in bedrooms to enhance sleep

Bathrooms

>> Grab bars in the tub or shower and near the toilet

>> Walk-in shower or bathtub with a nonslip floor

>> Shower seat

>> Elevated toilet seat

>> Conveniently accessible cabinet, sink, and countertop

Kitchen

>> Conveniently accessible cabinets and drawers

>> Lower countertops and sinks

In the kitchen, be sure to opt for lightweight pots, pans, and kitchenware. You may also want to look for a stove with controls on the front (instead of top) and a side-by-side refrigerator/freezer or one with a bottom freezer.

REMEMBER

Keep mobility and accessibility in mind when arranging furniture, such as coffee tables, and locating cables and cords to allow for unimpaired movement within and between rooms and eliminate any trip hazards.

Exploring Your Housing Options

Housing comes in a variety of sizes and styles — from efficiency apartments and tiny homes to mansions. When you're in the market for a place to live, consider your options carefully. In this section, we describe many housing styles, though we can't possibly cover all of them.

Traditional house

Traditional houses, often referred to as single-family homes, typically have a front and rear entrance, a garage, and a front and back yard. They come in a variety of styles. Here are a few styles that are more conducive to downsizing:

>> **Ranch:** These single-story houses are great for mobility because they have no stairs to climb. They also tend to be easier and more efficient to heat and cool. They're very popular with downsizers, often a top choice, and they tend to retain their value.

>> **Cabin/cottage:** These small, compact, affordable homes are often perfect for downsizers. They cost less than the typical home to heat and cool, maintain, furnish, decorate, and insure. They may feel cramped to some or cozy to others.

TIP

If you want to get away from it all and live in the woods or on the water, a cabin or cottage may be the perfect choice. You may pay extra for the location and views, but you'll probably save money on the house itself and on cleaning, repairs, and maintenance.

>> **Bungalow:** These homes are typically small, rectangular, and single-story with a low-pitched roof. Sometimes a second story is built into the attic space. They commonly have a large front porch or wraparound porch. Because bungalows are compact and economical, they're usually a good choice for downsizers.

>> **Townhouse:** A townhouse is typically a two- or three-story home that shares a wall with one or more other townhouses. However, single-level townhouses may also be available. They typically cost less than single-family homes in the same area, but because of their proximity to the neighbors, they generally come with less privacy and independence.

>> **Duplex/triplex:** A duplex or triplex is a single building with two or three separate units, which can be the perfect solution if you're downsizing and want some rental income to supplement your social security and pension payments or need room for family members or a caregiver to live right next door.

You may want to omit a few architectural styles from your search. Some styles are simply too large or too difficult and costly to maintain. Here are a few styles that you'll probably want to cross off your list:

>> **Classical (Colonial, Federal, or Georgian):** These two- or three-story homes with large rooms and high ceilings were popular in the 1700s through the 1800s. They're spacious, elegant, and durable, but they can be costly to heat, cool, and maintain.

>> **Victorian:** Victorian homes are typically large two- or three-story homes with intricate trim that are very ornate and solidly built. They come in a variety of styles, including Italianate, Gothic, and Queen Anne, to name only a few. They're beautiful and usually good investments, but if you need any work done, it can get expensive. They're also typically humongous, so probably not the best choice when you're downsizing.

>> **Greek Revival:** These homes are elegant and spacious — usually two or three stories with large rooms, high ceilings, and huge porches (not to mention lots of columns) — making them a great choice for homeowners who regularly host large gatherings. The cost (both in time and money) of cleaning, repairs, and maintenance make Greek Revival homes a poor choice for downsizers.

Apartment

An *apartment* is a room or suite of rooms generally located in a building occupied by more than one household. Apartments are usually rental units, but in some cases, you can buy them. If you're in the market for an apartment, think about the type you want.

>> **Conventional:** Conventional apartments have one or two bedrooms, a full bathroom, a separate kitchen and living room area, and sometimes a dining room.

>> **Studio:** A studio apartment has an open floor plan that combines the kitchen, bedroom, and living room, and a separate full bathroom.

>> **Loft:** A loft is like a studio apartment. It has one large room with high ceilings, usually large, tall windows, and exposed brick and support beams. Lofts are often located in commercial buildings that have been converted into residential units.

>> **Efficiency:** An efficiency is a small apartment with a combined bedroom and living area and a tiny kitchen and bathroom — the perfect apartment for a minimalist who rarely entertains guests.

Some apartment complexes may offer valuable amenities, such as a community pool, clubhouse, gym, and laundry facilities.

TIP

You're usually better off buying than renting, but renting an apartment may be the best option if you're between homes or you want to spend a trial period in a new location before buying a home there.

You may be able to trim your heating bill by renting a unit on one of the upper floors or trim your cooling bill by renting a unit on one of the lower floors.

Condo

A *condominium* (*condo* for short) is a building or complex in which individuals own their residential units and jointly own the grounds and the overall building or complex. In some ways, a condo provides the best of both worlds: home ownership and apartment living. You own your unit but have less upkeep and monthly maintenance. Typically, you're responsible only for repairs and maintenance of anything inside your unit.

Condo living isn't for everyone. Carefully weigh the pros and cons.

Pros

>> Less maintenance

>> Better security in some cases

>> Amenities (a condo may have a pool, fitness center, clubhouse, pond, community activities, and other perks)

>> Affordability (a condo typically costs less than a traditional home, although condo association fees can make condo living more expensive)

Cons

>> Condo association fees, which can be substantial and increase considerably over time

>> Potential for mismanaged condo association funds

>> Potential for other residents not paying their condo association fees

>> Less privacy

>> More rules and restrictions

WARNING

Before buying a condo, do your research. Read the condo association's covenants and restrictions, so you fully understand what you're getting yourself into. Also find out how much the fees are, what they're used for, how and when they're collected, and how much and under what conditions they can be increased. Request a copy of the association's financial statements — you're entitled to these documents.

Granny pod (aka mother-in-law cottage)

If you want to live with your adult children and your grandchildren but want the privacy and independence of your own living quarters, consider building a granny pod in your backyard (or on your children's property). A granny pod is a modern version of the old mother-in-law college, except that it's totally mobile — if you move, you can take it with you. It typically includes a kitchenette, bathroom, and bedroom/living room and often comes equipped with a monitoring system and other safety, security, and accessibility features built in.

Another option, if you're not ready to sell your property is to place a granny pod or build a small home or cottage on your land, move into it, and rent out the big house.

Tiny home

If you're striving to become a minimalist, consider downsizing into a tiny home. It's all the rage! A *tiny home* is a freestanding residential unit that's no larger than about 400 square feet, excluding a loft. The average tiny home is about 200 square feet. It's basically no larger than a shed. In fact, sheds are often converted into tiny homes.

A tiny home may be on wheels or set on a foundation. Some are placed on a lot with other buildings or a larger home, or they may be placed on a lot of their own or on family land (for example, a farm or ranch). They come in a variety of shapes and sizes. You can spend an entire day looking at photos and videos of tiny homes online (not that we did that).

TIP

If you're thinking that a tiny home may be the right choice for you, we encourage you to try before you buy (or build) one. Rent a tiny home for a month and see if you can handle living in a minimal amount of space. If you love it, you can then move forward with confidence, along with plenty of ideas about how to build your tiny home.

Mobile home

A *mobile home* is a prefabricated structure that's built in a factory on a permanently attached chassis before being transported to a site. It may be placed on a foundation on a lot of its own or in a trailer park, where it serves as a permanent dwelling, like a traditional home.

Some mobile homes, called *park models,* are no larger than tiny homes, maxing out at about 400 square feet. They're often parked in permanent or semipermanent locations in trailer parks, campgrounds, or RV parks. Like RVs, in many jurisdictions, park models aren't permitted as residential living units on private lots.

RV or van

When gas was cheap, more and more people were drawn to living a nomadic lifestyle, traveling across the U.S. and sometimes into other countries in an RV or converted van. Given the unpredictability of gas prices and growing concerns over climate change, we're wondering if interest in this lifestyle will begin to wane.

REMEMBER

This is another lifestyle option we recommend you try before you buy. Rent the type of RV or van you've always dreamed of and spend a month or two on the road in it. That's usually sufficient time to get the nomad lifestyle out of your blood or discover that you truly love it. In most cases, after living in cramped quarters, cooking and washing dishes in a dinky kitchen, spending quality time at the laundromat, and not seeing friends or family for a couple months, people lose their passion for living on the road.

55-and-older community

If you're 55 or older and you're looking for a safe, quiet, and well-established community of peers along with a host of amenities, check out some *55-and-older communities,* which typically offer the following advantages:

>> A safe, stable neighborhood

>> Community and camaraderie

>> A rich social life with plenty of events and activities

>> Desirable amenities, such as a pool, hot tub, clubhouse, and fitness center

>> Transportation, such as a shuttle service

Beware of the potential drawbacks of 55-and-older communities, such as the following:

» One-time buy-in fee, which may be substantial and may have refund restrictions

» Homeowner association fees or other fees

» Lack of diversity

» A culture that clashes with your desire for independence and privacy

» Separation from friends and family

» Excessive rules and restrictions

» Financial risk related to whether you own your unit and whether the organization that manages the community is financially sound

Perform your due diligence before buying into a 55-and-older community. Talk to residents to find out what they like and dislike about living there. If you know anyone who lived there and moved out, find out why. Read the community's rules and regulations. Read ratings and reviews online.

Barndominium

A *barndominium* is a metal pole barn with a steel frame and sheet metal siding that's converted into a home. It's easier, faster, and less expensive to build or assemble than a traditional home, and its interior is completely customizable, so the floor plan is whatever you want it to be.

Barndominiums are usually dual purpose — intended for both business and residential use or suitable if you need a lot of space for a hobby you're passionate about, such as woodworking or collecting classic cars. You can use part of it as your home and another part as your art studio. They're also typically large enough to store cars, boats, and RVs inside.

Barndominiums are spacious, so they're usually not at the top of the list for downsizers. They're affordable in terms of building, maintenance, and repair, but they may be expensive to heat and cool.

Shipping container home

Can you imagine living in a *shipping container* — one of those metal boxes you see riding atop a train car or being pulled behind a semitruck? Well, people are doing it, and they're doing it in style and comfort, sometimes stacking two, three, or more shipping containers and converting them into large compounds with kitchens, bathrooms, living rooms, and office space. A single shipping container can be used as a tiny house, or they can be combined to create massive structures.

Because of their size and versatility, they're certainly a consideration for downsizers. The biggest challenge is finding a buildable lot in an area that permits container homes. If you have a friend or family member who owns some extra land and is willing to make it available to you, problem solved.

Houseboat or cruise ship

If you're healthy, fit, love the water, and like to travel, living on a houseboat or cruise ship may be an option for you. We have a friend who packed up his belongings and moved to Florida to live on a sailboat. It's sort of like living in an RV but on the water.

People who live full-time on houseboats are called *liveaboards*, and they claim that living on a houseboat is typically cheaper than buying or renting a traditional home, assuming you're not paying a daily dock fee. You can buy a houseboat for less than a traditional home, and then all you have to pay for is drinking water, fuel, insurance, and license/registration. Of course, you're usually getting significantly less living space — it's more like a tiny home.

Downsizing to life on a cruise ship may not be as affordable, but if you have the money and you love to travel, it may be the perfect post-downsizing lifestyle for you. No cleaning, no maintenance, no meal prep, and everything is included — food, housing, housekeeping, entertainment, transportation, and more. The only complication may be health insurance for lengthy stays outside the country.

WARNING

Living on a houseboat or cruise ship does have some potential drawbacks, including the following:

>> Cramped quarters

>> Limited mobility (you can't just hop in a car and drive wherever you want)

>> Rough weather (storms, hurricanes)

>> Limited access to loved ones

>> Restricted or expensive communication (phone and internet service)

Assisted living facility

If you need help caring for yourself or a loved one, an *assisted living facility* may be the best option. These facilities are created for people who can't or choose not to live on their own — those who need various levels of medical or personal care. Services provided typically include the following:

>> Meals

>> Medication monitoring

>> Personal care, including help with personal hygiene and getting dressed

>> Housekeeping

>> Laundry

>> Social and recreational activities

>> Transportation

>> Limited medical services

REMEMBER

Different facilities deliver different levels of care, so talk with loved ones to determine the level and types of care needed along with how often help is needed before choosing a facility and care plan. If all you need is someone to check in on a loved one and do some housecleaning and meal prep, your loved one may be able to get by with some level of in-home care instead of having to transition to an assisted living facility. However, be realistic when making that assessment.

Accounting for Additional Costs

When you're comparing housing options, don't focus solely on the purchase price. One property may have a lower purchase price but additional costs that can make it a more expensive option over time. In this section, we cover costs that many homeowners often overlook.

Utilities

Regardless of where you live, you'll need to pay for utilities and basic services — gas, electricity, water, sewer/septic, and trash removal. However, when you're downsizing, one goal is to reduce these expenses substantially, typically by moving to an area where they're more affordable and living in a smaller space.

REMEMBER

Before renting or buying a place, find out how much the previous owner or renter paid in monthly utility bills. They should be able to provide copies of the bills or a spreadsheet showing you what they paid. If they won't provide documentation, contact the utility companies and ask.

Maintenance and repairs

Maintenance, repairs, and updates can be costly, so when you're comparing housing options, consider the cost of any work required to bring a property up to the market standard. Get the home inspected by a reputable and knowledgeable individual, someone in construction, to reduce the likelihood of getting blindsided by a big repair bill shortly after moving in — such as a bill for replacing the roof, furnace, or air conditioning unit or for mold remediation.

TIP

Here are a couple other ways to avoid large, unexpected repair and maintenance bills:

>> Buy a condo, so the condo association will at least be responsible for exterior repairs and maintenance.

>> When you buy a home, purchase a home warranty to cover major repairs, such as replacing the furnace or air conditioner. A home warranty is always a good idea for the first year you own a home until you have more knowledge of the mechanicals in your home.

Homeowner or condo association fees

If you buy a condo or a home that's part of a homeowner association (HOA), you'll be subject to annual or monthly fees. In both cases (HOA or condo association), fees cover maintenance and repairs of common areas, such as a clubhouse, community pool, park, and sometimes roads. In the case of a condominium, the fees also commonly cover the costs of external repairs and renovations to residential buildings, such as the cost of replacing the roof or siding.

Association fees can vary considerably — from a few hundred to thousands of dollars annually — and they tend to increase over time to keep pace with inflation. What the fees cover may also vary. Some associations merely cut the grass and clear snow from roads, walkways, and driveways. Others handle retention pond maintenance, pool maintenance, clubhouse repairs, all exterior building repairs and maintenance, and more. You usually get what you pay for.

REMEMBER

If you're opting for a nomadic lifestyle, living in an RV or on a boat, you may avoid association fees, but you're likely to be subject to similar expenses in the form of RV park fees or dock fees. Some RV parks have associations that allow you to buy a space and contribute time, money, or both to maintaining the grounds.

Property taxes

Whether you buy a home or a condo, one expense is a sure thing: property taxes. Unfortunately, the amount you'll be charged can present you with an unpleasant surprise in areas where property values are soaring. When you close on the property, you file a *transfer affidavit* notifying the county that the property is being transferred to you. This notification also contains the purchase price, which can trigger a reassessment of the property's value and a significant increase in property tax.

To avoid an unpleasant surprise, whenever you're buying a home, check with the county assessor's office to find out what the property tax rate is for your area and how it's calculated. You may even want to tell your county assessor what you're thinking of buying and ask for a ballpark estimate of what the property tax will be.

TIP

To simplify your monthly budget, consider setting up an escrow account through your lender for paying homeowner's insurance and property taxes. With an escrow account, you have a larger monthly payment, but what you pay in excess of your mortgage and interest payment is deposited into your escrow account. When your homeowner's insurance or property taxes are due, your lender pays those bills out of your escrow account, so you don't get hit with large, unexpected bills.

Chapter **16**

Buying and Selling a Home

A forever real estate agent understands that the concept of home is predicated on the many changes life can bring, and it doesn't start — or end — with the transaction.

— GINO BLEFARI

ownsizing doesn't necessarily involve selling a large home and buying a smaller one. It may involve staying in your current place, moving to a smaller apartment, moving in with a relative, couch surfing, living in an RV or houseboat, or even cruising the Seven Seas. However, downsizing *usually* involves selling a large home and moving into a smaller one, and you want to do this as efficiently and profitably (or at least cost-effectively) as possible.

In this chapter, we lay out your options, including keeping your current home and using it as a rental property. We explore issues related to the timing of a sale and purchase to help you steer clear of common mistakes that can cost you thousands of dollars. We provide guidance on how to find the best real estate agents in a given market. And we offer insights on how to keep more of your profit from the sale of your home by paying less in capital gains tax.

WARNING

If you have a partner who's on the fence about moving, consider waiting until you're both in agreement. Selling a home can be a very emotional decision, especially if you've created fond memories in that home. It's also a "together decision." If you're on board and your spouse isn't, selling the home can generate bitterness and resentment that tend to fester over time. Sometimes waiting until you're both ready is the wisest approach.

Deciding Whether to Sell or Keep Your Current Home as a Rental

When most homeowners move, they sell their current home, but that's not always the most financially savvy move, especially when real estate values are soaring. Sometimes holding onto your current home and renting it out is the smarter move, assuming you can handle a rental property and charge enough to cover the mortgage payment along with the cost of any repairs and maintenance. You can outsource the heavy lifting to a property management company if that option is affordable.

To decide whether to sell or keep your current home as a rental property, answer the following questions:

>> **Do I need to sell my house to buy my next one?** If your current home is already paid off or you have the funds to secure a mortgage on a second home, you may not *need* to sell your current home to buy another one. Talk with a lender to find out what's possible.

>> **Am I allowed to lease my home to renters?** If the property is part of a homeowner association or condo association, the association's rules and regulations may not permit owners to lease their property. The decision may have already been made for you. The association may also limit the number of properties that are rentable.

>> **Is now a bad time to sell?** If property values in your area are down, you may want to wait before selling your property. You may want to rent it out at least until property values recover.

>> **Can I lease the property for the amount of money I would need to make it worth the trouble?** Is your property in an area that would be attractive to renters? Is it the type of property that would be appealing to renters? For

example, a furnished home near a college or downtown area may be in high demand as a rental property, whereas you may have trouble finding someone to rent a large home in a rural area.

>> **Am I landlord material?** Do you have the time, energy, and patience to be a landlord? Consider worst-case scenarios: renters who can't or won't pay the rent or who trash your property. Will you worry about the property even if you have responsible tenants? Will that worry affect your health?

Having one or more rental properties can help you build wealth and may be very rewarding, but be sure the responsibility is something you're willing and able to take on. One of the main reasons people downsize is for the added peace of mind. Adding a rental property to your investment portfolio may be counterproductive to achieving that goal.

Deciding Whether to Buy First or Sell First

Ideally, when you're selling a home to buy a new one, you want to coordinate the sale and purchase so they happen at nearly the same time. You can close on both proper-ties in quick succession and then simply move from your old home to your new one. You don't have to store anything or secure temporary lodging. Unfortunately, the ideal scenario rarely unfolds according to plan. Your current home may sell before you have time to find a new place, or you may submit an offer on a new home and have it accepted only to discover that nobody seems interested in buying yours.

What's worse? Should you try to sell your current home before buying your next one or make an offer on a new place before listing yours for sale? In this section, we help you answer those questions and determine the best course of action.

Keeping your finger on the pulse of the housing market

Deciding whether to sell first or buy first depends a great deal on whether you're making the decision in a seller's market or a buyer's market.

>> In a *seller's market,* the number of buyers exceeds the number of homes available, real estate prices are rising, and homes are easy to sell. In a seller's market, you should generally consider buying a new home first, trusting that demand is so high, you won't have any trouble selling yours. With this approach, you won't feel rushed to find a new place or end up without a place to live if you list your home and it sells within days.

>> In a *buyer's market,* the number of homes available exceeds the number of people looking to buy homes, so real estate prices may be stagnant or dropping, and homes are more difficult to sell. In a buyer's market, you should generally consider listing your home for sale as you look for a new place so that you're less likely to get stuck with a home you can't sell or — worse — two mortgage payments.

Keep in mind that markets may differ based on location. For example, if you're planning to relocate somewhere across town or across the country, your home may be in a buyer's market while the home you want to buy is in a seller's market. In these cases, your decision about whether to sell or buy first becomes more complicated.

>> **Selling in a seller's market while buying in a buyer's market:** This scenario is the most favorable because you can list your home for top dollar, knowing it'll sell fast and for a good price, while you should have no trouble finding an affordable place where you're planning to move.

>> **Selling in a buyer's market while buying in a seller's market:** This scenario is the worst because you'll face challenges both with selling your home and finding a new place. In this situation, selling your home first may be even more compelling, especially if you're not in a financial position to cover the cost of two mortgage payments for at least a few months.

Keeping an eye on interest rates

Interest rates can also influence your decision about when to buy and sell. If interest rates are high and you have reason to believe they'll drop soon, you may want to hold off on buying or selling until they're more favorable. However, interest rates can always increase from their current levels and remain high for a considerable amount of time.

If you buy when interest rates are high, monitor interest rates and look for an opportunity to refinance at a lower rate. If interest rates drop a couple percentage points, refinancing at the lower rate may significantly reduce your mortgage payment and save you tens of thousands of dollars over the life of the loan. However, if you're planning to sell soon, think twice about refinancing. You usually need to hold the property for at least two or three years to recoup the up-front costs of a new mortgage loan.

Buying before selling

If you're leaning toward buying a new home before selling your current home, consider the pros and cons of doing so and read through our tips for executing this strategy.

Pros

You can gain several advantages by buying a home first, including the following:

>> You have somewhere to move — you won't have to move in temporarily with friends or relatives, rent a place, or store your belongings.

>> You move only once — you won't have to move your belongings to storage and then move them later to your new place.

>> You won't feel pressured to a buy a home you don't really like just so you'll have a place to live.

Cons

Buying before selling does have some potential drawbacks, including these:

>> If the money you need to purchase a new home is tied up in your current home, you may not have enough cash to make a competitive offer on your dream home.

>> After having your purchase offer accepted, you may feel pressured to sell, which can result in accepting a lower offer than you would otherwise accept.

>> You may end up with two homes and two mortgage payments, which can be very stressful and put even more pressure on you to lower your asking price.

>> You may be forced to rent out your home (instead of selling it) — and selling a home with tenants in it can be challenging and complicated.

Tips

Here are a few ways to make buying before selling go more smoothly:

>> **Pay cash for the new home.** If you have enough cash in savings, you can make a cash purchase and then take your time selling your current home.

>> **Use a home equity line of credit (HELOC) to help finance the purchase.** If you have enough equity built up in your current home, you can use a HELOC to convert the equity to cash to help buy the new home and then pay off the HELOC when you sell your place. For more on HELOCs, see the later section "Getting a Home Equity Line of Credit (Just in Case)."

>> **Take out a bridge loan to finance the purchase.** A *bridge loan* is a short-term (usually no longer than about six months), high-interest loan that can be ideal for situations like this. You can use a bridge loan to cover the down payment on a new home until you close on the sale of your current home.

>> **Make your offer to buy contingent upon the sale of your current home.**
The trouble with this approach is that the sellers can continue to wait for better
offers, in which case you stand a good chance of losing the home you bid on.
This strategy typically is best in a buyer's market. If you're dealing with new
construction, the builder won't take the risk, and they won't let you buy on
contingency.

>> **Negotiate an extended closing.** An extended closing (beyond the typical
30–45 days) on the house you're buying gives you more time to sell your
home. However, this strategy is a bit of a gamble. We recommend trying it
only if you're buying into a buyer's market and you're fairly certain you can sell
your current home within the extended period.

REMEMBER

Not everybody is in a strong enough financial position to own two homes at the
same time. Most people rely on money from the sale of their current home to
finance the purchase of their next home. Consult a reputable mortgage lender in
your area to evaluate your finances and explore your options before deciding
whether to sell your current home or buy a new home first. You may have more
resources and options available than you realize.

Selling before buying

If you're leaning toward selling your current home before buying a new place,
consider the pros and cons of doing so and read through our tips for executing this
strategy.

Pros

Selling before buying offers several potential advantages, including the
following:

>> Assuming you profit from the sale, you now have cash in hand to buy a new
place, which makes you an attractive and competitive cash buyer.

>> You'll know exactly how much money you have available to put toward your
new place.

>> You'll feel less stressed about the possibility of getting stuck with two homes
and two mortgage payments.

Cons

Selling before buying isn't ideal. Expect the following potential drawbacks:

>> Unless you find a new place before the scheduled closing, you'll need to find temporary living quarters — you'll have to rent a place or stay with friends/relatives.

>> Likewise, if you can't find a place before the scheduled closing on the home you're selling, you'll need temporary storage for your belongings.

>> You'll have to move twice — from your current home to your temporary digs and then to your new place.

REMEMBER

If you sell first when property values are rising rapidly, you're selling for less and potentially buying for more with each passing day as prices continue to climb.

Tips

Selling before buying can create some discomfort. Here are a few ways to execute this strategy more smoothly:

>> **Make the sale of your home contingent upon getting a new home under contract.** However, this tactic runs the risk of discouraging potential buyers from submitting an offer.

>> **Plan on renting a place.** If renting is part of your plan, it can be a positive, giving you plenty of time to find your dream home.

>> **Negotiate a rent-back agreement with your buyer.** A *rent-back agreement* enables you to lease the property for an agreed-upon period, giving you more time to find a place. This may be a great option if you're selling to a real estate investor or if the buyers need more time to sell their home.

REMEMBER

Don't make these decisions alone. Consult a leading real estate agent (a seller's agent for the home you're selling, and a buyer's agent in the market you're interested in moving to) to help you decide whether to list your current home for sale first or purchase a new home first. Your agents can help you evaluate your options based on your financial profile, market conditions, interest rates, and other factors. See the later section "Picking the Right Real Estate Agents for You" for details.

Choosing Whether to Pay Cash or Finance Your Purchase

If you have cash or enough equity built up in your current home to cover the cost of the downsized home you want, you have the option of paying cash for the home or financing the purchase with a mortgage loan. If you don't have cash, you have no choice but to take out a mortgage — assuming, of course, that you can qualify for a mortgage loan.

To decide whether to pay cash or finance the purchase, consider the advantages of each option, which we explain in the following sections.

REMEMBER

Paying cash or financing with a mortgage loan isn't necessarily an either/or choice. In fact, most purchases involve both: a down payment (in cash) and financing (a mortgage loan). Your lender may require a minimum down payment, but they don't specify a maximum.

Advantages of paying cash

Paying cash (or a significant down payment) for a property has several advantages over financing the purchase, including the following:

>> **Sellers prefer cash offers.** A cash offer gives sellers the confidence that you can close the deal — that you won't back out of the deal and leave them hanging because your financing fell through. As a result, your purchase offer is more likely to be accepted.

>> **Cash buys are faster and smoother.** All-cash transactions eliminate the time-consuming procedures and paperwork required to qualify for a mortgage loan.

>> **Cash buys slash closing costs.** A good chunk of closing costs is in the form of loan origination fees and other fees related to the mortgage loan. When you're paying cash, the mortgage loan and its associated fees are nonexistent.

>> **You'll pay no interest.** When you pay cash, you don't need to worry about rising interest rates or paying interest on a loan, which can save you a considerable amount of money. For example, a 30-year, $350,000 mortgage loan at 5 percent interest will end up costing you $326,396.80 just in interest over that 30-year period. Paying cash would cost you $0 in interest.

Advantages of financing the purchase

Even if you have the cash to pay for a property, financing the purchase may be the better choice. Financing with a mortgage loan offers the following potential advantages:

>> **Gives you more cash to cover other expenses.** You'll also have additional spending money for enjoying life.

>> **Frees up cash to invest elsewhere.** If you can earn a return on other investments that's higher than the interest you're paying on the mortgage loan, you may be better off financing the purchase of your home.

>> **Reduces your tax liability.** If itemizing your deductions on your tax return gives you a total deduction that's higher than the standard deduction, paying mortgage interest will lower your taxes.

>> **Helps you build credit.** Having mortgage payments can help you establish good credit, making it easier to borrow money for other things. However, if you already have stellar credit, having a mortgage isn't going to improve your credit score significantly.

REMEMBER

Finances, including taxes, can get complicated, especially if you're retired. You want to make sure you don't outlive your money and have to rely on loved ones or government programs. At the same time, how you liquidate assets (convert property and other investments into cash) to cover expenses can have a significant impact on your tax liability. Consult your financial advisor or an accountant who specializes in serving clients in retirement for advice and guidance.

Picking the Right Real Estate Agents for You

First things first: You're going to need two real estate agents — a seller's agent to help you sell your existing home, and a buyer's agent to help you find your next home. Yes, real estate agents, like doctors, specialize. You want someone who specializes in selling homes to list your home for sale and someone who specializes in finding properties for sale to guide you in finding and buying a home that fits your downsizing needs and goals. You also want someone who specializes in the location — a seller's agent who works in your neighborhood, and a buyer's agent whose focus is on the location you're moving to.

Second, we strongly recommend that you hire a licensed *Realtor* — a member of the National Association of Realtors — with the Graduate, Realtor Institute (GRI) designation. All Realtors are real estate agents, but only a select group of real estate agents qualify as Realtors. The GRI designation indicates that the Realtor has successfully completed more than 90 hours of comprehensive training. It's like the CPA designation for accountants. Realtors with the GRI designation have received training in legal and regulatory issues, technology, and professional standards, as well as the sales process. They're also well versed on homeowner and condo association rules and regulations.

Third, if you're downsizing as part of your retirement planning, look for Realtors who have a Seniors Real Estate Specialist (SRES) designation. The SRES designation shows that the Realtor has received special training to understand the types of properties and mortgages that are best suited for retirement and later stages of life. A Realtor with this training may have a better understanding of what you need in a home than you do and is likely to bring up issues that you hadn't considered or thought of asking about.

Finally, narrow your search to the most active, best-performing Realtors in the area. You can do a search on Realtor.com. Go to `www.realtor.com/realestateagents`, type your city and state or zip code in the designated box, and press the Search button. The search results include not only the names of Realtors in your area but also their certifications, the number of current listings they have, the number of homes they've sold, their years of experience, and more. If you already have the names of agents in your area, you can search for them by name to verify that they're licensed and active.

The best agent charges the same commission as the worst one.

REMEMBER When you have the names of several Realtors who have made the initial cut, schedule meetings with each one, so you can interview them and see how you feel about them. We recommend interviewing at least three agents to sell your current home and three agents to find your new home. Here are a few key questions to ask:

>> **How many transactions have you done in the past 12 months?** Fewer than ten is a warning sign that the person isn't very successful or is working only part-time.

>> **Are you a full-time agent?** Hire a full-time Realtor, never a part-timer. Hiring a part-time real estate agent is like hiring a part-time heart surgeon.

>> **How long have you been a Realtor?** You want a Realtor with a few years' experience, not one who recently entered the profession. Let someone else break in the novices.

>> **Do you work with buyers or sellers?** "Both" isn't an acceptable answer. You want an agent who specializes in helping clients sell their home or buy one, not both. Work with a *team* — sometimes, the best teams have buyer's and seller's agents that work under the same roof for the same organization.

>> **Do you have references or referrals from past clients?** Make sure the agent can provide you with the names and contact information for at least three references and then contact them to find out how satisfied those clients are with the service they received.

>> **What's your availability for answering questions, showing my home, or meeting with me to look at properties?** If the agent can show homes only on nights and weekends or isn't available on certain days or during certain times, you may want to continue your search.

WARNING

Listing your home For Sale By Owner (FSBO, commonly pronounced fizz-bo) is never a good idea. Homes sell faster and for more money when listed by a certified Realtor. In fact, the increase in sales price (over what you'd get by selling it yourself) will likely more than cover the Realtor's commission. As a buyer, you have nothing to lose — the seller pays the 6 percent commission. As a seller, you're likely to profit more by using a Realtor. According to recent data, the typical FSBO home sold for $217,000 compared to $242,300 when sold by an agent — that's a difference of $25,000 — while the agent's commission on a $242,300 home is only $14,538. In addition, an agent simplifies and streamlines the process and can keep you from making costly mistakes.

Timing the Market (or Not)

Ideally, you'd like to sell your home in a strong seller's market and buy when the market bottoms out, but timing the housing market is about as easy as timing the stock market or buying a jackpot-winning Powerball ticket. The market can change nearly overnight, and if you need to sell or buy in a hurry when market conditions aren't favorable, you can end up losing tens of thousands of dollars.

During the writing of this book, the U.S. housing market was booming, especially in the Sunbelt (which includes Tampa and Jacksonville, Florida; Raleigh, North Carolina; and San Antonio, Texas). However, as inventory grows and interest rates rise, the housing market is likely to cool. It may even experience a bubble followed by a crash, as occurred in 2008.

REMEMBER

We don't recommend trying to time the market. Price your home to sell at the market value and look to buy your new home at market value. If the market is up, the higher prices for the home you buy and the one you sell will essentially cancel each other out. Likewise, if the market is down — you'll lose out by having to sell your home for less, but you'll also pay less for your new home.

If you do try to time the housing market, here are a few strategies to consider:

>> **In a seller's market, sell high, secure temporary housing, and then buy low when prices drop.** If the housing market is sizzling, sell your current home, rent a place (or move in with a friend or family member), wait for the market to crash, and then buy a home. You run two risks with this approach:

- In a sizzling market, finding an affordable rental property can be a challenge.

- Housing prices may continue to rise or they may just level off. Worse, any potential profit you were hoping to gain may get eaten up in rent.

>> **In a buyer's market, buy low and hold onto the house you want to sell until the market recovers.** If you get lucky, the market will magically recover shortly after you buy, and you'll get a higher price for your current home. To mitigate the risk, you may be able to rent out the house you want to sell, but when the market recovers, you'll face the complexity of selling a home that has tenants in it.

>> **Sell when the market's hot and buy into an area that's less popular.** Even when the housing market is hot overall, you can find areas where it's not. Of course, you don't want to buy into a neighborhood that's run-down or shows little promise of ever recovering, but if you can find a home in an area that's in a temporary slump, and it's an area you like, it may be a wise move.

STAYING AHEAD OF A FALLING MARKET

During the housing crisis of 2008, Ralph was working with a client, Maria, who needed to sell her place as housing prices were tumbling. Every time we lowered the price, it was time to lower the price again.

We lowered the price by 35 percent in the course of six months. Values were disintegrating.

In a down market, you need to adjust your price ahead of the market. Set a price that's as attractive as you can afford so that you have offers to say no to. Price it right and adjust quickly.

Getting a Home Equity Line of Credit (Just in Case)

If you're going to apply for a mortgage loan to buy a place soon, you shouldn't be taking out any other loans, applying for new credit cards, transferring large sums of money, or making any other financial moves that can be interpreted as a sign of financial desperation. You may end up being turned down for your mortgage loan as a result.

However, if you're in the early stages of thinking about downsizing, you own a home, and you have considerable *equity* built up in it (meaning the home's value greatly exceeds the amount of money you owe on it), you should consider taking out a home equity line of credit (HELOC).

REMEMBER

Secure your HELOC before listing your house for sale. If your house is listed for sale, no lender is going to give you a HELOC, because they know you're going to sell the house soon and pay off the loan and, as a result, they won't make any money on that loan.

With a HELOC, you can qualify to borrow up to 80 percent of the equity you have built up in the home, and then you draw that money only when you need it. You pay interest only on the money you draw.

Suppose, for example, that your home is worth about $400,000, and you owe $100,000 on it. You can borrow up to $240,000 ($300,000 × 0.80). You find a new place for $350,000 and want to move quickly on it. You now have access to $240,000 cash that you can use to make a substantial *earnest money deposit (EMD)* and down payment on the new place. Suppose you make an EMD of 10 percent — that's $35,000. You start accruing interest only on that $35,000. (You make an EMD when you submit a purchase offer on a house to show that you're committed to buying it. The higher the EMD, the more attractive your purchase offer is to a seller. If the seller accepts your offer and you back out of the deal, the seller gets to keep the EMD.)

Here's a list of reasons why you should secure a HELOC:

>> Closing costs are minimal (possibly $0).

>> You borrow the money only when you need it, sort of like a credit card with a much lower interest rate.

>> You can use the HELOC as an emergency fund to get through tough times, such as a temporary job loss or unexpected medical bills. A HELOC has saved many homeowners from losing their home in foreclosure or being forced into bankruptcy.

>> Interest accrues only on the amount of money you draw. If you have a $240,000 HELOC and never draw money from it, you won't pay a penny in interest.

>> Your lender places no restrictions on how you use the money.

>> You're borrowing against your home, which means any interest you pay may be tax-deductible if you itemize deductions on your tax return.

>> Lenders rarely charge *usage fees* (fees to access the money).

WARNING

The only drawback of a HELOC is that they typically come with a *variable interest rate,* meaning the rate can go up or down based on the *prime interest rate* (the rate the government charges banks). When you're shopping for a HELOC, find out the maximum the rate can go up or down each period and the highest it can go (the rate cap). Borrowers often get burned with variable interest rate loans when interest rates rise and their monthly payments become surprisingly unaffordable.

REMEMBER

Don't use a HELOC as your personal ATM, drawing money to cover daily expenses like groceries and dining out, or buying a fancy new vehicle. Use it only for emergencies and for executing financial strategies in profitable ways. You don't want to be cashing out the equity in your home to cover living expenses, because then you won't have any equity in your home when you really need it. People who use their homes as ATMs often end up in foreclosure or bankruptcy when times are tough.

Accounting for Taxes on the Sale of Your Home

One aspect of home ownership that makes it a particularly attractive investment is that the federal government offers a huge tax break on profits from the sale of a primary residence. Assuming you lived in your primary residence for at least two of the past five years, when you sell it, $250,000 of the profit is tax-exempt. If you're married, $500,000 is tax-exempt. However, taxes related to the sale of a home are often more complicated than that, and you should be aware of the rules so you know what to expect and can plan accordingly.

Three types of taxes may come into play when you're selling a home:

>> Capital gains tax (a tax on investment profits)

>> Property tax

>> Real estate transfer tax

In the following sections, we cover each of these taxes.

Capital gains tax

A *capital gain* is the profit you earn from the sale of an asset. Basically, if you buy a home for $250,000 and sell it for $400,000, you have a capital gain of $150,000. However, if you invested in repairing or renovating the property, your investment value (or *cost basis* in the property) will be more than $250,000, in which case your capital gain will be lower. Agent commissions and other fees also increase your cost basis and reduce your capital gain. Your accountant can give you a precise dollar value of any capital gain subject to tax.

Your capital gain on the sale of a property may be subject to a capital gains tax. Capital gains taxes come in two types:

>> Short-term capital gains tax on assets owned for less than one year

>> Long-term capital gains tax on assets owned for at least one year

The difference in short- and long-term capital gains taxes is considerable, as shown in Tables 16-1 and 16-2.

REMEMBER

As explained earlier, if you're selling your primary residence and you owned it and lived in it for two of the past five years, $250,000 of your capital gain is exempt from capital gains tax, and $500,000 is exempt if you're married and filing a joint tax return. This is known as a *Section 121 exclusion*.

TABLE 16-1   ## Short-term Capital Gains Tax Rates (2022)

Rate	Single Filers	Married Filing Jointly	Head of Household
10%	Up to $10,275	Up to $20,550	Up to $14,650
12%	$10,275–$41,775	$20,550–$83,550	$14,650–$55,900
22%	$41,775–$89,075	$83,550–$178,150	$55,900–$89,050
24%	$89,075–$170,050	$178,150–$340,100	$89,050–$170,050
32%	$170,050–$215,950	$340,100–$431,900	$170,050–$215,950
35%	$215,950–$539,900	$431,900–$647,850	$215,950–$539,900
37%	Over $539,900	Over $647,850	Over $539,900

TABLE 16-2　**Long-term Capital Gains Tax Rates (2022)**

Rate	Single Filers	Married Filing Jointly	Head of Household
0%	Up to $41,675	Up to $83,350	Up to $55,800
15%	$41,675–$459,750	$83,350–$517,200	$55,800–$488,500
20%	Over $459,750	Over $517,200	Over $488,500

TIP

If the property you're selling doesn't qualify as your primary residence but is an investment property, you may be able to avoid having to pay a capital gains tax by performing a *1031 exchange*. With a 1031 exchange, you sell one investment property (such as a vacation home) and use the proceeds to buy another property of equal or greater value. You pay capital gains only when you cash out your chips at the end and collect your profit.

Property tax

When you sell your home, you may owe property taxes or receive a refund of property taxes you already paid. In most states, homeowners pay property taxes in *arrears*. For example, you receive a bill for the previous six months you lived on the property, so when you close on the sale of your home, you're likely to be required to pay the prorated portion of the tax bill for the time you owned the home up to the closing date. Your buyer will then take over paying property taxes from that date forward.

Property taxes vary considerably from state to state, from as low as 0.28 percent of the assessed property value in Hawaii to 2.49 percent in New Jersey.

Real estate transfer tax

Some areas of the U.S. charge a real estate transfer tax or title fee, which can range from next to nothing to several thousand dollars. Seattle, Washington, has one of the steepest transfer fees at $8,749. Check with your real estate agent to determine whether your area has a transfer tax and, if it does, how much it is. In most areas, the buyer is expected to cover the cost — think of it as a sales tax. However, who pays the transfer tax can become a point of negotiation.

IN THIS CHAPTER

» **Deciding whether to hire professional movers or do it yourself**

» **Finding, choosing, and working with a professional mover**

» **Stocking up on moving supplies**

» **Taking a room-by-room approach to packing**

Chapter **17**

Packing Your Belongings

Instead of cleaning my house, I'm just going to move to a new one!

— UNKNOWN

The key to a smooth move is an impeccable packing job. With your belongings arranged neatly in labeled boxes, all that's required is moving items from home to truck and truck to home, where they can be easily directed to the rooms they belong in.

Packing isn't rocket science, but a quality packing job does involve some skill and tender loving care. You want to pack your belongings so they take up as little space as possible and are protected from damage. And if you're outsourcing the job, you want to be sure the firm you hire has the requisite skill and will treat your treasures with the care they deserve.

This chapter is all about packing prior to a move — whether you're moving your belongings to a new residence or to a storage facility and whether you're outsourcing the task or doing it yourself. Here, you discover the tricks and the tools of the trade — the moving supplies that enable you to do the job right. We also provide specific guidance for packing room by room.

REMEMBER

The goal of packing is to make loading and unpacking as easy and straightforward as possible while protecting your possessions from getting damaged or broken. Taking care to do it right can save you both time and money.

Taking the Easy Way Out: Hiring a Professional

The best way to pack right is to hire experienced professionals to do it for you. Unfortunately, that approach is also the most expensive. Not everyone can afford to pay professional movers thousands of dollars to pack up and move their belongings, but if you can afford it, we strongly recommend hiring a moving company both to pack and to move. We were fortunate; we have friends in the moving business and could afford to pay professionals to pack everything for us.

Recognizing the advantages of hiring a moving company

A moving company offers the following benefits:

>> **Less hassle:** The moving company packs and moves for you. You don't need to buy packing supplies, box up all your stuff, find people to help you move, rent a truck, pick it up, drive the truck, and return it. In addition, the moving company coordinates the entire process.

>> **Faster results:** Experts who know the tricks of the trade can pack and move far more efficiently than you can, saving a significant amount of time and ensuring the move proceeds as scheduled.

>> **Less breakage:** Skilled movers pack fragile items to survive the move, whether you're relocating across town or across the country.

>> **Less risk of injury:** You're not teetering on step stools to empty cupboards or lifting or carrying heavy, bulky items and loading them into a truck. The amount of money you save on doctor visits after moving can cover the cost of a skilled mover. Professional movers know how to lift heavy, bulky items and use special equipment to move it. They may also be able to pack boxes heavier than you can lift, which can increase their efficiency.

>> **Fewer unpleasant surprises:** Experienced movers can take a brief tour of your current home and tell you exactly how many packers and movers you'll need, the size of the truck required, and the number of trips it'll take. In addition, a reputable firm will show up on schedule. You won't find out the night before that your cousin with a truck who was so eager to help broke out in monkeypox the night before and will be a no-show.

>> **Less stress and worry:** When you outsource packing and moving tasks, you eliminate the stress and worry that accompany those tasks. The movers you hire won't stress about it — they enjoy it and are happy to have the work. In

fact, professional movers love the challenge of a complicated move — it's like putting together a puzzle for them, with the added goal of not damaging anything in the process.

REMEMBER

When you're in your 20s and 30s, friends and family are typically readily available and eager to help you move, especially if you've helped them move. When you hit 50, finding people willing and able to help with a big move becomes increasingly difficult. You're likely to discover that, strangely enough, everyone you ask for help already has plans for that weekend. What a coincidence!

Choosing a reputable moving company

Anyone can start and run a moving company and hire unskilled labor to do the heavy lifting, but not everyone has the skills and know-how to move items safely and efficiently without damaging anything. Do your research and choose a firm that has a strong reputation and long track record of providing quality service.

Start your search by asking friends, neighbors, and family members for recommendations. You can also find potential candidates by searching the web for "moving companies near me" or "moving companies" followed by your zip code or state and city.

TIP

Consider searching for a moving company via a homeowners' referral service such as Angi (www.angi.com), Thumbtack (www.thumbtack.com), or HomeAdvisor (www.homeadvisor.com). Service providers on these sites have already been screened by customers, giving you better leads to start with.

When you have a list of candidates, you're ready to start vetting them. Use the following criteria:

>> **Affordability:** Get estimates from at least three moving companies, so you can compare quotes. We recommend using a company that does free on-site estimates. An on-site estimate provides you with a golden opportunity to meet with a customer rep to get a better feel for the company.

REMEMBER

Although we prefer in-person on-site estimates, many moving companies now do virtual estimates. Using a smartphone app such as Facetime, you take a moving company rep on a virtual tour of your home to show them everything you'll be moving, and they provide an estimate based on what you show them. Don't rule out a company just because it prefers virtual to in-person estimates; a company that's comfortable with technology may even be the better choice.

TIP

>> **License and insurance:** Consider only companies that are licensed and insured. Check the company's website, business card, or advertising for a statement like "Licensed and Insured," and if you're still unsure, ask. Don't hire a company that's not licensed and insured, because if anyone is injured in the process or anything gets damaged, you can be on the hook for paying the bills.

You can find out whether a moving company is licensed by looking up its U.S. Department of Transportation number in that agency's database at `li-public.fmcsa.dot.gov/LIVIEW/pkg_carrquery.prc_carrlist`.

>> **Better Business Bureau (BBB) rating:** Search for the moving company by name on the BBB's website at `www.bbb.org`. Here, you can see how long the company has been in business, its BBB rating, customer reviews, and the number of complaints filed against it in recent months and years. Look for a company with an A+ rating that has been in business for at least a few years.

>> **Years in business:** A moving company that's been in business for 20 years is generally a better choice than one that's been in business for a year or less. Companies that disappoint their customers don't stay in business very long.

>> **Customer ratings and reviews:** Search the web for the company by name and look for links to sites such as Yelp, Yellow Pages, and Move.org that contain customer ratings and reviews. The more ratings and reviews, the better, so long as they're mostly positive. If a company has only one or two positive ratings, they probably haven't been in business very long or may have recruited a friend, relative, or employee to post a glowing review.

WARNING

Don't choose a moving company merely because it quotes you the lowest price. You may end up paying far more in the end if the company underestimated the work, property is damaged, or someone gets hurt and the company isn't fully insured or cooperative in addressing issues.

REMEMBER

Movers are required by law to deliver your belongings for no more than 10 percent above the price of a nonbinding estimate. This is known in the industry as the *110 percent rule*. Take the estimated amount and multiply it by 1.10 to determine the maximum you can be charged.

Teaming up with your moving company for best results

Your movers will do the heavy lifting, but you can help make the process smoother by doing the following:

- » **Be open about everything that needs to be moved.** Your movers base their plan on the information you provide them. If you try to make the move seem easier than it will be by forgetting to mention the items in the attic or basement, for example, your movers can't account for those items in terms of time, labor, and cost.

- » **Review the list of items the movers won't move.** These items typically include firearms, medications, and anything highly flammable or combustible. Set these items aside and move them yourself.

- » **Pack your cash, jewelry, and prescription medications yourself.** Packers and movers don't want to deal with these items. Or they do want to deal with them, in which case it's even more important that you keep their hands off them.

- » **Be there when the packers/movers show up.** Movers have tight schedules and don't appreciate having to wait around, so be there on time to let them in.

- » **Be courteous.** Introduce yourself and your family members and ask if your packers/movers need anything. Providing refreshing beverages and possibly snacks or lunch can help keep them energized and motivated. Tell them which bathroom they can use. Try to remember their names and then address them by name throughout the day.

- » **Be available but stay out of their way.** You need to be available to answer questions and provide direction, but give them space to do their work. Don't hover or try to micromanage. Your job is to facilitate their job.

- » **Set a comfortable temperature.** While you may be comfortable sitting around your house on moving day, the people doing all the work may get overheated. Set the thermostat at a temperature that's comfortable for *them*.

- » **Communicate throughout the day.** Check in with your packers/movers every hour or so to see if they need anything or have any questions. Check more frequently at first and less frequently as the day goes on. Be sure that by the end of the day all boxes are labeled to describe their contents and where they go in the new residence. For more about labeling boxes, see the later section cleverly titled "Labeling boxes."

REMEMBER

If you're doing the packing yourself, make sure everything is packed the night before the movers are scheduled to load it into the trucks. Being packed before moving day is the number one way you can team up with your movers to ensure a smooth operation. In the next section, we take a deeper dive into packing your own belongings.

Doing the Packing Yourself

Even if you're hiring movers to do the heavy lifting, you have the option of handling the packing on your own. Packing can save you loads of money and gives you total control over how stuff gets packed.

In this section, we provide a checklist of moving supplies you'll need, room-by-room guidance on how to pack, and suggestions for labeling boxes that can save time and effort when you move and unpack.

Gathering your moving supplies and equipment

Before you even think about packing, gather the supplies and equipment to do the job right and as efficiently as possible. Here's a list of what you'll need:

❏ **Sturdy boxes:** We recommend using professional moving boxes, which are available at most hardware stores. Get a variety of sizes, so you have extra-large boxes for packing light, bulky items (such as bedding) and small boxes for packing dense, heavy items (such as books and hand tools). Also consider buying specialty boxes — for example, a wardrobe box that has a rod across the top for hanging clothes, a dish pack with partitions for cups and plates, TV boxes, lamp boxes, and file boxes (for office items).

REMEMBER

If you're buying boxes, buy more than you'll need and save the receipt so you can return the ones you don't use.

❏ **Cushioning:** Before placing any fragile items in a box, you need to wrap them or place some sort of cushioning between them. Many cushioning options are available, including bubble wrap, cardboard or foam plate separators, foam packing peanuts, and even newspapers (free, but less effective). Get some antistatic bubble wrap for electronic devices.

❏ **Corner protectors:** Corner protectors are cardboard or plastic shields that fit around the corners of tabletops, TV screens, picture frames, and other items to protect them from damage. Some are created more for furniture; others are for picture frames.

❏ **Plastic stretch wrap:** Stretch wrap comes in handy for keeping dresser and nightstand drawers closed, keeping parts of disassembled furniture together, and protecting the surfaces of wood furniture from scratches and other damage.

❏ **Packing tape and dispenser:** Get some quality (thick) packing tape and a dispenser that's easy to use. Don't buy cheap, flimsy tape, which is difficult to handle and doesn't hold up in a move. And don't skimp on the tape dispenser, either.

- ❏ **Painter's tape or masking tape:** You'll use this tape on the glass surface of any framed pictures to keep cracked or broken pieces together if the glass breaks during the move.

- ❏ **Scissors or utility knife:** You'll be cutting tape, bubble wrap, stretch wrap, cardboard, and other items, so be sure you have a reliable cutting tool.

- ❏ **Labels:** You can simply write on the boxes or write on labels and stick them to the boxes, whichever you prefer.

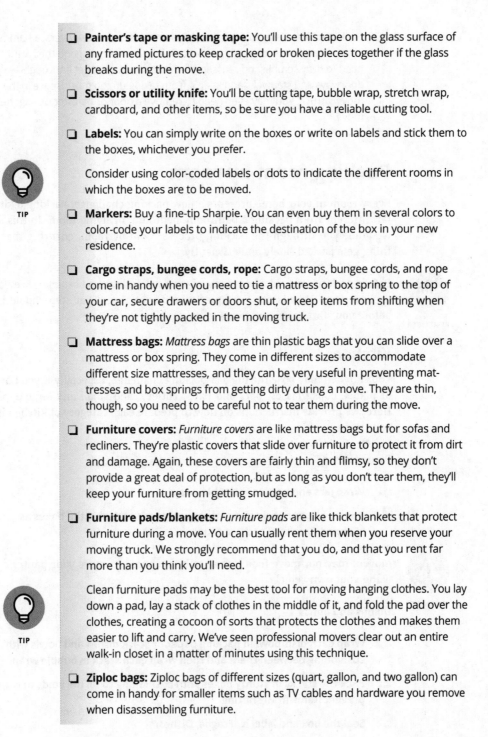

TIP

Consider using color-coded labels or dots to indicate the different rooms in which the boxes are to be moved.

- ❏ **Markers:** Buy a fine-tip Sharpie. You can even buy them in several colors to color-code your labels to indicate the destination of the box in your new residence.

- ❏ **Cargo straps, bungee cords, rope:** Cargo straps, bungee cords, and rope come in handy when you need to tie a mattress or box spring to the top of your car, secure drawers or doors shut, or keep items from shifting when they're not tightly packed in the moving truck.

- ❏ **Mattress bags:** *Mattress bags* are thin plastic bags that you can slide over a mattress or box spring. They come in different sizes to accommodate different size mattresses, and they can be very useful in preventing mattresses and box springs from getting dirty during a move. They are thin, though, so you need to be careful not to tear them during the move.

- ❏ **Furniture covers:** *Furniture covers* are like mattress bags but for sofas and recliners. They're plastic covers that slide over furniture to protect it from dirt and damage. Again, these covers are fairly thin and flimsy, so they don't provide a great deal of protection, but as long as you don't tear them, they'll keep your furniture from getting smudged.

- ❏ **Furniture pads/blankets:** *Furniture pads* are like thick blankets that protect furniture during a move. You can usually rent them when you reserve your moving truck. We strongly recommend that you do, and that you rent far more than you think you'll need.

TIP

Clean furniture pads may be the best tool for moving hanging clothes. You lay down a pad, lay a stack of clothes in the middle of it, and fold the pad over the clothes, creating a cocoon of sorts that protects the clothes and makes them easier to lift and carry. We've seen professional movers clear out an entire walk-in closet in a matter of minutes using this technique.

- ❏ **Ziploc bags:** Ziploc bags of different sizes (quart, gallon, and two gallon) can come in handy for smaller items such as TV cables and hardware you remove when disassembling furniture.

❏ **Basic tool kit:** Make sure you have a tape measure, screwdrivers, a hammer, pliers, wrenches, Allen wrenches, and a drill. Chances are good that you'll need to disassemble and reassemble some furniture to get it through doorways and stairwells and keep it from taking up too much space in the moving truck. You may even need to remove a door or banister during the move.

Packing room by room

Every room in your home presents a new packing challenge. Packing a kitchen is far different from packing a bathroom, bedroom, or living room. In this section, we guide you through the packing process room by room, ensuring that everything gets packed safely and efficiently.

REMEMBER Before packing, get rid of as many of your belongings as possible. (See Part 3 on decluttering.) Now is not the time to be downsizing. That step should be done before you start boxing up items to move them.

Kitchen

Your kitchen may pose the biggest packing challenge, especially if you have loads of plates, cups/glasses, pots and pans, cutlery, and small and large appliances. Here, we provide instructions on how to prepare each category of kitchen item for your move.

Pantry items

1. **Wrap jars and bottles in bubble wrap.**

2. **Box up all your packaged and canned goods and label the boxes as "Canned Goods," "Food," or "Pantry."**

WARNING

Movers may not move food items, so be prepared to move your pantry contents using your own vehicle.

Dishes and bowls

1. **Wrap each dish/bowl in packing paper or stack dishes and bowls with cushioning between them and then wrap each stack in bubble wrap.**

2. **Pack the stacks in sturdy boxes with cushioning to fill the voids to prevent items from shifting.**

3. **Seal the box and label it "Fragile, Dishes."**

Cups/mugs

1. Wrap cups/mugs individually with packing paper.

2. Placed wrapped cups/mugs upside down in a sturdy box.

3. Place a sheet of cardboard on top of the wrapped cups/mugs to create another layer and repeat Steps 1–3 until the box is full.

4. Seal the box and label it "Fragile, Cups."

Glasses

1. Stuff glasses with crumpled paper.

2. Wrap any stemmed glasses in bubble wrap and any glasses without stems in packing paper.

3. Set the glasses mouth down in a sturdy box. Use a dish pack box (with separators) for fragile glasses.

4. Stuff cushioning into any open spaces to prevent shifting.

5. Space permitting, create another layer of glasses separated with a piece of cardboard.

6. Seal the box and label it "Fragile, Glasses." You may also want to mark on the top of the box "This Side Up."

Pots and pans

1. Place a large pot or pan on the bottom of a box.

2. Place bubble wrap, a foam sheet, or a kitchen towel on top of it.

3. Put a smaller pot or pan inside it and cover it with bubble wrap or another foam sheet or kitchen towel.

4. Repeat Step 3 until the box is full.

5. Wrap additional small pots and pans, lids, or other kitchen items in bubble wrap and place them in the box to fill any spaces. Add cushioning, if necessary, to prevent shifting.

6. Seal the box and label it "Pots/Pans."

Cutlery and silverware

1. Wrap kitchen knives in thick towels or paper.

2. Stack forks/spoons of the same length and wrap them in bubble wrap.

3. Wrap irregularly shaped utensils in paper or bubble wrap.

4. Arrange wrapped items in a packing box, seal it, and label it "Kitchen Utensils."

Junk drawer

1. Empty your junk drawer into a small box or a large Ziploc bag.

2. Seal the box or bag and label it "Kitchen, Junk Drawer." If you use a bag, you can place it in a box with other items.

Cookbooks

1. Wrap any cookbooks you cherish in bubble wrap, a kitchen towel, or several layers of paper.

2. Lay your cookbooks flat, on edge (like on a shelf), or spine down.

3. Seal the box and label it "Kitchen, Cookbooks."

Small kitchen appliances

1. **Clean and dry the item if you haven't already done so.** This is particularly important if you're packing a toaster, which is typically loaded with crumbs.

2. Remove any detachable parts, such as a removable power cord, glass coffee pot, or ceramic mixing bowl, and wrap it separately in paper or bubble wrap.

3. Wrap the appliance itself in paper or bubble wrap and place it in its original box or a box that's not too big.

4. Add cushioning to prevent shifting and breakage.

5. Seal the box and label it with the item's name, such as "Coffeemaker," "Blender," "Mixer," or "Toaster."

Large kitchen appliances

1. Empty, defrost, and clean your refrigerator/freezer a couple days before the planned move.

2. Wrap large appliances in stretch wrap to secure doors/drawers and prevent scratches.

3. Tape any loose cables or hoses to the appliance.

REMEMBER

If you're moving a large appliance yourself, consider wrapping a furniture pad or blanket around it to prevent dents and scratches when loading it on the dolly and for its ride in the truck.

Dining room

Your dining room may be one of the first rooms you pack, because it's not essential living space. You can postpone any gatherings until after you move. Here, we provide instructions on how to prepare each category of dining room item for your move.

REMEMBER

Downsizers often downsize their way out of a formal dining room. If you belong to this group, congratulations — you can safely skip this section.

China, glassware, and silverware

Follow the instructions we provide in the "Kitchen" section for packing dishes, bowls, glasses, cups, mugs, and silverware. If you have fine china, expensive, fragile glassware, and fancy silverware, you'll want to be even more careful and use additional cushioning to prevent damage.

Paintings, photographs, and mirrors

1. Apply painter's tape or masking tape to the glass surface of each item (framed picture or photograph or mirror) in the shape of an X to hold the pieces in place if the glass breaks during the move.

2. Place foam or cardboard around the corners of each item and wrap it in stretch wrap to keep the corner cushioning in place.

3. Place a piece of thick cardboard over the front of the item to prevent scratches or other damage and use packing tape or stretch wrap to hold it in place.

4. Wrap the item in bubble wrap, using packing tape, if necessary, to secure the bubble wrap in place.

5. (Optional) Place the items in a suitable box, separating them with additional cushioning to prevent shifting. You can buy special boxes or crates for paintings, photos, mirrors, and similar items.

6. Seal the box and label it "Fragile, Pictures."

Vases and statues

Vases and statues are difficult to move without breaking them. If you have only a few and a short move, you may be wise to load them separately into your vehicle instead of putting them on a moving truck.

If you need to pack them, get custom crates or boxes and use plenty of bubble wrap or other cushioning to prevent damage. Seal the boxes and label them "Fragile, Handle with Care" followed by the item type, such as "Vase" or "Sculpture."

Dining room table

1. Remove any leaves and wrap them in furniture blankets.

2. Lower the drop sides (if present) and secure them in place with stretch wrap.

3. **Flip the table over onto a furniture blanket or carpet, remove the legs, wrap them individually in bubble wrap, and tape them together.** Place any hardware in a plastic bag and tape the bag to the legs.

4. Wrap the tabletop in a furniture blanket and wrap packing tape or stretch wrap around it to keep the blanket in place.

If your table doesn't have legs or disassembling and reassembling the table is more hassle than it's worth, you can pack around it when you get it on the truck. Just be sure to protect the tabletop and legs from damage.

Dining room chairs

1. Wrap the arms and legs in bubble wrap.

2. Wrap the chair backs and seats in stretch wrap.

3. Cover the chairs with furniture blankets when loading them onto the moving truck.

Dining room cabinet

Assuming you already packed everything that was inside the dining room cabinet, it's now empty. If it's not, do that first. Then, take the following steps:

1. Remove any removable shelves and wrap them separately in bubble wrap.

2. Wrap the entire piece (or pieces) in stretch wrap to protect against dust and scratches and secure all doors and drawers shut.

3. **Cover the entire piece (or pieces) in furniture blankets when loading them onto the truck.** You can use packing tape, stretch wrap, bungee cords, ropes, or cargo straps to hold the blankets in place.

Chandelier

The best way to handle a chandelier is to leave it for the new owners. If that's not an option, make sure the electricity to the chandelier is off, disconnect it, and disassemble it as much as possible — remove light bulbs, chains, candle cups, and so on, and wrap them individually in foam or bubble wrap. Place the chandelier in a box that isn't too large but is large enough, place the individually wrapped items in the box, and add cushioning to prevent shifting. Seal the box and label it "Fragile, Dining Room."

Living room/den

A living room can absorb a huge amount of stuff, so hopefully before you reach the packing phase, you've cleared out most of it. Here, we provide guidance on how to pack what's left.

Television

1. **Take photos of all TV connections and label the cables, so you'll know where everything plugs in.**

2. **Disconnect all cables and place them in a large sealable bag.** You can place your remote controls in the same bag.

3. **If your TV is mounted to a wall, carefully remove it from the mount (usually a two-person job).** Anything that's attached to real estate stays with the real estate, so you're not allowed to take the mount. Remove the hardware from the TV, as well, and leave it for the people who bought your house.

4. **Place a large piece of clean cardboard over the screen and tape it in place.**

5. **Wrap the TV in a large blanket or in bubble wrap and place it in a large, sturdy cardboard box.**

6. **Seal the box and label it "Fragile, TV."**

WARNING

The best way to move a TV is screen side up, wrapped in a thick blanket, in the back of your vehicle. Avoid hitting any potholes or running over any curbs on the way to your new home. Placing a TV on a moving truck is a recipe for disaster.

TV cabinet or stand

1. **Empty your TV cabinet.**

2. **Secure the doors in place with stretch wrap or remove them and wrap them separately.** Place the hardware in a Ziploc bag and tape it to one of the doors.

3. **Wrap the cabinet in a moving blanket as soon as it's on the truck.**

Other electronics

1. **Pack CD and DVD players and game consoles according to the manufacturer's instructions.** Some have transport screws you're advised to use to secure the laser readers when moving these sensitive devices.

2. **If you have a stereo turntable, lock the arm in place to prevent it from moving and secure the turntable following the manufacturer's instructions.**

3. **Wrap the devices, including any speakers, in antistatic bubble wrap or in towels or blankets to keep them safe, and, depending on their size, place them in sturdy boxes.** Fill any space with cushioning for added protection.

4. **Seal any boxes you used and label them "Fragile, Electronics."**

Discs and tapes

1. **Place a layer of foam or thick paper at the bottom of a small or medium-size box and place discs and tapes (in their cases), narrow side down, into the box (in other words, don't lay them flat).** You can place a piece of cardboard atop a layer of discs and tapes and create another layer if space allows.

2. **Place a foam sheet or a sheet of bubble wrap on top for added protection, and then seal the box and label it "Fragile, Discs."**

Books

1. **Sort books by size.**

2. **Wrap valuable books in packing paper or bubble wrap.**

3. **Line the bottom of a small or medium-size box with packing paper or foam.**

WARNING

Don't pack books in large boxes. The boxes will be too heavy, and the bottoms may fall out. No box should exceed 50 pounds.

4. **Lay the books flat inside the box, upright (like on a shelf) with their openings facing the sides of the box, or spine down at the bottom of the box.**

5. **Fill any spaces with cushioning.**

6. **Seal the box and label it "Books."**

Upholstered furniture

1. **Remove the cushions.** Cushions are great for slipping between items on the truck to prevent contact and for filling open spaces.

TIP

If you have a sleeper sofa, dump it. (Half kidding — these are beasts to move.) If you can't part with it, at least remove the mattress to lighten the load.

2. **Remove any detachable legs or other appendages, wrap them separately in stretch wrap, and then bundle them together with stretch wrap.** Place any hardware you remove in a Ziploc bag and tape it to the bundle.

3. **Wrap the remaining (large) piece in a moving blanket as soon as it's on the truck.**

Coffee and end tables

1. **Wrap the table legs with bubble wrap secured in place with packing tape.**

2. **Place corner protectors on all the corners of the tabletop and secure them in place with stretch wrap.**

3. **Wrap the table in a moving blanket as soon as it's on the truck.**

Bookshelves

1. **Remove all items, including the shelves if they're likely to come loose.**

2. **If you removed the shelves, wrap them separately in bubble wrap or a blanket secured in place with packing tape.**

3. **Place corner protectors on all corners of the bookshelf and secure them in place with stretch wrap.**

4. **Wrap the bookshelf in a moving blanket as soon as it's on the truck.**

Rugs

Roll up all rugs and wrap each one in stretch wrap to keep it from unrolling and protect it from dirt and dust.

Home office

If you have a home office, it likely has a desk, chair, computer, and one or more filing cabinets and bookshelves. Here, we provide some guidance on how to prepare all those items for a move.

Computer, printer, and accessories

1. **Perform a full backup of the computer's drives to the cloud or an external drive.**

2. **Take photos of all connections to the computer and label the cables, so you'll know where everything plugs in.**

3. **Disconnect all cables and place them in a large sealable bag.**

4. **Remove the monitor from its stand, place a sheet of cardboard over the screen and tape it in place, wrap the monitor in bubble wrap, place it in a sturdy box, and add cushioning to fill any open spaces.** (If your monitor is actually an all-in-one desktop computer, you're done with the computer-packing part of this process and can skip to Step 6.)

5. Wrap the system unit in antistatic bubble wrap, towels, or a blanket secured in place with packing tape or stretch wrap, place it in a sturdy box that's not too large, and add cushioning to fill any open spaces.

6. Remove any paper, toner, or ink cartridges from your printer.

7. Wrap peripherals (printer, speakers, mouse, keyboard, and so on) individually in antistatic bubble wrap, arrange them in sturdy boxes, and add cushioning to fill any open spaces.

8. Seal all boxes and label them "Office, Fragile, Computer."

TIP

For a short move, if you have space in your vehicle, we recommend moving your computer and peripherals yourself, in which case you can save time by not wrapping and packing everything. Just be careful when loading and unloading these sensitive items from your vehicle.

Desk and chair

1. Empty all desk drawers and pack items in a separate box labeled "Office, Desk."

2. Use corner protectors at all corners of the desktop and stretch wrap to hold them in place.

3. Wrap the desk in stretch wrap to keep any drawers or doors from popping open.

4. Wrap the desk in a furniture blanket as soon as it's on the moving truck.

5. Disassemble the desk chair and pack it in a box with plenty of cushioning, if possible, or wrap the chair in a furniture blanket using bungee cords or packing tape to hold it in place. Put any hardware you removed in a Ziploc bag and place it in the box.

Books and bookshelves

Check out the "Living room/den" section for details on packing books and preparing bookshelves for a move.

Filing cabinets

The big problem with filing cabinets is that the drawers tend to pop open during a move. Lock the drawers if you still have the key or wrap the filing cabinet in stretch wrap to keep them from sliding open. You may also want to use corner protectors, secured in place with stretch wrap, along with a furniture blanket, to prevent the corners from getting dinged or (more likely) damaging something else on the moving truck.

Bedrooms

You can pack up guest bedrooms early in the process, but you may want to hold off on packing your main bedroom until the night before moving day. You'll need at least one bed to sleep in and a change of clothes set out for moving day.

Photos, paintings, and mirrors

See the earlier "Dining room" section for guidance on packing framed photos and paintings and mirrors.

Beds, mattresses, and box springs

1. **Remove all pillows and bedding, pack them in large boxes or heavy-duty trash bags, and label them "Bedding."** If you have more than one bedroom in your new place, label the box/bag to indicate which bedroom these items belong in — for example, "Bedroom 1" or "Main Bedroom."

2. **If your bed frame has shelves or drawers, empty them and wrap and pack those items in a separate box.**

3. **Remove the mattress and pack it in a mattress bag.**

4. **Remove the box spring and (optionally) pack it in a mattress bag.**

5. **Disassemble the bed frame as much as possible.** Wrap larger parts in furniture blankets and smaller parts in bubble wrap, using stretch wrap or packing tape to secure the cushioning in place. Put hardware in a sealable bag and tape it to the frame. If you have more than one bedroom in the new place, label all parts to indicate which bedroom they belong in.

Dressers and wardrobes

Depending on their size and weight and whether they have any glass parts, such as mirrors, you need to exercise some judgment in deciding how best to move each dresser. Here are a few guidelines that can help you make the right call:

>> If your dresser or wardrobe has a mirror, remove it, wrap it in bubble wrap secured in place with packing tape, place it in a sturdy box, add cushioning to fill up any open spaces, seal the box, and label it "Dresser, Mirror" or "Wardrobe, Mirror" along with an indication of the bedroom it belongs in.

>> You may be able to move small, light, sturdy dressers and wardrobes with their drawers and contents in place.

>> You can either empty the drawers or leave everything inside large or heavy dressers. You can then remove the drawers, move the dresser onto the moving truck, and replace the drawers.

>> Regardless of the size and weight of the dresser or wardrobe, use corner protectors secured in place with stretch wrap to prevent them from getting dinged in transit. Wrap the entire piece in stretch wrap to keep drawers and doors from popping open. And cover the entire piece with furniture blankets after loading it on the truck.

Vanity tables

1. **If the vanity has a mirror, remove it, cover it with a piece of cardboard, and wrap it in bubble wrap secured in place with packing tape.** Place the mirror in a sturdy box, add cushioning to fill any open spaces, seal the box, and label it "Fragile, Vanity Mirror."

2. **Empty the drawers, wrap any delicate items in packing paper, foam, or bubble wrap, and pack the items in a Ziploc or box labeled "Fragile, Vanity."**

3. **Wrap the legs and any ornamentation with bubble wrap.**

4. **Use corner protectors secured in place with stretch wrap to prevent them from getting dinged in transit.**

5. **Wrap the vanity in stretch wrap to keep doors and drawers from popping open.**

6. **Cover the vanity with a furniture blanket after it's loaded onto the truck.**

Nightstands

1. **Remove items from the surface of the nightstand.**

2. **Use corner protectors secured in place with stretch wrap to prevent them from getting dinged in transit.**

3. **Wrap the nightstand in stretch wrap to keep any doors and drawers from popping open.**

4. **Cover the nightstand with a furniture blanket after it's loaded onto the truck.**

Clothes

How you pack your clothing for a move is a personal decision. Here are a few options:

>> Leave some clothes in dresser drawers.

>> Wrap hanging clothes in clean furniture blankets, as explained in the earlier section "Gathering your moving supplies and equipment."

>> Pack clothes in boxes, suitcases, or large, heavy-duty trash bags.

>> Pack delicate garments and hanging clothes in a wardrobe box.

Shoes

1. **Stuff your shoes with crumpled paper, wrap each shoe in packing paper, and then wrap each pair in packing paper with the shoes facing opposite directions to save space.**

2. **Pack your shoes in a separate box and add cushioning to fill any open spaces.**

3. **Seal the box and label it "Shoes."**

Bathrooms

Packing a bathroom can be a challenge, mostly because of the diversity of items: everything from toothpaste and medications to towels and blow-dryers. In this section, we offer some guidance for packing up your bathrooms.

REMEMBER

Pack an essentials bag or box with everything you'll need up to and including the first day you'll be in your new residence: toothbrush, toothpaste, deodorant, comb/brush, razor, soap, shampoo, conditioner, towels, everyday makeup, medications, and whatever else you'll need.

Hazardous products

Box up any potentially hazardous products that aren't permitted on a moving truck, such as aerosols (for example, hair spray), rubbing alcohol, nail polish, nail polish remover, and noxious cleaning products. You need to move these products in your vehicle or get rid of them.

Medications

Another item that shouldn't be loaded onto a moving truck is medication. Load all your medications in a separate box or bag to take with you in your vehicle.

Combs, brushes, blow-dryers, and other tools

You can bag or box combs, brushes, blow-dryers, toothbrushes, and other accessories. If an item is fragile, wrap it in bubble wrap.

Cosmetics

Cosmetics typically include many small, breakable bottles or jars containing liquids or gels, so the focus is on preventing items from shattering or leaking. You have a few options here:

>> Carefully place your cosmetics in bags or boxes and move them yourself.

>> Wrap breakable items in packing paper or bubble wrap, place them in Ziploc bags in case they leak, and pack them in boxes, adding extra padding to prevent breakage.

>> Pack cosmetics in padded makeup bags or boxes that have several padded pouches or compartments.

Liquid products

To pack liquid products other than cosmetics, such as shampoos, conditioners, lotions, and perfumes, take the following precautions:

>> Tighten the lids on all bottles and jars and wrap them in stretch wrap.

>> Wrap all glass bottles and jars with bubble wrap or towels.

>> Place tubes and small bottles or jars containing liquids into Ziploc bags.

>> Pack everything in a box, adding cushioning between items to further prevent breakage, seal the box, and label it "Bathroom."

Towels

Towels are easy, assuming you want to pack them. In most cases, you're better off using towels to cushion other items you're packing — sort of as a substitute for bubble wrap. If you don't like that idea, you can pack towels in a box or a large, heavy-duty trash bag labeled "Bathroom Towels."

Laundry room

Assuming you've packed all your clothes, towels, and bedding, perhaps all that's left in your laundry room is laundry products and one or two clothes baskets. You can probably load the laundry products into your own vehicle instead of placing them on the moving truck. Consider putting them in a plastic trash bag and then inside a box just in case they leak in transit.

Clothes baskets are great for moving loose items. They're sort of like boxes. You can use them at the last minute for packing things from your pantry, towels, shoes, and other assorted items.

Garage/shed

We moved from a home where we maintained everything to a condo that requires virtually no exterior maintenance on our part, so we were able to nearly empty our garage before our move. However, if you need to keep items that you have in storage areas such as your garage, basement, shed, or attic, here's some guidance on how to pack it up.

Hazardous materials

Movers won't move hazardous materials: fuel, oil, paints, solvents, pesticides, fertilizers, and so on. You have four options for dealing with these materials:

>> Use them up.

>> Give them away (to a neighbor, for example).

>> Move them yourself.

>> Dispose of them properly. Your area may have a ToxDrop site or Tox Away Day.

Gas-powered equipment

To prepare gas-powered equipment for a move, take the following steps:

REMEMBER

Before you go through all the trouble of preparing gas-powered equipment for a move, have a plan in place for moving or selling these items. Check with your moving company to find out whether they'll move these items (some won't for safety reasons). Will they fit in your vehicle? Do you want them in your vehicle? Even if properly prepared, they may be dirty and smelly and may still leak a little gas and oil. You may be better off selling any large items and buying new or used ones after you move into your new home.

1. **Drain the fuel into a suitable fuel container and run the engine until it dies out.**

2. **Disconnect the spark plug cable.**

3. **Drain the oil into a suitable container following the manufacturer's instructions and take it to your local auto supply store for disposal.** Be sure to add oil when you get the equipment to your new place.

4. **Place protective covers on lawn mower and chain saw blades to prevent injury.**

5. **If you have any space-saving models, such as a mower with a foldable handle, fold the item according to the manufacturer's instructions.**

Power tools

1. Remove any detachable parts, such as drill bits, saw blades, or batteries, and pack them separately.

2. Wrap each item in nonstatic bubble wrap or an old towel.

3. Place items in a sturdy box and fill any open spaces with extra cushioning.

4. Seal the box and label it "Garage" or "Shed."

Hand tools

If all your hand tools are in a toolbox, you're set. Just be sure to secure any drawers or doors that may pop open during the move. Use stretch wrap, packing tape, duct tape, bungee cords — whatever works.

If you have loose hand tools, wrap any that may get damaged or pose a safety hazard in bubble wrap, towels, or another suitable packing material, pack them in small or medium-size sturdy boxes, seal them, and label the boxes "Garage" or "Shed."

Garden tools

1. Wrap any sharp-edged tools in bubble wrap or old towels, using packing tape or stretch wrap to hold the cushioning in place.

2. (Optional) Bundle large garden tools with long handles, using stretch wrap, packing tape, or bungee cords to bind the handles together.

3. Place smaller garden tools into small or medium-size boxes, fill any empty spaces with extra cushioning, seal the boxes, and label them "Garden Tools."

Patio furniture

1. Remove any cushions and pack them in separate boxes or large, heavy-duty trash bags. Alternatively, you can use cushions to keep other items from getting damaged on the truck and to fill small spaces.

2. Clean the furniture. If you have a patio umbrella, remove the cloth part, wash it, and pack it separately or with your cushions.

3. Disassemble each piece of furniture as much as possible so it'll take up less space on the truck. Place any hardware you removed during the disassembly into a Ziploc bag and tape the bag securely to the piece from which the hardware was removed.

4. **Wrap each piece of furniture in a blanket, if necessary, to prevent damage.** If you have stackable chairs or tables, stack them and throw a blanket over them after loading them on the truck.

Motor vehicles

If you have any motorized vehicles, such as a golf cart, motorcycle, boat, or extra car, you'll need to connect a trailer or tow bar to your vehicle or hire an auto transport company to move it for you.

Safe

If you have a portable safe, empty it and carry those items (passports, jewelry, firearms, and so on) with you instead of placing them on the moving truck.

Movers will not move firearms. If you're moving your firearms yourself, check the laws in the areas you're moving from, to, and through to ensure compliance with all the laws.

Labeling boxes

Labeling boxes may seem like busywork, but it will save you loads of time and frustration later when you move your belongings to your new residence. A quick glance at a label tells you and any helpers exactly where to put the box. Labeling is especially important for boxes that don't allow you to see what's inside.

Here are a few tips for labeling boxes:

>> Label each box with the name of the room and a description of what the box contains.

>> Consider using color-coded stickers to save time. You can use a different color sticker for each room.

>> Before sealing a box, take a photo of its contents, print the photo, and tape it to the outside of the box.

>> If a box contains anything fragile, label the box "Fragile" and write "This Side Up" on the top and sides, along with an arrow showing the "up" direction.

If you're packing before putting your home up for sale, we strongly encourage you to hide your boxes or (better) remove them entirely from the premises before any

OUR LABELING SYSTEM

When you're packing boxes, you tend to assume you'll remember what's in each box. You won't. As soon as you seal that box, your memory will begin to fade, and all your boxes will begin to look the same.

Write on the boxes. Write the name of the room where the box needs to go, along with a description of the contents. Be as detailed as possible.

We took pictures of everything in each box, printed the pictures, and taped them to the outside of the box. We then labeled the box with the name of the room where it needed to go: Main Bedroom, Guest Bedroom, Garage, Storage Room, Kitchen.

We used our garage at our new condo as the staging area. All boxes were placed in the garage and later moved from the garage to their final resting place.

prospective buyer enters your home. You can stack boxes in your garage or basement to get them out of the way, load them into a portable storage unit (see Chapter 13), or place them on a moving truck until you're ready to move.

We tried to show our home with the boxes in it, but that was just too difficult for buyers. We weren't getting many offers, and the offers we were getting were low. We think the people who looked at our home didn't like seeing it in the middle of a move.

We eventually moved our boxes off premises and placed them in a storage unit while we showed the house. Ultimately, this was a much better option, because many people appreciated being able to really take in the full breadth of the space they would have at their disposal.

> » Scheduling a moving truck or portable containers for moving day
>
> » Lining up movers to do the heavy lifting
>
> » Making sure your gas, electricity, and water are turned on
>
> » Unpacking without cluttering your new home

Chapter **18**

Executing a Successful Move

It is only through labor and painful effort, by grim energy and resolute courage, that we move on to better things.

— THEODORE ROOSEVELT

If you're like most people, you dread moving — and for good reason. Although moving can be exciting, it's often overwhelming. You have so much to do and so little time, and you'd better be ready when the moving truck shows up, or you'll be in for a chaotic and aggravating experience.

Imagine showing up at the truck rental site at 8:00 Saturday morning to find out that they have no record of your reservation after you scheduled a crew to meet you at your house at 9:00 a.m. Imagine the movers showing up at 10:00 a.m. when you're only halfway through your packing. Imagine showing up at your new place on Friday and discovering that everything has been turned off — you have no water, gas, or electricity. These aren't just imaginary scenarios; they've happened, probably more often than anyone likes to admit.

Avoiding these and other moving fiascos requires careful planning, coordination, and communication. You need to schedule everything in advance and then check and double-check that everyone's in sync leading up to moving day. In this chapter, we explain how to prepare in advance to execute a smooth and successful move and prevent any unpleasant surprises.

Changing Your Mailing Address

A week or so before your scheduled moving date, submit a change of address notification to the postal service to have your mail forwarded to your new home and then start letting everyone know that you're moving. The post office will forward your mail for only a few months, so you need to give all your personal contacts your new address and change it on all your accounts/profiles, such as your bank accounts, health insurance accounts, credit card accounts, and so on.

In this section, we lead you through the process of changing your mailing address to prevent or mitigate any interruption in mail service.

Avoiding hurt feelings

Before you announce your plans publicly, consider how your friends, neighbors, and family members will respond to your move. Eventually, everyone will be supportive and happy for you, but initially they may feel hurt, especially if your announcement comes as an unpleasant surprise.

To avoid hurting anyone's feelings, consider taking the following precautions:

>> Start talking about your potential move with loved ones sooner rather than later, so they can ease into the transition psychologically and emotionally.

>> Notify loved ones individually and privately in person or over the phone. Finding out through a Facebook or Twitter post that a loved one is moving away can come as a shock. Take a more personal approach.

>> Assure loved ones that you value them and plan to keep in touch. Don't assume that they'll be overjoyed with your moving plans. They may take it personally.

Notifying the postal service of your change in address

You can submit a change of address notification to the U.S. Postal Service (USPS) to have your mail forwarded from your old address to your new one. In the U.S., you can pick up a change of address form at your local post office, complete it, and mail it in (or return it to the post office) for free. Or you can file your notification online at USPS.com for a small identity verification fee ($1.10 at the time of this writing).

Having your mail forwarded for 3 months is free. You can pay more to have it forwarded for an extended period — 6, 12, or 18 months.

Whether you're filling out a paper form or submitting your notification online, you'll need to enter the following information:

>> Your current mailing address

>> Your new mailing address

>> Whether the change in address is just for you or for everyone at your current address

>> Your contact info (name, email address, and phone number)

>> Whether you plan to return to your current address within six months (whether the change of address is temporary or permanent)

>> The date on which mail forwarding is to begin

WARNING

If you're the only one in your household who's moving, be sure to choose Individual instead of Family when you fill out the form, or the postal service will forward all your family members' mail to your new address and they'll need to file forms to reverse the process.

And don't submit a change of address request if you're only going to be gone for a couple weeks. Instead, submit a mail hold request. The postal service will hold your mail for up to 30 days and then deliver it when you return, or you can pick it up at your local post office.

REMEMBER

The post office doesn't forward magazines, so if you have any magazine subscriptions, be sure to change the address on your subscription account, as explained in the next section.

Changing your address on all your accounts

As soon as you move into your new place, start changing your address on all your accounts, including the following:

- » Bank accounts (savings and checking)
- » Credit card accounts
- » Lenders (mortgage and car loans)
- » Investment accounts
- » Cell phone service
- » Magazine and other subscription services
- » Insurance providers (health care, car, homeowners)
- » Social Security Administration (www.ssa.gov)
- » Online shopping sites

REMEMBER

Whenever you receive a piece of mail, check whether it was sent to your old address and then notify the sender of your new mailing address if you haven't done so already. Do this for about a month, and you'll have notified most of your providers of your change of address.

WHEN YOUR NEW ADDRESS IS TOO NEW

When you build a home instead of buying an existing home, you may run into novel problems with mail and other delivery services. For example, because our condo had a brand-new address, our location wasn't established in the known universe. When we moved in, we called three pizza places, none of which had our address in their system.

Even the USPS struggled to acknowledge our new address in its system. As a result, some mail sent to our new home was delayed. For example, we didn't receive a water bill for the longest time. We noticed that money was being transferred from our checking account to pay our bill, but we received no bill from the water company. Surely, they know our address — the same address they're pumping the water to — but somehow, the bills keep getting lost in the mail.

Keep in mind that physical mail delivery still has a human element to it. We have a full-time and a part-time mail carrier, and we suspect that may have something to do with our missing or delayed items.

Sending change of address notifications to everyone you know

The USPS used to provide free change of address postcards (though you had to pay the postage when you mailed them). You'd simply send these postcards to everyone you knew, and they'd change your address in their address books. Well, things have changed since the 1970s. Now, you can notify people of your change of address by blasting a single text to everyone on your cell phone's contact list or sending a message to all your email contacts.

If you want to go old school and send change of address cards to all your contacts, you can order custom cards through online services such as Zazzle, VistaPrint, Etsy, and even Amazon.

CHANGING OUR ADDRESS

To inform everyone we knew about our change of address, we used a combination of texts, emails, and cards. We made calling cards with our picture on one side and our contact information on the other side — email addresses, cell phone numbers, and new address — and we passed them along to everyone we knew. Also, because we were moving near the holidays (Christmas and New Year's Day), we added a change of address notification to our Christmas cards.

Kathleen had to go through her planner to find contact information for people who weren't on our cell phone or email contact lists. We also had to go online and start changing addresses for all our accounts. In some cases, we couldn't find anywhere on the site to change our address, so we had to call the support line and do it over the phone.

Our change in zip code caused an unexpected problem. When we swiped, inserted, or tapped one of our credit cards and were prompted to enter our zip code for verification, the system sometimes required our former zip code and other times required our new zip code. The credit card companies took some time sorting that out.

Arranging Transportation: Trucks or Portable Containers?

If you're hiring a moving company to pack and move everything, you don't need to arrange transportation — the moving company takes care of that for you. On the other hand, if you're moving yourself, you need to reserve one or more trucks or have moving containers delivered to your home so you can load your belongings into them. Then, you need to recruit or hire some helping hands to assist you in loading your stuff (as discussed in the next section, "Scheduling movers").

First things first: trucks or portable containers? While a moving truck is generally the lower-cost option, moving containers offer the following advantages:

>> You load the containers at your leisure as opposed to having a limited time to load a truck or pay for additional days.

>> Portable containers feature ground-level loading as opposed to having to lift items into a truck, although some trucks come with lifts or ramps or have low decks for easy loading.

>> Moving containers double as storage units, which comes in handy if you need to store your belongings between moves.

>> The container service does all the driving.

Whether you're reserving a truck or portable containers, call the provider several weeks before you're planning to move to ensure availability. When making your reservation, you need to have some idea of the size and number of trucks or containers you'll need. Professional movers are experts at making these assessments, but most people underestimate the space they'll need, often because they can't pack a truck as tightly as skilled movers can.

Details in the following table can help you estimate the truck size you'll need. If a large truck doesn't have the capacity you need, you'll have to make more than one trip or hire a moving company with one or more semis. However, most people who are doing any serious downsizing won't need a semi — a 26-foot truck or smaller is usually sufficient.

Truck Size	Cubic Feet	Recommended For	Number of Medium-Size Boxes	Number of Furniture Items	Maximum Weight in Pounds
Cargo van	357	Efficiency or studio apartment	40	1–2	3,400
12 feet	380	Studio apartment up to a 1- or 2-bedroom apartment	120	1–5	3,610
16 feet	658	3–4 rooms or a 1-bedroom house	250	1–10	4,460
26 feet	1,698	5–8 rooms or a 2- or 3-bedroom house	500	1–15	10,000

WARNING

If you have a king-size bed, you'll need at least a 16-foot truck. The mattress/box spring won't fit in a cargo van or a 12-foot truck.

TIP

When renting a truck or portable containers, you'll have the option of renting furniture pads or blankets, hand trucks, and an appliance dolly (for moving heavy appliances such as a refrigerator/freezer). Be sure to rent plenty of furniture pads/blankets, and if you have a refrigerator or freezer, pay the extra $20 or so to rent the appliance dolly. It's well worth it. A hand truck is also useful for moving heavier items and stacks of boxes instead of having to carry one or two at a time.

Scheduling movers

If you're reserving a truck or portable containers, you'll need your own moving crew. You have two choices: friends and relatives or hired hands. Sometimes you can use both, but if you're hiring helpers, they usually expect you to stay out of their way. They may be required, for safety reasons, to not let you help, they may not want your free help cutting into their hours, or both.

Friends and relatives are the most affordable option, assuming they're physically fit, they show up, they're careful not to damage your property, and they don't get injured. If you have reliable help, using volunteers isn't a bad choice. However, if someone gets injured, they or you will be paying the price, and you'll probably feel bad about it. It's a gamble, but one that many people feel is worth it.

The higher-cost option is to hire helpers, and the easiest approach is to go through the moving truck or container rental company. Most companies that lease moving trucks and portable containers have an option on their website or app for hiring helpers. You choose whether you want loading help, unloading help, or both, and specify the loading and unloading dates and addresses, and the service provides a list of third-party helpers along with rates, ratings, and reviews. You then have the option of booking available crews online.

Assuming all goes as planned, you pick up the truck (or the container is delivered), and your moving crew arrives at your home to load it. They load the truck (or container), and then you drive it to your new place (or the container is picked up by the rental company).

Moving crews vary in their level of expertise. Ideally, the team leader is highly skilled in packing a truck or container and overseeing the other members of the crew doing the loading. In some cases, though, you can end up with a crew that's careless and does a poor job of loading the truck, which may result in damage to your home and your belongings and the need for additional trips when the crew is unable to fit everything on the truck.

TIP

Choose a moving crew that asks lots of questions and provides an on-site or virtual estimate. An experienced crew can take a quick look at everything that needs to be moved and give a very accurate estimate of the size and number of containers/trucks you'll need and the number of helpers to meet your goals. Our movers showed up at 8:00 a.m., and by 2:37 p.m. they were beeping the horn on their way down the driveway.

REMEMBER

Hire only helpers who are insured. If they get injured on the job and decide to file a lawsuit, you may be on the hook for some expensive bills depending on what your homeowner's insurance covers. Spending extra for quality helpers who carry their own insurance is a wise investment. Our movers were great. Not one thing was broken, no walls or doorways were scratched or dinged, and nobody was injured. They created a detailed inventory of everything they packed and they were fully insured, giving us complete confidence and peace of mind.

Being available on moving day

When moving day arrives, your job is to answer questions and direct traffic. Regardless of whether your crew is volunteers or hired hands, avoid any temptation to help with the lifting, carrying, or loading unless you absolutely have to. You will be more useful answering questions and directing traffic, especially when the time comes to unload everything and carry it into your new place.

REMEMBER

If you're busy packing, carrying, and loading, you'll either be getting in the way and slowing others down, or you'll have a lot of people standing around not doing anything because they don't know what to do.

If your crew is composed of hired help, a team leader will usually supervise. If you have any questions or concerns, address them to the team leader. Otherwise, just stand back and let the crew do its job. Don't try to micromanage the process.

On the other hand, if you have a crew of volunteers, you'll be required to provide more direction — which items and rooms you want loaded first and next, and which areas you want specific people to work on. For example, you may have a couple friends who are built more for moving heavy, bulky items and others who are more suited to carrying boxes and transporting fragile items such as lamps and TVs in their vehicles. In these cases, you should be telling people what to do.

TIP

When unloading the truck, consider stationing yourself at the entrance where items will be moved in and directing traffic from there. In some cases, you'll need to decide on the fly where a specific item needs to go, especially if rooms at your old place don't match up with rooms at your new place. For example, if your old place had a den but the new place doesn't, something that was in the den at the old place may need to be moved to the living room or office at the new place.

Switching Your Utilities

Some utility companies (gas, electric, water, sewer, and trash) are very responsive in providing uninterrupted service to their customers. Others are not. If you treat utilities as an afterthought, you'll almost certainly experience a service interruption, especially if you move on or close to a weekend, so you need to be proactive. Take the following steps:

1. **Make a list of services you'll need at the new place, such as the following:**

    - Gas
    - Electricity
    - Water
    - Sewer
    - Trash
    - Cable TV
    - Internet

TIP

If you're moving into a community that has a homeowner association, check with the association to determine whether any services, such as water, sewer, and trash pickup, are covered.

2. **Research your destination location to obtain contact information for providers of each service.** You may want to ask the previous homeowner, one of your future neighbors, or the agent who showed you the property for recommendations. In some cases, such as water and sewer, you have only one choice.

3. **Contact your utility providers 2–3 weeks in advance to let them know when you're moving in.** If you need equipment installed, you may need to call up to a month in advance.

REMEMBER

Consider having utilities turned on in your name a day before you're scheduled to move in and having them switched from your name (at your previous residence) on the day, or day after, you close on the sale. The best approach usually involves the buyer and seller calling the utility companies together right after the closing to have services switched over.

4. **Contact the water and sewer service providers to be certain you'll have these essential services the day you move in.** You usually get water and sewer through the town or city, and they're generally closed on weekends.

When you're moving out, notify the utility companies that were providing service to your old home to remove your name from those utilities or, better yet, transfer service to the names of the new owners. Let the utility companies know the date you're moving out, so they won't charge you for services you didn't receive. And check any bills you receive in the future to make sure they didn't charge you.

TIP

When you're stopping a service, consider telling the utility company rep something like, "I'm going to be moving in on such and such date, and so-and-so is going to be moving in on this date, and they'll be calling to give you their information." Most utility companies are flexible and will try to work with buyers and sellers to prevent any interruption in service. Communication is key.

REMEMBER

In some areas, you may have a choice of trash and recycle services, but the community as a whole may have a preference for using one particular service. Large trucks put a lot of wear and tear on roads, so having one company service the entire area can help reduce the need for costly road maintenance. In addition, everyone can put their trash out on the same day, and the neighborhood won't have that eyesore several times a week. Some trash services offer a neighborhood discount as well. Check with your neighbors before choosing trash and recycle services.

Unpacking: Decluttering, Round 2

Unpacking may seem like a no-brainer: You just arrange the furniture, remove items from boxes, and put them where you want them. However, unpacking goes more smoothly and you end up with a more organized home when you have a system in place. In this section, we provide guidance on unpacking that can save you time and energy while preventing clutter.

Here are a few overall suggestions before we lead you through the process room by room:

>> Unpack your essentials first — the boxes or bags containing your changes of clothes, towels, toiletries, medications, phone chargers, and so on.

>> Prep rooms before unpacking. If a closet needs an organizer, install it before unloading anything you're planning to put in the closet. If cabinets or drawers need liners or organizers, do it now.

>> Focus on unpacking the kitchen and the main bedroom first. You can then take your time with the other rooms.

>> In every room that contains furniture, arrange the furniture before unpacking any boxes.

>> Start with a plan for each room. For example, in your main bedroom, you may want to unpack your bedding and pillows first and make the bed before unpacking anything else. If you have a photo or inventory of each box's contents, refer to those documents to determine the best sequence for unpacking the boxes. Otherwise, open all the boxes before you start unpacking them.

OUR UNPACKING EXPERIENCE

The same movers who packed for us helped us reassemble and arrange our furniture and unpack at our condo. We paid them by the hour. The same guy who packed up everything we had in our crystal cabinet unpacked it when we moved in. The same guys who disassembled the bedroom furniture and loaded it on the truck moved it into the main and guest bedrooms and reassembled it. Each nightstand has three drawers, and it took them a few tries to get the drawers back into the right openings so they'd open and close properly.

(continued)

(continued)

Because our condo was still partially under construction when we moved in, we had to hold off on unpacking the kitchen. We left several boxes of kitchen items in the great room and unpacked them about a month later.

We prioritized our unpacking based on where we were spending most of our time — the kitchen, great room, and main bedroom. That way, we had everything we really needed and could take our time unpacking and putting items where we wanted them. If you're in a rush, you'll spend a lot of time rearranging things later.

We continued to downsize after the move. We even got rid of our second vehicle because it wouldn't fit in the new garage.

Kitchen

You don't have to put everything away in the kitchen all at once, but you probably want to at least start with the following high-priority items:

» Make sure the refrigerator/freezer is empty, clean, plugged in, and set to the desired temperature.

» If you have any items in a cooler, unload those first and place them in the refrigerator/freezer.

» Line the cabinets and drawers if they aren't lined already and you want them to be. Lining cabinets and drawers is always a good idea to prevent scratches and water damage.

» Place any small appliances you want out on the counters, such as your coffeemaker and toaster, and plug them in.

» Put away your pots and pans.

» Put away your dishes, cups, glasses, utensils, knives, and silverware.

» Put away any pantry items you brought with you.

» Unload and put away everything else that belongs in the kitchen, including all those refrigerator magnets you can't live without.

Bedrooms

After the kitchen, arrange and unpack the main bedroom so you have a place to sleep. You can then arrange and unpack any other bedrooms at your leisure or the day before your first guests arrive. Take the following steps:

1. **Assemble and make the bed.** Be sure it's in the spot where you want it and oriented in the direction that feels right for you — feng shui, anyone?

2. **Place the dressers and other furniture where you want them and put the drawers back in, if necessary.**

3. **Install closet organizers, if needed/desired, and put your clothes, shoes, and any extra bedding away.**

Bathrooms

You'll need at least one bathroom the night you move in. Focus on the main bathroom first.

REMEMBER

Don't put anything away in your bathroom until you're sure all the plumbing is working properly. Flush the toilet, run the faucets and shower, and check for any leaks under the sink. Call a plumber to address any issues before you put anything away.

When you're ready to unpack, take the following steps:

1. **Make sure you have toilet paper near the toilet.**

2. **Hang the bath towels and hand towels you're going to use.**

3. **Place soap, shampoo, conditioner, and other items you use in the shower or bath area.**

4. **Unpack your medicine cabinet items and put them away.**

5. **Lay out the items you'll keep on the countertop and around the sink — hand soap, toothbrushes, combs, swabs, and so on.**

6. **Unload and put away all the items you store under the sink or in the bathroom closet.**

Living room

The big challenge related to the living room is figuring out how to arrange the furniture and where to put the TV/entertainment center. If you already have that worked out, then it's simply a matter of reassembling furniture, connecting all the electronics, putting away any discs/tapes and books, setting out your knick-knacks, and hanging pictures.

REMEMBER

Don't do anything in the living room until you have a clear idea of how you want the large items arranged — the sofa, recliners or armchairs, and TV/entertainment center. Otherwise, you're going to subject yourself to a lot of unnecessary rearranging. Draw a plan on a piece of paper first if you need to.

Dining room

People usually downsize their way out of a formal dining room, so chances are good that you don't have to deal with a dining room. However, if you do, moving into it is usually simply a matter of reassembling the table and placing your dining room chairs around it. If you have a dining room cabinet, you'll have some dishes and silverware to put away as well.

Garage/basement

Most people use their garage and basement as self-storage, but for many people these are important work areas for crafts and hobbies. Before unpacking anything in your garage or basement, organize the area. You can find shelving, cabinets, toolboxes, and garage organizers at your local hardware store to make maximum use of your available space while placing everything within easy reach.

REMEMBER

One of the key goals of downsizing is to reduce clutter. You don't want to be digging through a pile of stuff in your garage, basement, or closets to find what you need or, worse, buying items you already have because you can't find them. Follow the adage "A place for everything and everything in its place."

5

The Part of Tens

Discover ten good reasons that inspire you to arrive at your own *why* for downsizing.

Find out ten ways to make the downsizing process less stressful and aggravating and more successful.

Explore ten ways to reduce your living expenses so you have more money to spend on what matters most to you.

Find ten solutions for supplementing your income if your cash flow isn't keeping pace with your bills.

Chapter **19**

Ten Good Reasons to Downsize

My choice of a lighter lifestyle has brought me a great sense of well-being. In a world that often seems stressful and chaotic, that's a feeling I cherish.

— *LISA J. SHULTZ, AUTHOR OF* LIGHTER LIVING

Downsizing is demanding, and it can be the source of a great deal of frustration, disappointment, and conflict, so we encourage you to keep your eyes on the prize. When you're done downsizing, you'll be ready to reap the benefits of all the time and effort you put into it.

In the meantime, you need to stay motivated, and one of the best ways to motivate yourself is to remind yourself of the many benefits of downsizing. In this chapter, we present ten of those benefits — ten good reasons to downsize.

Reduce Your Cost of Living

Downsizing doesn't necessarily reduce your cost of living, but it has the potential to do so if you make that your goal. All other factors being equal, a smaller house equates with a smaller mortgage payment (or, better yet, no mortgage payment), reduced homeowner's insurance premiums, lower utility bills, lower property taxes, and lower costs for maintenance and repairs. If you move to an area where everything you need is a convenient distance from your home, you may also save on transportation costs.

WARNING

Although downsizing typically saves a person money, expect some short-term costs, such as the cost of repairs to prepare your home for sale, moving expenses, storage costs, potential increased living expenses in your new location (depending on where you move), and the cost of furniture, appliances, and furnishings for your new home.

Spend Time and Money on What Really Matters

For many people, downsizing is a transition from living to work to working to live. Instead of working overtime to accumulate and maintain physical possessions, including a large home, by downsizing, they're able to spend more time and money on what really matters to them — travel, adventure, health and fitness, innovation, learning, family, community, causes, and so on.

REMEMBER

We encourage you to envision a richer, fuller life with fewer possessions weighing you down and dictating what you do with the time, money, and other assets you have. Imagine how you can use the assets at your disposal to live a more fulfilling life. Think of it as downsizing your possessions to upsize your life.

Save Time and Effort Cleaning, Maintaining, and Repairing Property

People who are filthy rich can afford to buy and maintain large homes packed with possessions, because they can afford to pay other people to clean, maintain, and repair everything they own. If you're not filthy rich, all the time and effort required to clean, maintain, and repair what you own falls on you. You must do it yourself or work longer hours so that you can hire someone to do it for you. In many ways, you become a servant to your possessions.

Downsizing provides a path to freedom from possessions. With a smaller home and fewer possessions, you have less to clean, maintain, and repair and more time and energy to spend on enjoyable and rewarding activities. Even if you hire someone to do the work for you, you'll be paying less for housecleaning services, maintenance, and repairs. Time is money!

Become More Mobile and Flexible

When you downsize, you become more mobile, more flexible. Maybe it's because you're in a smaller living space, so you feel the urge to get out more and explore the world, or simply because now you have more time, money, and energy to do whatever you want. Also, you're probably at a stage in your life when your children (if you have children) are living on their own, and you no longer feel responsible for them. If you have pets, you may be a little less mobile and flexible than you'd be without them, but with the right boarder, doggie day care, or pet sitter, you're still relatively free to do what you want, when you want.

Reduce Stress

After our children left the nest and before we downsized, we experienced persistent low-level stress knowing that we eventually needed to downsize. We were living in far too much house for two people. The stress was mostly self-imposed. We could've continued to live in our 7,000-square-foot house for the foreseeable future, but we couldn't help but worry about the mess our children would have to deal with if anything happened to either of us.

Downsizing was stressful, but as soon as it was over, we felt as though a huge weight had been lifted from our shoulders. We're now in our forever home, and we don't need to think about ever moving again. We have far fewer possessions, and everything we have is well organized. If anything happens to either of us, the other can continue to live comfortably in the condo, and while we're living here together, we're close to everything we love.

Spend More Time with Loved Ones

Ideally, downsizing frees up your time, money, energy, and other resources, and one way to redirect those resources is to spend more time with loved ones. With a smaller house and fewer possessions, your mind is also freer, which gives you the opportunity to be more present than you've ever been with your family and friends.

REMEMBER

Having a smaller home may require that you take a different approach to family gatherings. You may need to gather at someone else's home or arrange to meet at restaurants or parks. Don't let that get you down. You may find that your family gatherings are even more enjoyable when you're not focused on cooking, cleaning, and entertaining others.

Alleviate the Future Burden on Loved Ones

If you own a ranch like John Dutton in the hit series *Yellowstone*, you may want to preserve it for future generations. Otherwise, maintaining a large home that's packed with belongings beyond the age of 70 or 80 is probably a disservice to your heirs. They're the ones who will be stuck with disposing of your belongings when you pass away or downsizing you when you're no longer able to live on your own.

TIP

If you're retired or nearing that age, we encourage you to downsize even if you choose to remain in your current home. Reduce the clutter, sort your possessions, get rid of anything you don't need, and organize everything, so that if you die or become incapacitated, the person in charge of dealing with your home will have a much easier job.

Optimize Your Health and Fitness

Many people sacrifice their health and fitness for their homes and family. They're so singularly focused on supporting their family that they neglect diet, exercise, leisure, and even sleep. Downsizing provides an opportunity to make diet and lifestyle changes that can have a huge positive impact on your health and fitness and even extend your life. Seize that opportunity.

The largest room in our condo is our fitness room. It has a weight machine, treadmill, stationary bicycle, battle ropes, and more. If you don't have space for a fitness room, don't let that discourage you. Move into a community living center that has a shared fitness room, join a gym, or designate a small area of your home as an exercise space. You can go online to find plenty of exercises for building strength and endurance that require no specialized machinery or even much space. Walking is also an excellent form of exercise.

Focus on Quality Over Quantity

Downsizing drives home the fact that bigger isn't necessarily better. More isn't necessarily better, either. Health and fitness, freedom to do what you want to do, and having more disposable income can significantly increase the quality of your life. Material possessions don't necessarily improve the quality of your life, although they certainly can if they're used for self-development and to create great experiences and memories.

REMEMBER

Life is all about being, doing, and having. Sometimes, by having less, you have the potential to be more and do more. You have more time, energy, and resources to work on self-development and on enjoying memorable experiences and adventures. As you downsize, look for opportunities to create a more fulfilling balance among who you are, what you do, and what you have, with less emphasis on what you have.

Work Less

Perhaps the biggest benefit of downsizing is that it provides an opportunity to work less — not that we have anything against work. We love to work, and we will continue working for the rest of our lives, but retirement has made it so that we're no longer compelled to work by a need to earn a lot of money. This freedom enables us to do the work we love and to find fulfillment in other ways. We have more time and freer minds to travel, explore, and experience more of what life has to offer.

For some people, downsizing actually results in more work. The freedom they experience from not having to work makes them more creative and innovative and gives them the confidence they need to try something new. You may use your new-found freedom to develop and market an invention or start a new business. Many people are *serial retirees* — retiring from one line of work only to enter another.

The point is, when you don't need to work for a living, the field is wide open to try new things and experiment with new endeavors.

Chapter **20**

Ten Tips to Make Downsizing Less Stressful

For me, decluttering and downsizing has caused shifts in my thinking and my habits. I don't have to declutter; I choose to declutter.

— *LISA J. SHULTZ,* AUTHOR OF LIGHTER LIVING

Ultimately, downsizing relieves stress. Living in a smaller space with less clutter and reduced expenses lightens your load. However, the process of downsizing can subject you to excessive short-term stress. Any major life change is accompanied by both positive and negative emotions — fear, excitement, regret, hope, sadness, happiness, feeling overwhelmed, and so on. Add to that the difficult decisions you're facing, the challenges of communicating and collaborating with loved ones, and the impact a big move can have on your personal relationships, and you're looking at some major stress.

If downsizing is giving you the jitters, you've come to the right place. In this chapter, we present ten ways to alleviate stress and make downsizing more manageable. We can't guarantee a stress-free experience, but these tips will help make your downsizing journey at least a little less nerve-wracking.

Focus on What to Keep, Not What to Get Rid Of

One of the biggest challenges and most stressful aspects of downsizing is deciding what to get rid of. If you're like most people, you've developed strong emotional attachments to much of what you own, even if that attachment can be attributed to something as basic as wondering whether you'll eventually need a particular item someday. If you get rid of it now and you need it later, you'll have to buy it *again*, and nobody wants to do *that*.

Instead of mulling over what you're going to get rid of, focus solely on what you need — or what you're going to keep — such as the following:

>> Two weeks of clothing plus a couple outfits for special occasions

>> Toiletries and beauty supplies

>> A bed, a couch or recliner, and a table

>> A medium and a large pot, a large frying pan, and a small set of cooking utensils

>> A good set of dishes, mugs, glasses, and silverware

>> Tools you use regularly, such as screwdrivers, pliers, and a wrench

>> Essential documents

>> A small collection of photos

>> A few of your more cherished memorabilia

TIP

If you know where you're moving, sketch out a floor plan and include a list of everything you need and want in each room, so you'll know ahead of time what'll fit and what won't.

Follow the One-Year Rule

Another way to simplify the decision-making process for what to keep and what to get rid of is to follow the *one-year rule* — if you haven't used something in the past year, you're very unlikely to use it in the next year. This rule is simple and effective, and it applies to a broad range of items — everything from clothing, to furniture, to pots, pans, and plates.

You may encounter a few exceptions, but even in those cases, carefully consider your options. Is the item you're thinking of keeping something you can borrow or rent for the short time you'll need it? If it is, then you're probably better off getting rid of it.

Downsize One Room at a Time

If the mere thought of downsizing your entire home makes you break out in hives, think smaller — one room at a time. If that's too much, break down the task even further — one area of one room or one cabinet or a single drawer at a time. What's important is that you get started and build on your success. Making a little progress is always better than freezing up and doing nothing, and as you get 'er done, you build momentum.

Consider taking out the trash first. For example, if you're sorting bathroom items, discard old meds and products first, so you'll have less to sort.

Set a Manageable Deadline and Milestones

Some downsizing experts advise giving yourself plenty of time, but that approach can be counterproductive. If you have too much time, you may not feel any sense of urgency to complete the task. Procrastination is far too easy when you have no firm deadline.

Choose a reasonable deadline and mark it on your calendar. Then set reasonable milestones leading up to that deadline. You can set milestones by room, by percentage (for example, 25, 50, 75, and 100 percent dates), or by some other metric, but be sure to set milestones — they help ensure that you stay on track to meet your deadline. They also alleviate stress by providing a structured schedule to follow.

Follow the OHIO Rule

You can waste a lot of time, energy, and thought by being indecisive about which items you want to keep and which ones you want to get rid of. The purpose of the *only handle it once (OHIO)* rule is to discourage such indecisiveness. As you sort items, you make a final decision of what to do with each item: Keep it, donate it, or throw it away. You don't change your mind. You place the item in its designated box, and that's the last time you touch it.

TIP

Make the OHIO rule a part of your daily routines. For example, when you open the mail, pay your bills as they arrive instead of setting the bill aside and then paying it later. By dealing with issues as they arise, you move past them immediately so they're not cluttering your mind.

Host a Sorting/Packing Party

Flying solo when downsizing isn't fun, nor is it efficient. As you're sorting through items, having family members and other loved ones available to consult about what to keep and what to get rid of can simplify that decision-making process and alleviate a great deal of stress. For example, if you're able to ask your daughter whether she wants your wedding dress as she's standing in the room, you can immediately make the call of whether to give the dress to your daughter or take it to the consignment shop.

TIP

Host two or more sorting/packing parties. You may want to schedule your first party for immediate family members — to give them the pick of the litter. Then, schedule additional parties for friends, neighbors, and former coworkers. You can host a final giveaway for hired help, such as your housekeeper or gardener. Have food and beverages available, play music, anything to make the experience more fun and less stressful for everyone, especially you.

Pack an Essentials Box

An *essentials box* is the last box you pack at your old place and the first box you unpack at your new place. It's also the box you keep with you instead of sending with the movers. In this box, you pack everything you'll need for the last night at your old place, any time you'll spend between places, and the first night at your new place.

Here's a checklist of items to consider packing in your essentials box:

- ❏ Toilet paper
- ❏ Toothbrush, tooth-paste, floss
- ❏ Bath soap and antiperspirant/deodorant
- ❏ Bath towel, face towel, and washrag for each family member
- ❏ Shampoo, conditioner, and comb or brush
- ❏ Beauty supplies

- ❏ Clothing, including socks and underwear
- ❏ Medicines
- ❏ Dish soap and towel
- ❏ Coffeemaker, coffee, and mugs
- ❏ Snacks
- ❏ Beverages
- ❏ Plate, fork, knife, spoon, and cup/glass for each family member
- ❏ All-purpose knife
- ❏ Can opener and wine key (corkscrew)
- ❏ Scissors
- ❏ Small emergency/medical kit
- ❏ Flashlight, candles, and matches
- ❏ Garbage bags
- ❏ Portable tool kit
- ❏ Electronics (smartphone, laptop, chargers)
- ❏ Valuable jewelry
- ❏ Essential or important documents
- ❏ Pet food and dishes

Have Your Adult Children Clear Out Their Belongings

Children often move out of their parents' house but continue to use it as their informal self-storage unit. Downsizing provides the perfect opportunity to put an end to that practice. Give your children reasonable notice that you are downsizing and they need to come and get their stuff by a specified date or it will end up in the dumpster or shredder. If they don't retrieve their belongings by that date, follow through with your plan.

REMEMBER

Don't let your adult children make their problems your problem.

Create a Yes and No Pile (No Maybe Pile)

In Chapter 9, we recommend that you sort items into six categories — keep, store, sell, give away, donate, and toss — but it really boils down to two categories: what to keep and what to get rid of, a yes and a no pile. Don't make the common mistake of creating a third category for items that you can't decide about. That pile will only get bigger and bigger, and the likelihood that you'll end up deciding to keep it all will increase substantially. At the same time, your stress over having to make the decision of whether to keep or get rid of an item in the maybe pile will continue to build.

Opt for Amenities Over Square Footage

Living in a smaller space can cause stress as well as alleviate it. You must adapt to living in more confined quarters. However, certain amenities can reduce the negative impact of having less living space, such as the following:

>> Location near restaurants, stores, entertainment venues, parks, walking/biking paths, and public transportation

>> Laundry facilities

>> A community swimming pool, hot tub, clubhouse, or tennis courts

>> A community gym or workout room

>> Designated areas for grilling out

>> Easy access to lakes or ponds for fishing or boating

REMEMBER

Having less living space is likely to make you feel the urge to get out more, so choose a home where more is available to get out to.

IN THIS CHAPTER

» Eliminating some bills while reducing others

» Using credit cards to your advantage

» Selling a car and vacating your storage unit

» Reducing health-care costs by becoming healthier

» Capitalizing on senior discounts

Chapter **21**

Ten (or So) Ways to Reduce Your Living Expenses

Beware of little expenses. A small leak can sink a great ship.

— BENJAMIN FRANKLIN

By downsizing, you're taking a big step toward reducing your living expenses. With a smaller house, you typically have a smaller mortgage payment (if any), and you pay less in property taxes, homeowner's insurance, utilities, and maintenance. If you took our advice and moved to a more convenient location, you're also saving in travel costs.

However, you can save even more. In this chapter, we present 11 ways to reduce your cost of living.

REMEMBER

Your cost of living is tied directly to your *standard of living*, which is defined as "the level of material comfort measured by the goods, services, and luxuries available to an individual, group, or nation." But cost of living has very little to do with *quality* of life. Some people can have more fun with an old fishing pole and a can of worms they plucked from the dirt in their garden than people who spend tens of thousands of dollars on an exotic vacation. You don't need a lot of money to live a rich life.

Slash Your Insurance Costs

Homeowner's and car insurance can take a chunk out of your income or savings. Here are a few ways to reduce your premiums:

>> Stay with the same company to benefit from loyalty discounts. Many insurance companies reward loyal customers with lower rates. However, shop around every few years, just to be sure you're not missing out on a policy that's much better and less costly. Ask about discounts periodically.

>> Consult an independent insurance agent to compare rates for you. You can compare rates online, but an independent agent is likely to have better tools and a broader selection of insurance providers from which to choose.

>> Look into *bundling* your home and auto insurance — insuring your home and vehicles through the same company.

>> Check whether you can get a discount by paying your annual premium all at once.

>> Check your coverage and deductibles (consult your agent if you have one). You can save money by increasing your deductible or dropping coverage you don't need, such as comprehensive coverage on a car that's not worth much.

Reduce Cable TV, Internet, and Phone Costs

Cable TV, internet, and phone services can cost hundreds of dollars a month. If you're spending $300 a month on all three, that's $3,600 annually. If you can trim $100 or more off that bill, you save $1,200. Here are a few ways to reduce your costs for these services:

>> Bundle cable TV, internet, and phone — get all three through the same provider.

>> Shop around. In many areas, you have multiple options — Comcast/Xfinity, Verizon, AT&T, DISH, DirecTV.

>> Cancel cable TV. Install a TV antenna to get channels locally and stream additional content through your internet connection, if desired.

REMEMBER

As we explain in Chapter 6, contacting your current provider for anything other than bundling is more likely to increase your monthly fees than reduce them. You have leverage only if you're willing to cancel your current service or change service providers.

Cancel Subscriptions

You can start subscriptions for all types of products and services these days — newspapers, magazines, software, video streaming, wines, craft beers, meat, and the list goes on. Subscribing is easy. Unsubscribing can be a pain.

Review your list of regular expenses and highlight the ones that are subscription services. Then whittle down the list to only the ones you really need/love and cancel the rest.

Reduce or Eliminate Vehicle Expenses

Vehicles can become very expensive when you total the cost of the vehicle itself, maintenance and repairs, insurance, license and registration, and fuel. If you have a low-maintenance vehicle that's paid off, congratulations — your vehicle expenses are probably already minimal for what you need. On the other hand, if your vehicle is costing you hundreds or thousands of dollars a month just to own it or if you don't drive it very often, this expense category may be ripe for cutting. Here are a few options to consider:

>> If you have more than one vehicle, consider getting rid of one.

>> If you drive very little, consider sharing a car with a neighbor, friend, or family member or borrowing a car when you need one. Or use public transportation, rideshare services such as Uber or Lyft, and taxis to get around.

>> If maintenance and fuel costs are blowing your budget every month, consider buying or leasing a newer, more fuel-efficient vehicle.

REMEMBER

Deciding when to pull the plug on an old car can be challenging, but do the math: Total your repair and maintenance costs over the past year and divide that number by 12 to determine the monthly costs. If that's more than a monthly loan or lease payment, you're better off buying or leasing a new vehicle.

Clear Out Your Storage Unit

If you have a storage unit packed with belongings you haven't touched in more than a year, the time has probably come to clear it out and turn in your lock and keys. Depending on your location and the size of your unit(s), eliminating your reliance on storage may save you $100–$200 per unit per month. And if you have anything of value in there, you can sell it for some additional cash.

Take Better Care of Yourself

Health care is expensive, even if you're healthy. If you're sick, medical bills can send you to the poorhouse. In fact, nearly 65 percent of all bankruptcies in the U.S. are tied to medical issues. The solution — don't get sick. By taking better care of yourself, you can reduce several expenses related to health care, including insurance premiums, doctor visits, medications, testing, and medical procedures.

In Chapter 6, we provide details on how to take better care of yourself. Here's that guidance in a nutshell:

>> Lay off the nicotine, alcohol, marijuana, caffeine, illegal drugs, junk food, fast food, and sweets.

>> Eat mostly whole foods, mostly plants.

>> Drink enough water.

>> Get off your butt.

>> Sleep 7–8 hours per night.

>> Silence the stress.

>> Consult a doctor who practices functional, integrative medicine to deal with any chronic health conditions.

Shed Your Consumer Debt

Taking on debt can be a smart move if you're using it to build wealth; for example, you borrow $250,000 at 6 percent interest to buy a home that's probably going to appreciate 3–5 percent annually. Otherwise, debt is just another expense. If you've racked up a lot consumer debt, such as credit card debt, work toward paying it down or paying it off. Here are a few options to explore:

» Transfer your balances to a balance transfer credit card account with a promotional zero percent interest rate for 12 months or longer and pay off the balance before the introductory period expires.

» Get a low-interest debt consolidation loan. For example, if you owe $10,000 in credit card debt with an APR of 22 percent, you may be paying nearly $400 per month just in minimum payments. With a debt consolidation loan at 11 percent, you can reduce your monthly payments to about $200, pay off the balance in about one-third the time, and save yourself over $5,000 in interest.

» Negotiate a debt management plan with your creditors. Call your lenders and let them know that you're struggling to pay your bills. They don't want you to file for bankruptcy because it will erase what you owe them. They may be willing to reduce the balance, lower your interest rate, reverse any fees, or all of the above. You can do this alone or with the help of a nonprofit credit counseling agency.

Use Cash-Back Credit Cards

Cash-back credit cards are useful for wringing another 1 or 2 percent discount out of every purchase. You buy something for $100, and you get a dollar or two back. Consider using cash-back credit cards for all your expenses — your monthly utility bills; cable, internet, and phone bills; online and in-store purchases; fuel for your car; and so on.

WARNING

People tend to spend more when paying with plastic instead of cash, so be careful. If you have trouble controlling your spending when using credit cards, the 1 or 2 percent you get back with a cash-back credit card may not be worth it. You may be better off just putting your autopay items (such as utilities) on your cash-back credit card and using cash for groceries and other consumer purchases.

Buy Your Groceries Online

How many times have you gone to the grocery for a few small items and walked out pushing a cartful of stuff you had no intention of buying? These impulsive purchases can really add up. It's why so many stores now have checkout lanes that force you through a maze of awesome products as you wait in line. By the time you reach the counter, you're practically salivating.

The solution is to shop online and order only what you need. Before paying, review your shopping cart and remove anything that qualifies as an impulse purchase.

TIP

If you can't bring yourself to shop for groceries online, we get it. We love shopping at Whole Foods and Trader Joe's. Just make a list beforehand and enter the store with a firm commitment to buy only what's on your list. No cheating — don't simply add to your list based on what appeals to you as you wander the aisles.

Set Spending Caps

Spending caps can keep you from going overboard in certain categories, such as groceries, clothing, or travel. You commit to spending only so much in each category, and when you've reached your limit, that's it — you cut yourself off. No raising the spending limit like they do in Washington, D.C.!

TIP

If you have a partner, consider separating your finances. What often happens with couples is that they both overspend and then blame each other. By separating your finances, each of you has more control and accountability individually. Try it for six months. If it doesn't work for you, you can always go back to your previous arrangement.

Ask About Senior Discounts

If you're over the age of 55, ask about senior discounts wherever you go — restaurants, theaters, motels, retail stores, cruises, concerts, sports events, and more. In most cases, you need to be over the age of 62 or 65, but some places offer discounts to people as young as 55.

For additional discounts, consider joining a senior organization such as AARP (www.aarp.org) or AMAC (amac.us).

IN THIS CHAPTER

» Getting a part-time job or starting a business

» House-sitting and pet walking

» Tutoring or substitute teaching

» Driving for dollars

» Freelancing online for extra cash

Chapter **22**

Ten Ways to Supplement Your Income

You can only be financially free when your passive income exceeds your expenses.

— T. HARV EKER

People often downsize to work less or not at all. They make their lives more affordable so they have more time for themselves — more time to enjoy life. However, after a few months or years of this newfound freedom, they may suddenly discover that their money is running out or they miss working. They miss the structure, purpose, and social opportunities that work provides.

Returning to the rat race isn't an option, of course. They want something less structured. They want to be their own boss and set their own hours. In many cases, they want to be able to work wherever their spirit carries them — they want portable employment.

In this chapter, we present ten work options that check all the boxes: You can be your own boss, set your own hours, work anywhere, and earn the income you need to support your more freewheeling lifestyle.

Find a Part-Time Job

As we're writing this book, the U.S. is suffering a labor shortage. Everywhere you turn, you see Help Wanted signs in a variety of places — restaurants, grocery stores, retail stores, factories, insurance agencies, real estate firms, law offices, schools — you name it. Whether you're skilled or unskilled often doesn't matter. In many cases, the sole requirement for landing a position is coming in and submitting an application.

And in many cases, employers are looking for part-time help — they want to avoid having to provide health-care and other benefits. For a downsizer like you, that may be the perfect fit.

REMEMBER

Don't let age or any other self-perceived limitation discourage you from applying for part-time jobs. Even if you've been out of the workforce for several years, somebody will hire you.

TIP

One often overlooked area of employment is entertainment venues — sports arenas and concert venues. The pay is decent, and you get to attend entertaining events for free.

Manage Property

If you live in or near an apartment or condominium complex, you may be able to find gainful employment as a property manager or groundskeeper and earn enough to cover your rent or monthly mortgage payment. People who own apartment complexes in particular need property managers to collect rent, handle minor repairs, give professionals like plumbers and electricians access to the property, mow the grass, keep an eye on things, and make sure the residents are happy and well-behaved.

TIP

You can earn even more money by offering cleaning services to residents. You can do the cleaning yourself or hire a third party and mark up the price to earn a reasonable profit. Remember, you don't need to do all the heavy lifting yourself — focus on your role as manager.

Start a Business

If you truly want to be your own boss, start your own business. Visit the U.S. Small Business Administration's website (www.sba.gov) for a ten-step guide to starting your own business and for additional information and resources. Here's a short list of the most profitable small businesses in 2022 to spark your imagination:

>> Food truck

>> Day care

>> Electronics repair

>> Personal wellness (personal trainer, yoga or Pilates instructor)

>> Accounting firm

>> Landscaping service

Watch Other People's Pets

People love to have pets but often lack the time or flexibility in their schedule to care for them properly, so they hire people to look in on their pets and walk their dogs. If you're available and reliable, you can make watching other people's pets a full-time occupation or even build a business around it and hire others to help.

To find work as a pet sitter/dog walker, you basically have two options:

>> **Advertise locally.** Let everyone know that you're available to walk dogs and care for pets. Hand out your business card to everyone you meet. Post about your service on neighborhood websites, such as Nextdoor.com, and on more general-purpose social media sites, such as Facebook.com. And don't forget to advertise at your local pet stores and veterinary clinics.

>> **Register with a pet-sitting service.** You can register with an online pet-sitting service where pet owners commonly go to find sitters, such as Rover.com, PetSitter.com, and the National Association of Professional Pet Sitters at PetSitters.org.

House-Sit

If you travel light, you can find plenty of free places to stay and earn a decent income by house-sitting for people who are going to be away from home for extended periods (and usually need someone to watch their pets, too). The added benefit is that you can house-sit nearly anywhere in world.

As with pet sitting, discussed in the previous section, you can advertise your service, register with a house-sitting service online, or do both. Here are a few online house-sitter registries you may want to check out:

>> MindMyHouse.com

>> TrustedHousesitters.com

>> HouseSittersAmerica.com

>> TheTravellingHousesitters.com

Sell Your Crafts

If you have a hobby that involves making something that people value, you may be able to turn it into a business. Here are some craft/hobby items that people commonly sell:

>> Photographs

>> Soaps

>> Candles

>> Jewelry

>> Paintings (originals or prints)

>> Scarves

>> Pottery

>> Woodwork projects

You can sell all these items at local farmers' markets and art festivals, on your own website and social media accounts, and through third-party sites, such as ShutterStock.com (for photos), Etsy.com, and Shopify.com.

Tutor or Substitute Teach

Educators are always in demand, and you can find plenty of opportunities both as a substitute teacher and, if you're strong in a particular subject area (math, science, foreign language), as a tutor. Many school districts require substitute teachers to have a college diploma and, in some cases, classroom experience, but they may be flexible depending on the availability of people to fill these positions.

If you're a retired teacher in a high-demand subject, such as math or a foreign language, you can earn a good income as a tutor. Let local teachers in your subject area and homeschoolers know you're available, and you'll start getting calls. Also, advertise locally in case any adult students are interested. Hand out your business card to everyone you meet and post your card or a flyer on public bulletin boards (for example, at the library and grocery stores). You may also want to spread the word at local businesses.

Become a Driver

To qualify for some jobs, all you need is a valid driver's license and a decent vehicle. You can then find plenty of work driving people around or delivering food, groceries, and other essentials. Plenty of work is available through the leading ride-sharing and delivery platforms, including the following:

>> Uber.com

>> Lyft.com

>> Grubhub.com

>> DoorDash.com

However, your driver/delivery options aren't limited to these newfangled services. Also consider the following more traditional opportunities:

>> Driving a school bus

>> Driving a shuttle bus (or creating your own shuttle service)

>> Starting a pet taxi service

>> Driving the Amish

>> Delivering pizzas

Build a Career as a Social Media Influencer

If you're charismatic, like to talk, and have specialized knowledge and interest in just about anything (makeup, fashion, health care, interior design, landscaping, carpentry — you name it), you can build a successful career as a *social media influencer* — an individual who has gained popularity and trust among an audience of online followers. Influencers typically generate income in the following ways:

>> **Sponsored content:** A company pays an influencer to feature their product in a blog post or podcast, for example.

>> **Paid brand ambassador or spokesperson:** A company pays the influencer to represent and support its brand.

>> **Affiliate marketing:** The influencer promotes a company's products and earns a commission from sales resulting from those promotional activities.

>> **Advertising:** Companies pay the influencer to include an advertisement on the influencer's website or blog. (Many influencers earn advertising money by posting videos on YouTube.)

>> **Tipping, donations, and subscriptions:** Some influencers earn income from their followers in the form of tips, donations, or subscriptions.

Become a Virtual Assistant

A *virtual assistant* is a self-employed individual who specializes in offering administrative services to clients from a remote location. Here are some of the tasks often outsourced to virtual assistants:

>> Scheduling and calendar management

>> Data entry

>> Research

>> Event planning

>> Basic bookkeeping

>> Customer support

- » Blogging and social media management
- » Transcription
- » Website creation/management
- » General paperwork and filing

You can find work as a virtual assistant through previous employers or by networking — for example, by marketing your services on LinkedIn.com (in an appropriate way). You can also find plenty of work on freelance services marketing sites such as Fiverr.com, Upwork.com, and Freelancer.com.

TIP

For more about working remotely, check out *Digital Nomads For Dummies* by Kristin Wilson.

Index

living room, 323–324

party for, 95

upholstered furniture, 300–301

upsizing, 31

Upwork website, 351

urban areas, 56

U.S. Legal Wills, 128

U.S. News and World Report, 55

USB flash drives, 184, 186

user guides, 190

Userfeel website, 123

utilities, 268–269, 319–320

V

valuables

determining worth of, 200–203

insuring, 238

protecting, 235–238

home safes, 236–237

safety-deposit boxes, 237–238

valuation, business, 142

valuation websites, 201

ValueMyStuff website, 201

vanity, 168–169, 304

vans, 24, 52, 265

variable expenses, 110

variable interest rate, 284

vases, 297

vehicle expenses, 341

Victorian homes, 262

video collection, 196–198

do-it-yourself option, 196–197

hiring professionals, 197–198

reducing collection, 192

videocassette players, 197

Vietnam Veterans of America (VVA), 181, 223–224

virtual assistants, 350–351

virtual mail service, 114

vision, 46–50

lifestyle questionnaire, 46–48

lists of interests and concerns, 48

vision board, 14, 48–49

vision folders, 49–50

Vrbo, 44, 66, 153

VVA (Vietnam Veterans of America), 181, 223–224

W

Walgreens Photo, 195, 197

walkability, 60

Walmart, 197

warranties, 190

water, 120

waterfront property, 55

whole foods, 120

whole life insurance, 143

wills, 127–132

joint will, 130–131

living will, 131

simple will, 129–130

testamentary trust will, 132

Wills and Trusts Kit For Dummies (Larson), 129

window treatments, 93

World Collectors Net, 201

World Economic Forum, 54

Worldwide Opportunities on Organic Farms (WWOOF), 24

Worst Roommate Ever (series), 124

WorthPoint, 201

Y

yard sale

overview, 206

tips for, 214–215

YNAB (finance management program), 111

yurts, 24

Z

Ziploc bags, 293

Zippy Shell, 232

About the Authors

Ralph R. Roberts's success in real estate sales is legendary. He has been profiled by the Associated Press, CNN, and *Time* magazine and has done hundreds of radio interviews. Ralph is a seasoned professional in all areas of real estate investing and has helped hundreds of clients meet their downsizing goals. He has penned several successful titles, including *Flipping Houses For Dummies* (Wiley), *Foreclosure Investing For Dummies* (Wiley), *52 Weeks of Sales Success* (Wiley), and *Protect Yourself from Real Estate and Mortgage Fraud* (Kaplan). In *Downsizing For Dummies,* Ralph reveals the tips and techniques he discovered while downsizing himself and other family members. For more about Ralph, visit RalphRoberts.com.

Kathleen Roberts has always loved books. Between fifth and sixth grade, she and her classmates were challenged with reading as many books as possible. Kathleen won the challenge! Now, she's excited to be a part of writing a book with her husband, son, and writer extraordinaire Joe Kraynak!

Kathleen married the King of Real Estate and raised their three children in their newly built home in the '90s. Since that time, they've enjoyed hosting parties of all kinds — family gatherings, sporting events, sleepovers, homecoming and prom pictures, and holiday parties. The best party they ever threw was for their daughter, Kaleigh, and her husband, Scott, who held their wedding reception in the backyard of the family home.

Kathleen and Ralph began their downsizing journey in 2019. It's been a whirlwind ride, but not one that she would change for anything! She hopes this book is helpful for readers going through their own downsizing.

Kyle Roberts works as a manager in the field of human resources. In his HR career, he has supported field operations, talent management, and talent development teams. Kyle was present throughout his parents' downsizing journey to observe and offer input and assistance, and he played a key role in managing the content development of this book.

Dedication

Ralph would like to dedicate this book to Joe Sirianni, a 30-year friend and accomplished CPA. Up until his recent retirement, Joe was Ralph's CPA. Joe has never faltered in his friendship with Ralph and has stood by his side his entire career. Ralph attributes much of his success to Joe's wisdom, support, and knowledge. To this day, they are great friends, and Joe continues to share wisdom and advice with Ralph.

Authors' Acknowledgments

Although we wrote the book, dozens of other talented individuals contributed to its conception, development, and perfection. Special thanks go to senior editor Jennifer Yee, who performed the numerous initial tasks required to get this project rolling in the right direction. We're also indebted to our project manager and development editor, Tracy Brown Hamilton, for ensuring the breadth, depth, and accuracy of the content and for acting as a very patient choreographer — shuffling chapters back and forth, shepherding the text and photos through production, and keeping the project on track. Thanks also to Kelly Brillhart, our copy editor, who read through everything — forward and backward — to identify and obliterate our many grammatical goofs and typos.

Throughout the writing of this book, we relied heavily on a knowledgeable and dedicated support staff, who provided expert advice, tips, and research, so we could deliver the most comprehensive and useful information. We owe special thanks to our technical editors, Lowell Pierce and Theresa Tucciarelli, for ferreting out technical errors in the manuscript, helping guide its content, and offering their own insights and guidance. Special thanks also to photographer Marty Medvedik, who supplied the before-and-after photos of our recent downsizing journey.

We also want to thank the following people who provided valuable insight into the downsizing process, called our attention to important things to consider, and helped make this book the best it could be: Lance and Joanne Avery, Jessica Lutz, Gregg Potvin, Dominic Alessi, Kaylie Alessi, Noel Jonescue, Jane and Steve Saigh, Al Caicedo, Cindy Dorman, Tracy L. Aldea, Mike Sugg, Jimmy Cole, Gary Beams, Norm Forster, Greg and Kathy Woods, John Pliva, Mike Murray, Paul Rettig, John (Augi) Augugliaro, Jon Angell, Tom Palmer, James Babcock, Fred Foley, James Hackney, Jeremiah Campbell, John Schluessler, Marty Medvedik, Jose Manuel Espitia Sanchez, and Courtland and Mary Lou Munroe.

Publisher's Acknowledgments

Senior Acquisitions Editor: Jennifer Yee

Project Manager and Development Editor:
Tracy Brown Hamilton

Copy Editor: Kelly Brillhart

Technical Editors:
Lowell Pierce and Theresa Tucciarelli

Production Editor: Mohammed Zafar Ali

Photographer: Marty Medvedik

Cover Image: © Jeremy Poland/Getty Images